الْقُرآنُ الْكَرِيمُ

بِالرَّسْمِ الْعُثْمَانِي

وَتَرْجَمَةُ مَعَانِيهِ إِلَى اللُّغَةِ

الْإِنْكِلِيزِيَّة

THE HOLY QUR'AN
WITH
ENGLISH TRANSLATION

First edition
İstanbul 01/07/1992

Forth edition
İstanbul 1998

Second edition (revised)
İstanbul 17/11/1994

Fifth edition
İstanbul 1999

Third edition (revised)
İstanbul 1/2/1996

Sixth edition
İstanbul 2000

All rights reserved

Seventy edition
İstanbul 2002

Eighty edition
İstanbul 2003

Typesetting   : Hasan Alioğlu, Yelda Yıldız
Proof reading : Dr. Abdulhakim Winter (lecturer in Cambridge University)

Prof.Dr. Ali Özek, teaching the interpretation of the Holy Qur'an at the Faculty of Theology in Marmara Üniversity - İstanbul, TÜRKİYE

Prof.Dr. Nureddin Uzunoğlu, professor and author of International Law and Islamic Studies in Nebraska U.S.A.

Doç.Dr. Tevfik Rüştü Topuzoğlu, teaching Arabic at the Faculty of Arts in İstanbul University, also working as a writer and editor of Arabic Language and Literature in DIA (Türkiye Diyanet Vakfı İslâm Ansiklopedisi The Turkish Religious Foundation Encyclopedia of İslam). TÜRKİYE

Prof.Dr. Mehmet Maksutoğlu, teaching Islamic History at the Faculty of Theology in Marmara University, İstanbul - TÜRKİYE

PUBLISHED BY:

Printed By:
ACAR MATBAACILIK YAYINCILIK HİZMETLERİ
AMBALAJ SANAYİİ VE TİCARET A.Ş.

1-877-WHY-ISLAM
www.WhyIslam.org
P. O. Box 1054
Piscataway, NJ 08855-1054
An ICNA Project

Tel&Fax: 1707 215 15 85 E-Mail: website@asirmedia.com
www.asirmedia.com

human race, or that human beings can find their way to the Truth on their own, are both untenable arguments. It is inconceivable that the Creator has bestowed on human beings an abundance of blessings to facilitate their physical existence but has left them clueless about their basic spiritual and emotional needs. The human race has on its own, invented a plethora of philosophies and "isms" that are often mutually contradictory.

When Allah settled his creation on this earth, he promised to send messengers from time to time, who would guide people to the right path. The Glorious Qur'an says:

"O Children of Adam! Whenever messengers of your own come to you who narrate to you My revelations, then whosoever refrains from evil and amends, there shall no fear come upon them neither shall they grieve.

But, they who deny Our revelations and scorn them; such are rightful owners of the Fire; they will dwell therein forever."

[Al-Qur'an: Surah 7, verses 35-36]

Indeed prophets did proclaim the Divine Message at various points in history. Prophets Noah, Abraham, Moses, David and Jesus (peace be on them all), were some of the Prophets who are mentioned in the Glorious Qur'an. The Divine revelations given to the prophets were known by different names. Prophet Abraham (p)[2] was given the Scrolls, Prophet Moses (p) was given the Torah, Prophet David (p) the Psalms and Prophet Jesus (p) the Gospel. None of these books however, are to be found in their original, unaltered form today. The last revelation for the human race is the Glorious Qur'an which was revealed to Prophet Muhammed (p), and which will always be found in its original form. The Glorious Qur'an says:

"We have, without doubt, sent down the Reminder, and We preserve it (from corruption)."

[Al-Qur'an: Surah 15, verse 9]

All the prophets preached the same fundamental truths of this life and the hereafter. Each prophet gave glad tidings of the prophet who would come after him and urged his followers to accept the new prophet. Thus, it is incumbent on every human to accept each and every prophet of God. To reject any one of them implies in effect rejecting all of them.

There existed two great nations that possessed earlier Divine revelations while the Qur'an was being revealed. They were exhorted, to accept the Qur'an in light of the fact that the Qur'an actually confirmed the fundamental teachings of their Divine books, and even fulfilled the prophecies mentioned therein.

The Qur'an was revealed with the open announcement that Prophet Muhammed (p) who received this revelation, was the last and final Messenger to be sent by Allah and that no messenger or prophet would follow him. The Glorious Qur'an says:

"Muhammad is not the father of any man among you, but he is the messenger of Allah and the Seal of the Prophets; and Allah is Aware of all things."

[Al-Qur'an: Surah 33, verse 40]

The greatness of the Qur'an lies in the fact that this is the last revelation from the Creator to humankind, and that it is through the Qur'an that the Way of Life prescribed by God, has been perfected. The Creator says in the Glorious Qur'an:

"This day have I perfected your religion for you and completed My favor upon you, and chosen for you as religion al-Islam."

[Al-Qur'an: Surah 5, verse 3]

---

[2] (p) stands for "pea ce be upon him", which is an invocation of respect for all Prophets.

**In the name of Allah,
the Most Compassionate, the Most Merciful,
Praise be to Allah, Lord of the Universe,
and Peace and Prayers be upon
His final Prophet and Messenger.**

PREFACE

A brief reflection on the world around us makes it clear that the human race has been chosen for an abundance of Divine blessings. Indeed, human beings have the highest stature among all of Allah's[1] creation.

We have been blessed with the faculties of speech, intelligence and understanding. We have the ability to assimilate facts, and to delve deep into various sciences. We adorn ourselves with fine clothing and harness the resources of this universe to our benefit. Wholesome food that nourishes our bodies and the beautiful flora and fauna found in nature are a part of the beautiful mosaic of creation that clearly bears the signs of the Creator.

We have been blessed with creativity and a variety of talents that enable us to invent modern conveniences. Thus, we can now ride on the winds or the waves to travel large distances, and transmit information across the globe in the blink of an eye. Allah has also bestowed mankind with a special gift - that of free will.

The Glorious Qur'an says:

"We have honored the children of Adam, and carried them on land and sea, and provided them with good things, and preferred them greatly over many of those We created."

[Al-Qur'an: Surah 17, verse 70]

The reality of the human being however is not confined to his physical existence alone. Rather, every human being is also blessed with a soul, and the soul too has certain needs. The existential need of every human then, is to identify the pattern of existence she should live out during her lifetime. Questions of identifying Truth v/s Falsehood, Good v/s Evil, Righteous v/s sinful, about the nature of our relationship to our Creator, and to His creation are what distinguish human beings from other creatures that walk the earth. The need to pursue success and everlasting happiness, and to seek the meaning of Life, are part of the primordial human instinct, that manifests in every normal human being, unless early conditioning suppresses this innate aspect of human nature.

The contention of the Glorious Qur'an is that the Creator has indeed fulfilled His responsibility of providing guidance and the correct worldview for the human race. All the other blessings of Allah merely fulfill the material needs that human beings have, by virtue of being a kind of superior animal. However if the innate instinct to seek the reality and meaning of life is unfulfilled, the human existence is rendered meaningless, while repulsive forms of materialism and nihilism that plague modern society, find fertile ground.

Allah has fulfilled this human need by means of prophets that came from time to time to convey Divine guidance. These prophets were among the greatest blessings of Allah to the human race. To reject prophethood is to reject the Mercy and Wisdom of the Creator. To say that the Creator has not established any means for guiding the

---

[1] Allah, is the Arabic word for the Creator and Sustainer of the Universe, and the Master of the Day of the Judgement. It is loosely translated into English as "God", but actually has far greater connotations.

One can only access the divine message of the Glorious Qur'an, if four things are borne in mind:

a. The Qur'an repeats its claim that it is a Divine revelation, and not a human product.

"Those who disbelieve say: 'If only the Qur'an would be sent down upon him all at one time!' Thus do We establish your heart with it, and We have recited it in a distinct recitation."

[Al-Qur'an: Surah 25, verse 32]

The Qur'an thus addresses each reader, by inviting him to follow the Divine Guidance that it carries.

b. You should free your mind from bias and preconceived notions when reading this book. You should approach the Qur'an with sincerity, and read it to understand its message. Only those who approach the Qur'an with humility and a sincere heart, can benefit from the Divine Message.

c. If you feel that the Truth is dawning on you while reading this book, it is quite natural that you will want to change your inner and outward life, and mould it according to the injunctions mentioned therein.

d. Whenever you sit down to read this book or have just finished reading it, pray that Allah makes your heart receptive to the Truth. It is the Creator alone who can guide, and without His guidance none can be guided. One is recommended to memorize the following supplication:

"O Allah, inspire me to reflect on all that I have read from your Book. Give me the wisdom to understand its meanings, and the ability to appreciate its greatness and miraculous nature. As long as I live, give me the ability to follow its teachings. Verily You have Power over all things."

The Glorious Qur'an is a fountainhead of knowledge and wisdom to those who seek the Truth with a sincere heart. I invite you to read and study this Divine book, and ponder over it. Humanity, now more than ever, is in need of its message of peace and hope.

Maulana Muhammed Yusuf Islahi,
Patron, 877-Why-Islam Project, New Jersey, USA
Rector, Jamiatus Salehat University, Rampur, India

Important Guidelines

1. Please remember, the Glorious Qur'an is sacred scripture, and should be treated as such.

2. Please handle this copy of the Glorious Qur'an respectfully, and in a state of personal cleanliness.

3. If you wish to dispose off this copy, do not throw it away. Please call the nearest Islamic Center or dial 1-877-WHY-ISLAM, and we will arrange to get the copy from you.

Translators' Forward to the Second Edition

As we pointed out in the first edition, our aim in preparing this English translation with explanations was to assist those reading this translation of the Qur'ân to understand the meaning of God's divine message as revealed in the Holy Qur'ân. In addition to using everyday English whenever possible, some explanations and brief commentaries were added in parentheses among the verses so that the connections between the verses are more apparent and the verses so that the connections between the verses are more apparent and the verses can be read more smoothly. Without this help, we feared that not only would some verses not be understood, but that understanding the Qur'ân as a whole would be difficult. It has not been our aim to provide a full commentary of the Qur'ân, though. There are many commentaries that can be turned to if more complete information is desired. However, in order to provide still more assistance of the type mentioned above, this edition contains more explanations than were in the first edition.

Finally we would like to thank Nurettin Uzunoğlu for the explanations he added especially in the last two sections, Tevfik Topuzoğlu and Halûk Ersoy for revising the text, Bilâl Başar for generously sponsoring the project, and lastly Zekeriya Acar and his staff for the care they took in printing this edition.

May Allah All-Mighty enable us all to walk on the "Right path" (Sirât Mustaqim) through the guidance of His Noble Messenger and forgive our shortcomings. Amen.

The translation Commitee
17.11.1994 İstanbul

Translators' Foreword

Praise be to God, the Most High, our Cherisher and Sustainer. And may peace and blessings be upon His Messenger!

Over thirty English translations of the Holy Qur'an have been made, many of which continue to serve people all over the world. Many of them are of high quality, and have filled a vital gap in conveying something of the Book's message to English speakers.

Nonetheless, there is a generally-felt belief that the gap has not been completely filled. Among the reasons for this dissatisfaction, apart from the obvious one of the Qur'an's inherent untranslatability, one could cite the following: -

Firstly, the most commonly-reprinted translations are written in an archaic, Biblical style, which, while dignified and melodious, is sometimes difficult for a new generation which has not been regularly exposed to premodern literature.

Secondly, the growing number of conversions to Islam in the English-speaking world, particularly in countries such as the United States, South Africa and Fiji, together with increased interest in Islam among non-Muslims, has created an urgent need for a wider range of translations, to suit all orientations and educational levels.

Thirdly, a number of translations have been done by non-Muslims with no direct experience of Islam, or by members of sectarian groupings suc as the Qadiyanis. Many offerings of this type contain interpretations which are eccentric and speculative, and in any case do not reflect the mainstream understanding of the text which most readers wish to know.

Fourthly, the existing translations are usually bereft of any commentary or explanation, leaving the text almost unintelligible in many places. In the present work, we have tried to include some explanations from a number of classical commentaries in Arabic and Turkish, as well as the English-language commentary of Abdallah Yusuf Ali. These exegetic remarks have been included in the text both through the insertion of italicised expansions in parenthesis, and by adding notes after those verses which seem in need of comment. Needless to say, only the most basic explanations have been included from the enormous traditional material available for the Qur'an (some classical commentaries would occupy over a hundred volumes if translated); but it is hoped that the reader's understanding and appreciation of the text may nonetheless be deepened as a result.

Under the chairmanship of Ali Özek, the Translation Committee has divided its labours as follows:

Nurettin Uzunoğlu	Suras 1 to 8	Pages 1 - 185
Tevfik R. Topuzoğlu	Suras 9 to 20	Pages 186 - 320
Ali Özek	Suras 21 to 39	Pages 321 - 465
Mehmed Maksudoğlu	Suras 40 to 114	Pages 466 - 603

The Translation Committee would like to express its gratitude to Mr. Bilâl Başar, who inaugurated this project and generously sponsored it.

We thank God Who has made this work possible, and pray Him to render this humble service of ours a means of understanding, guidance and salvation for people throughout the world. May the Lord forgive our unwitting shortcomings, and give us the chance to rectify them in the future, by means of reader's comments and corrections, which we will be happy to receive. May He gather us all under the banner of Hiss noble Messenger. Amen.

The Translation Committee.

PREFACE

What is the Qur'an? One may answer this question with the following definition: "The Qur'an is a Book of Guidance which is itself a miracle." It is a "Book of Guidance" because it was sent to direct mankind along the path to happiness and salvation, and it is a miracle (in fact, the greatest of all miracles) because it was vouchsafed as a revelation to the blessed Prophet of Islam. An understanding of the Book, therefore, demands an understanding of these two concepts.

The Arabic word "*qur'ân*" is a verbal noun which gives the sense of "reading and reciting". The word is used thus inside the Qur'anic text itself: "Do not move your tongue with it (i.e. the Qur'an) in order to hasten it. It is for Us to gather it and to convey it. But when We have conveyed it, follow its recital (*qur'an*); then it is for Us to explain it." (Sura al-Qiyama, 16-19.)

Although it has this general meaning, the word Qur'an in the course of time came to be applied to the *Mushaf*, the entirety of the revealed text which is composed of Sûras ("chapters") and Âyats ("verses"), and which begins with Sûra al-Fâtiha and ends with Sûra al-Nâs.

The word "Qur'an" is applied to the Book in its entirety, and also to any individual component thereof. Although the Qur'an has a considerable number of names, including the Book (*al-Kitâb*), the Criterion (*al-Furgân*), the Remembrance (*al-Dhikr*), and the Sending-Down (*al-Tanzil*), the best known name is "the Qur'an". The word Qur'an is also used in conjunction with a range of adjectives, including the Clear/Clarifier (*al-Mubîn*), the Light (*al-Nûr*), the Guidance (*al-Hudâ*), the Mercy (*al-Rahma*), the Cure (*al-Shifâ'*), Mercy

(*al-Rahma*), the Cure (*al-Shifâ'*), the Admonition (*al-Maw'iza*), the Good News (*al-Bushrâ*), the Bringer of Good News (*al-Bashîr*), the Warner (*al-Nadhîr*), the Precious/Noble (*al-Azîz*).

In its specific, technical meaning, the "Qur'an" is "the Book progressively revealed to the Prophet Muhammad (upon whom be peace) over a period of 23 years, which constitues a miracle both in its language and sense, and by the recitation of which, God is worshipped."

The Qur'anic text is distinguished by the following five characteristics:

1 Gradualness of revelation

2 Revealed status

3 Status as a miracle, both in its text and concepts

4 Status as an instrument of worship

5 Status as God's own speech

The fact that the Holy Qur'an was revealed gradually, over a 23-year period, reflects the human need for gradual, progressive education and gudinace. To grow accustomed to something radically new, and then to adopt it, requires a good deal of time and energy, both for habituation and reflection. More than anything, a new religion should give people time to grow used to its injunctions and norms. Hence the Qur'an's gradual revelation.

The Qur'an is a revelation from Heaven, cast by the Archangel Gabriel into the heart of Muhammad (upon whom be peace). It is hence the Word of God, not of man. The Blessed Prophet received it as revelation, and he, in turn, recited it to his people without the least addition or subtraction. Every word and letter is hence from God.

Both the words and the concepts of the Qur'an are miraculous. In Islam, a miracle is defined as an event which cannot be emulated by man. In all the specific features of the Book: its revelation, recitation, writing, preservation, arrangement, style of addressing issues, fur

nishing of information about the Hereafter, and the accuracy of the facts it brings to mankind, it differs from the works of literature which are produced by human minds. The ancient Arabs used to call a poetic anthology a *dîwân*, whose parts were termed *gasîda*, its lines bayt, and its rhyme, *gâfiya*. But the Book sent from God to His messenger is called *Qur'ân*, its parts are called *sûra*, its verses *âya*, and the ends of its *âyas*, fâsila.

Human literary productions are either in poetry or prose. The Holy Qur'an, however, is in neither of these genres. Neither can it be termed music, although it possesses a system of tonality and rhythm that is aesthetically superb, being of Divine authorship.

Another feature of the Qur'an is that it is a Book the recitation of which is itself an act of worship. In addition to its liturgical use in the *Salât* (the indispensable 5-times a day worship of the Muslims), it is recited independantly as a devotional act. To teach it, to learn it, to hear it; even to look at its writing, is an act of worship. As the *Salât* is a duty upon every Muslim, male and female, and reciting passages from the Qur'an is an indispensable part of the *Salât*, it is necessary for every Muslim to learn and be able to recite at least a few verses of the Book. And this must be done in the Arabic of the original Revelation.

The Qur'an is the eternally pre-existent Speech of God. The text, and its constituent verses, which we recite with our tongues, listen to with our ears, write with our hands, look at with our eyes, and tuch with our fingers, is a manifestation of God's pre-existent Speech in this material world. The source-book of the Qur'an is called *al-Lawh al-Mahfûz* (the "Well-preserved Tablet"). The first stage in its manifestation took place when God revealed it collectively (*inzâl*) to the metaphysical location known as *Bayt al-'Izza* (the "Abode of Glory"). From there it was revealed to our Prophet through Gabriel individually (the process known as *tanzîl*). Words revealed by God literally to His prophet are thus called Qur'an, and are distinguished from words revealed in meaning only, not in literal form, which are called *Hadîth Qudsî* ("Sacred Tradition"). Words, acts and affirmations proceeding from the Belassed Prophet are called *Hadîth Nabawî* ("Prophetic Tradition").

The Prophet Muhammed (upon whom be blessings and peace) described the Holy Qur'an in the following terms:

"The Qur'an is the Book of God. It contains the story of those
who lived before you, news of those who will come after you,
and a Law which judges between you. It is definitive; it is not a
est.Whoever abandons it because of a tyrant will be destroyed
by God, and whoever seeks guidance apart from it will be
caused to stray by Him. It is God's strong rope. It is the Wise
Reminder. It is the Straight Path. It is that whic carpice cannot divert, and tongues cannot pervert. The scholars are never
sated of it. It does not wear thin following much repetition. Its
marvels are unceasing. It is the Book concerning which the
Jinns said, when they heard it: 'We have heard an amazing
Qur'an, which guides to correctness.' [1]

Whoever speaks with it is given to speak the truth. Whoever
acts by it is rewarded. Whoever judges by it is just. Whoever
summons to it guides men to a Straight Path." [2]

The Qur'an was sent in Arabic. Was this because the Blessed Prophet was
sent among the Arabs, who were the best-equipped nation to follow a
new religion, or is there another reason? It would seem futile to attempt a precise answer to this question, since had it been sent in another language, an identical question would have arisen. Such matters
belong to the Unseen, and can be known only imperfectly by the limited human mind.

The Qur'an is sent to all mankind, despite the fact of its Arabic
revelation; and its Prophet, while an Arab, is a prophet for all mankind. How, then Book's message be proclaimed to the
world? Either mankind may be asked to study and master Classical
Arabic - an unfair demand - or the attempt should be made to convey
its concepts in other languages.

Hence the Holy Qur'an's impact on mankind takes place through
two channels:

   ·1 As a revealed text, the repetition of whose words brings grace, the
     Arabic Qur'an is memorised, read and listened to, and recited in
     prayers, thereby affecting the souls of mankind.

   2 The Holy Qur'an has been translated into hundreds of languages,
     in some of which commentaries have also been written.

---

1 Sura 72, vv, 1-2.
2 *Sunan al-Tirmidhī*, Bâb mâ Jâ'fī fadl *al-Qur'an*.

The influence of the Book on today's world is incalculable. It appears that in almost every country, young people are finding new inspiration in its message. And in the West, too, our experience is that conversions take place in many cases through the channel of the Qur'an, often in the most unexpected ways. Here again we are faced with the Book's miraculous nature, which seems certain to continue its influence in our age, and, God willing, until the Day of Judgement.

Prof. Dr. Ali Özek
İstanbul

سُورَةُ الفَاتِحَة

بِسْمِ اللهِ الرَّحْمَنِ الرَّحِيمِ ۝ الْحَمْدُ لِلَّهِ رَبِّ الْعَالَمِينَ ۝ الرَّحْمَنِ الرَّحِيمِ ۝ مَالِكِ يَوْمِ الدِّينِ ۝ إِيَّاكَ نَعْبُدُ وَإِيَّاكَ نَسْتَعِينُ ۝ اهْدِنَا الصِّرَاطَ الْمُسْتَقِيمَ ۝ صِرَاطَ الَّذِينَ أَنْعَمْتَ عَلَيْهِمْ غَيْرِ الْمَغْضُوبِ عَلَيْهِمْ وَلَا الضَّالِّينَ ۝

سُورَةُ البَقَرَةِ

بِسْمِ اللَّهِ الرَّحْمَٰنِ الرَّحِيمِ

الٓمٓ ۝ ذَٰلِكَ الْكِتَابُ لَا رَيْبَ ۛ فِيهِ ۛ هُدًى لِّلْمُتَّقِينَ ۝ الَّذِينَ يُؤْمِنُونَ بِالْغَيْبِ وَيُقِيمُونَ الصَّلَاةَ وَمِمَّا رَزَقْنَاهُمْ يُنفِقُونَ ۝ وَالَّذِينَ يُؤْمِنُونَ بِمَا أُنزِلَ إِلَيْكَ وَمَا أُنزِلَ مِن قَبْلِكَ وَبِالْآخِرَةِ هُمْ يُوقِنُونَ ۝ أُولَٰئِكَ عَلَىٰ هُدًى مِّن رَّبِّهِمْ ۖ وَأُولَٰئِكَ هُمُ الْمُفْلِحُونَ ۝

SÛRAH I

AL-FÂTIHA (THE OPENING)

Revealed at Makka

This is known as the "Opening Chapter , since it inaugurates the Book. It has several other names, including "Umm al-Kitâb (the "Mother of the Book), "al-Asâs ("The Foundation), and "al-Wâfiya , and "al-Kâfiya , and also "al-Sab' al-Mathânî ("The Seven Oft-repeated Verses).

Our Prophet taught that "The Salât (prayer) of anyone who does not recite Sûrah al-Fâtiha is not valid, and for this reason it is recited in each cycle (rak'a) of every prayer. If the Fâtiha is recited for the sick, they derive benefit from it. Additionally, Sûrah Fâtiha is the most important Muslim supplication and prayer, used in every occasion of life.

The guiding principles of the Qur'an, which was revealed to help mankind along the Straight Path, are summed up in this Sûrah.

The Basmala

The *Basmala* comprises the words "In the name of Allah, the Compassionate, the Merciful. According to the Hanafî School of thought, this formula is to be recited silently in prayers, because it does not form part of the Fâtiha or other Sûrahs, with the exception of a verse occurring in Sûrah al-Naml. According to the Shâfi'î school of thought, however, the Basmala is part of the Sûrahs, and hence should be recited aloud.

According to another hadith, "Everything which does not begin with a Basmala falls short (of the blessing of Allah). All Muslims believe in beginning everything with it, so that the Lord's blessings may be bestowed on them. According to Sûrah al-Nahl, verse 98, it is also necessary to recite the "Isti'âdha , a formula by which one seeks Allah's protection, before starting to recite the Basmala and the Holy Qur'an.

THE OPENING

In the name of Allah, the Compassionate, the Merciful

1. Praise be to Allah, the Lord of the Worlds;

2. The Compassionate, the Merciful;

3. Master of the Day of Judgement;

4. You alone do we worship, and to You alone we pray for help;

5. Guide us to the Straight Path;

6. The way of those whom You have favoured;

7. Not of those who have incurred Your wrath. Nor of those who go astray.

(The Arabic words "Rahmân and "Rahîm can be roughly translated as "Compassionate and "Merciful . "Al-Rahmân is one of the Names of God, Whose bounties are open to anyone, even without asking, whether they be believer or disbeliever, righteous or sinner. "Al-Rahîm is also one of the Names of God. In the hereafter His bounties are open only to the believers.

The Arabic word "Mâlik can be translated either as "owner or "master, or both; therefore Allah is the Owner and Master of the Day of Judgement.

The Arabic word "al-'Âlamîn is a plural of "'Âlam . There are many worlds in the Universe. There is the world of "Nâsût , the human world knowable by the senses. There is the "Malakût , which is the invisible world of angels and of other spiritual entities, such as jinn. Finally, "Lâhût is the world of the Divine Reality. Every planet in the Universe, too, may be a "world . There are also astronomical and physical "worlds , spiritual worlds, metaphysical worlds, and others. Most are known only to God.

The Arabic word which means "guide here yields the meaning, "Guide us to the Straight Path, and keep us there without swerving . According to certain of the Qur'an's commentators, the Straight Path is the way of the Prophets and those who follow them truly: not those who are cursed by the Lord, like the Jews, or those who simply deviated from the Straight Path, like the Christians. The two major nations which preceded Islam are held up as examples to the Muslims, so that the latter may pay attention, lest they too deviate from the truth, and tread the path of misguidance.)

The Patriarch Abraham (*Ibrâhîm*) is mentioned as a most righteous man and leader; he was the progenitor of the Arabs (Ishmael's line) and the Jews (Israel's line). Ibrahim (peace be upon him), aided by his son, built the Ka'ba (the House of Worship at Makka), and purified it. Finally he established the universal religion of Islam for all mankind.

In this chapter, issues of prayer, fasting, jihâd, charity, patience and endurance under cruelty, gambling, and wine-drinking, divorce, contract, pilgrimage, the abolition of usury, the good treatment of orphans and women, are also discussed.

The Verse of the Throne (*Âyat al-Kursî*) is also to be found in this Sûrah: a famous passage where Allah's sublime and transcendent nature is called to mind. The Sûrah ends with a prayer for forgiveness of shortcomings.

The period of revelation of this Sûrah was the years 1 and 2 A.H.)

THE COW

In the name of Allah, the Compassionate, the Merciful.

1. Alif. Lâm. Mîm.

(The true meaning of initials of this type is only known to Allah.

These mystical letters are called *al-Hurûf al-Muqatta'ât*, and are placed at the beginning of several Sûrahs, of which they are an integral part. Different interpreters and commentators have ascribed a range of different meanings to them, without, however, arriving at any consensus.)

2. This is the Book in which there is no doubt, in it is guidance for those who fear God.

3. Who believe in the unseen, establish the Salât-prayer, and spend out of what We have given them.

4. And who believe in that which is sent down to you (*Muhammad*), and that which was sent down before you (*the Books and the Prophets*), and have certain faith in the Hereafter.

5. These are the people on true guidance from their Lord, and such are (*the people who are truly*) successful.

SÛRAH II
AL-BAQARA (THE COW)
Revealed at Madîna

(This Sûrah, which is 286 verses long, is the longest Sûrah in the Holy Qur'an. It takes its name from the cow which was mentioned in verses 67-71. The Jews were ordered to slaughter this cow, but they disobeyed. When the Jews lost the true faith, they disobeyed Moses, inventing various excuses.

This Sûrah also deals with the establishment of the "Umma, the Islamic Brotherhood of Believers, together with the main principles of the Islamic law, and lays down ordinances for the ordering of society.

The Ka'ba was now to be the centre of the universal worship and the symbol of the Islamic Community, the *Umma.*

The story of man's creation is told, and that of the Children of Israel, of the privileges they received and how they refused them. There are references to Moses and Jesus, and their struggle with injustice and cruelty, and their persevering endeavours to establish the true faith.

6. As for the disbelievers, it is the same whether you warn them, or warn them not (*of the final punishment*). They will not believe.

7. Allah has set a seal on their hearts and on their hearing, and on their eyes there is a covering. For them there is a great penalty (*both in this world, and the hereafter*).

8. And there are some who say, "We believe in Allah and the Last Day , yet they believe not.

9. They think to deceive Allah and the believers, but they deceive no-one except themselves, though they realise it not.

10. In their hearts is a disease, so Allah has increased their disease. Because of their lies there is a great penalty for them.

11. When it is said to them: "Make not mischief in the earth , they say: "We are only peacemakers.

12. Nay, they are the ones who make mischief, but they realise it not.

13. And when it is said to them, "Believe as people believe , they say: "Shall we believe as the fools believe? They themselves are the fools, though they realize it not.

14. And when (*these hypocrites*) meet those who believe, they say: "We believe! but when they are alone with their evil ones, they say: "We are with you, we were only mocking.

15. Allah (*Himself*) does mock at them (*in reality, whether they realise it or not*), leaving them to wander blindly in their rebellion.

16. These are the people who have purchased error at the price of guidance, but their trade is profitless, and they are not guided.

(Having announced at the beginning of this Sûrah that the Holy Qur'an is without doubt the Book and the guidance, Allah proceeds to categorise men into three main types of attitude to faith.

(I)   The believers, whose attributes are discussed in the first five verses of the Sûrah.

(II) The disbelievers, whose qualities are discussed in the sixth and seventh verses.

(III) The Hypocrites, whose qualities, or signs, are discussed in detail from verses eight to twenty one.

Because the Holy Qur'an is the Book which is sent down to help mankind to the Straight Way, its subject matter is man, and his beliefs, whether correct or incorrect. An explanation is given of the consequences of the belief that man chooses and adopts within himself.

In reading the Qur'an, one must keep in mind the fact that the Speaker is always the Almighty Himself. Sometimes He lets His creation speak also, and sometimes He punctuates the text with goodly examples for our reflection.)

them, they stand still. Indeed, if Allah willed, He could take away their sight and hearing. Allah has power over all things.

(As we notice from the above verses, the disbelievers and the hypocrites suffer from a confusion in the mind. Sometimes they act as though they see the truth; sometimes they are hesitant with fear and excitement, and sometimes they are in complete darkness. In spite of this inner turbulence, Allah preserves their sanity. Those who want to believe, believe; while those who wish to disbelieve, disbelieve and prepare themselves for eternal punishment.

The next verses explain that Allah is the Creator of all things, and He alone is worthy of worship. Allah the Exalted is the sole Creator of everything man needs in order to exist. Men are obligated to know this fact, and act accordingly.)

21. O mankind, worship your Lord, who created you and those before you, so that you may protect yourselves.

22. It is your Lord who made the earth a bed, and the sky a canopy; and it is He Who sends down rain from above for the growth of every kind of food for your sustenance. And do not set up rivals to Allah, while you know better.

23. And if you are in doubt concerning that which We reveal unto Our slave (*Muhammad*), then produce a Sûrah of the like thereof, and call your witnesses who are apart from Allah, if you are truthful.

24. But if you cannot do it, and you can never do it, then guard yourselves against the fire whose fuel is men and stones, prepared for the disbelievers.

(In the above verses, mankind is called to believe in Allah. It is explained that it is Allah who created man, and gave him life and death and sustenance. They were challenged to produce a Qur'an similar to this. The impossibility of producing a second Qur'an was explained and stressed, and the consequent principle that those who do not believe in the Prophet and in his messages will be punished with hellfire. In the next verses, the glad-tidings to the believers of Heaven and their condition there will be explained.)

17. Their condition (*the hypocrites*) is the condition of one who kindles a fire, and, when it illuminates all around him, Allah takes away their light and leaves them in darkness, where they cannot see (*anything at all*).

(Here the inner state of the Hypocrites is described. When they embrace Islam, they benefit from its light as if they had languished in a dark night, but when they turn away from faith back to unbelief (kufr), that light vanishes. They return to their previous condition, for without light they are blind.)

18. They are deaf, dumb and blind, they will not return (*to the right way*).

19. Or as though when a heavy rain is fallen from the sky, accompanied by darkness, thunder, and lightning, they press their fingers into their ears for fear of death; but Allah encircles the disbelievers.

20. The lightning terrifies them as if it would snatch away their eyesight. When they see light, they walk a little, and when it becomes dark for

25. And give glad tidings to those who believe and do good deeds. For them there will be gardens beneath which rivers flow. Their fruits will resemble what had been given them before (*in the world.*) Every time they are served with such fruits they will say, "This is what was given to us aforetime! And there will be pure spouses for them, and they will abide there for ever.

(In this verse, the prophet Muhammad (*peace be upon him*) is told that those who believe and do good deeds in the world will receive a reward in the hereafter. Although some of those blessings or rewards will be similar to those available in the world, they are greatly superior. According to a hadith narrated by Bukhârî: "the people of the Garden will be rewarded with what no eye has seen, no eye heard, and which has never occurred to mortal mind.)

26. Allah does not disdain to coin even a gnat as a parable, or a larger creature. As for those who believe, they know that it is the Truth from their Lord. But those who disbelieve say, "What does God wish to teach by such a parable? He leads astray many thereby, and guides many. And He leads astray only the corrupt.

27. Those who break Allah's Covenant after ratifying it, who cut asunder what Allah has ordered to be joined, and who commit evil in the earth. These are indeed the losers.

28. (*O disbelievers!*) How can you deny Allah. when you were dead, and He gave you life? Then He will cause you to die and then restore you to life, and you will return to Him (*to give an account*)?

(In this verse the idea of death refers to the condition of man (either all men or individuals). A soul's life passes through three stages: (1) "Creation from death (creation from nothing or creation from lifelessness); (2) Death itself; (3) Restoration to life after death. The verse also explains that individuals will be required to account for themselves on the day of judgement. In this way, incidentally, the theory of reincarnation is repudiated.)

29. He created for you all that there is on Earth; then He turned to the sky and fashioned it into seven heavens. He has full knowledge of all things.

secrets of heaven and earth, and all that you conceal and all that you reveal?

(After this, Allah "tested the angels in another way.)

34. And when We said to the angels: "Prostrate yourselves before Adam! they all prostrated themselves, except Iblis, who in his pride refused, and turned his face away, and become a disbeliever.

(After this the real test came, this time to man "Adam": whether to obey Satan.)

35. We said: "O Adam! Dwell with your wife (Eve) in paradise, and eat of its fruits to your hearts' content, whenever you will, but never approach this tree, or you shall both become transgressors.

36. But Satan caused them to swerve from it (the Garden), and expelled them from their former state. "Go down, We said, "your offspring enemies to each other. The earth will for a while provide your sustenance, and a dwelling place.

37. Then Adam received words from his Lord, and his Lord relented towards him. He is the Forgiver, the Merciful.

(There are various interpretations of the "words that Adam received from his Lord. They may have been either warnings or advice to Adam. According to Ibn Mas'ûd, the recitation of the "Subhânaka prayer before the Fâtiha is the prayer and supplication made by Adam to his Lord. Although only the name of Adam is mentioned, Eve is also included in this.)

30. Recall the time when your Lord told the Angels "I am setting a man (Adam) on the Earth as a vicegerent. They asked: "Will you put there one that will work evil and shed blood, when we praise you and sanctify Your name? He replied, "Surely I know what you know not.

(The Angels could not grasp man's function, for he is not a simple being, but God's vicegerent on the Earth, who is to live in a state of constant trial until the day of judgement.)

31. He taught Adam the names (of all things, and their usefulness), and then showed them to the Angels: "Tell me the names of these, if you are truthful.

32. "Glory be to You they replied. "We have no knowledge except that which You have given us. You alone are the Knower, the Wise.

33. Then He said: "O Adam, tell them their names; and when Adam had informed them of them, He said, "Did I not tell you that I know the

38. We said "Go down, all of you, from here; yet Guidance shall come unto you from Me; and whoever follows My guidance, no fear shall come upon him, neither shall he grieve.

39. But those who disbelieve, and reject Our revelations, shall be doomed to the Fire, where they will remain forever.

40. O Children of Israel, remember My favour which I did bestow upon you, and fulfill your Covenant with Me and I shall fulfill My covenant with you; and fear Me alone.

41. And believe in the Book *(The Holy Qur'an)* I have now sent down, which confirms the Scripture which you already possess, and be not the first to reject it. Sell not My revelations for a paltry price; and fear Me alone.

42. Do not confound truth with falsehood, nor knowingly conceal the truth.

43. Establish Salât, and pay Zakât, and bow with those who bow down.

44. How is it that you enjoin others to follow the Right Way, but forget it yourselves, though you read the Scriptures *(the Torah)*! Have you no sense?

45. Seek help in patience and with Salât; and truly it is hard save for the humble-minded.

(What is meant by patience *(sabr)* here is: fasting and salât, for these strengthen faith, teach a man to be humble, put an end to laziness and idleness, and make a man strong enough to face all other kinds of difficulties. According to the historian al-Tâbari, whenever the Prophet Muhammad faced any kind of difficulty he immediately offered two rak'âts of Salât; Ibn Abbâs used to do the same thing. The "humble-minded are those whose hearts are filled with the fear of Allah. They find no difficulty in praying, fasting, and telling the truth under all circumstances.)

46. Those *(who are humble-minded)* who know that they will meet their Lord and that to Him they will return.

47. O Children of Israel! Remember My favour that I bestowed upon you and how I preferred you above all the worlds *(for My message, during a certain historical period)*.

(For a nation to which a prophet is sent is certainly a "chosen one. A Prophet, and then his family and nation, are in an honourable position. Yet their responsibility toward the Lord is equally great, for they have been blessed with a Prophet and Scriptures sent down by Allah. The Nation of Israel, although "chosen as indicated in the above verse, because of their subsequent deviation and disobedience to Allah, were reduced to a position of disgrace, as will be explained in verse 61. The wrath of the Lord descended upon them because of their ingratitude.)

48. And guard yourselves against a day when no soul shall aid another, and no intercession or ransom, or any compensation shall be accepted from it. Nor will they be helped.

49. (*Remember*) how We delivered you from Pharaoh's people, who afflicted you with dreadful torment, slaying your sons and sparing your women. Surely that was a great trial from your Lord.

(Pharaoh is the generic name given to the ancient Egyptian rulers. Before the advent of Moses, scholars foretold that a child from the Children of Israel would destroy the throne of Pharaoh. After learning this, Pharaoh gave orders to slay the sons of the Children of Israel and spare the daughters.)

50. And (*remember when*) We parted the sea for you, and, taking you to safety, drowned Pharaoh's followers before your eyes.

(A reference to a body of water, probably the Gulf of Suez, which was parted in two so that the people of Moses could passed into safety; and the army of Pharaoh was drowned.)

51. And when We appointed for Moses forty nights (*of communing*), and then you adopted the calf, and worshipped it, and thus became wrongdoers.

(The story is told in Sûrah Tâ Hâ of Moses' visit to mount Tûr, at which time a man by the name of Sâmiri brought a golden calf, and asked people to worship it, saying, "This is your Lord. Moses forgot to tell you to worship this. Moses' brother Aaron (*Hârûn*) could not prevent this.)

52. Then after that, We pardoned you, in order that you might give thanks.

53. And when We gave Moses the Scripture and the criterion (*between right and wrong*) that you might be led a right.

54. Moses told his people: "O my people, you have wronged yourselves by taking the calf. Turn in repentance to your Creator, and kill your (*lower*) selves. That will be best for you with your Creator, and He will relent towards you. He is the Forgiving, the Merciful.

55. And when you said to Moses: "We will not believe in you until we see Allah with our own eyes, a bolt of lightning struck you while you were looking on.

56. Then We revived you after your extinction, that you might give thanks.

(The people that were struck by lightning were revived, and realized that what they had asked for was wrong. In the above verse this is described in terms of [dying] and [reviving].)

57. And We caused the clouds to shade you, and sent down upon you manna and quails, saying, "Eat of the good things We have given you. Indeed, they did not wrong Us, but they wronged themselves.

(In these verses the mischief of the Children of Israel is explained, that we may derive a lesson, and not be among those upon whom Allah's wrath descends. The best conduct of man lies in keeping himself from evil acts, being tolerant to others, not forgetting that all men are human beings; all of which he does by disobeying his own selfish desires. There are two reasons why the Jews have been condemned and put down throughout history and in all cultures. Not only are they a major cause of mischief and evil throughout the world, but they think that they are better than others. They misinterpret the fact that they were the chosen people to mean that they are superior to all others.)

58. And when We said, "Go into this town and eat where you will, to your hearts' content. Make your way through the gates by bowing down, saying: "We repent. We shall forgive you your sins and bestow abundance on the right-doers among you.

(The town mentioned in the above verse is either Jerusalem or Jericho. The right-doers (muhsinîn) are those who do their tasks thoroughly without any shortcomings. A person who has the qualities of Muhsin is praised very highly. In the famed Hadith of Gabriel, he is described as being "he who acts as though the Lord is seeing him".)

59. But the wrongdoers changed the words which had been said to them for another saying, and We sent down upon the wrongdoers wrath from Heaven as a punishment for their misdeeds.

60. And when Moses asked for water for his people, We said to him: "Strike the rock with your staff! And there gushed out therefrom twelve springs. Each tribe know its drinking-place. (We said) "Eat and drink of that which Allah has provided, and do not make mischief in the earth.

(The stone mentioned in this verse was a special one that Moses (Mûsâ) carried with him. According to some traditional accounts, Adam had brought this

stone from Heaven, and it was passed down the generations, coming finally to Moses.)

61. And when you said, "O Moses! We cannot endure only one kind of food, so call on your Lord to give us some of the varied produce of the earth, green herbs, cucumbers, garlic, lentils and onions! He said "Would you exchange that which is higher for that which is lower? Go down to the settled country. There you shall obtain what you have asked for. Shame and misery were stamped on them, and they incurred the wrath of Allah, because they disbelieved His signs and slew His prophets unjustly. That was for their disobedience and transgression.

(The Children of Israel assassinated Jethro, Zachariah, John and Jesus. No matter how intelligent they might be, they are not intelligent enough to see the Truth. And they have not used their intelligence to control their evil yearnings within themselves. And so it is that they shall never have peace on earth. As the next verse shows, however, if they are true in faith, they are acceptable to the Lord.)

62. Those who believe *(in the Qur'an and the Prophets sent before you)*, Jews, Christians, and Sabaeans; whoever believes in Allah and the Last Day and does what is right; shall be rewarded by their Lord; no fear shall come upon them, neither shall they regret.

(The name "Jew" was given to the Jews after they had repented of worshipping the golden calf. According to another narration it is a name which comes from Jahuza who was the oldest son of the prophet Jacob *(Ya'qub)*. Nasara, in turn, is the name given to Christians, perhaps because Jesus *(Isa)* came from Nazareth, although according to certain other accounts it is taken from Sûrah Al 'Imrân 52 and Sûrah al-Saff 14, where the words *"man ansârî ila'llâh* are used.)

63. *(O Children of Israel! Remember)* when We made a Covenant with you, and caused the Mount to tower above you, *(saying)*: "Hold firmly to what We have given you, and remember that which is therein, that you may guard yourselves *(against evil)*."

64. Then, after that, you turned away, and if it had not been for the grace of Allah and His mercy you would have been among the losers.

65. And you know of those of you who broke the Sabbath, how We said unto them: "You shall be detested apes.

66. We made their fate *(changing into the state of detested apes)* an example to their own generation and to those who followed them, and a lesson to the God-fearing.

(Allah set the Jews into the condition of detested apes, and later on destroyed them because of their persistence in rebellion and creating mischief on earth.)

67. And when Moses said to his people: "Allah commands you to sacrifice a cow, they replied: "Are you making fun of us? He answered: "Allah forbid that I should be among the ignorant!

(According to certain accounts, a man among the Children of Israel killed his uncle, in order to acquire his wealth. Moses attempted to identify the killer, but could not. Praying for divine aid, he received the command to sacrifice a cow. When Mûsâ announced this sacrifice to the Israelites they treated it as a jest, and attempted to find all kinds of excuses in order to evade the command. The more questions they asked, the more answers they received; finally they ran out of excuses and obeyed. The Israelites used a piece of meat taken from the sacrificed cow to strike the dead person, who was revived and then disclosed the name of his killer.)

68. They said, "Pray for us to your Lord that He make clear to us what kind of cow she shall be. Moses answered: "He says that she should neither be old nor immature but a cow between the two conditions; so do that which you are commanded.

69. Then they asked, "Pray for us to your Lord that He make clear to us of what colour she should be. Moses answered: "He says that she is a yellow cow; bright her colour, pleasing to the eye.

بِسْمِ اللّٰهِ الرَّحْمٰنِ الرَّحِيْمِ

قَالُوا ادْعُ لَنَا رَبَّكَ يُبَيِّنْ لَنَا مَا هِيَ اِنَّ الْبَقَرَ تَشَابَهَ عَلَيْنَا وَاِنَّا اِنْ شَاءَ اللّٰهُ لَمُهْتَدُوْنَ ۝ قَالَ اِنَّهٗ يَقُوْلُ اِنَّهَا بَقَرَةٌ لَّا ذَلُوْلٌ تُثِيْرُ الْاَرْضَ وَلَا تَسْقِى الْحَرْثَ مُسَلَّمَةٌ لَّا شِيَةَ فِيْهَا قَالُوا الْـٰٔنَ جِئْتَ بِالْحَقِّ فَذَبَحُوْهَا وَمَا كَادُوْا يَفْعَلُوْنَ ۝ وَاِذْ قَتَلْتُمْ نَفْسًا فَادّٰرَءْتُمْ فِيْهَا وَاللّٰهُ مُخْرِجٌ مَّا كُنْتُمْ تَكْتُمُوْنَ ۝ فَقُلْنَا اضْرِبُوْهُ بِبَعْضِهَا كَذٰلِكَ يُحْىِ اللّٰهُ الْمَوْتٰى وَيُرِيْكُمْ اٰيٰتِهٖ لَعَلَّكُمْ تَعْقِلُوْنَ ۝ ثُمَّ قَسَتْ قُلُوْبُكُمْ مِّنْ بَعْدِ ذٰلِكَ فَهِيَ كَالْحِجَارَةِ اَوْ اَشَدُّ قَسْوَةً وَاِنَّ مِنَ الْحِجَارَةِ لَمَا يَتَفَجَّرُ مِنْهُ الْاَنْهٰرُ وَاِنَّ مِنْهَا لَمَا يَشَّقَّقُ فَيَخْرُجُ مِنْهُ الْمَاءُ وَاِنَّ مِنْهَا لَمَا يَهْبِطُ مِنْ خَشْيَةِ اللّٰهِ وَمَا اللّٰهُ بِغَافِلٍ عَمَّا تَعْمَلُوْنَ ۝ اَفَتَطْمَعُوْنَ اَنْ يُّؤْمِنُوْا لَكُمْ وَقَدْ كَانَ فَرِيْقٌ مِّنْهُمْ يَسْمَعُوْنَ كَلٰمَ اللّٰهِ ثُمَّ يُحَرِّفُوْنَهٗ مِنْ بَعْدِ مَا عَقَلُوْهُ وَهُمْ يَعْلَمُوْنَ ۝ وَاِذَا لَقُوا الَّذِيْنَ اٰمَنُوْا قَالُوْا اٰمَنَّا وَاِذَا خَلَا بَعْضُهُمْ اِلٰى بَعْضٍ قَالُوْا اَتُحَدِّثُوْنَهُمْ بِمَا فَتَحَ اللّٰهُ عَلَيْكُمْ لِيُحَاجُّوْكُمْ بِهٖ عِنْدَ رَبِّكُمْ اَفَلَا تَعْقِلُوْنَ ۝

١٠

70. *(O Moses),* they said: "Pray for us to your Lord, that He make known to us the exact type of cow she should be, for to us cows look alike. And if Allah wills, we shall be rightly guided.

71. He answered, "Your Lord says: 'She should be a cow which has not been yoked, nor has ploughed the land or watered the fields, a cow free from any blemish.' "Now you have told us the truth, they answered; and they sacrificed it, although they almost did not.

72. And *(remember)* when you slew a man and began to accuse one another, but Allah made known what you concealed.

73. So We commanded "Strike *(the corpse)* with a piece of it *(the sacrificed cow).* Thus Allah restores the dead to life and shows you His signs *(the miracles given to the Prophets),* that you may understand.

74. After all this your hearts became as hard as rock, or even harder; for from some rocks rivers burst forth, while others split asunder so that water gushes from them, while others fall down for fear of Allah. And Allah is not unaware of what you do.

75. Now *(O company of believers),* do you then hope that they will believe in you, when some of them have already heard the word of Allah and knowingly perverted it, after they had understood its meaning?

(Rabbis subsequent to Moses changed the Torah, and interpreted it according to their own desires. Even today there are some Muslims who like to interpret Scripture according to their own preference. According to a *hadith* we are told that whoever interprets the Qur'an according to his own human opinion shall enter hellfire.)

76. When they *(the hypocrites)* meet with the believers they declare "We are believers. But when they are alone they say to each other: "Will you tell them what God has revealed to you, that they might contend with you before your Lord concerning it? Have you then no sense?"

77. Do they really not know that Allah has full knowledge of all they hide and all that they reveal?

78. There are illiterate men among them who are ignorant of the Scripture (the Torah), and depend on nothing but conjecture and guesswork.

(The word here rendered as "illiterate may, according to some authorities, instead denote some Arabs that were neither Jewish nor Christian.)

79. Woe to those who write the Scripture with their own hands, and then declare, "This is from Allah, in order to sell it for a paltry price. Woe unto them because of that their hands have written, and woe unto them for what they have gained (from their trade)!

(Some Jewish rabbis used to append their own interpretations to the Torah and claim that these formed part of it, and used to sell these to people in exchange for money.)

80. They also say, "The Fire is not going to touch us, and (even if it does), it will be only for a few days! Say (to them): "Did Allah make such a promise, for Allah will not break His promise, or do you attribute to Allah things you do not know?

81. No, but whoever earns evil and becomes surrounded in his sin shall be doomed to Hell, and abide therein for ever.

82. And those who believe and do good works, shall be dwellers of the Garden, and live therein forever.

83. And (remember) when We made a covenant with the Children of Israel, We said: "Serve none but Allah, show kindness to your parents and to your relatives, to the orphans and the needy; speak kindly to mankind, establish the Prayer and and pay the Zakât. But with the exception of a few, you turned away and paid no heed.

(This information about the Jews was given because they had concealed the coming of the Prophet (Muhammad) announced in the Torah. At the time of the Prophet Muhammad there were a considerable number of Jews living around Yathrib, the city which is today known as Madînah. When the expected prophet appeared among the Arabs instead of the Jews they grew wildly jealous, which is one reason why so much is told about the Jews in the Qur'an. Because of their treason, the Final Prophet was often at odds with the Jews, many of whom, convinced that no revelation could come after the Hebrew prophets, continue to bear a grudge against Muslims today.)

84. *(O Children of Israel, remember)* when We made a Covenant with you, saying: "You shall not shed blood among yourselves, nor expel one another from your homes. And you confirmed it, and were witnesses thereto.

85. But in spite of this *(the solemn promise you made),* you were slaying your own brethren and driving them out from their homes and helping others against them with sin and aggression. And when they come to you as captives you ransom them, although the expulsion *(itself)* was unlawful for you. Do you believe in one part of the Scripture and disbelieve in another? Those of you that act thus shall only be rewarded with disgrace in this world, and with the most grievous punishment on the Day of Resurrection. Allah is not unaware of what you do.

86. Such are they who buy the life of this world at the price of the hereafter. Their punishment will not be lightened, nor will they be helped.

(The above verses explain the sundry mischiefs caused by the Jews. Before Islam, the Jews of Madîna were divided into two warring groups. When they took each other prisoner they would pay an indemnity for them and take them back, explaining, when asked the reason: "This is the commandment of Allah.)

87. And assuredly We gave Moses the Scripture, and after him We sent messenger after messenger. We gave Jesus son of Mary the clear miracles *(to serve as proofs of Allah's sovereignty.)* and strengthened him with the Holy Spirit *(the Angel Gabriel).* Is it so, that whenever a Messenger whose message does not suit your desires, comes to you, you grow arrogant, denying some of them, and slaying others?

88. They *(the Jews)* say: "Our hearts are wrappings *(which are enough to preserve the divine word),* but Allah has cursed them for their unbelief. Little faith do they have.

89. And now that a Scripture from Allah confirming their own (the Torah) - though before they were asking for a victory over the disbelievers - has come they deny it, although they know it to be the truth. May Allah's curse be on disbelievers.

90. Evil is that for which they have sold their souls: to deny Allah's own revelation, grudging that He should reveal His bounty to whom He chooses from His servants! They have incurred wrath upon wrath. For disbelievers there is a humiliating punishment.

91. And when it is said to them: "Believe in what Allah has revealed, they say: "We believe in what was revealed to us (the Torah). But they deny what has since been revealed, although it is the truth, confirming that which they possess. Say (to them, O Prophet): "Why then did you kill the messengers of Allah aforetime, if you are indeed believers?"

92. Moses came to you with clear signs, but in his absence you chose the calf, and you were wrongdoers.

93. And (remember) when We made a covenant with you, and raised the Mount above you, (saying), "Hold fast to what We have given you, and hear (Our commandments), you said, "We hear and disobey. For their disbelief, they were made to drink into their hearts (the love of) the Calf. Say (to them), "Evil is that which your belief enjoins you to, if you are believers.

(Some central points are discussed in the above verses. Although the Jews knew that there was a prophet coming at some future date, they rejected Muhammad because he was not from the Jews, but from the Arabs (verse 89). They had not really believed even in Moses, although he brought many miracles, for they regressed to the worship of the "golden calf. To admonish them, the Lord made the Mount tower above them. At first they were afraid, and said: "We hear and obey ; yet soon they returned to disobedience. These stories, while ancient and specific to one people, retain their relevance to all mankind.)

94. *(O Muhammad)*, say to them, "If the abode of the Hereafter with Allah is exclusively reserved for you, and not for the rest of mankind, then long for death, if you are sincere in your claim!"

95. But they will never long for death, because of what their hands have wrought. And Allah is Aware of the wrongdoers.

(The Jews claimed that "the Hereafter is only for Jews. And yet due to their weak faith, they will never wish to die. These verses show the racist attitude of the Jews, which shall abide until the Day of Judgement.)

96. You will find that, of all mankind, they are the greediest for life; greedier, even, than the polytheists. Each one of them would love to live a thousand years, although to do so would by no means remove them from the punishment. Allah is Seer of all that they do.

97. Say *(O Muhammad, to them)*: "Who is an enemy to Gabriel? For it is he who has revealed *(this scripture)* to your heart by Allah's leave, confirming that which was *(revealed)* before it, and a guidance and glad tidings to believers.

(According to an account, a rabbi of the Arabian town of Fadak, named Abdullah ibn Suriya, argued with the Prophet Muhammad and asked him: "Who brings you the revelations? When the Prophet answered that it was the Archangel Gabriel he grew angry, and said: "He is our enemy. If somebody else brought it, we would believe. The next verse was revealed following this incident.)

98. Who is an enemy to Allah, and His Angels and His Messengers, and to Gabriel and Michael? Thus is Allah *(Himself)* an enemy to the disbelievers.

99. *(O Muhammad)*, We have sent down to you clear signs *(in the revelation)*, and none but miscreants will deny them.

100. Is it not so that whenever they make a covenant a party of them set it aside? Nay, most of them do not believe.

101. And whenever a Messenger comes to them from Allah, confirming that Scripture which they already possess, a group from among those who had received the Book threw the book of Allah behind their backs as though they knew nothing.

(According to some accounts the Jews are of four categories:

1. Those who believe in the Torah and accept it. These, who are called "the People of the Book, are few in number.

2. Those who rejected the Scriptures and caused schism and mischief. This is the group referred to in these verses.

3. The ignorant, who do not know what they are doing.

4. The hypocrites who, although feigning faith, in reality strive to work mischief in the earth.)

١٥

1. The witchcraft of the Chaldeaens, who worshipped the stars, which, they held, direct the universe. Both good and evil comes from them, and when the forces of the sky are united with the forces of the earth miracles occur. In order to deliver a message to these people, the patriarch Abraham was sent by God to tell them the truth.

2. The witchcraft that depends on quasi-spiritualist forces. According to the exponents of this type, man can eliminate the spirit, create, kill, and bring back to life, and by spiritualist means effect certain changes in the human body.

3. Witchcraft that depends for its operation on mediums and spiritual beings such as the jinns.

4. Prestidigitation.

The Islamic scholars are unanimously agreed that the first and the second group are to be reckoned forms of disbelief. However, as long as a man believes in Allah as the sole Creator, there can sometimes be justification for learning certain categories of magic. Magical techniques were current among the Jews to a considerable extent, and because of this many people believed that the Prophet Solomon *(Sulaymân)* was a great magician, whose arts aided him to govern his kingdom, and also the realm of the animals and jinn. When Solomon was recognized as a prophet in the Qur'an, the Jews said "Muhammad thinks Solomon was a Prophet, but he was not, he was a magician.)

102. They followed that which the devils had falsely attributed to the kingdom of Solomon. Yet Solomon did not disbelieve, but the devils disbelieved, teaching people magic, and that which was sent down to Hârût and Mârût, the two angels at Babylon. Nor did they *(the two angels)* teach it to anyone until they had said; "We are only a temptation, therefore do not disbelieve *(in Allah's guidance)*. And from these two, people learn that by which they cause division between man and wife; but they injure no-one thereby save by Allah's leave. And they learn that which harms them, and profits them not. And surely they do know that he who traffics therein will have no *(happy)* portion in the Hereafter; and surely evil is the price for which they sell their souls, if they but knew.

(The ancient clans used to believe in witchcraft, by means of which their magicians used to deceive the masses.

Several kinds of witchcraft. exist:

103. And if they had believed in Allah and protected themselves from evil, a recompense from Allah would have been better, if they had but known.

104. *(O believers!)* do not say: *"Râ'inâ,* but say *"Unzurnâ* and listen; and for the disbelievers there is a painful punishment.

(*Râ'inâ,* meaning "look at us , could easily be distorted by enemies to give a derisory sense. Hence the believers were counselled to use a form which could not be thus distorted.)

105. *(O Believers!)* Neither the disbelievers among the people of the Book nor the polytheists would like it that there should be sent down to you any good thing from your Lord. But Allah chooses for His mercy whom He Wills, and Allah is of tremendous favour.

106. If We abrogate any verse or cause it to be forgotten, We replace it by a better or a similar one. Do you not know that Allah has power over all things?

(When a verse is revealed to cancel out an earlier provision of revelation, this is called *naskh.*, or "abrogation. Allah has over the centuries sent new prophets and books to fulfill the needs of a world whose culture and civilisation is in constant change. The verses abrogated within the Qur'anic text itself, however, are very few in number.)

107. Do you not know that it is to Allah that the sovereignty of the heavens and the earth belongs, and that there is none besides Him to protect or help you?

108. Or would you then question your Prophet as Moses was once questioned? He who changes belief for disbelief surely strays from the right path.

109. Many of the People of the Book wish through their envy to lead you back to disbelief, now that you have embraced faith and the truth has become manifest to them. Forgive and be indulgent (*towards them*), until Allah makes known His will. He has power over all things.

110. Establish the Prayer, and pay Zakât, and whatever good you send before (*you*) for our souls, you will find it with Allah. He is Watcher over all your actions.

111. And they say, "None will enter the Garden unless he be a Jew or a Christian. These are their own desires. Bring your proof (*of what you state*), if you are truthful.

112. Whoever surrenders himself to Allah, while doing good, shall receive his reward from his Lord, and no fear shall come upon him, neither shall he grieve.

(To be an obedient servant to the Lord one needs to be "*Muhsin* . a doer of good: just worshipping the Lord is not enough for salvation. A *muhsin* is a person who does everything for the sake of Allah, and has no fear of anyone else. Whatever he does, he does in the most satisfactory way. It is told that a group of Christian Arabs once came to visit the Prophet. Following a debate, the following verses were revealed.)

113. The Jews say the Christians are misguided; and the Christians say it is the Jews who are misguided; although both are readers of the Scripture. Even thus speak those who know not. Allah will judge between them on the Day of Resurrection concerning that wherein they differ.

114. Who does greater wrong than he who forbids the approach to Allah's sanctuaries, and seeks to destroy them, and forbid His name to be mentioned in them? As for such people, they do not deserve to enter the place of worship unless it be with fear in their hearts. They will be held to shame in this world, and a painful punishment in the Hereafter shall be theirs.

(According to the Muslim scholars, the "sanctuaries referred to here are: al-Masjid al-Haram in Makka, and al-Masjid al-Aqsa in Jerusalem. The Jews, the Christians and the polytheists have all tried to prevent the Muslims from using them. Instead of doing this, the Jews, Christians, and polytheists should be entering the sanctuaries with fear of Allah; thus shall the divine wrath not fall upon them.)

115. To Allah belongs the East and the West. Whichever way you turn, there is the face of Allah. Allah is All-Embracing, and Allah is All-Knowing.

(One reason why every Muslim turns his face in one direction is to establish unity in worshipping Allah; Who, nonetheless, is present at all times and locations.)

116. They say: "Allah has taken a son . Allah is far above such things! To Him belongs all that is in the heavens and on the earth. All things are subservient to Him.

(The Jews claimed that Uzair was the "son of God, the Christians made the same claim for Jesus, while the polytheists claimed that the angels are the daughters of God. Yet it takes only a little intelligence to realise that He is transcendant, far above such things.)

117. Originator of the heavens and the earth: when He decrees a thing, He merely says "Be! - and it is.

(When Allah wishes something, He merely says "Be! and it appears, all at the time and place decreed in His wisdom.)

118. And those who have no knowledge say, "Why does Allah not speak to us, or give us a sign? The people before them demanded the same thing. Their hearts are similar. We have already shown clear signs to those whose faith is firm.

119. We have sent you *(O Muhammad)* with the truth, and as a bringer of glad tidings and a warning. You shall not be questioned about the people of the Flame.

120. Neither the Christians nor the Jews will be pleased with you until you follow their faith. Say, "the guidance of Allah is the (only) guidance. And if, after all the knowledge you have received, you yield to their desires, there shall be none to help or protect you from the wrath of Allah.

(Neither the Jews nor the Christians can be real friends to Muslims. Both the Jews and Christians were happy to exploit the Muslim countries for centuries.)

121. Those to whom We have given the Scripture, and who read it the way it should be read, truly believe in it. And those who deny it, they are the true losers.

(This verse was revealed when a certain Jewish scholar named Abdullâh ibn Salâm, together with his friends, believed in the Qur'an and testified to it. According to another account, it refers to a group of forty People of the Book who came from Ethiopia under the leadership of Ja'far ibn Abî Tâlib, having accepted Islam.)

122. O Children of Israel! Remember that I have bestowed favours on you and preferred you above all the other worlds (in that you have received the divine message so frequently).

123. And guard yourselves against a day when no soul will avail against another, nor shall compensation be accepted from it, nor will intercession be of use to it, nor will they be helped.

(Intercession depends on certain conditions, the most important of which is to have faith in God's unity and justice.)

124. And (remember) when his Lord tried Abraham with certain words (commandments), and he fulfilled them. He said "I have appointed you a leader of mankind. Abraham asked "And of my descendants? He answered, "My covenant does not extend to the transgressors.

125. And we made the House (the Holy Ka'ba at Makka) a place of assembly for mankind and a place of safety, (saying):"Adopt the place where Abraham stood, as a place of worship. And We imposed a duty upon Abraham and Ishmael to purify Our house for those who walk around and those who meditate in it, and those who bow down and prostrate.

126. And when Abraham prayed: "Make this city a city of peace, and bestow fruits upon its people, such of them as believe in Allah and the Last Day , He answered: "As for those who disbelieve, I shall leave them in contentment for a while, then I shall compel them to the punishment of the Fire; and that is the worst abode.

(In this world both believers and disbelievers have their portion of the blessings of this world, which do not depend on being religious or having a certain creed. Those who use their wealth and other blessings that Allah has bestowed on them in what is good and just, shall be successful both in this world and the Hereafter. If men do not use their wealth and blessings in the right way, they are gone astray, and will be losers both in this world and the Hereafter.)

127. And when Abraham and Ishmael were raising the foundations of the house, (they prayed): "Our Lord! Accept from us (this act); You are indeed the All-Hearing, the All-Knowing.

(The following account has come down to us about the building of the Ka'ba. When Adam and Eve were expelled from Heaven they met each other at the great plain known as Arafât, and walked towards the west, until they came to the valley-floor where the present Ka'ba is located. Adam endeavoured to thank his Lord, desiring to have a place similar to the column of light which was given to him to make walk around (tawaf). He thus elected to build a simple building of four walls, setting a black stone in one corner of this building. Today the black stone, which remains from the original structure of Adam, is called "al-Hajar al-Aswad. After the great Deluge of the prophet Noah (Nûh), this building was lost beneath the sands. The Prophet Abraham, following a commandment from his Lord, left his bondsmaid Hagar with son Ishmael at the Ka'ba. Abraham and Ismael together dug the sands, and found the foundation of the original edifice, and built the Ka'ba upon it. The Qur'anic reference to Abraham and Ishmael's "raising the foundation of the House denotes the building of the present day Ka'ba.)

128. O our Lord! Make us submitters to You! And raise from among our offspring a community which will be submitters to You. Show us our ways of worship, and relent towards us. You are indeed the Forgiving, the Merciful.

129. Our Lord! And raise up from among them a Messenger who shall recite Your revelations to them and teach them the Scriptures and the wisdom, and purify them (or: make them grow). You are the Powerful, the Wise.

130. Who but a foolish man would renounce the faith of Abraham? We chose him in the world, and in the Hereafter he is among the righteous.

131. When his Lord said to him, "Surrender! he responded, "I have surrendered to the Lord of the Worlds.

132. Abraham enjoined the same upon his children, and so did Jacob: "O my children, Allah has chosen for you the true faith (of Islam), so do not die except in the faith (of Islam)."

133. Or were you present when death came to Jacob? He said to his sons, "What will you worship when I am gone? They answered: "We shall worship your God and the God of your forefathers Abraham, Ishmael and Isaac: the one (true) God. To him we are submitted."

134. Those are a people who have passed away. Theirs was what they did, and yours is what you do. You will not be questioned about their actions.

135. They say: "Be Jews or Christians, and you will be rightly-guided. Say (*O Muhammad*): rather the religion of Abraham, the upright, and he was not of the idolators."

("Upright (*hanîf*) means following the true and ancient Faith which is free of all superstition and idolatry.)

136. Say (*O Muslims*): "We believe in Allah and that which is revealed to us, and in what was revealed to Abraham, Ishmael, Isaac, Jacob, and the tribes; to Moses and Jesus and the (*other*) prophets by their Lord. We make no distinction between any of them, and to Allah we have surrendered ourselves.

(The "tribes (*asbât*) referred to here are the descendants of the prophet Jacob).

137. If they believe in the likes of what you believe, they shall be rightly-guided; yet if they reject it, they shall surely be in schism. Allah will suffice you *(for defence)* against them. He is the Hearer, the Knower.

138. (*We take our*) colour from Allah; and who is better than Allah at colouring? Allah it is that we worship.

(According to the commentary of al-Zamakhsharî, some Christians used to baptise their new-born babies with yellow coloured water, believing this to be a process of purification. So the Muslims in this verse are commanded to say, "We take our colour from Allah, meaning that involuntary rites can be of no avail, and that the only "colouring possible for the soul is that induced by purity and the conscious recovery of man's primordial nature.)

139. Say (*to the people of the Book)*: "Do you dispute with us concerning Allah, when He is our Lord and your Lord? We are responsible for our works and you for yours. We look to Him alone."

140. Or do you say that Abraham, Ishmael, Isaac, Jacob, and the Tribes, were Jews or Christians? Do you know better, or does Allah? Who is more unjust than the man who hides a testimony which he has received from Allah? Allah is not unaware of what you do.

(The truth that the Jews and the Christians were hiding was the fact that the prophet Abraham was true in religion and worshipped one Almighty God. And they also hid the fact that the prophet Muhammad was also true in religion, being a *Hanîf* (see above, to verse 135).)

141. Those are a people who have passed away; theirs is that which they earned and yours that which you earn. And you will not be asked of what they used to do.

(After the Migration (*hijra*) of the prophet Muhammad and his companions from Makka to Madîna, the Muslims faced Jerusalem for about sixteen or seventeen months to worship. This fact annoyed the Jews, who started saying that the Prophet did not know which way to face, and thus had accepted the guidance of the Jews. Then the prophet prayed to Allah that his own direction of prayer (*qibla*) might be granted him. After this, the commandment of Allah came, the following verse indicating that the Muslim community should now turn to face the Holy Ka'ba. Yet after this commandment was given, the Jews and the hypocrites still continued to talk, as is narrated below.)

142. The foolish among the people will ask: "What has made them change their *Qibla*? Say: "To Allah belongs the east and the west. He guides whom He will to a straight path.

143. Thus have We made you a middle nation (*umma*), so that you may be witnesses against mankind, and that the Messenger may be a witness against you. And we decreed your former *Qibla (Jerusalem)* only so that We might know the Messenger's true followers and those who would turn their backs to him. It was indeed a (*hard*) test, except for those whom Allah guided. He would not cause your faith to be in vain. He is Kind and Merciful to mankind.

(According to tradition, it is said that many nations will deny the fact that their prophets ever conveyed a divine message. Allah will ask the prophets for "proof that they had indeed delivered the messages with which they had been entrusted. When the Nation of Muhammad is called, they will testify that he did indeed convey the message.)

144. *(O Muhammad!)* We have seen turn your face towards heaven *(hoping for guidance from the Lord)*. We will surely turn you towards a *Qibla* that will please you. Turn towards the Inviolable Sanctuary (*al-Masjid al-Haram in Makka*); and wherever you may be, turn your faces towards it. Those to whom the Scriptures were given know this to be the truth from their Lord. And Allah is not unaware of what they do.

145. But even if you gave those who have received the Scriptures every sign, they would not follow your *Qibla*, nor would you follow theirs; nor will they follow each other's *Qibla*. If, after all the knowledge you have been given you follow their desires, then you would surely become amongst the evil-doers.

(In this verse the stubbornness of the Jews and Christians is recalled. The Holy Prophet Muhammad did not fulfill their desires; and even if he had acceded to them, they would still have been displeased. So he was ordered by the Lord not to follow their desires, lest he fall into some transgression. Their desires were of the sort that are unregulated by faith, and as such were uncontrolled and dangerous.)

146. These to whom We gave the Scriptures know it (*the Prophet, or the Qur'an*) as well as they know their own sons. But some of them knowingly conceal the truth.

(The Jews and Christians had read in their scriptures that another Prophet would someday come, possessed of specific qualities by which he could be recognised. This awareness was passed on from generation to generation, and the advent of the new Messenger was eagerly awaited. However, when he finally appeared as a poor Arab orphan they immediately rejected him, because of snobbery and racism. In reality many of them were certain that he was the true Prophet foretold in their books. Yet so great was their pride and stubbornness that they swerved aside.)

147. This is the truth from your Lord; therefore do not be of those who doubt.

148. Each one has a goal toward which he turns; so vie with one another in good works. Wherever you may be, Allah will bring you all together. Allah is over all things. Powerful.

149. So from whencesoever you depart, turn your face towards the Inviolable Sanctuary. This is surely the Truth from your Lord. Allah is not unaware of what you do.

150. From whencesoever you depart, face towards the Inviolable Sanctuary. And wherever you are (*O Muslims*), face towards

it (*when you pray*), so that men may have no argument against you, except the unjust - fear them not, but fear Me! - so that I may complete my favour upon you, and that you may be rightly-guided.

151. Thus We have sent to you a Messenger from among you, who will recite to you Our signs (*revelations*) and purify you (*or: cause you to grow*), who will teach you the Scripture and wisdom, and teach you that of which you have no knowledge.

152. Remember Me; and I will remember you. Give thanks to Me and deny Me not.

153. O Believers, seek help in steadfastness and in the Prayer. Allah is with those that are steadfast.

(Such are the two best weapons against his "*nafs* : the lower soul which urges man towards immediate gratification.)

soul will eventually taste death, the Qur'an reminds us. The person who understands and learns from this is an intelligent believer, should he proceed to act in accordance with his knowledge.)

158. As-Safâ and al-Marwa are among the sacred indications of Allah. It shall be no sin for him who is on Hajj or Umra to the House (*the Ka'ba*) should he walk between them. He that does good of his own volition; truly Allah is Responsive, Aware.

(al-Safâ and al-Marwa are two small hills to the eastern side of the Ennobled Ka'ba. When Hagar was searching for water for her child, she ran between these two hills seven times. Today, those who go to Makka to perform Hajj and Umra (the Greater and Lesser Pilgrimages) perform the rite of "*sa'y* between these two hills. In this text we are specifically told that there is no sin in running between the two hills, although previously there were two idols standing on both hills during the *Jâhiliyya* (the Age of Ignorance in Arabia before Islam). Certain people still had doubts about this tradition, forgetting its origin, until this verse came.)

159. Those that hide the clear proofs and the guidance We have revealed, after We have proclaimed them in the Scriptures, shall be cursed by Allah, and by those who have the power to curse.

160. Except those that repent and amend and make known (*the truth*). These it is towards whom I relent. I am the Relenting, the Merciful.

161. As for those who disbelieve, and die as disbelievers, they shall incur the curse of Allah, and of the angels, and of all mankind.

162. Under (*this condemnation*) they shall remain forever; their punishment shall not be lightened, nor shall they be reprieved.

163. Your God is One God; there is no god but Him. He is the Compassionate, the Merciful.

154. And do not say that those who were slain in the cause of Allah are dead; rather, they are alive; but you do not perceive (*their life*).

155. We shall surely test you with fear and hunger, and loss of property and lives and crops; but give glad tidings to the steadfast.

156. Who say, when a misfortune comes to them: "We belong to Allah, and to Him we shall return.

157. On such will be blessings from their Lord and mercy; and such are the rightly- guided.

(These verses concern the fourteen people who were martyred at the Battle of Badr, which was the first major clash between the aggressive polytheists of Makka and the new Muslim community, following the emigration to Madîna the Radiant. The martyrs are not dead, for their spirits live among us. This is also a proof-text for punishment or reward in the grave. Fear, hunger, famine, poverty, sickness, death of loved ones. these are all tests for us, to purify our souls and to see how we conduct ourselves. These are the common problems of mankind that none of us can avoid. Every

(In the above verses we have been told how man can be ungrateful to his Lord and how awful his end will be. The next verses will explain how a man can use his intelligence to obey Him, and can learn lessons from the natural phenomena he observes around him. Those who think clearly and logically can work out the truth and come to know the Maker.)

164. In the creation of the heavens and the earth; in the alternation of night and day; in the sailing of the ships through the ocean for the benefit of mankind; in the water which Allah sends down from the sky and with which He revives the earth after its death, and dispersing over it all kinds of beasts; in the ordinance of the winds and clouds that are driven between earth and sky: are signs for people who have sense.

165. Yet there are some who set up equals with Allah and adore them with the adoration due to Allah. Those who believe are stauncher in love of Allah. If only the unrighteous could see (on the day) when they behold the punishment, that might is His alone, and that Allah is severe in punishment!

166. Then would those who are followed declare themselves innocent of those who follow

(them); they would see the punishment, and all that unites them will be broken asunder.

167. Those who followed (them) will say: "Would that we were given a chance to return (to life in the world); then we would disown them even as they have disowned us (since we are in Hell). Thus will Allah show them their own deeds as anguish for them, and they will not emerge from the Fire.

168. O mankind! Eat of that which is lawful and clean in the earth, and follow not the footsteps of the devil, for he is indeed an open enemy to you.

169. He enjoins upon you evil and indecency, and to say concerning Allah that which you know not.

(The Evil One arouses and aggravates evil thoughts and desires in man, and makes him love them. Hazrat Abû Bakr has remarked that "The greatest of men is he who disobeys his own self-oriented desires.)

170. And when it was said to them: "Follow what Allah has sent down , they said: "We will follow that wherein we found our forefathers. What! Even if their forefathers comprehended nothing, nor were they guided?

171. The condition of the disbelievers (in relation to the messenger) is the condition of the (shepherd) who calls on (beasts) that can hear nothing except a shout and a cry. They are deaf, dumb, blind, therefore they do not understand.

(In these verses Allah condemns those who follow the traditions of their forefathers blindly. In this connection more than any other, those who can think logically should use their own wisdom and intelligence.)

172. O you who believe! Eat of the good and clean things which We have provided for you, and be grateful to Allah, if it is He whom you worship.

173. He has only forbidden you carrion, blood, and swine, and that which has been consecrated (to the name of) any other than Allah. But he who is driven by necessity, neither craving nor transgressing, it is no sin for him. For Allah is Forgiving, Merciful.

(Since "Islam is the religion of ease", absolute necessity renders permissible certain things which are normally forbidden, for as long as such conditions continue. Hence a man may eat of swine-flesh or other impurities if he will otherwise be in real danger of starvation; for "Allah is Forgiving, Merciful .)

174. Those who conceal any part of the Scripture which Allah has sent down and barter it for a paltry price, simply fill their bellies with fire. Allah will not speak to them on the Day of Resurrection, nor will He purify them (or: make them grow). Theirs will be a painful torment.

(The Rabbis of the Jewish tribes settled in Arabia concealed the signs of the anticipated prophet Muhammad which are mentioned in their scriptures, afraid that their authority would be undermined by the arrival of a new Prophet.)

175. Those are they who purchase error at the price of guidance, and torment at the price of pardon. How steadfast they are in their efforts to reach the Fire!

176. That is because Allah had revealed the Scripture with the truth. And those who seek differences in the Scriptures are in open schism.

(Those who seek to make changes in the Holy Qur'an and try to advance interpretations which accord with their own preferences without the benefit of any solid evidence or proof cause themselves to fall into schism.)

177. Righteousness is not whether you turn your faces to the East or to the West; but righteous is he who believes in Allah and the Last Day and the angels and the Scripture and the Prophets; and gives his wealth for the love of Allah to relatives, orphans and the needy, and the wayfarer, and those who ask, and for (*the liberation of*) slaves; and establish the Prayer and pay the Zakât; and those who keep their pledges when they make them, and show patience in hardship and adversity, and the time of distress. Such are the true believers; and such are the Godfearing.

178. O you who believe! The law of retribution is prescribed for you in the matter of the murdered; the freeman for the freeman, the slave for the slave, and the female for the female. For him who is forgiven somewhat by his (*injured*) brother, prosecution shall be according to usage, and payment to him in kindness. This is an alleviation and a mercy from your Lord. He who transgresses after this shall have a painful doom.

(All religions unanimously agree that murder is a mortal sin. Islam tries to eradicate the conditions which stimulate crimes, endeavoring to perfect man by strengthening his faith, improving his worship and nurturing his innate ethical values, which are founded on a sense of accountability to Allah. Yet crimes will always exist in society, and thus He provides legislation to deal with it, for universal pardon provides no deterrent. Those relatives who under certain circumstances may prefer the payment in the form of a fine, for instance, instead of the death penalty, are given the right to request the comminution of the sentence.)

179. In (*this law of*) retribution there is life for you, O people of understanding, that perhaps you shall be Godfearing.

(That "there is life for you here is an important point. Through this legislation, not only do relatives exercise the right to leniency, but by establishing a major deterrent, other murders are prevented, thereby "giving life .)

180. It is prescribed for you, when one of you approaches death, if he leaves wealth, that he bequeath it to parents and near relatives according to reasonable usage. This is a duty for all who fear Allah.

181. And those who change (*the will*) after they have heard it, the sin thereof is only upon those who change it. Assuredly, Allah hears and knows all things.

182. And he who fears from a testator some unjust or sinful clause, and makes peace between the parties incurs no guilt. Allah is Forgiving, Merciful.

(In the following verses, the text turns to the obligatory fast to be observed during the sacred month of Ramadan. Fasting is one of the five pillars of Islam. One of the greatest virtues of this month is that it contains a night called the Lailat al-Qadr. The "Night of Power , or the "Night of Destiny . In this night the Holy Qur'an began to be sent down from al-Lawh al-Mahfuz to Bayt al-'Izza. In the cave of Hira, the Prophet, upon whom be blessings and peace, received the first verse. Aware of the significance of this time, Muslims commemmorate it with fasting, good works, and special prayers.)

183. O you who believe! Fasting is prescribed for you, as it was prescribed for those who came before you; that you will perhaps guard yourselves (against evil).

(Here the function and benefit of fasting is explained: by cutting ourselves off from our worldly requirements for a period, our awareness of our dependance on Allah increases, and we are more able to guard ourselves against evil.)

184. (Fast) a certain number of days, but if any one of you is ill or an a journey, let him (break his fast, and) fast the same number of days later on. And for those who can afford it there is a ransom: the feeding of a man in need. But he that does good of his own accord, it is better for him, but to fast is better for you, if you did but know.

185. The month of Ramadan in which the Qur'an was revealed, a guidance for mankind, (a book of) clear proofs of guidance and the criterion (distinguishing right from wrong). Therefore whoever of you is present in that month let him fast; but he who is ill or on a journey shall fast (a same) number of days later on. Allah desires for you ease; He desires not hardship for you; and (He desires) that you should complete the period, and that you should magnify Allah for giving you His guidance, and that perhaps you will be thankful.

(There is no difficulty in the religion of Islam. While Allah has ordained an obligatory fast for men and women, those who are ill or on a journey for a period of time, which might render the fast difficult, are excused from fasting, and permitted to make up an equivalent number of days at some later point in the year. Those who are unable to fast at all because of old age or chronic illness can feed the poor instead, if they can afford it.)

186. When My servants question you about Me, (tell them) I am surely near. I answer the prayer of the suppliant when he prays to Me; therefore let them hear My call and put their trust in Me, that they may be rightly guided.

(The Prophet, peace be upon him, was once asked: "Is our Lord close to us or far away? If He is close we will whisper in our prayers; while if He is far away then we should shout! A verse was thus revealed explaining that Allah promises to fulfill the prayers of those who believe and obey, and that He, being Omnipotent, can hear them even if they pray quietly. Prayers will surely be accepted by Him, as He promises, of those who are believers and His good servants.)

187. It is made lawful for you to go unto your wives (*in sexual relations*) on the night of the fast. They are a garment for you and you are a garment for them. Allah is aware that you were deceiving yourselves in this respect, and He has turned in mercy toward you and pardoned you. Therefore you may now have intercourse with them and seek what Allah has ordained for you. Eat and drink until the white thread becomes distinct to you from the black thread of the dawn. Then resume the fast till nightfall, and do not approach them, but stay at your devotions in the mosques. These are the limits set by Allah, so do not approach them. Thus He makes known His revelations to mankind, that they may guard themselves (*against evil*).

(In the early days of Islam, the Muslims held to a strict rule of fasting from the evening meal of one day until the evening meal of the next. If they fell asleep before they had taken their meal they thought it necessary to abstain from it, with the result that some people fainted from hunger. Intercourse with their wives had been similarly restricted. By the revelation of this verse, the present, definitive practice of fasting from first light (as defined by the ability to tell between a white and black thread) until sundown, was established.)

188. Do not eat up one another's property among yourselves by unjust means, nor bribe with it the judges in order that you may knowingly and wrongfully deprive others of their possessions.

189. They question you (*O Muhammad*) about the (*phases of*) the moon. Say: "They are seasons fixed for mankind and for the pilgrimage. And it is not righteousness that you go to dwellings by the backs thereof (*as is the pagan custom*). The righteous man is he who fears Allah. Enter houses by their doors, and fear Allah, so that you may prosper.

(The Blessed Prophet was asked why the moon begins as a very thin crescent, gradually becomes full, and then gradually returns to a thin crescent again. They were answered with the above verse. The movements of the moon determine the lunar calendar, as well as determining the pilgrimage days. The verse also contains a condemnation of the pagan Arab custom by which, when they were in their "*Ihram* (the state of consecration required for the Makka pilgrimage) they would avoid entering their houses by the front door upon their return. The provision has a more general application, defining the need to observe proper manners, and, metaphorically, to carry out one's affairs in a straightforward and open fashion)

190. Fight for the sake of Allah those that who fight against you, but do not attack them first. Allah does not love the aggressors.

(Here the general Islamic commandment about armed combat is presented. Wars of aggression are specifically forbidden, but to fight in self-defence is not only allowable, but is an obligation, to prevent the occurrence of tumult and persecution in the land.)

191. Kill them wherever you find them *(those who fight against you); drive them out of the places from which they drove you, for tumult and persecution are worse than killing. But do not fight them at the Inviolable Sanctuary (al-Masjid al-Harâm) until they first attack you there, but if they attack you (there), then kill them. Such is the reward of the disbelievers.*

192. But if they desist, then *(know that)* Allah is Forgiving, Merciful.

193. And fight them until tumult and persecution are no more, and religion is for Allah. But if they desist, then let there be no hostility except against the evil-doers.

194. A sacred month for a sacred month, and sacred things *(too are subject to)* reciprocity. If anyone attacks you, attack him with the like of that with which he attacked you. And fear Allah, and know that Allah is with the Godfearing.

(In the 6th year of the Muslim calendar, our Blessed Prophet left Madîna for Makka with the intention of performing the Lesser Pilgrimage (*'Umra*), but his path was blocked by the pagans at a place called Hudaibiya. There were bitter arguments there, but in the end, the Treaty of Hudaibiya was signed. According to the articles of this Treaty, the Muslims in that year were to return back to Madîna without performing the *'Umra*, but the following year in the same sacred month they were to be permitted to perform it. The Pagans thought this a great success, although the Muslims were successful in visiting the Inviolable Sanctuary the following year. Hence the establishment of the rule of the "sacred month for the sacred month . Sacred things too are subject to reciprocity.)

195. Spend generously for the cause of Allah, and do not cast yourselves into destruction by your own hands. And know that Allah loves the doers of good.

(The "doers of good in the above verse are those who are honest, and accomplish their labours to perfection. According to a hadith, the Prophet Muhammad was asked to define this quality, known as "*ihsan* , and he replied that it was "to worship God as though you saw Him, and, if you do not see him, still, He sees you . Social justice and justice in general are also included in the concept.)

196. Perform the Greater and Lesser Pilgrimage *(Hajj and 'Umra)* for Allah. If you are prevented, then send such offerings as you can afford. And do not shave your heads until the offerings have reached their destination. But whoever among you is ill or has an ailment of the head must pay a ransom, either by fasting or by almsgiving, or by offering a sacrifice. And if you are in safety, then whosoever combines the *'Umra* with the *Hajj (by relaxing the state of consecration in between)* must offer such offerings as he can afford; but if he cannot find *(such offerings)* then let him fast three days while he is on pilgrimage and seven days when he has returned; that is, ten in all. That is for him whose family are not present *(residents nearby)* at the Inviolable Sanctuary. And fear Allah; and know that Allah is severe in punishment.

197. The pilgrimage is (in) the appointed months. Whoever intends to perform it therein must abstain from sexual intercourse, obscene language, abuse and angry conversation while on the pilgrimage. And whatever good you do, Allah knows it. So make provisions for yourselves (for the journey to the hereafter), and the best provision is piety (fear of Allah and observance of His law); therefore keep your duty to Me, O people of understanding!

(The old pagan Arabs used to hold street bazaars during the pilgrimage season, where all kinds of merchandise would be displayed. Since the affairs of these bazaars were conducted according to the usages of the pagan Arabs as these prevailed before Islam, the Muslims considered them unlawful. But Allah legalised the practice of sale during the Pilgrimage in the following verse.)

198. It is no sin for you to seek the bounty of your Lord (by trading during the Hajj season). When you come hastening from 'Arafât with the multitude, remember Allah at the Sacred Monument. Remember Him that gave you guidance, although before you were of those gone astray.

('Arafât and the Sacred Monument are two of the main ritual sites of the Pilgrimage ceremonies. Like the other forms of worship, Hajj also benefits society in numerous ways, for instance:

1. The pilgrimage dress, or 'Ihram', comprising two seamless pieces of cloth, symbolises the fact that the pilgrims have left behind all worldly things, their possessions, title, position, nobility and the like, and stand equal before Him Who created them equal.

2. The Ihram dress resembles the shroud in which the dead are interred. And the mass gathering at the plain of 'Arafât recalls the Day of Judgement.

3. People from all over the world, of every race and culture, gather together in order to exchange both material and spiritual things, and to seek solutions to their common problems. Thus are the divergences between mankind reduced.)

199. Then hasten on from the place whence the multitude hastens onward, and ask forgiveness of Allah. Allah is Forgiving, Merciful.

200. And when you have completed your sacred rites, then (continue to) remember Allah as you remember your forefathers, or even more. Among mankind there are some who say: "Our Lord! Give us what is good in this world! and in the Hereafter they have no share.

201. And there are others who say: "Lord! Give us what is good in this world and in the Hereafter; and keep us from the fire of Hell!

202. For them there is an abundant reward which they have earned. Assuredly, Allah is Swift at reckoning.

203. Remember Allah on the Appointed Days (*the three days which close the Hajj*). Whoever hastens (*his departure*) on the second day, there is no sin upon him. And whoever delays, there is no sin for him; for him who fears Allah. Have fear of Allah, then, and know that you will be gathered unto Him.

(The following three verses were revealed in connection with a man named al-Ahnas ibn Shurayk. Although a handsome and well-spoken man, al-Ahnas was a hypocrite. He used to come to visit the Prophet like a Muslim and speak politely, yet he was feigning his faith, his heart being filled with poison and conniving. His sole purpose was to harm the Muslims. One should not be deceived by the aspect and words of a man, but should investigate his case before entrusting him with important affairs.)

204. There are some men whose conversation on the life of this world pleases you (*O Muhammad*) and they call on Allah to vouch for that which is in their hearts; whereas they are the most rigid of opponents.

205. And when he turned away (*from you*) his effort in the land is to make mischief therein, and to destroy the crops and the cattle; and Allah does not love mischief.

206. When it is said to him, "Have fear of Allah, pride takes him into sin. Hell shall be enough for him, an evil resting-place.

207. But there are others who would give away their lives and their belongings in order to seek the pleasure of Allah. Allah is Compassionate to His servants.

(The above verse was sent down because of a man named Suhayb ibn Sinân ar-Rûmî. The pagans of Makka had captured and persecuted this man, and attempted to make him renounce Islam. Suhayb told his persecutors that he was an old man possessed of some wealth, and that if he gave them all he owned, his continuing allegiance to Islam would not harm them. The pagans agreed to this, and released him. When he was on his way to Madîna the above verse was revealed. When Hazrat Abû Bakr saw him he greeted him by remarking, "The trade that you have completed will bring you good profits! Suhayb then quoted the above verse to him.)

208. O you who believe! Submit, all of you, to Allah, and do not walk in Satan's footsteps; assuredly he is an open enemy to you.

209. If you slide back after the clear signs have come to you, then know that Allah is Mighty, Wise.

210. Are they waiting for anything other than Allah's coming to them in the shadow of a cloud with all the angels, and the question is (*thus*) settled? To Allah shall all things return.

211. Ask the Children of Israel how many clear signs We gave them! But he who alters Allah's blessing after it has reached him: assuredly Allah is severe in punishment.

212. For the disbelievers the life of this world is adorned; and thus they mock at believers. Yet those that fear Allah will be above them on the Day of Judgement. Allah gives without measure to whomsoever He will.

(Abû Jahl, a pagan aristocrat of Makka, together with his friends, mocked the believers, and in this connection the above verse was revealed. But the verse has a more universal application, decrying those who, not having tasted the sweetness of faith, find the things of this base world delightful.)

213. Mankind were once one nation. And Allah sent to them Prophets, to give them good news and warning, and with them He sent down the Scripture with the truth, that it might judge the disputes between mankind. And only those to whom *(the Scripture)* was given differed concerning it, after clear signs had come to them, through hatred of one another. And Allah by His will guided those who believed to the truth of what they had disputed. Allah guides whom He will to a straight path.

(The human race, the descendants of the Prophet Adam, was once united. As time passed, however, they fell into dispute, and the Prophets were sent to end their differences.)

214. Or do you think that you will enter the Garden while untouched by the like of (*the suffering which was endured by*) those who were before you? Affliction and adversity befell them, and they were shaken as though with an earthquake, until the Messenger and those who believed along with him said: "When will the

help of Allah come? Assuredly, the help of Allah is near.

(The way to success for Muslims both in this world and in the next is to strive with faith and enthusiasm, to endure all kind of difficulties, never to feel defeated, and always to prefer spiritual pleasures over the pleasures and self-indulgences constantly whispered by Satan and the lower self.

According to some narrations the above verse describes the conditions of the Muslims during the Battle of the Trench (*al-Khandaq*), or, according to another narration, at the Battle of Uhud. Yet another narration holds it to refer to the Muslims who left their homes, belongings and their families in Makka and migrated to Madîna. The above verse was revealed as a kind of reward, to console the suffering Muslims.)

215. They ask you *(O Muhammad)* about what they will spend. Say: "Whatever you spend for good must go to parents, and to your near relatives, orphans and to the poor and the wayfarer. Allah is Aware of whatever good you do.

216. Fighting is obligatory for you, though it be disliked by you; but it may be that you hate a thing although it is good for you, and love a thing although it is bad for you. Allah knows, but you know not.

(War is not something people like. Except for some individuals who are born mentally sick, people do not enjoy killing or destroying, or harming others in any way. However, some unpleasantnesses are sometimes necessary, as in the case of a gangrenous limb which has to be cut off in order to save a human life, or in the case of breaking into a burning house in order to save a child trapped inside. To establish freedom of religion and conscience it is at times necessary to wage wars against oppression and cruelty. In these kind of cases it is a source of honour and pride to defend freedom and justice. In Islam, *jihâd* (struggle) has been established to further this end. *Jihâd* is not aggression. Non-Muslims are guaranteed freedom of worship and conscience in a Qur'anically-based state. Only if they refuse to pay their taxes can war be declared on them. When some nations deserve punishment, Allah punishes them with many kinds of disasters, and war is one of them. In fact, there is a verse

in which it is indicated that if Allah did not deflect people with each other, law and order would break down. The Prophet Muhammad once sent a platoon of soldiers to Makka under the command of Abdullah ibn Jahsh in order to acquire information about a trade caravan belonging to the Quraish, which was at war with the Muslims. They waylaid the caravan, and brought it to the Prophet. That was on the first day of the month of Rajab according to the Islamic calender. The pagans accused the Prophet of fighting during the sacred months recognised in Arabia; and in consequence the following verse was revealed.)

217. They ask you about the sacred month. Say: To fight (*in a sacred month*) is a grave matter; but barring people from the path of Allah, denying Him, and expelling people from the Inviolable Sanctuary is far graver in His sight. Tumult and persecution are worse than killing. They will not cease to fight against you until they force you to renounce your faith, if they can. But whoever of you turns away from his religion and dies in disbelief, his works will come to nothing in this world, and in the world to come. Such are the companions of the Fire, where they will stay forever.

218. Assuredly, those who believe and emigrate (*to escape persecution because of their religion*) and fight in the way of Allah, may hope for Allah's mercy. Allah is Forgiving, Merciful.

219. They ask you about drinking and gambling. Say: "There is great harm in both, although there is some benefit for men, but their sin is greater than their benefit. And they ask you what they should spend; say: "What is superfluous. Thus Allah makes plain to you His revelations, so that you may ponder.

(Drinking wine or any other kind of alcoholic beverage is, in the Islamic vision, a prohibited vice. However, just because it has been prohibited does not mean that it has no benefit, but only that its harm outweighs its benefit. Similarly with gambling: the one who gains something in gambling appears to gain some benefit, but since the practice as a whole yields, on balance, more suffering than advantage, the Lord has forbidden it.

The beginning of verse 220 is related to the end of verse 219, the sense being that if you think about the affairs of this world as well as affairs of the Hereafter you will be successful in both.)

220. In this world and in the Hereafter. They question you concerning orphans. Say: "To deal with them in goodness is best. If you mix their affairs with yours, remember that they are your brothers. Allah knows the spoiler from the improver. If He wills he truly can put you into difficulties. He is Mighty, Wise.

(Muslims are to treat orphans justly, so that they never feel that they are without father or mother. The person who is a guardian to an orphan is being tested, and Allah surely knows whether he is a spoiler or and improver. Those who do not treat them justly must remember that they are under the unceasing scrunity of their Creator.)

221. Do not marry polytheist women unless they believe *(in Islam)*. A believing slavegirl is better than an idolatress, though the latter please you. Nor marry *(your daughters)* to polytheists unless they believe in Islam. A believing slave is better than a *(free)* polytheist, though the latter please you. These call you to the Fire, but Allah calls you, by His will, to the Garden and to forgiveness. He makes plain His revelations to mankind, that perhaps they will think.

(According to Islam, man is judged by the degree of his faith. In the eyes of Allah a believing slave and servant are far better and purer; hence for a Muslim to marry an idolater is prohibited.)

222. They ask you about menstruation. Say: It is a hurt, so let women alone during their menstruation periods, and do not touch them until they are clean again. Then go into them as Allah enjoined you. Assuredly, Allah loves those that turn to Him in repentance, and strive to keep themselves clean.

(In this verse there is good news for believing women. Because to have sexual relations with a

woman during her courses is unpleasant for her, and unclean - Islam being the religion of cleanliness - men must abstain from such relations at this time.)

223. Your wives are a tilth for you. Go, then, into your tilth as you will. Advance good deeds for yourselves, and fear Allah, and know that you shall meet Him. And (*O Muhammad*), give glad tidings to believers!

(In the above verse the importance of spiritual closeness and preparation before intercourse is discussed. Muslims are here enjoined to avoid anal intercourse.)

224. Make not Allah, by your oaths, a hindrance to your being righteous and observing your duty to Him and making peace among mankind. Allah is All-Hearing, All-Knowing.

(In this verse it is emphasized that where there is a chance of keeping one's duty to Allah and making peace among mankind, oaths taken previously should not be a hindrance. Such an oath may be broken without any expiation being required.)

225. Allah will not call you to account for that which is unintentional in your oaths. But He will call you to account for that which is intended in your hearts. Allah is Forgiving, Clement.

226. Those who swear to abstain from their wives must wait four months, and if they change their minds, Allah is Forgiving, Merciful.

227. But if they decide upon divorce, then know that Allah is Hearer, Knower.

(The pagan Arabs had a custom by which a man could deprive his wife of conjugal rights, but at the same time keep her tied to him indefinitely, so that she could not marry again. If the husband was reproached, he would say that an oath sworn to God restrained him. In these verses the Islamic principle of divorce is laid down, which establishes a four month "cooling-off period, after which a husband is obliged either to retain or to divorce his wife. If he refuses to abide by this, the wife may raise the matter before a magistrate, who will force him to take a decision.)

228. Divorced women must wait, keeping themselves from men for three menstrual courses. It is unlawful for them, if they believe in Allah and the Last Day, to hide what Allah has created in their wombs. In that case, their husbands would do well to take them back, if they both desire a reconciliation. And (*women*) have rights similar to those of (*men*), in kindness; and men are a degree above them. Allah is Mighty, Wise.

229. Divorce may be pronounced twice, (*and then a woman must be*) retained in honour or allowed to go with kindness. It is not lawful for you (*husbands*) to take from them anything you have given them, unless both fear that they may not be able to keep within the limits set by Allah; in which case it will be no offence for either of them if the wife ransom herself. These are the limits set by Allah; do not transgress them. Those that transgress the bounds of Allah; such are the wrongdoers.

(Here the laws of divorce are elaborated. According to Islamic law a man can divorce his wife with two pronouncements, after which he can return to his wife. But when he utters the divorce statement for the third time he cannot return to his wife unless she has married someone else after the divorce, and then been divorced again. Lack of marital harmony is considered a justification for divorce. The basic form of divorce is by mutual consent; but there are ways in which it can be instigated at the man's behest, and others in which it can be instigated at the woman's behest, depending on circumstance.)

230. If a man divorce his wife (*for the third time*), then she is not lawful to him until she has married another man. If (*the latter*) divorce her, in which case it is no sin for either of them to return to the other, if they think that they can keep the limits set by Allah. Such are the limits of Allah. He makes them plain to people who have knowledge.

Divorce

231. When you have divorced your wives, and they have reached the end of their waiting periods, then either retain them in kindness or let them go with kindness. But do not retain them in order to harm them or wrong them, lest you transgress. Whoever does this wrongs his own soul. Do not make the revelations of Allah a mockery. Remember the favours He has bestowed on you and the Book and the wisdom which He has revealed, wherewith He does exhort you. Fear Allah, and know that He has knowledge of all things.

232. When you divorce women and they reach the end of their waiting-periods, do not prevent them from remarrying their husbands if it is agreed between them in kindness. This is a counsel for him among you who believes in Allah and the Last Day. That is more virtuous for you, and purer. Assuredly, Allah knows, and you do not.

(The incident which accompanied the revelation of this verse concerned a man named Ma'qil ibn Yasâr. This man had prevented his sister from remarrying her former husband, until this verse was revealed. The Prophet sent for Ma'qil who, when he came into the presence of the Blessed Prophet, obeyed the order of Allah and let his sister remarry her former husband, declaring that the divine Command had done away with his pride. A similar incident is related of Jabir ibn Abdullah. Although these verses were sent down in connection with particular incidents, the laws they enact are binding on all believers.)

233. Mothers shall give suck to their children for two whole years, for those who wish the suckling to be completed. They must be maintained and clothed in a reasonable manner (according to the tradition of that particular country, assessed if necessary by a magistrate) by the father of the child. No one should be charged beyond his capacity. A mother should not be made to suffer because of her child, nor should a father because of his child. The same duties devolve upon the father's heir. If, after consultation, they choose by mutual agreement to wean the child, it is no offence for them. If you wish to give your children out to nurse (by a wet-nurse), it is no offence for you, provided that you (the father) pay what is due from you in kindness. Have fear of Allah, and know that Allah is Seer of what you do.

(The following subjects are discussed in the above verses: divorce, remarriage, the period of waiting before remarriage, the nursing rights of the child, the duties of mother and father in regard to nursing. For details, one is required to turn to the Sunna, and the classical texts of Islamic Law.)

234. Widows shall wait, keeping themselves apart *(before they remarry)* for a period of four months and ten days, after their husbands' death. When they complete the period of waiting, it shall be no sin for you to let them do whatever they choose for themselves in decency. Allah is Aware of what you do.

(The reason for this waiting period is to ensure that the woman is not pregnant. In the case of the husband's decease, it also constitutes a period of quiet mourning. Within this period a woman should not be bothered before the period is over, unless this be absolutely inescapable; the object being to ensure her peace of mind. Whether the waiting-period is for divorce or death, it is psychologically very useful, both to console the widow and her close relatives, and to prepare her for a possible new marriage. It also prevents certain types of harm that might be instigated by the woman's relatives.)

235. It shall be no offence for you to propose marriage to women *(who are waiting for their period of four months and ten days),* or to hold it in your hearts. Allah knows that you will remember them. Do not make a secret contract with them, except that you speak to them in honourable terms. Do not resolve on the tie of marriage before the end of their waiting period. Know that Allah knows what is in your hearts, so beware of Him; and know that Allah is Forgiving, Clement.

(Once a woman becomes a widow, then provided she is not pregnant she may remarry after four months and ten days. There might be more than one man interested in marrying the widow, so there is no harm if one of them shows his intentions of marriage with her during her waiting period; or he may prefer to keep these feelings in his heart.)

236. It shall be no offence for you to divorce your wives before the marriage is consummated or the dowry settled. Provide for them with fairness; the rich man according to his means and the poor man according to his. This is a binding duty upon righteous men.

237. If you divorce them before the marriage is consummated but after their dowry has been settled, give them the half of their dowry, unless they *(the women)* agree to forgo it or *(the man's half)* is remitted by him in whose hand is the marriage tie *(the bridegroom).* It is more proper that the husband should forgo it. Do not forget to show kindness to each other. Allah is Seer of what you do.

Remarriage

238. Attend regularly to your prayers, including the middle prayer. Stand (in your salât) with devotion to Allah.

(Salât is one of the main "Pillars of Islam", as is explained in a hadith. The "middle prayer" mentioned in the verse is said to be the midafternoon prayer ('Asr). The Prophet, peace be upon him, stated during the Battle of al-Ahzâb that: "They have prevented us from the middle prayer! May Allah fill their house with fire! On the basis of this, according to the view of Ibn 'Abbâs, the middle prayer is the midafternoon prayer ('Asr). According to Ibn 'Umar's opinion, however, the "middle prayer" is the Noon (Zuhr) Prayer.)

239. If you are exposed to danger, (pray) while riding or on foot; and when you are restored to safety remember Allah (and pray), as He has taught you what you did not know.

240. Those of you who are about to die and leave behind wives should bequeath to their wives a year's provision, without causing them to leave their homes, but if they leave (on their own accord), there is no sin for you in that which they do of themselves within their rights. Allah is Mighty and Wise.

241. For divorced women a provision in kindness should be made, a binding duty for those who are Godfearing.

242. Thus Allah makes known to you His revelations that you may grow in understanding.

243. Have you not seen those who fled their habitations in thousands for fear of death. Allah said to them: "Perish! and then He brought them back to life. Surely Allah is bountiful to mankind, but most men do not give thanks.

244. Fight for the cause of Allah, and know that Allah is Hearer, Knower.

245. Who will grant Allah a generous loan? He will multiply it many times over. It is Allah who gives you want or plenty, and to whom you will all be returned.

247. Their prophet said to them: "Allah has appointed Saul to be your King. But they replied: "Should he be given the kingship, when we are more deserving of it than he? Besides, he is not rich at all. He said: "Allah has chosen him to rule over you, and increased him in knowledge and stature. Allah gives His sovereignty to whom He will. He is All-Embracing, All-Knowing.

(According to a habitual belief of the Israelite elite, the right to rule belongs to the people of wealth and capital: a view contrary to the correct, Prophetic teaching, which is that governance should be given on the basis of merit, knowledge, experience, physical strength and courage, not of wealth.)

248. Their prophet also said to them: "The sign of his kingship is that there shall come to you the ark wherein is peace of reassurance from your Lord, and a remnant of that which the house of Moses and the house of Aaron left behind, the angels bearing it. Behold; in this shall be a sign for you, if you are believers.

(According to some accounts, the Ark of the Covenant was a kind of chest, made of acacia wood and lined with gold, which contained the Tablets of the Ten Commandments. The Prophet Moses used to carry this in times of war, sending it in front of the army. In time, when the Israelites become weak, this Ark was carried away by Goliath. And, challenging the authority of Saul's kingship, they said: "If he is a true ruler let him bring true signs about it. He gave proof of his kingship by bringing the Ark of the Covenant, carried by angels.)

246. Think of the leaders of the Children of Israel, how they demanded of one of their prophets after (the death of) Moses: "Set up for us a king they (their council of elders) said, "and we will fight for the cause of Allah. He replied: "What if you refuse to fight, when ordered so to do? "Why should we refuse to fight for the cause of Allah, they replied, "when we and all of our children have been driven away from our habitations? - but when they were ordered to fight, they all refused, except a few of them. And Allah is Aware of the wrongdoers.

(The Amalekites dwelling in Midian, under the command of Goliath (Jâlût) had attacked the Israelites and subdued them. The Israelites proposed to a prophet of theirs that he appoint a commander to lead their defence. The prophet chose Saul (Tâlût), a son of Jacob (Ya'qûb). They refused this choice, on the grounds of his extreme poverty, and only relented when the prophet proclaimed that he was Allah's choice because of his good qualities, wisdom and physical power, which would qualify him to win the war.)

فَلَمَّا فَصَلَ طَالُوتُ بِالْجُنُودِ قَالَ إِنَّ اللّٰهَ مُبْتَلِيكُم بِنَهَرٍ فَمَن شَرِبَ مِنْهُ فَلَيْسَ مِنِّى وَمَن لَّمْ يَطْعَمْهُ فَإِنَّهُ مِنِّىٓ إِلَّا مَنِ اغْتَرَفَ غُرْفَةًۢ بِيَدِهِ فَشَرِبُوا مِنْهُ إِلَّا قَلِيلًا مِّنْهُمْ فَلَمَّا جَاوَزَهُ هُوَ وَالَّذِينَ ءَامَنُوا مَعَهُ قَالُوا لَا طَاقَةَ لَنَا الْيَوْمَ بِجَالُوتَ وَجُنُودِهِ قَالَ الَّذِينَ يَظُنُّونَ أَنَّهُم مُّلَـٰقُوا اللّٰهِ كَم مِّن فِئَةٍ قَلِيلَةٍ غَلَبَتْ فِئَةً كَثِيرَةًۢ بِإِذْنِ اللّٰهِ وَاللّٰهُ مَعَ الصَّـٰبِرِينَ ۝ وَلَمَّا بَرَزُوا لِجَالُوتَ وَجُنُودِهِ قَالُوا رَبَّنَآ أَفْرِغْ عَلَيْنَا صَبْرًا وَثَبِّتْ أَقْدَامَنَا وَانصُرْنَا عَلَى الْقَوْمِ الْكَـٰفِرِينَ ۝ فَهَزَمُوهُم بِإِذْنِ اللّٰهِ وَقَتَلَ دَاوُۥدُ جَالُوتَ وَءَاتَىٰهُ اللّٰهُ الْمُلْكَ وَالْحِكْمَةَ وَعَلَّمَهُ مِمَّا يَشَآءُ وَلَوْلَا دَفْعُ اللّٰهِ النَّاسَ بَعْضَهُم بِبَعْضٍ لَّفَسَدَتِ الْأَرْضُ وَلَـٰكِنَّ اللّٰهَ ذُو فَضْلٍ عَلَى الْعَـٰلَمِينَ ۝ تِلْكَ ءَايَـٰتُ اللّٰهِ نَتْلُوهَا عَلَيْكَ بِالْحَقِّ وَإِنَّكَ لَمِنَ الْمُرْسَلِينَ ۝

٤٠

249. And when Saul marched out with his army, he said: "Allah will put you to the test by means of a river: whoever, therefore, drinks from it shall not be of me, and whoever does not drink shall be of me, except him who takes a sip out of the hollow of his hand. But they all drank of it, except a few of them. And when he crossed it together with those who believed him, they said: "We have no power this day to face Goliath and his soldiers. But those of them who knew that they would meet their Lord replied: "Many a small company has defeated a mighty company by Allah's leave. Allah is with those who endure with patience.

250. When they met Goliath and his soldiers they cried: "Our Lord bestow on us steadfastness. Make our feet firm, and help us against the disbelieving people.

251. By Allah's will they routed them. David slew Goliath, and Allah bestowed on him the Kingship and wisdom and taught him what He pleased. Had Allah not defeated some by the might of others, the earth would have been utterly corrupted. But Allah is Bountiful to His creatures.

(In this verse, something of the importance of the divine Law is explained. Allah has established a balance in the social order. Some of the people are rich and some are poor, some are powerful and others are weak; some are healthy and others sick. Some are believers and some are not. The relations which evolve between these groups will determine the progress of the world. In the realm of physics, the interaction of positive and negative forces produces both light and energy. Thus, too, wars that take place between nations bring a new order into the world.)

252. Such are the signs of Allah. We recite them to you (O. Muhammad) with Truth, for you are one of the messengers.

(In the above verses, military discipline is discussed. The army's success depends how well the soldiers obey their commander and believe in their cause, rather than on the size of the army. David, we are told, was only seven years old when he slew Goliath. Allah informed the prophet that Goliath would be killed by David, and hence he took David with him to the war. On the way, David saw three stones that talked to him, saying: "Pick us up, David, you will kill Goliath with us. Picking them off the ground, he used them in his sling to kill the enemy chief.)

253. Of those messengers We have exalted some above others *(in degree)*. To some Allah spoke directly; others He raised to a lofty status. We gave Jesus son of Mary clear signs, and strengthened him with the Holy Spirit *(the archangel Gabriel)*. Had Allah so willed, those who succeeded them would not have fought against one another after the clear signs had come to them. But they disagreed among themselves; some believed, and others did not. Yet had Allah willed, they would not have fought against one another; but Allah does what He will.

254. O you who believe! Spend a part of what We have given you before that day arrives when there shall be neither trading, friendship nor intercession. Truly, it is the disbelievers who are the wrongdoers.

255. Allah! there is no god but Him, the Living, the Eternal. Neither slumber nor sleep overtakes Him. His is what is in the heavens and what is in the earth. Who can intercede with Him except by His permission? He knows what is

before them and what lies behind them, and they can grasp only that part of His knowledge which He will. His Throne embraces the Heavens and the earth, and it tires Him not to uphold them both. His is the High, the Tremendous.

(This is the celebrated Throne Verse (*Âyat al-Kursî*). It describes certain of the divine attributes, and indicates the exalted degree of Allah, which is properly known only to Himself. The great spiritual advantages of reciting this verse have been explained in many hadiths. Our Blessed Prophet has stated in one such account: "The greatest (or the most significant) verse in the Qur'an is the Verse of the Throne. Whoever recites it, Allah sends a special angel for him who records this good deed in his Book. Satan flees from the house in which it is recited, and will not return within thirty days, while no magic or magician can enter the house for forty days. O 'Alî! Teach this to your family, your children and your neighbours. The king of days is Friday; the king of words is the Qur'an, the Master of the Qur'an is the Sûrah of the Cow, and the master of this Sûrah is the Verse of the Throne. It is said that those who recite this verse with sincerity and devotion are preserved from all manner of disasters. "*Hayy*" means "Living . It is one of the unique attributes of God that He is Eternal and Living at all times. "*Kayyûm* is also one of His attributes, indicating that He upholds and administers all creation, and is the Judge on the Day of Resurrection.)

256. There is no compulsion in religion. True guidance is distinct from error. But whoever disbelieves in *Tâghût* and believes in Allah has grasped the strong handhold that will never break. And Allah is All-Hearing, All-Knowing.

("*Tâghût* denotes anything worshipped rather than Allah. Man, being subject to the inner promptings of the devil, is easily misled. By self-discipline and restraint, and the assistance of a guide, man can teach himself to combat these promptings, and hence save himself from committing wrong actions. Life is thus a struggle against *tâghût*, for when we do not serve God, we are assuming that others are more worthy of service than our Maker.

The verse also contains the teaching that in genuine religion, truth is clearly discernable, and that constraint of any kind in the propagation of faith is to be renounced.)

257. Allah is the Protecting Friend of those who believe. He brings them out of darkness into light. As for those who disbelieve, their supporters will be *Tâghût*, who bring them out of light into darkness. Such are the rightful dwellers of the fire. They will abide there for ever.

(In the above verse we are given a different kind of comparison between men of belief and infidelity. The former are rightly guided to "light, while the latter are lured by the devil and their own caprices into darkness, so that they can only end their days in the archetype of all darkness: the Fire.)

258. Have you not heard of him *(Nimrod)* who argued with Abraham about his Lord because he had bestowed on him the kingdom? Abraham said: "My Lord is He who gives life and death. He answered: "I give life and death! (*by slaying or sparing my subjects.*) Abraham said: "Allah causes the sun to rise from the East, so cause it to come from the West! Thus was the disbeliever baffled. And Allah does not guide a wrong-doing people.

259. Or *(have you heard)* of him who, when passing by a ruined and desolate city, exclaimed: "How can Allah give life to this city, now that it is dead? And Allah caused him to die, and after a hundred years, brought him back to life. He said: "How long have you stayed away? "A day, he answered, "or part of a day. Then Allah said "Know then that you have stayed away a hundred years. Yet look at your food and drink: they have not rotted; and look at your donkey! We will make you a sign to mankind: See how We will raise them and clothe them with flesh! And when *(the matter)* became clear to him, he said: "I know now that Allah is Able to do all things.

(The commentators on the Holy Qur'an are mostly agreed that the person discussed in verse 258, and the

man who visited the ruined city were both disbelievers. But according to certain traditions,the visitor to the ruined city was Uzair. Picking up some food, he travelled on his donkey until he came to a ruined city, where he settled. Looking about him, he wondered if the past inhabitants of the place could ever come to life again. While he contemplated this, he fell asleep, only to be brought back to life by God after a hundred years. His food had not rotted, but his donkey was dead; only its bones remaining. The ruined city, however, had been revived and rebuilt. Allah then brought back his donkey to life in front of his eyes. At this, he was humbled, and realised the infinite power of the Divine. The moral of the story is the superiority of the believer over all who are in ignorance of truth.

The person who argued with Nimrod was the prophet Abraham. Some commentators, however, hold that the episode took place in Egypt between Abraham and Pharaoh, who also claimed, "I am the one who causes life and death. But the lesson to remember is that God supports His spokesmen with all manner of miracles, and may enable them to overcome seemingly insuperable odds.)

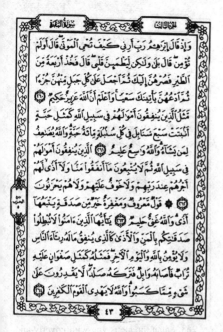

grains. Allah gives increase manifold to whom He will. He is All-Embracing, All-Knowing.

260. When Abraham said: "Show me, my Lord, how You give life to the dead! He asked, "Do you not believe? Abraham answered, "Yes indeed, I do believe; but I wish to set my heart at rest. Then Allah said: "Take four birds, draw them to you and cut their bodies to pieces and place a part of them on each hill, then call them: they will come to you in haste. And know that Allah is Mighty, Wise.

(The holy Prophets sent by God for the guidance of erring mankind may, as the previous few verses have intimated, be possessed of miraculous powers to further their divinely-appointed missions. Yet it is God Alone who has granted them these powers; they are not, therefore, to be accounted magical. Here we see the holy Prophet Abraham admonished by his own miracle, which was deployed not to gratify him, but rather, as is the case with all authentic miracles, to guide and remind mankind.)

261. The likeness of those who spend their wealth in Allah's way is as the likeness of a grain which grows seven ears, in every ear a hundred

262. Those that spend their wealth for the cause of Allah and do not follow their spending (charity) with taunts and insults: no fear shall come upon them, neither shall they grieve.

263. A kind word with forgiveness is better than charity followed by injury. Allah is Self-Sufficient, Clement.

264. O you who believe! Render not vain your almsgiving by taunts and injury, like those who spend their wealth only for ostentation, and believe neither in Allah nor in the Hereafter. Such men are like a rock covered with earth; a shower of rain falls upon it and leaves it hard and bare. They will gain nothing from their works. Allah does not guide the disbelievers.

(In the above verses we are encouraged to give out of our wealth in charity without following our charity with patronising taunts or injury, or showing off, or scolding or belittling the plight of the needy. Otherwise, instead of gaining good deeds from one's charity, one might receive God's wrath and punishment.)

265. And the likeness of those who spend their wealth in search of Allah's pleasure and for the strengthening of their souls, is as the likeness of a garden on a hilltop. If abundant rain falls upon it, it yields up twice its normal crop; and if no heavy rain falls upon it, it is watered by a light shower. Allah is Seer of what you do.

266. Would any one of you like to have a garden of palm-trees and vines, with rivers flowing beneath it, with all kinds of fruit for him therein, and old age had stricken him and he has helpless children to support; and a fiery whirlwind strikes it and it is (all) consumed by fire? Thus Allah makes plain the signs to you, so that you may perhaps think.

(This image addresses the problems that man may face in the life of this world: position, wealth, and other worldly gains are no guarantee for anyone. Many states and empires have been wiped out from the face of the earth, so that only eloquent ruins remain. Many rich people have become poor, and many nations because of internal crises have collapsed. But man always plans many beautiful dreams, never knowing how matters will end. The only certain thing, and the only consolation, is to have faith and trust in the One Lord and Sustainer.)

267. O you who believe! Spend of the good things which you have earned, and of that which We have brought out of the earth for you. And seek not the bad (with intent) to spend of it (in charity); and know that Allah is Self-Sufficient, and Worthy of Praise.

268. Satan threatens you with poverty and commands you towards immorality. But Allah promises you His forgiveness and His bounty. Allah is All-Embracing, All-Knowing.

269. Allah gives His wisdom to whomsoever He pleases; and whoever is given wisdom, has truly been given abundant good. But none remember except men of understanding.

(The "Wisdom discussed in the above verse denotes knowledge of the Qur'an. The first to receive this wisdom was the Blessed Prophet, followed by his heirs, the scholars who act in accordance with the knowledge that they possess. The most knowledgeable person is the one who is most useful to mankind. Our prophet, in a well-known hadith, teaches: "Ask (from God) knowledge that useful, seek refuge in Him from knowledge that is not useful. Honesty, justice, sincerity, love, respect, humbleness, to be useful to others, generosity, compassion and similar good traits characterise the people who posses this wisdom. He who learns the Qur'an well and practices it, keeping himself from evil things, is also a man of wisdom, and is thus "given abundant good .)

270. Whatever charity you give and whatever vows you make are known to Allah. The wrongdoers shall have none to help them.

271. To give charity in public is good, but to give alms to the poor secretly is better for you, and will atone for some of your sins. Allah has knowledge of all that you do.

("Alms-giving is either obligatory or optional. Zakât is the obligatory form, being possessed of two functions: (1) To purify wealth and render it blessed; (2) To improve one's own faith. Whether it be obligatory or optional, to give it secretly is considered better than to give it openly, for thus will it be less exposed to the danger of ostentation. To give in secret also saves face for the needy, whose dignity is preserved.)

272. (O Muhammad!) It is not for you to guide them. Allah gives guidance to whom He will. Whatever good thing you spend, it is for your own soul, and you shall do so only for Allah's sake. And whatever good you spend, it will be repaid to you in full, and you will not be wronged.

273. (Alms) are for the poor who are restrained in the cause of Allah, unable to travel in the land. The ignorant man accounts them wealthy because of their restraint. But you will know them by their appearance. They never beg of people with importunity. And whatever good things you spend, surely Allah knows them well.

(These verses refer to people fighting for the cause of Allah, and those who are spending their lives to acquire knowledge and spread this knowledge in the world. Because of this honourable work, they are unable to make a sufficient living, and are hence worthy recipients of this type of Zakât.)

274. Those who spend their wealth by night and day, in private and public, shall be rewarded by their Lord. No fear shall come upon them, neither shall they grieve.

(The above verses serve to institute the Islamic tithe - the Zakât. Were the Zakât to be given in conformity to Allah's injunctions there would be no poverty left on the face of the earth. Only certain people are qualified to receive Zakât. There are, of course, other forms of charity over and above the obligatory, which can be donated to such recipients as seem appropriate.)

275. Those who swallow usury shall rise up *(from their graves)* before Allah like the men whom Satan has bewitched and maddened by *(his)* touch, for they assert that usury is just like trading, although Allah has permitted trade and forbidden usury. He that receives an admonition from his Lord and mends his ways may keep what he has already earned; his affair will be determined by Allah. But those that return *(to usury)* will be the rightful owners of the Fire. They will abide there forever.

276. Allah blights usury and makes almsgiving fruitful; He does not love the impious and guilty.

(Taking or giving money at interest in any way is an unjust practice forbidden in Islam. When Islam is fully applied in any place there is no need for such loans, which can lean to hopeless debt and exploitation. Islamic economics encourages partnership-based investment, in which participants share directly in the profit or loss of a venture. The prohibition of interest reduces the cost of such ventures, and also suppresses inflation. Money is a means of exchanging goods. To make money itself a subject of trade without any risk is illogical, exploitative, and generates a host of essentially parasitic activities.)

277. Those that believe, and do good works, and establish the Prayer and pay the Zakât, will be rewarded by their Lord; and no fear shall come upon them, neither shall they grieve.

278. O you who believe! Have fear of Allah, and give up what is still due to you from usury, if you are true believers.

279. And if you do not, then be warned of war *(against you)* by Allah and His messenger. If you repent, you may retain your principal *(without interest)*. Wrong not, and you shall be not wronged.

280. And if the debtor is in straitened circumstances, then grant him a postponement until a *(time of)* ease; but if you remit the debt as almsgiving it would be better for you, if you did but know.

281. And guard yourselves against a day in which you will be brought back to Allah. Then every soul will be paid in full that which it had earned, and they will not be wronged.

282. O you who believe! When you contract a debt for a fixed period, record it in writing. Let a scribe write it down for you with equity. No scribe should refuse to write as Allah has taught him, so let him write; and let the debtor dictate, fearing Allah his Lord, and not diminishing (*the sum he owes*). If the debtor be a feeble minded or weak person, or unable to dictate, let his guardian dictate for him in fairness. Call in two witnesses from among your men, and if two men (*are not at hand*), then one man and two women of such as you approve as witnesses, so that if either of the (*women*) commit an error, the other will remind her. Witnesses must not refuse if called upon to do so. Do not fail to record (*your debts*) in writing, be they small or large, together with the date of payment. This is more just in the sight of Allah; it ensures accuracy in testifying and is the best way to remove all doubt. But if the transaction in hand be a bargain concluded on the spot, it is no offence for you if you do not record it in writing. See that witnesses are present when you trade with one another, and let no harm be done to either scribe or witness. If you (*harm them*) it shall be a wickedness in you. Have fear of Allah. Allah is teaching you; and He is Knower of all things

(This is the longest verse in the Qur'an. It contains the rules necessary for the establishment of the office of Notary Public, for the first time in history. The law of Islam is founded on the principle of protecting the rights and interests of mankind, and in the area of debts this is spelt out in detail. In order to protect the rights of citizens, the necessary witnessed documents and proofs are needed in courts of law, a requirement which is acknowledged even in modern secular legal practice. The Holy Qur'an requires believers to serve as witnesses when they are called, no matter how busy they may be, because participating in the legal processes which uphold the stability and equity of society is a duty upon all citizens, and one that merits God's generous reward.)

بِسْمِ اللهِ

283. If you are on a journey and a scribe cannot be found, then let pledges be taken. If any one of you entrusts another with a pledge, let the trustee restore the pledge to its owner; and let him fear Allah, his Lord. You must not withhold testimony. He that withholds it, surely, his heart is doing wrong. Allah is Aware of what you do.

284. To Allah belongs all that the heavens and the earth contain. Whether you make known what is in your souls or hide it, Allah will bring you to account for them. He will forgive whom He will and punish whom He pleases; He has power over all things.

285. The Messenger believes in what has been revealed to him by his Lord, and so do the believers. They all believe in Allah and His angels, His scriptures and His messengers: "We make no distinction between any of His messengers - and they say: "We hear and obey. Grant us Your forgiveness, our Lord; to You is the journeying.

286. Allah does not charge a soul with more than what it can bear. It shall be requited for whatever good and whatever evil it has done. "Our Lord! Do not condemn us if we forget, or err! Our Lord! Do not lay on us a burden like that which You laid on these before us! Our Lord! Do not charge us with more than we can bear! Pardon us, forgive us, and have mercy upon us. You are our Protector. Give us victory over the disbelieving people!

(The last two verses of Sûrah al Baqarah reflect the faithfulness and loyalty of believers, and their obedience to the divine laws. Because of the enormous responsibility implied by the preceding verse ("Whether you make known what is in your minds or hide them; Allah will bring you to account for them.) those Companions who first heard these words were terrified and alarmed. The following passage consoles the Muslims and lessens their burden. The verse, which announces that obedience to Allah yields delightful fruits, was revealed to the Blessed Prophet on the night of the "Mi'raj ; directly, and without the intermediary role of the Angel Gabriel. The Prophet, peace be upon him, praised this verse in various hadiths, and encouraged the Muslims to recite it always, and especially before going to bed at night. For it contains the essence of Islam, which is loving submission to the Divine will, and satisfaction with the just decrees of Heaven. As such, it is the perfect conclusion to the Sûrah.)

Don't think?

SÛRAH III

ÂL ‘IMRÂN (THE FAMILY OF ‘IMRÂN)

Revealed at Madîna

(This Sûrah, which includes two hundred verses, takes its title from verses 34 through 37, where the family of ‘Imrân (the father of Moses) and the ancestor of the Blessed Virgin Mary are mentioned. It is also a generic name for all the Jewish prophets from Moses (*Mûsâ*) to John (*Yahyâ*) the Baptist and Jesus Christ (*‘Îsâ*), peace be upon them all. As the previous Sûrah dwelt at length on the Jews, much of the present Sûrah addresses itself to the Christians, and speaks of the prophetic glory of Jesus Christ (*‘Îsâ*), upon whom be peace.)

THE FAMILY OF ‘IMRÂN

In the name of Allah, the Compassionate, the Merciful.

1. Alif. Lâm. Mîm.

2. Allah! There is no god but Him, the Living, the Self-Subsistent.

3. He has revealed to you *(Muhammad)* the Scripture with truth, confirming that which was revealed before it, even as He revealed the Torah and the Gospel.

4. Previously, for a guidance to mankind, and had revealed the Criterion *(Furqân: the distinction between right and wrong, a name of the Qur'an)*. Those who deny the signs of Allah shall receive a heavy penalty; and Allah is Mighty, Able to Requite.

5. Nothing in the earth or in the heavens is hidden from Allah.

6. It is He Who fashions you in the wombs as pleases Him. There is no God but Him, the Almighty, the Wise.

7. It is He Who has revealed to you the Qur'an. Some of its verses are precise and clear in meaning; they are the Mother of the Book; while others are allegorical. Those with a swerving in their hearts pursue the allegorical, to seek to create dissension by seeking to explain it. Yet no-one knows their explanation except Allah. Those who are firmly grounded in knowledge say: "We believe in it; it is all from our Lord, but only man of understanding really heed.

(According to some of the Qur'an's interpreters, the words "firmly grounded in knowledge imply that some of the Qur'an's meanings will only become apparent as human knowledge changes in nature.

The Mother of the Book and the "allegorical are terms which denote the fundamental distinction in the Qur'anic text between expressions which are self-explanatory, and others which appear to require a degree of deeper interpretation, since their literal meaning is not readily apparent.)

8. *(Those people pray)* "Our Lord, do not cause our hearts to go astray after You have guided us, and bestow upon us mercy from Your Presence. Assuredly, You are the Bestower.

9. Our Lord! It is You Who shall gather mankind together to a Day of which there is no doubt. Allah does not fail the promise.

10. As for the disbelievers, neither their riches nor their progeny will save them from the wrath of Allah. They will become fuel for the Fire.

11. As with Pharaoh's people and those before them, who denied Our signs, so that Allah seized them for their sins. And Allah is severe in punishment .

12. Say *(O Muhammad)* to those who disbelieve: "You will be overcome and gathered into Hell, an evil resting-place!

(In this verse Allah gives glad tidings to His prophet Muhammad about the forthcoming defeat of the idolators and the Jews, who had oppressed them so fiercely. Shortly after this verse was revealed the Muslims were able to defeat both opponents.)

13. There was a sign for you in the two armies which met on the battlefield *(the Battle of Badr)*. One army fighting for the cause of Allah, and another disbelieving, whom they saw as twice their number, clearly, with their very eyes. Thus does Allah strengthen with His aid whom He will. Surely in this there is a lesson for those who are able to see.

14. Made beautiful for mankind is the love of desires, for women and offspring, of hoarded treasures of gold and silver, of branded horses, cattle and plantations. These are the comforts of this life; yet with Allah is the best of all goals.

15. Say *(O Muhammad:)* "Shall I tell you of better things than that? For those who are Godfearing shall be gardens with their Lord, beneath which rivers flow, and pure wives, and the good-pleasure of Allah. Allah is Seer of His servants.

(Verse 14 is an explanation of the blessings of this world and the excessive weakness of man for them. Although instinct is necessary for man to survive, and is hence a natural and right part of his disposition, he should not lean towards excess, lest he become enslaved to his desires. The path of Islam is the middle course in all things, including the course between the things of this world, which must perish, and those of God, which will abide forever.)

16. Those who say: "Our Lord! Assuredly we believe; therefore forgive us our sins, and keep us from the punishment of the Fire!

17. The steadfast, and the truthful, and the obedient, those who spend (*in charity, hence those who do not hoard*), and those who ask forgiveness at the time before dawn.

18. Allah bears witness that there is no god but Him, and so do the angels and the men of learning. He is the Upholder of Justice. There is no deity save Him, the Almighty, the Wise.

19. The (*true*) religion in the sight of Allah is Islam. Those who (*formerly*) received the Scripture disagreed among themselves through jealousy only after knowledge came to them. Whoever disbelieves in the signs of Allah should know that Allah is swift in reckoning.

(The word "*dîn*, here rendered "religion, can be possessed of several meanings, including [obedience], [punishment], [nation], and [God-given Law]. The word *islâm*, in turn, can mean "submission and "obedience, in addition to its more specific reference to the Islamic religion. It denotes inner peace, realised through total sincerity and a life of devotional prayer. As is also suggested in the above verse, *islâm* means believing in the Oneness of God, which becomes perfect when belief is affirmed in the way of life that has been perfected by the prophet Muhammad, who has brought the final Law from our Creator.)

20. And if they argue that with you (*O Muhammad*), say: "I have surrendered myself to Allah, and (*so have*) those who follow me. And say to those who have received the Scripture and those who read not: "Will you too surrender yourselves to Allah? If they become Muslims they shall be rightly guided; if they turn away, then your duty is only to inform them. Allah is Seer of all His servants.

(The Arabic word "*Ummî* usually connotes an unlettered person who cannot read or write, although some interpreters interpret it as a reference to the Arabs, who, having been idolaters, had never received a Book from God.)

21. Those who disbelieve in the revelations of Allah and slay the prophets unjustly and kill the men who enjoin equity: warn them of a painful scourge.

22. Those are they whose works have failed in this world and in the Hereafter; and there shall be none to help them.

(What could be more natural and just, for those who fail to believe, and prevent the propagation of truth and justice, that they should turn out at the end to be losers? Despite all their efforts they are unable to prevent the spread of the religion of truth and mercy. Despite the efforts of persecutors and tyrants, this just religion will gain victory over the others by the grace of God. The deeds of wrongdoers will be vain because their capital, namely, their life in this world, will have been wasted. And those who refuse to store up good works in the world cannot expect to receive anything at the Judgement.)

23. *(O Muhammad!)* Have you not seen how those who have received a portion of the Scriptures, when called upon to accept the judgement of Allah's Book between them, some turn their backs and pay no heed?

24. That is because they declare: "The fire will not touch us save for a certain number of days." That which they used to invent has deceived them concerning their religion.

25. How will it be with them when We gather them all together upon a Day which is sure to come, when every soul will be given what it had earned, and there shall be no injustice?

26. *(O Muhammad,)* say: "O Lord God, Owner of sovereignty! You bestow sovereignty on whom You will, and take it from whom You will; You exalt whom You will and abase whom You will. In Your hand lies all that is good; You have power over all things.

27. You cause the night to pass into the day, and the day to pass into the night. You bring forth the living from the dead and the dead from the living; and You give sustenance to whom You choose, without stint.

28. Let not the believers take disbelievers for their friends in preference to the believers. He who does this has no help from Allah, unless you guard yourselves against them, taking a precaution. Allah admonishes you to fear Him. To Him you shall all return.

(The type of friendship forbidden in the above verse is a friendship of believers with disbelievers which requires the desertion of other believers. An Islamic state, however, is able to carry out mutual agreements with disbelievers in regard to trade, diplomatic and other matters, as long as they are not harmful to other Muslim states.)

29. *(O Muhammad)* say: "Whether you hide what is in your breasts or reveal it, Allah knows it. He knows all that the heavens and the earth contain; and He has power over all things."

(In his interpretation of the above verse, Qadi Baydâwî states: "If you have an inclination in your hearts of love and friendship towards the disbelievers, then whether you hide it or not, Allah is Aware of it. Allah, Who is able to know of all things between Heaven and earth, also knows what is hidden in your hearts, or made public. Those who deal with unbelievers in preference to believers, and against the latter's interests, God shall take them to task.)

which is in my womb. Accept it from me; You alone are the Hearer, the Knower."

36. And when she was delivered of the child, she said: "My Lord, I have given birth to a female child. Allah knows best of what she was delivered: the male is not like the female; "and I have named her Mary. Protect her and her descendants from Satan, the outcast.

37. And her Lord accepted her with full acceptance, and vouchsafed to her a goodly growth, and entrusted her to the care of Zachariah. Whenever Zachariah went into the chamber where she was, he found that she had food. He said: "O Mary! Where is this food from? She answered: "It is from Allah. Allah gives without stint to whom He will.

(Zachariah, peace be upon him, was the husband of Mary's aunt. As is explained in the above verse, Zachariah took upon himself the responsibility to be Mary's guardian. He set aside a special chamber for her, a "mihrâb , a word which ordinarily denotes "a path to war . Here, however, it signifies a chamber in which one may enter a retreat, to devote oneself to all kinds of prayers and acts of divine remembrance. This mihrâb mentioned above has nothing to do with the Mihrâb which is a niche let into the qibla wall of mosques where the imam stands and leads the prayers. Every time Zachariah entered Mary's chamber he saw various kinds of fruits, including some which were out of season at that time. Zachariah was surprised, and asked her who sent them; she answered that she was sustained by her Lord. This is accounted one of her miracles.)

30. On the day when every soul will find itself confronted with whatever good it had done and whatever evil it had done, it will wish that there might be a mighty gulf between it and that evil. Allah admonishes you to fear Him; and He is Kind to His bondsmen.

31. Say (O Muhammad): "If you love Allah, then follow me; Allah will love you and forgive you your sins. Allah is Forgiving, Merciful.

32. Say: "Obey Allah and the Messenger. But if they turn away, assuredly Allah loves not the disbelievers.

33. Allah did prefer Adam and Noah and the Family of Abraham and the Family of 'Imrân above His creatures.

34. They were descendants of one another. Allah is Hearer, Knower.

35. (Remember) when the wife of 'Imran said: "My Lord! I dedicate to Your service that

38. Then Zachariah prayed to his Lord, and said: "O my Lord! Grant me of Your bounty, of upright descendants. You are the Hearer of prayer.

39. And the angels called to him as he stood praying in the *mihrâb*. "Allah gives you the glad tidings of a son whose name is John (*Yahyâ*), (*who comes*) to confirm a word from Allah, princely and chaste, a Prophet of the righteous.

(According to the interpreters of the Holy Qur'an, the person mentioned in this verse is Jesus Christ, upon him be peace. This will be explained further in verse 45.)

40. "Lord , said Zachariah: "How can I have a son when old age has overtaken me, and my wife is barren? "Such is the will of Allah, He replied, "Who does what He will.

41. He said: "My Lord! vouchsafe unto me a portent!" The answer was: "For three days you shall not speak to any man except by signs. Remember your Lord much, and praise Him in the early hours of night and morning.

42. And when the angels said: "O Mary! Allah has chosen you, and made you pure, and has preferred you above all the women of creation.

43. O Mary! Be obedient to your Lord, prostrate yourself, and bow with those who bow in worship.

44. This is of the tidings hidden, which We reveal to you (*O Muhammad*). You were not present with them when they cast lots to see which of them should be the guardian of Mary; nor were you present when they argued (*concerning this*).

(According to the interpreters of the Holy Qur'an, the children of Israel threw their pens into a river to know which one would be the guardian of Mary. They decided that the guardian of Mary would be the man whose pen floated. According to other accounts, arrows were used rather than pens.)

45. When the angels said: "O Mary! Allah gives the glad tidings of a word from Him, whose name is the Messiah, Jesus, son of Mary, illustrious in this world and the Hereafter, and one of those who shall be brought near (*to God*). · ·

(The word 'Messiah' is a Hebrew word, denoting "the anointed one . As one of the names of Jesus, upon whom be peace, it denotes his exalted and honoured status.)

46. He will speak to mankind in his cradle and in his manhood, and he is of the righteous.

(According to verses 27-33 of Sûrah Maryam, when Mary gave birth to Jesus, he began to talk in his cradle, announcing that he was a slave and servant of Allah, and a prophet sent by Him with a book.)

47. She said: "My Lord! How can I have a child, when no man has touched me? He replied: "Such is the will of Allah. He creates what He will. When He decrees a thing He only says: Be! and it is.

48. And he will teach him the Scripture and wisdom, and the Torah and the Gospel.

49. And will make him a Messenger to the Israelites. He will say: "I bring you a sign from your Lord. From clay I will make for you the likeness of a bird; I shall breathe into it and, by Allah's leave, it shall become a (living) bird. By Allah's leave I shall give sight to the blind, heal the leper, and raise the dead to life. I shall tell you

what you eat and what you store up in your houses. Surely that will be a sign for you, if you are believers.

50. (I come) to confirm the Torah that has already been revealed, and to make lawful to you some of the things you were forbidden. I bring a sign to you from your Lord. So fear Him, and obey me.

51. Allah is my Lord and your Lord; so worship Him. That is the straight path.

(Verse 160 of Sûrah al-Nisâ', verse 146 of the Sûrah al-An'âm, and verse 118 of Sûrah al-Nahl explain that because of the wrongdoings and cruelty of the Jews certain restrictions were placed on them, but with the coming of Jesus some of these were abrogated.)

52. But when Jesus become aware of their disbelief he said: "Who will be my helpers in God? The disciples said: "We will be Allah's helpers. We believe in Allah; and bear you witness that we have surrendered (ourselves to Him)!

(The word hawârî, here translated as "disciple , came into the Arabic language from Ethiopic, in which language it means "helper . Thus those who were the companions of the Prophet Jesus, and stood with his call, are known by this title.)

53. Our Lord! We believe in that which You have revealed, and we follow him whom You have sent. Account us among those who witness *(the truth; i.e. the oneness of God, and the truth of the prophets He has sent, including Jesus).*

54. And they *(the disbelievers)* schemed, and Allah schemed *(against them)*; and Allah is the best of schemers.

55. *(And remember)* when Allah said: "O Jesus! I am gathering you and causing you to ascend to Me, and am cleansing you of those who disbelieve, and am setting those who follow you above those who disbelieve until the Day of Resurrection. Then to Me you will all return, and I shall judge between you as to that in which you used to differ.

56. As for those who disbelieve, I shall punish them with a heavy chastisement in the world and the Hereafter; and they will have no helpers.

57. And as for those who believe and do good works, He will pay them their wages in full. And Allah loves not the wrongdoers.

58. *(O Muhammad!)* This which We recite to you is a revelation and a wise reminder.

59. The likeness of Jesus with Allah is as the likeness of Adam. He created him of dust, then He said to him: Be! and he was.

(Allah created Adam, peace be upon him, from clay without a father and mother; likewise He created Jesus without a father. This verse demonstrates the power of our Omnipotent Lord, as well as serving as a testimony to Mary's chastity, and as a refutation of those who believe that Jesus has existed from eternity.)

60. This is the truth from your Lord, so *(O Muhammad!)* do not be of those who waver.

61. And those who dispute with you concerning him *(Jesus)*, after the knowledge which has come to you, say *(to them)*: "Come! Let us summon our sons and your sons, and our women and your women, and ourselves and yourselves, then we will pray humbly and invoke the curse of Allah upon those who lie.

(This is known as the verse of *"Mubâhala .* According to some interpreters of the Holy Qur'an, a group of people from the Christians of Najrân in the Yemen came to visit the Prophet Muhammad, peace be upon him. They stated that since the Qur'an acknowledges the fact that Jesus was born without a father, then it would seem that Jesus was God. The Prophet invited them to take part in this procedure of *mubâhala.* They refused to accept the proposal; but instead signed a treaty with the Muslims, and accepted their protection.)

62. This is the whole truth *(about the mother of Jesus)*. There is no deity but Allah, and He is the Mighty, the Wise.

63. And if they turn away, Allah is Aware of the evildoers.

64. Say: "O People of the Scripture! Come to an agreement between us and you, that we shall worship none but Allah, that we shall assign no partner to Him, and that none of us shall take others for lords beside Allah. And if they turn away, then say: "Bear witness that we are the surrenders *(to Allah)*.

65. O People of the Scripture! Why do you argue about Abraham, when neither Torah nor Gospel were revealed until after him? Have you no sense?

66. Indeed, you are those who argue about that of which you have some knowledge; why then do you argue concerning that of which you have no knowledge? Allah knows, but you do not.

Abraham

(The ancient Jews and the Christians had a recurrent argument. The Jews claimed that Abraham was a Jew, whereas the Christians claimed that he was properly a Christian. Both sides tried to bring arguments to prove their point, but they were both wrong, as the above verse proves, because both religions came after him, and he was a follower of the primordial, true path of God.)

67. Abraham was neither a Jew nor a Christian, but was an upright man who had surrendered to Allah; he was not of the polytheists.

68. Surely, those of mankind who have the best claim to Abraham are those who followed him, and this Prophet, and those who are with him; and Allah is the Protecting Friend of the believers.

69. Some of the People of the Scripture wish to make you go astray; and they make none to go astray except themselves, but they do not perceive it.

70. O People of the Scripture! Why do you deny the signs of Allah, when you yourselves bear witness *(to their truth)*?

71. O People of the Scripture! Why do you confound the truth with the falsehood, and knowingly conceal the truth?

72. And some of the People of the Scripture say: "Believe in that which has been revealed to those who believe in the morning and deny it in the evening, so that they may turn away *(from their faith)*.

(The reference is to a group of twelve Rabbis of Khaybar, who, we are told, agreed to enter Islam in the morning and abondon it in the evening, by which device they hoped to detach some of the Muslims from Islam.)

73. And believe not except in one who follows your religion - Say *(O Muhammad!)*: "The *(only)* guidance is the guidance of Allah - that any one is given the like of that which was given to you or that they may argue with you in the presence of their Lord. Say *(O Muhammad!)*: The bounty is in the hands of Allah. He bestows it on whom He will. He is All-Embracing, All-Knowing.

74. He selects for His mercy whom He will. Allah's bounty is infinite.

75. Among the People of the Scripture there is he who, if you trust him with a weight of treasure, will return it to you. And among them there is he who, if you entrust him with a single dinar, will not return it to you, unless you keep standing over him. That is because they say: "We have no duty to the Gentiles. They speak a lie concerning Allah knowingly.

(The word "Gentiles" here means those Arabs who were not from the People of the Scripture. The word is also sometimes used to denote non-Jews)

76. Those *(are the chosen of God)* who fulfill their pledge and guard themselves against evil. For assuredly, Allah loves the righteous.

77. Those who purchase a small gain at the cost of Allah's covenant and their oaths, they have no portion in the Hereafter. Allah will neither speak to them nor look upon them on the Day of Resurrection, nor will He make them grow. Theirs will be a painful punishment

Elsewhere, in Sûrah al-Mâ'ida, 116-7, he repudiates
the idea that God could have "partners .)

78. And there is a party of them who distort
the Scripture with their tongues, that you may
think that what they say is from the Scripture,
when it is not from the Scripture. And they say:
"It is from Allah, when it is not from Allah, and
they speak a lie concerning Allah knowingly.

79. It is not possible for any human being to
whom Allah has given the Scripture and wisdom
and prophethood that he should afterwards have
said to mankind: "Be slaves of me instead of
Allah! He would rather say: "Be worshippers of
Allah by virtue of your constant study and
teaching of the Scripture .

(The Christians claimed that Jesus was identical
with God. This is diametrically opposed to the
teachings of Jesus, as recorded in history, and Islam: in
reality, he taught the absolute and undivided Oneness
of God. In many verses of the Holy Qur'an Jesus claims
only to be a prophet, not God. See for instance Sûrah
Maryam, 30-36, where he specifically denies the
extravagant claims made for him by later generations.

80. Nor would he command you that you
should take the angels and the prophets for Lords.
Would he command you to disbelieve after you
had surrendered to Allah?

81. When Allah made His covenant with the
Prophets, (*He said*): "Here are the Scriptures and
the wisdom which I have given you. And
afterwards there will come to you a messenger,
confirming that which you possess. You shall
believe in him, and shall help him. He said:
"Will you affirm this, and accept the burden I
have laid on you in this matter? They answered:
"We will affirm it He said: "Then bear witness; I
will bear witness with you.

82. Then whosoever after this shall turn away:
they will be transgressors.

83. Are they (*the Christians and Jews*)
seeking a religion other than the religion of Allah
when all that is in the heavens and earth submits
to Him, willingly or unwillingly, and they will be
returned to Him?

84. Say (*O Muhammad!*): "We believe in Allah and that which is revealed to us and that which was revealed to Abraham and Ishmael and Isaac and Jacob and the tribes; and that which was vouchsafed to Moses and Jesus and the Prophets from their Lord. We make no distinction between any of them, and to Him we have surrendered.

85. He who seeks a religion other than Islam, it will not be accepted from him, and he will be a loser in the Hereafter.

(The main principles of all religions that are based on divine revelation are identical, furnishing a tremendous basis for understanding and tolerance among believers. The only differences are in the form of worship prescribed for each people, which is modelled after their cultural needs. Islam accepts all the teachings of other religions, as long as these do not conflict with common sense, and the known principles of the Islamic revelation. Islam is the final link in the line of revelations, and hence meets all the needs of man in our time, whether these be spiritual, moral, social or other. Now that Islam, the definitive and summary religion, has been given to us, the others are obsolete, and have been entirely superseded.)

86. How shall Allah guide a people who disbelieved after their belief, and after they bore witness that the messenger is true, and after clear proofs had come to them? Allah does not guide a wrongdoing people.

87. As for such, their reward shall be the curse of Allah, the angels, and all mankind combined.

88. They will abide there forever. Their punishment shall not be lightened, nor shall they be reprieved.

89. Except those who afterwards repent and mend their ways, for Allah is Forgiving, Merciful.

90. But those who disbelieve after accepting the true faith and afterward grow more intense in disbelief, their repentance will not be accepted, and such are those who are astray.

91. As for those who disbelieve and die in disbelief, no ransom even if it was the earth full of gold would be accepted from them. Theirs will be a painful punishment, and they will have no helpers.

92. You will not attain to righteousness until you spend of what you love. And whatever you spend, Allah is aware of it.

(The word *birr* in this verse, here translated as "righteousness, denotes goodness and spiritual selflessness, the zenith of one's maturity from the point of view of religion.. This is also intimated in verse 177 of Sûrah al-Baqarah. In order to attain to *birr* one has to spend the things that one loves most. According to the interpreters of the Holy Qur'an; these things might be wealth, belongings, status, knowledge, good health, and other material and spiritual gifts with which the Lord blesses us. Only work done against one's own worldly interests is in our spiritual interests, provided that this is not done to excess, and does not endanger our health or families.)

93. All food was lawful to the children of Israel except what Israel forbade himself before the Torah was revealed. Say: "Produce the Torah and read it, if what you say be truth!

94. And whoever shall invent a falsehood about Allah, such are the wrong-doers.

95. Say: "Allah speaks the truth. So follow the religion of Abraham, the upright. He was not of the polytheists .

96. The first Sanctuary ever built for mankind was that at Bakka (*Makka*), a blessed place, a guidance to the peoples;

97. In it there are plain signs; the place where Abraham stood. Whoever enters it is safe. And pilgrimage to the House is a duty to Allah for mankind, for all who are able to make the journey. As for the disbelievers (*they should know that*) Allah is Independant of all creatures.

(Thus is the sacred obligation of the Hajj, the Fifth Pillar of Islam, ordained. The four orthodox Schools have different teachings on who exactly is obliged to go on Hajj. According to Imâm Mâlik, for instance, all who can earn and walk must go.)

98. Say: "O People of the Scripture! Why disbelieve you in the signs (*revelations*) of Allah, when Allah Himself is a witness to what you do?

99. Say: "O People of the Scripture! Why do you drive back believers from the Way of Allah, seeking to make it crooked, when you are witnesses (*to the Lord's guidance*)? Allah is not unaware of what you do.

100. O you who believe! If you obey some of those who have received the Scripture, they will make you disbelievers after your belief.

101. How can you disbelieve, when Allah's revelations are recited to you and His messenger is in your midst? He who holds fast to Allah shall be guided to a right path.

102. O you who believe! Fear Allah as He should be feared, and do not die unless you are submitted to Him (*in Islam*).

(According to the interpreters of the Holy Qur'an, to fear Allah means to obey Him wholeheartedly, being conscious of His scrutiny. 'Abdullah ibn Mas'ûd, may Allah be pleased with him, has explained this passage as meaning: "Not to be disobedient to Him, but to obey Him, not to be ungrateful, but to be thankful and praise Him at all times, without forgetfulness or neglect.)

103. And hold fast, all together, to the rope of Allah, and do not separate. And remember Allah's favour to you: how you were enemies and He made friendship between your hearts, so that you became brothers by His grace; and how you were on the brink of an abyss of fire, and He did save you from it. Thus Allah makes plain His signs to you, that perhaps you will be guided.

104. Let there arise from you a nation who invite to goodness and enjoin what is right, and forbid evil. Such are they who are successful.

(According to the interpreters, it is obligatory on Muslims to establish a social order which regulates the life of the Muslims, and carries out the injunction to enjoin what is good and forbid what is evil. Needless to say, those who perform these duties should have the appropriate qualifications.)

105. And do not be of those who deviated and disputed after the clear proofs had come to them. For such there is a stern punishment.

106. On the day when some faces will be bright and others blackened; and as for those whose faces have been blackened, it will be said (*to them*): "Did you disbelieve after having believed? Then taste the punishment for that you disbelieved.

107. As for those whose faces will be bright, they will abide forever in the mercy of Allah.

108. These are the signs (*revelations*) of Allah. We recite them to you in truth. And Allah wills no injustice to His creatures.

109. Whatever is between the heavens and earth belongs to Allah. To Him all things are returned.

110. You are the best community that has been raised up for mankind. You enjoin what is good and forbid what is evil, and you believe in Allah. And if the People of the Scripture had believed, it would have been better for them. Some of them are believers, but most of them are evildoers.

(The part of this verse which relates to the Muslims is taken as a proof-text for the doctrine of *ijma'*, which holds that the consensus of the believing community constitutes a binding source of law.)

111. They will not harm you except a little hurt, and if they fight against you they will turn and flee. And afterward they will not be helped.

112. Ignomiñy shall be their portion wherever they are found, unless they (*seize*) a rope from Allah and a rope from man. They have incurred the wrath of Allah, and wretchedness is laid upon them. That is because they used to disbelieve the revelations of Allah, and slew the prophets wrongfully. That is because they were rebellious and used to transgress.

113. (*Yet*) they are not all alike. Among the People of the Scripture there is an upright community who during the night recite the revelations of Allah and fall prostrate before Him.

114. They believe in Allah and the Last Day, and enjoin what is right and forbid what is evil, and vie with one another in good works. They are of the righteous.

115. And whatever good they do, its reward will not be denied them. Allah is Aware of those who are righteous.

(In some exegetical works we are told in connection with this verse that when 'Abdullah ibn Salâm, who was a Jew, embraced Islam the Jews criticised him, saying, "By accepting this new religion you have brought upon yourself a great harm. With this verse, the Lord affirms that on the contrary he did the right thing. For the act of embracing Islam, though often enraging to one's fellows, brings tranquillity in this world and salvation in the next. Allah proclaims that the good deeds of such converts will not go to waste, and that they will be rewarded.)

116. As for the disbelievers, neither their riches nor their progeny will protect them in the least against Allah. They are the rightful owners of the Fire, where they will abide forever.

117. The wealth they spend in the life of this world is like a biting, icy wind, which smites the harvest of people who have wronged themselves, laying it waste. Allah wronged them not, but they wronged themselves.

(When men of no faith spend their money, it brings them no true benefit; on the contrary, it resembles a wind which, rather than bringing fruitful rains, yields frost and deadly cold.)

118. O you believe! Take not for friends other than your own people, who would spare no pains to ruin you; they love to hamper you. Their hatred is made clear by (the utterance of) their mouths, but more violent is the hatred which their breasts conceal. We have made plain for you the signs, if you will understand.

119. See, you are those who love them though they love you not, and you believe in all the Scripture. When they meet you they say: "We believe; but when they are alone they bite their fingertips at you with rage. Say: "Perish in your rage! Allah is Aware what is hidden in your breasts.

120. If you are blessed with good fortune they grieve; if a disaster strikes you they rejoice. If you persevere and guard yourselves against evil, their guile will never harm you. Allah is Surrounding what they do.

121. And remember when you set forth at an early hour from your housefolk to assign to the believers their battle positions; Allah was Hearer, Knower.

122. When two parties of you became fainthearted, but Allah was their Protecting Friend. In Allah let the believers put their trust!

(During the Battle of Uhud, two sections of the Muslim army, the Banû Salama of the Khazraj tribe and the Banû Hâritha from the tribe of Aws, showed faintheartedness. Ibn 'Ubayd, who was commander of three hundred men, told them: "We do not want to cast ourselves and our children into danger! and he withdrew his troops.)

123. Allah had already given you the victory at Badr when you were a despised (small force). So have fear of Allah, in order that you may be thankful.

124. And when you said to the believers: "Is it not sufficient for you that your Lord should support you with three thousand angels sent down?

125. Yes: if you have patience, and guard yourselves against evil, Allah will send to your aid five thousand angels making a terrific onslaught, if they suddenly attack you.

126. Allah ordained this only as a message of good cheer for you, and that thereby your hearts might be at rest. Victory comes only from Allah, the Mighty, Wise.

127. That He may cut off a part of those who disbelieve (reduce their number), or overwhelm them so that they might withdraw, frustrated.

128. It is no concern of yours (O Muhammad whether He will relent towards them or punish them. They are assuredly wrongdoers.

(The phrase "a part of" mentioned in verse 127 may mean either the leaders, the commanders, or some of the well-known warriors.)

129. Whatever is in the heavens and the earth belongs to Allah. He forgives whom He will and punishes whom He will. Allah is Forgiving, Merciful.

130. O you who believe! Do not live on usury, multiplying your wealth many times over (as compound interest). Have fear of Allah, that perhaps you may be successful.

(In verses 275, 276 and 278 of Sûrah al-Baqarah, God outlaws lending money at interest, but renders trade lawful. Compound interest is mentioned in the present context because the pagan Arabs before Islam used to permit it.)

131. Guard yourselves against the Fire prepared for disbelievers.

132. And obey Allah and the Messenger, that you may find mercy.

133. And vie with one another for the forgiveness of your Lord and for a garden as vast as the heavens and the earth, prepared for the Godfearing.

134. Those who spend (*of that which Allah has given them*) in ease and adversity, those who control their anger and are forgiving toward mankind; for Allah loves the good.

135. And those who, when they do an evil thing or wrong themselves, remember Allah and seek forgiveness for their sins - Who can forgive sins except Allah only? - and will not knowingly persist (*in their misdeeds*).

(The above three verses summarise proper Islamic behaviour. Verse 133 explains the objective of the moral life: conformity with the objective scale of values established by the Unitive Principle of Existence, which must necessarily lead to final proximity to that Unity. And in verses 134 and 135, the specifics of this conformity are outlined in general terms: care for others, self-restraint and good character, and scrutiny of one's own conduct, coupled with the seeking of God's forgiveness for slips and errors. Thus may one liberate oneself from the shackles of worldly caprice and conformity, and achieve the highest standard of spiritual perfection.)

136. The reward of such will be forgiveness from their Lord, and gardens beneath which rivers flow, where they will abide forever. Blessed is the reward of those who work!

137. Many ways of life have passed away before you. Travel in the land and see how was the end of those who denied (*the Messengers who brought the reminder, or the reminder itself*).

138. This is a declaration for mankind; a guidance and an admonition to the Godfearing.

139. Faint not nor grieve. If you are true believers you will overcome them.

(This verse was revealed after the Battle of Uhud. Many Muslims, because of their apparent defeat, were in despair. In this verse Allah told them that if they were true believers they would win out in the end. This is also glad tidings to the Muslims, who are informed that they will have many victories in the future.)

140. If you have suffered a wound, so did the (*disbelieving*) people (*at Badr*). We alternate these vicissitudes among mankind so that Allah may know those that believe, and choose witnesses (*or: martyrs*) from among you. And Allah does not love the wrongdoers.

(There have been different interpretations of this passage, but the main point is that Allah, having knowledge of past and future, simply wishes to put the believers to the test in order that the real believers should become distinct from the hypocrites. Hence the ambiguity of the word *shuhadâ'*, which can mean "martyr" as well as "witness".)

141. And that Allah may prove those who believe, and blight the disbelievers.

142. Did you suppose that you would enter the Garden before Allah had tested (*known*) those of you who really strived (*for His cause*), and who endured with steadfastness?

143. And you used to wish for death before you met it (*on the battlefield*). Now you have seen it with your own eyes!

(The verse relates to an incident in which the Prophet Muhammad, peace be upon him, having admired the martyrs of the Battle of Badr, proposed that his companions should stay in Madîna to defend the city against the idolaters. Certain of his Companions, on the other hand, confident that martyrdom was the highest gain this life can offer, proposed to go out to Uhud and fight a battle there.)

144. Muhammad is but a messenger; and messengers have passed away before him. Will you, when he dies or is slain, turn back on your heels *(go back to your old religion)?* He who turns back does not hurt Allah. And Allah will reward the thankful.

(At the Battle of Uhud, an idolator named 'Abdullah ibn Qami' threw a stone which broke the Prophet's tooth and injured him, after which the idolator screamed that "Muhammad has been killed! This false rumour spread among the Muslim soldiers and they began to scatter. Realising this, the Blessed Prophet immediately called back the demoralised believers, and about 30 of the Companions formed around him and vigorously protected him. The above verse criticises those Muslims who were affected by the rumour, and states that although the Prophet Muhammad is only a mortal man, Islam will remain, even if he dies. The Muslims should accept this as a fact, and show steadfastness and endurance.

The passage also has a bearing on another famous incident: the morning in which the Blessed Prophet died, when Abu Bakr came out into the mosque of Madîna, and, finding the people distracted with grief, declared, "As for him that worshipped Muhammad, (let him know that) Muhammad is dead. But as for him that worshipped the Lord of Muhammad, He is Alive, and does not die.)

145. No soul dies without the permission of Allah, and at a term appointed. He who desires the reward of this world shall have it from Us; and he who desires the reward of the Hereafter shall have it from Us also. We will surely reward the thankful.

146. And with how many a prophet have there been a number of devoted men who fought (*beside him*). They quailed not despite what befell them in Allah's path, nor did they weaken, nor were they brought low. Allah loves the steadfast.

147. Their only words were: "Lord; forgive us our sins and anything we may have done that transgressed our duty, establish our feet firm (*on Your path*) and give us victory over the disbelieving people.

148. So Allah gave them the reward of this world and the excellent reward of the Hereafter. Allah loves those whose deeds are good.

149. O you who believe! If you obey those who disbelieve they will make you go back to your old religion *(idolatry):* and you will then turn back as losers.

150. But Allah is your Protector, and He is the best of helpers.

151. We will cast terror into the hearts of those who disbelieve because they ascribe partners to Allah for whom no warrant had been revealed. Their abode is the Fire. Evil is the dwelling of the unjust!

(This verse emphasizes the importance of the moral strength of the believers, something which disbelievers customarily lack. Although during the Battle of Uhud, many of the Muslims were demoralized, the idolaters were unable to finish them off: they hesitated, and did not have enough courage to come and press home their victory. They returned to Makka without any real gains.)

152. Allah fulfilled His pledge to you when by His leave you defeated them, until *(the moment)* when your courage failed you, and you disagreed about the order and you disobeyed, after He had shown you that for which you long. Some of you desired the world, and some of you desired the Hereafter. Therefore He made you flee from them, that He might try you. But now He has forgiven you; He is a Lord of Kindness to believers.

(The tide of battle turned against the Muslims when a detachment of them, which had been posted as archers upon a hillock, deserted their post to seek booty, thinking the battle won. This exposed the Muslim flank, and made the success of the idolators possible.)

153. When you climbed *(the hill)* and paid no heed to anyone, while the Messenger behind you was calling out to you. Therefore Allah rewarded you with grief after grief, so that you might not grieve for what you missed or what befell you. Allah is Informed of what you do.

154. Then, after grief, He sent down security for you. A sleep which overtook some, while others lay troubled on their own account, moved by wrong suspicions of Allah, the suspicion of ignorance. They said: "Have we any part in the cause? Say (O Muhammad): "The cause belongs wholly to Allah." They hide within themselves (a thought) which they reveal not to you, saying: "Had we had any part in the cause we should not have been slain here. Say: "Even though you had been in your houses, those appointed to be slain would have gone forth to the places where they were to lie. (All this had been) in order that Allah might try what is in your breasts and prove what is in your hearts. Allah is Aware of what is hidden in the breasts (of men).

(At the Battle of Uhud, the enemy soldiers were several times more numerous than the Muslim army. Since victory is in the hands of Allah the believers were sent down security in the form of a sleep which overtook them. 'Abdullah ibn Mas'ûd states that: "Slumber in time of battle is from Allah, and slumber during the time of prayer (Salât) is from Satan. Abû

Talha states: "I was among the fighting men during the Battle of Uhud; slumber also overtook me, so that I could not help myself; my sword fell from my hand, and I picked it up, and it fell out again; and this happened to me many times . The other group mentioned in the verse is the hypocrites.)

155. Those of you who turned back on the day the two hosts met, it was Satan alone who caused them to backslide, because of some of that which they have earned. But now Allah has forgiven them. Assuredly, Allah is Forgiving, Clement.

156. O you who believe! Do not be like the disbelievers, who said of their brothers when they went abroad in the land or were in battle: "Had they stayed here with us they would not have died or been killed. This that Allah may make it a cause of sighs and regrets in their hearts. It is Allah who gives life and death; and He is Seer of what you do.

157. If you should die or be slain in the cause of Allah, His forgiveness and His mercy would surely be better than all that they amass.

158. If you should die or be slain, before Him you shall all be gathered.

159. It was by the mercy of Allah that you were lenient with them (O Muhammad). Had you been stern and hard-hearted, they would have surely have dispersed from round about you. So pardon them and ask forgiveness for them and consult with them in the conduct of affairs (of the community); and when you are resolved, put your trust in Allah. Allah loves those that trust (in Him).

160. If Allah helps you, none can overcome you. If He abandons you, who then can help you? In Allah let believers put their trust.

161. It is not for any prophet to deceive (mankind); whoever deceives will bring his deceit with him on the Day of Resurrection. Then every soul will be paid in full what it had earned; and they will not be wronged.

(In the aftermath of the Battle of Badr some items from the war-spoils went missing. The hypocrites took advantage of this incident and accused the Blessed Prophet of stealing them, and hence this verse was revealed. Another interpretation applies the verse to those archers at Uhud who had deserted their posts in search of booty.)

162. Can one who seeks the pleasure of Allah be compared to him who has incurred His wrath? Hell shall be their habitation. Evil shall be their fate.

163. These are degrees (of grace and its opposite) with Allah; and Allah is Seer of what you do.

164. Allah has surely shown grace to the believers by sending to them a Messenger of their own who recites to them His revelations, and purifies them, and instructs them in the Scripture and in wisdom; although before they were in flagrant error.

165. When a disaster befell you after you had yourselves inflicted (losses) twice as heavy, you exclaimed: "Whose fault was that? Say (to them, O Muhammad): "It is from yourselves. Allah is Able to do all things.

(At the Battle of Badr, the Muslims killed seventy of the idolaters and took prisoners from them, but during the Battle of Uhud it was the exact opposite; the Muslims losing seventy martyrs. In the above verse, the disaster mentioned is related to the incidents just mentioned.)

166. That which befell you on the day when the two armies met was by permission of Allah; that He might know the true believers.

167. And that He might know the hypocrites, to whom it was said: "Come, fight for the cause of Allah, or defend yourselves. They answered: "If only we could fight, we would follow you. On that day they were nearer to disbelief than faith. They were saying a thing with their mouths which was not in their hearts. And Allah is best aware of what they hide.

168. Those who, while they sat at home, said of their brothers (who were fighting for the cause of truth): "If they had obeyed us they would not have been slain. Say: (to them, O Muhammad) "Then avert death from yourselves, if what you say be true!

169. Think not of those who are slain in the cause of Allah as dead. They are alive; with their Lord they have provision.

170. Joyful because of what Allah has bestowed on them of His grace; rejoicing for the sake of those who have not joined them but are left behind: that there shall be no fear for them neither shall they grieve.

171. They rejoice because of grace from Allah and kindness; and that Allah wastes not the wage of the believers.

172. As for those who heard the call of Allah and His Messenger after the harm befell them (in the fight), for such of them as do right and keep from evil, there is a great reward.

173. Those to whom men said: "The enemy have gathered against you, therefore fear them, but this increased their faith, and they cried: "Allah is sufficient for us! He is the best Protector.

(According to the historians, during the Battle of Uhud the enemy had not achieved the result that they hoped, even though the Muslim army had momentarily panicked. When Abû Sufyân, the commander of the enemy army, was ready to leave the battlefield he addressed the Prophet Muhammad as follows: "O Muhammad, we shall meet you again next year at Badr. And the Prophet Muhammad replied: "God willing. Next year, news of Abû Sufyân's efforts to gather a new army reached Madîna. The Blessed Prophet immediately prepared a force of cavalry, and left Madîna to meet the enemy. The above verse praises the faith of the believers, and their courage and determination.)

174. So they returned with grace and favour from Allah, and no harm touched them. They followed the good pleasure of Allah, and Allah is of infinite grace.

(The forces of the Prophet Muhammad came to the place where Abû Sufyân had proposed to meet them a year ago. And yet Abû Sufyân had grown afraid, and did not keep his promise. The Muslim army under the Prophet's command waited for him for about a week, and when he did not show up they engaged in trade for a while, and, having made a goodly profit, returned to Madîna triumphantly.)

175. It is only Satan who would make (men) fear his followers; but have no fear of them. Fear Me, if you are believers.

176. (O Muhammad,) let not their conduct grieve you, who run easily to disbelief. They will not harm Allah at all. He wills to assign them no share in the Hereafter, and theirs will be a terrible punishment.

177. Those who barter away their faith for disbelief will do Allah no harm. Theirs will be a painful punishment.

178. Let those who disbelieve not imagine that We prolong their time for the good of their own souls. We only give them respite that they may grow in sinfulness; and theirs will be a shameful punishment.

179. Allah will not leave the believers in the state in which you are now until He separates what is evil from what is good; nor will He disclose to you the secrets of the unseen. But He chooses of His messengers whom He will, so believe in Allah and His messengers. And if you believe in Allah and guard yourselves against evil, yours will be a reward without measure.

(Interpreters of the Holy Qur'an state that the above verse was revealed as a response to the disbelievers, who were enquiring of the Prophet Muhammad who had faith and who did not.)

180. And let not those who hoard up that which Allah has bestowed upon them of His bounty think that it is better for them. It is worse for them. That which they hoard will be their collar on the Day of Resurrection. Allah's is the inheritance of the heaven and the earth, and Allah is aware of what you do.

(The word "inheritance" (mîrâth) in the above verse is interpreted to mean everything that God shall one day inherit, when mankind has left this earth for good. There is no reason to hoard up that which God has given us, for one day we must die, and the sole heir, trustee and executor is the One Almighty God, Who has made us, and lent us all we possess.)

181. Allah has heard the saying of those who said: "Truly Allah is poor, and we are rich! We shall certainly record their saying with their slaying of the prophets wrongfully, and we shall say: "Taste now the torment of the Blaze .

(This blasphemous utterance of the Medîna Jews, whose obsession with wealth had made them hated by all, was hardly less heinous then the murder of God's prophets in previous generations.)

182. This is on account of that which your own hands have sent before you. Allah is no oppressor to His servants.

183. They (also) said: "Allah had commanded us that we believe not in any messenger until he bring us an offering which fire (from heaven) shall devour. Say (to them, O Muhammad): "Messengers came to you before me with miracles, and with that (very miracle) which you describe. Why then did you slay them? Answer, if you are truthful!

184. Then if they reject you, (know that) other messengers were rejected before you, who came with miracles, and with the Psalms, and with the Scripture giving light.

185. Every soul shall taste of death. And you shall be paid on the Day of Resurrection only that which you have fairly earned. Whoever is removed from the fire of Hell and is made to enter the Garden, he indeed is successful. The life of this world is nothing but the comfort of illusion.

186. You shall certainly be tried in your possessions and in your lives, and you shall certainly hear much wrong from those who were given the Scripture before you, and from the polytheists. But if you persevere patiently and guard yourselves against evil, that will be a determining factor in affairs.

187. And *(remember when)* Allah took a covenant from those who had been given the Scripture, to make it clear to mankind, and not to hide it. But they flung it behind their backs, and exchanged it for a miserable price. Assuredly, evil was what they purchased.

188. Think not that those who rejoice at what they have done, and wish to be praised for what they have not done - Do not think that they can escape from the punishment. For them there is a painful punishment.

189. To Allah belongs the sovereignty of the heavens and the earth. Allah has power over all things.

190. In the creation of the heavens and the earth, and in the alternation of night and day, there are signs for men of understanding.

191. Those that remember Allah standing, sitting, and lying down, and meditate upon the creation of the heavens and the earth. "Our Lord! You have not created this in vain. Glory be to You! Protect us from the punishment of the Fire.

192. Our Lord! Those whom you will admit to the Fire, you have abased them. For evil-doers there are no helpers.

193. Our Lord! We have heard a caller calling to faith: "Believe you in your Lord! So we believed. Our Lord! Therefore forgive us our sins and remit from us our evil deeds, and take our souls in death in the company of the righteous!

194. Our Lord! And grant us what You did promise to us through Your messengers, and do not abase us on the Day of Resurrection. You never break the promise!

195. And their Lord accepted (their prayers): "Never will I suffer to be lost the work of any of you, whether male or female; you are (the offspring) of one another. So those who emigrated, and were expelled from their homes, and suffered harm in My cause, and fought and were slain, assuredly, I will remit from them their sins, and admit them into gardens beneath which rivers flow; a reward from Allah, and with Allah is the best of rewards.

196. Let not the strutting of the disbelievers in the land beguile you.

(A number of the believers were given to speaking with one another about the material wealth and comfort of the disbelievers, and murmured that: "The enemies of Allah are rich; and we are poor. Because of this, the above verse was revealed. More generally, it provides a counsel to all those who would be beguiled by wordly distractions from God's remembrance, for such distractions are by no means a sign of favour; they may commonly be a curse.)

197. It is but a little enjoyment; and their abode is Hell; an evil bed.

198. For those who feared their Lord are gardens beneath which rivers flow; wherein they will dwell for ever. A gift of welcome from their Lord. Allah's reward is better for the good.

199. And there are certainly among the People of the Scripture some who believe in Allah and that which is revealed to you and that which was revealed to them, humbling themselves before Allah. They will not sell the revelations (signs) of Allah for a miserable gain! Verily their reward is in the presence of their Lord; and Allah is Swift in reckoning.

200. O you who believe! Endure, vie with each other in endurance, be ready, and fear Allah, that perhaps you may succeed.

(The words "be ready" refer to the loyal citizen's readiness to fight against aggressors, and in defence of justice and the revealed Law. And with this spectacular series of commandments and prayers closes the Sûrah.)

SÛRAH IV

AN-NISÂ' (THE WOMEN)

Revealed at Madîna

"*Nisâ* means "women . And much of this section of the Holy Book treats of the legal position and standing of women in sacred society.

In the name of Allah, the Compassionate, the Merciful

1. O mankind! Have fear of Allah, Who created you from a single soul, and from it created its mate and from the two of them spread abroad a multitude of men and women. Fear Allah in Whom you claim your mutual *(rights)*, and toward the wombs *(that bare you.)* Allah is ever Watching over you.

2. Give orphans the property which belongs to them. Exchange not the good for the bad *(in the way you manage their property),* nor absorb their wealth into your own wealth. Indeed, that would be a great sin.

3. And if you fear that you will not deal fairly with the orphans, marry women of your choice, two or three or four; but if you fear that you cannot deal justly *(with so many),* then one only, or *(the captives)* that your right hands possess. Thus it is more likely that you will not do injustice.

(By this verse the sacred institution of polygamy, recognised in the Mosaic law, practised by Solomon and Charlemagne, and defended by Martin Luther, is confirmed. From now on, however, a limitation is introduced: men must confine themselves to no more than four wives. Further, if they so much as fear that they may not be able to treat them justly, they are obliged to marry only one. Elsewhere, in the Traditions of the Blessed Prophet, Muslims are commanded to provide equally for each spouse, and to give them separate and equivalent accommodation; as a result, the institution, despite its advantages for both sexes, is often confined to the more prosperous sections of society.

4. And give to the women (whom you marry) their dower with a good heart; but if they of their own good pleasure, remit any part of it to you, take it, and enjoy it without fear of any harm (as Allah made it lawful).

5. Do not give the weak of understanding *(minors, and the mentally deficient)* the property which Allah has given you to maintain, but clothe them from it, and speak kindly to them.

6. Put orphans to the test until they reach the age of marriage; then, if you find them of sound judgement, deliver over to them their property, and devour it not by squandering and in haste lest they grow up. If the guardian is rich, let him claim no remuneration, but, if he is poor, let him have for himself what is just and reasonable. When you release their property to them, have *(the transaction)* witnessed in their presence. Allah is sufficient as Reckoner.

7. From what is left by parents and those nearest related there is a share for men and a share for women, whether the property be small or large; a legal share.

8. If at the time of division other relatives, orphans, or poor, are present (exist), give them out from the property, and speak to them kindly.

(The above two verses are typical of the sort of social amelioration brought by Islam. In the pagan period before the Blessed Prophet came, women were deprived of the right to inherit; and this verse established their rights in this regard. Secondly, we note that provision is made not simply for close relatives, but also for more distant kinsfolk, as well as neighbours and the local poor, in order to dispel any ill-feelings that might have been generated during a person's lifetime, especially concerning the means by which the property was acquired.)

9. Let those fear (in disposing of an estate) as they would fear for their own if they left behind a helpless family: let them fear Allah, and speak correctly.

10. Those who devour the wealth of orphans wrongfully, do but swallow fire into their bellies, they will be exposed to blazing flame!

11. Allah thus commands you concerning (the division for) your children: to the male, a portion equal to that of two females, and if there be women more than two, then their share is two-thirds of the inheritance; and if only one her share is a half. And to his parents, a sixth of the inheritance, if the deceased left children; if he has no children, and the parents are the (only) heirs, the mother has a third; if he left brothers (or sisters) the mother has a sixth. (The division in all cases is) after the payment of legacies and debts. You know not which of your parents or your children are more beneficial to you. These are settled portions commanded by Allah; and Allah is Knowing, Wise.

(In this verse, it is to be noted how a balance is carefully struck between shares and responsibilities. Those who are charged with the responsibility of taking care of other people are to receive a larger share. Under Islamic Law, the party which provides the dowry at marriage is the man, not the woman, and he too is legally obliged to take care of expenses incurred during the wedding, and the marriage itself, such as expenditure on food, clothing and shelter of the wife, children, and near relations. In the light of this, Islamic law grants men a larger share in most cases of inheritance.)

12. And you will inherit half of your wives' share if they leave no child; but if they leave a child then to you the fourth of that which they leave, after payment of legacies they may have bequeathed, or debt. And to them belongs the fourth of that which you leave if you have no child; but if you have a child then the eighth of that which you leave, after any legacy you may have bequeathed, or debt. And if a man or woman (*whose inheritance is in question*), has left neither ascendants nor descendants, but has left a brother or a sister, each one of the two shall have a sixth; but if they be more than two, they shall share in the third; after any legacy which may have been bequeathed, or debt; so that no loss is caused *(to anyone)*. This is the ordinance of Allah. Allah is Knowing, Gentle.

(The Arabic word *kalâla*, here rendered "neither ascendants nor descendants was nowhere defined authoritatively in the lifetime of the Blessed Messenger. 'Umar, may God be pleased with him, later remarked that there were three terms which he wished had been defined in the Blessed Prophet's lifetime: *khilâfa*, *ribâ* and *kalâla*.

On the accepted definition, which we follow in the translation, we are concerned with the inheritance of a person who has left no descendant or ascendant (however remote), but only collaterals, with or without a widow or widower. If there is a widow or widower surviving, she or he takes the share as already defined, before the collaterals come in.)

13. These are the limits set by Allah. Whoever obeys Allah and His messenger, He will make him enter Gardens beneath which rivers flow, where such will dwell for ever. That will be the great success.

14. And whoever disobeys Allah and His Messenger and transgresses His limits; Allah will make him enter fire, to dwell there forever; his will be a humiliating punishment.

(The legal systems of the world have adopted different arrangements in regard to inheritance laws. In many secular systems, we find that the testator has the right to deprive his immediate family of any inheritance whatsoever, even if he be old and cantankerous. While a portion of the deceased's funds may indeed be disposed as he specifies in a will, a fixed percentage must be distributed to relations, according to the shares specified in detail in the preceding passages.)

15. As for those of your women who are guilty of adultery (*or fornication*), call to witness four of you against them. And if they testify (*to their guilt*) then confine them to the houses until death takes them or till Allah finds another way for them (*through new legislation*).

16. As for the two of you who are guilty of it, punish them both; and if they repent and mend their ways, leave them alone. Allah is Forgiving, Merciful.

(The above two verses relate to the crimes of adultery and fornication. The first verse deals with adultery proper, where one of the parties or both are married, whereas in the second verse the parties are unmarried people. In another Sûrah, new rules are laid down which replace and abrogate the present passage, which was of a provisional nature. According to the interpretation of verse 2 of Sûrah al-Nûr, if the person who commits this crime is a married person, the punishment of stoning is applied, whereas if he or she is single and has not been married 100 lashes are administered, on the (*rather difficult*) condition that four witnesses to the actual act are forthcoming.

According to other interpreters of the Holy Qur'an, however, the present passage is not abrogated: rather than adultery being the theme, it deals with inversion: the first verse dealing with lesbianism, whereas the second addresses male homosexuality.)

17. Allah accepts the repentance of those who do evil in ignorance and then quickly turn to Allah in repentance, Those are they whom Allah pardons, and Allah is ever Knower, Wise.

18. Forgiveness is not for those who do ill deeds until, when death comes upon one of them, he says: "Now I repent! ; nor yet for those who die while they are disbelievers. For such We have prepared a painful punishment.

19. O you who believe! It is not lawful for you to inherit women against their will, nor to put constraint on them that you may take away a part of that which you have given them, unless they are guilty of open lewdness. Treat them with kindness, for even if you hate them it may be that you hate a thing in which Allah has placed much good.

(Before Islam it was customary among the Arab tribes to treat woman like chattels. If a woman's husband died she would become part of his estate. She would be forced to marry against her will or would be sold as though she were a commodity, or be used for any other material gain. With the revelation of this verse this practice come to an end, and women, who were candidates for salvation too, were given the dignity and respect they deserved.)

20. If you wish to divorce a woman in order to wed another, and you have given her a (whole) treasure as dowry, take not the least part of it back. Would you take it by way of calumny and open wrong?

(It is an obligatory customary in Islamic marriage that when a man marries a woman, he gives her a certain amount as a "gift in the form of gold, jewelry, currency, or property, or other material good, as specified by her and her family. This is called *mahr*. This can be given in advance before the marriage once they decide to get married; or alternatively it can be postponed, to be paid either in case of a divorce or on the death of the husband, the option being in the bride's hand. Under Islamic Law, it is illegal for men to deprive their wives of this money, the purpose of which is to give her a degree of financial independance. All kinds of abuse, pressure and harrassment are prohibited, and are actionable in a court of law.)

21. How can you take it (back) when one of you has gone in to the other, and they have taken a strong pledge from you?

(A man who marries a woman and has sex with her, and later decides to divorce her, is obligated to give her *mahr* in full, however brief the marriage may have been. If the marriage contract has been completed but the man did not consummate the marriage, then the woman takes half of the dowry, whatever it might be.)

22. And marry not those women whom your fathers married, except what has already happened (of that nature) in the past. It was always a foulness and an abomination, and an evil way.

(The above verse also abrogates the practice whereby a stepson would marry a man's widow, as was sometimes the case in the pre-Islamic Days of Ignorance. The next verse specifies the forbidden degrees of marriage.)

23. Forbidden to you are your mothers, and your daughters, and your sisters, and your father's sisters, and your mother's sisters, and your brother's daughters, and your sister's daughters, and your foster-mothers, and your foster-sisters, and your mothers-in law, and your

step-daughters who are under your protection (born) of your women unto whom you have gone in - but if you have not gone in to them, then it is no sin for you (to marry their daughters) - and the wives of your sons who (spring) from your own loins. And (it is forbidden to you) that you should have two sisters together, except what had already happened (of that nature before Islam) in the past. Surely, Allah is ever Forgiving, Merciful.

(Concerning the part of the above verse which reads "your women to whom you have gone in - but if you have not gone in to them, then it is no sin for you (to marry their daughters), the meaning is that you cannot marry the daughter of a woman you have made a contract to marry. If the marriage contract is performed but the actual consummation has not taken place, and a divorce follows he is not barred from marrying any daughter the woman might have had by another man. Although there are some distant relatives who are able to marry with each other, marriage with close relatives is forbidden both by the Holy Qur'an and the Noble Hadiths.)

right hands possess. Allah knows best your faith. You are one from another, so wed them by permission of their families, and give them their portions in kindness, they being honest, not debauched or of loose conduct. And if when they are honourably married they commit adultery, they shall incur the half of the punishment (*prescribed*) for a free woman (*in this case*). This is for him among you who fears to commit sin. But to have patience would be better for you. Allah is Forgiving, Merciful.

(Adultery and fornication are forbidden in all the higher religions. Neither is it lawful, as some suppose, for a couple to marry for a fixed period of time at a certain price. The intention has to be permanent. To keep a mistress in secret is no more than a form of adultery. A Muslim man, when he marries, should prefer a believing free woman. A Muslim man can also marry from among the people of the Book; i.e., the Jews and Christians. The above passage which states that "you are one from another" shows the importance of treating slaves kindly. The dignity of man or woman, whether slave or free, is immensely important. By means of the kind treatment of captive slaves in times of war, captives can be led to Islam, appreciating its emphasis on compassion and justice. There can be no greater contrast than the difference of emphasis between an Islamic order, in which temporary enslavement is possible for some, and the modern nation-state, in which permanent slavery is obligatory for all.)

24. And all married women (*are forbidden to you*) except those your right hands possess. It is a decree of Allah for you. Lawful to you are all beyond those mentioned, so that you seek them with your wealth in honest wedlock, not in fornication. And those of whom you seek content (*by marrying them*), give to them their portions as a duty. And there is no sin for you in what you do by mutual agreement after the duty (*has been done*). Allah is ever Knower, Wise.

(Among some religions, the custom exists of giving a dowry to the husband, not the wife. This practice is known among the Hindus, Armenians, Jews and Greeks. In these cultures, this is regarded as a means by which a woman can attract a man. Islam, however, enacts the opposite. It is assumed that a Muslim man will not prefer wealth, but chastity and dignity. Because of this it is the man who gives a financial gift to the woman.)

25. And if any of you is not able to afford to marry from the free, believing women, let them marry from the believing women whom your

26. Allah would explain to you and guide you by the examples of those who were before you, and would turn to you in mercy. Allah is Knower, Wise.

27. And Allah would turn to you in mercy; but those who follow their caprice would have you go far astray.

28. Allah would make the burden light for you, for man was created weak.

(The counsels and obligations of religion are not a burden; on the contrary, they are necessary measures to prevent man from going astray and harming himself and others. By recognising that the revealed Law exists to protect and guide us, man attains to serenity and happiness in both worlds.)

29. O you who believe! Do not devour your property among yourselves in vanity; except it be a trade by mutual consent, and kill not one another. Surely Allah is ever Merciful to you.

30. Whoever does that through aggression and injustice, We shall cast him into Fire, and that is ever easy for Allah.

(It is useful for societies to do trade, and exchange goods and services, as long as they are within the boundaries of justice and equality and respect each others' rights. All these activities are lawful from the Islamic point of view. But forms of trade done between people illegally do not bring permanent happiness; on the contrary, they bring disaster and poverty for many, even though they might bring temporary success to certain groups of people. Such unjust economic activities can also give rise to rebellions, strife, revolution and other forms of chaos. The words "your property mentioned in verse 29 might aso connote the wealth of the community as a whole, which is held in trust from God. Another injustice committed against humanity is the killing of another man without just cause.)

31. If you avoid the great sins which you are forbidden, we will remit from you your evil deeds, and make you enter a Gate of Honour.

(Man, unlike the angels, is not created free from the will to sin. The virtues come from striving against the evil instincts and selfish tendencies which we bear within our souls. When one strives in this way, which is the essence of the moral life, God will surely remit the sins one had previously committed, from His grace, and grant us increasing proximity to Him, in this world and the next.)

32. And do not covet the things in which Allah had made some of you excel others. To men is

allotted a share of what they earn, and to women a share of what they earn. (*Do not fall prey to envy*),but ask Allah of His bounty. For Allah has full knowledge of all things.

(Since the Lord has blessed every individual with certain abilities and talents, there is no reason for a person to be jealous of others. It is a miserable way of passing one's life to yearn for things that one does not possess; instead one should be content with the blessings that Allah has bestowed on him and ask directly from Allah's bounty for the things that he does not possess. And the things of the Spirit are finer still.)

33. And to each We have appointed heirs of that which parents and near kinsmen leave; and as for those with whom your right hands have made a covenant, give them their due. Assuredly, Allah is ever Witness over all things.

(The "covenant here means the practice of certain heirs under contract to inherit from the estate of the deceased. This practice, according to some commentators, discontinued upon the revelation of verse 75 of Sûrah al-Anfâl. According to other scholars, however, it simply denotes "wives .)

34. Men are the protectors of women, because Allah has given the one more than the other (*strength*), and because they spend of their property (*to maintain them*). So righteous women are the devoutly obedient, guarding in secret that which Allah had guarded. As for those from whom you fear disloyalty, admonish them and banish them to beds apart, and beat them (*lightly, without visible injury*). Then if they obey you, seek not a way against them. For Allah is High, Sublime.

(Because of the role customarily exercised by man in society, which gives him a certain degree of experience and foresight, he is the natural head of the family. The family is the smallest building block of society, and on its health all else depends. No community, not least the complex one that is a family, can endure long without a leader. In Islam, every leader, head or administrator has to rule according to the Divine Law, and to disobey such a leader, while they rule with justice and compassion, is to disobey the Lawgiver, and merits punishment.)

It should be observed that the sanction in the case of marriage is a last resort. The Blessed Prophet never hit any of his wives. In fact, he warned the Muslim community that it is a donkey who beats his wife. If a man has to administer physical correction to a wife, his strokes should be symbolic, as they must leave no bruises or other marks. A wife with a complaint against her husband's treatment may apply to a magistrate to deal with the problem.)

35. And if you fear a breach between them (*man and wife*), then appoint an arbiter from his people and an arbiter from her people. If they desire reconciliation, Allah will make them of one mind. Allah is ever Knower, Aware.

36. Serve Allah, and do not ascribe partners to Him. And show kindness to your parents, and to your close kindred, and orphans, and the needy, and to the neighbour who is of kin, and the neighbour who is not of kin, and the fellow-traveller and the wayfarer and (*the bondsmen*) whom your right hands possess. Surely Allah does not love the arrogant, the boastful.

(A true servant of Allah possesses a beautiful character. He who prays, fasts, and is learned, but remains stingy and harsh, is not among the Lord's true servants.)

37. Who hoard their wealth and enjoin avarice on others, and hide that which Allah has bestowed upon them of His bounty. For disbelievers We prepare a shameful doom.

38. And those who spend their wealth in order to be seen of men, and believe not in Allah nor the Last Day. Whoever takes Satan for a friend, an evil friend has he.

39. What have they *(to fear)* if they believe in Allah and the Last Day and spend *(aright)* of that which Allah had bestowed upon them, when Allah is ever Aware of them *(and all that they do)?*

40. Surely, Allah wrongs not even in the extent of an atom; and if there is a good deed, He will double it, and will give *(the agent of the good deed)* from His presence a great reward.

41. How will it be when We bring a witness from every nation, and We bring you *(O Muhammad)* as a witness against these?

(All messengers of Allah came with the same purpose: to convey the Lord's message. Altough principles and moral absolutes do not change, nonetheless, since civil and social conditions change constantly, their application must sometimes vary. The prophet Muhammad Mustafâ, being the Last Messenger, sent for the time of advanced civilisation, came to remind erring man of the ancient message, presenting it in the most appropriate form. People who tamper with the message, or deny it completely with the claim that the universe has no unitive principle, will be brought to trial on the Last Day, and their messengers will bear witness against them. And the Final Prophet, Muhammad, will testify in favour of all the Messengers that came before him.

According to a hadith narrated by Bukhârî, the Prophet once asked Ibn Mas'ûd to recite the Holy Qur'an, and he enquired: "Should I be the one to recite to you, altough it has been revealed to you? The Prophet answered, "Yes, it pleases me a great deal to hear someone else reciting Ibn Ma'sûd continued: "Then I recited Sûrah an-Nisâ', and when I came to verse 41, he said, 'Enough for now.' He told me to stop, and when I looked at him, tears were streaming from his eyes.)

42. On that day those who disbelieved and disobeyed the Messenger will wish that they were level with the ground, and they can hide no fact from Allah.

43. O you who believe! Do not approach prayers when you are drunk, until you know what you say, nor when you are in a state of impurity *(following sexual relations and before bathing)* except when you are on a journey, till you have

bathed. And if you be ill, or on a journey, or one of you comes from the privy, or you have touched women *(lain with them)*, and you find not water, then take yourselves to clean earth and rub your faces and your hands. Surely, Allah is Benign, Forgiving.

(When ablution is necessary to clean oneself for divine worship, and no water can be found in the surrounding area, the practise of "*tayammum* may be implemented. In Islam, strict cleanliness and purity both of mind and body are required, especially at the time of prayer, and when actual physical hygiene is impossible, a symbolic gesture, activated by God's grace, can supply for it. *Tayammum*, which is a facilitation, or dispensation, can only be resorted to in certain circumstances. The water might be too far away, or a person might be ill and cannot walk any distance, he might suffer from a disease which renders the use of water hazardous, or, being on a journey, he might have limited supplies, or fear an enemy or wild beasts.)

44. Do not you see that those to whom a portion of the Scripture had been given, how they buy error, and seek to make you *(Muslims)* err from the right path?

45. Allah knows best (who are) your enemies. Allah suffices as a Friend, and Allah is sufficient as a Helper.

46. Some of those who are Jews change words from their context and say: "We hear and disobey; hear you as one who hears not; and "listen to us! distorting with their tongues and slandering religion. If they had said: "We hear and we obey; hear you, and look at us it had been better for them, and more upright. But Allah has cursed them for their disbelief, so they believe not, except a few.

(The Jews mischievously changed the Scriptures that were given to them by Allah. They mutilated the words which they had received from Moses and the later Prophets. They even hid the passages which predicted the coming of the Blessed Prophet Muhammad. Whenever they had an opportunity to insult and show their ill-will to the new dispensation, they did not hesitate to do so. For example, the Arabic word râ'inâ used in the above verse, if used respectfully, means "please attend to us . And yet the Jews, with a twist of their tongues, implied an insulting meaning such as "O you that takes us to pasture; or, in Hebrew, "Our bad one! The above verse is a condemnation of their behaviour.)

47. O you to whom the Scriptures have been given! Believe in what We have revealed confirming that which you possess, before We destroy countenances so as to confound them, or curse them as We cursed the Sabbath-breakers (of old). The commandment of Allah is always enforced.

48. Allah will not forgive those who assign partners to Him. He forgive all except that to whom He will. Whoever ascribes partners to Allah is guilty of a monstrous sin.

49. Have you not seen those who praise themselves for purity? Allah purifies whom He will, and they will not be wronged, even (in a measure as trivial as) the hair upon a datestone.

50. See how they invent lies about Allah! That of itself is a most flagrant sin.

51. Have you not seen those to whom a portion of the Scripture had been given, how they believe in idols and false deities, and how they say of those who disbelieve: "These are more rightly guided than those who believe?

(A Madîna Jew named Ka'b ibn al-Ashraf was intriguing against the Holy Prophet, endeavouring to cement the alliance between the Jews and the pagans of Makka against the Prophet. On occasion, the idolaters would ask the Jews: "Who is on the right track: we or the Muslims? And the Jewish response came: "You are. The above verse was revealed about this attitude.)

52. Those are they whom Allah has cursed, and he whom Allah has cursed, you *(O Muhammad)* will find for him no helper.

53. Or have they even a share in the Sovereignty? Then in that case they would not give mankind even the speck on a datestone.

54. Or are they jealous of mankind because of that which Allah of His bounty has bestowed upon them? For We bestowed upon the house of Abraham the Scripture and Wisdom, and We bestowed on them a glorious kingdom.

55. And of them were *(some)* who believed, and *(some)* of them averted their faces from him *(Abraham)*. Hell is sufficient for *(their)* burning.

56. Surely, those who disbelieve in Our revelations, We shall expose them to the Fire. As often as their skins are roasted We shall exchange them for fresh skins, that they may taste the torment. Surely, Allah is ever Mighty, Wise.

57. And as for those who believe and do good deeds, We shall make them enter Gardens beneath which rivers flow, to dwell therein for ever; there for them are pure spouses, and we shall make them enter spreading shade.

(The above thirteen verses give a series of comparisons between three human possibilities: idolatry, unbelief, and Judaism. These possibilities are very much alive today, and the intelligent should be fully aware of them.)

58. Surely, Allah commands you to render back things held in trust to their rightful owners, and if you judge between mankind, that you judge justly. Assuredly, excellent is the teaching which Allah gives you! For Allah is He who hears and sees all things.

(Although this verse lays down the timeless principle of taking care of trusts and covenants, it also reflects a specific occasion of revelation. When the blessed Prophet Muhammad conquered Makka, a man named 'Uthmân ibn Talha was the caretaker of the Ka'ba, whose keys he held.

Refusing to surrender the keys to the monotheists, he climbed onto the roof of the Ka'ba, paying attention to no-one, but saying to the Blessed Prophet: "If I really knew that you are the prophet, I would certainly give the keys to you." Yet Hadrat 'Alî, may God be pleased with him, took the keys from him by force, and opened the Ka'ba's door. The Prophet entered into the Ka'ba, offered two rak'as of prayer, and went out again. Then the uncle of the Prophet, al-'Abbâs, asked him to entrust him with the keys of the Ka'ba, and to appoint him its caretaker. This was the reason for the revelation of the above verse. But the Blessed Prophet refused his uncle, and asked 'Alî to return the keys to the original caretaker, and asked him to apologise. Having seen and heard this, 'Uthmân ibn Talha embraced Islam.)

59. O you who believe! Obey Allah and obey the Messenger and those of you who are in authority; and if you have a dispute concerning any matter, refer it to Allah and the Messenger, if you are true believers in Allah and the Last Day. That is better and more suitable for final determination.

(The above verse establishes a hierarchy, or order of priority, in the utilisation of sources of sacred authority, whether in matters of law, or state, or the running of individual Islamic enterprises. The ranking is as follows: (1) The Holy Qur'an; (2) The pattern of life (*sunna*) of the Blessed Prophet; (3) the consensus of administrative, legislative or academic bodies which represent the Muslim community; (4) Analogy, whereby rulings for issues not ascertainable through the previous three methods may be derived by identifying the rationale behind known rulings, and applying it to the new situation to establish a judgement. Whenever Muslims disagree over a matter, they are required to abide by this fourfold ranking of priorities. The occasion for the revelation of this verse is said to have been an incident in which one of the hypocrites declared, "We should seek the opinion of Ka'b ibn al-Ashraf .

60. Have you not seen those who pretend that they believe in that which is revealed to you and that which was revealed before you? They seek the judgement of false gods (*tâghût*), although they are ordered to reject them. Satan would mislead them far astray.

Reference to the word *tâghût* in the Glossary will show its meaning more exactly. But the following five verses deal with it, and show that Satan is tâghût, as is anything in rebellion against the Truth or His prophets.)

61. And when it is said to them: "Come to that which Allah has revealed and to the Messenger, you see the hypocrites turn from you with aversion.

62. How would it be if a misfortune seized them because of that which their own hands have sent before them? Then would they come to you, swearing by Allah that they were seeking nothing but goodwill and conciliation.

63. Those are they the secrets of whose hearts Allah knows. So keep clear of them, but admonish them, and speak to them in plain terms about their souls.

64. We sent no Messenger except that he should be obeyed by the permission of Allah. And if, when they wronged themselves, they had but come to you and asked forgiveness of Allah, and asked forgiveness of the messenger, they would have found Allah Forgiving and Merciful.

(This is an indication that the prayers of the Blessed Prophet were especially acceptable to God.)

65. But no, by your Lord, they will not believe (*completely*) until they make you judge of what is in dispute between them, and find within themselves no dislike of that which you decide, and submit with full submission.

(Faith in Islam does not consist merely in a verbal affirmation. One must believe in one's heart, and believe wholeheartedly. It is not enough simply to say, "I believe in God and His prophet : one has to accept the divine commandments, and the teachings and example of the Prophet, with full sincerity.)

66. If we had decreed for them: "Sacrifice your lives or leave your homes , few of them would have done so; though if they did what they are exhorted to do it would be better for them, and more strengthening (*for their faith*).

67. And then We should bestow upon them from Our presence an immense reward.

68. And should guide them to a straight path.

(According to a hadith narrated by the Lady 'A'isha, may God be pleased with her, a man once came to the Prophet and said to him: "O Prophet of Allah, I love you more dearly than my wife and my children. When I am at home I remember you, I immediately come to see you. When I remember that you and I will both die, I know that you will go to the Garden with the rest of the prophets, while as for me, even if I can enter the Garden, I will not be able to see you! On this occasion the prophet did not answer at once, but waited, and the following verse was revealed.)

69. Whoever obeys Allah and His messenger, they are with those to whom Allah had shown favour, of the Prophets and the sincere (*saints or lovers of the Truth*), and the martyrs, and the righteous. The best of company are they!

70. Such is the bounty of Allah, and Allah is sufficient as Knower.

71. O you who believe! Take your precautions, then go forth in parties (*to jihâd*), or go forth all together.

(It is one of the ironies of life on earth that peace can often only be secured through violent means. If good men do not fight for what is true and good, then evil men will surely triumph, and it is hence the duty of those who uphold God's truth to take up arms from time to time, however much they may be averse to doing so. Islam encourages mankind to fight just wars, in order to prevent oppression, cruelty, and injustice, and to establish the truth and freedom of religion. But it prohibits any form of combat embarked upon without just cause, for its objective is peace, not strife and dissension.)

72. There are certainly some men among you who tarry behind; and if misfortune befell you, he would say: "Allah has been gracious to me since I was not present with them.

(The above verse is a characterisation of the hypocritical mind. There are men who proclaim their allegiance to the cause, for their own convenience, but whose true indifference becomes plain when they are called upon to risk their lives in the defence of truth and goodness.)

73. And if a bounty from Allah befell you, he would surely to say, as if there had been no love between you and him: "Oh, would that I had been with them, then should I have achieved a great success!

74. Let those fight for the cause of Allah who sell the life of this world for the Hereafter. Whoever fights for the cause of Allah, be he slain or be he victorious, on him We shall bestow a great reward.

75. And why should you not fight for the cause of Allah and of the weak among men and of the women and the children who are crying: "Our Lord! Rescue us from this town of which the people are oppressors! Oh, give us from Your presence some protecting friend! Oh, give us from your presence some defender!

(Before Makka was conquered by the Muslims, those who embraced Islam and were unable to emigrate to other places were ill-treated and persecuted by the idolators of Makka. Hence they prayed humbly to Him, for His support, that He might deliver them from the cruel persecution. The above verse commands Muslims to fight injustice and oppression in whatever part of the world it might exist. No matter who the oppressed might be, Muslims or non-Muslims, it is our Islamic duty to liberate them.)

76. Those who believe fight for the cause of Allah; and those who disbelieve fight for the cause of tâghût. So fight the minions of Satan. Assuredly, the devil's strategy is ever weak.

77. Have you not seen those to whom it was said: "Hold back your hands from fighting, establish the Prayer and pay the Zakât , but when fighting was prescribed for them, behold! a party of them fear men even as they fear Allah, or with a greater fear, saying: "Our Lord! Why have You ordained fighting for us? If only You would give us respite for a while! Say (to them, O Muhammad): "The enjoyment of this world is short; and the Hereafter will be better for him who fears Allah; and you will not be wronged, even (in the weight of) a date-thread.!

78. Wherever you are, death will find you, even though you be in towers built up strong and high! Yet if some good befalls them, they say: "This is from Allah ; and if an evil befalls them they say: "This is of your doing (O Muhammad). Say: "All is from Allah. But what is wrong with these people, that they fail to understand a single fact?

79. Whatever of good befalls you (O mankind) is from Allah, and whatever ill befalls you is from yourself. We have sent you (Muhammad) as a Messenger to mankind; and Allah is sufficient as witness.

(All too often, we think of our successes as the fruit of our own special skills and talents, forgetting that all that is good, including our talents, is from the Creator. And when some disaster overtakes us, the most hateful thing for us is to accept blame, and remember our own incapacities. Instead we blame others, or outside conditions, or Fate. Now, Allah, blessed and exalted is He, judges all things, and distributes all things. He does not wish any harm for any of His creatures, for He loves his creation, and mercy is His special attribute. By giving His servants a form of free will, however, He makes it possible for them to suffer, should they abuse this trust. The Lord is Creator, and the creature is created, and it is he who earns, or "acquires, good and evil.)

80. He who obeys the Messenger obeys Allah, and whoever turns away: We have not sent you as a warder over them.

81. And they say: "(*It is*) obedience ; but when they leave you a party of them spend the night in planning other than what you say. Allah records what they plan by night. So oppose them, and put your trust in Allah. Allah is sufficient as Trustee.

(There were hypocrites at Medîna who, although they did not believe, would pretend to obey the Prophet in his blessed presence, but, as soon as they were alone with each other, would hatch stratagems to confound God's new religion.)

82. Will they not ponder on the Qur'an? If it had been from other than Allah they would have found therein many contradictions.

(The Holy Qur'an, being of divine authorship, reflects a perfect consistency to all who are prepared to consider it carefully. To the extent that the reader's soul is pure, and filled with the reverential fear of the Lord, it will derive benefit from the Book. The more such a person reads it, the more its wonders are discovered to him, and the more his mind and heart are attuned to the its ineffable Source. This beauty, spiritual symmetry, and complete lack of error, are, to those who look carefully and with pure hearts, a sufficient proof of its divine origin.)

83. And if any tidings, whether of safety or fear, come to them, they spread it abroad; whereas if they had referred it to the Messenger or to those who are charged with authority, those among them who are able to think out the matter would have known it. If it had not been for the grace of Allah and His mercy you would have followed Satan, all but a few of you.

84. So fight (*O Muhammad*) for the cause of Allah. You are not responsible (*for anyone*) except for yourself, and rouse the believers.

Perhaps Allah will restrain the might of those who disbelieve. Allah is stronger in might and stronger in inflicting punishment.

85. Whoever mediates in a good cause will have the reward thereof, and whoever mediates in an evil cause will share its burden, and Allah oversees all things.

(No society can avoid the necessity of various forms of mediation, so as to secure the interests of justice. But this faculty must not be abused by interceding for wrongdoers, whoever they may be, and whatever their claims may be on one.)

86. When you are greeted with a greeting, give a greeting better than it or return it. Surely, Allah takes account of all things.

(By greeting someone else first, we show our good intention, and hence deserve an even better response. Mutual greeting is a Prophetically confirmed custom among Muslims, which spreads peace and love among them, and puts an end to any sense of alienation.)

87. Allah! There is no God save Him. He gathers you all to a Day of Resurrection about which there is no doubt. Who is more true of speech than Allah?

88. What ails you that you are divided into two groups regarding the hypocrites, when Allah cast them back *(to disbelief)* because of what they earned? Would you guide those whom Allah has sent astray? He whom Allah has sent astray, for him *(O Muhammad)* never can you find a way.

(According to Tradition, the reference here is not to the lukewarm section of the Muslims of Medîna, but to a particular group of alleged converts from among the Arabs, who afterwards relapsed into idolatry, and concerning whom there were two opinions among the Muslims.)

89. They yearn that you should disbelieve even as they disbelieve, that you may be upon a level *(with them)*; so take not friends from them until they migrate from their homes in the cause

of Allah; and if they turn back to *(to enmity)* then seize them and slay them wherever you find them, and choose no friend or helper from among them.

90. Except those who seek refuge with a people between whom and you there is a treaty *(of peace)*, or *(those who)* come to you because their hearts forbid them to make war on you or make war on their own people. Had Allah willed He could have given them power over you so that assuredly they would have fought you. So, if they keep away from you and wage not war against you and offer you peace, Allah allows you no way against them.

91. You will find others who desire that they should have security from you, and security from their own people. As often as they are returned to hostility they are plunged therein. If they keep not aloof from you nor offer you peace, nor cease their hostilities against you, then seize them and slay them wherever you find them. Against such We have given you clear authority.

(The people discussed in the above verse are disbelievers located outside of Medîna. Some of them stayed in Makka and did not emigrate and collaborated with the idolaters of Quraish. Since these people were the enemies of Islam, fighting ruthlessly against the Muslims, it was necessary to fight against them. Some of these people sought refuge with groups with which the Muslims had peace treaties. Others wished to stay neutral and, although they would not fight against their own people, they wanted to live in peace with the Muslims. These two latter categories were to be left alone.)

92. Never may a believer kill a believer unless *(it be)* by mistake. He who has killed a believer by mistake must set free a believing slave, and pay the blood-money to the family of the slain, unless they remit it as a charity. If he *(the victim)* be of a people hostile to you, and he is a believer, then *(the penance or compensation)* is to set free a believing slave. And if he comes of a people between whom and you there is a treaty, then the blood-money must be paid to his people, and *(also)* a believing slave must be set free. And those who find this beyond their means must fast two consecutive months. Such is the penance imposed by Allah; and Allah is Knowing, Wise.

93. He who slays a believer intentionally, his reward is Hell forever, and the wrath and curse of Allah are upon him, and for him He has prepared a dreadful penalty.

(According to Islamic Law *(Shari'ah)*, the penalty for intentional murder is known as *"Qisâs .* This means that a life should be taken for a life destroyed, in conformity with justice. The right to remit the death penalty is vested in the family of the victim, who, if they wish, can ask for compensation from the murdered, or, if they wish, can remit both out of compassion. In this latter case the state has the right to punish the killer to a lesser degree. The matter of Qisâs has been discussed in Sûrah II verses 178-9, where the spiritual punishment is stated. Accidental killing, or manslaughter, which can come about, for instance, by mistaking the victim for game during a hunt, or as an enemy in times a war, does not carry the death penalty, but renders the agent liable to payment of the blood-money, as follows:

1. The compensation the killer, or his family, has to pay to the slain, is set at two hundred camels, or their equivalent monetary value. In cases where the killer or his family are poor, the state may be asked to pay all or part of it on their behalf;

2. He has to free a slave, thereby contributing something to society. If he is unable to do this then he has to fast two consecutive months.

If the slain person's family belongs to a nation at war with the Muslims, payment of compensation is not required, lest the enemy gain in strength thereby.)

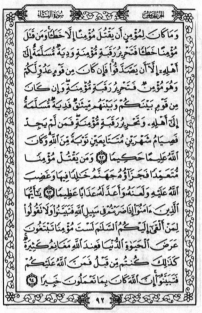

94. O you who believe! When you go out to fight for the cause of Allah, investigate carefully, and say not to anyone who offers you peace: "You are not a believer, seeking the chance profits of this life *(so that you may despoil him)*. With Allah profits and spoils are abundant. Even thus *(as he now is)* were you before; but Allah has since then been gracious to you. Therefore take care to investigate. For Allah is well aware of what you do.

(During one of the battles, the Islamic forces under Usâma ibn Zayd, encountered a group of enemy who saluted them with words indicating a desire to accept Islam. Despite this, Usâma was unconvinced, and killed the commander of the group and captured his men. When the Blessed Prophet heard this he grew intensely angry with Usâma, demanding of him "Did you split his heart in half to see whether the words "There is no deity save Allah, and Muhammad is the Messenger of Allah were written in his heart? Usâma said that the man had declared his interest in Islam only out of deceit. But the Prophet reproached him, and ordered him immediately to free a slave.)

95. Those of the believers who sit *(at home in Medina)*, other than those who have a *(disabling)* hurt, are not equal with those who strive for the cause of Allah with their wealth and their lives. Allah has conferred on those who strive with their wealth and their lives a rank above the ones who sit *(at home)*.

96. Degrees of rank from Him; and forgiveness and mercy, Allah is ever Forgiving, Merciful.

97. Assuredly, as for those whom the angels take *(in death)* while they wrong themselves, *(the angels)* will ask: "In what were you engaged? They will reply: "We were oppressed in the land. *(The Angels)* will say: "Was not Allah's earth spacious enough for you that you could have migrated therein? As for such, their habitation will be hell, an evil journey's end.

98. Except those who are weak among men, and the women, and the children, who are unable to devise a plan and are not shown a way.

99. As for such, it may be that Allah will pardon them. Allah is ever Clement, Forgiving.

100. Whoever emigrates for the cause of Allah will find much refuge and abundance in the earth, and whoso leaves his home, a fugitive to Allah and His messenger, and is overtaken by death, his reward is incumbent upon Allah. Allah is ever Forgiving, Merciful.

(Before the great Emigration to Madîna, Muslims were oppressed, persecuted, and mistreated, so much so that the Blessed Prophet instructed some to emigrate to Ethiopia. In the year 622, the Prophet Muhammad and his companions undertook the greater Emigration to the city of Madîna, a month's journey to the north. The Muslims left everything behind for the cause of Allah and His messenger, and proceeded to organise a new society and new state in Madîna. After this it was obligatory on every believing man and woman to flee from idolatry and disbelief, with the exception of those who are weak, disabled or unable to emigrate, who were obliged to stay behind. Those who were unwilling to sacrifice their homes, their businesses, their properties, and their relations were warned by the revelation of the above verse that their end would be hellfire. There were also some who attempted the journey, but died before completing it, and the verse indicates that Allah will reward them. According to a hadith narrated by Imâm Bukhârî, after the conquest of Makka emigration was no larger obligatory, but if the same conditions returned in future years, it would become obligatory again.)

101. And if you travel in the land, it is no sin for you to shorten your prayers, if you fear that those who disbelieve may attack you. In truth, the disbelievers are an open enemy to you.

102. And when you *(O Muhammad)* are among them and arrange their worship for them, let only a party of them stand with you *(for prayers)*, and let them take their arms. Then when they have performed their prostrations, let them fall to the rear and let another party come that has not prayed and let them pray with you, and let them take their precaution and their arms. Those who disbelieve wish for you to neglect your arms and your baggage, that they may attack you in a single charge. It is no sin for you to lay aside your arms if rain impedes you or you are ill. But take your precaution. Surely, Allah prepares for the disbelievers a shameful punishment.

103. When you have performed the *(congregational)* prayers, then remember Allah standing, sitting and reclining. And when you are in safety, observe proper worship. Worship at fixed hours has been enjoined on the believers.

(The above three verses describe how the mandatory prayers should be performed by the Muslims during times of danger and on journeys. During journeys of over 80 or 90 kilometres, the noon, afternoon and night prayers can be shortened even though no danger exists, as a facilitation for travellers. During times of war the obligatory prayers should be abbreviated also, as the verses state. As for the question of how the congregational prayers should be performed, according to the Hanafi school of thought, the congregational prayer in danger in face of the enemy is performed by dividing the worshippers into two groups; one prays while the other watches the enemy. Then the second group stands up to pray while the first falls back to face the enemy. Each party does only one or two rak'as, or about half the normal congregational prayer. Details can be varied according to circumstances, and according to the school of thought that the soldiers follow.

Prayer is the best form of remembering Allah and praising Him. A mentally sound person should never abandon the Prayer. In times of difficulty and danger Allah has given permission to make things easy for the believers, but the obligation remains, which demonstrates its force. For Prayer is the pillar of religion, and when it falls, the religion falls also. It connects the individual to God, and also to his brothers in the faith. Remove these two bonds, and nothing of faith remains.)

104. Relent not in pursuit of the enemy. If you are suffering hardships, they too are suffering similar hardships, and you hope from Allah that for which they cannot hope. Allah is ever Knower, Wise.

105. And We reveal to you the Scripture with the truth, that you may judge between mankind by that which Allah shows you. And be not a pleader for the treacherous;

106. And seek forgiveness of Allah. Surely Allah is ever Forgiving, Merciful.

107. And plead not an behalf of (people) who deceive themselves. Surely Allah loves not one who is treacherous and sinful.

108. They seek to hide from men and seek not to hide from Allah. He is with them when by night they hold discourse displeasing to Him. Allah ever surrounds all that they do.

109. Ah! you are the ones who pleaded for them in the life of the world. But who will plead with Allah for them on the Day of Resurrection, or who will then be their defender?

110. Yet whoso does evil or wrongs his own soul, then seeks Allah's forgiveness, will find Allah Forgiving and Merciful.

111. Whoever commits sin commits it only against his own soul. Allah is ever Knower, Wise.

112. But whoever commits an offence or a crime, then throws (the blame) on to one who is innocent, has burdened himself with falsehood and a flagrant sin.

113. But if it were not for the grace of Allah and His mercy to you (O Muhammad), a party of them had resolved to mislead you, but they will mislead only themselves, and they will hurt you not at all. Allah reveals to you the Scripture and wisdom, and teaches you that which you knew not. The grace of Allah toward you has been mighty.

(There are good lessons to be learned from the incidents in connection with which the above verse was revealed. A Muslim named Ta'ima ibn Ubayraq from the tribe of Zafar was suspected of having stolen a suit of armour. When he feared detection, he planted the stolen property in the house of a Jew, where it was found. The Jews denied the charge and accused Ta'ima, but the sympathies of the Muslim community were with Ta'imah on account of his nominal profession of Islam. When the case came for trial, pressure was exerted to convict the Jew, but Islamic impartiality prevailed, and the case seemed to be turning against Ta'ima. Realising that his punishment was imminent, he fled and left Islam.)

114. There is no good in much of their secret conferences except *(in)* him who enjoins charity and kindness and peace-making among the people. Whoso does that, seeking the good pleasure of Allah, We shall bestow on him an immense reward.

115. And whoso opposes the Messenger after the guidance *(of Allah)* has been conveyed to him, and followed other than the believers' way, We appoint for him that to him which he himself had turned, and expose him to hell - a hapless journey's end!

(The above verse also refers immediately to the episode of Ta'ima. His sympathisers were holding secret meetings, hoping to prejudice the Prophet to use his authority to favour Ta'ima. The Prophet, however, was unmoved. When Ta'ima fled and apostasised, he travelled to Makka, where he continued his thieving. It is said that he died there when a wall from an old building collapsed onto him.)

116. Surely, Allah forgive not that partners should be ascribed to him. He forgives all save that to whom He pleases. Whosoever ascribes partners to Allah has strayed far indeed.

(This verse, and also a number of sayings of the Blessed Prophet on the same subject, expound the Muslim doctrine of God's mercy towards all sinners, save only those who were guilty of the greatest sin of all: polytheism and idolatry. If a man or woman dies with faith, he may be punished for his sins, or, because of his good deeds he may be saved, or Almighty God may forgive him absolutely. Believers may spend some time in hellfire before they are purged of their sins and impurities, and are admitted into the Garden by God's grace. But disbelievers will never have this chance.)

117. They *(the idolators)* call upon female deities, but they call upon no-one but Satan, the persistent rebel!

(To pray and to ask certain things from Allah is a noble and necessary part of servanthood to Him. But to ask from deities apart from Him is the worst of all crimes: it is *shirk*, or polytheism.)

118. Whom Allah cursed, and he said: "Surely I will take of your slaves an appointed portion.

119. And surely I will lead them astray, and surely I will arouse desires in them, and surely I

will command them and they will cut the cattle's ears, and surely I will command them and they will change Allah's creation. Whoever chooses Satan for a friend instead of Allah is assuredly a loser, and his loss is manifest.

(To change the creatures of Allah from their natural ways by unnecessarily cutting some part of their bodies, or marking or burning or branding them is not allowed in Islam. Instead, the teaching of the Blessed Prophet was that man should be kind to animals, and would be called to account for his treatment of them. Pagan and magical practices often involve cruelty to animals, and in this case it becomes especially hideous. Neither is it permitted for human beings to mutilate themselves, for they are thereby tampering with God's creation, and the repository of His trust.)

120. Satan makes them promises, and stirs up in them false desires. But what Satan promises them is nothing but beguilement.

121. For such their dwelling-place will be hell, from which they will find no refuge.

122. But as for those who believe and do good deeds, We shall bring them into gardens beneath which rivers flow, wherein they will abide for ever. It is a promise from Allah in truth; and who can be more truthful than Allah in utterance?

123. It will not be in accordance with your desires, nor the desires of the People of the Scripture. He who does wrong will have the recompense thereof, and will not find against Allah any protecting friend or helper.

124. And whosoever does good works, whether male or female, and is a believer, such will enter the Garden, and they will not be wronged (so much as) the spot on a datestone.

(In this verse, Almighty God proclaims that man's worth is according to his deeds, not his wealth, status, or gender. Hence, in Islamic teaching, no-one may pass judgement upon another, for the only object of judgement is what lies in the heart, which is visible only to the Lord. The next verse continues the theme.)

125. Who can be better in religion than one who surrenders himself to Allah, does good and follows the way of Abraham the upright in faith? Allah (Himself) chose Abraham for a friend.

(Although the prophets of Allah are all messengers, and are all the same in terms of general function, they have been sent to widely differing cultures and spiritual conditions. Thus it is that their inner reality has differing aspects, for example, the prophet Moses is called "Kalîmullâh - the speaker with Allah - because he spoke with Allah; on Sinai; similarly, the Prophet Jesus is called "Rûhullâh - the spirit of Allah - because Allah blew His spirit into him. And the Prophet Muhammad is "Habîbullâh - the Beloved of Allah, for he was loved by Allah even more than the other Prophets, and because his is the way of love.)

126. To Allah belongs whatsoever is in the heavens and the earth. It is Allah that encompasses all things.

127. They consult with you concerning women. Say: Allah gives you the decree concerning them, and the Scripture which has been recited to you (gives decree), concerning female orphans to whom you give not that which is ordained for them though you desire to marry them, and (concerning) the weak among children, and that you should deal justly with orphans. Whatever good you do, surely Allah is well-acquainted with it.

128. If a woman fears ill-treatment from her husband, or desertion, it is no sin for the two of them if they make terms of peace between themselves. Peace is better. But greed has been made present in the minds (of men). If you do good and keep from evil, surely Allah is well-acquainted of what you do.

(In order to work, marriage must be worked at by both partners, who must be prepared to make the necessary sacrifices. Although, as the verse teaches, to be greedy is innate in men, so that they expect the other party to make the sacrifices, peace can only be attained by the efforts of both parties to the union. Peace is, after all, better than pride.)

129. You will never be able to deal equally between (your) wives, however much you may desire (to do so). But incline not altogether away (from one wife), leaving her as though suspended. If you do good, and keep from evil, surely Allah is ever Forgiving, Merciful.

(A man who has entered upon a plural marriage is obliged both ethically and at law to treat them equally. Of course, this is hard to achieve all the time, for it is natural to love one more than the other, or to be unhappy with certain traits in one or more of one's wives. A happy polygamous relationship demands even more sacrifices than a monogamous one. Thus the Law has intervened, demanding equal treatment in as much as this can be assured by law: housekeeping allocations, the kind of accommodation, food, and other normal accoutrements of life, must be divided on an equal basis between the co-wives.)

130. But, if they (the couples) separate, Allah will compensate each out of His abundance. Allah is ever All-Embracing, All-Knowing.

(If a marriage is not working out, despite all efforts and precautions, and the home has become a kind of hell, the couple should separate, and not live in that condition. Fear of poverty, or lack of resources or savings should not prevent the couple from separation. Allah will provide for each of them from His infinite kindness.)

131. To Allah belongs whatsoever is in the heavens and the earth. And We charged those

who received the Scripture before you, and (We charge) you, to have fear of Allah. And if you disbelieve, surely, to Allah belongs whatsoever is in the heavens and the earth. Allah is ever Rich, Praiseworthy.

132. To Allah belongs whatsoever is in the heavens the earth. And Allah is sufficient as Trustee.

133. If He will, He can destroy you, O mankind, and produce others (instead of you). Allah is Able to do that.

(Eternity and Absoluteness are attributes only present in Allah. The very existence of man depends on His grace and Mercy. If man betrays His trust and disobeys Him, His blessings are likely to be withdrawn from him, and he may be destroyed and replaced with others more worthy of God's earth.)

134. Whoso desires the reward of the world, (let him know that) with Allah is the reward of the world and the Herafter. And Allah is ever Hearer, Seer.

135. O you who believe! Stand out firmly for justice, as witnesses to Allah, even though it be against yourselves, or your parents, or your kindred, and whether it be against rich or poor, for Allah is nearer to both *(than you are)*. So follow not caprice, lest you lapse *(from truth);* and if you lapse or fall away, then surely Allah is ever Informed of what you do.

(In the above verse, mankind is warned not to deviate from justice, whether for economic, social, psychological, or other reasons. When dispensing justice, man should remember that he is the viceroy of Allah, Who is the Just.)

136. O you who believe! Believe in Allah and His Messenger and the Scripture which He has revealed to His messenger, and the Scripture which He revealed before *(you).* Whoever disbelieves in Allah and His Angels and His Scriptures and His messengers and the Last Day, he assuredly has gone far astray.

137. Those who believe, then reject faith and then again believe, then reject faith, and then increase in disbelief, Allah will never pardon them, nor will He guide them unto a way.

(Thus does the Lord characterise those whose faith wavers with the changing fortunes of the believers. Such hypocrites, for that is what they are, will eventually be expelled from faith definitively, and shall wander forever in misguidance.)

138. Give to the hypocrites the tidings that for them there is a grievous penalty.

139. Those who choose disbelievers for their friends instead of believers! Do they seek honour among them? Surely all honour belongs to Allah.

140. He *(Allah)* has already revealed to you in the Scripture that when you hear the revelations of Allah rejected and ridiculed you sit not with them until they engage in some other conversation. If you did *(remain with them)* you would be like them. Surely, Allah will gather hypocrites and disbelievers, all together, in Hell.

(When we hear truth held in low esteem, we ought to protest and withdraw from such company, not out of arrogance, as if we thought ourselves superior to other people, but out of real humility, lest our own nature be corrupted in such company. It is possible that our protest or sincere reproach will change the subject under discussion. In that case, we have done good to those who were inclined to belittle Truth, if we have saved them from ridiculing it.)

141. Those who wait and watch you closely, if a victory comes to you from Allah, they say: "Are we not with you? - and if the disbelievers meet with a success they say: "Had we not gained advantage over you, and did we not protect you from the believers? Allah will judge between you at the Day of Judgement, and Allah will not give the disbelievers any way *(of success)* against the believers.

142. The hypocrites seek to deceive Allah, but it is Allah who deceives them. When they stand up to pray they stand up lazily, and to be seen of men, and remember Allah only a little.

143. Wavering between this and that, belonging neither to these or to those. He whom Allah has left to go astray, you will not find any way for him.

144. O you who believe! Choose not disbelievers for friends rather than believers. Would you wish to offer Allah an open proof against yourselves?

(The Holy Qur'an emphasises on several occasions the risks involved in taking friends among unbelievers rather than one's co-religionists. To associate affectionately with a people is to become one of them, and to acquire something of their self-form. Those who have rejected Islam, whatever they may say to one's face, have chosen to reject the underpinnings of one's moral and spiritual life, and it is unreasonable to expect them to be sincere friends.)

145. Surely, the hypocrites will be in the lowest deep of the Fire, and you will find no helper for them.

146. Except those who repent and amend, and hold fast to Allah, and make their religion pure for Allah *(only)*. Those are with the believers. And Allah will bestow on the believers a reward magnificent.

(So even hypocrites can obtain forgiveness, on four conditions: (1) sincere repentance, which purifies their minds; (2) amendment of their conduct, which purifies the outer life; (3) steadfastness and devotion to Allah,

which strengthens their faith and protects them from the onslaughts of evil; and (4) sincerity in their religion, or their whole inner being, which retrieves them as full members of the global brotherhood of faith.)

147. Why should Allah punish you if you render thanks to Him, and truly believe in Him? It is Allah that is Recogniser *(of all your good actions)*, and Knower *(of all things)*.

(Allah the Exalted can gain nothing by punishing His creatures, over whom He watches with affection and concern. On the contrary, He recognises any good - however little - which He finds in us, and gives us a reward beyond all measure. His recognition of us is compared by a bold metaphor to our gratitude to Him for His favours. The epithet *shâkir* is applied here to Allah, as at 2:158, and elsewhere. At 16:121 it is applied to Abraham, who had showed himself grateful. Allah, too, can be *shâkir*, in spite of His absolute independance of us.)

148. Allah loves not the utterance of harsh words except by one who has been wronged. Allah is ever Hearer, Knower.

(Harsh words spoken against others are a breach of the ethics of Islam. Yet for those who have been wronged, and who can only hope to effect redress or remonstrance, there is a dispensation: it is not an insult or an act of slander to critice vocally one who has done wrong. For instance, in a court of law, criticism of others can be not only permissible, but required.)

149. If you do good openly or keep it secret, or forgive evil, surely Allah is Forgiving, Powerful.

150. Those who disbelieve in Allah and His messengers, and seek to make distinction between Allah and His messengers, and say: "We believe in some and disbelieve in others, and seek to choose a way in between them.

151. Such are disbelievers in truth; and for disbelievers We prepare a humiliating punishment.

152. But those who believe in Allah and His messengers and make no distinction between any of them; to them Allah will soon give their *(due)* rewards; and Allah was ever Forgiving, Merciful.

153. The People of the Scripture ask of you that you should cause an *(actual)* Book to descend upon them from heaven. They asked a greater thing *(miracle)* of Moses aforetime, for they said: "Show us Allah plainly. The storm of lightning seized them for their wickedness. Yet they worshipped the calf even after clear signs had come to them. And even so We forgave them that! And We bestowed on Moses a clear authority.

154. And We caused the Mount *(of Sinai)* to tower above them at *(the taking of)* their covenant, and We bade them: "Enter the gate prostrate! and We bade them, "Transgress not the Sabbath! and We took from them a firm covenant.

(During the time of the Prophet Muhammad the Jews and the Christians demanded many miracles from him. Even though many miracles were in fact showed them, many still rejected the faith. But, as this passage points out, thus had been the case with the people of Moses, long before)

155. Then because of their breaking of their covenant, and their disbelieving in the revelations of Allah, and their slaying of the prophets wrongfully, and their saying: "Our hearts are hardened, - No, but Allah has set a seal on their hearts for their disbelief, so that they believe not, except a few.

156. And because of their disbelief and of their speaking against Mary a tremendous calumny.

157. And because of their saying: "We slew the Messiah, Jesus son of Mary, Allah's messenger. They slew him not, nor crucified him, but it appeared so to them; and those who disagree concerning it are in doubt thereof; they have no knowledge thereof except pursuit of a conjecture; they slew him not for certain.

(Allah saved Noah from the flood; Abraham from the fire, Muhammad from the traps of the idolaters, and Jesus from the wickedness of the Jews, who wished to crucify him. It was Judas Iscariot, who sought to betray Jesus, who was arrested instead, and crucified instead of the Prophet Jesus, upon whom be peace.)

158. But Allah raised him up to Himself. Allah is Mighty, Wise.

159. There is not one of the People of the Scripture but will believe in him before his death, and on the Day of Resurrection he will be a witness against them.

(Allah protected His prophet Jesus from the Jews so that they could not slay him, and then raised him to Himself. There are different interpretations about how and when he was raised to Heaven. According to the majority opinion, Allah lifted him up to Heaven, and placed him in a special place there. Before the Day of Resurrection he will return to the world, and the People of the Scripture will believe that he was indeed the prophet of Allah, and they will renounce their disbelief in the final dispensation of Islam. During his second stay on the earth, Jesus (upon whom be peace), will rule the world with the Holy Qur'an. He will put an end to all kinds of superstitions, and will break the cross, forbid the eating of pork, and rectify other violations of the Law which had been introduced by later generations of Christians.

It is interesting to note that the doctrine of Jesus' torture by crucifixion was not accepted by a number of early Christian churches, including the Basilideans and Docetians. Its source is probably to be identified in

Greco-Roman ideas of incarnation, blood-sacrifice and redemption, which, although offensive to the Jewish monotheism of the messengers, filtered in during the first few centuries. The Gospel accounts of the supposed crucifixion do not, of course, stand up to historical analysis: their authors are unknown.)

160. Because of the wrongdoings of those who were Jews We made unlawful for them certain good things which were (before) made lawful to them, and because they hindered many from Allah's way.

161. And of their taking usury when they were forbidden it, and of their devouring people's wealth by wrongful means. We have prepared for those of them who disbelieve a painful punishment.

162. But those of them who are firm in knowledge, and the believers, believe in that which is revealed to you, and that which was revealed before you, especially the diligent in prayer and those who pay the Zakât, the believers in Allah and the Last Day. To them We shall bestow a great reward.

163. We send revelation upon you, as We sent it upon Noah and the prophets after him, and as We sent revelation upon Abraham and Ishmael and Isaac and Jacob and the tribes, and Jesus and Job and Jonah and Aaron and Solomon, and as We gave David the Psalms.

(Prophecy is the highest human condition, for the Prophet is a bridge between man and God, who helps the world to recall its primal source and ultimate return. "Revelation is the condition of contact, vouchsafed by God and not acquired by man, which may be imparted through the intermediary of an angel, or directly from Allah.

The word "tribes in the above verse means the grandchildren of the prophet Jacob.

As the next verse explains, although Allah has enumerated several of the greatest Prophets sent in former ages, there are many He has not mentioned. According to some accounts, He has sent 124,000 Prophets since the creation of man.)

164. And messengers We have mentioned to you before and messengers We have not mentioned to you; and Allah spoke directly with Moses.

165. Messengers of good news and of warning, in order that mankind might have no argument against Allah after the messengers. And Allah was ever Mighty, Wise.

166. But Allah (Himself) bears witness concerning that which He has revealed to you; in His knowledge has He revealed it; and the angels also testify. And Allah is sufficient for a witness.

167. Those who reject faith and hinder (others) from the road of Allah, they assuredly have strayed far from the path.

168. Those who reject faith, and do wrong, Allah will never forgive them, either will He guide them to a road.

169. Except the road of hell, where they will abide for ever. And that was ever easy for Allah.

170. O mankind! The messenger has come to you with the truth from your Lord. Therefore believe; (it is) better for you. But if you disbelieve, still, assuredly to Allah belongs whatsoever is in the heavens and the earth. Allah was ever Knower, Wise.

171. O People of the Scripture! Commit no excess in your religion, nor say nothing but the truth about Allah. The Messiah, Jesus son of Mary, was only a messenger of Allah, and His word which He conveyed to Mary, and a spirit from Him. So believe in Allah and His messengers, and say not "three Cease! *(it is)* better for you! Allah is only One God. Far is it removed from His transcendent majesty that He should have a son. His is all that is in the heavens and all that is in the earth. And Allah is sufficient as Defender.

(Many Christians have never accepted the theory of pure monotheism advanced by Judaism and Islam, since their love for their Messenger, upon whom be peace, caused them to deify him, just as the Romans deified their emperors. Although Jesus, like all the Holy Prophets, brought the message of absolute Divine Unity, later generations of Christians developed a theory of "trinity . According to this doctrine, God is one, but also three, and one entity of this three has two distinct personalities. He is Father, Son, and Holy Ghost, which are separate entities, but together are not separate but entirely united; just as the human and divine natures of Christ are united but separate. When the trinitarian Christian prays, he can pray to any of these five; or to all together. So the error of the Jews, the Qur'an explains, was excessive formalism, and the error of the Christians, metaphysical confusion and deification of one who never claimed to be God, for only "He is good, Who is in Heaven . We ask God to preserve us from both extremes.)

172. The Messiah will never disdain to be a slave to Allah, nor will the favoured angels. Whoso disdains His service and is proud, all such will He assemble to Him.

173. Then, as for those who believed and did good works, to them will He pay their reward in full, adding unto them of His bounty; and as for those who were disdainful and proud, them will He punish with a painful doom. And they will not find for them, against Allah, any protecting friend or helper.

174. O mankind! Assuredly has a proof from your Lord come to you; and We have sent down to you a clear light.

(Here "Proof denotes the Prophet Muhammad, upon whom be peace, and the "clear light refers to the Holy Qur'an.)

175. As for those who believe in Allah, and hold fast to Him, them He will cause to enter into His Mercy and grace, and will guide them to Him by a straight road.

176. They ask you for a legal judgement. Say: "Allah has granted you a judgement concerning distant kindred. If a man die childless, and have a sister, hers is half the heritage, and he would have inherited from her had she died childless. And if there be two sisters, then theirs are two-thirds of the heritage, and if they be brethren, men and women, to the male is the equivalent of the share of two females. Allah makes it clear to you, lest you err. And Allah is Knower of all things.

SÛRAH V

AL-MÂ'IDA (THE TABLE SPREAD)

Revealed at al-Madîna

The great bulk of this Sûrah was revealed at Madîna in the sixth year of the Muslim calendar. Verse 3, however, was the last of all the Qur'an's verses to be revealed, for it announces the completion of their religion for the Muslims, and the choice for them of

Islam (the surrender to Allah) as their religion. This verse was revealed during the Prophet's Farewell Pilgrimage to Makka, and spoken by him during his sermon to the assembled thousands at Arafat, when all Arabia had accepted Islam, only a little while before his death. The Sûrah derives its name from vv.112ff., where it is told how the disciples of Jesus asked for a table spread with food to be sent down from Heaven, and their prayer was granted. The general theme of the Sûrah is observance of religious duties, and the Muslims are urged not to violate their covenant with God as did followers of earlier prophets.

AL-MÂ'IDA (THE TABLE SPREAD)

In the name of Allah, the Compassionate, the Merciful

1. O you believe! Fulfill your undertakings! It is lawful for you to eat the flesh of all beasts except that which is (*here*) announced to you. Game is forbidden to you while you are in the state of consecration (*for pilgrimage*).

(Fulfillment of undertakings, promises and contracts, is a pillar of the Islamic social, legal and political order. Here it is proclaimed as an absolute obligation.)

2. O you who believe! Violate not the sanctity of the symbols of God, nor of the Sacred Month, nor of the animals brought for sacrifice, nor the garlands (*that mark out such animals*), nor the people resorting to the Sacred House, seeking of the bounty and good pleasure of their Lord. But when you leave the state of consecration (*and the sacred precincts around the City*), you may hunt. Let not the hatred of a people (*who once*) obstructed you from the Sacred Mosque lead you to transgress (*and hostility on your part*). Help one another in goodness and piety, and help not one another in sin and transgression. And fear God, for He is strict in punishment.

3. Forbidden to you *(for food)* are carrion and blood and swineflesh, and that which has been dedicated to any other than Allah, and the strangled, and the dead through beating, and the dead killed by *(the goring of)* horns, and the devoured of wild beasts, saving that which you make lawful *(by slaughtering decently before they die)*, and that which has been sacrificed to idols. And *(forbidden)* also is settling matters with gambling-arrows. That is an abomination. This day are those who disbelieve in despair of *(ever harming)* your religion; so fear them not, and fear Me! This day have I perfected your religion for you and completed my favour upon you, and chosen for you as religion *al-Islam*. Whoso is forced by hunger, not by will, to sin: *(for him)* Allah is Forgiving, Merciful.

(All the world's religions, recognising man's inability to work out the truth for himself, establish certain guidelines to show him what is lawful and what is not. These laws serve the individual as well as society. Islam, by its dietary regulations, which, although simpler, in many ways reflect those given by Allah to ancient Israel, seeks to protect the individual from the spiritual dirt which proceeds from consuming animals which are themselves dirty. All scavenging animals, therefore (as opposed to grazing ones), are forbidden. Similarly, animals slain in accordance with non-monotheistic principles, are seen as unjustly killed, and hence cannot be consumed. In these regulations, too, we find a hint of asceticism and renunciation reminiscent of the Islamic rules of fast. To renounce the world with the soul, and hence to address oneself to God, one does not have to renounce everything in the world, but only some things, as a symbol and reminder.)

4. They ask you *(O Muhammad)* what is made lawful for them. Say: *"(All)* good things are made lawful for you. And those beasts and birds of prey which you have trained as hounds are trained, you teach them that which Allah taught you; so eat of that which they catch for you and mention Allah's name upon it, and observe your duty to Allah. Indeed, Allah is swift to take account.

5. This day are *(all)* good things made lawful for you. The food of those who have received the Scripture is lawful for you, and your food is

lawful for them. And so are the virtuous women of the believers, and the virtuous women of those who received the Scripture before you *(lawful for you)* when you give them their marriage portions and live with them in honour, not in fornication, nor taking them as secret concubines. Whoso denies the faith, his work is vain, and in the Hereafter he will be among the losers.

(Muslims can eat, and will be blessed in, all foods which are both inherently wholesome, and permitted in the Sacred Law. The verse indicates, too, that the food slaughtered by Jews and Christians, despite the distorted and abrogated status of their scripture, is permissible, if it is slaughtered correctly (the flesh of the pig is an exception: it was never authorised as a food in either Judaism or Christianity, despite later interference. Muslim men are likewise permitted to marry believing Jewish and Christian women. Muslim women, however, cannot marry non-Muslim men. For while Muslims recognise the prophets of the other faiths, Jews and Christians do not acknowledge Muhammad. Hence a woman should not be set under a man who utterly rejects her religion, and does not share her love of all the Prophets.)

١٠٧

6. O you who believe! When you rise up for prayer, wash your faces, and your hands up to the elbows, and lightly rub your heads, and (*wash*) your feet up to the ankles. And if you are unclean, purify yourselves. And if you are sick or on a journey, or one of you comes from the privy, or you have touched (*had sexual relations with*) women, and you find not water, then go to clean earth, and rub your faces and your hands with some of it. Allah would not place a burden on you, but He would purify you, and would perfect His grace upon you, that you may perhaps give thanks.

(Prayer for a Muslim is to commune intimately with the Lord. As is the case before every important meeting, one must prepare for it in the proper way. The practice of *wudâ'*, the minor ablution required before most devotional acts, purifies the outward, symbolises the purification of the inward, and serves to wake us up, and redirect us towards Almighty God. When water is not readily obtainable, clean earth may be used as a temporary substitute.)

7. Remember Allah's favour upon you, and His covenant by which He bound you when you said: "We hear and we obey ; and keep your duty to Allah. Indeed Allah knows what is in the breasts (*of men*).

(The "covenant here referred to denotes the spiritual obligation of the creature towards the Creator, Who has given us reason, the higher faculties of the soul, and the position of His vicegerent upon the earth. The verse was revealed also in connection with the Pledge made to the Blessed Prophet by two groups of new Muslims from Madîna at al-'Aqaba and al-Hudaybiya, the first about fourteen months before the Hijra, and the second a little later.)

8. O you who believe! Be steadfast witnesses for Allah in equity; and let not hatred of any people make you swerve from justice. Deal justly; that is nearer to Godfearing. Observe your duty to Allah. Indeed Allah is Informed of what you do.

9. Allah has promised those who believe and do good deeds: Theirs will be forgiveness and an immense reward.

10. And those who disbelieve and deny Our signs, such are the rightful owners of hell.

11. O you who believe! Remember Allah's favour to you, how a people formed the design to stretch out their hands against you but He withheld their hands from you; and keep your duty to Allah. In Allah let believers put their trust.

(This verse was revealed in connection with a man who, during the time of the Blessed Prophet, was incited by the idolators and hypocrites to murder the Prophet. Yet he was confounded by God's will, and was unable to fulfill his evil intentions. While the plot was against the Prophet only, nonetheless, by implication, it threatened the very existence of the believers.)

12. Allah made a covenant of old with the Children of Israel, and We raised among them twelve chieftains, and Allah said: "I am with you. If you establish worship and pay the poordue, and believe in My messengers and support them, and lend to Allah a goodly loan, surely I shall remit your sins, and surely I shall admit you into gardens beneath which rivers flow. Whosoever among you disbelieves after this has gone astray from a straight path.

(When Allah saved the Children of Israel from the oppression of Pharaoh, Allah guided them toward the Holy City of Jerusalem. Moses called the chieftains of the people, who all assembled together, declaring to Moses: "All that the Lord had spoken we will do. The chieftains of the twelve tribes each sent agents to spy out the land of Canaan. When they all returned from

their mission, they alarmed the Israelites by stating that the inhabitants of the land were strong and prepared to fight. Unwilling themselves to fight for their inheritance, they thus broke the promise that they given to their Lord in the presence of Moses.)

13. And because of their breaking their covenant, We have cursed them and made hard their hearts. They change words from their context and forget a part of that wherewith they had been reminded. You will not cease to discover treachery among them, all save a few. But bear with them, and pardon them. Surely, Allah loves those who are kind.

(During the time of Moses and his successors, only one copy of the Torah was made. When the Israelites fought with the Babylonians, and were taken captive by them, this copy was lost. When the Israelites regained their freedom, they tried to write it out again. Yet in the process, they began to distort the text, contriving to forget a good part of God's commandments to them. Today's Torah is a late, incomplete anthology of earlier material.)

14. And with those who say: "Surely, we are Christians, We made a covenant, but they forgot a part of that whereof they were admonished. Therefore We have stirred up enmity and hatred among them till the day of Resurrection, when Allah will inform them of what they have done.

(The early Christians suffered much persecution from the Romans and the Jews, and the Christians became widely scattered. The Christian Covenant which was given by Jesus to his apostles was lost in the process, and although a variety of gospels were written by various hands, they contained only an oblique reference to the fact that God's messages to man had not come to an end, and that the Comforter, Ahmad, would come to reestablish monotheism. See the Gospel of John, xv.26, and xvi.7, where an echo has been preserved. True Christians are those who have accepted not just Jesus, but all of Allah's prophets, and affirm His absolute unity. The verse is also a reminder of the enmity which Allah has set between Christians and Jews, and which shall abide until the Last Day.)

15. O people of the Scripture! Now has Our messenger come, to you, expounding to you much of that which you used to hide in the Scripture, and forgiving much. Now there has come to you light from Allah, and a plain Scripture.

16. Whereby Allah guides all who seek His good pleasure to ways of place and safety, and leads them out of darkness, by His Will, to light, and guides them to a straight path.

17. They indeed have disbelieved who say: "Allah is the Messiah, son of Mary. Say: "Who then has the least power against God, if He had willed to destroy the Messiah son of Mary, and his mother and everyone on earth? Allah's is the Sovereignty of the heavens and the earth, and all that is between them. He creates what He will. And He has power over all things.

18. The Jews and the Christians say: "We are the sons of Allah, and His loved ones. Say: "Why then does He chastise you for your sins? Surely, you are but mortals of His creating. He forgives whom He will, and chastises whom He will. Allah's is the Sovereignty of the heavens and the earth and all that is between them, and to Him is the journeying.

19. O people of the Scripture! Now has Our messenger come to you to make things plain after an interval (*between*) messengers, lest you should say: "There come not to us a messenger of glad tidings and warner. Now has a messenger of glad tidings and warner come to you. Allah has Power over all things.

20. And (*remember*) when Moses said to his people: "O my people! Remember Allah's favour to you, how He placed among you Prophets, and He made you kings, and gave you that (*which*) He gave not to any (*other*) of (*His*) creatures.

21. O my people! Go into the holy land which Allah has ordained for you. Turn not in flight, for surely you would then turn back as losers.

22. They said: "O Moses! In this land are a people of exceeding strength (*and oppression*); never shall we enter it until they leave it. When they leave, then we shall enter.

23. But among their Godfearing men were two on whom Allah had bestowed His grace; they said: "Enter in to them by the gate, for if you enter by it, surely you will be victorious. So put your trust in Allah, if you are indeed believers.

(Among those who returned after spying out the land were two men who had faith and courage. They were Joshua and Caleb. Joshua was the successor to Moses in Prophethood. These two true followers of Moses asked for an immediate entry through the proper gate. They had no fear from the strength of the Canaanites. The advice of Joshua and Caleb, and the proposals of Moses were unpalatable to the ordinary Israelites, whose prejudices were further encouraged by the ten other men who had been on the spying mission with Joshua and Caleb. The crowd was in open rebellion, and was prepared to stone Moses, Aaron, Joshua and Caleb, and return to Egypt.)

them and was not accepted from the other. *(The one)* said: "I will surely kill you! *(The other)* answered: "Allah accept only from those who are righteous.

28. Even if you stretch out your hand against me to kill me, I shall not stretch out my hand against you to kill you, for I fear Allah, the Lord of the Worlds.

29. Surely! I would rather you should bear the punishment of the sin against me and your own sin, and become one of the owners of the Fire. That is the reward of wrongdoers.

30. The *(selfish)* soul of the other *(Cain)* lead him to the killing of his *(own)* brother, so he slew him and become one of the losers.

31. Then Allah sent a raven scratching up the ground, to show him how to hide his brother's naked corpse. He said: "Woe unto me! Am I not able to be as this raven and so hide my brother's naked corpse? And he become repentant.

(Pride, selfishness and jealousy can so overmaster a man as to cause him to murder his own brother. In this story, which recounts the first human conflict and murder, we are reminded of the lethal power of the *nafs*, which, in its lower, instinctive condition *(al-nafs al-ammâra)*, perpetually enjoins man to sin. When this is disciplined somewhat, it becomes *al-nafs al-lawwâma:* the soul which blames itselfs, but is still not purified. Finally, by divine grace, one can attain to the station of *al-nafs al-mutma'inna,* or "the soul at peace , which is free of selfish impulses.

The story of Cain and Abel is here briefly told in order to represent the story of Israel. Israel rebelled against the Lord, slew and insulted the righteous, and, when Allah transferred His favour to another nation, was overcome by jealousy.)

24. They said: "O Moses! We will never enter *(the land)* while they are in it. So go, you and your Lord, and fight! We will sit here.

25. He said: "My Lord! I have control of none but myself and my brother, so separate us from the wrongdoing people.

26. *(Their Lord)* said: "For this the land will surely be forbidden them for forty years that they will wander in the earth, bewildered. So grieve not over the wrongdoing people.

(Allah punished the people, who had rebelled ten times or more, by leaving them to wander in the wilderness for forty years. That rebellious generation was not to see the Holy Land. All those that were twenty years old and upwards were to die in the wilderness. And so it happened. Forty years afterwards they crossed the River Jordan opposite what is now Jericho, but by that time Moses, Aaron, and the whole of the older generation had died.)

27. But recite to them with truth the tale of the two sons of Adam, how they offered each a sacrifice, and it was accepted from the one of

32. For that cause We ordained for the Children of Israel that whosoever kills a human being for other than manslaughter or corruption in the earth, it shall be as if he had killed all mankind, and whoso saves the life of one, it shall be as if he had saved the life of all mankind. Our messengers came to them of old with clear signs (*of Allah's sovereignty*), but afterwards many of them became evildoers in the earth.

(Throughout the history, all nations have known that the Jews have striven against Allah's revealed order. By their unreasonable denial of Jesus and Muhammad, and their belief that they are God's chosen people, they have earned the astonishment and condemnation of all intelligent people.)

33. The only reward of those who make war upon Allah and His messenger and strive after corruption in the land will be that they will be killed or crucified, or have their hands and feet on alternate sides cut off, or will be expelled out of the land. Such will be their degradation in the world, and in the Hereafter theirs will be a severe punishment.

34. Save those who repent before you overpower them, for in that case Allah is Forgiving, Merciful.

(In Islam, to kill someone without just cause, thereby repeating the crime of Cain, is considered a crime against all humanity; it is as if the murdered had killed not just one man, but everyone. To commit acts

of terror is treason both against society and against Allah and His prophet. Although the Islamic jurists differ somewhat on the interpretation of these provisions, it is acknowledged that those who commit armed robbery combined with murder are to be punished with one of the four penalties specified above. The actual penalty applicable is decided upon by the legislature in accordance with what is deemed suitable for the region's culture and norms.)

35. O you who believe! Be mindful of your duty to Allah, and seek the way of approach to Him, and strive in His way in order that you may succeed.

(One of the ways of "approaching Allah is to strive in His cause, as is stated in the above verse. Other ways include worshipping and obeying Him, and doing other acts of goodness for His sake.)

36. As for those who disbelieve, if all that is in the earth were theirs, and as much again therewith, to ransom them from the doom on the Day of Resurrection, it would not be accepted from them. Theirs will be a grievous penalty.

sensibilities are more comfortable with a form of punishment which leaves no physical marks, and draws no unsightly blood, forgetting that to torture the soul by locking a man up in the company of criminals does far more lasting damage. Neither is incarceration just, for there are certain types of man who thrive in prison, and others who suffer immeasureably. The former is likely to learn the criminal arts while behind bars, while the latter will be permanently traumatised. As for its deterrent value, while prison is widely regarded as unpleasant, for certain individuals to have a criminal record is seen as a mark of manhood. And while physical punishment is comprehensible beforehand, the miseries of prison life are known only to those who have experienced them. These inadequacies in the penal system are one reason why secular countries are experiencing a rapidly increasing incidence of crime.

Having said this, it is important to recall that the punishment for theft cannot be applied if the defendant stole out of hunger, or from some other dire necessity. For God does not will injustice for His servants.)

40. Do you not know that to Allah alone belongs the sovereignty of the heavens and the earth? He punishes whom He will, and forgives whom He will. Allah has power over all things.

41. O messenger! Do not be grieved by those who vie with one another in the race to disbelief, of such as say with their mouths: "We believe," but their hearts believe not, and of the Jews: listeners for the sake of falsehood, listeners on behalf of other people who come not to you, changing words from their context and saying: "If this be given to you, receive it, but if this be not given to you, then beware! He whom Allah dooms to sin, you *(by your own efforts)* will avail him naught against Allah. Those are they for whom the will of Allah is that He cleanse not their hearts. Theirs in the world will be ignominy, and in the Hereafter a heavy punishment.

(There were men among the Jews who were eager to spread any lie about the Blessed Prophet. They had their ears open to catch tales even from those who had not come near to him. And yet whenever they attempted to show that the Chosen One was violating the Sacred Law, it was proved that he was in fact applying it meticulously.)

37. They will wish to come forth from the Fire, but they will not come forth from it. Theirs will be a lasting penalty.

38. As for the thief, both male and female, cut off their hands. It is the reward of their own deeds, an exemplary punishment from Allah. Allah is Mighty, Wise.

39. But whosoever repents after his wrongdoing and amends his conduct, Allah will turn to him in forgiveness. Indeed Allah is Forgiving, Merciful.

(One of the masterstrokes of Islamic legislation is its punishment for theft, which is here laid down with great clarity. It is increasingly being acknowledged in prison-based penal systems that prison is neither just, nor effective as a deterrent or a punishment. The high levels of suicide in prisons in modern countries are a mute testimony to the fact that death itself is often seen as preferable to the psychological tortures which prisons inflict. It would appear, however, that liberal

سورة المائدة

سَمّٰعُوۡنَ لِلۡكَذِبِ اَكّٰلُوۡنَ لِلسُّحۡتِ ۚ فَاِنۡ جَآءُوۡكَ
فَاحۡكُمۡ بَيۡنَهُمۡ اَوۡ اَعۡرِضۡ عَنۡهُمۡ ۚ وَاِنۡ تُعۡرِضۡ عَنۡهُمۡ فَلَنۡ
يَّضُرُّوۡكَ شَيۡئًا ۚ وَاِنۡ حَكَمۡتَ فَاحۡكُمۡ بَيۡنَهُمۡ بِالۡقِسۡطِ ؕ
اِنَّ اللّٰهَ يُحِبُّ الۡمُقۡسِطِيۡنَ ۝ وَكَيۡفَ يُحَكِّمُوۡنَكَ وَعِنۡدَهُمُ
التَّوۡرٰىةُ فِيۡهَا حُكۡمُ اللّٰهِ ثُمَّ يَتَوَلَّوۡنَ مِنۡۢ بَعۡدِ ذٰلِكَ ؕ
وَمَآ اُولٰٓئِكَ بِالۡمُؤۡمِنِيۡنَ ۝ اِنَّآ اَنۡزَلۡنَا التَّوۡرٰىةَ فِيۡهَا
هُدًى وَّنُوۡرٌ ۚ يَحۡكُمُ بِهَا النَّبِيُّوۡنَ الَّذِيۡنَ اَسۡلَمُوۡا لِلَّذِيۡنَ
هَادُوۡا وَالرَّبّٰنِيُّوۡنَ وَالۡاَحۡبَارُ بِمَا اسۡتُحۡفِظُوۡا مِنۡ كِتٰبِ
اللّٰهِ وَكَانُوۡا عَلَيۡهِ شُهَدَآءَ ۚ فَلَا تَخۡشَوُا النَّاسَ
وَاخۡشَوۡنِ وَلَا تَشۡتَرُوۡا بِاٰيٰتِيۡ ثَمَنًا قَلِيۡلًا ؕ وَمَنۡ لَّمۡ يَحۡكُمۡ
بِمَآ اَنۡزَلَ اللّٰهُ فَاُولٰٓئِكَ هُمُ الۡكٰفِرُوۡنَ ۝ وَكَتَبۡنَا عَلَيۡهِمۡ
فِيۡهَآ اَنَّ النَّفۡسَ بِالنَّفۡسِ ۙ وَالۡعَيۡنَ بِالۡعَيۡنِ وَالۡاَنۡفَ
بِالۡاَنۡفِ وَالۡاُذُنَ بِالۡاُذُنِ وَالسِّنَّ بِالسِّنِّ وَالۡجُرُوۡحَ
قِصَاصٌ ؕ فَمَنۡ تَصَدَّقَ بِهٖ فَهُوَ كَفَّارَةٌ لَّهٗ ؕ وَمَنۡ
لَّمۡ يَحۡكُمۡ بِمَآ اَنۡزَلَ اللّٰهُ فَاُولٰٓئِكَ هُمُ الظّٰلِمُوۡنَ ۝

١١٤

42. They listen to falsehoods and devour what is unlawful. If they come to you, either judge between them or decline to interfere. If you decline, they cannot hurt you in the least. If you judge, judge between them with equity. Surely Allah loves those who judge with equity.

(The people of the Scripture are free to refer their disputes among themselves to the Prophet if they wish to do so. The Prophet himself is also free to judge the matters referred to him by them, but when he does so, he must do so by the Holy Qur'an.)

43. How come they come to you for judgement when they have their own law (Torah) wherein Allah delivered judgement (for them)? Even after that, they turn away. They are not (truly) people of faith.

44. Indeed, We did reveal the Torah wherein there was a guidance and a light, by which the prophets who surrendered (to Allah) judged the Jews, and the rabbis and the priests (judged) by such of Allah's Scripture as they were bidden to observe, and thereunto were they witnesses. So fear not men, but fear Me. And sell not My

revelations for a miserable price. Whoever judges not by that which Allah has revealed; such are disbelievers.

45. And We ordained for them therein: The life for the life, and the eye for the eye, and the nose for the nose, and the ear for the ear, and the tooth for the tooth, and for wounds retaliation. But, if any one remit the retaliation (by way of charity), it is an act of atonement for himself. And whoever judges not by what Allah had revealed, such are the wrongdoers.

(Those who do not judge by what Allah has revealed can be classified into three groups: (1) Those who reject the faith, thereby becoming kuffâr: "disbelievers ; (2) Those who know the truth but diverge from it and judge with iniquity, thereby becoming zâlimûn : "wrongdoers ; (3) As is stated in verse 47 below, they may be fâsiq: "corrupt .)

46. And in their footsteps We sent Jesus son of Mary, confirming that which was (revealed) before him, and We bestowed on him the Gospel wherein is guidance and a light, conforming that which was (revealed) before it in the Torah - a guidance and an admonition to the Godfearing.

47. Let the People of the Gospel judge by that which Allah had revealed therein. Whoever judges not by that which Allah had revealed; such are the corrupt.

48. And to you have We revealed the Scripture with the truth, conforming whatever Scripture was before it, and a watcher over it. So judge between them by that which Allah has revealed, and follow not their desires away from the truth which has come to you. For each We have appointed a (divine) law and a traced-out way. Had Allah willed He could have made you one community, but that He may try you by that which He has given you (He has made you as you are). So vie with one another in good works. To

Allah you will all be returned, and He will then inform you of that wherein you disputed.

(Those nations who have believed in Allah and followed the teachings of His prophets should not dispute with each other because of differences of opinion on personal and political matters. They should be competing with each other to attain the goals that their Prophets have shown them.)

49. So judge between them by that which Allah has revealed, and follow not their desires, but beware of them lest they seduce you from some part of that which Allah has revealed to you. And if they turn away, then know that Allah's will is to smite them for some sin of theirs. Indeed many of mankind are evildoers.

(Those who refuse to live in the Divinely-revealed way of life, may be smitten for their sin, either in this world, through a catastrophe such as massacre, exile, enslavement or incarceration; or, alternatively, their chastisement may be postponed to the Hereafter.)

50. Is it a judgement of ignorance that they are seeking? Who is better than Allah for judgement to a people who have certainty (in their belief)?

("Ignorance (jahiliyya) here refers to the state of pagan ignorance which prevailed before Islam. As such, it remains a problem in many societies and regions, where the simple message of Divine unity and the obligation to serve others has not penetrated.)

51. O you who believe! Take not the Jews and Christians for friends. They are friends to each other. He among you who takes them for friends is *(one)* of them. Assuredly Allah guides not wrongdoing people.

52. And you see those in whose heart is a disease race toward them, saying: "We fear lest a change of fortune befall us! And it may happen that Allah will vouchsafe *(to you)* the victory, or a commandment from His presence; then will they repent of their secret thoughts.

(Muslims are advised not to look to Christians and Jews for help and comfort. They are more likely to combine against you than to help you. And this happened more than once in the lifetime of the Prophet, and in later ages again and again. He who associates with them and shares their counsels must be counted as one of them. One of the most serious problems of the Muslim world today is the admiration of many professed Muslims for the ways of the Jews and Christians, which, despite their profanity and indifference to all spirituality, carry with them a certain superficial glitter, being associated with the technical cleverness of the age. But Allah is indifferent to machinery; for in His sight the only greatness is greatness in the Spirit.)

53. Then will the believers say *(to the people of the Scripture)*: "Are these they who swore by Allah their most binding oaths that they were surely with you? Their works have failed, and they have become the losers.

54. O you who believe! If any from among you turn back from his religion, Allah will bring a people whom He loves and who love Him, humble toward believers, stern toward disbelievers, striving in the way of Allah, and fearing not the blame of any blamer. Such is the grace of Allah which He gives to whom He will. Allah is All-Embracing, All-Knowing.

(Throughout history, in spite of the miscreancy and short-sightedness of the worldly, Allah has always caused a group of the righteous to rise up and bear aloft the banner of Islam.)

55. Your friend can be only Allah; and His messenger and those who believe, who establish the Prayer and pay the Zakât, and bow down *(in prayer).*

56. And whosoever takes Allah and His messenger and those who believe for friends *(will know that)* assuredly, the party of Allah, they are the victorious.

57. O you who believe! Choose not for friends such of those who received the Scripture before you, and of the disbelievers, as make a mockery and sport of your religion. But keep your duty to Allah if you are true believers.

58. And when you call to prayer they take it only for a jest and a sport. That is because they are a people who do not understand.

59. Say: "O People of the Scripture! Do you blame us for no other reason than that we believe in Allah and that which is revealed unto us and that which was revealed before, and because most of you are evil-livers?"

(A group of Jews attacked the Muslims by declaring that "we do not know any community worse than you, or any religion worse than yours. . Allah answered their accusations by revealing the following verse.)

60. Shall I tell you a worse *(case)* than theirs for retribution with Allah? Worse *(is the case of him)* whom Allah had cursed, him on whom His wrath has fallen! Worse is he of whose sort Allah has turned some to apes and swine, and who serves idols. Such are in a worse plight and further astray from the even path.

61. When they come to you *(Muslims)*, they say: "We believe ; but in fact they enter with unbelief and they go out with unbelief; and Allah knows best what they were hiding.

62. And you see many of them racing with each other in sin and rancour, and their devouring of things forbidden. Evil indeed are the things that they do.

63. Why do not the rabbis and the priests forbid their evil speaking, and their devouring of things forbidden? Evil indeed is their handiwork.

64. The Jews say: "Allah's hand is fettered. Be their hands fettered, and be they cursed for saying so. Nay, but both His hands are outstretched. He gives as He pleases. But the revelation which has been revealed to you from your Lord is certain to increase in most of them their obstinate rebellion and disbelief; and We have cast among them enmity and hatred till the Day of Resurrection. As often as they light a fire for war, Allah extinguishes it. Their effort is for corruption in the land, and Allah loves not those who work corruption.

(Disbelievers have always tried to create wars and spread mischief on earth. Through the centuries they have not only quarrelled among themselves, but have also united with each other to attack the Muslims. In the same spirit, they have regularly contrived to sow discord and friction between Muslims. Despite all this, however, they have never been able to extinguish the light of Allah. Fortunately, among the disbelievers there is division also; even among members of the same religion there may be thousands of squabbling sects.)

وَلَوْ أَنَّ أَهْلَ الْكِتَابِ ءَامَنُوْا وَاتَّقَوْا لَكَفَّرْنَا عَنْهُمْ سَيِّئَاتِهِمْ وَلَأَدْخَلْنَاهُمْ جَنَّاتِ النَّعِيمِ ۝ وَلَوْ أَنَّهُمْ أَقَامُوا التَّوْرَاةَ وَالْإِنْجِيلَ وَمَا أُنْزِلَ إِلَيْهِمْ مِنْ رَبِّهِمْ لَأَكَلُوا مِنْ فَوْقِهِمْ وَمِنْ تَحْتِ أَرْجُلِهِمْ مِنْهُمْ أُمَّةٌ مُقْتَصِدَةٌ وَكَثِيرٌ مِنْهُمْ سَاءَ مَا يَعْمَلُونَ ۝ يَا أَيُّهَا الرَّسُولُ بَلِّغْ مَا أُنْزِلَ إِلَيْكَ مِنْ رَبِّكَ وَإِنْ لَمْ تَفْعَلْ فَمَا بَلَّغْتَ رِسَالَتَهُ وَاللَّهُ يَعْصِمُكَ مِنَ النَّاسِ إِنَّ اللَّهَ لَا يَهْدِي الْقَوْمَ الْكَافِرِينَ ۝ قُلْ يَا أَهْلَ الْكِتَابِ لَسْتُمْ عَلَى شَيْءٍ حَتَّى تُقِيمُوا التَّوْرَاةَ وَالْإِنْجِيلَ وَمَا أُنْزِلَ إِلَيْكُمْ مِنْ رَبِّكُمْ وَلَيَزِيدَنَّ كَثِيرًا مِنْهُمْ مَا أُنْزِلَ إِلَيْكَ مِنْ رَبِّكَ طُغْيَانًا وَكُفْرًا فَلَا تَأْسَ عَلَى الْقَوْمِ الْكَافِرِينَ ۝ إِنَّ الَّذِينَ ءَامَنُوا وَالَّذِينَ هَادُوا وَالصَّابِئُونَ وَالنَّصَارَى مَنْ ءَامَنَ بِاللَّهِ وَالْيَوْمِ الْآخِرِ وَعَمِلَ صَالِحًا فَلَا خَوْفٌ عَلَيْهِمْ وَلَا هُمْ يَحْزَنُونَ ۝ لَقَدْ أَخَذْنَا مِيثَاقَ بَنِي إِسْرَائِيلَ وَأَرْسَلْنَا إِلَيْهِمْ رُسُلًا كُلَّمَا جَاءَهُمْ رَسُولٌ بِمَا لَا تَهْوَى أَنْفُسُهُمْ فَرِيقًا كَذَّبُوا وَفَرِيقًا يَقْتُلُونَ ۝

۱۱۸

65. If only the People of the Scripture would believe and keep from evil, surely We would bring them into Gardens of Bliss.

66. If they had observed (practiced) the Torah and the Gospel and that which was revealed to them from their Lord, they would surely have been nourished from above them and from beneath their feet. Among them there are people who are moderate, but many of them are of evil conduct.

(Those who leave their religion and live by the philosophy of self survival and personal gain, feel no compunction in exploiting other nations; they cause oppression, poverty, unhappiness, and are a major cause of wars. If all submitted to the Creator, the Almighty, there would be no oppression, cruelty, or poverty in the world. Every individual would earn what is rightfully theirs, there would be abundance in the world and the blessings of the Lord would be showered upon mankind from all directions. And yet how far we have become from all this, rendering religion a source of discord rather than harmony, and devising secular ideologies which slaughter and maim in unprecedented numbers.)

67. O Messenger! Make known that which has been revealed to you from your Lord, for if you do it not, you will not have conveyed His message. Allah will protect you from men (who mean mischief). Surely, Allah guides not the disbelieving people.

68. Say: "O People of the Scripture! You have nothing (of true guidance) till you observe the Torah and the Gospel, and that which was revealed to you from your Lord. That which is revealed to you (Muhammad) from your Lord is certain to increase the obstinate rebellion and disbelief of many of them. But grieve not for the disbelieving people.

69. Those who believe (in the Qur'an), and those who are Jews, and Sabaeans, and Christians, whoso believes in Allah and the last Day and does right, no fear come upon them, neither shall they grieve.

(See also II:62. Regardless of the religion one may have followed in the past, and the sins one may have accumulated, once a man accepts Islam, and practices it in a fashion pleasing to God, he shall triumph in both worlds.)

70. We took the Covenant of the Children of Israel, and We sent to them messengers. As often as a messenger came to them with that which their souls desired not (they became rebellious). Some (of them) they denied, and some they slew.

71. They thought to harm would come of it, so they were willfully blind and deaf. And afterward Allah turned (in mercy) toward them. Now (even after that) are many of them willfully blind and deaf.

72. They surely disbelieve who say: "God is the Messiah, the son of Mary. The Messiah (himself) said: "O children of Israel, worship Allah, my Lord and your Lord. Whoever ascribes partners to Allah, for him Allah has forbidden paradise: His abode is the Fire. For evildoers there will be no helpers.

73. They surely disbelieve who say: "Allah is the third of three; when there is no God save One God. If they desist not from so saying, a painful doom will fall on those of them who disbelieve.

74. Will they not rather turn to Allah and seek forgiveness of Him? For Allah is Forgiving, Merciful.

75. The messiah, son of Mary, was no other than a messenger, messengers (the like of whom) had passed away before him. And his mother was a saintly woman. And they both used to eat (earthly) food. See how We make the revelations clear for them, and see how they are turned away!

(The Jews never believed that Jesus was born from a virtuous woman, but slandered her by claiming that she bore an illegitimate child. The Holy Qur'an here shows that the birth of Jesus was miraculous. Mary never claimed that she was the "mother of God , or that her son was God. She was a pious, virtuous woman. On the other hand, the slander of the Christians is refuted here by pointing out the human nature of the Messiah, for he needed food, which, although the most basic human requirement, is not needed by God, Who cannot be sustained by anything. So God is one; His Message is one; yet how easily does man's perversity transforms truth into falsehood, and religion into superstition.)

76. Say: "Do you worship in place of Allah that which possesses for you neither harm nor benefit? Allah it is who is the Hearer, the Knower.

77. Say: "O People of the Scripture! Exceed not in your religion the bounds, and do not follow the vain desires of people who erred in times gone by and led many astray, and strayed from the plain road.

78. Those of the Children of Israel who went astray were cursed by the tongue of David, and of Jesus, the son of Mary. That was because they rebelled and used to transgress.

79. They restrained not one another from the wickedness they did. Assuredly, evil was what they used to do.

80. You see many of them making friends with those who disbelieve. Surely evil for them is that which they themselves send on before them: (*with the result*) that Allah's wrath will be upon them, and in torment will they abide.

81. If they believed in Allah and the Prophet and that which is revealed to him, they would not choose them for their friends, but many of them are wrongdoers.

82. You will find the most vehement of men in enmity to those who believe *(to be)* the Jews and the idolaters. And you will find the nearest of them in affection to those who believe *(to be)* those who say: "We are Christians. That is because there are among them priests and monks, and because they are not proud.

(According to certain interpreters of the Holy Qur'an, the above verse refers to the Christians of Abyssinia (Ethiopia) who welcomed the early Muslims who emigrated to their land. According to others, it denotes the Christians of Najrân, who signed a treaty with the Prophet Muhammad. More generally, the meaning is that sincere Christians will be able to appreciate Muslim virtues. Let us not, however, forget that many fanatic so-called Christians have waged war against Muslims, as during the Crusades, and ransacked Muslim lands. While Muslims are by this and other verses enjoined to look with compassion upon Christians, they should not forget the crimes which some of them have committed.)

83. When they listen to that which has been revealed to the Messenger, you see their eyes overflow with tears because of their recognition of the Truth. They say: "Our Lord, we believe! so inscribe us among the witnesses!

84. How should we not believe in Allah and that which has come to us of the truth? And *(how should we not)* hope that our Lord will bring us in along with the righteous people?

85. Allah has rewarded them for their saying with Gardens beneath which rivers flow, wherein they shall abide forever. That is the reward of those who do good.

86. But those who disbelieve and deny Our signs *(revelations)*, they are owners of hellfire.

87. O you who believe! Forbid not the good things which Allah has made lawful for you, and do not transgress. Assuredly, Allah does not love the transgressors.

88. Eat of that which Allah has bestowed on you as food lawful and good, and keep your duty to Allah in Whom you are believers.

(In one of his talks, the holy Prophet Muhammad discussed with some of his companions, including 'Alî, Ibn Mas'ûd, and al-Miqdâd (may Allah be pleased with them!) some important aspects of renunciation and the devotional life, and they were deeply affected by his words. Afterwards, they gathered together at the home of 'Uthmân ibn Maz'ûn, and resolved to fast every day, to pray throughout everyt night, to renounce sexual relations, to renounce meat, and to wear shabby clothes for the remainder of their lives. When the Holy Prophet heard about this he immediately came to visit them, saying: "Your body has rights over you, your eye has rights over you, and your wife has rights over you. You should fast and pray, but also eat and sleep. I pray some of the time, and I also sleep; I fast, and I break my fast; I eat meat, and I have relations with my wives. He who leaves my Way, he is not of me. It was in this connection that the above two verses were revealed.)

89. Allah will not call you to account for what is unintentional in your oaths, but He will call you to account for the oaths which you swear deliberately. The expiation thereof is the feeding of ten of the needy with the average of that with which you feed your own people, or the clothing of them, or the liberation of a slave, and for him who finds not *(the wherewithal to do so)* then a three day's fast. This is the expiation of your oaths when you have sworn; and keep your oaths. Thus Allah expounds to you His revelations, in order that you may give thanks.

(Vows of penance or abstention may sometimes be unintentional, or stand in the way of a good or virtuous act. The general principles established here are: (1) take no unintentional oaths; (2) do not use God's name, literally or in intention, to fetter yourselves against doing a lawful or good act; (3) keep to your solemn oaths to the utmost of your ability; (4) Where you are unable to do so, expiate your failure by feeding or clothing the poor, or obtaining someone's freedom; or, if you have not the means, by fasting. This pertains to the spiritual side of the question. If anyone suffers damage from your failure, compensation will be due to him, but that would be a question of law.)

90. O you who believe! Intoxicants and gambling, and *(occult dedication of)* stones and divining arrows are only an infamy of Satan's handiwork. Leave them aside in order that you may succeed.

91. Satan seeks only to cast among you enmity and hatred by means of strong drink and gambling, and to turn you from remembrance of Allah and from *(His)* worship. Will you not then abstain?

(During the period of ignorance before Islam the pagan Arabs were given to drinking wine and other alcoholic drinks. The Islamic prohibition was effected in three stages. Allah first discouraged the believing Muslims from drinking wine, drawing to their attention the fact that there was more evil than benefit in intoxicants. Later they were forbidden from praying while under the influence of alcohol. With the above verse, the practice was definitively forbidden. At the same time, gambling was also outlawed, the two vices having many of the same properties. The "arrows referred to were used for the division of meat by a sort of lottery or raffle. They were also used for divinition, for example, in ascertaining lucky or inauspicious moments, or learning the wishes of the heathen gods, as to whether men should undertake certain actions or not. All superstitions, whether or not they seem to have an occult reality, are outlawed by God's law.)

92. Obey Allah and obey the messenger, and beware! But if you turn away, then know that the duty of Our messenger is only plain communication *(of the message)*.

93. These shall be no sin *(imputed)* to those who believe and do good deeds for what they may have eaten *(in the past)*; so be mindful of your duty *(to Allah)*, and believe and do good works; and once again: be mindful of your duty, and believe; and once again: be mindful of your duty, and do good. Allah loves those who do good.

94. O you who believe! Allah will surely try you somewhat *(in the matter)* of the game which you take with your hands and your spears, that Allah may know him who fears Him in secret.

Anyone who transgresses after this, for him there is a painful punishment.

95. O you who believe! Kill no wild game while you are in the state of consecration. If any of you kills it intentionally he shall pay its forfeit in the equivalent of that which he had killed, of domestic animals, the judge to be two men among you known for justice, *(the forfeit)* to be brought as an offering to the Ka'ba; or, for expiation, he shall feed poor persons, or the equivalent thereof in fasting, that he may taste the evil consequences of his deed. Allah forgives whatever *(of this kind)* may have happened in the past, but whosoever relapses, Allah will take retribution from him. Allah is Mighty, Able to Requite *(the wrong)*.

(While in the state of consecration for pilgrimage *(ihrâm)*, or in the Sacred Territory around Makka, it is forbidden to harm any living thing, with the exception of certain dangerous reptiles and insects. Thus does Allah remind man of the sacrosanct nature of His city, which is a place of peace and security for all.)

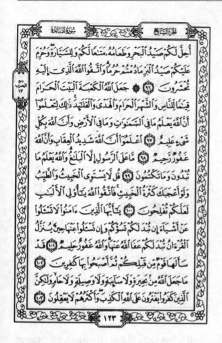

be mindful of your duty to Allah, O men of understanding, that you may succeed.

(Islam emphasises quality rather than quantity. The intelligent man will not be dazzled by numbers, or allow his heart to be captured by what he sees everywhere around him. Instead he knows that the best is likely to be uncommon, and that he must exert himself if he is to find it.)

101. O you who believe! Ask not of things which, if they were made known to you, would trouble you; but if you ask of them when the Qur'an is being revealed, they will be made known to you. Allah pardons this, for Allah is Forgiving, Clement.

102. A people before you asked (for such disclosures), and then disbelieved therein.

103. Allah has not appointed anything in the nature of a Bahîra or a Sâ'iba or a Wasîla or a Hâm, but those who disbelieve invent a lie against Allah. Most of them have no sense.

(The above verse is related to the pagan tradition of the pre-Islamic Arabs. The pagan mind, not understanding the hidden secrets of nature, attributed certain phenomena to divine anger, and were assailed by superstitious fears which haunted their lives. If a she-camel or other female domestic animal had a large number of young, at least five times, then after the fifth time she had her ear slit and was dedicated to a god; such an animal was Bahîra. On a safe return from a journey, or a recovery from an illness a she-camel was similarly dedicated, and let loose pasture freely, being known as a Sâ'iba. Where an animal bore twins, certain sacrifices or dedications were made to idols: an animal so dedicated was a Wasîla. A stallion camel dedicated to the gods by certain rites was a hâmi. The particular examples lead to the general truth: that superstition is due to ignorance, and is degrading to man and dishonouring to God.)

96. To hunt and to eat the fish of the sea is made lawful for you, a provision for you and for seafarers; but to hunt on land is forbidden you so long as you are in the state of consecration. Be mindful of your duty to Allah, to whom you will be gathered.

97. Allah has appointed the Ka'ba, the Sacred House, a standard for mankind, and the sacred month and the offerings and the garlands. That is so that you may know that Allah knows whatever is in the heavens and whatever is in the earth, and that Allah is Knower of all things.

98. Know that Allah is severe in punishment, but that Allah (also) is Forgiving, Merciful.

99. The duty of the Messenger is only to convey. Allah knows what you proclaim and what you hide.

100. Say: "The evil and the good are not alike, even though the plenty of the evil attract you; so

104. And when it is said to them: "Come to that which Allah had revealed and to the messenger, they say: "Enough for us is that wherein we found our fathers. What! Even though their fathers had no knowledge whatsoever, and no guidance?

105. O you who believe! Guard your own souls. If you follow right guidance, no harm can come to you from those who stray. To Allah you will all return; and then He will inform you of what you used to do.

(Our souls are what our lives are about. Everything we do should be directed towards their purification from forgetfulness and ugly traits of character, so that we will be protected from the insinuations of those whose hearts are in a worse condition than ours. But it is part of tending one's soul to ensure the wellbeing of others, particularly those who are in one's charge.)

106. O you who believe! Let there be witnesses between you when death draws near to one of you, at the time of bequest - two witnesses, just men from among you, or two others from another tribe, in case you are on a journey through the land and the calamity of death befall you. You shall detain them after the prayer, and if you doubt, they shall be made to swear by Allah (saying): "We will not take a bribe, even though it were (on behalf of) a near kinsman, nor will we hide the testimony of Allah, for then indeed we should be of the sinful.

107. But then, if it is afterwards ascertained that both of them merit (the suspicion of) sin let two others take their place of those nearly concerned, and let them swear by Allah, saying: "Assuredly, our testimony is truer than their testimony, and we have not transgressed (the bounds of duty), for then indeed we should be of the evildoers.

108. Thus it is more likely that they will bear true witness or fear that after their oath the oath (of others) will be taken. So be mindful of your duty (to Allah) and listen (to His counsel). Allah guides not the corrupt people.

(In order to deal with the liabilities of the deceased as well as his assets, certain principles are established to ensure that after a man's death his obligations are carried out honourably. The close relatives of the deceased, or the individuals appointed as executors of his will, are required to see that debts and other liabilities are discharged and no money is wrongfully diverted. The above verses discuss these responsibilities, and how to address them.)

109. In the day when Allah will gather the messengers together and ask: "What was the response you received *(from the people you were assigned to teach)?* They will say: "We have no knowledge: it is You, only You, who knows in full all that is hidden.

110. Then will Allah say: "O Jesus, son of Mary! Remember My favour to you and to your mother; how I strengthened you with the holy spirit *(the archangel Gabriel)* so that you spoke to mankind in the cradle as in maturity; and how I taught you the Scripture and Wisdom and the Torah and the Gospel; and how you did shape of clay as it were the likeness of a bird by My permission, and did blow upon it, and it was a bird by My permission, and you did heal him who was born blind and the leper by My permission; and how you did raise the dead, by My permission; and how I restrained the Children of Israel from *(harming)* you when you came to them with clear signs, and those of them who disbelieved exclaimed: "This is nothing but clear magic!

(Both the above verse and the verses to come discuss the miracles of the prophet Jesus. In order to make things easy for the mankind Allah empowered all His messengers with the ability to work certain kinds of miracles, in order to help men to believe in Allah and in the teachings of His messengers. These miracles took place only with the permission of Allah.)

111. And when I inspired the disciples, *(saying)*: "Believe in Me and in My messenger, they said: "We believe. Bear witness that we have surrendered *(to You as Muslims)* .

(The "disciples (*hawâriyyûn*) were the closest followers of Jesus. Like the Companions of the Prophet Muhammad, they believed in Allah and followed the teachings of their master with loyalty, and surrendered themselves to Allah, in the state known in Arabic as *islâm*: the entire submission to God.)

112. When the disciples said: "O Jesus, son of Mary! Is your Lord able to send down for us a table spread with food from heaven? He said: "Observe your duty to Allah, if you are true believers.

113. They said: "We wish to eat thereof, that we may satisfy our hearts and know that you have spoken truth to us, and that thereof we may be witnesses.

114. Jesus, son of Mary, said: "O Allah, our Lord! Send down for us a table spread with food from heaven, that it may be a feast for us, for the first of us and for the last of us, and a sign from You. Give us sustenance, for you are the Best of Sustainers.

115. Allah said: "I will send it down for you. But if any of you disbelieves afterward, him surely will I punish with a punishment wherewith I have not punished any of my peoples.

116. And when Allah said: "O Jesus, son of Mary! Did you say to mankind: "Take me and my mother for two gods beside Allah? he said: "Be glorified! It was not mine to say that to which I had no right. If I used to say it, then You knew it. You know what is in my mind, and I know not what is in Your mind. Assuredly, You, only You, are the Knower of things hidden."

117. I spoke to them only that which You commanded me, (saying): "Worship Allah, my Lord and your Lord. I was a witness of them while I dwelt among them, and when You took me You were the Watcher over them. You are Witness over all things.

118. If You punish them, they are Your slaves, and if You forgive them, You, only You, are the Mighty, the Wise."

119. Allah will then say: "This is a day in which their truthfulness profits the truthful, for theirs are Gardens beneath which rivers flow, wherein they are secure for ever, Allah is well-pleased with them and they with Him. That is the great triumph.

120. To Allah belongs the sovereignty of the heavens and the earth and whatsoever in therein, and He is Able to do all things.

(Man's successes in this world mean nothing, for he and it are transitory. Only Allah the Exalted is real, and the permanent Owner of all. When we compare our planet, in which our endeavours unfold, to the known universe, which is 10 billion light-years, it seems less significant than a grain of sand in a desert. What, then, is real success for man? It is to seek the pleasure of Allah. For while to materialists the world is all, and man's actions therein are his only actions, to believers in Almighty God, the world is of worth only as a Divinely designed arena of tests and signs, which give us the opportunity of acknowledging Him. For as He says, "I created men and jinn only that they may worship Me. His perfection is manifested in its recognition by those who are capable of imperfection and ignorance, but yet overcome their lower possibilities, and know Him. Hence the believer's best prayer is, "May Allah be well-pleased with you, and may you be well-pleased with Him .)

١٢٧

SÛRAH VI
AL-AN'ÂM (THE CATTLE)

Revealed at Makka

This is a Sûrah of the late Makkan period, although verses 91, 92, 93, 151, 152, and 153 were perhaps revealed at Madîna. The name of the Sûrah derives from verse 137, where a theme emphasised here, the condemnation of the pagan sacrifice of animals, is recalled. More generally, the Sûrah is a vindication of the Divine Unity, and hence follows on from the subjects of the previous Sûrahs. The note of certain triumph is remarkable in the circumstances of its revelation, when the Blessed Prophet, after thirteen years of effort, saw himself obliged to leave Makka and seek help from strangers.

THE CATTLE

In the name of Allah, the Compassionate, the Merciful.

1. Praise be to Allah, Who has created the heavens and the earth, and has appointed darkness and light. Yet those who disbelieve ascribe rivals to their Lord.

2. He it is who has created you from clay, and has decreed a term for you. A term is fixed with Him, yet still you doubt!

3. He is Allah in the heavens and in the earth. He knows both your secret and your utterance, and He knows what you earn *(by your deeds).*

4. Never came there to them a revelation of the revelations of Allah but they did turn away from it.

5. And they denied the truth when it came to them. But there will come to them the tidings of that which they used to deride.

("The Truth mentioned in the above verse is the Holy Qur'an, and the other miracles that were given to the Prophet.)

6. See they not how many a generation We destroyed before them, whom We had established in the earth more firmly than We have established you, and We shed on them abundant showers from the sky, and made the rivers flow beneath them. Yet We destroyed them for their sins, and created after them another generation.

7. Had We sent down to you *(Muhammad)* an *(actual)* writing on parchment, so that they could feel it with their hands, those who disbelieve would have said: "This is nothing but mere magic.

(The Holy Qur'an was revealed to the Prophet Muhammad both by the Archangel Gabriel and other means. In both cases, the revelations were not revealed to him on paper but rather through teaching and memorizing. The rejecters of the "Truth did not accept this, and, as materialists, they wanted to see written messages. Almighty Allah is here telling mankind that even if he did send written messages, the rejecters of the faith would still automatically reject it. After all, the Jews rejected the revelation of Moses, even when he brought it to them on stone tables given by God.)

8. They say: "Why has an angel not been sent down to him? If We sent down an angel, then the matter would be judged; no further time would be allowed them *(for reflection).*

(An angel is a heavenly being, created by the divine Omnipotence, a manifestation of Allah's glory, invisible to men who live gross material lives. Such men are given plenty of respite in which to turn in repentance to Allah and make themselves worthy of His light. But if their prayer to send an angel were granted, it would do them no good, for they would be destroyed as darkness is destroyed by light.)

9. Had We appointed an angel *(as Our messenger)*, We assuredly had made him *(as)* a man *(that he might speak to men)*; and *(thus)* confused them in a matter which they have already covered with confusion.

(If the prophet appeared in the form of an angel, they would say: "You are a man like us! and would not believe in him. For if one appeared to them, he could only do so in human form, further confusing their present confused notions about spiritual life.)

10. Messengers *(of Allah)* have been mocked at before you, but that at which they scoffed surrounded such of them as mocked.

11. Say *(to the disbelievers):* "Travel in the land, and see the nature of the consequence for the rejecters!

12. Say: "To whom belongs whatsoever is in the heavens and the earth? Say: "To Allah. He has prescribed for Himself mercy, that He may bring you all together to a Day in which there is no doubt. Those who ruin their own souls will not believe.

13. To Him belongs whatsoever rests in the night and the day. He is the Hearer, the Knower.

14. Say: "Shall I choose for a protecting friend other than Allah, the Originator of the heavens and the earth, who feeds and is not fed? Say: "I am ordered to be the first to surrender *(to Him)*, and be not you of the polytheists.

15. Say: "I fear, if I rebel against my Lord, the retribution of an Awful Day.

16. He from whom *(such retribution)* is awarded on that day, *(Allah)* has in truth had mercy on him. That will be the signal triumph.

17. If Allah touches you with affliction, there is none that can relieve from it save Him; and if He touches you with good fortune *(there is none that can impair it)*; for He is Able to do all things.

18. He is the Omnipotent over His slaves, and He is the Wise, the Knower.

19. Say (O Muhammad): "What thing is most weighty in testimony? Say: "Allah is witness between you and me. And this Qur'an has been inspired in me, that I may warn with it you and whomsoever it may reach. Do you truly bear witness that there are other deities beside Allah? Say: "I do not bear witness! Say: "He is only One God. I am innocent of that which you associate (with Him).

(The people of Makka had accused the prophet that there is no witness to his prophethood, and hence the above verse was revealed.)

20. Those to whom We gave the Scripture recognize (this Revelation) as they recognize their (own) sons. Those who ruin their own souls will not believe.

21. Who does greater wrong than he who invents a lie against Allah and denies His signs (revelations)? Assuredly, the wrongdoers will not succeed.

22. And on the day We gather them together, We shall say to those who assigned partners (to Allah): "Where (now) are those partners that you claimed?

23. Then will they have no contention save that they will say: "By Allah, our Lord, we never were polytheists.

(The word here rendered as "contention is fitna, which is from a root meaning "to try, to test, to tempt . By extension it often denotes trouble, sedition and tumult, or a false and contentious answer to a trial (as here).)

24. See how they lie against themselves, and (how) the thing which they devised had failed them!

25. Of them are some who listen to you, but We have placed upon their hearts veils, lest they should understand, and in their ears a deafness. If they saw every sign they would not believe in it; to the point that, when they come to you to argue with you, the disbelievers say: "This is nothing else than the legends of the ancients.

26. And they forbid (men) from it and avoid it, and they ruin only themselves, though they do not realise.

27. If you could see when they are set before the Fire and say: "Oh, if only we could return! Then we would not deny the revelations of our Lord, and would be of the believers!

28. No, but that which they before used to hide has become clear to them. And if they were sent back they would return to that which they are forbidden. Certainly they are liars.

29. And they say: "There is nothing save our life of the world, and we shall not be raised *(again)*.

30. If you could see when they are set before their Lord! He will say: "Is this not real? They will say: "Yes, verily, by our Lord! He will say: "Taste now the retribution for that you used to disbelieve.

31. They indeed are losers who deny their meeting with Allah until, when the hour comes on them suddenly, they cry: "Alas for us, that we neglected it! They bear upon their backs their burdens. Ah, evil is that which they bear!

32. The life of the world is nothing but a pastime and a play. But best is the home in the Hereafter for those who keep their duty *(to Allah)*. Have you then no sense?

(Abû Jahl, the arch-enemy of Islam, once told the Holy Prophet: "We are not saying that you are lying. We truly believe that you are honest and trustworthy; it is only that we do not believe in the revelations . The Prophet was saddened by these words from Abû Jahl. Then the Lord revealed the following verse to console him.)

33. We know well how their talk grieves you, though in truth they deny not you *(Muhammad)*; but it is the signs *(revelations)* of Allah that the wicked condemn.

34. Messengers indeed have been denied before you, and they were patient under the denial and the persecution till Our aid reached them. There is none to alter the decisions of Allah. Already there has reached you *(something)* of the tidings of the messengers *(We sent before)*.

35. And if their aversion is grievous to you, then, if you can, seek a way down into the earth or a ladder to the sky that you may bring to them a sign *(to convince them all)*! If Allah willed, He could have brought them all together to the guidance, so do not be among the foolish ones.

(As we understand from the above verse, it is not within the ability of the prophet to cause miracles. The prophet asks for a miracle, and, if the Lord wills, he will be granted one. The ability to overturn natural laws belongs to the Lawmaker alone.)

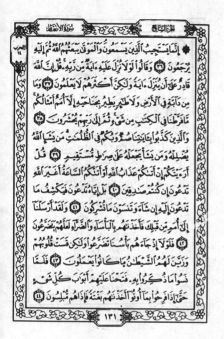

36. Only those who listen to the truth can respond. As for the dead, Allah will raise them up; then to Him they will be returned.

37. They say: "Why has no sign been sent down upon him from his Lord? Say: "Allah is certainly able to send down a sign. But most of them know not.

38. There is not an animal in the earth, nor a flying creature flying on two wings, but they are peoples like unto you. We have neglected nothing in the Book *(of Our decrees)*. Then to their Lord they will be gathered.

(All living creatures live a life, social and individual, as we do, and all life is subject to the Plan of Allah. In 6:59 we are told that not a leaf falls but by His will, and things dry and green are recorded in His Book. In other words, they all obey His archetypal Plan, the Book which is also mentioned here.)

39. Those who deny Our revelations are deaf and dumb in darkness. Allah sends astray whom He will, and whom He will He places on a straight path.

40. Say: "Can you see yourselves, if the punishment of Allah come upon you or the Hour come upon you, calling upon other than Allah? Do you then call *(for help)* to any other than Allah? *(Answer that)* if you are truthful.

41. No, but to Him you call, and He removes that because of which you call to Him, if He will, and you forget whatever partners you ascribe to Him.

42. We have sent already to peoples that were before you, and We visited them with suffering and adversity, in order that they might grow humble.

(Allah sent many prophets to other nations before the Prophet Muhammad, but some of those nations rejected them. Because of this Allah punished them with all kinds of catastrophes.)

43. If only, when Our disaster came on them, they had been humble! But their hearts were hardened, and the devil made all that they used to do seem fair to them.

44. Then, when they forgot that whereof they had been reminded, we opened to them the gates of all things till, even as they were rejoicing in that which they were given, We seized them unawareness, and lo! they were plunged in despair.

(Learning the inner truth of ourselves and the world presupposes a certain advanced stage of sensitiveness and spiritual development. There is a shallower stage, at which prosperity and the good things of life may teach us sympathy and cheerfulness. In such cases, the Message can take root. But there is another type which is made proud and arrogant by prosperity, for whom it is a trial or a punishment. They go deeper and deeper into sin, until they are pulled up all of a sudden and then, instead of being contrite, they merely become desperate.)

45. So of the people who did wrong the last remnant was cut off. And praise be to Allah, Lord of the Worlds!

(Instead of thanking Allah, they disobeyed Him and did wrong, hence their Maker destroyed them. For He is the Lord, Who is just in retribution, and Who will not torment His righteous servants with the company of the evil.)

46. Say: "Have you imagined, if Allah should take away your hearing and your sight and seal your hearts, who is the God who could restore it to you save Allah? See how We display the revelations to them? Yet still they turn away.

47. Say: "Can you see yourselves, if the punishment of Allah come upon you unawares or openly? Will any perish save the wrongdoing people?

48. We send the messengers only to give good news and to warn. So those who believe and do right, no fear shall come upon them, neither will they grieve.

49. But as for those who deny Our revelations, torment will afflict them for that they used to disobey.

50. Say (O Muhammad), to the disbelievers): "I say not to you (that) I possess the treasures of Allah, nor that I have knowledge of the Unseen; and I say not to you: "I am an angel. I follow only that which is inspired in me. Say: "Are the blind man and the seer equal? Will you not then think?

(The idolators told the Prophet Muhammad: "If you are truly a messenger of Allah, then tell your Lord to shower us with His blessings so that we can believe in you; otherwise we will not. Because of their disbelief the above verse was revealed. For the mission of a prophet is not to make men rich with worldly blessings, but is to convey the message of eternity to them.)

51. Warn with this those who fear (because they know) that they will be gathered to their Lord, for whom there is no protecting friend nor intercessor beside Him, that they may guard against evil.

52. Send not away those who call upon their Lord at morning and evening, seeking only to gain His favour. You are not by any means accountable for them, nor are they accountable for you, that you should turn them away, and thus be of the wrongdoers.

(Some of the rich and influential people of Quraish thought it beneath their dignity to listen to the Blessed Prophet's teaching in company with the poor believers who were gathered around him. Because of the wish of these people, the Prophet thought to send them away, but in the above verse he was reminded not to do so, for those lowly disciples were the sincere seekers of God.)

53. And even so do We try some of them by others, that they say: "Are these they whom Allah favours among us? Is not Allah best aware of those who are grateful?

(The idolators couldn't stomach the equal treatment of the lowly believers with themselves in the presence of the prophet. In the eyes of Allah there is no discrimination of His creatures except inwardly, on the basis of belief and piety. The idolators were tried by God's justice, and were found wanting.)

54. And when those who believe in Our revelations come to you, say: "Peace be upon you! Your Lord has prescribed for Himself mercy, that whoso of you does evil and repents afterward and does right, *(for him)* assuredly Allah is Forgiving, Merciful.

55. Thus do We expound the revelations that the way of the unrighteous may be manifest.

56. Say: "I am forbidden to worship those on whom you call instead of Allah! Say: "I will not follow your desires, for then I would go astray, and would not be of the rightly-guided.

57. Say: "I am *(relying)* on clear proof from my Lord, while you deny Him. I do not have that for which you are impatient. The decision is for Allah only. He tells the truth and He is the Best of Deciders.

58. Say: "If I had that for which you are impatient *(the punishment they mockingly desired)*, the matter would be settled at once between you and me. But Allah knows best those who do wrong.

(Thus the Blessed Prophet is taught to deploy four arguments against the pagans of Makka. (1) I have received Light, and will follow it; (2) I prefer my Light to your fantasies and desires; (3) your challenge, 'if there is a God, why does He not finish the blasphemers all at once', is not for me to take up; punishment rests with Allah; (4) if it rested with me, it would be for me to take up your challenge; all I know is that Allah is aware of the existence of folly and wickedness, and many other things beside, that no mortal can know; you can see little glimpses of His plan, and you can be sure that He will not be late in calling you to account.)

59. And with Him are the keys of the unseen. None but He knows them. And He knows what is in the land and the sea. Not a leaf falls but with his knowledge, not a grain amid the darkness of the earth, nothing of wet or dry but *(it is noted)* in a clear record.

(Every movement and stillness in the vast expanses of the universe is fully know to Him, and has been since before its creation, for He is the All-Knowing. If this is His providence in the natural world, how can His attention to man be any less?)

60. He it is who gathers you at night and knows that which you commit by day. Then He raises you again to life therein that the term appointed (*for you*) may be accomplished. And afterward to Him is your return. Then He will proclaim to you what you used to do.

61. He is the Omnipotent over His slaves. He sends guardians over you until, when death comes to one of you, Our messengers (*angels assigned for this special duty*) receive him, and they neglect not.

62. Then are mankind returned to Allah, their Lord, the Just. Surely His is the judgement, and He is the most swift of reckoners.

63. Say: "Who delivers you from the darkness of the land and the sea? You call upon Him humbly and in secret, (*saying*): "If we are delivered from this (*fear*) we truly will be of the thankful.

64. Say: "It is Allah who delivers you from this and from all other afflictions. Yet you attribute partners to Him.

65. Say: "He is able to send punishment upon you from above you or from beneath your feet, or to bewilder you with dissension and make you taste the violence one of another. See how We display the revelations so that they may understand.

(It is only by the grace of Allah that the immediate punishment is withheld from you. In the past, cities with crimes like yours were destroyed utterly.)

66. Your people (*O Muhammad*) have denied it, though it is the Truth. Say: "I am not put in change of you.

(The meaning is that it is the function of a prophet only to bring the reminder to his people, not to force them to accept it.)

67. For every message there is a term, and you will come to know.

68. And when you see those who meddle with Our revelations, withdraw from them until they meddle with another topic. And if the devil cause you to forget, sit not, after the remembrance, with the congregation of wrongdoers.

(During the Makkan period, the believers were not allowed to fight; the idolaters took advantage of this situation, and mocked at the believers, and the revelations that were being revealed by Allah. Because of this, Allah commanded the Blessed Prophet to leave their company. Although this revelation was directly specifically to the Blessed Prophet in the first instance, its implications are applicable to all Muslims who find themselves in the company of blasphemy and evil, and yet have not the power to prevent it.)

69. Those who ward off *(evil)* are not accountable for them at all, but it is *(their duty)* to remind them that they may perhaps fear Allah.

70. And forsake those who take their religion for a pastime and an amusement, and whom the life of the world deceives. Remind *(mankind)* with this, lest a soul be destroyed by what it earns. It has beside Allah no friend nor intercessor, and though it offer every compensation it will not be accepted from it. Those are they who perish by what they have acquired. For them is drink of boiling water and a painful punishment, because they disbelieved.

71. Say: "Shall we indeed call on others beside Allah, to that which neither profits us nor hurts us, and shall we turn back after Allah has guided us, like one bewildered whom the devils have infatuated in the earth, who has companions who invite him to the guidance *(saying):* "Come to us? Say: "Surely, the guidance of Allah is

Guidance, and we are ordered to surrender to the Lord of the Worlds.

(This verse clearly describes the inner turmoil of a soul which has accepted the One True God as Lord, and then retreats to the worship of many gods. Confused and bewildered, his heart in ruin, the devils have taken hold of him and drag him further and further into the wilderness. And yet the voices of the prophets and saints still come towards him, calling him back to the true and only guidance. A person who is intelligent, and has the strength to fight off the devils, will respond to the call, and return to the Way of the Prophets, ultimately gaining the peace and security that he most desires.)

72. To establish regular prayers and to fear Allah, and He it is to Whom you will be gathered.

73. He it is who created the heavens and the earth in truth. In the day when he says: "Be! it is. His word is the truth, and His will be the sovereignty on the day when the trumpet is blown. Knower of the Unseen and the Witnessed. He is the Wise, the Aware.

(The trumpet mentioned here is a body of light, which resembles a horn, and is blown by the Archangel Seraphiel to signal the end of the world. He shall blow it twice. The first time, all the living creatures in the earth shall be slain, and only the One True God shall abide. Then he shall blow it again, and they shall return to life, and await the Judgement.)

74. (*Remember*) when Abraham said to his father Azar: "Do you take idols for gods? Assuredly, I see you and your people in manifest error.

(The nation that Abraham was sent to as a prophet were the ancient Chaldeans, who lived in northern Iraq. When Abraham saw his father and his people worshipping idols he condemned them ardently, convinced that immobile statues made by human hands could neither be nor represent divinity.)

75. Thus did We show Abraham the kingdom of the heavens and the earth that he might be of those possessing certainty.

(The word *malakût,* here translated "kingdom", means the realities behind the outward creation: Allah showed him the spiritual glories which underlie the magnificent powers and laws of the physical universe.)

76. When the night grew dark upon him he saw a star. He said: "This is my Lord! But when it set, he said: "I love not things that set."

77. And when he saw the moon rising in splendour, he said: "This is my Lord But when it set, he said: "Unless my Lord guide me, I surely shall become one of the people who are astray."

78. And when he saw the sun rising in splendour, he cried: "This is my Lord! This is greater! - and when it set he exclaimed: "O my people! Assuredly, I am free from all that you associate *(with him).*

79. Assuredly, I have turned my face toward Him who created the heavens and the earth, as one by nature upright *(or righteous),* and I am not of the polytheists.

(The word *hanîf* used in the original text, and here translated as "one by nature upright", denotes someone who recognizes only one God, even if he has not received a religion from Him. There are differences of opinions between the translators of the Holy Qur'an as

to whether Abraham, upon him be peace, is here searching for the one true God, or rhetorically demonstrating the absurdity of worshipping heavenly bodies. The latter opinion seems to be the more acceptable.)

80. His people argued with him. He said: "Dispute you with me concerning Allah, when He has guided me? I fear not at all that which you set beside Him unless my Lord wills. My Lord includes all things in His knowledge. Will you not then remember?

81. How should I fear that which you set up beside him, when you fear not to set up beside Allah that for which He has revealed to you no warrant? Which of the two factions has more right to safety? *(Answer me that)* if you have knowledge.

(The two factions mentioned here are (1) those who recognise one almighty God, and (2) those who worship several gods, and are devoted to idols. Which group is more worthy of God's protection from Hellfire? The next verse gives the response.)

82. Those who believe and obscure not their belief by wrongdoing, theirs is a safety; and they are rightly guided.

83. That is Our argument. We gave it to Abraham against his people. We raise to degrees of wisdom whom We will. Verily your Lord is Wise, Aware.

("Argument (*Hujja*) here could also be translated as wisdom, knowledge, dignity, and the ability to see and compare.)

84. And We bestowed upon him Isaac and Jacob; each of them We guided; and Noah did We guide aforetime; and of his seed *(We guided)* David and Solomon and Job and Joseph and Moses and Aaron. Thus do We reward the good.

85. And Zachariah and John and Jesus and Elias. Each one was of the righteous.

86. And Ishmael and Elisha and Jonah and Lot. Each one of them did We prefer above all creatures *(or nations)*.

(The reason why these prophets were thus favoured is explained in verse 89 below. Some Prophets received only revelation. Others received political authority and judgement as well.)

87. With some of their forefathers and their offspring and brethren; and We chose them and guided them to a straight path.

88. Such is the guidance of Allah with which He guides whom He will of His bondmen. But if they had set up *(for worship)* anything beside him, *(all)* that they did would have been vain.

89. Those are they to whom We gave the scripture and command and prophethood. But if these disbelieve therein, then indeed We shall entrust it to a people who will not be disbelievers therein.

90. Those are they whom Allah guides, so follow their guidance. Say *(O Muhammad, unto mankind)*: "I ask of you no reward for it. Assuredly, it is nothing but a Reminder to *(His)* creatures.

(Thus is the mission of the Blessed Prophet Muhammad set in context: Islam is not a departure from God's way with mankind, and the Prophet is simply sent to remind humanity of the message taught by earlier Prophets, which was then forgotten.)

91. And they measure not the power of Allah its true measure when they say: "Allah has revealed nothing to a human being. Say *(to the Jews who speak thus)*: "Who revealed the book which Moses brought, a light and guidance for mankind, which you have put on parchments which you show, but you hide much *(thereof)*, and by which you were taught that which you knew not yourselves nor did your fathers *(know it)?* Say: "Allah . Then leave them to their plunge into their games.

92. And this is a blessed Scripture which We have revealed, conforming that which *(was revealed)* before it, that you may warn the Mother of Cities *(Makka)* and those around her. Those who believe in the Hereafter believe herein, and they are careful of their Prayers.

(The city of Makka is the spiritual centre of Islam, being built around man's first house of worship. Located at the axis of three continents, it is surrounded by the whole world. Thus it is that one of the names of Makka is "the Mother of Cities .)

93. Who is guilty of more wrong then he who forges a lie against Allah, or says: "I am inspired , when he is not inspired in anything; and who says: "I will reveal the like of that which Allah has revealed? If you could see, when the wrongdoers reach the pangs of death and the angels stretch their hands out, saying: "Deliver up your souls! This day you are awarded the punishment of degradation for having spoken concerning Allah other than the truth, and having scorned His Signs.

(It is said that this verse was revealed in condemnation of false prophets like Musaylima al-Kadhdhab and al-Aswad al-Ansi, who, seeing the Blessed Prophet's success, falsely claimed that they too were prophets. They came to an evil end.)

94. Now have you come to Us alone as We did create you at the first, and you have left behind you all that We bestowed upon you, and We behold not with you those your intercessors of whom you claimed that they possessed a share in you. Now is the bond between you severed, and that which you presumed has failed you.

95. Assuredly, it is Allah who splits the grain and the datestone. He brings forth the living from the dead, and is the bringer-forth of the dead from the living. Such is Allah. How then are you deluded?

96. He is the Cleaver of the daybreak, and He has appointed the night for stillness, and the sun and the moon for reckoning. That is the measuring of the Mighty, the Wise.

(The night, the day, the sun, the moon - the great astronomical universe of God: how far, and yet how near to us! His universe is boundless, and we can hardly comprehend its relation to us. But this we must try to do, if we are to be numbered among "those who have knowledge.)

97. And He it is Who has set for you the stars, that you may guide your course by them amid the darkness of the land and the sea. We have detailed Our revelations for a people who have knowledge.

98. And He it is Who has produced you from a single soul, and *(has given you)* a habitation and a repository. We have detailed the signs (*revelations*) for a people who have understanding.

(The word "habitation here means either the place of human habitation on the face of the earth, or the seed of the father. And the "repository is either the womb of the mother, or the grave.)

99. He it is who sends down water from the sky, and therewith We bring forth vegetation of every kind; We bring forth the green blade from which We bring forth the thick-clustered grain; and from the datepalm, from the pollen thereof, spring pendant bunches; and *(We bring forth)* gardens of grapes, and the olive and the pomegranate, alike and unlike. Look upon the fruit thereof, when they bear fruit, and upon its ripening. Herein assuredly are signs for people who believe.

100. Yet they ascribe as partners to Him the jinn, although He did create them, and impute falsely, without knowledge, sons and daughters to Him. Glorified be He, and high exalted above what they attribute to Him!

101. The Originator of the heavens and the earth! How can He have a child, when there is for Him no consort, when He created all things and is Aware of all things?

102. Such is Allah, your Lord. There is no God save Him, the Creator of all things, so worship Him. And He takes care of all things.

103. Vision comprehends Him not, but He comprehends all vision. He is the Subtle, the Aware.

(Human faculties of sense-perception cannot perceive He who by definition transcends them. But in the next life, we are promised that the pure of soul will experience a vision of Him, this being the supreme delight granted to the indwellers of the celestial Garden.)

104. Proofs have come to you from your Lord, so whoso sees, it is for his own good, and whoso is blind, is blind to his own hurt. And I am not a keeper over you.

(Just as Allah has given human beings physical eyes to see physical things, He has also given us "eyes of the heart , faculties of intuition and physical realisation which enable us to recognise Him in a way which is direct and leaves no room for doubt.)

105. Thus do We deploy Our signs (revelations), that they may say (to you, Muhammad): "You have studied, and that We may make (it) clear for people who have knowledge.

106. Follow that which is inspired in you from your Lord; there is no God save Him; and turn away from the polytheists.

107. Had Allah willed, they had not been polytheists. We have not set you as a keeper over them, nor are you responsible for them.

108. Revile not those to whom they pray besides Allah, lest they wrongfully revile Allah

through ignorance. Thus to every nation have We made their conduct seem fair. Then to their Lord is their return, and He will tell them what they used to do.

(This verse lays it down as a principle of dialogue that Muslims should not insult the objects of devotion venerated by others. Here the case of idols is presented; so how much more important must it be to refrain from insulting the deities of others when those deities are those of a higher religion. When explaining the fallacies of a certain belief, one must not descend into abuse, for this will have no effect, and may cause the listener to be repelled, and even to curse the God to whom he is being called.)

109. And they swear a solemn oath by Allah that if there come to them a sign they will believe in it. Say: "Signs are with Allah and (so is) that which tells you that if such came to them they would not believe.

110. We confound their hearts and their eyes. As they believed not therein at the first, We let them wander blindly on in their contumacy.

111. And though We should send down the angels to them, and the dead should speak to them, and We should gather against them all things in array, they would not believe, unless Allah so willed. But most of them are ignorant.

(Those who go astray not because of an insufficiency of proofs but because of their obstinacy, are the most misled and satanically inspired of all rejecters of the Reminder.)

112. Thus have We appointed to every prophet an adversary: devils of humankind and jinn who inspire in one another with flowery discourses by way of deception. If your Lord willed, they would not do so; so leave them alone with their devising.

113. That the hearts of those who do not believe in the Hereafter may incline thereto, and that they may take pleasure therein, and that they may earn from it what they may.

114. Shall I seek other than Allah for a judge, when He it is who has revealed to you (this) scripture, fully explained? Those to whom We gave the scripture (previously) know that it is revealed from your Lord in truth. So be not you (O Muhammad) of those who waver!

(The intelligent man seeks no other standard of judgement but the Divine Will. How can he fail in this, when the Book explains His will in a fashion intelligible both to the simple and the intellectual?)

115. Perfected is the Word of your Lord in truth and justice. There is nothing that can change His words. He is the Hearer, the Knower.

116. If you obeyed most of those on earth they would mislead you far from Allah's way. They follow not but an opinion, and they do but guess.

117. It is your Lord Who knows best who strays from His way; and knows best (who are) the rightly guided.

118. Eat of that over which the name of Allah has been mentioned, if you are believers in His revelations.

119. How should you not eat of *(meats)* over which the name of Allah has been mentioned, when He has explained to you that which is forbidden to you, unless you are compelled by necessity. But many do mislead men by their own desires through ignorance. Your Lord knows best those who transgress.

120. Forsake all sin open or secret. Those who earn sin will be awarded that which they have earned.

121. And eat not of *(meats)* on which Allah's name has not been mentioned; that would be a foulness. The devils inspire their friends to dispute with you. But if you obey them, you will be in truth idolaters.

(If the name of God has not been mentioned during the slaughter of an animal, it's life has been taken wrongly, and no Muslim may eat of its meat.)

122. Is he who was dead and We have raised him to life, and set for him a light wherein he walks among men, as him whose similitude is in utter darkness from which he can never come out? Thus is their conduct made fair-seeming for the disbelievers.

123. And thus have We made in every city great ones of its wicked ones, that they should plot therein. They do but plot against themselves, though they perceive not.

124. And when a sign comes to them, they say: "We will not believe until we are given that which Allah's messengers are given. Allah knows best with whom to place His message. Humiliation from Allah and heavy punishment will smite the guilty for their plot.

125. He whom Allah wills to guide, He expands his breast to Islam, while with those whom He wills to leave straying, He makes their breast close and narrow as if they were ascending to the skies; thus Allah lays ignominy upon those who believe not.

(Above 20,000 metres man cannot breath without special equipment. As he rises to this height, his breath become laborious, and this provides a simile for those who endeavour to live properly without spiritual oxygen.)

126. This is the path of your Lord, a straight path. We have detailed Our revelations for a people who take heed.

127. For them is the home of peace with their Lord. He will be their Protecting Friend because of what they used to do.

128. In the day when He will gather them together (he will say): "O you assembly of the jinn! Many of humankind did you seduce, and their adherents among humankind will say: "Our Lord! We enjoyed one another, but now we have arrived at the appointed term which You appointed for us. He will say: "Fire is your home. Dwell therein forever, except him whom Allah wills (to deliver). For your Lord is Wise, Aware.

129. Thus We let some of the wrongdoers have power over others because of what they are wont to earn.

130. O assembly of the jinn and humankind! Did there not come to you messengers of your own who recounted to you My tokens and warned you of the meeting of this your Day? They will say: "We testify against ourselves. And the life of the World deceived them. And they testify against themselves that they were disbelievers.

131. This is because your Lord destroys not the cities for their wrongdoing while their occupants were unwarned.

132. For all there will be ranks from what they did. Your Lord is not unaware of what they do.

133. Your Lord is the Self-Sufficient, the Lord of Mercy. If He will, He can remove you and can cause what He will to follow after you, even as He raised you from the seed of other people.

134. That which you are promised will surely come, and you cannot escape.

(A reference to the Day of Judgement.)

135. Say (O Muhammad): "O my people! Work according to your power. Surely, I too am working. Thus you will come to know for which of us will be the (happy) outcome. Surely, the wrongdoers will not be successful.

136. They assigned to Allah, of the crops and cattle which He created, a portion, and they say: "This is Allah's -in their make-believe, "and this is for (His) partners in regard to us. Thus that which (they assign) unto His partners in them does not reach Allah, and that which (they assign) to Allah goes to their (so-called) partners. Evil is their ordinance.

(In the Time of Ignorance, the pagan Arabs used to divide their harvest between their animals and their idols. They would say "This is the share of the animals, this is the share of the idols. The shares assigned to the "partners went to the priests and hangers-on of the "partners who were many and clamorous for their rights. The share assigned to Allah possibly went to the poor, but more probably went to the priests who had the cult of the "partners , for the Supreme God had no separate priests of his own. It is also said that when heaps were thus laid out, if any portion of Allah's heap fell into the heaps of the "partners the priests greedily and promptly appropriated it, while in the contrary case the "partners priests were careful to reclaim any portion from what they called "Allah's heap . The absurdity of the whole thing is here ridiculed.)

137. Thus have their (so-called) partners (of Allah) made the killing of their children to seem fair to many of the polytheists, that they may ruin them and make their faith obscure for them. Had Allah willed (it otherwise), they had not done so. So leave them alone with their devices.

140. They are losers who wantonly have slain their children without knowledge, and have forbidden that which Allah bestowed upon them, inventing a lie against Allah. They indeed have gone astray, and are not guided.

(The reference is to the burial alive of female children who were deemed superfluous and the practice of human sacrifice to idols.)

141. He it is who produces gardens trellised and untrellised, and the datepalm, and crops of diverse flavours, and the olive and the pomegranate, like and unlike. Eat you of the fruit thereof when they are in season, and pay the due thereof upon the harvest day, and waste not in excess. Assuredly, Allah loves not the wasters.

142. And of the cattle *(He produces)* some for burdens, some for food. Eat of that which Allah has bestowed upon you, and follow not the footsteps of the devil, for he is an open enemy to you.

138. And they say: "Such cattle and crops are forbidden. No-one is to eat of them except whom We will - in their make-believe - cattle whose backs are forbidden, cattle over which they mention not the name of Allah. *(All that is)* a lie against Him. He will repay them for that which they invent.

(Cf. 5:103.)

139. And they say: "That which is in the bellies of such cattle is reserved for our males and is forbidden to our wives; but if it born dead, then they *(all)* may be partakers thereof. He will reward them for their attribution *(of such ordinances)* to Him. For He is Wise, Aware.

143. Eight pairs: Of the sheep a pair, and of the goats a pair. Say: "Has he forbidden the two males or the two females, or that which the wombs of the two females contain? Expound to me *(the case)* with knowledge, if you are truthful.

144. And of the camels a pair and of the oxens a pair. Say: "Has He forbidden the two males or the two females, or that which the wombs of the two females contain; or were you there to witness when Allah commanded you *(all)* this? Then who does greater wrong than he who devises a lie concerning Allah, that he may lead mankind astray without knowledge. Surely, Allah guides not a wrongdoing people.

145. Say: "I find not in that which is revealed to me anything *(of meat)* prohibited to an eater that he eat thereof, except it be carrion, or blood poured forth, or swineflesh, for that assuredly is foul, or the abomination which was immolated to the name of other than Allah. But whoso is compelled *(thereto)*, neither craving nor transgressing, *(for him)* surely your Lord is Forgiving, Merciful.

(Cf. v.119 above.)

146. To those who were Jews We forbade every animal with claws. And of the oxen and the sheep forbade We to them the fat thereof save that upon the backs of the entrails, or that which is mixed with the bone. That We awarded them for their rebellion. And We assuredly are Truthful.

(Cf. Leviticus, vii.23: "ye shall eat no manner of fat, of ox, or of sheep, or of goat. As regards the exceptions, it is to be noticed that priests were enjoined (Leviticus, vii.3, 6) to eat of the fat in the trespass offering, which was considered holy, that is, "the rump and "the fat that covereth the inwards .)

147. So if they give the lie to you (*Muhammad*) say: "Your Lord is a Lord of all-embracing mercy, and His wrath will never be withdrawn from guilty people.

148. Those who ascribe partners (*to Allah*) will say: "If Allah had wished, We should not have ascribed partners to Him, nor would our fathers: nor should we have had any taboos. Thus did those who came before them argue falsely, until they tasted of Our wrath. Say: "Have you any (*certain*) knowledge? If so, produce it before us. You follow nothing but conjecture. You do nothing but guess.

149. Say: "For Allah's is the final argument. Had He willed He could indeed have guided all of you.

(As used by the pagans, the argument is false, for it implies (1) that men have no personal responsibility; (2) that they are victims of a determinism against which they are helpless; (3) that they might therefore go on doing just as they liked. It is also inconsistent, for if 2 is true, 3 cannot be true. Nor is it meant to be taken seriously.)

150. Say: "Come bring your witnesses who can bear witness that Allah forbade (*all*) this. And if they bear witness, do not you bear witness with them. Do not follow the whims of those who deny Our revelations, those who do not believe in the Hereafter, and deem (*others*) equal with their Lord.

151. Say: "Come, I will recite to you that which your Lord has made a sacred duty for you: that you ascribe nothing as partner to Him and that you do good to parents, and that you slay not your children on a plea of want - We provide for you and for them - and that you draw not near to shameful things whether open or concealed. And that you slay not the life which Allah has made sacred, except in the course of justice. This He has commanded you, in order that you may learn wisdom.

152. And approach not the wealth of the orphan save with that which is better, until he reach maturity. Give full measure and full weight, in justice. We burden not any soul beyond its scope. And if you give your word, do justice thereunto, even though it be *(against)* a kinsman; and fulfil the covenant of Allah. This He commands you that you may perhaps remember.

153. And *(He commands you, saying):* This is My straight path, so follow it. Follow not other ways, lest you be parted from His way. This has He ordained for you, that you may fear Him.

(Verses 151-3 contain the famous "Ten Commandments , which has been given to all prophets from Adam to the Prophet Muhammad.)

154. Again, We gave the Scripture to Moses, complete for him who would do good, an explanation of all things, a guidance and a mercy, that they might believe in the meeting with their Lord.

155. And this is a blessed Scripture which We have revealed. So follow it and fear Allah, that you may find mercy.

156. Lest you should say: "The Scripture was revealed only to two peoples *(Christian and Jews)* before us, and we in fact were unaware of what they read .

157. Or lest you should say: "If the Scripture had been revealed to us, we surely had been better guided than they. Now has there come to you a clear proof from your Lord, a guidance and a mercy; and who does greater wrong than he who denies the revelations of Allah, and turns away from them? We award to those who turn away from Our revelations a severe penalty because of their aversion.

all have you with them. Their case will go to Allah, who will tell them what they used to do.

("Divide their religion : i.e. (1) make a distinction between one part of it and another, take the part which suits them and reject the rest; (2) do religion one day in the week, and plunge into the world for the other six; (3) "keep religion in its right place , as if it did not claim to govern and uplift all of life, thereby making a distinction between the secular and the religious; (4) show a sectarian bias, seeking differences of views in order to attempt to destroy Islam's unity.)

160. Whoso brings a good deed will receive tenfold the like thereof, and whoso brings an evil deed will be awarded but the like thereof; and they will not be wronged.

161. Say: "As for me, my Lord has guided me to a straight path, a right religion, the community of Abraham the upright, who was not one of the polytheists."

162. Say: "Truly, my worship and my sacrifice and my living and my dying are for Allah, Lord of the Worlds.

(The word *nusuk* commonly means a sacrifice, but here bears the more general sense of "worship .)

163. He has no partner. This am I commanded, and I am first of those who surrender *(to Him)*.

164. Say: "Shall I seek another than Allah for Lord, when He is Lord of all things? Each soul earns only on its own account, nor do any laden bear another's load. Then to your Lord is your return, and He will tell you that wherein you differed.

165. He it is who has placed you as vicegerents of the earth and has exalted some of you in rank above others, that He may try you by *(the test of)* that which He has given you. Assuredly, your Lord is swift in punishment, and assuredly, He is Forgiving, Merciful.

158. Do they wait for nothing less than that the angels should come to them, or your Lord should come, or there should come one of the signs from your Lord? In the day when one of the signs from your Lord comes, its belief will do no good to a soul which previously believed not, nor in its belief earned good *(by works)*. Say: "Wait you! Assuredly! We (too) are waiting.

(The signs of the "end of the world" would prove Islam to them, but by then it would be too late. According to the Qur'an and our blessed Prophet, the principal such signs are: the appearance of a Smoke, the appearance of a Beast creeping upon the earth, the appearance of the Antichrist *(dajjâl)*, the rising of the sun from the west, the appearance of Gog and Magog, and the appearance of a Fire in Aden.)

159. As for those who divide their religion and become divided into different sects, no concern at

SÛRAH VII

Al-A'RÂF (THE HEIGHTS)

Revealed at Makka

This Sûrah takes its name from a word occurring in verse 46: "And on the Heights are men who know them all by their marks. Al-A'râf is a Sûrah which revealed in the later period of Makka, though some consider vv. 163-167 to have been revealed at Madîna. The subject may be said to be the opponents of God's will and purpose, from Satan onward, through the history of Divine Guidance.

THE HEIGHTS

In the name of Allah, the Compassionate,
the Merciful.

1. Alif. Lâm. Mîm. Sâd.

2. *(It is)* a Scripture that is revealed to you *(Muhammad)* - so let there be no heaviness in your heart therefrom - that you may warn thereby, and *(it is)* a Reminder to believers.

3. *(Saying):* Follow that which is sent down to you from your Lord, and follow no protecting friends beside Him. Little do you recollect!

4. How many a township have We destroyed! As a raid by night, or while they were resting at midday, Our terror came to them.

5. No plea had they, when our terror came to them, except that they said: "Assuredly, we are wrongdoers!

6. Then verily We shall question those to whom *(our message)* has been sent, and assuredly We shall question the messengers.

(In the final reckoning, the warners and teachers will give evidence of their preaching the truth, and the evildoers will themselves have to acknowledge the truth.)

7. Then We shall narrate to them *(the event)* with knowledge, for assuredly We were not absent *(when it came to pass).*

8. The weighing on that day is the true *(weighing).* As for those whose scale is heavy, they are the successful.

9. And as for those whose scale is light: those are they who lose their souls because they disbelieved Our revelations.

10. And We have given you *(mankind)* power in the earth, and appointed for you therein a livelihood. Little thanks do you give!

11. And We created you, then fashioned you, then told the angels: "Fall prostrate before Adam! and they fell prostrate, all save Iblîs, who was not of those who prostrate.

(Iblîs not only refused to prostrate to his Maker, he refused to be among those who prostrate. In other words, he arrogantly despised the angels who prostrated themselves, as well a man, to whom they were prostrate. He committed the triple crime of arrogance, jealousy and disobedience.)

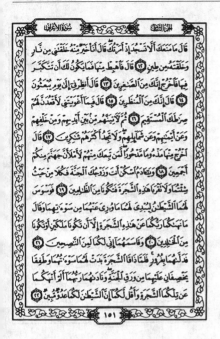

12. He said: "What hindered you from falling prostrate when I bade you? *(Iblîs)* said: "I am better than him. You created me of fire while you created him of mud.

13. He said: "Then go down hence! It is not for you to show pride here, so go forth! Verily you are of those degraded.

14. He said: "Reprieve me until the day when they are resurrected!

15. He said: "Assuredly, you are of the reprieved.

16. He said: "Now, because You have sent me astray, assuredly I shall lurk in ambush for them on your straight path.

17. Then I shall come upon them from before them and from behind them and from their right hands and from their left hands, and You will not find most of them, thankful *(for Your mercies)*."

(The devil's success is that he renders us forgetful of who we are, and who our Maker is, so that we become thankless for His gift of life and provision. And such ill-manners cannot be allowed to endure for ever.)

18. He said: "Go forth from this, degraded, banished. As for such of them as follow you, surely I will fill hell with you all.

(Next the story turns to man. He was placed in a spiritual Garden of innocence and bliss, but it was the Lord's plan to give him a limited faculty of choice. The only forbidden thing in the Divine Law of that time was to approach the Tree, but he succumbed to Satan's suggestion. Note that the name of the Evil One now changes from Iblîs to Satan: the former conveys the idea of desperateness and retreat, while the second implies perversity or enmity. Cf. II:34-6, where the same transition may be observed.)

19. *(Then Allah commanded)*: "O Adam! Dwell you and your wife in the Garden, and enjoy *(eat from good things)* as you wish, but come not near to this tree, lest you become wrongdoers.

20. Then Satan whispered to them that he might manifest to them that which was hidden from them of their shame, and he said: "Your Lord forbade you this tree only lest you should become angels or become of the immortals.

21. And he swore to them *(by saying)*: "Truly, I am a sincere adviser to you.

22. Thus did he lead them by a deceit; and when they tasted of the tree their shame was manifest to them and they began to hide *(by heaping)* on themselves some of the leaves of the Garden. And their Lord called them *(saying)*: "Did I not forbid you from that tree and tell you: 'assuredly Satan is an open enemy to you?'

23. They said: "Our Lord! We have wronged ourselves. If you forgive us not and have not mercy on us, surely we are of the lost!

24. He said "Go down *(from hence)*, one of you a foe unto the other. There will be for you on earth a habitation, and provision for a while.

25. He *(Allah)* said: "There shall you live, and there shall you die, and thence shall you be brought forth.

26. O Children of Adam! We have revealed to you raiment to conceal your shame, and splendid vesture; but the raiment of piety, that is best. This of the signs *(revelations)* of Allah, that perhaps they may remember.

(The "raiment of piety is defined by some scholars of Islam as a "sense of shame , "good deeds , "rough and ordinary clothing that expresses a modest and humble attitude , and "the armour that a fighter for Truth wears in time of war . One could also add the observation that the traditional dress worn in sacred societies reminds the wearer of his viceregal function, and renders triviality and play an absurdity. The dress of every society reflects its understanding of man.)

27. O Children of Adam! Let not Satan seduce you as he seduced your *(first)* parents to go forth from the Garden and tore off from them their robe *(of innocence)* that he might manifest their shame to them. Assuredly, he sees you, he and his tribe, from whence you see them not. Indeed, We have made the devils protecting friends for those who do not believe.

(Satan, resembling the jinn, cannot usually be seen by the human eye; hence the efficacy of his counsels. He can, however, appear to certain human beings in a wide variety of forms.)

28. And when they do some foulness they say: "We found our fathers doing it, and Allah has enjoined it on us . Say: "Allah, assuredly, does not enjoin foulness. Do you relate concerning Allah that which you know not?

29. Say: "My Lord enjoins justice. And set your faces, upright *(toward Him)* at every place of worship, and call upon Him, making religion pure for Him *(only)*. As He brought you into being, so do you return.

30. A group has He led aright, while error has a just hold over another, for surely, they have chosen the devils for protecting friends instead of Allah, and consider that they are rightly guided.

(Guidance is for all. But in some it takes effect, while in others the doors are closed against it, because they have taken Evil as a friend. If they have lost their way, they have richly deserved it; for they deliberately took their choice, even though, in their self-righteousness, they may think that sin is their virtue, and that their evil is the good.)

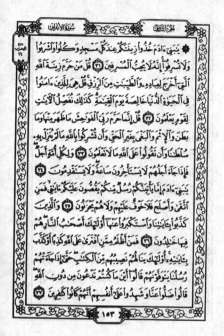

31. O Children of Adam! Wear your beautiful adornment at every (*time and*) place of worship, and eat and drink, but do not be prodigal. For Allah loves not the prodigal.

(In the religion of Islam. cleanliness and proper appearance is very important. Men and women should wear clean and sufficient attire. At times of worship every Muslim should wear the most beautiful and the most clean clothes he possesses, as long as he is not extravagant.)

32. Say: "Who has forbidden the adornment of Allah which He has brought forth for His servants, and the good things of His providing? Say: "Such, on the Day of Resurrection, will be only for those who believed during the life of the world. Thus do We detail Our revelations for people who have knowledge.

(The beautiful and good things of the world should really be for those who recognise and understand their divine origin. But the world, as the locus of imbalance, sometimes sets blessings in the hands of those who appear not to deserve them. Such is the confusion induced by Satan. But in the Next World, beauty will be the exclusive property of beautiful souls, while dark, distracted souls shall experience only foulness. Thus will the universe's equilibrium, disturbed by the Fall, reaffirm itself in the end.)

33. Say: My Lord forbids only indecencies, such of them as are apparent and such as are within, and sin and wrongful oppression, and that you associate with Allah that for which no warrant has been revealed, and that you tell concerning Allah that which you know not.

34. And every nation has its term, and when its term comes, they cannot put it off an hour nor yet advance (*it*).

(Nations and governments are like individuals: they are born and grow, become vigorous, and ultimately enter a period of senility before they die. Their term, whether short or long, depends on the solidity of their early upbringing, and upon God's grace.)

35. O Children of Adam! Whenever messengers of your own come to you who narrate to you My revelations, then whosoever refrains from evil and amends, there shall no fear come upon them neither shall they grieve.

36. But, they who deny Our revelations and scorn them; such are rightful owners of the Fire; they will dwell therein forever.

37. Who does greater wrong than he who invents a lie concerning Allah or denies Our signs? (*For such*) their appointed portion of the Book (*of destiny*) reaches them till, when Our messengers (*the angels*) come to gather them, they say: "Where (*now*) is that to which you cried beside Allah? They say: "They have departed from us. And they testify against themselves that they were disbelievers.

38. He said: "Enter into the Fire among nations of the jinn and men who passed away before you. Every time a nation enters, it curses its sister *(nation);* till, when they have all been made to follow one another there, the last of them says to the first of them: "Our Lord! These led us astray, so give them a double torment of the Fire." He says: "For each one there is double *(torment),* but you know not.

(Those who mislead the people on a wrong path will have double punishment: firstly for having rejected the Reminder, and secondly for misleading others. Those who disbelieve and follow unjust leaders will also have double punishment: firstly for being disbelievers, and secondly, for their allegience to the unjust.)

39. And the first of them says to the last of them: "You were not better than us, so taste the punishment for what you used to earn.

40. Those who deny Our revelations and scorn them, for them the gates of Heaven will not be opened nor will they enter the Garden until the camel goes through the eye of the needle. Thus do We reward the guilty.

(Some interpreters of the Holy Qur'an hold that the word *jamal* is not to be translated as "camel", but rather as a "heavy rope". In any case, however, the meaning is plain: the doors of Heaven are too small for those who are puffed up with pride, and the rejection of their Maker's reminders.)

41. Theirs will be a bed of Hell, and over them coverings *(of Hell).* Thus do We requite the wrongdoers.

42. But *(as for)* those who believe and do good works - We burden not any soul beyond its scope - such are the rightful owners of the Garden. They shall dwell therein forever.

(The road to God's forgiveness may sometimes seem hard, but He has promised that it is never impossible. We must simply do what we can, and be confident in His overwhelming love and compassion.)

43. And We remove whatever rancour may be in their hearts. Rivers flow beneath them, and they say: "Praise is for Allah, who has guided us to this. We could not have been led aright if Allah had not guided us. Assuredly the messengers of Lord brought the Truth. And it is cried to them: "This is the Garden; you inherit it for what you used to do.

44. And the dwellers of the Garden cry to the dwellers of the Fire: "We have indeed found what our Lord promised us *(to be)* true. Have you *(also)* found what your Lord promised to be true? They say: "Yes, assuredly ; and a crier between them cries: "The curse of Allah is on the evildoers.

45. Who hinder *(men)* from the path of Allah and would have it crooked, and who are disbelievers in the Hereafter.

46. Between them is a veil. And on the Heights are men who know them all by their marks. And they call to the dwellers of the Garden: "Peace be upon you! They enter it not, although they hope.

(The *A'râf*, or "heights , form a limbo between Heaven and Hell, where those who have an equal quantity of good and evil works shall stand, waiting for the time when their Lord will have mercy upon them, and admit them to the Garden.)

47. And when their eyes turn toward the dwellers of the fire, they say: "Our Lord! Place us not with the wrongdoing people!

48. And the dwellers on the Heights call to men whom they know by their marks, *(saying)*: "What did your multitude and that in which you took your pride avail you?

49. Are these they of whom you swore that Allah would not show them mercy? Enter the Garden; no fear shall come upon you, neither shall you grieve.

50. And the dwellers of the Fire cry out to the dwellers of the Garden: "Pour some water upon us, or some of that wherewith Allah has provided you! They say: "Allah has forbidden both to disbelievers *(in His guidance).*

51. Who took their religion for a game and pastime, and whom the life of the world beguiled. So this day We have forgotten them even as they forgot the encounter of this Day, and as they used to deny Our Signs.

52. Assuredly We have brought them a scripture which We expound with knowledge, a guidance and a mercy for a people who believe.

53. Are they waiting for anything except its fulfillment? On the day when its fulfillment comes, those who were forgetful of it will say: "The messengers of our Lord did bring the Truth! Have we any intercessors, that they may intercede for us? Or can we be returned *(to life on earth),* that we may act differently to the way we acted? They have lost their souls, and that which they devised has failed them.

(If those without faith want to wait and see what happens in the Hereafter, they will of course learn the truth, but by then it will be too late to be of any use. All the false ideals and deities which they had preferred will leave them in the lurch. If they thought that the goodness and greatness of others would help them, they will be undeceived on the day when their personal responsibility will be enforced. There will be no salvation except on their own record. How they will then wish they had another chance! But their chance will be gone.

Such is the destiny of disbelievers. For the believers, however, who, despite their faith, committed enough sins to bring them to Hell, there will indeed be an intercession by the Blessed Prophet, who will save them from the trials of the Day of Judgement, and deliver them from hell by God's permission.)

54. Assuredly your Lord is Allah, who created the heavens and the earth in six days, then was established upon the Throne. He covers the night with the day, which is in haste to follow it, and has made the sun and the moon and the stars subservient by His command. His assuredly is all creation and commandment. Blessed be Allah, the Lord of the Worlds!

(Before the heavens and the earth were created there was no conception of time. The Creation in "six days is of course an expression for "stages , for before the universe existed, there were no "days . In Sûrah 22:47 we are told that a day in the sight of Allah is like a

thousand years of our reckoning, while in Sûrah 70:4 a "day is considered to be 50,000 of our years. The word is hence figurative, for our purposes. As for God's "being established on the Throne, this denotes His assumption of authority of His created world, the throne being a symbol of dominion.)

55. *(O Mankind!)* Call on your Lord with humility and in secret. For Allah loves not those who trespass the bounds.

56. Work not corruption in the earth after it has been set in order, and call on Him in fear and hope. Assuredly, the mercy of Allah is near to those who do good.

57. And He it is who sends the winds as tidings heralding His mercy, till, when they bear a cloud heavy *(with rain),* We lead it to a dead land, and then cause water to descend thereon and thereby bring forth fruits of every kind. Thus bring We forth the dead. Perhaps you will remember.

58. As for the good land, its vegetation comes forth by permission of its Lord; while as for that which is bad, only evil comes forth *(from it)*. Thus do We explain the signs for those people who give thanks.

(This parable contains a triple significance: (1) In the physical world the winds go like heralds of glad tidings; they are the advance guard, behind which comes a great army of winds driving heavily laden clouds before it: divine Providence is their field-marshal, who directs them towards a parched land, which with the rain of mercy they convert to a fruitful garden; (2) In the spiritual world, the winds are the great motive forces in the mind of man, or the world around him, that bring the clouds of instruments of God's mercy, which descend and fertilise souls which were spiritually dead; (3) If we can see and experience such things in our life here-below, how can we doubt the Resurrection? But all depends on the state of the soil, for a rich harvest cannot grow on poor ground.)

59. *(Of old)*, We sent Noah to his people, and he said: "O my people! Worship Allah! You have

no other god except Him. Assuredly, I fear for you the retribution of a dreadful Day!

60. The leaders of his people said: "We see you surely wandering in mind!

61. He said: "O My people! No wandering is there in my mind; but I am a messenger from the Lord of the Worlds.

62. I convey to you the messages of my Lord and give good counsel to you, and know from Allah that which you know not.

63. Do you wonder that there should come to you a Reminder from your Lord by means of a man among you, that he may warn you, and that you may keep from evil, and that perhaps you may find mercy?

64. But they denied him, so We saved him and those with him in the ship, and We drowned those who denied our signs. They were indeed a people in blindness.

65. And to *(the tribe of)* Aad *(We sent as a prophet)* their brother, Hûd. He said: "O my people! Serve Allah. You have no other God except Him. Will you not fear *(Allah)*?

66. The leaders of his people, who were disbelieving, said: "We see you surely in foolishness; and we think you are among the liars!

67. He said: "O my people; There is no foolishness in me, but I am a messenger from the Lord of the Worlds.

68. I convey to you the messages of my Lord, and am for you a true adviser.

69. Do you wonder that there should come to you a Reminder from your Lord by means of a man among you, that he may warn you? Remember how He made you inheritors after Noah's people, and gave you growth of stature. Remember the favours of your Lord, that perhaps you may be successful.

70. They said: "Have you come to us that we should serve Allah alone, and forsake what our fathers worshipped? Then bring upon us that with which you threaten us, if you are of the truthful!

71. He (the prophet Hûd) said: "Terror and wrath from your Lord have already fallen on you. Would you wrangle with me over names which you have named, you and your fathers, for which no warrant from Allah has been revealed? Then await (the consequence), indeed I (also) am of those awaiting (it).

72. And We saved him and those with him by a mercy from Us, and We cut the root of those who denied Our revelations and were not believers.

73. And to (the ancient tribe of) Thamoud (We sent) their brother Sâlih. He said: "O my people! Serve Allah! You have no other God save Him. A wonder from your Lord has come to you. This is the she-camel of Allah, a token unto you; so let her feed in Allah's earth, and touch her not with hurt, lest a painful torment seize you.

(When Allah sent Sâlih to the people of Thamoud as a prophet, his people asked him: "If you are indeed a prophet of Allah, ask your Lord to bring a she -camel out of this rock. Then we will truly believe in you. Sâlih duly prayed, and Allah immediately granted his wish, and a she-camel came out of the rock. Some of those who saw this miracle at once believed, but the rest continued to disbelieve, despite this proof. Although the Prophet Sâlih asked his people not to touch the camel, and to allow her to graze freely, they hamstrung and killed her. After this incident the prophet Sâlih left his home-town, and Allah destroyed the arrogant people by sending a mighty earthquake against them.)

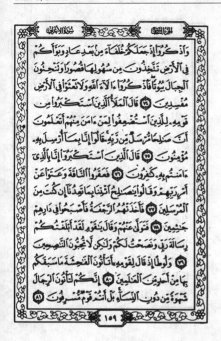

74. And remember how He made you inheritors after Aad, and gave you habitations in the earth. You choose palaces and castles in the plains and carve out the mountains into houses. So remember *(all)* the bounties of Allah and do not do evil, working corruption in the earth.

(The Thamoud, who were the successors to the Aad, lived somewhere between Damascus and Hijaz *(Makka)*, in a place called "al-Hijr . Descendants of Shem, they attained a high level of material civilisation and used to carve out mountains, and build homes, palaces, castles, and ponds. It is said that they were the fist people in history who carved out rocks, and created one thousand seven hundred settlements of this type.)

75. The arrogant leaders of his people said to those whom they reckoned powerless, to such of them as believed: "Do you know that Salîh is one sent from his Lord? They said: "We are believers in that with which he has been sent.

76. Those who were arrogant said: "We are disbelievers in that which you believe.

77. So they hamstrung the she-camel, and insolently defied the commandment of their Lord, and they said: "O Sâlih! Bring upon us what you threaten if you are indeed of those sent *(from Allah)*.

78. So the earthquake seized them, and morning found them prostrate in their dwelling-place.

79. And Sâlih turned from them and said: "O my people! I delivered my Lord's message to you and gave you good advice, but you love not good advisors!

(His speech here may be either a parting warning, or a soliloquy lamenting the destruction of his people for their sin and folly.)

80. And Lot! *(Remember)* when he said to his people: "Will you commit foulness such as no creature ever did before you?

81. For you come with lust to men instead of women: you are indeed a people transgressing the bounds.

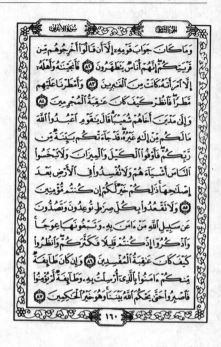

82. And his people gave no response but this: "Drive them out of your city! They are people who keep themselves pure!"

83. And We rescued him and his household, except his wife, who was of those who stayed behind *(being a disbeliever)*.

84. And We rained a rain upon them. See how was the upshot of the criminals!

(The prophet Lot was a grandson of the prophet Abraham, upon them be peace. He was sent as a prophet to the people of Sodom and Gomorrah, places now located in Syria somewhere in the plain east of the Dead Sea. The people of this city committed a offense which no other nation had indulged in - the unspeakable crime of homosexuality. The people of Sodom and Gomorrah did not pay heed to the counsel of Lot. Allah punished them with a rain of brimstone, and a devastating earthquake, so that none of the inverts survived.)

85. And to Midian *(We sent)* their brother Shu'ayb. He said: "O my people! Serve Allah. You have no other God save Him. Indeed, a clear sign has come to you from your Lord; so give full measure and full weight, and wrong not mankind

in their goods, and work not corruption in the earth after it has been set in order. That will be best for you, if you are believers.

(Midian were descendants of a son of the prophet Abraham. They are sometimes believed to have dwelt in a city located on the shore of the Red Sea between Palestine and the Hijâz. Other historians locate them in South Yemen.)

86. Lurk not on every road to threaten *(wayfarers),* and to turn away from Allah's path him who believes in Him, and to seek to make it crooked. And remember, when you were but few, how He did multiply you. And see the nature of the consequence for the corrupters!

87. And if there is a group of you which believes in that wherewith I have been sent, and there is a group which believes not, then have patience until Allah judge between us. He is the best of judges.

88. The arrogant leaders of his people said: "Surely we will drive you out, O Shu'ayb, and those who believe with you, from our city, unless you return to our religion. He said: "Even though we hate it?

89. We should have invented a lie against Allah if we returned to your religion after Allah has rescued us from it. It is not for us to return to it unless Allah should (so) will. Our Lord encompasses all things in knowledge. In Allah do we put our trust. Our Lord! Decide with truth between us and our people, for you are the best of deciders.

(Here, the Prophet Shu'ayb refuses point blank to return to the religion of his ancestors and asks them: "Do you want us to lie against our consciences and our Lord, after we have seen the evil of your ways? Neither bribes nor threats, nor specious appeals to patriotism or ancestral religion can move us: the matter rests with Allah, Whose will and pleasure we obey, on Whom alone we rely. His knowledge will search out all your specious pretenses.)

90. But the leaders of his people, who were disbelieving, said: "If you follow Shu'ayb, then truly we shall be the losers.

91. So the earthquake seized them, and morning found them prostrate in their dwelling-places.

92. Those who denied Shu'ayb became as though they had not dwelt there. Those who denied Shu'ayb, they were the losers.

93. So he turned from them and said: "O my people! I delivered my Lord's messages to you and gave you good advice; then how can I sorrow for a people that rejected?

94. And We sent no prophet to any city but We did afflict its people with suffering and adversity in order that they might grow humble.

95. Then We changed the evil plight for good until they grew affluent and said: "Suffering and distress did touch our fathers. Then We seized them unawares, when they perceived not.

96. And if the people of the cities had believed and kept from evil, surely We should have opened for them blessings from the sky and from the earth. But *(to every messenger)* they gave the lie, and so We seized them on account of what they used to earn.

97. Are the people of the cities then secure from the coming of Our wrath upon them as a night-raid while they sleep?

(Verses 97-99 should be read together. They furnish a commentary on the stories of the five Prophets that have already been related. Allah's wrath may come by night or day, whether people are arrogantly defying Allah's laws or are sunk in lethargy and vain dreams of reality. Who can escape the Maker's plan, and who can feel themselves outside it?)

98. Or are the people of the cities then secure from the coming of Our wrath upon them in the daytime while they play?

99. Are they then secure from Allah's plan, except people that perish?

100. Is it not an indication to those who inherit the land after its people *(who thus reaped the consequence of evildoing)* that, if We will, We can punish them for their sins and seal up their hearts so that they hear not?

101. Such were the cities. We relate some tidings of them to you *(Muhammad)*. Their messengers assuredly came to them with clear signs *(of Allah's sovereignty)*, but they could not believe because they had before denied. Thus does Allah seal up the hearts of disbelievers *(that they hear not)*.

102. We found no *(loyalty to any)* covenant in most of them. Nay, most of them We found to be wrongdoers.

(Having reviewed the stories of peoples who denied God and were destroyed, we now turn to the story of a people that just managed to escape Allah's destruction: the people of Moses.)

103. Then, after them, We sent Moses with Our Signs to Pharaoh and his chiefs, but they repelled them. Now, see the nature of the consequence for the corrupters!

104. Moses said: "O Pharaoh! Indeed, I am a messenger from the Lord of the Worlds.

(The serpent played a large role in Egyptian mythology; hence Allah chose it as a symbol to display His mastery. And to show that this was no occult accomplishment, he was given the second miracle: the shining hand, radiant with a light which could only come from the Divine.)

109. The chiefs of Pharaoh's people said: "This is indeed a learned magician.

110. Who would expel you from our land. Now what do you command?

111. They said (to Pharaoh): "Put him off (for a while), him and his brother, and send into the cities summoners.

112. To bring you every learned magician."

113. And all the sorcerers came to Pharaoh, saying: "Surely there will be a reward for us if we are the victors.

114. He answered: "Yes, and surely you shall be of those brought near (to me).

115. They said: "O Moses! Will you throw first or shall we be the first to throw?

116. He said: "Throw! And when they threw they cast a spell upon the people's eyes, and overawed them, and produced a mighty spell.

117. And We inspired Moses (saying): "Throw your rod! and behold! it swallowed up the falsehoods which they fake!

118. Thus was the Truth vindicated and that which they were doing was made vain.

119. Thus were they there defeated, and brought low.

120. And the sorcerers fell down prostrate.

105. Approved upon condition that I speak concerning Allah nothing but the truth. I come to you (O lords of Egypt) with a clear sign from your Lord. So let the children of Israel go with me.

(When Joseph was a Minister of Finance in Egypt, the children of Israel led by their father Jacob immigrated from Palestine to Egypt. In due course, the Egyptians used the children of Israel as slaves, and persecuted them. The time had come, it seemed clear, for them to attempt to escape.)

106. (Pharaoh) said: "If you come with a sign, then produce it, if you are of those who speak the truth.

107. Then (Moses) threw down his rod and behold! it was a serpent plain (for all to see).

108. And he drew forth his hand (from his bosom), and behold! it was white for the beholders.

121. Crying: "We believe in the Lord of the Worlds.

122. The Lord of Moses and Aaron.

123. Pharaoh said: "You believe in Him before I give you leave! Surely, this is a ruse that you have contrived in the city that you may drive its people from here. But you shall come to know!

124. Surely I shall have your hands and feet cut off upon alternate sides. Then I shall crucify you every one.

(Pharoah and his court were doubly angry: first because they were made to look small when confronted by the divine Power; and secondly, because their magicians had been snatched away from them. These men, the sorcerers, at once recognised the authentic miracle, and in their case the mission of Moses and Aaron was fulfilled. But as usually happens, hardened sinner resent all the more the saving of any of their companions from sin and error. Judging other people's motives by their own, they accuse them of duplicity, and, if they have the power, they take cruel revenge.)

125. They said: "Surely, we are about to return our Lord!

126. You take vengeance on us only since we believed the signs of our Lord when they came to us. Our Lord! Vouchsafe to us steadfastness, and make us die as men who have surrendered to You!

127. The chiefs of Pharaoh's people said: "(O King), will you suffer Moses and his people to make mischief in the land, and abandon you and your gods? He said: "We will slay their sons and spare their women, for we are in power over them.

128. And Moses said to his people: "Seek help in Allah, and endure. Verily, the earth is Allah's. He gives it for an inheritance to whom He will. And the end is for those who are righteous.

129. They said: "We suffered hurt before you came to us, and since you have come to us. He said: "It may be that your Lord is going to destroy your adversary and make you inheritors in the earth, that He may see how you behave.

(The Israelites, despite their perilous situation, were to be delivered and given authority in Canaan. They would be granted sacerdotal kingship, as with David and Solomon, and material power, upon Joshua's conquest of Jerusalem.)

130. And We grasped Pharaoh's people with famine and the dearth of crops, that they might take heed.

131. But whenever good befell them, they said: "This is ours"; and whenever evil befell them, they ascribed it to the evil auspices of Moses and those with him. Surely their evil auspice was only with Allah. But most of them knew not.

132. And they said: "Whatever sign *(miracle)* you bring to bewitch us, we shall not put faith in you.

133. So We sent them the flood and the locusts and the vermin and the frogs and the blood: a succession of clear signs. But they were arrogant and became guilty.

(At 17:101, the reference is to nine signs. These were: (1) the Rod (7:107); (2) the Radiant Hand (7:108); (3) the years of drought (7:130); (4) short crops (7:130); and the five mentioned in this verse.)

134. And when the terror fell on them they cried: "O Moses! Pray for us to your Lord, because He has a covenant with you. If you remove the terror from us we assuredly will trust you, and will let the Children of Israel go with you.

135. But when We did remove from them the terror for a term which they must reach, behold! They broke their covenant.

136. Therefore We took retribution from them; therefore We drowned them in the sea; because they denied Our revelations and were heedless of them.

137. And We caused the people who were despised to inherit the eastern parts of the land and the western parts thereof which We had blessed. And the fair word of the Lord was fulfilled for the Children of Israel because of their endurance; and We annihilated *(all)* that Pharaoh and his people had done and that they had contrived.

(Under the command of Moses, the Children of Israel stayed in the Sinai Peninsula for a while. Later on they captured Jerusalem and Damascus. Many interpreters of the Holy Qur'an interpret the "eastern parts and the "western parts of the land as Damascus and Egypt; but others identify them with the Sinai Peninsula, Palestine and Damascus, pointing out that the Israelites never had authority in Egypt.)

138. And We brought the Children of Israel across the sea, and they came to a people who were given up to idols which they had. They said: "O Moses! Make for us a god even as they have gods! He said: "Surely you are an ignorant people.

(After crossing the Red Sea, the Children of Israel came in contact with the idolatrous Amalekites of the Sinai Peninsula. The Israelites asked Moses to make an idol for them to worship, so that they might resemble them. Thus is the imitative nature of the Jews.)

139. As for these (people), their way will be destroyed, and all that they are doing is vain.

140. He said: "Shall I seek for you a god other than Allah, when He has favoured you above (all) nations?

(Allah then goes on to remind Israel through the mouth of Moses. There was a double trial: (1) while the bondage lasted, the people were to learn patience and constancy in the midst of affliction; (2) when they were rescued, they were to learn humility, justice and righteousness.)

141. And (remember) when We did deliver you from Pharaoh's people who were afflicting you with dreadful torment, slaughtering your sons and sparing your women. That was a tremendous trial from your Lord.

142. And when We did appoint for Moses thirty nights (of solitude), and added to them ten, and he completed the whole time appointed by his Lord of forty nights; and Moses said to his brother: "Take my place among the people. Do right, and follow not the way of mischief-makers.

143. And when Moses came to Our appointed place, and His Lord had spoken to him, he said: "My Lord! Show me (Yourself), that I may gaze upon you. He said: "You will not see Me, but gaze upon the mountain! If it stands still in its place, then you will see Me. And when his Lord revealed (His) glory to the mountain He sent it crashing down. And Moses fell down in a swoon. And when he woke he said: "Glory to You! I turn to You repentant, and I am first of (true) believers.

(Even the reflected glory of Allah is too great for the grosser substance of matter. The peak on which it shone became as powder before the ineffable glory, and Moses could only live by being taken out of his physical senses. When he recovered, he saw the true position, and the distance between sense-perception and the fulgurating Splendour of the Divine. He at once repented to Allah, and confessed his faith.)

144. He said: "O Moses! I have preferred you above mankind by My messages and by My speaking *(to you)*; so hold that which I have given you, and be among the thankful.

145. And We wrote for him, upon the tablets, an admonition and the detailing of all things, then *(bade him)*: "Hold fast to it; and command your people to take the better course therein. I shall show you the homes of the evil-livers.

(The Tablets of the Law, now lost, contained the essential spiritual Truth, from which were derived the positive injunctions and prohibitions which it was the function of the prophetic office to hold up for the people to follow. Note now the following feature, characteristic of the Qur'an, in which Allah's speech switches from the "We of authority and honour, to the "I of personal concern.)

146. I shall turn away from My revelations those who magnify themselves wrongfully in the earth; and if they see each sign believe it not, and if they see the way of righteousness choose it not for *(their)* way, and if they see the way of error choose it for *(their)* way. That is because they denied Our revelations and used to disregard them.

147. Those who deny Our revelations and the meeting of the Hereafter, their works are fruitless. Are they *(to be)* rewarded for anything except what they used to do?

148. And the people of Moses, after *(he had left them),* chose a calf *(for worship), (made)* out of their ornaments, of saffron hue, which gave a lowing sound. Saw they not that it spoke not to them nor guided them to any way? They chose it, and became wrong-doers.

(When the absence of Moses was extended for another 10 days on Mount Sinai, a man named Sâmirî from the Children of Israel had melted all the people's gold ornaments, and made the image of a calf like the bull of Osiris located in the city of Memphis in Egypt. Sâmirî told the people: "This the Lord of Moses and of you. So great a craftsman was he that when the wind blew through the golden calf it bellowed like a live bull.)

149. And when they feared the consequences thereof and saw that they had gone astray, they said: "Unless our Lord have mercy on us and forgive us, we assuredly are of those who will perish.

150. And when Moses returned to his people, angry and grieved, he said: "Evil is that *(course)* which you took after I had left you. Would you hasten on the judgement of your Lord? And he cast down the tablets, and he seized his brother by the head, dragging him toward him. He *(Aaron)* said: "O son of my mother! Indeed the people did judge me weak and almost killed me. Oh, make not enemies to triumph over me and count me not among the evildoers!

(Aaron addresses Moses as "son of my mother , an affectionate term. He explains how the turbulent people nearly killed him for resisting them. And he states that the idolatry neither originated with him, nor had his consent. Cf. 20:85.)

151. He said: "My Lord! Have mercy on me and on my brother; bring us into Your mercy, You are the Most Merciful of all who show mercy.

152. Those who took the calf *(for worship),* terror from their Lord and humiliation will come upon them in the life of the world. Thus do We recompense those who invent a lie.

153. But those who do ill deeds and afterward repent and believe - for them, afterward, Allah is Forgiving, Merciful.

154. Then, when the anger of Moses abated, he took up the tablets, and in their inscription there was guidance and mercy for all those who fear their Lord.

(Since the Children of Israel regretted having worshipped the golden calf, Allah ordered Moses to choose seventy men among his tribe and bring them together to the presence of Lord to repent. The following verse explains this.)

155. And Moses chose of his people seventy men for Our appointed tryst and, when the trembling came on them, he said: "My Lord! If You had willed You had destroyed them long before, and me with them. Will you destroy us for that which the ignorant among us did? It is but Your trial *(of us).* You send astray whom You will, and You guide whom You will. You are our protecting friend; therefore forgive us and have mercy on us, You are the best of all who show forgiveness.

(Seventy of the elders were duly taken up to the mount, but left at some distance from the place where Allah spoke to Moses. They were to be silent witnesses, but their faith was not yet complete, for they said, "We will not believe in you unless We see your Lord in person. (2:55) A powerful trembling took place, and they all fainted. Moses prayed to his Lord to forgive them, and to deliver them, and this He did.)

156. And ordain for us in this world that which is good, and in the Hereafter *(that which is good),* surely, we have turned to You. He said: "I smite with My punishment whom I will, and My mercy embraces all things, therefore I shall ordain it for those who ward off *(evil)* and pay the Zakât, and those who believe Our signs *(revelations).*

157. Those who follow the messenger, the prophet who can neither read nor write, whom they will find described in the Torah and Gospel *(which are)* with them. He will enjoin on them that which is right, and forbid them that which is wrong. He will make lawful for them all good things and prohibit for them only the foul; and he will relieve them of their burden and the fetters that they used to wear. Then those who believe in him, and honour him, and help him, and follow the light which is sent down with him: they are the successful.

(The word "Ummî" used in the above verse is commonly taken to mean that he could neither read nor write. This emphasises his "virginal status as the recipient of the Divine Word.)

158. Say *(O Muhammad):* "O Mankind! Surely I am the messenger of Allah to you all; *(the messenger of)* Him to whom belongs the sovereignty of the heavens and the earth. There is no God save Him. He quickens and He gives death. So believe in Allah and His messenger, the prophet who can neither read nor write, who believes in Allah and in His words, and follow him that you may be rightly-guided."

159. And of the people of Moses, there is a community who lead with truth and establish justice therewith.

(The "community mentioned in the above verse might be the Jews who believe in the prophecy of Muhammad, or those Jews who, during the time of Moses, remained faithful to the Lord, and continued to guide others along the straight path.)

160. We divided them into twelve tribes, nations; and We inspired Moses, when his people asked him for water, saying: "Smite with your staff the rock! And there gushed forth therefrom twelve springs, so that each tribe knew their drinking place. And We caused the white cloud to overshadow them and sent down for them the manna and the quails *(saying)*: "Eat of the good things with which We have provided you. They wronged us not, but they were wont to wrong themselves.

(The word "*Asbât* mentioned in the above verse is the plural of the word "*sibt* , translated normally as "tribe . The Children of Israel were the descendents of Jacob from his twelve sons. They multiplied and in time became tribes.)

161. And when was said to them: "Dwell in this township and eat therefrom whence you will, and say "Repentance and enter the gate prostrate; We shall forgive you your sins; We shall increase *(reward)* for the right-doers.

162. But those of them who did wrong changed the word which had been told them for another saying, and We sent down upon them wrath from heaven for their wrongdoing.

(This "wrath was a plague which the Lord sent upon them.)

163. Ask them *(O Muhammad)* of the township that was by the sea: how they did break the Sabbath, how their big fish came to them visibly upon their Sabbath day and on a day when they did not keep Sabbath came they not to them. Thus did We try them because they were evil-livers.

(Allah commanded the Israelites not to fish on Saturdays, a day which was to be observed as the Sabbath. As a trial to them, on Saturday He sent large shoals of fish swimming towards them. The Israelites disobeyed the commandment of Allah, and fished on the Sabbath, so they became evil-livers.)

164. And when a community among them said: "Why preach you to a people whom Allah is about to destroy and punish with an awful doom? they said: "In order to be free from guilt before your Lord, and that haply they may fear Him.

165. And when they forgot that whereof they had been reminded, We rescued those who forbade wrong, and visited those who did wrong with dreadful punishment because they were evil-livers.

166. So when they took pride in that which they had been forbidden, We said to them: "Be you apes, despised and rejected!

. (Because of their disrespect to the Sabbath, they became like apes and pigs. There is a difference of opinion among our commentators over whether these Israelites were transformed physically into apes, or whether they were merely led to behave like them. In any case, it was a punishment from Allah, Who made manifest in their outward something of that which had entered their inward reality.)

167. And (remember) when your Lord proclaimed that He would raise against them till the Day of Resurrection those who would lay on them a cruel torment. Assuredly your Lord is swift in prosecution and assuredly He is Forgiving, Merciful.

168. And We have broken them up in the earth as (separate) nations. Some of them are righteous and some far from that. And We have tried them with good things and evil things that perhaps they might return.

169. And a generation has succeeded them who inherited the scriptures. They grasp the goods of this low life (as the price of evil-doing) and say: "It will be forgiven us. And if there came to them (again) the offer of the like, they would accept it (and would sin again). Has not the covenant of the scripture been taken on their behalf that they should not speak aught concerning Allah except the truth? And they have studied that which is therein. And the home of the hereafter is better, for those who fear Him. Have you then no sense?

170. And as for those who make (men) keep the Scripture, and establish the Prayer: never do We squander the wages of reformers.

بِسْمِ اللّٰهِ الرَّحْمٰنِ الرَّحِيْمِ

۞ وَإِذْ نَتَقْنَا الْجَبَلَ فَوْقَهُمْ كَأَنَّهُ ظُلَّةٌ وَظَنُّوٓا أَنَّهُ وَاقِعٌ بِهِمْ خُذُوا مَآ ءَاتَيْنٰكُمْ بِقُوَّةٍ وَاذْكُرُوا مَا فِيهِ لَعَلَّكُمْ تَتَّقُونَ ۝ وَإِذْ أَخَذَ رَبُّكَ مِنْ بَنِيٓ ءَادَمَ مِنْ ظُهُورِهِمْ ذُرِّيَّتَهُمْ وَأَشْهَدَهُمْ عَلَىٰٓ أَنْفُسِهِمْ أَلَسْتُ بِرَبِّكُمْ قَالُوا بَلَىٰ شَهِدْنَآ أَنْ تَقُولُوا يَوْمَ الْقِيَامَةِ إِنَّا كُنَّا عَنْ هٰذَا غَافِلِينَ ۝ أَوْ تَقُولُوٓا إِنَّمَآ أَشْرَكَ ءَابَآؤُنَا مِنْ قَبْلُ وَكُنَّا ذُرِّيَّةً مِنْ بَعْدِهِمْ أَفَتُهْلِكُنَا بِمَا فَعَلَ الْمُبْطِلُونَ ۝ وَكَذٰلِكَ نُفَصِّلُ الْآيَاتِ وَلَعَلَّهُمْ يَرْجِعُونَ ۝ وَاتْلُ عَلَيْهِمْ نَبَأَ الَّذِيٓ ءَاتَيْنٰهُ ءَايَاتِنَا فَانْسَلَخَ مِنْهَا فَأَتْبَعَهُ الشَّيْطَانُ فَكَانَ مِنَ الْغَاوِينَ ۝ وَلَوْ شِئْنَا لَرَفَعْنٰهُ بِهَا وَلٰكِنَّهُ أَخْلَدَ إِلَى الْأَرْضِ وَاتَّبَعَ هَوَاهُ فَمَثَلُهُ كَمَثَلِ الْكَلْبِ إِنْ تَحْمِلْ عَلَيْهِ يَلْهَثْ أَوْ تَتْرُكْهُ يَلْهَثْ ذٰلِكَ مَثَلُ الْقَوْمِ الَّذِينَ كَذَّبُوا بِآيَاتِنَا فَاقْصُصِ الْقَصَصَ لَعَلَّهُمْ يَتَفَكَّرُونَ ۝ سَآءَ مَثَلًا الْقَوْمُ الَّذِينَ كَذَّبُوا بِآيَاتِنَا وَأَنْفُسَهُمْ كَانُوا يَظْلِمُونَ ۝ مَنْ يَهْدِ اللّٰهُ فَهُوَ الْمُهْتَدِي وَمَنْ يُضْلِلْ فَأُولٰٓئِكَ هُمُ الْخَاسِرُونَ ۝

۱۷۲

171. And when We shook the Mount above them as it were a covering, and they supposed that it was going to fall upon them *(and We said)*: "Hold fast that which We have given you, and remember that which is therein, that you may fear Allah.

172. And *(remember)* when your Lord brought forth from the Children of Adam, from their reins, their seed, and made them testify of themselves, *(saying)*: "Am I not your Lord? They said: "Yes, assuredly. We testify! That was lest you should say at the Day of Resurrection: "Of this we were unaware.

173. Or lest you should say: "*(It is)* only that our fathers ascribed partners to Allah of old and we were *(their seed)* after them. Will you destroy us on account of that which those who follow falsehood did?

(In this verse is revealed the doctrine of the primordial covenant, by which every soul, before its birth, was made to declare its recognition of the Divine Existence and Unity. There is a debate over whether this took place before the Creation, or in the mothers' womb.)

174. Thus We detail Our revelations, that perhaps they may return.

175. Recite to them *(the Jews)* the tale of him to whom We gave Our revelations, but he sloughed them off, so Satan overtook him and he became of those who lead astray.

(Interpreters of the Qur'an or the commentators differ over whether this story or parable refers to a particular individual, and if so, who is intended. Some identify him with a Jewish scholar whose name was Balaam, who lived during the time of Moses, and with the encouragement of certain rich Jews worked against the prophet Moses. He was a man of talents and position, to whom great opportunities of spiritual insight came, but he perversely passed them by, preferring the opportunities presented by his material wealth and standing. There was a triangle established between Pharaoh, who was ruler of Egypt, Korah, who represented the rich elite, and Balaam, who represented the corrupt and mercenary scholars. They all worked against Moses, forming an archetype whose manifestations continue to repeat themselves in all ages.)

176. And had We willed We could have raised him by their means, but he clung to the earth and followed his own lust. Therefore his likeness is as the likeness of a dog; if you attack him he pants with his tongue out, and if you leave him he pants with his tongue out. Such is the likeness of the people who deny Our revelations. Narrate to them the history *(of the men of old),* that perhaps they may think.

177. Evil as an example are the people who denied Our revelations, and were wont to wrong themselves.

178. He whom Allah leads, he indeed is led aright, while he whom Allah sends astray - they indeed are losers.

181. And of those whom We created there is a nation who guide with the Truth and establish justice therewith.

182. And those who deny Our revelations - step by step We lead them on from whence they know not.

(The blessing given to the evil by Allah are not immediately cut off because they have rejected the signs; sometimes Allah continues to give His blessing up to a certain time so that they can continue to enjoy themselves. His punishment may come to them in the midst of the surfeit-inspired forgetfulness, when they least expect it. The tactic is called *istidrâj*.)

183. I give them rein *(for a while) (but)* My scheme is strong.

184. Has it not ever occurred to them *(that)* their compatriot is no madman? He is but a plain warner.

185. Have they not considered the dominion of the heavens and the earth, and what things Allah has created, and that it may be that their own term draws near? In what fact *(revelation)* after this will they believe?

186. Those whom Allah sends astray, there is no guide for them. He leaves them to wander blindly on in their contumacy.

187. They ask you of the *(destined)* Hour, when will it come to pass. Say: "Knowledge thereof is with my Lord only. He alone will manifest it at its proper time. The heavens and the earth are heavy with it. It comes not to you save unawares. They question you as though you could be well informed thereof. Say: "Knowledge of it is with Allah only, but most of mankind know not.

179. Already have We urged to hell many of the jinn and humankind, having hearts wherewith they understand not, and having eyes wherewith they see not, and having ears wherewith they hear not. These are as the cattle. No, but they are worse! These are the neglectful.

180. Allah's are the most beautiful Names; so call on Him by them! And leave the company of those who blaspheme His names. They will be requited for what they do.

(According to a hadith "Allah has ninety-nine names, and whoever memorises them (or acts in awareness of them) will enter into Heaven. Examples of His names are The Compassionate, The Merciful, The Loving, The Kind, The Guide, The Great, The Eternal, and others. But this hadith does not put a restriction on the number of Allah's names. There are many other beautiful names of Allah. The idolaters used to blaspheme His names by mutilating them, giving some to their idols like "al-'Uzzâ .)

188. Say: "For myself I have no power to benefit, nor power to hurt, except that which Allah wills. Had I knowledge of the Unseen, I should have abundance of wealth, and adversity would not touch me. I am but a warner, and a bearer of glad tidings unto people who believe .

189. He it is who did create you from a single soul, and therefrom did make his mate that he might take rest in her. And when he covered her she bore a light burden, and she passed (unnoticed) with it. But when it became heavy they cried unto Allah, their Lord saying: "If you give into us aright we shall be of the thankful.

190. But when He gave unto them aright (a goodly child), they ascribed unto Him partners in respect of that which He had given them. High is He exalted above all that they associate (with Him).

(The solemn fact of new life growing in the womb should render us more conscious of the guiding providence of the One True God. Instead, however, childbirth is often surrounded with absurd superstitions, of a magical or astrological nature,

which compromise the doctrine of monotheism. The parallel process is for men to attribute offspring to the Almighty, or to their supposed gods. Thus is the miracle or procreation perverted by lack of sense.)

191. Attribute they as partners to Allah those who created not, but are themselves created.

192. And cannot give them help, nor can they help themselves?

193. And if you call them to the Guidance, they follow you not. Whether you call them or silent, it is the same to them.

194. Those on whom you call beside Allah are slaves like unto you. Call on them now, and let them answer you, if you are truthful.

195. Have they feet wherewith they walk, or have they hands wherewith they hold, or have they eyes wherewith they see, or have they ears wherewith they hear? Say: "Call upon your (so-called) partners (of Allah), and then contrive against me, spare me not!

196. My Protecting Friend is Allah, who revealed the scripture. He befriends the righteous.

197. They on whom you beside Him have no power to help you, nor can they help themselves.

198. And if you *(Muslims)* call them to the Guidance they hear not; and you *(Muhammad)* see them looking toward you, but they see not.

199. Keep to forgiveness *(O Muhammad)*, and enjoin kindness, and turn away from the ignorant.

(The Arabic word *'urf*, or *ma'rûf*, denotes customs acceptable to the monotheistic creed and just social patterns of the new Revelation. The ways of the pagan Arabs were largely supplanted by the Islamic norm, although a few harmless traditions were not proscribed.)

200. And if a temptation from the devil wound you, then seek refuge in Allah. He is Hearer, Knower.

(Even a prophet of God is human. He might think that revenge or retaliation, or a little tactful silence when evil stalks abroad, or some compromise with ignorance, might be best for the cause. He is to reject such suggestions. And if such is the case with the Blessed Messenger of God, what must it be with us, who hear the devil's whispering with such frequency?)

201. Those who ward off *(evil)*, when a passing notion from the devil troubles them, they remember, and behold! they see!

(Spiritual vision can only be attained when the insinuations of the devil are suppressed, for they are like rust on the heart, which prevents it from beholding the Divine Truth.)

202. Their brothers plunge them further into error, and cease not.

203. And when you bring not a verse for them they say: "Why have you not chosen it? Say: "I follow only that which is inspired in me from your Lord. This *(Qur'an)* is insights from your Lord, and a guidance and a mercy for a people that believe.

204. And when the Qur'an is recited, give ear to it and pay heed, that you may obtain mercy.

(When the Holy Qur'an is recited, whether during the prayers or at other times, one should pay the utmost attention , listen with reverence to the Speech of God, and attempt to grasp its meaning, so that one may benefit from it and practice it in one's life.)

205. And *(O Muhammad!)* remember your Lord within yourself humbly, and with awe, below your breath, at morning and evening. And do not be among the neglectful.

206. These who are with your Lord are not too proud to worship Him, but they praise Him, and fall down in prostration.

SÛRAH VIII

AL-ANFÂL (THE SPOILS)

Revealed at Madîna

This Sûrah takes its name from the first verse by which it is proclaimed that property acquired in war from the enemy belongs "to Allah and His messenger - that is to say, to the Islamic State where the *Sharî'a* is applied, to be used for the welfare of the people. Of its seventy-five verses, most were revealed at Madîna during the second year of the Islamic calendar. Some authorities hold that verses thirty to thirty-six were revealed at Makka just before the Hijra.

SPOILS OF WAR

In the name of Allah, the Compassionate, the Merciful.

1- They ask you *(O Muhammad)* about the spoils of war. Say: "The spoils of war belong to Allah and the messenger, so keep your duty to Allah, and adjust the matter of your difference, and obey Allah and His messenger, if you are *(true)* believers.

2- They only are the *(true)* believers whose hearts feel fear when Allah is mentioned, and when the revelations of Allah are recited unto them their faith increases, and who trust in their Lord;

3- Who establish the Prayer and spend of that We have bestowed on them.

4. Those are they who are in truth believers. For them are grades (of honour) with their Lord, and pardon, and a generous provision.

(Before the "Battle of Badr some of the believers were restless and not happy about the war. Some of them were concerned with how the spoils should be divided. Allah responded by revealing the following verse.)

5. Even as your Lord caused you *(Muhammad)* to go forth from your home with the Truth, and yet a group of the believers were averse *(to it)*.

6. Disputing with you of the Truth after it had been made manifest, as if they were being driven to death visible.

7. And when Allah promised you one of the two bands *(either the caravan or the army of*

Quraish) that it should be yours, and you longed that other than the armed one might be yours. And Allah willed that He should cause the Truth to triumph by His words, and cut the root of the disbelievers;

(Just before the battle of Badr there were two alternatives open to the Muslims in Madîna, to save themselves from being overwhelmed by the Quraish of Makka, with all their resources from the rich Syrian trade. One, which was for the moment less dangerous, and promised much booty, was to attack the rich Quraish caravan returning from Syrian to Makka, accompanied by only forty men. The other alternative, which the Blessed Prophet, following the Divine command, adopted, was to march out boldly against the well-armed Quraish army of 1,000 men. The Muslims had no more than 300 men, who were, moreover, poorly equipped. Yet by choosing the latter course, the Muslims triumphed over the worldly aristocracy of Makka, whose power was shaken, never to recover.)

8. That He might cause the Truth to triumph and bring vanity to naught, however much the guilty might hate it.

9. When you sought help of your Lord and He answered you *(saying)*: "I will help you with a thousand of the angels, rank on rank.

(When the Blessed Prophet Muhammad saw the number of the enemy soldiers, which seemed likely to overwhelm the Muslim army, he raised his hands and prayed to Allah: "O Lord God! Fulfill Your promise that you have given me; for if you destroy this small group of believers no-one will remain to worship You. He repeated this prayer several times, and then the Lord sent an army of angels against the idolaters, and a mighty victory for truth and goodness was assured.)

10. Allah appointed it only as glad tidings, and that your hearts thereby might be at rest. Victory comes only by the help of Allah. Assuredly Allah is Mighty, Wise.

11. When He made the slumber fall upon you as a reassurance from Him and sent down water from the sky upon you, that thereby He might purify you, and remove from you the fear of Satan, and make strong your hearts and firm *(your)* feet thereby.

(The army of the Quraish had arrived first, and secured the use of the Badr wells. But God favoured the Muslims, firstly by sending them a drowsiness which calmed their nerves, and secondly by sending rain, which not only relieved them of their want of water, but made the ground firm, and more suitable for close combat.)

12. When your Lord inspired the angels, *(saying)*: "I am with you. So make those who believe stand firm. I will throw fear into the hearts of those who disbelieve. Then smite the necks and smite of them each finger.

13. That is because they opposed Allah and His messenger. Whoso opposes Allah and His messenger, *(for him)* assuredly! Allah is severe in punishment.

14. That *(is the award)* so taste it, and *(know)* that for disbelievers is the torment of the Fire.

15. O you who believe! When you meet those who disbelieve in battle, turn not your backs to them.

16- Whoso on that day turns his back to them, unless manoeuvering for battle or intending to join a company, he truly has incurred wrath from Allah, and his habitation will be hell, a hapless journey's end.

17. You *(Believers)* slew them not, but Allah slew them. And you *(Muhammad)* did not throw when you threw, but Allah threw, that He might test the believers by a fair test from Him. Truly Allah is Hearer, Knower.

(When the army of Quraish came to fight the Muslims, the Prophet raised his hands again and prayed to Allah: "Those disbelievers who reject Your messenger are come to fight me with their leaders, in whose hearts is nothing but conceit. I implore You to fulfill the promise that You have given me. And when the two armies met together, he picked up a handful of dirt from the ground and threw it at the enemy, mentioning the name of Allah. The enemies' eyes were blinded, and they could see nothing.)

18. That *(is the case)*; and *(know)* that Allah *(it is)* who makes weak the plan of disbelievers.

19. *(O Disbelievers!)* If you sought a judgement, now has the judgement come to you. And if you cease *(from persecuting the believers)* it will be better for you, but if you return *(to the attack)* We also shall return. And your host will avail you naught, however numerous it be, and *(know)* that Allah is with the believers *(in His guidance)*.

20. O you who believe! Obey Allah and His messenger, and turn not away from him when you hear *(him speak)*.

21. Be not as those who say, "We hear! and they hear not.

22. Assuredly the worst of beasts in Allah's sight are the deaf, the dumb, who have no sense.

(Cf. 2:18. The implication is clear: ignorance of man's true nature, his origin and his place of return, reduces him to an infra-human level. In fact, he is worse than the animals, for they at least are fulfilling their part in the created order. Man can be God's viceroy on earth, crowned with glory and honour, or can be a creature lower than the animals.)

23. Had Allah known of any good in them He would have made them hear, but had He made them hear they would have turned away, averse.

24. O you who believe! Obey Allah, and the messenger, when He calls you to that which gives you life, and know that Allah comes in between a man and his own heart, and that He it is to Whom you will be gathered.

(The essence of man is his soul, which is, by a common metaphor, located in his heart, the spiritual faculty by which he may know God. Following on from the previous verse, we are told that acceptance and recognition of the Divine Principle behind all life, gives life to the soul, which otherwise would be cold and dead. In another verse, the Lord tells us that He is closer to man than his jugular vein. Here He states that it is He who intervenes between us and our hearts. In every case, it is He who guides the heart when it is illuminated with the love and knowledge of Him, granting it life in this world, and eternal Life in the next, when all are gathered once more unto Him.)

25. And guard yourselves against a chastisement which cannot fall exclusively on those of you who are wrongdoers, and know that Allah is severe in punishment.

26. And remember, when you were few and reckoned feeble in the land, and were in fear lest men should extirpate you, how He gave you refuge, and strengthened you with His help, and made provision of good things for you, that perhaps you might be thankful.

27. O you who believe! Betray not Allah and His messenger, nor knowingly betray your trusts.

(Trusts may be of various kind: (1) property, goods, credit, and so forth; (2) plans, confidences, secrets, etc., (3) knowledge, talents, opportunities, etc., which we are expected to use fruitfully in the service of our fellow men. Men may betray the trust of Allah and His prophet by misusing property, or abusing the trust reposed in them, or the knowledge or talents given to them. On that special occasion, when the plans for the protection of Allah's worshippers against annihilation were of special importance, the Prophet's trust and confidence had to be guarded with special care. Occasions for scrupulously respecting the trust and confidence of other human beings occur every day in our lives, and few of us can claim anything like perfection in this respect. Hence the special distinction of the Blessed Prophet of God, who earned the title of *al-Amîn*, the one who was true to every trust reposed in him.)

28. And know that your possessions and your children are a test, and that with Allah is immense reward.

29. O you who believe! If you keep your duty to Allah, He will give you discrimination *(between right and wrong)* and will rid you of your evil thoughts and deeds, and will forgive you. Allah is of infinite bounty.

30. And when those who disbelieve plot against you *(O Muhammad)* to wound you fatally, or to kill you or to drive you out; they plot, but Allah *(also)* plots; and Allah is the best of plotters.

31. And when Our revelations are recited to them they say: "We have heard. If we wish we can speak the like of this. Assuredly! This is nothing but fables of the men of old.

32. And when they said: "O Allah! If this be indeed the truth from You, then rain down stones on us or bring on us some painful doom.

33. But Allah would not punish them while you were with them, nor will He punish them while they seek forgiveness.

34. What *(plea)* have they that Allah should not punish them, when they debar *(His servants)* from the Inviolable Mosque, though they are not its fitting guardians. Its fitting guardians are those only who keep their duty to Allah. But most of them know not.

35. And their worship at the *(holy)* House is nothing but whistling and hand-clapping. Therefore *(it is said to them)*: "Taste of the doom because you disbelieve!

(The pagan Arabs used to circumambulate the Holy Ka'ba naked, both men and women together. At the same time, they used to whistle through their fingers, and clap their hands, believing that this was a form of prayer.)

36. Those who disbelieve spend their wealth in order that they may debar *(men)* from the way of Allah. They will spend it, then it will become an anguish for them, then they will be conquered. And those who disbelieve will be gathered to Hell.

(The Pagan Arabs expended vast sums in their attempts to suppress monotheism in the Peninsula,

both at the Battle of Badr and thereafter; yet it made no difference. Islam won out.)

37. That Allah may separate the wicked from the good. The wicked will He place piece upon piece, and heap them all together, and consign them to hell. Such are the losers.

38. Tell those who disbelieve that if they cease *(from their persecution of the believers)* that which is past will be forgiven them; but if they return *(thereto)* then the example of the men of old has already gone *(before them, for a warning)*.

39. And fight them until persecution is no more, and religion is all for Allah. But if they cease, then assuredly Allah is Seer of what they do.

40. And if they turn away, then know that Allah is your Befriender. The best to befriend, and the best to help!

41. And know that whatever you take as spoils of war, a fifth thereof is for Allah, and for the messenger and for the kinsman *(who has need)* and orphans and the needy and the wayfarer, if you believe in Allah and that which We revealed to our slave on the Day of Discrimination, the day when the two armies met. And Allah is Able to do all things.

(The scholars have debated the identity of the House of the Prophet - the *Ahl-al-Bayt* - who have a special position in Muslim affection. According to Imam Shafi'i they are the descendants of Hashim, or al-Muttalib, while others define them as all those who, because of their blood-relationship with the Holy Prophet, are not entitled to receive Zakât. A third group identifies them with the entire tribe of Quraish. Spoils which may result from military action will be divided fairly, so as to avert chaos: one fifth going to those who are mentioned in the above verse, and the rest belonging to the veterans of the campaign.)

42. When you were on the near bank *(of the valley on the Madîna side)* and they were on the farther side, and the caravan was below you *(on the coastal plain).* And had you set a time to meet one another you surely would have failed to keep it, but *(it happened, as it did, without the forethought of either of you)* that Allah might conclude a thing that must be done; that he who perished *(on that day)* might perish by a clear proof *(of His sovereignty)* and he who survived might survive by a clear proof *(of His sovereignty).* Assuredly, Allah in truth is Hearer, Knower.

43. When Allah showed them to you *(O Muhammad)* in your dream as few in number, and if He had shown them to you as many, you *(Muslims)* would have faltered and would have quarrelled over the affair. But Allah saved *(you).* Assuredly, Allah knows what is in the breasts *(of men).*

44. And when He made you *(Muslims),* when you met *(them),* see them with your eyes as few, and lessened you in their eyes, *(it was)* that Allah might conclude a thing that must be done. Unto Allah all things are brought back.

45. O you who believe! When you meet an army, hold firm and think of Allah much, that you may be successful.

46. And obey Allah and His messenger, and dispute not with one another lest you falter and your strength depart from you; but be steadfast! Assuredly, Allah is with those who are steadfast.

47. Be not as those who came forth from their dwelling boastfully and to be seen of men, and debar (men) from the way of Allah, while Allah is surrounding all they do.

48. And when Satan made their deeds seem fair to them and said: "No one of mankind can conquer you this day, for I am your protector. But when the armies came in sight of one another, he took flight, saying: "Assuredly, I am guiltless of you. Assuredly, I see that which you see not. Surely, I fear Allah. And Allah is severe in punishment.

49. When the hypocrites and those in whose hearts is a disease said: "Their religion had deluded these. Whoso puts his trust in Allah (will find that) assuredly, Allah is Mighty, Wise.

50. If you could see how the angels receive those who disbelieve, smiting their faces and their backs and (saying): "Taste the punishment of burning!

51. This is for that which your own hands have sent before (to the Judgement), and (know) that Allah is not a tyrant to His slaves.

52. (Their way is) as the way of Pharaoh's people and those before them; they disbelieved the revelations of Allah, and Allah took them in their sins. Assuredly Allah is Strong, Severe in punishment.

they betrayed them, and joined the idolators. Later the Jews claimed that they had simply forgotten about the treaty, and a new treaty was signed between the prophet and the Jews. They again broke the treaty during the "Battle of the Trench and helped the idolaters, and joined them. Finally, Ka'b ibn al-Ashraf, their chief, went to Makka, and signed a formal treaty with the idolaters against the Muslims.)

57. If you come on them in the war, deal with them so as to strike fear in those who are behind them, that perhaps they may remember.

58. And if you fear treachery from any people, then throw back to them *(their treaty)* fairly. Assuredly, Allah loves not the treacherous.

59. And let not those who disbelieve suppose that they can outstrip *(Allah's purpose)*. Assuredly, they cannot escape.

60. Make ready for them all you can of *(armed)* force and of horses tethered, that thereby you may dismay the enemy of Allah and your enemy, and others beside them whom you know not. Allah knows them. Whatsoever you spend in the way of Allah it will be repaid to you in full, and you will not be wronged.

61. And if they incline to peace, incline also to it, and trust in Allah. Assuredly, He is the Hearer, the Knower.

(While we must always be ready to fight for justice when need be, even in the midst of the fight we must always be ready for peace if the other side shows any inclination towards it. There is no merit in fighting for its own sake; rather, it is a sin. It should be a duty, contentedly engaged in for the sake of justice, tolerance, and the revealed Law.)

53. That is because Allah never changes the grace He has bestowed on any people until they first change that which is in their hearts, and *(that is)* because Allah is Hearer, Knower.

54. *(Their way is)* as the way of Pharaoh's people and those before them; they denied the revelations of their Lord, so We destroyed them in their sins. And We drowned the people of Pharaoh. All were evil-doers.

55. Assuredly, the worst of beasts in Allah's sight are the ungrateful who will not believe.

56. Those of them with whom you made a treaty, and then at every opportunity they break their treaty, and they do not fear *(Allah)*.

(The people mentioned in the above verse are the Banû Qurayza, a Jewish tribe of Madîna that had entered into a treaty agreement with the Muslims. Yet believing that the Muslims were lost,

62. And if they would deceive you, then surely, Allah is sufficient for you. He it is who supports you with His help, and with the believers.

63. And *(As for the believers)* He has attuned their hearts. If you had spent all that is in the earth you could not have attuned their hearts, but Allah has attuned them. Surely, He is Mighty, Wise.

(Human souls resemble radio transmitters, whose frequency is often not even detectable, let alone heard clearly. The grace of God, however, can attune souls with great precision, so that they are united in an astonishing degree of understanding and love. The two Arab tribes of Madîna, the Aws and Khazraj, were constantly fighting with each other before the advent of the Blessed Prophet, and much blood was spilt in endless skirmishing and revenge attacks. But when Allah chose them to bless with Islam, the blood-feud between them evaporated and vanished without trace. The two tribes became close friends. The above verse refers to this incident.)

64. O Prophet! Allah is sufficient for you and those who follow you of the believers.

65. O Prophet! Urge the believers to fight. If there be of you twenty steadfast they shall overcome two hundred, and if there be of you a hundred steadfast they shall overcome a thousand of those who disbelieve, because they *(the disbelievers)* are a people without intelligence.

66. Now has Allah lightened your burden, for He knows that there is weakness in you. So if there be of you a steadfast hundred they shall overcome two hundred, and if there be of you a thousand *(steadfast)* they shall overcome two thousand by permission of Allah. Allah is with the steadfast.

(In early period of Islam the Muslims were few, and were thus forced to fight at a ratio of one to ten. But later on, when the number of Muslims increased, Allah the Exalted lessened the burden of the Muslims, commanding them to fight if the odds were one to two, or better. They were also told that if they were steadfast the victory would be theirs.

During the Battle of Badr, the Muslim took 70 prisoners from the idolaters. The prophet consulted with his companions as to what to do with these prisoners of war. At the end they decided to ransom them and to relieve them. Upon this incident the following verse was revealed.)

67. It is not for any prophet to have captives until he has made slaughter in the land. You desire the lure of this world and Allah desires for you the Hereafter, and Allah is Mighty, Wise.

(Cf. Matthew, x:34: "Think not that I am come to send peace on earth. I came not to send peace, but a sword. While a prisoners-of-war are to be treated honourably, (cf. 76:8), in battle one should not be afraid to make slaughter among the enemy.

Verses 67-9 were revealed when the Blessed Prophet had decided to spare the lives of the prisoners taken at Badr, and hold them to ransom, against the wishes of 'Umar, who wished them to be executed for their past crimes. The Blessed Prophet took the verses as a reproof, and they are generally understood to mean that no quarter ought to have been given in that first battle.)

68. Had it not been for an ordinance of Allah which had gone before, an awful doom would have come upon you on account of what you took.

69. Now enjoy what you have won, as lawful and good, and keep your duty to Allah. Surely, Allah is Forgiving, Merciful.

their homes, you have no duty to protect them till they leave their homes; but if they seek help from you in the matter of religion then it is your duty to help *(them)* except against a people between whom and you there is a treaty. Allah is Seer of what you do.

(The reference is to the Muhâjirûn and the Ansâr (the Emigrants from Makka and the new Muslim "helpers of Madîna, the people who forsook their homes and adopted voluntary exile with their blessed Leader, and their brethren in the Illuminated City, who gave them refuge and every kind of assistance, moral and material.) Under the magnetic personality of the Blessed Prophet, these two groups became like blood-brothers, and they were so treated in matters of inheritance during the period when they were cut off from their families.)

73. And those who disbelieve are protectors of one another - if you do not so, there will be confusion in the land, and great corruption.

74. Those who believed and left their homes and strove for the cause of Allah, and those who took them in and helped them - these are the believers in truth. For them is forgiveness, and a generous provision.

75. And those who afterwards believed and left their homes and strove along with you, they are of you; and those who are akin are nearer one to another in the ordinance of Allah. Surely, Allah is Knower of all things.

(Temporary rights of mutual inheritance established between the early Emigrants and Helpers would not apply to later recruits, who would come under entirely different circumstances.)

70. O Prophet! Say to those captives who are in your hands: "If Allah knows any good in your hearts He will give you better than that which has been taken from, you, and will forgive you. Surely, Allah is Forgiving, Merciful.

(This is a consolation to the prisoners of war. In spite of their previous hostility, Allah will forgive them in His mercy if there was any good in their hearts, and confer upon them a far higher gift than anything they have ever lost. In its highest sense, this would be the blessing of Islam; but even in a material sense, there was great good fortune awaiting them, for instance in the case of al-'Abbâs, the uncle of the Blessed Prophet, who was among them.)

71. And if they would betray you, they betrayed Allah before, and He gave *(you)* power over them. Allah is Knower, Wise.

72. Those who believed and left their homes and strove with their wealth and their lives for the cause of Allah, and those who took them in and helped them; these are protecting friends of one another. And those who believed but did not leave

SÛRAH IX

AT-TAWBA (REPENTANCE)

Revealed at Madîna

(Verse 104 is about repentence; whence the usual name of the Sûrah. But it has other names, the most common of them being "Immunity *(barâ'a).* As it is not clear whether this is a separate Sûrah at all, or should rather be considered an extension of the Sûrah preceding it, it is not prefixed with the *Basmala.*

In the ninth year of the Hijra, Hadrat Abû Bakr was given the task of taking the pilgrims to Makka. At that time, the Sûrah began to be revealed. The Prophet appointed Hadrat 'Alî to announce verses 1-29 to the pilgrims, for these contained the proclamation that the idolaters were not to be permitted to enter the Inviolable Sanctuary at Makka. The Lord then gave them four months in which to repent, and change their evil ways, after which they would be in a state of war with the Muslim community. The beginning of the Sûrah is hence a kind of ultimatum to the idolaters of Makka. The rest of the Sûrah concerns the Tabûk campaign against the Byzantines.)

REPENTANCE

1. A declaration of immunity from Allah and His messenger to those polytheists with whom you have made treaties:

2. So, you may travel in the land for four months *(more),* but know that you cannot frustrate Allah's will; and that He will degrade the disbelievers.

3. And a proclamation from Allah and His Messenger to all people on the day of the Greater Pilgrimage that Allah and His Messenger are free from obligation to the polytheists. So if you repent it will be better for you; but if you turn away know that you cannot frustrate Allah. Proclaim a woeful punishment to those who disbelieve.

4. Excepting those of the polytheists with whom you *(Muslims)* have made a treaty, and who have not later violated it, nor have supported anyone against you. So fulfil their treaty to them till their term. Surely Allah loves the righteous.

5. When the sacred months are over, slay the polytheists wherever you find them, and take them *(captive)* and besiege them, and lie in ambush for them everywhere. But if they repent and establish the Prayer and pay the Zakât, let them go their way. Allah is Forgiving and Merciful.

6. If any polytheist seeks your protection, then protect him so that he may hear the word of Allah, then convey him to a place where he can be secure. That is because they are a people who do not know.

7. How can there be a treaty with Allah and His Messenger for the polytheists except those with whom you have made treaties at the Inviolable Mosque? So long as they are true to you, be true to them. For Allah loves the Godfearing.

8. How *(can there be a treaty)* when, if they have an advantage over you, they will not respect ties of kinship or covenant with you? They *(try to)* please you with their tongues but their hearts refuse; for most of them are corrupt.

9. They have sold the signs *(revelations)* of Allah for a trifling price, hence they debar *(men)* from His path. Evil, indeed, is what they do.

10. They do not respect either kinship nor covenant towards a believer. These are the transgressors.

11. Yet if they repent and establish the Prayer and pay the Zakât, then they shall become your brothers in religion. *(Thus)* We explain the revelations in detail for those who know.

12. And if they break their oaths after their treaty and assail your religion, then fight the heads of disbelief. For they have no binding oaths, and so that they may desist.

13. Will you not fight people who have broken their oaths and purposed to drive out the messenger and attacked you first? What! Do you fear them? Surely Allah is more worthy of your fear, if you are believers.

14. Fight them! Allah will punish them by your hands and humble them and give you victory over them and heal the breasts of a believing people.

15. And He will remove the anger of their hearts. Allah accepts the repentance of whom He will. Allah is Knowing, Wise.

(People from other countries used to come to the city of Madîna, embrace Islam, and return to their countries. The idolaters, however, would intercept them, and torture them. In this verse Allah warns them. Yet if they should repent, and enter into Islam, their repentence will be accepted.)

16. Or, did you think that you would be left (without a trial) before Allah had known which of you fought valiantly, and chose none as intimate friend other than Allah and His messenger and the believers? Allah has full knowledge of what you do.

17. It is not for the polytheists to attend (and maintain) Allah's houses of worship bearing witness against themselves of disbelief. As for such, their works are in vain, and in the Fire they shall abide forever.

18. None should visit and maintain Allah's houses of worship except those who believe in Allah and the Last Day, establish the Prayer and pay the Zakât, and fear none but Allah. For such (only) it is possible that they be rightly-guided.

(The above verses explain why the pagans are no longer to be permitted in the vicinity of the holy places. Now that Makka was conquered (8 A.H.), and the sanctuary was once more dedicated to the worship of the One True God, and the idols had been destroyed, their presence would be an abomination testifying to their own disbelief.)

19. Have you made the (mere obligation of) giving water to the pilgrims and the maintenance of the Inviolable Mosque as (equal to the works of) those who have believed in Allah and the Last Day and fought for His cause? They are not equal in the sight of Allah. He does not guide the wrongdoers.

20. Those who believe and have left their homes and fought for Allah's cause with their wealth and their lives are of much greater worth in Allah's sight . They are the triumphant.

21. Their Lord gives them good tidings of a mercy from Him, and His pleasure, and of gardens wherein is everlasting bliss for them.

22. There they will dwell for ever. In Allah's presence is a reward tremendous.

23. O you who believe! Do not take your fathers and brothers to be your friends if they prefer disbelief to belief. Whoever of you takes them for friends; such are the wrongdoers.

24. Say: If your fathers, your sons, your brothers, your wives, your tribe, the wealth you have gained, the commerce you fear may slacken and the homes you love are dearer to you than Allah and His messenger and the struggle in His way, then wait until Allah brings about His command. Allah does not guide the evildoing people.

(Having conquered Makka the Prophet marched, with a sizeable number of soldiers, about twelve thousand, all enthusiastic and confident men - upon the Hawâzin and the Thaqîf tribes around the city of Tâ'if, who, alarmed at Islam's victory, were preparing an army of about 4,000 men to march against Makka. The battle took place at Hunayn, a valley in the mountainous area between Tâ'if and Makka. At first, the battle seemed to be going the way of the Muslims, because of their number, as well as the strength of their belief. But the Muslims were over-dependent on this fact, and forgot the enemy's advantage of knowing the hilly ground thoroughly. Many Muslims were slain in ambush, and many others turned back in confusion and retreat. As for the Blessed Prophet, who always relied upon Allah, he was calm. He rallied his forces, and dealt the enemy a crushing defeat, with the help of Allah.)

25. Allah has already helped you on many fields, and on the day of Hunayn; while you were pleased with your great numbers, it availed you nothing; the earth, with all its vastness seemed to close in, and you turned your backs in retreat.

26. Then Allah sent down His tranquillity upon His messenger and the believers, and sent (to your aid) invisible warriors and punished the disbelievers. Such is the reward of disbelievers.

بِسْمِ اللّٰهِ الرَّحْمٰنِ الرَّحِيْمِ

ثُمَّ يَتُوْبُ اللّٰهُ مِنْ بَعْدِ ذٰلِكَ عَلٰى مَنْ يَّشَاءُ ۗ وَاللّٰهُ غَفُوْرٌ رَّحِيْمٌ ۝ يٰۤاَيُّهَا الَّذِيْنَ اٰمَنُوْۤا اِنَّمَا الْمُشْرِكُوْنَ نَجَسٌ فَلَا يَقْرَبُوا الْمَسْجِدَ الْحَرَامَ بَعْدَ عَامِهِمْ هٰذَا ۚ وَاِنْ خِفْتُمْ عَيْلَةً فَسَوْفَ يُغْنِيْكُمُ اللّٰهُ مِنْ فَضْلِهٖۤ اِنْ شَاءَ ۗ اِنَّ اللّٰهَ عَلِيْمٌ حَكِيْمٌ ۝ قَاتِلُوا الَّذِيْنَ لَا يُؤْمِنُوْنَ بِاللّٰهِ وَلَا بِالْيَوْمِ الْاٰخِرِ وَلَا يُحَرِّمُوْنَ مَا حَرَّمَ اللّٰهُ وَرَسُوْلُهٗ وَلَا يَدِيْنُوْنَ دِيْنَ الْحَقِّ مِنَ الَّذِيْنَ اُوْتُوا الْكِتٰبَ حَتّٰى يُعْطُوا الْجِزْيَةَ عَنْ يَّدٍ وَّهُمْ صٰغِرُوْنَ ۝ وَقَالَتِ الْيَهُوْدُ عُزَيْرُۨ ابْنُ اللّٰهِ وَقَالَتِ النَّصٰرَى الْمَسِيْحُ ابْنُ اللّٰهِ ۗ ذٰلِكَ قَوْلُهُمْ بِاَفْوَاهِهِمْ ۚ يُضَاهِئُوْنَ قَوْلَ الَّذِيْنَ كَفَرُوْا مِنْ قَبْلُ ۗ قَاتَلَهُمُ اللّٰهُ ۚ اَنّٰى يُؤْفَكُوْنَ ۝ اِتَّخَذُوْۤا اَحْبَارَهُمْ وَرُهْبَانَهُمْ اَرْبَابًا مِّنْ دُوْنِ اللّٰهِ وَالْمَسِيْحَ ابْنَ مَرْيَمَ ۚ وَمَاۤ اُمِرُوْۤا اِلَّا لِيَعْبُدُوْۤا اِلٰهًا وَّاحِدًا ۚ لَاۤ اِلٰهَ اِلَّا هُوَ ۗ سُبْحٰنَهٗ عَمَّا يُشْرِكُوْنَ ۝

١٩٠

27. Then afterward Allah guides to repentance whom He will; for Allah is Forgiving, Merciful.

28. O you who believe! The polytheists are unclean. Let them not approach the Sacred Mosque after this year of theirs *(is ended)*. If you fear poverty Allah will enrich you through His bounty if He will. He is All-Knowing All-Wise.

29. Fight against those from among the People of the Scripture who do not believe in Allah nor the Last Day; who do not forbid what Allah and His messenger have forbidden, and who do not adopt the religion of truth until they pay the tribute out of hand, utterly subdued.

30. The Jews say Uzair *('Uzayr)* is the son of Allah, and the Christians say the Messiah is the son of Allah. Such are their sayings by which they imitate those who disbelieved of old. May Allah assail them. How perverse they are!

(The Torah, the book which Moses received from Allah, is frequently referred to in the Qur'an and is recognised in Islam as having been an inspired Book. But the Torah today is not the one which was revealed to Moses, nor does it contain any of the Tablets which he had received. When it became apparent that the Torah was in need of reconstruction, certain priests and scribes headed by Uzair promulgated a new code.

Uzair *(or Esdras, in Arabic, 'Uzayr)* who lived in the fourth century B.C., was an able scribe who had been an astrologer during the Babylonian captivity. It is said that he was inspired to rewrite the Torah. So indebted did the Jews feel to him for this service, that some of them regarded him as a son of God.

Some Christians, too, still call Christ the "son of God .)

31. They have made their rabbis and their monks, and the Messiah the son of Mary, as Lords besides Allah; though they were only ordered to worship one God. There is no god but Him! Transcendent is He above what they associate *(with Him)*.

32. They desire to extinguish the light of Allah with their mouths, and Allah refuses but to perfect His light, though the disbelievers detest it.

33. It is He who has sent His messenger with the guidance and the religion of truth to make it triumphant above all religion though the idolaters may dislike it.

34. O you who believe! indeed many of the rabbis and the monks devour the wealth of people by false means, and debar them from the way of Allah. Those who hoard up gold and silver and do not spend it in the way of Allah; give tidings unto them of a painful punishment.

(Falsehood or vain things always capture man's mind and make him give up elevated and high feelings. People may sometimes abandon their belief in Allah for this. In the history of mediaeval Europe this was most strikingly exemplified. Rabbis and priests made their office a stepping-stone to worldly power and possessions. The Monastic Orders for example which took vows of poverty for individuals became so rich with corporate property that their wealth became a scandal, even among their own people. Such are the dangers of creating official religious hierarchies.)

35. The day shall come when their treasures shall be heated in the fire of Hell; and their foreheads, sides and backs shall be branded with them (saying) "Here is that treasure you hoarded up for yourselves; taste, now what you were hoarding up.

36. The number of the months with Allah has been twelve since the time He created the heavens and the earth. Four of them are sacred. That is the right religion. So do not wrong yourselves during them. And fight the polytheists altogether just as they themselves fight against you altogether. Know that Allah is with the righteous.

(There was a long-established custom among Arabs that four of the twelve months of the year were a period in which fighting of any kind was forbidden. These were Dhu'l-Qa'da, Dhu'l-Hijja, Muharram and Rajab. Since the first three come one after the other, resulting in a long period without fighting, those Arabs who were accustomed to raid other tribes and maintain themselves through this, used to change the months about, or added to or deducted from them when it suited them, in order to get an unfair advantage over the enemy. Islam, while condemning all internecine strife, took steps to ensure that the especial sanctity of the Sacred Months was preserved, especially since at this time the pilgrim caravans would be on the move.)

37. Postponement of a sacred month is only an excess of disbelief, whereby the disbelievers go astray. They allow it one year, and forbid it the next, that they might make up the number of months which God has made sacrosanct, so that they allow that which Allah has forbidden. The evil of their deeds is made to seem fair to them. Allah does not guide the disbelieving people.

(The Sûrah now turns to affairs in the North. The Byzantines, who, since the time of the Edict of Theodosius, had put to death all who refused to follow the Orthodox faith, were preparing to invade Arabia and massacre the Muslims. Despite the hypocrites' propaganda, the Prophet collected about 30,000 soldiers and marched to Tabûk, a place near the Byzantine frontier. He was expecting to confront an army of 40,000 soldiers, but the enemy had fled. The Blessed Prophet made some alliances with certain Christian and Jewish tribes in the area before he returned to Madîna.

The next few verses relate to the attitudes of the hypocrites.)

38. O you who believe! What is the matter with you that when you are asked to go forth in the cause of Allah you cling heavily to the earth? Do you prefer the life of this world to the Hereafter? But little is the comfort of this life as compared with the Hereafter.

39. If you do not go forth, He will punish you sternly and replace you by other people. You will in no way harm Him. Allah has power over all things.

(Although many hesitated about the Tabûk campaign, many more joined in. But a more striking example of faith was provided during his famous Hijra. When the pagans plotted for his life, he was ordered by

Allah to move to Madîna where he had already sent his followers, and Hadrat 'Alî volunteered to face his enemies in his house. When the Prophet was on the way his single companion was Abû Bakr. When the pagans realised that he had slipped out of Makka, they began to search the vicinity for him, and the two men concealed themselves in the Cave of Thawr. Abû Bakr, being very anxious of the Prophet's life, said: "We are but two. "Nay, said the Prophet, "for Allah is with us. This strength of faith gave their souls peace, and Allah enabled them to reach Madîna unchallenged. The help of Allah was not immediately visible, but it was there and always will be.)

40. If you do not help him *(the Prophet Muhammad)* Allah did help him before when the disbelievers expelled him. When the two were in the Cave he said to his companion: "Do not despair, for Allah is with us. Then Allah caused His tranquillity to descend upon him and supported him with invisible forces and humbled to the depths the word of the disbelievers. But the word of Allah is exalted to the heights. And Allah is Mighty, Wise.

(The hypocrites produced false excuses not to join the Tabuk campaign, which took place in the summer heat, and at the time of the date-harvest in Madîna. The Blessed Prophet knew that all their oaths were false, but he let them remain, as he also knew that their attendance would bring no benefit for the cause.)

43. May Allah give you grace! Why did you give them leave (*to stay behind*), until it became clear to you who spoke the truth and until you knew who were the liars?

44. Those who believe in Allah and the Last Day will never ask you to exempt them from fighting with their wealth and their lives. Allah knows well the righteous.

45. Only those ask you leave, who do not believe in Allah and the Last Day and whose hearts doubt, so that they waver in their doubt.

46. If they had wished to go forth they would surely have made some preparation for it, but Allah disliked their being sent forth, and held them back and they were told to stay behind with those who stay behind (*like women and children*).

47. If they had gone forth with you they would have added nothing but mischief to you and they would have hurried through your ranks, seeking to cause sedition among you. And there would have been some among you who would have listened to them. Allah knows the wrongdoers.

41. March forth, lightly armed and heavily, and strive with your wealth and your lives in the way of Allah. That is best for you if you but knew it.

(This commandment is to be taken literally, in which case it denotes the type of armament one should take, and that one may go out on foot and mounted, and also metaphorically, where it means that every one is called. All people can and should join, whether experienced (for dangerous activities) or less experienced (for other duties). Those who were too poor or elderly to contribute were later exempted: see verse 91.)

42. Had it been an immediate gain or a moderate journey they would have followed you, but the distance seemed too far to them. Yet they will swear by Allah (saying): "If we had been able we would surely have set out with you. They destroy their souls, and Allah knows that they are certainly liars.

48. Indeed they had plotted sedition before and upset matters for you until the Truth arrived and the decree of Allah gained mastery, though they disliked it.

49. There is one among them who says, "Give me leave *(to stay behind)* and do not expose me to temptation. Surely they have already fallen into temptation. Hell is surrounding the disbelievers.

(Some hypocrites claimed exemption from service in the Tabûk campaign, pleading that they could not withstand the charms of the women of the enemy. By making such pleas, however, they merely announced that they had fallen into a different kind of temptation: that of cowardice and sloth.)

50. If a good thing comes to you it grieves them, but if a disaster befalls you, they say, "We took indeed our precautions beforehand! and they turn away rejoicing.

51. Say: "Nothing will befall us except what Allah has ordained. He is our Guardian. In Him let the believers put their trust.

52. Say: "Are you waiting for anything to befall us except one of the two best things *(martyrdom or victory)?* But we expect for you that Allah will send His punishment from Himself, or by our hands. So wait, if you will; we too, are waiting with you.

53. Say: "Whether you give willingly or with reluctance it will not be accepted from you, because you are a corrupt people.

(The Hypocrites, who secretly plotted against the believers, from time to time made a show of contributing something to the Islamic cause, in order to maintain their pretence. Their contributions, however, were not acceptable, because there was sickness in their hearts. Three reasons are given for their rejection, in the next verse.)

54. The only reason why their offerings shall not be accepted from them is because they have denied Allah and His Messenger, and they come to the Prayer halfheartedly, and they offer contributions unwillingly.

55. So let neither their wealth nor their children please you (O Muhammad). For Allah wills to punish them through these things in the life of the world, and that their souls shall pass away while they are disbelievers.

56. They swear by Allah that they are (believers) like you, yet they are not at all. But they are people who are afraid.

57. If they find a shelter, or caves, or any hiding-place, they would run in frantic haste to seek (refuge in) it.

58. There are some among them who find fault with you in the matter of alms. If a share is given them they are pleased but if they receive nothing, behold, they grow resentful.

(Sadaqa: alms, that which is given in God's name, mainly to the poor and needy, and to the associated purposes specified in verse 60 below. Zakât is the regular and binding charity in an organised Muslim community, usually one-fortieth of merchandise and one tenth of fruits of the earth. Further details are given in the Hadiths of the Blessed Prophet, and in the classical works of Islamic law.)

59. If only they had been content with what Allah and His Messenger have given them, and would say, "Allah is Sufficient for us. He will provide us in abundance out of His Own bounty, and so will His messenger. To Allah we turn our hopes.

60. Alms are only for the poor and the needy, and those who collect them and for those whose hearts are to be reconciled, and for the ransom of captives and debtors and for the way of Allah and for (the hospitality of) the wayfarers. This is an obligatory duty from Allah, and Allah is Knowing, Wise.

61. There are some among them who injure the Prophet, saying, "He listens (to everyone, and is disposed to believe) . Say: "He hears only what is best for you. He believes in Allah and trusts the believers. He is a mercy to the (true) believers among you. Those who injure the Messenger of Allah, there is a painful punishment for them .

62. They swear in the name of Allah in order to please you *(Muslims)*. But it is more just that they should please Allah and His messenger, if they are *(true)* believers.

63. Do they not know that whoever opposes Allah and His Messenger there shall be the fire of Hell for him, wherein he shall abide forever? That is the great humiliation.

64. The hypocrites are afraid lest a Sûrah should be sent down about them, telling them what is in their hearts. Say: "Go on mocking. Allah will surely bring to light that *(the disclosure of which)* you fear.

65. If you question them, they will say: "We were only jesting and making merry. Ask them: "What, then, were you mocking at: Allah, His signs *(revelations)*, and His Messenger?

(When hypocrites mocked the Prophet for his attempt to conquer the Byzantines a revelation came down concerning them. When they were questioned they said, "We were only trying to increase morale for the war. They lied, and this verse was revealed.)

66. Do not invent excuses now; you have indeed disbelieved after your *(confession of)* belief. Even if We pardon some of you We will surely punish others of you, for they are the guilty ones.

67. The hypocrites, both men and women, proceed from one another *(are all alike)*. They enjoin the wrong and forbid the right, and they withold their hands *(from spending for the cause of Allah)*. They have forgotten Allah, so He has forgotten them. Indeed the hypocrites are the evildoers.

68. Allah has promised the hypocrites, both men and women, and the disbelievers, the fire of Hell wherein they shall abide forever. That is a sufficient recompense for them. The curse of Allah is upon them, and theirs shall be a lasting torment.

(A "curse , here as elsewhere, is the deprivation of grace and mercy, brought about by the rejection of the Lord.)

69. As in the case of those before you: they were mightier than you in power and possessed more wealth and children. They had enjoyed their portion (*of the good things*), and you too have enjoyed your portion (*of the good things*) as did those who were before you. And you indulge in idle talk as they did. But their works are in vain in this world and in the Hereafter. They are assuredly the losers.

70. Has not the story reached them of those who had gone before them the people of Noah and Aad and Thamoud, the people of Abraham and the dwellers of Midian and of the overturned cities? Their messengers came to them with clear signs; then Allah would not wrong them; but they wronged themselves.

(The "overturned cities were Sodom and Gomorrah, to whom Lot had preached in vain. Cf. 7:80-4.)

71. And the believers, men and women, are friends to each other; they enjoin what is good and forbid what is evil, and they establish the Prayer and pay the Zakât, and obey Allah and His messenger. On these, Allah will have mercy. Allah is Mighty, Wise.

72. Allah has promised the believers, men and women, gardens beneath which rivers flow, to dwell therein, and beautiful mansions in Gardens of Paradise. But the good pleasure of Allah is greater still. That is the supreme triumph.

(The explicit repetition of "men and women" in the previous verses is proof, if any were needed, of Islam's recognition of the spiritual potential of both sexes.)

73. O Prophet! Strive against the disbelievers and hypocrites. Be harsh with them. Their ultimate abode is hell; an evil destination.

74. They swear by Allah that they said nothing (evil) yet they did say the word of disbelief and did disbelieve after entering Islam. They intended to do what they were not able to carry out. Yet they had no reason to be spiteful; except perhaps because Allah and His Messenger had enriched them. If they repent it will indeed be better for them; but if they turn away, Allah will afflict them with a painful punishment in the world and in the Hereafter, and they have none on earth to protect or help them.

(The specific reference here is to a plot made by the Blessed Prophet's enemies to murder him when he was returning from Tabûk. The plot failed. But it was all the more evil in that some of the conspirators were among the men of Madîna, who were enriched by the general prosperity that followed the peace and good government established through Islam in Madîna. Trade flourished, justice was firmly administered with an even hand. Yet the only return that these men could make was the return of evil for good. That was their revenge, because Islam aimed at suppressing selfishness, stood for the rights of the poorest and humblest, and judged human worth on spiritual rather than material or social grounds.)

75. Some of them made a covenant with Allah (saying): "If He gives us of His bounty we will give alms and live like righteous men.

76. But when Allah did bestow of His bounty, they grew niggardly, turning their backs, hurrying away.

77. So He has caused hypocrisy to reign in their hearts until the day when they shall meet Him, because they broke their word to Allah that they promised Him, and because they lied.

78. Are they not aware that Allah knows their secret (thoughts) and secret counsels, and that Allah knows what is hidden?

79. As for those that slander the believers who give freely in charity, and scoff at those who find nothing to give except their own endeavours, Allah will scoff at them. Theirs shall be a painful punishment.

('Abdullâh ibn Ubayy, the chief of the hypocrites was ill and was about to die. His son asked the Prophet to pray for him. Since the son was a very sincere Muslim, the Prophet could not refuse him, and pleaded God's forgiveness for the father. Then the following verse was revealed.)

80. Whether you ask forgiveness for them or not *(their sin is unforgivable)*; if you ask forgiveness for them seventy times, Allah will not forgive them. That is because they have denied Allah and His messenger, and Allah does not guide a people who are corrupt.

81. Those who were left behind rejoiced at sitting still, *(remaining far)* behind the messenger of Allah, for they did not like to fight in the way of Allah with their wealth and their lives. They said "Do not go forth in this heat. Say to them: "The fire of Hell is far hotter . If only they could understand!

82. Then let them laugh a little; much will they weep, as the reward of what they used to earn.

83. If Allah brings you back *(from the war)* unto a group of them, and they ask leave to march with you, say: "You shall not march with me, nor shall you fight with me against an enemy. You were content with sitting still on the first occasion, so sit still with those who remain behind.

84. And never *(O Muhammad)* pray for one of them who dies, nor stand by his grave. For they denied Allah and His Messenger, and died while they were corrupt.

85. So let neither their wealth nor their children please you *(O Muhammad)*; for Allah wills to punish them through these things in this world, and that their souls shall pass away while they are disbelievers.

(Except for the absence of the word "life , this verse repeats verse 55 above. The repetition indicates the harmonious closing of the same argument in two aspects. In 9:55 it occurred in connection with the reasons for refusing to receive the contributions of such persons to the expenses of an enterprise which, though vital to Islam's defence, was secretly opposed by them. Here, in verse 85, it is a question of refusing to participate in the obsequies of such persons after their death; whence the ommission of the word "life .)

86. Whenever a Sûrah is revealed saying: "Believe in Allah and fight along with His Messenger , the men of wealth among them still ask you to excuse them, saying "leave us with those who sit *(at home)* .

87. They were content to be with those who stayed behind: a seal was set upon their hearts, therefore they do not understand.

88. But the Messenger and the believers with him have struggled with their possessions and their lives. These shall be rewarded with good things. They are the successful.

89. Allah has prepared for them gardens beneath which rivers flow, in which they shall abide forever. That is the supreme triumph.

(There is another echo here, this time of verse 72 above. This balances the parallel repetition, or reminiscence in verse 85 above. The symmetry of the argument is completed; as regards the Hypocrites of Madîna, before we pass on to consider the case of the Hypocrites of the desert Bedouin tribes.)

90. Some Arabs of the desert come with excuses, begging leave to stay behind, while those who lied to Allah and His messenger sat at home. The disbelievers among them will be afflicted with a painful chastisement.

91. It shall be no offense for the feeble, the sick, and those lacking the means to contribute (to the war, to stay behind), if they are true to Allah and His messenger. There is no way (of blame) against those who do good. Allah is Forgiving and Merciful.

(For those who are weak in body, on account of age, sex, infirmity, or illness, there can be no blame for not taking part in military action for the Cause. Neither are they who are too poor to contribute worthy of any blame. But they are expected to keep calm, not to cause any panic, to help the wounded and support the families of those who are fighting at the front. Such services can play an important role in an army's victory.)

92. Nor (is there any blame) on those who came to you, to be provided with mounts, and when you said to them, "I am unable to provide you with mounts, they returned with tears streaming from their eyes, grieving that they could find no means to contribute.

(Some companions of the Prophet were too poor to own a horse or camel, suitable clothes or even the necessary food to share in the expedition to Tabûk. They came and begged the Prophet to obtain all these things for them. But such was impossible for the Prophet. Their disappointment was in proportion to their eagerness to serve.)

93. The way of blame is only against those who ask you exemption although they are rich. They are content to remain with those who stay behind. Allah has sat a seal upon their hearts, therefore they do not know (what the consequences might be).

94. They will apologize to you, when you return to them. Say: "Make no excuses: we will not believe you. Allah has revealed to us the tidings about you. Allah and His messenger are watching over all your actions, then you shall be returned to Him Who knows the unseen and the visible, and He will declare to you what you used to do.

95. When you return they will appeal to you in Allah's name to leave them alone. So leave them alone. For they are unclean. Hell shall be their home, the punishment for their misdeeds.

96. They will swear to you that you may be pleased with them. But (even) if you are pleased with them, Allah will not be pleased with the corrupt.

97. The desert Arabs are the worst in disbelief and hypocrisy, and the more fitted to be ignorant of the limits which Allah has revealed to His messenger. But Allah is All-Knowing, All-Wise.

98. Some desert Arabs regard what they give for the cause of Allah as a compulsory fine and wait for some misfortune to befall you. May ill-fortune befall on them. Allah hears all and knows all.

99. But some of the desert Arabs believe in Allah and the Last Day, and regard what they expend as a means of bringing them close to Allah and the prayers of the messenger. Surely they are an (acceptable) offering for them, and Allah will admit them to His mercy. Allah is Forgiving, Merciful.

100. As for those who led the way *(to respond to the invitation to the Faith)*, the first of the Emigrants *(Muhâjirs)* and the Helpers *(Ansâr)*, and those who followed them in goodness, Allah is pleased with them and they, too, are pleased with Him. He has prepared for them gardens beneath which rivers flow, where they shall dwell for ever. That is the supreme triumph.

101. Some of the desert Arabs around you are hypocrites and some of the people of Madîna; they are grown bold in hypocrisy. You do not know them, but We know them. Twice We will chastise them, then they shall be sent to a tremendous punishment.

102. Others have confessed their sins; they have mixed a righteous deed with another evil. Perhaps Allah will turn to them in mercy. He is Forgiving, Merciful.

(Some who stayed at home during the Tabûk expedition felt ashamed afterwards and repented. They had themselves tied to the columns of the mosque and vowed to remain there unless the Prophet come and untie them. On his return from Tabûk when he was informed about what happened the Prophet said: "I, too, vow that I will not untie them until I receive my Lord's command. Then the following verse was revealed.)

103. Take alms of their wealth so that you may purify and sanctify them thereby, and pray for them: for your prayers are a comfort for them. Allah is Hearer, Seer.

104. Have they not known that Allah accepts the repentance of His servants and receives *(approves of)* their alms, and that Allah is the Forgiving, the Merciful?

105. Say: "Work, Allah will surely see your work, and His messenger and the believers, and you will be returned to Him Who knows the unseen and the visible, and He will tell you what you were doing.

106. There are *(yet)* others held in suspense for the command of Allah. He will either punish or pardon them. Allah is Wise, Knowing.

(Three categories of hypocrites did not join the Tabûk expedition. (1) Those who made excuses whenever they could; so much so that it became their habit. For such there was no hope. (2) Those who had lapsed into evil but later felt guilt-stricken and ashamed, then repented. They spent their wealth afterwards as a compensation. (3) Doubtful cases, for whom Allah's judgement came in verse 118.

Some other incidents are related of this nature. A man in Madîna by the name of Abû 'Âmir was so jealous of the Prophet that he converted to Christianity and became a priest. He fought against the Prophet at Uhud and Hunayn, after which he fled to Damascus, where he asked the population to build him a church, and to supply him with soldiers and weapons to defeat the Muslims. There was a well-known group of hypocrites who built a mosque in order to steal the congregation of the Qubâ Mosque at Madîna, which was the first mosque built by the Muslims. When the Prophet returned from Tabûk they invited him to lead the prayers in the newly-built mosque. The Blessed Prophet was about to accept their invitation in order to win them over, when the following verse was revealed.)

107. And there are those who built a mosque by way of mischief and unbelief, to disunite the believers, and in expectation of him who had made war on Allah and His messenger. They swear: "We desired nothing but good , but Allah bears witness that they are liars.

108. Never stand (to pray) there. A place of worship founded on piety from the very first day is more worthy that you should stand (to pray) therein. For there are men in it who would like to make themselves pure. Allah loves those that purify themselves.

109. Who is the best, he who founds his building on the fear of Allah and His good pleasure, or he who builds on the brink of a crumbling precipice so that his house will fall with him into the fire of Hell? Allah does not guide the wrongdoers.

110. The building they have built will never be free from suspicion in their hearts until their

hearts are cut into pieces. Allah is Wise, Knowing.

111. Allah has bought from the believers their lives and their wealth because the Garden will be theirs. They shall fight in the way of Allah, kill and be killed; that is a promise binding upon Allah in the Torah and the Gospel and the Qur'an. Who is more faithful to His promise than Allah? Rejoice then in the bargain you have made with Him. That is the supreme triumph.

(When 70 men from among the *Ansâr*, the people of Madîna who had received the Makkan emigrants, swore allegiance to the Blessed Prophet, one of them, 'Abdullâh ibn Rawâha asked him, "O messenger of Allah! What are your Lord's conditions, and yours? The Prophet replied: "The condition of allegiance to my Lord is that you believe in Him, and do not associate anyone with Him, and worship Him. As for my condition, it is to regard me and my cause as your cause, and to defend it to the end. They asked: "If we so act, what then will we receive in return? "The Garden, in eternal life, replied the Messenger. They exclaimed: "What a profitable trade! Never will we turn away from this covenant, nor will we want it to be broken.

This is a promise binding upon Allah in the Torah, that is, the original Law of Moses; and the Gospel, that is, the original Gospel of Jesus, and in the Qur'an itself. Any other view of redemption is rejected by Islam, especially of that corrupted form of Christianity which thinks that "some other person suffered for our sins, and we are redeemed by his blood . It is only our self-surrender, and not the merit of others merit that counts. This self-surrender may take the form of both physical and spiritual service to the cause of Allah, so that our hearts are made pure, and we are deserving of His grace.)

112. The repenters, the worshippers, the praisers, the fasters, the bowers, the prostraters, the commanders of good and the forbidders of evil, and the observers of Allah's limits (commandments). And give good news to the believers!

(Sâ'ihûn, rendered here as "the fasters", is also interpreted to mean "those that wander in devotion to the cause of Allah, admiring and taking admonition from all around them, living in austerity, increasing their knowledge of the works of Allah, and worshipping Him in gratitude for His blessings.)

113. It is not fitting for the Prophet and the believers to pray for the forgiveness of the polytheists, even though they be near of kin *(to them)* after it has become clear to them that they are the owners of hellfire.

(This is usually understood to refer to the prayer for the dead, (1) if they died unrepentant after Islam was preached to them; (2) if they actively resisted or opposed the Faith to the last; and (3) if the person praying knows that because of his persistent sin, the deceased may be said to have had the doors of mercy closed to him. How is he to know? The knowledge must come from special commands as declared by the Blessed Prophet in his lifetime concerning individuals. Where no light is available from this source, we must follow the best judgement we can.)

114. The prayer of Abraham for the forgiveness of his father was only because of a promise he had made to him; but when it had become clear to him that he *(his father)* was an enemy to Allah he *(Abraham)* disowned him. Assuredly, Abraham was tender-hearted and forbearing.

115. Allah would never lead a people astray after He has guided them until He has made clear to them what they should avoid. Allah has knowledge of all things.

116. Surely to Allah belongs the kingdom of the heavens and of the earth. He gives life and death. You have none besides Allah to protect or help you.

117. Allah has turned in mercy to the Prophet, and the Emigrants *(Muhâjirin)* and the Helpers *(Ansâr)* who followed him in the hour of hardship, when some of them were on the point of losing heart, then He turned to them in mercy. He is Gentle for them, and Merciful.

118. And to the three also *(did He turn in mercy)* who were left behind. *(They felt guilty)* to such a degree that the earth seemed constrained to them for all its vastness and their own souls seemed straitened to them. And they perceived that there is no shelter from Allah but to Himself. Then He turned unto them in mercy that they might repent. Allah is the Accepter of repentance, the Merciful.

(A reference to three of the believers of Madîna who had found reasons for not marching with the Tabûk expedition, and who afterwards deeply regretted their decision.)

119. O you who believe! Have fear of Allah, and be with the truthful ones.

120. It was not fitting for the people of Madîna and the desert Arabs who dwell around them to fail to follow Allah's Messenger and prefer their lives to his life, because nothing could they suffer or do, but was reckoned to their credit as a deed of righteousness, whether they suffered thirst, or fatigue, or hunger in the way of Allah, or took a step which provoked the disbelievers or received from the enemy a gain. Allah does not lose the wages of the good.

121. Nor do they spend any sum, small or great, nor do they cross a valley but it is recorded for them, that Allah repay them the best of what they used to do.

(Since so many verses had been revealed condemning those who did not take part in the Tabûk expedition, thereafter hardly a single Muslim failed to march with the army. Then, the following verse was revealed. It is not correct to go to war leaving no-one behind. Some people who have knowledge and a craft should stay and teach the youngsters. For of what use is it to win battles at the front, while the battle for culture is being neglected?)

122. It is not right that the believers should go out to fight altogether. A band from each community should stay behind to instruct themselves in religion and warn their people when they return to them so that they may take heed.

123. O you who believe! Fight the disbelievers who are near to you, and let them find a harshness in you; and know that Allah is with the righteous.

124. And whenever a Sûrah is revealed some of them ask: "Whose faith will this increase? It will surely increase the faith of the believers and they rejoice.

125. But as for those whose hearts are diseased *(with disbelief and hypocrisy)* it will add more filth to their filth, and they shall die in a state of disbelief.

126. Do they not see how every year they are tried once or twice? Yet they neither repent nor take warning.

127. And whenever a Sûrah is revealed they glance at each other *(asking)*: "Does anyone see you? Then they depart. Allah has turned their hearts *(away)*, because they are people who do not understand.

(Even the disbelievers, in their hearts and conscience, feel uncomfortable when they turn aside from faith and truth, and therefore their turning aside is figured by furtive glances, such as we may suppose literally to have been the behaviour of the hypocrites in the assemblies of the Blessed Prophet.)

128. There has come to you a messenger from among yourselves, grievous to whom is your burden, concerned for you; for the believers full of compassion, merciful.

(Almighty God has given two of His beautiful names, al-Ra'ûf *(The Compassionate)* and al-Rahîm *(The Merciful)* to his beloved messenger, Muhammad. No messenger before him had received this honour.)

129. Now if they turn away, say: "Allah is Sufficient for me. There is no God but Him. In Him have I put my trust, and He is the Lord of the Tremendous Throne.

SÛRAH X

YÛNUS (JONAH)

Revealed at Makka

(This takes its name from the Prophet Jonah, whose people were nearly perished for their sins, but repented and were saved by the Lord.

The Arabs had known Muhammad as an orphan brought up by his uncle Abû Tâlib, but when the divine message came through him, they never accepted the fact. They never even believed that a human could have been the carrier of the celestial Message. They said: "Such a man should at least have been rich and possesed of high position, a mighty leader, a king . But confronted with his honesty, and willingness to suffer for his Lord's cause, they were confounded, and could only attribute it to sorcery. Much of the Sûrah is taken up with this absurd attitude.

With the exception of a three verses, which came at Madîna, this Sûrah was revealed late in the Makkan period.)

JONAH

In the name of Allah, the Compassionate, the Merciful

l. Alif. Lâm. Râ. These are the signs of the Wise Book.

(*Âyât* - signs, or verses of the Qur'an. The next few verses are about the wonders of Allah's creation. But we should observe man's position in the eyes of the Creator, Who chooses man for Himself to speak to, through His messengers, in man's own tongue, in order to give him His message.)

2. Does it seem strange to mankind that We should have revealed to a man from among them, saying: "Warn the people *(of their danger)* and give to those who believe good tidings that they have a sure footing in the sight of their Lord? The disbelievers say: "This man is clearly a magician .

3. Surely your Lord is Allah, Who created the heavens and the earth in six days, then established Himself upon the Throne *(of authority)* directing all things. There is no intercessor *(with Him)* except after His permission. That is Allah, your Lord, so worship Him. Will you not take heed?

(For the creation of the heavens and earth in six "days see VII:54.)

4. To Him you shall all return. Allah's promise is true and sure. It is He Who begins (*the process of*) creation, then brings it back *(to life)* again, so that He may justly reward those who have believed in Him and done good works. As for those who disbelieve, theirs will be a seething drink, and a painful doom for their disbelieving.

5. It is He Who made the sun a radiance and the moon a light, and determined for her stages, that you might know the number of the years and the reckoning. Allah has not created all this but in truth, distinguishing the signs to a people who understand.

6. In the alternation of night and day and what Allah has created in the heavens and the earth, surely there are signs for a people who fear Him.

بِسْمِ اللّٰهِ الرَّحْمٰنِ الرَّحِيمِ

إِنَّ الَّذِينَ لَا يَرْجُونَ لِقَاءَنَا وَرَضُوا بِالْحَيٰوةِ الدُّنْيَا وَاطْمَأَنُّوا بِهَا وَالَّذِينَ هُمْ عَنْ اٰيٰتِنَا غَافِلُونَ ۞ أُولٰٓئِكَ مَأْوٰىهُمُ النَّارُ بِمَا كَانُوا يَكْسِبُونَ ۞ إِنَّ الَّذِينَ اٰمَنُوا وَعَمِلُوا الصّٰلِحٰتِ يَهْدِيهِمْ رَبُّهُمْ بِإِيمَانِهِمْ تَجْرِي مِنْ تَحْتِهِمُ الْأَنْهٰرُ فِي جَنّٰتِ النَّعِيمِ ۞ دَعْوٰىهُمْ فِيهَا سُبْحٰنَكَ اللّٰهُمَّ وَتَحِيَّتُهُمْ فِيهَا سَلٰمٌ وَاٰخِرُ دَعْوٰىهُمْ أَنِ الْحَمْدُ لِلّٰهِ رَبِّ الْعٰلَمِينَ ۞ وَلَوْ يُعَجِّلُ اللّٰهُ لِلنَّاسِ الشَّرَّ اسْتِعْجَالَهُمْ بِالْخَيْرِ لَقُضِيَ إِلَيْهِمْ أَجَلُهُمْ فَنَذَرُ الَّذِينَ لَا يَرْجُونَ لِقَاءَنَا فِي طُغْيَانِهِمْ يَعْمَهُونَ ۞ وَإِذَا مَسَّ الْإِنْسٰنَ الضُّرُّ دَعَانَا لِجَنْبِهِ أَوْ قَاعِدًا أَوْ قَائِمًا فَلَمَّا كَشَفْنَا عَنْهُ ضُرَّهُ مَرَّ كَأَنْ لَمْ يَدْعُنَا إِلٰى ضُرٍّ مَسَّهُ كَذٰلِكَ زُيِّنَ لِلْمُسْرِفِينَ مَا كَانُوا يَعْمَلُونَ ۞ وَلَقَدْ أَهْلَكْنَا الْقُرُونَ مِنْ قَبْلِكُمْ لَمَّا ظَلَمُوا وَجَاءَتْهُمْ رُسُلُهُمْ بِالْبَيِّنٰتِ وَمَا كَانُوا لِيُؤْمِنُوا كَذٰلِكَ نَجْزِي الْقَوْمَ الْمُجْرِمِينَ ۞ ثُمَّ جَعَلْنٰكُمْ خَلٰٓئِفَ فِي الْأَرْضِ مِنْ بَعْدِهِمْ لِنَنْظُرَ كَيْفَ تَعْمَلُونَ ۞

٢٠٨

7. These who do not look to come before Us, and are well pleased with the life of the world, and find rest in it, and those who are heedless of Our revelations,

8. Those - their refuge is the Fire, because of what they used to earn.

9. Surely those who believe, and do deeds of righteousness, their Lord will guide them for their belief. Rivers will flow beneath them in gardens of delight.

10. Their call therein (will be): "Glory be to you, O Allah , and their greeting therein will be: "Peace . And the close of their call will be: "Praise be to Allah, the Lord of the Worlds!

11. If Allah were to hasten for men the ill (they have earned) as they would hasten on the good, their term (allowed to them) would already have expired. But We leave those who do not look to the meeting with Us, to, in their trespasses, wandering blindly.

(Some of the idolaters said: "O God! If Muhammad is really Your messenger, send down upon us stones from the sky, or punish us right away! The above verse was revealed as a response to this foolishness.)

12. When misfortune befalls a man he calls Us (lying down) on his side, or sitting or standing, but when We have relieved him of the misfortune he goes his way as if he had never called Us for a misfortune that afflicted him. Thus are their (foul) deeds made to seem fair to the transgressors.

13. We destroyed the generations before you when they did wrong, and their messengers came to them with clear signs, but they would not believe. Thus do We reward the guilty.

14. Then we appointed you viceroys in the earth after them, that We might see how you behave.

15. When Our clear revelations are recited unto them, those who do not look to the meeting with Us say, "Bring a Qur'an other than this, or change it." Say: "It is not for me to change it of my own accord. I follow nothing except what is revealed to me. Truly I should myself fear, if I were to disobey my Lord, the penalty of a tremendous Day."

(The duty of the messengers is to deliver the Divine message as revealed. No change whatsoever can be made by human hands. The idolaters of Makka wanted the Prophet to either change the Qur'an's rules or to bring another Book. Most of the corruptions of religion arise when people desire to use religion for their own ends.)

16. Say: "If Allah had so willed I would not have recited it to you, neither would He have given you any knowledge of it. I dwelt among you a whole lifetime before it *(came to me)*. Have you then no sense?"

(The Chosen One had lived his whole life of purity and goodness amongst his people, and they knew and acknowledged it before he received his mission. They knew he loved his people, and was loyal to them. Why should they turn against him when he had to point out under inspiration their ignorance and wrongdoing? And he had to plead again and again with them: "Will you not understand, and see what a privilege it is for you to receive a revelation from the Lord?")

17. Who is more wicked than the man who invents a lie about Allah and denies His revelations? Truly the evil-doers shall not succeed.

18. They worship beside Allah that which neither harms nor profits them, and they say: "These are our intercessors with Allah". Say "Do you indeed inform Allah of something He does not know in the heavens or on earth?" Glory be to Him and far is He above all that they associate with Him.

19. Mankind were only one nation, then they fell into variance; and had it not been for a word that had already gone forth from your Lord their differences would have been settled between them.

(Cf. 6:115, 9:40 and 4:171. The "Word" is the decree of God, the expression of His universal will or wisdom in a particular case. When men began to diverge from one another, and their primordial brotherhood was disrupted by selfishness and egotism, Allah made their very differences subserve the higher ends by increasing their emulation in virtue and piety, and thus pointing back to the ultimate Unity and Reality.)

20. They say: "Why has a sign not been sent down upon him from his Lord?" Say: "The unseen belongs only to Allah. Then *(watch and)* wait; I too will wait with you."

21. And when We cause the people to taste of mercy after some misfortune has afflicted them, behold! they have some plot against Our revelations. Say: "Allah is more swift in plotting. Surely, Our angels are recording your intrigues.

(This verse is about the people of Makka. It is related that for seven consecutive years not a single drop of rain came down, and many men and beasts perished in the subsequent famine. Then Allah sent abundant rain, bestowed His blessings, and made the country prosperous again. Yet the disbelievers took this as the work of idols and stars, and denied the unitary signs of Allah.)

22. It is He Who enables you to travel on the land and the sea; and when you are in the ship, and the ships run with a favourable wind and they rejoice in it, there comes upon them a strong wind, and waves come on them from every side and they think they are encompassed. Then they cry unto Allah, making their faith pure for Him only, (saying): "If You deliver us from this, we truly will be thankful!

(All the great inventions and discoveries on which man prides himself are the fruit of that genius and talent which the Lord has freely given of His grace. But the spirit of man remains small, as is illustrated by the famous parable from the sea. How smug is man when a ship beneath him glides effortlessly through the waves! But how helpless he feels, when the divine rigour is manifested on the sea, and he recalls that all his devices are shields of straw which cannot protect him from the immense forces of chaos. Only the Lord does that, although for the most part we do not know.)

23. But when He has delivered them, they rebel in the earth wrongfully. O mankind! Your rebellion is only against yourselves. (You have) the enjoyment of the life of the world, then unto Us you shall return. Then We shall tell you all that you used to do.

24. The likeness (or parable, similitude) of the life of the world is that of water which We send down from the sky, then the plants of ornaments and is embellished, and her people think they have power over her, the earth of which men and cattle eat mingle with it, until, when the earth has taken on her Our command comes down upon it by night or day, and We make it as reaped corn as if it had not flourished the previous day. Thus We make plain Our revelations for a people who reflect.

(The same lesson is here taught with a second parable, this time set on dry land. Man's cleverness can lead him to believe that in his scratching on the earth's surface he has become master of it. Yet he remains utterly dependant on the environment which the Lord has created. If he does not give thanks for His gifts, the gifts may be taken away, leaving him with the ruined and poisoned landscape which he in fact deserves.)

25. Allah invites to the Abode of Peace, and guides whom He will to a straight path.

26. For those who do good is the greatest good, and even more. Neither darkness nor shame shall cover their faces. They are the owners of the Garden, dwelling there forever.

(Goodness (or ihsân, husnâ) is to act in accordance with the wise commandments of the Lord. The Prophet defined it as being a servant to God as though one saw Him. From such a degree, all the virtues must flow abundantly, rendering those who attain to it lights for the guidance and salvation and mankind. The greatest good shall be for them, and also "even more": the delight of gazing upon the ineffable and blessed Countenance of God, the reward of the pure in heart, to be granted in the Abode of Peace.)

27. As for those who have acquired evil deeds, the recompense of an evil deed shall be the like of it; abasement shall cover (their faces). They shall have no protector from (the wrath of) Allah. It is as though their faces are veiled with pieces of the darkest night. They are the owners of the Fire, dwelling in it forever.

28. On the day when We gather them all together, then We shall say to those who ascribed partners unto Us: "Stand back, you and your (pretended) partners (with Allah)!" And We will separate them one from the other, and their (pretended) partners will say to them: "It was not us that you worshipped.

(The sources of final power other than God, that they had imagined, were imaginary. But the prophets, or the great or good men whose names were vainly taken in competition with the name of God, and the personified ideas treated in the same way would themselves protest against their names being used in that way, and show that the worship was paid not to them, but to the ignorance, superstition or overwhelming lusts of the false worshippers.)

29. Allah is a sufficient witness between us and you; assuredly we were unaware of your worship of us."

30. Thereupon each soul will experience what it had done, and they are returned to Allah, their rightful Lord, and that which they invented will forsake them.

31. Say (to them, O Prophet): "Who is it that provides for you from the sky and the earth, or who possesses hearing and sight; and who brings forth the living from the dead and the dead from the living, and who directs all affairs?" They will surely say: "Allah". Then say: "Will you not then fear Him"?

32. Such then is Allah, your rightful Lord. What is there, after the truth, but error? How, then, do you turn away?

33. Thus has the word of your Lord (O Prophet) proved true in regard to the corrupt; that they do not believe.

34. Say: "Is any one of your partners (*that you ascribe to Allah*) able to originate creation then bring it back again? Say: "It is Allah Who originates creation and brings it back again. How, then are you misled?

35. Say: "Is any one of your partners (*that you ascribe to Allah*) able to guide to the Truth? Say: "It is Allah who guides to the truth. Is He who guides to the truth more worthy to be followed, or he that cannot find it, and is himself in need of guidance? What, then, is the matter with you? How you judge?

36. Most of them follow nothing but a mere conjecture. But a conjecture is no substitute for truth. Allah is well aware of what they do.

37. This Qur'an could not have been invented (*by one*) apart from Allah, but it is a confirmation of that (*series of revelations*) which was before it, and a (*fuller*) explanation of the Book - wherein there is no doubt - from the Lord of the Worlds.

(The Lord's revelation throughout the ages and to all peoples is one. The Qur'an confirms, fulfils, completes and further explains the one true revelation.)

38. Or do they say he (*the Prophet*) invented it? Say: "Then bring a Sûrah like it, and call (*to your aid*) anyone you can other than Allah, if you speak the truth.

39. No, but they have denied that the knowledge of which they could not compass, and the interpretation of which (*i. e. Qur'an*) has not yet come to them. Thus did those that were before them also deny. So see what was the end of the wrong-doers.

(The Message of God not only gives us rules of our everyday conduct, but speaks of exalted matters of religious significance, which require elucidation in

three ways: (1) by instruction from spiritual teachers; (2) by experience of the actualities of life, and (3) by the final fulfillment of the hopes and warnings which we now take on trust through our faith. Disbelievers reject the divine Reminder simply because they cannot understand it, and without giving it even a chance of elucidation in any of these ways.)

40. Some among them believe in it (*the Holy Qur'an*) while others do not. Your Lord is best aware of the workers of corruption.

41. And if they deny you, say: "I have my works, and you have yours. You are quit of what I do; I am quit of what you do.

42. Some of them listen to you. But can you make the deaf to hear, incapable as they are of understanding?

(If a man in whose heart is hypocrisy and a deep-seated resistance to faith goes to hear some great spiritual teacher, he will receive no benefit, because he is not sincerely seeking the truth. He is like a blind or a deaf man, or an imbecile. Where the will to be guided is absent, the guidance will be absent also.)

43. Some of them look upon you. Yet can you show the way to the blind, deprived as they are of sight?

(The five senses of man are not sufficient to receive the truth. Rather, man must use his will to understand, and his inner, spiritual faculties of perception. Ignorance of these inner faculties is the worst of all deformities.)

44. Indeed, Allah does not wrong mankind in any way; but mankind wrong themselves.

(Every individual has been created with the ability to know God, and is supplied with abundant opportunities for reflection throughout his life. Yet many use their abilities for material ends, or in the working of evil. Thus do they wrong themselves, and deny the purpose for their creation, which is to recognise and proclaim the Unity of the Source.)

45. The day will come when He will gather them again, as though they had remained only an hour of the daytime, recognizing one another. Those will surely have perished who denied the encounter with Allah, and were not guided.

46. Whether We let you (*O Muhammad*) witness a part of that *(punishment)* which We promise them, or *(whether We)* cause you to die *(before it falls upon them)*; unto Us they shall return. And Allah is witness to what they do.

47. For every nation there is a messenger. And when their messenger comes, justice is done among them; they are not wronged.

(It is of the absolute justice of the Lord that He has sent reminders to every people and in all ages. The message was one, although tailored in some details of social and ritual practice to meet local cultural needs. When the Messengers died, the messages were gradually forgotten, or horribly distorted. The final Rectifier is our prophet Muhammad, upon whom be blessings and peace. His message must everywhere be heard, and all that hear it must respond. Those who hear and respond positively will receive joy on the day when God's justice is done. It will be observed that this is a tolerant and universal doctrine, which allows for the working of God's grace throughout history, rather than being confined to one people or period, as is the belief of some religions, such as Christianity and Judaism.)

48. They say: "When will this promise *(of punishment)* be fulfilled, if what you say be true?"

49. Say: "I have no power to hurt or benefit myself, except by the will of Allah. A term is fixed for every nation. When their term comes, they cannot put it off an hour, nor can they hasten it."

50. Say: "Have you considered? If His punishment should come to you by night or by day, which part of it would the sinners wish to hasten?

51. What, (*is it only*) when it has come to pass that you will believe in it? (*It will be said:*) 'Is it now (*you believe*), yet *(till now)* you have been hastening it on!'

52. Then it will be said to wrongdoers: 'Taste the torment of eternity! Shall you be rewarded for anything other than what you acquired?'"

53. They ask you to tell them, "Is it true?" Say: "Yes, by my Lord, it is the truth, and you cannot frustrate it."

54. If every would which sinned were to possess all that is in the earth, she would give it for a ransom. When they face the punishment they will avow repentance. But judgement shall be fairly passed between them; they shall not be wronged.

(The verb in "avow repentance is *asarrû*, which may mean either "declare or "reveal , or "conceal . The commentators are divided as to the meaning to be adopted here. If it is the first, then the present translation is appropriate, if the second, then the sense would be that they would give anything in order to escape the punishment, but the hardest thing of all for them is to confess and repent, and so they conceal their sense of shame and ignominy.)

55. Assuredly, to Allah belongs everything that is in the heavens and earth. Assuredly, Allah's promise is true; but most of them do not know.

56. He gives life and death, and to Him you shall be returned.

57. O mankind! There has come to you an advice from your Lord, and a healing for what is in the hearts, and a guidance and a mercy to the believers.

(No joy is greater than that of spiritual activity, of prayer and recollection of the One. And there is no sickness which can afflict our hearts, no sorrow, agitation or bitterness, which cannot be cured thereby. The word of God must be poured upon our wounds, and left to work its miracle.)

58. Say: "Let them rejoice in Allah's grace and mercy. That is better than *(the worldly riches)* which they collect.

59. Say: "Have you considered the provision Allah has sent down for you, and you have made some of it unlawful and some lawful? Say: "Has Allah permitted you, or do you invent a lie about Him?

60. And what think those who lie against Allah upon the Day of Judgement? Allah is kind to mankind, but most of them do not give thanks.

61. In whatever activity you may be, and whichever part of Qur'an you recite, and whatever deed you do, We are witness over you when you are deeply engrossed therein. Not an atom's weight in the earth and in the heaven escapes your Lord, nor is there anything smaller or greater, but that it is *(written)* in a clear Book.

(The Lord's knowledge comprehends all things. Nothing can be hidden from the omniscient One. In His knowledge there is no ambiguity or imprecision, nor is it confined on the basis of space or time, or any other circumstance. It is pre-existent, and endures for ever.)

62. Assuredly, the Friends of Allah: no fear shall come upon them, neither shall they grieve.

63. Those who believe, and feared Him.

64. Theirs is the good news in this world and in the Hereafter. No change can there be in the words of Allah. This is the supreme triumph.

(The "glad tidings in this world are Allah's promises of eternal life in His proximity, and other things which the human mind cannot imagine, but will nonetheless come to pass.

Such good news is brought to us in the Qur'an and the Sunna. Also, righteous dreams may bring such news, for they are glimpses of the divine world. As the Blessed Prophet taught, the righteous dream is a fraction of Prophethood. Finally, the angels, coming to a man at the moment of his decease, may bring him the glad tidings of Allah's mercy upon him.

As for the glad tidings in the Hereafter, this includes the announcements made by the angels after the soul has left the world, about its future bliss in the Garden.)

65. Let their words not grieve you (O Muhammad), for all power belongs to Allah. He is the Hearer, the Knower.

66. Assuredly, to Allah belong all who dwell in the heavens and on earth. Those that follow (alleged) partners apart from Allah follow nothing but a conjecture. They do nothing but lie.

67. It is He who made the night for your rest and (rendered) the day a source of light. Surely in this there are signs for a people who listen.

68. They say: "Allah has taken to Himself a son. Glory be to Him (and high exalted above that)! He is Self-subsistent. To Him belongs all that is in the heavens and in the earth. You have no authority for this. Are you saying concerning Allah that which you do not know?

69. Say: "Those who invent falsehoods about Allah shall not succeed.

70. Some enjoyment in this world; then to Us is their return, and then We shall make them taste the severe penalty for their disbelief.

71. Relate to them the story of Noah when he said to his people: "O my people! If my dwelling here *(with you)* and my reminding you of Allah's signs *(revelations)*, are burdensome upon you, in Allah have I put my trust, so decide upon your course of action, you and your partners. Then let not your affair be a worry to you, pass your sentence on me, and give me no respite.

(Since Noah knew that Allah would protect him, he challenged the idolaters, as here, in order to make them realise their inability to deal with him. His story is mentioned here only to illustrate the special theme of the Sûrah; for a fuller narration, see 11:25-49.)

72. If you turn away *(from my message, consider, for)* no reward have I asked of you. My reward is only due from Allah, and I am commanded to be of those who surrender *(to Him in Islam)*.

73. But they denied him, so We saved him and those with him in the Ark, and made them inherit *(the earth)*, while We drowned those who denied Our signs *(revelations)*. See then how was the fate of those who were given warning *(but never heeded)*.

74. Then after him We sent *(many)* messengers to their peoples, and they brought them clear signs, but they were not men to believe in what they denied before. Thus do We seal up the hearts of the transgressors.

75. Then after them, We sent Moses and Aaron with Our revelations to Pharaoh and his nobles, but they rejected with scorn, for they were a sinful people.

76. When the truth came to them from Us, they said: "This is clear sorcery!

77. Moses said: "Do you speak of the truth *(like this)* when it has come to you? Is this *(at all)* magic, *(though)* magicians never prosper?

78. They said: "Have you come to turn us away from the ways we found our fathers practising, and that you two may have greatness in the land? We will not believe in you two.

79. And Pharaoh said: "Bring every skilled magician to my presence!

80. When the magicians came, Moses said to them: "Throw what you will throw .

81. And when they had thrown, Moses said: "What you have brought is magic. Allah will surely make it vain. Allah never upholds the work of those who cause corruption.

(Magic is mere manipulation, and has no ultimate reality. But in materialistic civilisations such as Pharaoh's, it can take the place of religion, for it deals with matter and power, and the exaltation of the ego, rather than the service of the One True God. All materialistic cultures have a thriving magical subculture.)

82. And Allah, by His words, does prove and establish His truth, however much the sinners may hate it.

83. But, none believed in Moses, except some children of his people, for the fear of Pharaoh and his nobles that they would persecute them; and *(in fact)* Pharaoh was assuredly a tyrant on earth, and one of those who those who extravagantly transgress the bounds.

84. Moses said: "O my people; if you believe in Allah, *(and)* if you have surrendered yourselves to Him *(in Islam)*, in Him *(alone)* put your trust.

85. They said: "In Allah we have put our trust. Our Lord! Do not make us a *(cause of)* temptation for the people of the wrongdoers!

86. And deliver us through Your mercy from the disbelievers.

87. And We revealed *(Our will)* to Moses and his brother saying: "Build houses in Egypt for your people and make your homes places of worship, Conduct prayers and give good news to the believers.

(Probably this instruction was given after the confounding of the state magicians, and when some of the Egyptians believed. Moses was for a little while to remain in Egypt, so that his message would have time to work, before the Exodus. They were to make their houses into places of prayer, as Pharaoh was unlikely to allow them to set up public houses of worship.)

88. Moses said: "Our Lord, you have bestowed on Pharaoh and his nobles splendour and riches in this life. Our Lord, *(is this)* that they may lead astray the people from your path? Our Lord, destroy their riches and harden their hearts so that they shall persist in disbelief until they face the painful chastisement.

89. Allah replied: "Your prayer is answered. Follow you two *(O Moses and Aaron)* the right path, and do not walk in the footsteps of those who do not know.

90. And We brought the Children of Israel across the sea, and Pharaoh and his legions followed them with wickedness and hate, until the drowning overtook him, and Pharaoh cried: "Now I believe that there is no god except Him in whom the Israelites believe, and I am of those who submit *(to Allah in Islam).*

91. Now *(do you believe)?* When previously you were disobedient, and were one of those who work corruption?

92. So, today We shall preserve your body that you may be a sign to those after you: although most men give no heed to Our signs.

(Pharaoh had claimed to be God, and used to torture those who denied him, especially the monotheistic Children of Israel, whose male offspring he slew. Moses and his brother purposed to leave Egypt. Having received a commandment from Allah, he came with his people to the shores of the Red Sea, and touched it with his staff, and a furrow opened across the sea. Pharaoh attempted to follow him, but was engulfed with his legions.)

93. We settled the Children of Israel in a beautiful dwelling-place and provided them with good things. They were not in disagreement among themselves until knowledge was given them. Your Lord will judge their differences on the Day of Resurrection.

94. If you are in doubt regarding what We have revealed to you, then ask those who have been reading the Book before you. The truth has come to you from your Lord, therefore do not doubt it.

95. Nor shall you deny the signs *(revelations)* of Allah, lest you be among those who lose.

96. Those concerning whom the word of your Lord *(concerning sinners)* has effect will not believe.

97. Even though every sign come to them until they see the painful penalty.

98. If only there had been a (*single*) city (*among those We warned*) that believed, it would have profited from its faith, (*but this had been so*) only with Jonah's people. When they believed We spared them the penalty of disgrace in the life of this world, and gave them comfort for a while.

(For the story of Jonah (Yûnus) see 37:139-148. Jonah was sent to the thriving city of Ninevah, near Mosul. If we calculate the date of his mission at around 800 BC, this would coincide with the dawn of the second Assyrian Empire. The Qur'anic story of Jonah is deployed as the archetype of a people that almost merited God's chastisement, but were saved.)

99. If it had been your Lord's will, all who are in the earth would have believed, altogether. Will you, then, force the people to become believers?

(If it had been Allah's Will not to grant the limited free will that he has granted to man, whereby he acquires his actions, His omnipotence could have made all mankind alike. All would have then had faith, but that faith would have reflected no merit on them. In the actual world as it is, man has been endowed with the capacity to forget, and to be reminded, and to purify his spiritual faculties so that his faith can receive Allah's direct grace, and become perfect. Hence faith becomes a moral and spiritual achievement, and to resist it becomes a sin. As a complementary proposition, people of faith must not grow angry if they have to contend against unfaith, neither must they succumb to the temptation of forcing faith, whether by physical compulsion, or through social pressure.)

100. No soul can have faith except by the will of Allah. He will place the filth (*of doubt*) upon those do not use their intelligence.

101. Say: "See all that is in the heavens and on earth. But neither signs nor warnings will benefit a people who do not believe.

102. Do they, then, wait for anything other than the fate of those who have gone before them? Say: "Then (*watch and*) wait. I shall be with you, (*watching and*) waiting.

103. Then We shall save Our messengers and those who believed. Thus, as is Our duty, We deliver the believers.

104. Say (*O Muhammad*): "O mankind! If you are in doubt concerning my religion then (*know that*) I do not worship those whom you worship instead of Allah, but I worship Allah who will cause you to die, and I have been commanded to be one of the believers.

105. And set your face towards religion, as a man of pure faith, and never in any case be of the disbelievers.

106. And do not call, other than Allah, on that which can neither help nor harm you, but if you do then, you will surely be of the evildoers.

107. If Allah afflicts you with a misfortune none can remove it but He, and if He desires any good for you none can keep back His favour. He favours whom He will. He is the Forgiving, the Merciful.

108. Say: "O mankind, the truth has come to you from your Lord. He that follows the right path follows it to the advantage of his soul, and he that goes astray does so against (*the interests of*) his soul. And I am not a guardian over you."

109. And (*O Muhammad*) follow that which is inspired in you, and be patient and steadfast until Allah gives judgement. And He is the best of judges.

SÛRAH XI

HÛD

Revealed at Makka

(This Sûrah takes it name from v,50, which begins the story of Hûd, one of the prophets sent to the ancient Arabians. The Sûrah also contains the stories of two other Arab prophets: Sâlih of the tribe of Thamoud, and Shu'ayb of the Midianites, which, with those of Noah and Moses, are quoted as part of the history of Divine Revelation, the truth of which is here vindicated, in a manner supplementary to the preceding Sûrah. Sûrah Hûd was revealed during the late period of Makka, with the exception of v.114f., which was revealed at Madîna the Radiant.)

In the name of Allah, the Compassionate, the Merciful

1. Alif. Lâm. Râ. (*This is*) a Scripture(book), the verses of which are perfected and then expounded. (*It comes*) from One who is All-Wise, All-Aware.

2. (*It teaches*) that you should worship none but Allah. I am to you a warner from Him and a bearer of glad tidings.

3. (*It invites you to*) seek forgiveness of your Lord and turn to Him in repentance. He will give you fair enjoyment until an appointed term, and will bestow His grace upon every one who is graceful. But if you turn away then I fear for you the retribution of a mighty Day.

4. To Allah you shall all return. He is Powerful over all things.

5. Now, they cover up their breasts to hide (*their thoughts*) from Him. But when they cover themselves with their garments He knows what they hide and what they reveal. He knows what is in the breasts.

6. There is not a beast in the earth but its sustenance depends on Allah. He knows its dwelling and its resting place. All is in a clear book.

7. He created the heavens and the earth in six Days - and His throne was upon the waters - that He might try you, which of you is best in conduct. When you *(O Muhammad)* say: "After death you shall indeed be raised to life," the unbelievers will then say: "This is nothing but plain magic."

(For the creation of the heavens and earth in six "days" see VII:54. All life, as the Qur'an also assures us, has been created out of water, while the Throne is the symbol of sovereignty.)

8. And if we delay the punishment until an appointed term, they ask; "Why is it delayed?" Assuredly, on the day when it comes to them, it cannot be averted from them, and that which they derided will surround them.

9. If We let man taste mercy from Us, and then deprive him of it, he is despairing, ungrateful.

10. But if We let him taste prosperity after some misfortune that had befallen him he says: "The evils have gone from me!" Behold, he becomes exultant, boastful.

11. Except those who are patient and do good deeds. They will have forgiveness and a great reward.

12. You may chance to *(feel the inclination)* to omit a part of that which is revealed to you and be distressed because they say: "Why has no treasure been sent to him? Why has no angel come with him?" You are *(there)* only to warn. Allah is the guardian of all things.

(Every prophet of God, when he encounters opposition and is accused of falsehood, may feel inclined, in his human weakness, to ask himself, "Supposing I omit this little point, will Allah's truth be accepted more readily?" Or he may think, "If only I had a little more money to organise my campaign, or something to attract their attention, like the company of an angel, how much more efficiently I could present my message!" But he is reminded that truth must be delivered as it is revealed, even though parts of it may be unpalatable, and that resources and other means are beside the point. He must use what he has been given, and leave the rest to the Lord.)

13. Or they say: "He has invented it! Say: "Then bring ten Sûrahs like it, invented. Call *(to your aid)* whomsoever you can, other than Allah, if what you say be true.

14. But if they *(your false gods)* do not answer your prayer, then know that it is revealed only in the knowledge of Allah; and that there is no god but Him. Will you then accept Islam?

15. Those that desire the life of this world with all its decoration, We shall reward their deeds in *(their life)* time, and they will not be diminished in this.

16. They are those for whom there is nothing in the Hereafter but the Fire. All that they contrive here is vain, and *(all)* that they do is fruitless.

17. Are they *(the worshippers of the world, to be counted equal)* with those who accept, from their Lord, a clear sign, recited by a witness from Him, and before this was the book of Moses, a guidance and a mercy? These believe in it, but for those of the factions that deny it, the Fire will be their promised place. Therefore do not doubt it. It is the Truth from your Lord, but most of mankind do not believe.

("A witness from Him; i. e. the Book which was given to the Blessed Prophet Muhammad, the Holy Qur'an which is compared to the original revelation given to Moses. Islam makes no difference between one true and genuine message and another, nor between one messenger and another. All of them called to Allah, the only God, the Creator of all. The clear witness that the Prophet held was the Qur'an itself, in which the divine books of the past were mentioned. As such, and in other ways, it is a miracle, clearly perceptible as such to those whose hearts are pure, and is a firm basis for faith.)

18. Who does more wrong than the man who invents a falsehood about Allah? Such will be brought before their Lord, and the witnesses will say: "These are they who lied about their Lord. Surely the curse of Allah is upon those who do wrong.

19. Who hinder *(men)* from the way of Allah and seek to make it crooked, and who deny the life to come.

20. Such are not able to frustrate Him on earth, nor have they protectors besides Allah. For them the torment will be doubled. They were unable to hear, neither did they see.

21. Such are they who have lost their souls, and all that they invented has vanished away from them.

22. Without a doubt, in the Hereafter they will be the greatest losers.

23. But those who believe, and do righteous deeds, and have humbled themselves before their Lord, they are the owners of the Garden, where they shall abide forever.

24. These two kinds *(of men)* may be compared to the blind and deaf, and those who can see and hear well. Are they equal in likeness? Will you not then take heed?

25. And We sent Noah to his people, *(and he said)*: "I am a plain warner to you.

26. That you serve none but Allah. Assuredly I do fear for you the penalty of a painful day.

27. But the chiefs of his people who disbelieved, said: "We regard you as a mortal like ourselves, nor can we see any among your followers but the lowliest of us, without reflection. We see in you no merit above us; rather, we think you are liars.

(The unbelievers were driven by three motives to reject truth: (1) jealousy, for they said, "We see in you no merit above us ; (2) contempt of the weak and lowly, who are often better morally and spiritually: "the lowliest of us ; (3) arrogance and imagined self-sufficiency. The claim made for Allah's Message was to attack all three of these attitudes, and their response was to abuse it impatiently, and call it a lie.)

28. He said: "Think, O my people, if I rely upon a clear sign from my Lord and He sent mercy unto me from His own presence, though it be hidden from you, shall we compel you to accept it while you dislike it?

(Noah's response is characteristic in its combined meekness and firmness. He gently informs his people that he has received a message from the Lord; then he tells them that it is a message of mercy, even though the fact be hidden from them; and finally he tells them that there can be no compulsion in religion, and all he will do is to warn.)

29. "O my people! I do not ask of you any money for this. My reward comes only from Allah. I will not drive away those who believe, they shall surely meet their Lord. But I can see that you are an ignorant people.

(The fourth point in Noah's address responds to the claim that he is a liar, implying that he was serving some selfish end of his own: on the contrary, he says, he seeks no reward from them, and will bear any insults they direct at him. But, fifthly, if they insult the poor and needy who come to him in faith, and think that he will send them away in order to attract the great ones of the land, he tells them that they are mistaken. In fact (sixthly), he has no hesitation in telling them that they themselves are the ignorant ones, and not the poor who come to seek the Lord's truth.)

30. "O my people, who would help me against (the penalty of) Allah if I drove them away? Will you not then take heed?

31. I do not say to you that I possess Allah's treasures nor do I know what is hidden. I do not claim to be an angel, nor do I say to those whom your eyes despise, that Allah will not grant them good. Allah knows best what is in their hearts. I should then (if I did drive them away) be among the wrongdoers."

32. They said: "O Noah, you have already argued with us and argued too much. Now bring upon us that (punishment) which you promise us, if what you say be true."

33. He said: "Only Allah will bring it on you if He wills, and then you will not be able to frustrate Him."

34. My counsel, if I wished to counsel you, cannot profit you if Allah has decided that you should go astray. He is your Lord, and to Him you shall be returned.

35. (O Muhammad!) Do they (the pagans of Makka) say, "He himself has forged this (Qur'an)?" Say to them: "If I have forged this myself, then upon me falls my sin; but I am free of the crimes that you commit."

(This verse is positioned here to show that the story of Noah is also a parable for the time and ministry of the Blessed Prophet Muhammad. It is related to verse 49, where the story is wound up.)

36. And it was revealed to Noah: "None of your people will believe in you except those who have already believed. Do not be distressed because of what they do.

37. Build the Ark under Our eyes and (in accordance) with Our revelation. And do not plead with Me for those who have been unjust. They shall be drowned."

38. And he was building the Ark, and whenever the chiefs of his people passed by him, they jeered at him. He said: "If you mock us, we shall mock you even as you mock.

39. And you shall know to whom will come a punishment that will disgrace him, and upon whom a lasting punishment will fall.

40. Until, when Our will was done and water welled out from the oven, We said to Noah: "Take into the Ark a pair from every kind, and your family, except those against whom the word has already gone forth, and those who believe. But only a few believed with him.

(The "oven (*tannûr*) is believed to have been that of the Prophet Adam, and several explanations are advanced for it. Another interpretation of the text would yield "fountains of the earth rather than "oven . The point is that the water gushed up from underground as well as falling from the sky.)

41. And he said: "Embark in it! In the name of Allah is its course and its mooring. My Lord is Forgiving and Merciful.

42. So the ark floated with them on waves like mountains, and Noah cried out to his son who stood apart: "O my son! Ride with us, and do not be with the disbelievers!

43. He replied: "I shall seek refuge in a mountain, which will protect me from the water. Noah cried: "None shall be protected this day from Allah's judgement, except those to whom He has shown mercy. And the wave came between them, and he was among the drowned.

44. Then it was said: "O earth, swallow up your waters; O sky, withold *(your rain)*! The floods were made to subside, and the commandment was fulfilled. The Ark came to rest upon al-Jûdî, and it was said: "A far removal for the wrongdoing people!

(According to Muslim tradition, the Deluge was local, confined to a region of the northern Tigris basin, rather than engulfing the entire world. And the Ark rested upon Mount Jûdî, not Mount Ararat - for the great height of Ararat would render the Flood a geographical impossibility. Mount Jûdî is located near the frontiers of modern Turkey, Syria and Iraq.)

45. Noah called out to his Lord, saying: "Lord, my son was of my family. Your promise was surely true. You are the Most Just of judges.

(Thus did Noah, despite his grief for his son, address the Lord in terms which avoid all hint of blame, but rather bespeak an exquisite satisfaction with His will.)

قَالَ يَٰنُوحُ إِنَّهُۥ لَيۡسَ مِنۡ أَهۡلِكَۖ إِنَّهُۥ عَمَلٌ غَيۡرُ صَٰلِحٖۖ فَلَا تَسۡـَٔلۡنِ
مَا لَيۡسَ لَكَ بِهِۦ عِلۡمٌۖ إِنِّيٓ أَعِظُكَ أَن تَكُونَ مِنَ ٱلۡجَٰهِلِينَ ﴿٤٦﴾
قَالَ رَبِّ إِنِّيٓ أَعُوذُ بِكَ أَنۡ أَسۡـَٔلَكَ مَا لَيۡسَ لِي بِهِۦ عِلۡمٞۖ وَإِلَّا
تَغۡفِرۡ لِي وَتَرۡحَمۡنِيٓ أَكُن مِّنَ ٱلۡخَٰسِرِينَ ﴿٤٧﴾ قِيلَ يَٰنُوحُ
ٱهۡبِطۡ بِسَلَٰمٖ مِّنَّا وَبَرَكَٰتٍ عَلَيۡكَ وَعَلَىٰٓ أُمَمٖ مِّمَّن مَّعَكَۚ
وَأُمَمٞ سَنُمَتِّعُهُمۡ ثُمَّ يَمَسُّهُم مِّنَّا عَذَابٌ أَلِيمٞ ﴿٤٨﴾ تِلۡكَ
مِنۡ أَنۢبَآءِ ٱلۡغَيۡبِ نُوحِيهَآ إِلَيۡكَۖ مَا كُنتَ تَعۡلَمُهَآ أَنتَ وَلَا قَوۡمُكَ
مِن قَبۡلِ هَٰذَاۖ فَٱصۡبِرۡۖ إِنَّ ٱلۡعَٰقِبَةَ لِلۡمُتَّقِينَ ﴿٤٩﴾ وَإِلَىٰ عَادٍ
أَخَاهُمۡ هُودٗاۚ قَالَ يَٰقَوۡمِ ٱعۡبُدُواْ ٱللَّهَ مَا لَكُم مِّنۡ إِلَٰهٍ
غَيۡرُهُۥٓۖ إِنۡ أَنتُمۡ إِلَّا مُفۡتَرُونَ ﴿٥٠﴾ يَٰقَوۡمِ لَآ أَسۡـَٔلُكُمۡ عَلَيۡهِ
أَجۡرًاۖ إِنۡ أَجۡرِيَ إِلَّا عَلَى ٱلَّذِي فَطَرَنِيٓۚ أَفَلَا تَعۡقِلُونَ ﴿٥١﴾
وَيَٰقَوۡمِ ٱسۡتَغۡفِرُواْ رَبَّكُمۡ ثُمَّ تُوبُوٓاْ إِلَيۡهِ يُرۡسِلِ ٱلسَّمَآءَ
عَلَيۡكُم مِّدۡرَارٗا وَيَزِدۡكُمۡ قُوَّةً إِلَىٰ قُوَّتِكُمۡ وَلَا تَتَوَلَّوۡاْ
مُجۡرِمِينَ ﴿٥٢﴾ قَالُواْ يَٰهُودُ مَا جِئۡتَنَا بِبَيِّنَةٖ وَمَا نَحۡنُ
بِتَارِكِيٓ ءَالِهَتِنَا عَن قَوۡلِكَ وَمَا نَحۡنُ لَكَ بِمُؤۡمِنِينَ ﴿٥٣﴾

46. He replied: "O Noah! He was not of your family; he was of unrighteous conduct. So do not question Me about things of which you have no knowledge. I admonish you that you should not behave as an ignorant man."

(Noah's son did not believe in his father's message. While his brothers Shem, Ham and Japheth boarded the Ark together with the other believers, this son stayed aloof, despite the evidence of the rain, and did not mount. The closest, most authentic tie among people is religion, not family or race. Hence, as the Holy Qur'an says, "Believers are brothers", while a son and a father of different faiths are not so regarded. Thus it was that Noah's son had left his family.)

47. Noah said: "O my Lord! I seek refuge with You lest I ask you for that of which I have no knowledge. And unless You forgive me and have mercy on me, I shall indeed be lost."

48. It was said to him: "O Noah! Go down *(from the mountain)* with peace from Us and blessings upon you and upon some nations *(that will spring)* from those with you. *(There will be other)* nations unto whom We shall give enjoyment a long while and then a painful doom from Us will overtake them.

49. Such are some of the narratives of the Unseen which We have revealed unto you *(O Muhammad)*. Before this neither you nor your people knew them. So have patience. For the end is for those who are righteous.

(The message is that the pure of heart, who work for Allah and their fellow-men, may be ridiculed and persecuted, but they will be sustained by His mercy. The outcome is for God's loved ones. Next the Sûrah turns to the comparable tale of the prophet Hûd, upon him be peace, who was sent to the people of Aad in Arabia. The story has been mentioned before, at 7:65-72, where the intention was to draw a parallel between the Blessed Prophet's treatment at the hands of the Makkan idolaters, and the life of the earlier prophet. Here, however, another point is emphasised: the insolence of Aad's blind adherence to their false gods, even when a Messenger from God had been sent to them. Patience, however, will be rewarded, as it was in Noah's case, and the outcome is for the righteous.)

50. And to the (tribe of) Aad *(We sent)* their brother Hûd. He said: "O my people! Serve Allah. You have no god other than Him. You do nothing but invent *(your other gods)*.

51. O my people, I ask of you no reward for this *(message)*. My reward is due from none but Him who created me. Will you not then understand?

52. And, O my people, ask forgiveness of your Lord, and turn to Him *(in repentance)*. He will send you the skies pouring abundant rain, and add strength to your strength. So do not turn away, guilty!"

53. They said: "O Hûd, you have brought no clear proof, and we are not going to forsake our gods on your *(mere)* say-so, and we are not believers in you.

54. We say nothing but that *(perhaps)* one of our gods has possessed you with some evil. He said: "I call Allah to witness, and you *(too)* bear witness, that I have nothing to do with what you ascribe *(as supposed partners to Him)*,

55. Beside Him. So *(try to)* circumvent me, all of you, give me no respite.

56. I have put my trust in Allah, my Lord and your Lord. There is no beast but that He is grasping its forelock. My Lord is upon a Straight Path.

(That is, the standard of all virtue and righteousness is the Will of Allah, the universal Will that controls all things in goodness and justice.)

57. And if you turn away, I *(at least)* have conveyed to you *(the message)* with which I was sent. My Lord will make another people to succeed you, and you cannot harm Him in the least. For my Lord is Guardian over all things.

58. And when Our commandment came, We saved Hûd and those who believed with him, through a mercy from Us. We saved them from a severe penalty.

59. Such were the Aad. They denied the revelations of their Lord and flouted His messengers, and followed the command of stubborn tyrant.

60. And a curse was made to pursue them in this life, and on the Day of Judgement. Surely Aad denied their Lord. A far removal for Aad, the people of Hûd!

(The Sûrah now progresses to the story of the prophet Salih, which has been cited already at 7:73-9. While the sin of Aad was pride and obstinacy, the sin of Thamoud was oppression of the poor, as illustrated by the test-case of the She-Camel.)

61. And unto *(the tribe of)* Thamoud, *(We sent)* their brother Sâlih. He said: "Serve Allah, my people; you have no god other than Him. It is He who produced you from the earth and gave you dwellings upon it. Seek forgiveness of Him and turn to Him in repentance. Surely my Lord is *(always)* Nigh, Responsive.

62. They said: "O Sâlih! Until now you were one in whom we placed our hopes. Do you forbid us to worship *(gods)* which our fathers worshipped? Indeed we are in grave doubt about that to which you are calling us.

الجزء الثاني عشر

قَالَ يٰقَوْمِ أَرَءَيْتُمْ إِنْ كُنْتُ عَلٰى بَيِّنَةٍ مِّنْ رَّبِّيْ وَاٰتٰنِيْ
مِنْهُ رَحْمَةً فَمَنْ يَّنْصُرُنِيْ مِنَ اللّٰهِ إِنْ عَصَيْتُهُ فَمَا تَزِيْدُوْنَنِيْ
غَيْرَ تَخْسِيْرٍ ۞ وَيٰقَوْمِ هٰذِهٖ نَاقَةُ اللّٰهِ لَكُمْ اٰيَةً
فَذَرُوْهَا تَأْكُلْ فِيْ أَرْضِ اللّٰهِ وَلَا تَمَسُّوْهَا بِسُوْءٍ فَيَأْخُذَكُمْ
عَذَابٌ قَرِيْبٌ ۞ فَعَقَرُوْهَا فَقَالَ تَمَتَّعُوْا فِيْ دَارِكُمْ
ثَلٰثَةَ أَيَّامٍ ذٰلِكَ وَعْدٌ غَيْرُ مَكْذُوْبٍ ۞ فَلَمَّا جَاءَ
أَمْرُنَا نَجَّيْنَا صٰلِحًا وَّالَّذِيْنَ اٰمَنُوْا مَعَهٗ بِرَحْمَةٍ مِّنَّا
وَمِنْ خِزْيِ يَوْمِئِذٍ إِنَّ رَبَّكَ هُوَ الْقَوِيُّ الْعَزِيْزُ ۞ وَأَخَذَ
الَّذِيْنَ ظَلَمُوا الصَّيْحَةُ فَأَصْبَحُوْا فِيْ دِيَارِهِمْ جٰثِمِيْنَ
۞ كَأَنْ لَّمْ يَغْنَوْا فِيْهَا أَلَا إِنَّ ثَمُوْدَا۟ كَفَرُوْا رَبَّهُمْ أَلَا بُعْدًا
لِّثَمُوْدَ ۞ وَلَقَدْ جَاءَتْ رُسُلُنَا إِبْرٰهِيْمَ بِالْبُشْرٰى قَالُوْا
سَلٰمًا قَالَ سَلٰمٌ فَمَا لَبِثَ أَنْ جَاءَ بِعِجْلٍ حَنِيْذٍ ۞ فَلَمَّا
رَاٰ أَيْدِيَهُمْ لَا تَصِلُ إِلَيْهِ نَكِرَهُمْ وَأَوْجَسَ مِنْهُمْ خِيْفَةً
قَالُوْا لَا تَخَفْ إِنَّا أُرْسِلْنَا إِلٰى قَوْمِ لُوْطٍ ۞ وَامْرَأَتُهٗ قَائِمَةٌ
فَضَحِكَتْ فَبَشَّرْنٰهَا بِإِسْحٰقَ وَمِنْ وَّرَاءِ إِسْحٰقَ يَعْقُوْبَ ۞

٢٢٨

63. He said: "O my people! Do you not see, if I have a clear sign from my Lord and He has sent mercy upon me from Himself, who then can help me against Allah If I were to disobey Him? You would do nothing for me, except increase my loss!

64. O my people, this is the she-camel of Allah, to be a sign for you. Leave her to eat in Allah's earth and inflict no harm on her, lest a swift penalty seize you.

(Since the she-camel was a miracle created by Allah from a rock, as Sâlih's people demanded, the Prophet Sâlih warned and told them not to harm her at all, lest Allah's wrath descend upon them. Yet they paid no attention.)

65. But they hamstrung her. He *(Sâlih)* said: "Enjoy yourselves in your homes for three days *(more, then will be your ruin)*. This is a threat that will not prove false."

66. So when Our commandment came to pass, We saved Sâlih, and those who believed with him, by a mercy from Us, from the ignominy of that day. Your Lord is Strong, Mighty.

67. And the *(awful)* cry overtook the wrongdoers, and morning found them prostrate in their dwellings.

68. As if they had never dwelt there. Surely Thamoud disbelieved in their Lord. A far removal for Thamoud!

(According to the sequence of Sûrah 7, the next story should be that of Lot, which in fact commences at verse 77 below. It is introduced, however, by a brief episode in the life of his uncle Abraham. Abraham had by this time passed through the persecutions in the Mesopotamian valleys; having left behind him the ancestral idolatry of Ur of the Chaldees, had triumphed over the tyranny of Nimrod, and was now dwelling in Canaan. Thus prepared and sanctified, he was now ready to receive the Message that he was to be the progenitor of a great line of Prophets.)

69. And Our messengers came to Abraham with good news. They said: "Peace!" He answered "Peace!" and hastened to bring them a roasted calf.

70. But when he saw their hands not reaching towards it, he mistrusted them, and was afraid of them. But they said: "Do not fear. We are sent to the people of Lot."

71. And his wife, standing by, laughed when We gave her good tidings *(of the birth)* of Isaac, and after Isaac, of Jacob.

72. She said. "Alas for me! How shall I bear a child when I am old, and my husband is an old man? That is indeed a strange thing!"

(According to the commentators, the Prophet Abraham was 120 at this time, and Sarah was 90.)

73. They said: "Are you surprised at Allah's commandment? May the blessings and the mercy of Allah be upon you, O people of the house! He is indeed Glorious, Worthy of praise."

74. So when the fear departed from Abraham and the good tidings came to him, he pleaded with Us for the people of Lot.

75. For Abraham was indeed, mild, imploring and penitent.

76. O Abraham, turn away from this, (plead no more). Your Lord's command has surely come, and there is coming upon them a penalty which is not to be turned back.

77. When Our messengers came to Lot he was grieved on their account and felt himself powerless to protect them. He said: "This is a distressful day."

(The angels came as young handsome men. The Prophet Lût thought they were human and feared that his vicious people would act indecently towards them.)

78. And his people came rushing to him - and before then they used to commit abominations - He said: "O my people! Here are my daughters (among my people)! They are cleaner (more lawful) for you. Have fear of Allah and do not humiliate me by wronging my guests. Is there not among you one right-minded man?"

(The story present in some ancient sources, which asserts that Lot committed incest with his daughters, is a slur upon the prophetic office, and has no historical or theological foundation.)

79. They replied: "You know we have no need of your daughters. You know full well what we are seeking."

80. He said: "O would that I had strength against you, or had some strong support (among you)!"

81. (The messengers) said: "O Lot, we are messengers of your Lord. They shall not reach you. So travel with your people, without your wife, in a part of the night and let none of you turn around; (all) save your wife. That which smites them shall smite her (also). In the morning their hour will come. Is not the morning near?"

82. So when Our commandment came to pass, We overthrew (*that city*), and rained down on them brimstones as hard as baked clay, one after another.

83. Marked from your Lord (*for the destruction of the wicked*). And they are never far from the wrong-doers.

(Thus were the people of Lot destroyed for their sin, and their country turned to a pile of stones. Let all who commit like crimes take note.

Next we turn to the people of Midian. Midian is the archetype of a further type of evil: economic. Knowing not the One True God, they felt that they could do as they pleased with their wealth, and defraud others, and live in thoughtless luxury.)

84. And to Midian (*We sent*) their brother Shu‘ayb. He said: "O my people! Serve Allah. You have no other god but Him. Do not give short measure or weight. I see you in prosperity, but I fear for you the penalty of a day that will compass (*you*) all around.

85. And O my people! Give just measure and weight, nor withhold from the people the things that are their due. And do not commit evil in the land, causing corruption .

86. What Allah leaves with you is the best for you, if you are believers. And I am no guardian over you.

87. They said (*in sarcasm*): "O Shu‘ayb! Does your Prayer command you that we should leave that which our forefathers worshipped, or that we should cease doing what we like with our property? Truly, you are clement, right-minded!

88. (*Shu‘ayb*) said: "O my people! What do you think, if I stand upon a clear sign from my Lord, and He has sustained me with fair sustenance from Himself? (*how could I, then, be party to your evil and unlawful practices?*) I do not wish to oppose you and then to commit which I forbid you to do. I only wish to set things right so far as I am able. And my success (*in my task*) can only come from Allah. In Him do I trust, and unto Him do I turn (*repentant*).

89. And O my people! Let your disagreement with me not bring upon you the doom which overtook the peoples of Noah, Hûd and Sâlih. And the people of Lot are not far (in time) from you.

90. Ask forgiveness of your Lord and turn to him (in repentance). For my Lord is indeed Merciful, Loving.

91. They said: "O Shu'ayb; we do not understand much of what you say. In fact we see that you are powerless among us. Were it not for your family we would have stoned you, for you are not strong against us.

92. He said: "O my people! Is then my family of more consideration with you than Allah? And you put Him behind you, neglected! My Lord encompasses the things you do.

93. And, O my people! Do whatever you will; so shall I. You will soon know on whom will descend a penalty of ignomy, and who is a liar. And watch, for I, too, am watching with you.

94. And when Our commandment came to pass We delivered Shu'ayb and those who believed with him by a mercy from Us. And the (awful) Cry seized those who worked injustice, and the morning found them prostrate in their dwellings.

95. As if they had never dwelt there. A far removal for Midian, even as Thamoud was far removed!

(The people of Shu'ayb were destroyed by a disaster resembling that which encompassed Thamoud, evidently a deafening blast accompanied by volcanic explosions.

Before turning to general teachings, the narration now briefly recalls the story of Moses, which, as the classic emblem of the conflict between revelation and statist tyranny, is referred to several times in the Holy Qur'an. This time, the story is told in the context of the Sûrah's general theme: the danger of submitting to false leadership and blind tradition, and failure to recognise the signs of the Lord.)

96. And We sent Moses with Our revelations and a clear authority,

97. Unto Pharaoh and his nobles. But they followed the command of Pharaoh, and the command of Pharaoh was no right (guide).

98. *(For)* he shall go before his people on the Day of Resurrection and will lead them to the Fire. Evil is the place to which they are led.

99. And a curse is made to follow them in the world, and on the Day of Resurrection. Evil is the gift which shall be offered *(to them)*.

100. These are *(some)* of the stories of nations which We relate to you *(O Muhammad)*. Some are standing and others have been mown down.

101. We wronged them not; but they wronged themselves. The gods whom they plead beside Allah profited them nothing when the command of your Lord came. They added to them nothing but ruin.

102. Such is the seizing of your Lord when He seizes the communities while they are working iniquity. Assuredly, His seizing is painful, severe.

103. Surely in this is a sign for those who fear the penalty of the Hereafter. That is a day to which mankind shall be gathered together; that is a day to be witnessed.

104. We shall not delay it but for a term appointed.

105. When that day comes no soul will speak except by His leave. Among those *(gathered will be some)* wretched, *(some)* blest.

106. As for the wretched, they shall be in the Fire, wherein there shall be for them a moaning and a sighing.

107. Eternally therein, so long as the heavens and earth abide, unless your Lord ordains otherwise. For your Lord is Doer of what He wills.

(We are told by our blessed Prophet, upon whom be blessings and peace, that the day will come when the Lord shall rescue from the Fire everyone in whose heart there was so much as a mustard-seed's weight of faith. Monotheists, however much they may sin, shall not remain in the Hell for ever.)

108. And as for the blessed, they shall dwell eternally in the Garden as long as the heavens and the earth endure, unless your Lord ordains otherwise. A gift unfailing.

109. Have no doubt as to what they (*the idolaters*) worship. They worship nothing but what they fathers worshipped before *(them)*. We shall pay them back *(in full)* their portion *(of the penalty)* undiminished.

110. We certainly gave the Scripture to Moses, but differences arose about it. Had a decree not already gone forth from your Lord the case would have been judged between them. They are in grave doubt concerning it.

111. And, surely to all *(men)* your Lord will pay back in full *(the recompense)* of their deeds, for He is Knower of all that they do.

112. Therefore stand firm *(in the straight path)* as you are commanded, together with those who turn to Allah. And do not transgress. For He is Seer of all that they do.

(As the companions of the Prophet have told us, no verse made the Blessed Prophet more anxious than this. Once he said: "The Sûrah of Hûd has turned my hair grey . For this verse is the essence of religion. To recognise God demands that one follow His commandments, and walk His path. While for the Blessed Prophet, whose whole life was an act of sincere worship, this was not difficult, he is here commanded to stand firm "together with those who turn to Allah , namely, the believers. And not all such were firmly established on the path of light, purity and goodness. It was this anxiety which rendered his hair grey. Such was his concern for us. May the Lord bless him, and grant him peace!)

113. And do not incline towards those who work iniquity, or the Fire will touch you, and you will have no protecting friends other than Allah, and then you will not be helped.

114. And establish the Prayer at the two ends of the day and at the approaches of the night. Surely, good deeds will annul evil ones. This is a remembrance for the mindful.

(Prayer, as the Blessed Prophet taught his Companions, is like a river running by one's house. If one bathes in it five times a day, no dirt can remain.)

115. And have patience *(O Muhammad)*; Allah will not cause the reward of doers of good to be lost.

116. If only there had been among the generations before you, men possessing a remnant *(of sense)* to forbid people mischief in the earth! Only a few among them whom We delievered *(have done this)*. But the workers of iniquity pursued their luxurious pleasures, and thus were guilty.

117. Your Lord would not destroy cities without just cause, if their people were workers of righteousness.

118. If your Lord had so willed, He could have made mankind one nation, yet they do not cease to differ.

(Man's essential unity can be retrieved by a universal recognition that his Maker is One, and that He has sent reminders for our guidance. Then the purpose of his creation, to recognise Allah and seek the return to Him, would be completely fulfilled. This is one of the key messages of this Sûrah.)

119. Except those to whom your Lord has shown mercy. For this end He has created them. This word of your Lord shall be fulfilled: "I will fill Hell with jinns and men altogether."

120. And all the stories of the messengers that We relate to you are to make firm thereby your heart. And in them there comes to you the truth, as well as an admonition and a reminder to the believers.

121. Say to those who do not believe: "Do whatever you can, We shall do our part.

122. And wait if you will; we too are waiting."

123. To Allah belongs the Unseen of the heavens and the earth. To Him the whole affair shall be returned, so worship Him and put your trust in Him. Your Lord is not heedless of what you do.

SÛRAH XII
YÛSUF (JOSEPH)
Revealed at Makka

(This Sûrah differs from all the others in having only one subject, in this case, the life of the Prophet Joseph. It is said that it was revealed two years before the Hijra.)

In the name of Allah, the Compassionate, the Merciful

1. Alif. Lâm. Râ. These are the signs *(or "the verses")* of the Manifest Book.

2. We have sent it down as an Arabic Qur'an, in order that you may understand.

3. We recount to you the best of narratives in that We have inspired in you this Qur'an, although before this you *(too)* were among the heedless *(those who did not know them)*.

4. When Joseph said to his father: "O my father! I saw in a dream eleven stars, and the sun and the moon; I saw them prostrating themselves to me."

5. *(His father)* said: "My *(dear)* little son, say nothing of this dream to your brothers, lest they should plot against you. For Satan is an open enemy to man.

6. Thus your Lord will choose you and teach you the interpration of events, and will perfect His grace upon you and upon the family of Jacob as He perfected it to your forefathers Abraham and Isaac before you. Assuredly, your Lord is Knowing, Wise.

7. Surely in *(the tale of)* Joseph and his brothers there are signs for the seekers *(of truth)*.

(The Rabbis had told the pagan chiefs of Makka to question the Blessed Prophet, to discover whether he could say anything about which the Israelites had gone to Egypt. This Sûrah was revealed as a response to them.)

8. They said *(to each other)*: "Surely Joseph and his brother *(Benjamin)* are dearer to our father than ourselves, although we are a band. Truly, our father is much mistaken.

9. "Kill Joseph or cast him out in some *(other)* land, so that your father's attention should turn only to you, and thereafter you should again become righteous people.

10. One of them said: "Do not kill Joseph, but if you must act, cast him into the depth of the pit; some caravan will find him.

11. They said to their father: "Why do you not trust us with Joseph? Surely we are good friends to him!

12. Send him with us tomorrow that he may play and enjoy himself. We will take good care of him.

13. *(Jacob)* said: "It would much grieve me that you should take him with you, and I fear lest the wolf should devour him while you are inattentive of him .

14. They said: "If the wolf devour him while we are a band, then we should surely be lost!

15. And when they went with him *(Joseph)* and agreed to put him in the depth of the pit, We revealed to him: "You shall *(one day)* tell them of this deed of theirs when they will know you not.

16. At nightfall they returned weeping to their father.

17. They said: "O our father! We went racing and left Joseph with our goods and the wolf devoured him. But you will not believe us, though we tell the truth.

18. And they brought his shirt *(to Jacob)* with false blood on it. "No! he cried. "Your souls have tempted you to do something *(evil)*. *(For me)* comely patience *(is most fitting)*. Allah *(alone)* is He whose help can be sought *(to bear the misfortune of which you speak.*

(Joseph wore a garment of many colours. If the brothers could produce it bloodstained before their father, they thought he would be convinced that Joseph had been killed by a wild beast. But the stain was of "false blood , not the blood of Joseph, but the blood of a goat which the brothers had killed for this purpose. Their device was not quite convincing, because, as the commentators point out, the garment was intact, an unlikely thing if he had been savaged by a wolf.)

19. And there came a caravan, and they sent their water-drawer. He let down his pail *(into the pit).* He said: "Good luck! Here is a young man. And they hid him as a treasure, and Allah was aware of what they did.

20. And they sold him for a low price, a number of silver coins; and they attached no value to him.

21. The man who bought him in Egypt said to his wife: "Receive him honourably. Perhaps he may prove useful to us, or we may adopt him as a son. Thus we established in the land a home for Joseph and taught him to interpret events. Allah has power over all things, though most men do not understand.

22. And when Joseph reached his full manhood, We bestowed on him wisdom and knowledge. Thus do We reward those who do good.

23. Now, the woman in whose house he was *(his master's wife)* sought to seduce him; she bolted the doors and said: "Come! "Allah forbid! he replied. He *(your husband)* is my lord, and has treated me honourably. Assuredly, wrongdoers never prosper.

24. She assuredly desired him and he himself would have desired her, had he not seen the veritable sign of his Lord. Thus We warded off from him indecency and evil, for he was one of Our sincere *(and purified)* servants.

(The "sign refers to his intuitive knowledge of his Lord's omniscience.)

25. So they raced each other to the door, and she tore his shirt from the back, and they met her master near the door. She cried: "What shall be his punishment, who wishes evil to your family, save prison or a painful punishment?

26. Joseph said: "It was she who asked of me an evil act. And one of her household saw *(this)* and bore witness *(saying)*, "If his shirt is torn from the front she is speaking the truth, and he is a liar.

27. But if it is torn from behind then she is lying, and he speaks the truth .

(It is said that the witness was a small child, who had been present at the scene.)

28. So when he saw his shirt torn from behind *(her husband)* said: "This is of the guile of you women. Assuredly, your guile is great.

29. O Joseph, turn away from this; and you *(O woman)*, ask forgiveness for your sin, for you have done wrong.

30. And women in the city said: "The governor's wife has been asking of her boy an ill deed, he has smitted her with love. We see her in plain aberration.

31. When she heard of their malicious talk she invited them and prepared a banquet for them. She gave each of them a knife and said *(to Joseph)*: "Come out before them! When they saw him, they were amazed at him and cut their hands, exclaiming "Allah preserve us! This is not a human being. This is none but a gracious angel.

32. "This is the man she said, "on whose account you reproached me. I did seek to seduce him from his *(true)* self, but he did firmly save himself guiltless! And now, if he does not do my bidding he shall certainly be cast into prison and be of the company of the vilest.

33. He said: "O my Lord! Prison is more dear to me than that to which they invite me; and unless you turn their guile away from me I should feel inclined towards them and so become one of the ignorant.

34. So his Lord answered him and turned away from him their guile. He is the Hearing, the Knowing.

35. And it seemed good to the men after they had seen the signs *(of his innocence that it was best)* to imprison him for a time.

36. Now with him there came into the prison two young men. One of them said: "I dreamt that I was pressing grapes. The other said: "I dreamt that I was carrying upon my head loaves of bread of which the birds were eating. Tell us its interpretation, for we see that you are of the doers of good.

37. He said: "The food which you are given *(daily)* will not come to you before I shall have told the interpretation before it befalls you. This is a part of the *(knowledge)* that my Lord has taught me. I have abandoned the religion of people who do not believe in Allah and deny the Hereafter.

(Ancient Egyptian religion was steeped in polytheism, state-worship and idolatry. The Prophet, despite his situation, lost no opportunity to call men to the One True God. Here he does it simply, by appealing to his own experience. He had found that the One God had always aided him, however black the circumstance, and kept his hopes alive through his faith in Him.)

38. And I follow the religion of my fathers, Abraham, Isaac and Jacob; and it is not for us to associate anyone with Allah as a partner. This is the grace of Allah upon us and upon mankind, yet most people are not grateful.

39. O my two fellow-prisoners! Are many diverse lords better, or Allah, the One, the Almighty?

40. Those whom you worship other than Him are nothing but names which you and your fathers have named. Allah has revealed no authority for them. The judgement is for none but Allah. He has commanded that you worship none but Him: that is the right religion; but most men do not understand.

41. O my two fellow-prisoners! As for one of you he will pour out wine for his lord to drink, and as for the other he will be crucified, and birds will peck at his head. Thus is the case judged, concerning which you did inquire.

42. And (Joseph) said to the prisoner whom he knew would be freed: "Remember me in the presence of your lord! But Satan made him forget to mention him to his lord, and (Joseph) stayed in prison for several years (more).

43. And the king (of Egypt, one day) said: "I saw (in a dream) seven fat cows which seven lean ones devoured; and also seven green ears of corn and (seven) others dry. O my courtiers! Tell me the interpretation of my dream, if you understand the meanings of dreams .

44. They said: "A confusion of dreams; and we are not skilled in the interpretation of dreams.

45. Thereupon one of the two men who had been released *(from the prison)* and who, after a long time, remembered, said: "I will tell you the interpretation of it, send me *(to Joseph in prison).*

46. "O Joseph! *(he said)*: "O men of truth! Tell us *(the dream)* of seven fat cows which seven lean ones devoured; also of the seven green ears of corn and the other *(seven)* which were dry, that I may return to my people, so that they may know.

47. He said: "You shall sow, as usual, for seven years. Leave in the ear the corn you reap, except a little which you may eat.

48. Then will come after that seven years of severity, which will consume all but a little of that which you have stored for them.

49. Then will come after that a year in which the people will have abundant water and in which they will press *(wine and oil).*

50. So the king said: "Bring him to me. But when the messenger came to him, he *(Joseph)* said: "Go back to your master and ask him about the women who cut their hands. My master knows their guile.

51. He *(the king)* said *(to the women)*: "What happened when you asked an evil act of Joseph? They answered: "Allah forbid, we know no evil of him. The wife of the ruler said: "Now the truth has come to light. It was I who asked of him an evil act and he is indeed of those who are truthful .

52. *(Then Joseph said: I asked for)* this that he *(my lord)* may know I have never betrayed him in his absence and Allah will never guide the snare of the false.

57. And the reward of the Hereafter is the best for those who believe and are constant in righteousness.

(The Prophet Joseph was appointed as supreme authority over the internal affairs of Egypt, governing with the Pharoah's own authority. In the meantime, Potiphar, the erstwhile Minister of Finance, had died. The king married Joseph to his widow, Zulaykhâ. The Prophet Joseph took all necessary precautions for the drought, improving farming techniques, and establishing a system of stores for use in the difficult years ahead. During the years of drought, people from around the world came to Egypt to buy grain. Jacob, too, sent his sons - with the exception of Benjamin.)

58. Then came Joseph's brothers. They entered his presence and he recognized them, but they knew him not.

(The Prophet Joseph asked his brothers who they were. They said their father's name was Jacob the Prophet. They were once twelve brothers, but one had died in the desert, while another had stayed behind with their father.)

59. And when he had given them their provisions, he said: "Bring me the brother of yours from same father (but a different mother). Do you not see that I pay out full measure and I am the best of hosts?

60. But if you do not bring him to me you shall have no grain from me; nay, you shall not even come near me.

61. They said: "We will try to win him from his father, indeed we shall do it,

62. And (Joseph) told his servants to put their merchandise (with which they had bartered) into their saddle-bags, so that they should know it only when they returned to their people, in order that they might return.

63. So when they went back to their father they said: "O our father! No more measure of grain shall we get (unless we take our brother); so send our brother with us that we may obtain our measure, and we will indeed take every care of him.

53. I do not ever free my own self (of blame), the human (soul) is certainly prone to evil, unless my Lord bestows His mercy; indeed my Lord is Forgiving, Merciful.

54. So the king said: "Bring him before me so that I may attach him exclusively to myself. Therefore when he had spoken to him he said: "You shall hence forth dwell with us honoured and trusted.

(Feeling confident that Joseph's interpretation was a correct and an inspired one, the Pharoah then asked him for counsel.)

55. (Joseph) said: "Set me over the storehouses of the land, for I am a skilled custodian.

56. Thus We established Joseph in the land, to take possession of it where he pleased. We reach with Our mercy when We will, and We never cause to be lost the reward of those who do good.

بِسْمِ اللّٰه

قَالَ هَلْ اٰمَنُكُمْ عَلَيْهِ اِلَّا كَمَا اَمِنْتُكُمْ عَلٰى اَخِيهِ مِنْ قَبْلُ فَاللّٰهُ خَيْرٌ حٰفِظًا وَّهُوَ اَرْحَمُ الرّٰحِمِيْنَ ۞ وَلَمَّا فَتَحُوْا مَتَاعَهُمْ وَجَدُوْا بِضَاعَتَهُمْ رُدَّتْ اِلَيْهِمْ ۖ قَالُوْا يٰٓاَبَانَا مَا نَبْغِيْ ۖ هٰذِهٖ بِضَاعَتُنَا رُدَّتْ اِلَيْنَا ۖ وَنَمِيْرُ اَهْلَنَا وَنَحْفَظُ اَخَانَا وَنَزْدَادُ كَيْلَ بَعِيْرٍ ۖ ذٰلِكَ كَيْلٌ يَّسِيْرٌ ۞ قَالَ لَنْ اُرْسِلَهٗ مَعَكُمْ حَتّٰى تُؤْتُوْنِ مَوْثِقًا مِّنَ اللّٰهِ لَتَأْتُنَّنِيْ بِهٖٓ اِلَّآ اَنْ يُّحَاطَ بِكُمْ ۖ فَلَمَّآ اٰتَوْهُ مَوْثِقَهُمْ قَالَ اللّٰهُ عَلٰى مَا نَقُوْلُ وَكِيْلٌ ۞ وَقَالَ يٰبَنِيَّ لَا تَدْخُلُوْا مِنْۢ بَابٍ وَّاحِدٍ وَّادْخُلُوْا مِنْ اَبْوَابٍ مُّتَفَرِّقَةٍ ۖ وَمَآ اُغْنِيْ عَنْكُمْ مِّنَ اللّٰهِ مِنْ شَيْءٍ ۖ اِنِ الْحُكْمُ اِلَّا لِلّٰهِ ۖ عَلَيْهِ تَوَكَّلْتُ ۖ وَعَلَيْهِ فَلْيَتَوَكَّلِ الْمُتَوَكِّلُوْنَ ۞ وَلَمَّا دَخَلُوْا مِنْ حَيْثُ اَمَرَهُمْ اَبُوْهُمْ ۖ مَا كَانَ يُغْنِيْ عَنْهُمْ مِّنَ اللّٰهِ مِنْ شَيْءٍ اِلَّا حَاجَةً فِيْ نَفْسِ يَعْقُوْبَ قَضٰهَا ۖ وَاِنَّهٗ لَذُوْ عِلْمٍ لِّمَا عَلَّمْنٰهُ وَلٰكِنَّ اَكْثَرَ النَّاسِ لَا يَعْلَمُوْنَ ۞ وَلَمَّا دَخَلُوْا عَلٰى يُوْسُفَ اٰوٰى اِلَيْهِ اَخَاهُ ۖ قَالَ اِنِّيْ اَنَا اَخُوْكَ فَلَا تَبْتَئِسْ بِمَا كَانُوْا يَعْمَلُوْنَ ۞

٢٤٢

64. (*And Jacob said:*) "Am I to entrust him (Benjamin) to you as I once entrusted his brother (Joseph) to you before? But Allah is the best to take care (*of him*) and He is the Most Merciful of those who show mercy.

65. Then when they opened their baggage they found that their merchandise had been returned to them. They said, "O our father! what (*more*) can we ask? Here is our merchandise returned to us. So we shall (*again*) buy food for our family and we shall take care of our brother, also add a full camel's load (*of grain to our provisions*). This (*that we bring now*) is a small quantity.

66. He (*Jacob*) said: "I will never send him with you until you swear a solemn oath to me in Allah's name to bring him back to me, unless you are (*in some way*) prevented. And when they had brought their solemn oath, he said: "Allah shall be Guardian over all what we say.

67. (*Further*) he said: "O my sons! Do not, all of you, enter (*the capital of Egypt*) by one gate; enter by separate gates. I cannot help you as against Allah. The judgement is His alone, in Him have I put my trust and all who trust (*anyone*), should put his trust in Him alone.

(Had they entered all together, dressed in foreign garb, they might have attracted attention or suspicion.)

68. And when they entered in the manner their father had advised, it did not benefit them in the least against the decree of Allah. It was but a wish in Jacob's soul which he had thus fulfilled. For he was full of knowledge which We had given him, but most of mankind know it not.

69. And when they came into Joseph's presence, He received his (*full*) brother to stay with him. He said (*to him*): "I am your (*own*) brother; so do not grieve at what they did.

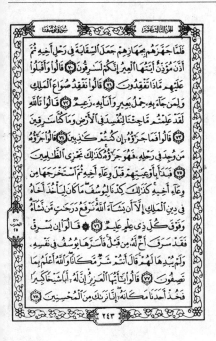

(According to the Egyptian law of the period, a thief was beaten and forced to pay double the value of what he stole. But in the Jewish law, as recorded in Exodus xxii:3, we read that if a thief has not the resources to make restitution, he is to be enslaved by the plaintiff.)

76. So he *(Joseph)* began *(the search)* with their baggage before the baggage of his brother; then he brought it out of his brother's baggage. Thus did We plan for Joseph. He could not have taken his brother according to the king's law, unless Allah so willed. Whomsoever We will, We raise in degrees. Over every man of knowledge is One who is All-Knowing.

77. They said: "If he has stolen, a brother of his has committed a theft before him. But Joseph kept his secret and did not reveal it to them. He said *(within himself)*: "You are in worse case; and Allah knows best the truth of what you are describing.

(When Joseph was a child, an aunt of his who loved him dearly wished him to stay with her, against the wishes of Jacob, who loved him also. The aunt devised a plan, by which she tied a belt inherited from Abraham around the waist of Joseph, and then announced to everyone that the belt was lost. After a short search, it was found on Joseph. According to the law, he was then obliged to stay with his aunt. Here we see the hatred of the ten brothers for Joseph and Benjamin again made manifest. Again they tell a lie, and they are ready to believe the worst of Benjamin. But they fear their father's wrath still more.)

78. They said: "O exalted sir, behold! He has a father, aged and venerable *(who will grieve for him);* so take one of us instead of him, for we see that you are one of the doers of good .

70. And when he had furnished them with provisions, he hid the drinking cup into his brother's saddlebag. Then shouted out a crier: "O camel-riders. You are surely thieves!

71. They said turning towards them: "What is it that you have lost?

72. They *(the royal servants)* said: "We do not find the king's cup; and *(their headman added)* he who brings it shall have a camel load, and I guarantee this.

73. They *(the brothers)* said: "By Allah, you well know that we did not come to make mischief in the land; and we are no thieves.

74. *(The Egyptians)* said: "What then shall be the penalty for it, if you are proved liars?

75. They said: "The penalty shall be the one in whose saddle-bag *(the cup)* is found. He is *(held as a bondsman for)* the penalty of it. Thus we punish the wrongdoers.

79. He said: "Allah forbid that we should seize any but him with whom our property was found, for then we should be unjust.

80. When they despaired of moving him *(Joseph),* they went aside to confer together. The eldest of them said: "Do you not know how your father did take a solemn oath from you in Allah's name and how before this you did fail concerning Joseph? Never will I leave this land until my father permits me or Allah judges for me. He is the Best of Judges.

81. Return to your father and say: "Father, your son has committed a theft. We testify only to that which we know but we cannot guard against the unseen .

82. "Enquire of the city where we have been, and the caravan in which we returned, and we are indeed telling the truth.

83. *(Jacob)* said: "No, but your souls have tempted you to *(such)* evil. So, a comely patience *(is most fitting for me).* Maybe Allah will bring them all *(back)* to me. For He is indeed Knowing, Wise.

(As Joseph's brothers had lied before, the Prophet Jacob was not disposed to believe their words now. He said: "You are liars; how can the great Minister of Egypt know our law, and punish my son this way?)

84. And he turned away from them and said "How great is my grief for Joseph! And his eyes turned white with the sorrow that he was suppressing.

85. They said: "By Allah! Will you not cease to think of Joseph until your health is ruined, and you die?

86. He said: "I only complain of my anguish and my sorrow unto Allah. And I know from Allah what you do not know.

87. "O my sons; go and seek news of Joseph and his brother, and never give up hope of Allah's Mercy. Truly, no-one despairs of Allah's Mercy except those who have no faith.

88. Then when they came back into Joseph's presence they said: "O exalted sir, we and our people are scourged with famine. *(Though)* we have brought but little capital, fill up for us the measure, and be charitable to us. Surely, Allah rewards the charitable.

89. He said: "Do you know what you did with Joseph and his brother in your ignorance?

90. They said: "Are you indeed Joseph? "I am Joseph , he said, "and this is my brother. Allah has indeed been gracious to us. Whosoever fears Allah and is patient, surely Allah does not waste the reward of those who do good.

91. "By Allah, they said; "Allah has indeed preferred you above us; and certainly we have been sinful .

92. He said: "No reproach, this day, shall be on you. Allah will forgive you. And He is the Most Merciful of those who show mercy.

(Joseph here shows true forgiveness, realising that his brothers are now contrite, and recognise that greatness is given by God alone. But an urgent task remains: the aged Jacob must be brought the good news.)

93. "Go with this shirt of mine and lay it on my father's face. He will recover his sight; then bring me your family, all together.

94. *(When the caravan departed (from Egypt)*, their father said (*in Canaan*): "Surely, I perceive Joseph's scent, though you think I am doting .

95. *(Those around him)* said: "By Allah truly you are *(still)* in your old aberration.

فَلَمَّآ أَن جَآءَ الْبَشِيرُ أَلْقَاهُ عَلَىٰ وَجْهِهِ فَارْتَدَّ بَصِيرًا قَالَ
أَلَمْ أَقُل لَّكُمْ إِنِّي أَعْلَمُ مِنَ اللَّهِ مَا لَا تَعْلَمُونَ ٩٦ قَالُوا
يَـٰٓأَبَانَا اسْتَغْفِرْ لَنَا ذُنُوبَنَآ إِنَّا كُنَّا خَـٰطِـِٔينَ ٩٧ قَالَ سَوْفَ
أَسْتَغْفِرُ لَكُمْ رَبِّيٓ إِنَّهُۥ هُوَ الْغَفُورُ الرَّحِيمُ ٩٨ فَلَمَّا
دَخَلُوا عَلَىٰ يُوسُفَ ءَاوَىٰٓ إِلَيْهِ أَبَوَيْهِ وَقَالَ ادْخُلُوا مِصْرَ
إِن شَآءَ اللَّهُ ءَامِنِينَ ٩٩ وَرَفَعَ أَبَوَيْهِ عَلَى الْعَرْشِ وَخَرُّوا
لَهُۥ سُجَّدًا وَقَالَ يَـٰٓأَبَتِ هَـٰذَا تَأْوِيلُ رُءْيَـٰيَ مِن قَبْلُ قَدْ جَعَلَهَا
رَبِّي حَقًّا وَقَدْ أَحْسَنَ بِىٓ إِذْ أَخْرَجَنِى مِنَ السِّجْنِ وَجَآءَ بِكُم
مِّنَ الْبَدْوِ مِنۢ بَعْدِ أَن نَّزَغَ الشَّيْطَـٰنُ بَيْنِى وَبَيْنَ إِخْوَتِىٓ إِنَّ
رَبِّي لَطِيفٌ لِّمَا يَشَآءُ إِنَّهُۥ هُوَ الْعَلِيمُ الْحَكِيمُ ١٠٠ رَبِّ
قَدْ ءَاتَيْتَنِى مِنَ الْمُلْكِ وَعَلَّمْتَنِى مِن تَأْوِيلِ الْأَحَادِيثِ فَاطِرَ
السَّمَـٰوَٰتِ وَالْأَرْضِ أَنتَ وَلِيِّى فِى الدُّنْيَا وَالْآخِرَةِ تَوَفَّنِى
مُسْلِمًا وَأَلْحِقْنِى بِالصَّـٰلِحِينَ ١٠١ ذَٰلِكَ مِنْ أَنۢبَآءِ الْغَيْبِ
نُوحِيهِ إِلَيْكَ وَمَا كُنتَ لَدَيْهِمْ إِذْ أَجْمَعُوٓا أَمْرَهُمْ وَهُمْ يَمْكُرُونَ
١٠٢ وَمَآ أَكْثَرُ النَّاسِ وَلَوْ حَرَصْتَ بِمُؤْمِنِينَ
١٠٣

٢٤٦

96. When the bearer of glad tidings came he laid it on his face, and once more his sight returned to him. He said: "Did I not tell you I know from Allah what you do not know?

97. They said: "O our father, ask forgiveness of our crimes for us; We have indeed been sinful.

98. He said: "I shall ask forgiveness for you of my Lord, for He is indeed Forgiving, Merciful.

99. When they entered the presence of Joseph, he provided accommodation for his parents with himself, and said: "Enter you (all) into Egypt, if Allah wills, in safety.

100. And he raised his parents (high) on the throne (of dignity) and they fell down in prostration (all) before him. He said: "O my father! This is the interpretation of my dream of long ago. My Lord has made it come true. He was indeed good to me when He took me out of the prison and brought you (all here) out of the desert (even) after Satan had sown enmity between me and my brothers. My Lord is tender unto whom He wills. He is Knowing, Wise.

101. "O my Lord! You have indeed bestowed on me some power and thought me something of the interpretation of the events (within dreams), O Creator of the heavens and the earth; You are my protector in this world and in the Hereafter, make me to die in submission to you (as a Muslim) and join me to the righteous.

(The famous prayer of Joseph is confirmation of his deep humility. In the moment of his greatest triumph, his rulership, spiritual gifts and family situation do not make him arrogant, for he knows that all is from the Lord.)

102. This is of the tidings of the unseen which We reveal to you (O Muhammad). You were not present with them when they fixed their plan and they were scheming (so that you could know all these).

103. And though you try so eagerly, the majority of men will not believe.

104. You demand of them no recompense for this, it is nothing but a reminder to the worlds.

105. Many are the signs in the heavens and the earth, yet they pass them by, and they turn away from them.

106. And most of them believe in Allah only if they can affirm other gods besides Him.

107. Do they feel secure that a pall of Allah's wrath will not come upon them, or that the Hour of Doom will not come upon them suddenly when they are unaware?

108. Say: "This is my path. On clear evidence, I call to Allah, I and all my followers. Glory be to Allah! And I am not among the idolaters.

109. We did not send before you *(any messengers)* except men whom We inspired, of the people of the townships. Have they not travelled through the earth and seen what was the end of those before them? But the home of the Hereafter is best for those who keep from evil. Will you not then use your intelligence?

110. And *(when at length)* the messengers despaired and thought that they were treated as liars, there reaches them Our help. And those whom We will, are delivered into safety. And never will Our punishment be averted from a people who are in sin.

111. In their stories there is a lesson for men of understanding. This *(Qur'an)* is no invented tale but a confirmation of the previous *(scripture)* and a detailed explanation of all things and a mercy to people who believe.

(The message and source of the Qur'an are not new. The story of Joseph: the "best of all stories", is known to the Christians and Jews, who have it in Genesis. The message of the Blessed Prophet of Islam is a joyful reminder of God's ancient truth, a source of mercy for all with faith.)

SÛRAH XIII

AR-RA'D (THE THUNDER)

Revealed at Makka

This Sûrah takes its name from a word occurring in verse 13. The subject is Divine guidance in relation to the law of consequences, it being explained here, as elsewhere in the Qur'an, that there is no partiality or aversion on the part of God, but that reward and punishment are the result of obeying or rejecting the laws which define and reflect our God-given nature. According to most authorities, it was revealed late in the Makka period, with the exception of two Madînan verses.

THE THUNDER

In the name of Allah, the Compassionate, the Merciful

1. Alif. Lâm. Mîm. Râ. These are the verses of the Book. That which is revealed to you from your Lord is the Truth; but most men do not believe.

2. Allah is He who raised the heavens without any pillars that you can see, then He established Himself upon the Throne *(of authority)*. He has subjected the sun and the moon *(to his Law)*; each one runs *(its course)* for an appointed term.

He regulates all affairs, explaining the signs, that you may believe with certainty in the meeting with your Lord.

3. And it is He who spread out the earth and placed upon it firm mountains and *(flowing)* rivers, and fruit of every kind in two pairs *(male and female)*. He draws the night *(as a veil)* over the day. Behold, assuredly in these things are signs for those who consider.

4. And on the earth are neighbouring tracts, vineyards and ploughed lands, and palms in pairs and palms single; watered with one water; and some of them We make more excellent than others to eat. Surely in these things there are signs for those who have sense.

5. And if you wonder, then wondrous is their saying *(that)*: "What! When we became dust, shall we then be raised to a new life again? Those are they who disbelieve in their Lord; on their necks are fetters; those shall be the owners of the Fire, dwelling there forever.

6. They demand from you to hasten on the evil rather than the good, even though, indeed, there have passed before them *(many)* exemplary punishments. But assuredly your Lord is forgiving to men for all their evil-doing, and your Lord is stern in retribution.

(The Makkan idolaters had said, "O Lord God! If this Qur'an is indeed a message from You, then rain down stones upon us at once, or punish us in some other way!")

7. And the unbelievers say: "Why has no sign been sent down to him from his Lord? But you are only a warner; and every people has a guide.

8. Allah knows what every female bears *(in her womb, and what takes shape in it)* and what the wombs decrease and increase *(of their time or number)*. Every single thing is before His sight, in *(due)* proportion.

(Only the Lord knows the destiny of children in the womb. But here the female is used only as an example, as an image of extreme secrecy. And it is God who

regulates all things in the world, just as He brings about the miracle of birth.)

9. He knows the unseen and the visible He is the Great, the Most High.

10. It is the same *(to Him)* whether any of you conceal his speech or declare it openly, whether he hides himself in the night or walks forth freely in the daytime.

11. For every *(such person)* there are guardian-angels before him and behind him. They guard him by the command of Allah. Allah never changes the condition of a people unless they themselves change what is in their souls. If Allah wills a misfortune, there can be no turning it back, nor will they find besides Him anyone to protect them.

(The angels mentioned, who are known as the *Mu'aqqibât*, both protect man and keep a record of his actions. Another point mentioned in the verse is that if people grow proud of their acquisitions, and turn away from the path of Allah, they will be deprived of those blessings and riches, all of which in fact were the generous gifts of the Creator to His creatures.)

12. It is He Who shows you the lightning *(to fill you)* with fear and with the hope *(of rain)*; and raises up the heavy clouds.

13. The thunder glorifies Him with His praise, as do the angels with awe of Him. He lets loose the thunderbolts and smites with them whomsoever He will, yet they *(dare to)* dispute about Allah, Who is Mighty in wrath.

14. To him *(alone)* is the call of truth. And those *(idols)* upon whom they call beside Allah, give them no answer, *(no more than)* if one stretched forth one's hands toward water *(asking)* that it may come unto his mouth, but it can never reach it. The prayers of the disbelievers can only go astray.

15. And unto Allah prostrate all who are in the heavens and the earth, willingly or unwillingly, and their shadows too, in the mornings and in the evenings.

16. Say: Who is the Lord of the heavens and the earth? Say: "(It is) Allah. Say: "Have you then taken, unto you, others beside Him to be your protectors, who can do neither good nor harm even to themselves? Say: "Are the blind and the seeing equal, or the shadows and the light? Or have the partners they have set up with Allah, created anything like His creation so that the creation *(which they made and His creation)* seemed similar to them? Say: "Allah is the creator of all things, and He is the One, the Almighty.

17. He sends down water from the sky, and the channels flow, each according to its capacity, then there happens a flood and a swelling foam comes to the surface. *(Likewise)* there arises a scum out of the metals which they melt in the fire for making ornaments and utensils. Thus Allah *(by such similitudes)* makes the truth distinct from falsehood. Then, as for the foam, it passes away as scum upon the banks, while what is beneficial for the people remains on earth. Thus Allah sets forth the similitudes.

(Several parables are contained in this verse. (1) Just as the ways in which God's rain are received and deployed by the earth, some flowing in channels, some used for irrigation, so too is His grace, which falls over the earth, but which is received and used very differently by different kinds of soul. (2) In the physical world, water is pure and beneficial. A froth may gather upon it, rendering it impure, but this can be carried away, just as God's grace and mercy purifies our spiritual lives, which can grow so polluted. (3) The froth may obscure the pure water, but it cannot last, being weak. Truth, also, cannot be obscured forever by falsehood, which is only its feeble perversion.)

18. Bliss is the reward of those who respond the call of their Lord. As for those who rejected His call, they would willingly give for their ransom all that is on earth, if they possessed it, and as much more besides *(in order to escape retribution)*. Those are the people who shall have a heavy reckoning: their abode shall be Hell: a wretched resting-place!

angels shall enter unto *(welcome)* them from every gate, *(saying):*

24. "Peace be upon you because you persevered. How excellent is the Final Abode!

25. But those who break the Covenant of Allah after accepting it and who cut asunder what Allah has commanded to be joined, and commit evil in the land, a curse shall be laid on them and they shall have an evil abode.

26. Allah enlarges provision for whom He will, and, *(strictly)* measures it; and they rejoice in the life of the world; whereas the life of the world is nothing but a brief enjoyment compared with the Hereafter.

27. Those who disbelieve say: "Why has a sign not been sent down upon him from his Lord? Say: "Allah leaves in error whom He will and guides to Him those who repent.

28. Those who believe, and whose hearts find tranquillity in the remembrance of Allah. Assuredly in the remembrance of Allah do hearts find tranquillity.

19. How can one who believes that *(this Book)*, which is sent down to you from your Lord, is the Truth, be like one who is blind *(to this fact)*? It is only men of inner wisdom who can take advice *(from this).*

20. Those who fulfil their Covenant with Allah, and do not break their pledge.

21. And those who join together what Allah has commanded to be joined, and fear their Lord and dread an evil reckoning.

22. And those who patiently persevere, seeking the countenance of their Lord, and establish the Prayer, and spend openly and secretly out of what We have bestowed upon them, and overcome evil with good. Theirs shall be the Final Abode.

23. Gardens of Paradise which they shall enter, together with the righteous from among their fathers, their wives and descendants, and the

٢٥٢

29. Those who believe and work righteous deeds; *(let every)* blessedness be for them, and a beautiful place of return.

30. Thus We have sent you to a nation before whom many others have passed away, that you may recite to them what we have revealed to you. Yet they disbelieve in the Compassionate God. Say: "He is my Lord, there is no god but He. In Him I have put my trust and to him I turn.

31. Had it been possible for a Qur'an to cause the mountains to move, or the earth to be torn asunder, or the dead to speak, *(this Qur'an would have done so).* Nay, but Allah's is the whole command. Did not the believers know that if Allah had willed, He would have guided men altogether? As for the disbelievers, disaster, because of what they do, will not cease to afflict them, or to dwell near their home until Allah's promise is fulfilled. Allah will not fail in His promise.

(When one day the Prophet Muhammad preached Islam to the people of Makka, one of them, called 'Abdullâh ibn Umayya, said: "These two hills of Makka trouble us greatly. Remove them from their places, and we will have sufficient room for cultivation

and farming. Let there be rivers flowing. Also let so-and-so among our forefathers come to life so that he may tell us whether you speak the truth. The above verse was then revealed.)

32. And assuredly *(many)* messengers *(of Allah)* were mocked before you: but though I bore long with the disbelievers, at last I seized them, and how *(awful)* was My punishment!

33. Is then He Who watches over every soul and *(all)* that it acquires *(like any other?)* And yet they ascribe partners to Allah. Say: "Name them! Or are you informing Him of what He does not know on earth, or is it *(just)* a show of words? Indeed, their foul devices seem fair to the disbelievers, and they are kept away from the *(right)* path. There can be no guide for those whom Allah leaves to go astray.

34. There shall be punishment for them in the life of the world, but more harder is the punishment of the life to come. There shall be none to protect them from Allah.

35. The likeness of the Garden which is promised the righteous *(is this):* Rivers flow beneath it, its fruits are eternal, and its shade *(also).* Such is the end of the righteous; but the end of the unbelievers is the Fire.

36. Those to whom We have given the Book rejoice in what has been sent down to you, while some factions deny a part of it. Say: "I have only been commanded to worship Allah and not to associate anyone with Him. To Him I call, and unto Him is my return.

37. Thus We have revealed it to be a judgement of authority in Arabic. And if you follow their desires after the knowledge that has come to you, you shall then have no protector against Allah, and no defender.

38. We have sent messengers before you, and appointed for them wives and children, yet none of them could bring a sign *(a miracle)* except by the leave of Allah. For every age is a book *(revealed).*

39. Allah blots out or confirms whatever He will, and with Him is the Mother of the Book.

(The archetypal Source of Revelation is in His presence. But He may, to suit changing spiritual needs, amend His law as time goes. He is the Omnipotent.)

40. Whether We let you witness a part of the *(punishment)* We promised them, or cause you to die *(before it is fulfilled),* your mission *(O Muhammad)* is only to give the message. It is for Us to do the reckoning.

41. Do they not see how We have come to land reducing it of its outlying borders? If Allah decrees a thing there is none to reverse it. Swift is He at the reckoning.

42. Those who were before them also plotted, but all plotting is *(in the hand)* of Allah. He knows the acquisitions of every soul. The disbelievers shall soon know for whom is the Final Abode.

43. The disbelievers say: "You are not a messenger of *(Allah)*. Say: "Allah, and those who have knowledge of the Book, are sufficient witnesses between me and you.

(Those who have knowledge of revelation generally will recognise Allah's revelation in the Holy Qur'an, and will be unable to prove that it contains a non-divine message. An alternative reading of the text would yield a slightly different translation: "And from Him is all knowledge of the Book.)

SÛRAH XIV

IBRAHIM (ABRAHAM)

Revealed at Makka

This Sûrah, which derives its name from Abraham's prayer in verses 35-41, at the time when he was establishing his son Ishmael, the ancestor of the Arabs, in the "uncultivable valley of Makka, deals, apart from this, with the same subject as the other Makkan Sûrahs revealed during the last three years before the Hijra. Verses 28-30, however, were revealed at Madîna.

ABRAHAM

In the name of Allah, the Compassionate, the Merciful.

1. Alif. Lâm. Râ. *(This is)* a Scripture which We have sent down to you *(O Muhammad)* so that you may lead men from darkness to the light by the leave of their Lord; to the path of the Mighty, the Praiseworthy.

2. Allah, unto Whom belongs whatever is in the heavens and on earth. But woe to the disbelievers from an awful penalty.

3. Those who love the life of the world more than the Hereafter, and hinder *(men)* from the path of Allah and seek to make it crooked: they have strayed far in error.

4. And We never sent a messenger except with the language of his people in order that he might make *(the message)* clear for them. But Allah leaves in error whom He will and guides whom He pleases. He is the Mighty, the Wise.

5. We assuredly sent Moses with Our revelations, *(saying)*: "Bring your people forth from darkness into the light, and remind them of the days of Allah. Surely in this there are signs for every steadfast, thankful man.

(The Days of Allah are the great days of a nation's history, when God's favour upon them is at its apogee.)

6. And *(remind them)* how Moses said unto his people: "Remember Allah's favour unto you, when He delivered you from Pharaoh's people who were oppressing you with dreadful torment, slaughtering your sons and sparing your women. That was a grievous trial from your Lord.

(The reference back to Israel and Moses serves a double purpose: as an appeal to the People of the Scripture, and as a reminder to the Quraish of the favour now conferred on them by the coming of a greater Prophet than Moses.

7. And when your Lord proclaimed: "If you are thankful I will add more *(favours)* unto you. But if you show ingratitude my punishment is terrible indeed.

8. And Moses said: "If you and all on earth show ingratitude, Allah is assuredly Independant, Worthy of praise.

9. Has there not come to you the story of those who were before you, the people of Noah, Aad, and Thamoud, and of those who came after them? None knows them but Allah. Their messengers came unto them with clear signs, but they thrust their hands into their mouths and said: "We deny the mission on which you have been sent. We strongly doubt the faith to which you invite us.

10. Their messengers said: "Is there any doubt about Allah, the Creator of the heavens and the earth? He calls you that He may forgive you your sins and respite you till an appointed time. They said: "You are but mortals like us! You wish to turn us away from what our fathers used to worship. So bring some clear authority!

قَالَتْ لَهُمْ رُسُلُهُمْ إِنْ نَحْنُ إِلَّا بَشَرٌ مِّثْلُكُمْ وَلَٰكِنَّ اللّٰهَ
يَمُنُّ عَلَىٰ مَنْ يَشَاءُ مِنْ عِبَادِهِ ۖ وَمَا كَانَ لَنَا أَنْ نَّأْتِيَكُمْ
بِسُلْطَانٍ إِلَّا بِإِذْنِ اللّٰهِ ۚ وَعَلَى اللّٰهِ فَلْيَتَوَكَّلِ الْمُؤْمِنُونَ ۝
وَمَا لَنَا أَلَّا نَتَوَكَّلَ عَلَى اللّٰهِ وَقَدْ هَدَانَا سُبُلَنَا ۚ
وَلَنَصْبِرَنَّ عَلَىٰ مَا آذَيْتُمُونَا ۚ وَعَلَى اللّٰهِ فَلْيَتَوَكَّلِ الْمُتَوَكِّلُونَ ۝
وَقَالَ الَّذِينَ كَفَرُوا لِرُسُلِهِمْ لَنُخْرِجَنَّكُمْ مِّنْ
أَرْضِنَا أَوْ لَتَعُودُنَّ فِي مِلَّتِنَا ۖ فَأَوْحَىٰ إِلَيْهِمْ رَبُّهُمْ لَنُهْلِكَنَّ
الظَّالِمِينَ ۝ وَلَنُسْكِنَنَّكُمُ الْأَرْضَ مِنْ بَعْدِهِمْ ۚ
ذَٰلِكَ لِمَنْ خَافَ مَقَامِي وَخَافَ وَعِيدِ ۝ وَاسْتَفْتَحُوا
وَخَابَ كُلُّ جَبَّارٍ عَنِيدٍ ۝ مِنْ وَرَائِهِ جَهَنَّمُ وَيُسْقَىٰ
مِنْ مَّاءٍ صَدِيدٍ ۝ يَتَجَرَّعُهُ وَلَا يَكَادُ يُسِيغُهُ
وَيَأْتِيهِ الْمَوْتُ مِنْ كُلِّ مَكَانٍ وَمَا هُوَ بِمَيِّتٍ ۖ وَمِنْ
وَرَائِهِ عَذَابٌ غَلِيظٌ ۝ مَّثَلُ الَّذِينَ كَفَرُوا بِرَبِّهِمْ ۖ
أَعْمَالُهُمْ كَرَمَادٍ اشْتَدَّتْ بِهِ الرِّيحُ فِي يَوْمٍ عَاصِفٍ ۖ لَّا يَقْدِرُونَ
مِمَّا كَسَبُوا عَلَىٰ شَيْءٍ ۚ ذَٰلِكَ هُوَ الضَّلَالُ الْبَعِيدُ ۝

11. Their messenger said unto them: "We are indeed only mortals like yourselves, but Allah gives grace unto whom He will of His servants. It is not for us to bring you a proof unless it be by the permission of Allah. In Allah let believers put their trust.

12. Why should we not put our trust in Allah, when He has guided us to our paths? We shall certainly endure all the hurt that you may cause us. In Allah let all the trusters put their trust.

13. And the disbelievers said to their messengers: "Be sure that we shall drive you out of our land unless you return to our religion. Then their Lord inspired them, (saying): "Assuredly We shall destroy the wrongdoers.

14. And assuredly We shall let you dwell in the land after them. This is for him who fears My majesty, and fears My threat.

15. And they sought help (from their Lord), and every obstinate tyrant was frustrated.

16. Hell is before him, and he is given to drink a festering water.

17. He will sip but can hardly swallow it, and death will come from every side, yet he cannot die. A dreadful torment is his.

18. The likeness of those who disbelieve in their Lord is this: their work are as ashes on which the wind blows hard on a stormy day; they have no power over what they acquired. That is the far misguidance!

(The works of the unspiritual are in themselves light and insubstantial, like ashes: they are the useless rubbish that remains out of the faculties and opportunities which they have misused by burning them up. The ashes are blown here and there: the ungodly have no compass, direction or purpose that can stand. The wind, too, which blows on them, is no ordinary wind, nor the day on which they seek to enjoy the fruits of their labours an ordinary day: a furious gale is blowing, for such is the divine Wrath. They have neither inner peace nor outer gain.)

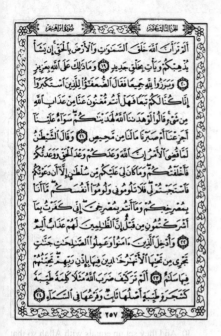

19. Do you not see that Allah has created the heavens and the earth with truth? If He will, He can remove you and bring *(into being)* a new creation.

20. That is no difficult thing for Him.

21. They all shall appear before Allah. Then those who were weak *(in the world)* will say to those who were arrogant: "We were your followers, can you now do anything to save us from the torment of Allah? They will reply: "Had Allah guided us, we would have guided you. It is all the same whether we rage or patiently endure. We have no place of refuge.

22. And when the matter has been decided, Satan will say: "It was Allah who gave you a promise of truth; I too promised, but I failed in my promise to you. I had no power over you except to call you, but you listened to me. So do not blame me, but blame yourselves. I cannot help you, nor can you help me. I disbelieved in your making me

a partner with Allah before this. The wrongdoers shall have a painful chastisement.

23. But those who have faith and do good works shall be admitted to gardens where running streams flow. They shall abide there for ever by their Lord's permission. Their greeting shall be: "Peace *(be upon you)*!

("Peace is a greeting, and also the expression of a wish, that one's companion may be free of every difficulty and illness. Among believers, it is both a greeting and a prayer.)

24. Do you not see how Allah likened a good word to a good tree whose root is firm and its branches are in heaven?

(The "good word is here interpreted as the Divine Word, the Divine Message, the True Religion. It may also be interpreted in a more general sense as a word of truth, a word of goodness or kindness, which follows from a true appreciation of religion. The "evil word is opposite to this: false religion, blasphemy, false speech, or preaching or teaching unkindness and wrongdoing.)

25. It yields its fruit at all times by the leave of its Lord. Thus does Allah set parables for men, in order that they may take heed.

(The goodly tree is known for: (1) its beauty: it gives pleasure to all who see it; (2) its stability: it remains firm and unshaken in storms, because its roots are firmly fixed in the earth; (3) its wide compass: its branches reach high, and it catches all the sunshine from heaven; (4) its abundant fruit, which it yields at all times. Thus, also, is the Good Word, in all its significations.)

26. But an evil word is like an evil tree, torn out of the earth, and with no stability.

27. Allah confirms those who believe with the Word of Steadfastness in the present life and in the Hereafter. Allah leads the wrongdoers astray. Allah does what He will.

28. Have you not seen those who gave the grace of Allah in exchange for unthankfulness, and caused their people to dwell in the Abode of Ruin?

29. Hell, wherein they shall burn. An evil abode!

30. And they set up equals with Allah so that they should lead men astray from His path. Say: "Enjoy (*life while you may*). For surely your journey's end will be the Fire.

31. Tell my servants who have believed that they shall establish the Prayer and spend in charity of that which We have given them, secretly and openly, before the coming of a Day when there shall be neither bargaining nor friendship.

32. It is Allah who has created the heavens and the earth, and sends down from the sky rain and with it He brings forth fruits to be your sustenance. And He makes the ships to be of service unto you that they may run upon the sea at His command, and has made of service unto you the rivers.

33. And makes the sun and the moon, both constant in their courses, to be of service unto you; and has made of service unto you the night and the day.

34. And He gives you of all that you ask Him; and if you reckon the favours of Allah, you can never count them. Surely man is a wrong-doer, ungrateful!

(After this invocation of God's blessings upon man, the text turns to the Prayer of Abraham, which here serves to illustrate the four preceding verses. It falls into four divisions: (1) verses 35-6 are spoken by the Patriarch on his own behalf ("My Lord!"); (2) verses 37-8 are spoken on behalf of his progeny ("Our Lord!"), but with special reference to the elder branch, the children of Ishmael; (3) verses 39-40 are again a personal appeal, but both branches of his family, namely the sons of Ishmael and Isaac, are expressly mentioned; (4) verses 41 is a prayer for himself, his parents and all believers in the One True God, typifying Islam's claim that in the universality of Islam all nations are to be blessed. Jerusalem, for the Mosaic Law and the Gospel of Jesus, was the centre and symbol for the Jews, altough of course God's truth is universal;Makka, the centre of the Arabs, was to throw off its tribal character and become universal in spite of the Makkans themselves.)

35. And when Abraham said: "My Lord! Make this land secure, and turn me and my sons away from serving idols!

36. My Lord! They have misguided many of the people. But whosoever follows me belongs to me, while whosoever rebels against me, surely You are Forgiving, Merciful.

37. Our Lord! I have settled some of my offspring in a barren valley near Your sacred house, in order, Our Lord, that they may establish the Prayer. So put in the hearts of some men kindness towards them, and provide them with fruits, so that they may give thanks.

(The Makkan valley is enclosed by hills on all sides. Precisely because of its natural isolation, it is fitted to be a centre of prayer and praise.)

38. Our Lord! You know all that we hide and all that we reveal. Nothing in the earth or in heaven is hidden from Allah.

(In Abraham's prophetic mind was the secret and open enmity or contempt which the Children of Israel were to have for the Children of Ishmael (the Arabs). He prays to Allah that they may be united in Islam, as indeed they were, except for a small remnant.)

39. Praise be to Allah, Who has given me in my old age, Ishmael and Isaac. My Lord is indeed the Hearer of prayer.

40. My Lord! Make me, and my descendants, steadfast in prayer. Our Lord! And accept this supplication!

41. O our Lord! Forgive me, and my parents, and the believers on the day when the Reckoning will be established!

42. Do not think that Allah is unaware of what the wicked do. He only gives them respite till a day when eyes will stare (in terror).

بِسْمِ اللَّهِ الرَّحْمَنِ الرَّحِيم

مُهْطِعِينَ مُقْنِعِي رُءُوسِهِمْ لَا يَرْتَدُّ إِلَيْهِمْ طَرْفُهُمْ وَأَفْئِدَتُهُمْ هَوَاءٌ ۞ وَأَنْذِرِ النَّاسَ يَوْمَ يَأْتِيهِمُ الْعَذَابُ فَيَقُولُ الَّذِينَ ظَلَمُوا رَبَّنَا أَخِّرْنَا إِلَى أَجَلٍ قَرِيبٍ نُجِبْ دَعْوَتَكَ وَنَتَّبِعِ الرُّسُلَ أَوَلَمْ تَكُونُوا أَقْسَمْتُمْ مِنْ قَبْلُ مَا لَكُمْ مِنْ زَوَالٍ ۞ وَسَكَنْتُمْ فِي مَسَاكِنِ الَّذِينَ ظَلَمُوا أَنْفُسَهُمْ وَتَبَيَّنَ لَكُمْ كَيْفَ فَعَلْنَا بِهِمْ وَضَرَبْنَا لَكُمُ الْأَمْثَالَ ۞ وَقَدْ مَكَرُوا مَكْرَهُمْ وَعِنْدَ اللَّهِ مَكْرُهُمْ وَإِنْ كَانَ مَكْرُهُمْ لِتَزُولَ مِنْهُ الْجِبَالُ ۞ فَلَا تَحْسَبَنَّ اللَّهَ مُخْلِفَ وَعْدِهِ رُسُلَهُ إِنَّ اللَّهَ عَزِيزٌ ذُو انْتِقَامٍ ۞ يَوْمَ تُبَدَّلُ الْأَرْضُ غَيْرَ الْأَرْضِ وَالسَّمَوَاتُ وَبَرَزُوا لِلَّهِ الْوَاحِدِ الْقَهَّارِ ۞ وَتَرَى الْمُجْرِمِينَ يَوْمَئِذٍ مُقَرَّنِينَ فِي الْأَصْفَادِ ۞ سَرَابِيلُهُمْ مِنْ قَطِرَانٍ وَتَغْشَى وُجُوهَهُمُ النَّارُ ۞ لِيَجْزِيَ اللَّهُ كُلَّ نَفْسٍ مَا كَسَبَتْ إِنَّ اللَّهَ سَرِيعُ الْحِسَابِ ۞ هَذَا بَلَاغٌ لِلنَّاسِ وَلِيُنْذَرُوا بِهِ وَلِيَعْلَمُوا أَنَّمَا هُوَ إِلَهٌ وَاحِدٌ وَلِيَذَّكَّرَ أُولُو الْأَلْبَابِ ۞

٢٦٠

43. As they come hurrying on in fear, their heads uplifted, their glances never returned to themselves, and their hearts as air.

44. So warn mankind of a day when the Chastisement will come upon them; then will the wrong-doers say: "Our Lord! Reprieve us for a little while, we will obey Your call and will follow the messengers! *(But a voice will say to them)*: "Did you not swear before, that there would be no end for you?

45. And you lived in the dwelling-places of those who wronged their own souls, and it became clear to you how We had dealt with them, and had given you many a parable about them.

46. Assuredly, they plotted their plot, and their plot is with Allah, though their plot was such as to shake the mountains.

47. Never think that Allah will fail in His promise to His messengers. Surely Allah is Mighty, Able to Requite.

(Here the Lord proclaims that just as He never failed in His promise to the prophets of old, He will never fail the Blessed Prophet Muhammad, and the Muslims. For He is Mighty, Able to Requite.)

48. On the day when the earth is changed into other than the earth, and the heavens *(into new heavens)*; and they *(mankind)* will come forth before Allah, the One, the Almighty.

49. And you will see the sinners that day, bound together in chains.

50. Their garments of liquid pitch, and their faces covered with fire.

51. That Allah may repay each soul what it has acquired. Allah is indeed Swift at Reckoning.

52. This is a message for mankind. Let them take warning from it, and let them know that He is only one God. And let men of understanding take heed!

SÛRAH XV

AL-HIJR

(THE ROCKY TRACT)

Revealed at Makka

(al-Hijr is the name of the area where the people of Thamoud dwelt. This Sûrah belongs to the middle group of Makkan Sûrahs.)

In the name of Allah, the Compassionate, the Merciful.

1. Alif. Lâm. Râ. These are the verses of the Book, and of a manifest Qur'an.

2. (*The day will surely come when*) the disbelievers will wish that they had been Muslims.

3. Leave them to eat and to take their entertainment, and to be beguiled by hope; for they will come to know.

4. Never have We destroyed a township but there was a known decree for it.

(Every nation has a lifetime which is known unto God; their faculty of choice gives them the chance to mould their will according to their Divinely-revealed spiritual natures. During that term, they are given much respite, but when it is justly concluded, neither the righteous nor the ungodly can hasten or delay the final end.)

5. No nation can outstrip its term, nor can they put it back.

6. They say: "O you, to whom the Reminder is sent down, you are surely possessed.

(Before Islam, poets were believed to be inspired by spirits known as jinns. The book the Prophet Muhammad brought seemed to them to be explicable in the same terms. They assumed that the Prophet, since he brought writings which far exceeded the best literary and poetic productions of their time, must have been possessed. They could not understand that he might have sincere, disinterested motives, and could have received a Revelation from the Lord.)

7. Why do you not bring down the angels unto us if you are of the truthful?

8. We do not send down the angels only with the truth. Then they will not be respited.

(If Angels appeared, there would be no moral and intellectual effort required in faith, and hence the purpose of the respite granted the Quraish would have been defeated.)

9. We have, without doubt, sent down the Reminder, and We preserve it.

(This promise has been realised in history. For fourteen hundred years the Book has been with us, yet not one word of its text has been deleted, added or mutilated.)

10. We sent forth messengers before you, to the older nations.

11. But never came a messenger to them but they did mock him.

12. Even so We cause it to enter into the hearts of the sinners.

13. They do not believe in it, despite the example of the men who have gone before.

14. Even if We opened for them a gate in Heaven through which they ascend,

15. They would still say: "Our eyes have been dazzled; nay, we have been bewitched!

16. And assuredly We have set in heavens mansions of stars, and We have beautified it for beholders.

(In the countless millions of stars in the universe which we see, we marvel at the beautiful order of the galaxies and star clusters, such as the Magellanic Clouds, the Orion Nebula and the Crab Nebula. The more man looks into the cosmos, the more astonishing and exquisite it becomes.)

17. And We guarded them from every accursed devil.

(The devil's sway is only over the animal soul. The Cosmos itself, despite the claims of some non-Muslim religions, is inherently good and beautiful, not "fallen". Any Satanic force which attempts to disrupt the cosmos itself is shot down, and the meteors visible on earth are emblematic of this.)

18. Except him who listens by stealth; and he is pursued by a manifest flame.

19. And the earth, We have spread it out, and set upon it immovable mountains, and caused to grow on it all kinds of things in due balance.

20. And We have provided therein livelihoods for you, and for those whom you do not provide for.

21. And there is not a thing but its (sources and) treasures are with Us. But We only send down each thing in an appropriate measure.

(No less astonishing than the heavens is the earth in which we live. Its endlessly complex network of forces and relationships is determined precisely to enable man, despite his fragility, and numerous wants, to live and thrive upon it.)

22. We let loose fertilizing winds, and bring water from the sky for you to drink; and it is not you who are the guardians of its stores.

(The wind performs the task of fecundating flowers and shrubs, by bringing the male pollen to the female ovary. Winds, too, determine the distribution of the clouds, with their stores of water-vapour, and set up atmospheric currents which result in the condensation and descent of rain, which gives life to the earth. Such is the miraculous garden into which man has been set.)

23. We ordain life and death. And We are the Inheritors.

24. We know those who have gone before you and those who lag behind.

(Either: (1) those who are foremost and deficient in faith, or (2) those who lived in the past, and those nations who are yet to appear.)

25. Assuredly it is your Lord Who will gather them together. For He is Wise, Knowing.

(Having spoken of the universe, and the earth, the divine narrative now turns to the recalcitrant pivot of creation: man himself.)

26. We created man of a clay of moulded mud.

27. And the jinn did We create aforetime of flaming fire.

28. And (remember) when your Lord said to the angels: "I am creating man of a clay of moulded mud.

29. When I have shaped him and breathed My spirit into him, kneel down and prostrate yourselves before him!

30. So all the angels prostrated themselves, all together,

31. Except Iblîs. He refused to be among the prostraters.

32. Allah said: "O Iblîs! What ails you, that you are not among the prostraters?

33. (Iblîs) said: "I am not one to prostrate myself to man whom you have created of a clay of moulded mud.

34. (Allah) said: "Then get you hence from here, for you are (rejected and) accursed.

35. And the curse shall be upon you until the Day of Judgment.

36. (Iblîs) said: "O my Lord! Grant me a respite until the day they (mankind) shall be resurrected.

37. (Allah) said: "You are among the ones that are respited,

38. Until the day of the Time Appointed.

39. (Iblîs) said: "I swear that because You have cast me astray, I shall adorn the path of error for them in the earth, and shall mislead them, every one,

40. Except Your perfectly devoted servants.

41. (Allah) said: "This is the right course incumbent upon Me.

42. For over My servants no authority shall you have, except those that follow you, being perverse.

43. And assuredly, Hell is the promised abode for them all.

44. It has seven gates; and for each gates there is an appointed portion.

45. But the righteous shall dwell amongst gardens and fountains.

46. (And it is said unto them): "Enter you here in peace and security!

47. And We shall remove from their hearts any lurking sense of injury. (They will be) brothers facing each other on thrones (of dignity).

(All past rancour, jealousy or sense of injury shall dissolve there, to be replaced by true brotherhood. For disharmony between men is caused by ignorance of God, and in the Garden, no such ignorance can remain.)

48. No fatigue shall touch them there, neither shall they ever be expelled.

49. Tell My servants that I am the Forgiving, the Merciful.

50. And that My penalty is the painful penalty.

(As He is the Absolute, His range of attributes is inconceivably vast. Just as His mercy to those who come near Him is tremendous, so is His penalty to those who turn their backs on His light of immeasurable severity.

Four illustrations of the gulf between Good and Evil are now given: (1) an incident from the life of Abraham; (2) an episode of his nephew Lot; (3) the Dwellers of the Wood; (4) the Dwellers of the Rocky Tract. As usual, the recital of God's grace comes first.)

51. And tell them of the guests of Abraham.

52. When they entered his presence and said, "Peace *(be upon you)*, Abraham said: "We feel afraid of you.

53. They said: "Be not afraid. We come to you with good news of a son endowed with wisdom.

54. He said: "Do you bring me such news in my old age? What news can this be?

55. They said: "We give you good news in truth. Do not be of those who despair.

56. He said: "Who could despair of Allah's mercy, save those who are astray?

57. He said: "And what then is your business, O messengers?

58. They said: "We have been sent to a people who sin,

59. Except the house of Lot; We shall deliver them all;

60. Excepting his wife. We have decreed that she should be among those who stay behind.

61. So when the messengers came unto the family of Lot,

62. He said: "You are a people unknown *(to me)*.

63. "Nay, they replied, "We have brought you that concerning which they have been doubting.

64. We have come to you with the truth, and assuredly we tell the truth.

65. So travel with your household in a portion of the night. Walk in their rear and let none of you turn round, but go where you are commanded.

66. And We decreed for him this commandment, that the root of them *(who did wrong)* was to be cut at early morn.

67. The inhabitants of the city came in *(mad)* joy at the news *(of the young men).*

68. Lot said *(to his people)*: "These *(young men)* are my guests. Do not disgrace me!

69. "Have fear of Allah, and do not degrade me!

70. They said: "Did we not forbid you *(to speak)* for any one?

(Or: "to entertain anyone?")

71. He said: "These are my daughters, *(the young girls of the city for you to marry)*, if you must act *(so)*.

72. Assuredly, by your life *(O Muhammad)*, they wandered blindly in their wild intoxication.

73. Then the Cry overtook them at sunrise.

74. And We turned *(the cities)* upside down, and rained down upon them stones of baked clay.

(See note to Sûrah 7:84 above.)

75. Surely in this there are signs for those who read the signs.

76. And *(the remains of)* those *(cities)* are upon a high-road, still uneffaced.

77. Surely in this there is a sign for believers.

(Now we turn to the Midianites. The Arabic word by which they are here described is *al-Ayka*, which has the sense of a thicket, or forest. For more on them, and their prophet Shu'ayb, upon whom be peace, see 26:176-191.)

78. And the Dwellers of the Wood were also evildoers.

79. So We took vengeance on them. They both *(the cities of the Plain and the Dwellers of the Wood)* are on a high road, plain to see.

80. The people of the Rocky Tract also denied the messengers.

(The "Rocky Tract" can be identified with the region of Mount Hijr, some 150 miles north of Madîna the Radiant. This was the land of Thamoud.)

81. We sent them Our signs, but they persisted in turning away from them.

82. And they used to hew out dwellings from the hills, feeling secure.

83. But the Cry overtook them at the morning hour,

84. And all that they used to acquire availed them not.

(Now comes the close of the Sûrah, where the discourse returns to the mission of our own Prophet.)

85. We have not created the heavens and the earth, and all that is between them, save with the Truth. And the Hour *(of Reckoning)* is surely coming. So overlook *(O Muhammad)* *(their faults)* with gracious forgiveness.

86. Surely your Lord is the Creator, the Knower!

87. And We have bestowed upon you the seven Oft-repeated *(Verses of the Fâtiha)*, and the Glorious Qur'an.

88. Do not regard *(with desire)* the good things We have bestowed on some of them, nor grieve on their account. But lower your wing *(in gentleness)* to the believers.

89. And say *(to those who reject you)*: "I am indeed a manifest warner.

90. Such as We send down for those who make division *(of the scripture into arbitrary parts)*,

91. And who have broken the Qur'an into fragments *(as they please).*

(Namely, those who believe in part of it, and reject the rest. Or, those who regard it as poetry or magic. Or, those Makkan pagans who took clay tablets of the Qur'an which had thus far been revealed, and gave it to people coming on the Makka pilgrimage, hoping thereby that they would slander God's messenger.)

92. Therefore, by the Lord, We shall surely question them altogether.

93. About what they used to do.

94. So proclaim openly what you are commanded, and turn away from the idolaters.

95. For We are sufficient unto you against the mockers.

96. *(Even)* against those who adopt with Allah another god; but soon will they come to know.

97. We do indeed know how your heart is distressed at what they say.

98. But glorify your Lord with His praise, and be of those who prostrate.

99. And worship your Lord until what is certain comes to you *(the Judgement, or death).*

SÛRAH XVI

AL-NAHL (THE BEE)

Revealed at Makka

(This takes its name from verse 68, where the activities of bees are mentioned as an example of duty and of usefulness. With the exception of verse 110, this Sûrah was revealed for the most part in the final Makkan period.)

In the name of Allah, the Compassionate, the Merciful

1. The Commandment of Allah comes to pass, so do not seek to hasten it. Glory be to Him,

and Exalted, above all that they associate *(with Him, in their polytheism).*

2. He sends down the Angels with the Spirit of His command unto whomsoever He will among His servants *(saying):* "Warn mankind that there is no god save Me, so fear Me.

3. He has created the heavens and the earth with Truth. Exalted is He, high above what they associate *(with Him).*

4. He has created man from a drop of fluid, and lo! he becomes an open disputer.

5. And the animals, He created them; which provide you with warm *(clothing),* and *(sundry)* benefits; and of them do you eat.

6. And there is beauty in them for you, when you bring them home to rest and when you bring them out to pasture.

7. And they bear your heavy loads to lands that you could not reach except with great trouble to yourselves. Surely your Lord is Kind, Merciful.

8. And *(He has created)* horses, mules and donkeys for you to ride and for ornament; and He creates that which you do not know.

(In mentioning means of transport, the text cannot confine itself to pack-animals alone, but specifies that God will bring into being things which man, at the time of the revelation, did not know.)

9. And unto Allah is the direction of the way, but some roads go not straight. If Allah had willed, He could have guided every one of you.

(Physical journeys are emblematic of the metaphysical Journey to the Homeland. There is a straight road, which is found by those who follow the guides, and can read the signposts pointing to the Destination in the scenery around them. And there are erratic, roundabout routes, for those that stray with little knowledge but in the end are compassed by God's mercy. The purpose of creation is the return of the creatures to the Creator, that His perfection may not only exist, but be known. Hence the size of the distance to be covered, and hence the difficulty, and moral and intellectual demands, of the journey.)

10. It is He Who sends down from the sky, water of which you drink; and brings forth the trees on which you feed your cattle.

11. And thereby He brings up for you corn, olives, date-palms, grapes and every kind of fruit. Surely in this there is a sign for a people who think.

12. And Hè subjected to you the night and the day, and the sun and the moon. And the stars are *(also)* in subjection *(to serve you)* by His command. Surely in this there are signs for a people who use their intelligence.

13. And whatsoever He has created for you in the earth in varying colours *(and qualities)*: Assuredly in this there is a sign for a people who take heed.

14. It is He who subjected to you the sea, so that you may eat of its fresh meat, and bring up from it ornaments which you wear. And you may see the ships cleaving through it. *(All this He has created)* so that you may seek His bounty and render thanks to Him.

15. And He has set up on the earth firm hills, lest it shake with you, and rivers, and roads, that you may guide yourselves,

(The mountains piled up on the earth's crust have a stabilising effect, and hinder the underlying plate from rapid movement.)

16. And landmarks *(too),* and by the star *(men)* guide themselves.

17. Is, then, He who creates like one who does not? Will you not take heed?

18. And if you would count the favours of Allah you will never be able to number them. Allah is Forgiving, Merciful.

19. Allah has knowledge of all that you hide and all that you reveal.

20. And those *(idols)* which they *(the pagans)* call upon apart from Allah, create nothing, and are themselves created.

21. *(They are things)* dead, not alive; nor do they know when they will be raised up.

22. Your God is one God. Those that do not believe in the life to come, their hearts refuse *(to know),* for they are arrogant.

23. Assuredly, Allah knows what they hide and what they reveal. Surely He does not love the arrogant.

24. When they are asked: "What has your Lord revealed? They say "Legends of the ancients!

25. That they may bear their burdens in full on the Day of Resurrection, and also some of the burdens of those that they lead astray without any knowledge. Alas, how grievous are the burdens they will bear!

26. Those before them did also plot *(against Allah's Way).* But Allah struck at the foundations of their building, and the roof fell down upon them from above, and the chastisement came upon them from where they did not perceive.

27. Then on the Day of Resurrection He will degrade them, saying: "Where are My partners, for whose sake you opposed *(My guidance)?* Those who have been given knowledge will say: "Disgrace and evil shall this day, *(fall)* upon the disbelievers.

28. Those whom the angels cause to die while they are wronging themselves will make full submission *(claiming):* "We did nothing evil . "Indeed *(the angels will reply),* "Allah knows all that you used to do.

29. So enter the gates of Hell, there to dwell forever. Woeful indeed will be the lodging of the arrogant.

30. But when those who were righteous are asked, "What has your Lord revealed? they will reply: "Goodness! Good is the reward of those that do good works in this world, but better is the reward of the life to come. And excellent indeed, is the home of the righteous.

31. Gardens of Paradise which they shall enter, rivers shall flow beneath them, wherein they shall have all that they desire. Thus Allah will reward the righteous.

32. *(Namely,)* those whom the angels cause to die while they are good *(and pure),* saying *(to them):* "Peace be upon you, enter the Garden because of *(the good)* which you did *(in the world).*

33. Are the unbelievers waiting for anything other than the descent of the angels, for the fulfillment of your Lord's judgement? Those who went before them also waited. Allah did not wrong them, but they used to wrong themselves.

34. But the evil results of what they did overtook them, and that which they used to mock surrounded them.

35. Those guilty of polytheism say: "If Allah had so willed, we would not have worshipped anything apart from Him, neither we nor our fathers, nor would we have forbidden anything other than with His *(sanction)*. So did those who went before them. But what is the mission of the messengers, other than to convey clearly?

36. And assuredly We have raised in every nation a messenger, proclaiming: "Serve Allah, and avoid false gods! Amongst them were some whom Allah guided and others justly destined to go astray. So travel in the land, and see the nature of the consequence for the deniers!

37. Even if you *(O Muhammad)* desire their right guidance, still, Allah assuredly will not guide those whom He leads astray. There shall be none to help them.

38. And they solemly swear by Allah that Allah will never raise the dead to life. Nay, but it is a promise binding upon Him in truth, but most of mankind do not realise it.

39. *(They must be raised up)* in order that He may manifest to them that in which they differ, and so that the disbelievers may know that they were liars.

40. The only word We say to a thing when We decree it, is that We say to it "Be , and it is.

(Allah's "word is itself the act. His promise is itself the Truth. There is no interposition of time or condition between His will and its consequences, for He is the Ultimate Reality. He is independant of proximate or material causes, for He Himself creates them and establishes their Laws as He pleases.)

41. And those that emigrated in the cause of Allah after they were wronged, We shall surely give them goodly lodging in the world, but truly the reward of the life to come will be greater if they only knew.

42. *(They are)* those who persevere in patience, and put their trust in their Lord.

43. The messengers We sent before you (*O Muhammad*), were not other than men to whom We gave revelation. Ask the people of the Remembrance if you do not know.

(If the pagan Arabs were unclear about the meaning of prophecy, let them ask the Jews, who had also received God's message, through Moses, whether Moses was a man, an angel or a god. "The people of the Remembrance may also denote any men of wisdom who were qualified to have an opinion on such matters.)

44. *(We sent them)* with clear signs and writings; and We have revealed to you (*O Muhammad*) the Remembrance *(the Qur'an)* that you may explain to mankind what was sent to them, that they may give thought.

45. Do those who devise evil *(plots)* feel secure that Allah will not cause the earth to swallow them, or that the chastisement will not come on them from whence they are not aware?

46. Or that He will not seize them in their going to and fro, and they will not be able to frustrate Him?

47. Or that He will not seize them with a gradual wasting? Surely your Lord is Clement, Merciful.

48. Have they not observed all things that Allah has created, how their shadows incline to the right and to the left, making prostration unto Allah in all humility?

49. To Allah is prostrated everthing that is in the heavens and every creature crawling on the earth, and the angels *(also)*, and they are not proud.

50. They all revere their Lord, High above them, and they do all that they are commanded.

51. Allah has said: "Do not take two gods. For He is but One God. So fear Me *(and Me alone).*

52. To him belongs all that is in the heavens and earth, and religion is His forever. Do you fear any other than Allah?

53. And whatsoever blessing you have, it is from Allah; then when misfortune reaches you, unto Him you cry for help.

54. Yet when He removes the distress from you, behold! some of you set up other gods beside Him.

55. *(As if)* to show ingratitude for the favours We have bestowed on them. Enjoy your entertainment, then, for you shall know the truth.

56. And they even appoint a share of what We have provided them to what they do not know. By Allah, you will surely be asked concerning what you used to invent.

(Before Islam some of the pagan Arabs used to divide their harvest or cattle, saying: "This are Allah's share, and this the share of our gods. Then they used to give what they called "Allah's share to the poor, the needy and their guests. They spent the other share in rituals performed in front of their idols.)

57. And they assign daughters to Allah. Be He glorified. and unto themselves *(sons)* that they desire *(to have)*.

58. When if one of them receives tidings of the birth of a female his face darkens and he is filled with inward grief.

59. With shame does he hide himself from his people, because of the bad news he has had, *(asking himself):* "Shall he keep it in contempt, or bury it beneath the dust? Assuredly, evil is their judgement!

(In many cultures, the birth of a female is regarded as a misfortune, an attitude which Islam condemns, as the above passage shows. It was even the practice in pagan Arabia to bury alive female babies.)

60. To those who do not believe in the Hereafter applies the similitude of evil: and to Allah applies the highest similitude, for He is the Mighty, the Wise.

61. If Allah were to punish men for their wrongdoing He would not leave on the earth a single living creature; but He reprieves them to an appointed term, and when their term comes they cannot put it back by a single hour, nor put it forward.

62. And they assign unto Allah that which they hate *(for themselves)* and their tongues expound the lie that the better portion is theirs. Assuredly theirs will be the fire, and they will be abandoned *(to it).*

63. By Allah! We have sent messengers before you to other nations. But Satan made their *(foul)* deeds seem fair to them. He is also their patron today. But theirs shall be a painful punishment.

64. We have sent down the Book to you only that you may explain to them those things in which they differ, and that it should be a guide and a mercy to a people who believe.

65. Allah sends down water from the sky with which He gives life to the earth after its death. Surely in this there is a sign for those who give ear.

66. And in the cattle *(too)* you have a lesson. We give you to drink of that which is in their bellies, between bowels and blood, pure milk, palatable for those who drink.

67. And of the fruits of the date-palm and grapes from which you derive strong drink and *(also)* good nourishment. Surely in this there is a sign for a people who use their intelligence.

(There are various wholesome and non-alcoholic drinks which can be produced from dates and grapes. But if the word "*sakar* is to be taken in the sense of fermented wine, it refers to the time before intoxicants were prohibited. This a Makkan Sûrah and the prohibition came in Madîna.)

68. And your Lord inspired the bee, saying: "Build your homes in the mountains and in the trees, and the *(hives)* which men shall make.

69. Then feed on every kind of fruit, and follow the paths of your Lord made smooth *(for you)*. There comes forth out of their bellies a fluid of many hues, wherein is healing for mankind. Indeed in this there is a sign for a people who give thought.

(The bee assimilates the juice of various kinds of flowers and fruit-blossoms, and forms within its body the honey which it stores in cells of wax. The types of blossom it frequents influence the colour of the honey. Honey is used in many medical traditions as a remedy for various ailments; as a rich source of nourishment it also helps to protect the body against disease.)

70. Allah created you; then He shall cause you to die; and some of you will be kept back unto the vilest state of *(old)* age, when all that they once knew they shall know no more. Allah is Knowing, Powerful.

(After directing our attention to the remarkable transformations in life and nature, by which the divine knowledge and power work out His Compassionate plans for His creatures, we are reminded that man is at best a feeble creature, but for God's grace. We now pass on to the differences in the gifts which men themselves enjoy, distinguishing them into so many categories. How much greater is the difference between the created things and the Creator!)

71. Allah has favoured some of you above others in provision, but those who have been thus favoured do not give away their provisions to those whom their right hand possesses, so as to be equal in this respect. Would they deny Allah's grace?

72. Allah has given wives from among yourselves, and has given you, through your wives, sons, daughters and grandchildren, and has provided you with good things. Is it then in falsehood that they believe, and in the grace of Allah that they disbelieve?

73. And they worship, beside Allah, those which do not have anything to provide them with from the heavens and the earth, nor do they (*whom they worship*) have any power (*to do so*).

74. Invent no similitudes for Allah. Allah knows, and you know not.

75. Allah cites a similitude: (*on the one hand*) a slave who has no power of anything, and (*on the other hand*) one whom We, from Ourselves, have provided with a fair provision from which he spends openly and secretly. Are they (*at all*) equal? Praise be to Allah; but most men do not know.

(This parable is of two men, one of whom is a powerless slave, and another a free man who is gifted in every way, and is most generous in sharing his substantial wealth. The first is like the imaginary gods which men set up: whether powers of nature, which have no independant existence but are manifestations of the Divine attributes, or deified heroes or men, who can do nothing of their own authority but are subject to God's will and power. The second describes in a faint way the position of Allah, the Self-Subsistent, to Whom belongs all dominion.)

76. And Allah cites (*another*) similitude: two men, one of them dumb, having no power over anything, and he is a burden upon his master: wherever he directs him he brings no good. Is he equal with one who commands justice and is on a straight path?

(In the second parable, one man is dumb, he can explain nothing, and he can certainly do nothing; he is

only a wearisome burden. Such are the idols (literal and metaphorical). The other man is in a position to command, and he commands what is just and righteous; not only his commands but his actions also are on the path of righteousness. Such are the qualities of Allah.)

77. And unto Allah belongs the unseen of the heavens and the earth. And the matter of the Hour (*of Doom*) is (*as short, and as imminent*) as a twinkling of the eye, or even quicker. For Allah has power over all things.

78. And it is He Who brought you forth from the wombs of your mothers when you knew nothing, and He gave you hearing and sight and hearts, that perhaps you may give thanks.

79. Do they not look at the birds made subservient (*to God's Laws*) in the sky's air? Nothing holds them up but Allah. Assuredly in this there are signs for a people who believe.

(All the laws of the cosmos are written by the Lawmaker. No causality is outside His decree.)

80. It is Allah Who made your habitations homes of rest for you, and made for you out of the skins of animals *(tents for)* dwellings which you find light when you travel and when you stop; and out of their wool, fur and hair, rich stuff *(to serve you)* for a time.

81. It is Allah Who made out of the things He created, shade; and has given you places of refuge in the mountains and has given you garments to protect you from heat, and coats *(of armour)* to save you from your own violence. Thus does He complete His favours on you that you may submit *(to His will, thereby entering Islam)*.

82. But if they turn away, then your duty *(O Muhammad)*, is only to convey clearly.

83. They recognise the favours of Allah and then they deny them. And most of them are ungrateful.

(All mankind recognise the value of God's favours, but in forgetting or disobeying their Source, men show gross ingratitude, for in practice they deny their obligation to Him for these blessings.)

84. And the day when We raise up of every nation a witness, then there is no leave for the ungrateful, nor are they allowed to make amends.

85. When the wrongdoers face their punishment it shall not be lightened for them nor shall they be reprieved.

86. And when those who ascribed partners to Allah see their partners, they will say: "Lord, these are our partners, to whom we used to pray apart from You. But they will throw back their word at them *(saying)*: "Indeed you are liars .

87. That day they *(openly)* proffer *(their)* submission to Allah, and all their inventions will forsake them.

88. Those who disbelieve and hinder *(men)* from the path of Allah: for them We will add penalty to penalty; because of the corruption which they used to work.

89. One day We shall raise from every nation a witness against them of their own people, and We bring you *(O Muhammad)* as a witness against these *(your people)*. And We have sent down to you the Book as an exposition of all things, a guidance, a mercy and glad tidings to the Muslims.

90. Allah commands justice and kindness and charity to one's kindred, and forbids indecency, wickedness and oppression. He admonishes you so that you may take heed.

91. Fulfil the covenant of Allah when you have entered into it, and do not break your oaths after you have confirmed them, and after you have made Allah surety over you. Indeed Allah knows all that you do.

(The immediate reference here may be to the oath of fidelity to the Blessed Prophet taken at al-'Aqaba fourteen months before the Hijra, and repeated a little later. But the general meaning is wider, and may be seen from two angles: (1) Every oath and covenant made is a Covenant before God, and should be faithfully observed (cf. 5:1). (2) In particular, every Muslim makes, by the profession of his faith, a Covenant with God, and he confirms that Covenant every time he repeats that profession. He is therefore bound faithfully to observe the duties taught him by his Lord.)

92. Do not behave like the woman who had spun yarn firmly and then had herself broken it into pieces, by taking your oaths as a means of mutual deceit in your affairs because of one nation being more numerous than another. Allah

only puts you to trial by these pledges. Allah will certainly reveal to you the truth about all your differences on the Day of Resurrection.

(The Covenant which binds us in the spiritual world makes us strong, like a thread made of individual strands of cotton, which was difficult to unite, and is far easier to unwind. We are forbidden from making our religion merely a game of making one's own party numerically strong by alliance cemented by oaths, which we readily break when a more numerous party offers us its alliance. The Quraish were addicted to this vice, and in international politics today this seems to be almost a standard of national self-respect and skill. Islam enjoins more rigorous standards, for a covenant is binding before both man and God, even if large numbers are ranged against it.)

93. If Allah so willed He would have made you *(all)* one nation, but He leaves straying whom He will and guides whom He will. And you shall certainly be questioned about what you used to do.

reward according to the best of what they used to do.

97. Whoever works righteousness, man or woman, and has faith, We shall assuredly give him to live a goodly life, and We will bestow upon them their reward according to the best of what they used to do.

98. When you recite the Qur'an seek refuge in Allah from Satan the accursed.

(Evil cannot dominate those who put their trust in Allah, and seek refuge in Him from the devil. The formal expression of it is contained in the following words: "I seek refuge in Allah from Satan the accursed . This must be recited whenever we wish for Divine protection from evil. It is also to be uttered before recitations of the Qur'an, lest demonic forces interfere with the recital of the Word of God.)

99. He has no power over those who believe and put their trust in their Lord.

100. His power is only over those who make a friend of him and those who ascribe partners unto Allah.

101. When We exchange a revelation in place of another revelation - and Allah knows best what He reveals - they say: "You are an impostor . Indeed, most of them have no knowledge.

102. Say: "The Holy Spirit brought it down from your Lord in truth, to strengthen those who believe, and as a guidance and good tidings to those who have surrendered (to Allah, thereby entering Islam).

(The wicked attribute to God's Messengers every possible devious motive. The Pagans of Arabia could not understand how such astonishing words could flow from the tongue of the Holy Prophet, and were obliged to postulate some human teacher. Unfortunately for this theory, any possible human teacher they could think of would be poor in Arabic speech, if he had all the knowledge that the Qur'an reveals of previous revelations. Apart from this, even the most eloquent Arab could not, and cannot, produce anything of the eloquence, width and depth of Qur'anic teaching, as is evident from every verse of the Book.)

94. Do not make your oaths a deceit between you with the result that someone's foot may slip after it has stood firm, and you may have to taste the evil (consequences) of having hindered (men) from the path of Allah. And a mighty punishment may descend on you.

(In verse 92 above the motive for false and fraudulent covenants was pointed out. Now the consequences are mentioned: (1) to others; if they had not been deceived, they might have walked firmly on the Path, but now they lose faith and perhaps commit frauds for which you will be responsible; (2) to yourselves; you have not only gone wrong yourselves, but by setting others on the wrong path deserve a twofold penalty.)

95. Nor sell the covenant of Allah for a small gain. Surely what is with Allah is better for you, if you only knew.

96. What is with you will waste away, and what is with Allah will endure. And We will certainly bestow on those who were patient their

103. We know very well that they say: "It is only a man that teaches him. But the man to whom they allude speaks a foreign tongue, while this is eloquent Arabic speech.

104. Allah will not guide those who disbelieve in the revelations of Allah; and theirs will be a painful punishment.

105. None invents falsehoods except those who disbelieve the revelations of Allah: they are the liars.

106. Whoever disbelieves in Allah after he has believed - excepting him who has been compelled and his heart is still firm in faith - but those who open their breast to disbelief, upon them shall rest anger from Allah, and there awaits them a mighty punishment.

('Ammâr ibn Yâsir and his parents were brutally tortured, and were forced to turn away from Islam. His father Yâsir and mother Sumayya were killed, thereby becoming the first martyrs of Islam. As for 'Ammâr, under extreme torture he uttered words of apostasy. But when this was conveyed to the Prophet, he said: "'Ammâr is a wholehearted believer; faith has been mixed with his very flesh. It is this that counts. If they force you again, and force you by every means, and you

again utter what they want you to utter, let your heart always be with Allah.

This was a special permission granted by the Blessed Prophet to 'Ammâr. But there will always be disbelievers to torture men of faith, and there will always be 'Ammârs prepared to be tortured for their belief in Islam. No-one should ever allow faith to vanish from his heart, although a compassionate dispensation to claim disbelief may sometimes be used, to end needless suffering.)

107. This is because they prefer the life of this world over the Hereafter, and because Allah does not guide those who disbelieve.

108. Such are they whose hearts and ears and eyes Allah has sealed. They are the forgetters.

109. And assuredly, in the Hereafter they will be the losers.

110. Then surely your Lord, unto those who emigrated after they had been persecuted and then fought and were steadfast, surely your Lord thereafter is Forgiving, Merciful.

111. On the day that every soul shall come disputing on its own behalf; and every soul shall be paid in full for what it did, and they shall not be wronged.

112. Allah has made an example of a city which was once safe and peaceful. Its provisions used to come in abundance from every quarter, yet its people denied the favours of Allah. Therefore He caused it to taste the garb of famine and fear as a punishment for what they did.

(The double metaphor here works as follows: (1) the "tasting of famine and fear after its previous abundance refers to the seven years of hardships suffered by the Makkan pagans after their expulsion of the Muslims, and their fear that their time was up; (2) the "garb is an Arabic expression denoting the complete surrounding of a thing, for the idolaters were increasingly isolated.)

113. And there came to them a messenger of their own, but they denied him. Therefore Our scourge smote them while they were evildoers.

114. So eat of the lawful and good things which Allah has provided for you, and give thanks for His favours, if it is He whom you serve.

(The Makkan food-supplies dried up when they lost the blessing of the Prophet's presence, and because they failed to thank their Lord.)

115. He has forbidden for you only carrion, blood and the flesh of swine; also any *(flesh)* consecrated in the name of any but Allah. But if one is forced *(by dire necessity to eat it)* without willful disobedience nor transgressing the limits, then Allah is Forgiving, Merciful.

116. Do not *(falsely)* declare: "This is lawful, and this is forbidden, in order to invent a falsehood about Allah. Those who invent falsehoods about Allah shall never prosper.

117. Brief is their enjoyment, and they shall have a painful punishment.

118. We have forbidden the Jews that which We have already related to you. We never wronged them but they wronged themselves.

119. Then, surely, your Lord, unto those who commit evil in ignorance and afterwards repent and amend, surely your Lord for them thereafter is Forgiving, Merciful.

120. Abraham *(being a paragon of piety)* was a community obedient to Allah, a man of pure faith. He was never of the polytheists.

(Abraham, upon whom be peace, was an *umma*, here translated as "community , but which also bears the sense of "model , "pattern , and "an example for imitation . He was the model and fountainhead for the doctrine of Divine Unity in Western Asia, and its spiritual descendants all over the world. Although born among the idolatrous Chaldean community, he was not of them, but was a monotheist community in himself.)

121. Showing thankfulness for His blessings; He chose him and guided him to a straight path.

122. And We gave him good in the world, and in the Hereafter he shall be among the righteous.

123. Then We revealed to you *(O Muhammad)* saying: "Follow the religion of Abraham, the upright in faith; he was not of the polytheists.

124. The Sabbath was ordained only for those who disagreed *(as to its observance)*; and your Lord will judge between them on the Day of Resurrection concerning that in which they used to differ.

(If Abraham's way was the right one, the Jews were ready with the taunt, "Why don't you then observe the Sabbath? The answer was: (1) the Sabbath has nothing to do with Abraham, it came with the Mosaic law because of Israel's hardness of heart (2:74); (2) The Jews and the Christians differ over which is the true Sabbath: Saturday or Sunday. They are to be left to their dispute, and God shall judge it on the Last Day. Meanwhile, the Muslims observe Friday as the special day of the week; they are, of course, emancipated from the stringent restrictions of the Jewish sabbath, as well as the traditional Christian Sunday.)

125. Invite (all) to the path of your Lord with wisdom and kindly exhortation, and reason with them in the most courteous manner. For your Lord knows best those who have strayed from His path, and those who are rightly-guided.

(The patience and self-restraint of the Blessed Prophet were sorely tested: at Uhud the disbelievers not only killed his uncle Hamza but cut his nose and ears, then they took out his liver and devoured it. When the Prophet saw his uncle's body thus disfigured, he felt impelled to declare that if Allah gave him a victory he would do the same to seventy-two disbelievers. Then the following verse was revealed, in which the restraint and gentleness which had always been the Islamic way were confirmed and emphasised. When he at last entered Makka in triumph, he caused astonishment by forgiving his enemies.)

126. If you punish, then punish with the like of that wherewith you were afflicted. But if you endure patiently, this is indeed better for those who are patient.

127. Endure patiently *(O Muhammad)*; your endurance is only by *(the help of)* Allah. Do nor grieve for them *(the disbelievers)*, nor distress yourself because of what they devise.

128. Allah is with those who keep from evil, and are workers of good.

SÛRAH XVII

AL-ISRÂ' (THE NIGHT JOURNEY)

Revealed at Makka

(This Sûrah is named after the mention in verse 1 of the Prophet's miraculous Night Journey, on which he was carried by night to the Temple Mount in Jerusalem, after which he was caught up through the seven heavens to the Presence of God. It is also known as Banû Isrâ'îl, or "the Children of Israel, since it begins and ends with references to the Israelites. It belongs to the middle group of Makkan Sûrahs, with the exception of verse 81, or verses 76-82, which according to some historians were revealed at Madîna.)

THE NIGHT JOURNEY

In the name of Allah, the Compassionate, the Merciful

1. Glory be to Him Who carried His servant by night from Sacred Mosque to the Farthest Mosque Whose surroundings We have blessed, that We might show him some of Our signs, for He the Hearer, the Seer.

2. We gave Moses the Book and made it a guide to the Children of Israel, (*saying*), "Take no guardian beside Me.

3. (*They were*) The seed of those whom We carried (*in the ship*) along with Noah. Assuredly He was a grateful servant.

(Those who were saved in the Ark but relapsed into idolatry and sin are reminded of the true and sincere devotion of Noah himself, as contrasted with the unworthiness of his descendants, especially the Children of Israel.)

4. And We forewarned the Children of Israel in the Scripture: "You shall verily work corruption in the earth twice, and shall become great tyrants.

5. When the time for the first of the two came, We roused against you the slaves of Ours of great might, who wrought destruction through the land; and it was a promise (*completely*) fulfilled.

(The Jews had once been the servants of Allah in the sense that they received His revelation, and some of them were righteous. Yet when they grew sinful and arrogant, the Lord's wrath was poured upon them: in 586 BC their Temple was destroyed, the Torah burnt, 70,000 rabbis were slain, and the rest were carried off into captivity.)

6. Then We gave back to you the turn as against them, and aided you with wealth and children and made you more numerous in man-power (*than before*).

(In about 520 BC the Jews returned from captivity, and began life afresh, rebuilding the Temple, and creating a new Judaism based on Uzair's attempted recreation of the Torah. But in 70 AD the Temple was finally and permanently destroyed by Titus, and the Jews were scattered through the earth.)

7. (*Saying to them*): "If you do good, you do good for your own souls, and if you do evil (*you do it*) against yourselves. So when the second (*of the promises*) came to pass, (*We roused against you others*) to disfigure your faces and to enter the temple as they had entered it before; and to destroy utterly all that fell into their power.

8. Your Lord may yet be merciful to you; but if you return *(to your sins)* We shall return *(to Our punishment)*. We have made the Hell a prison for the disbelievers.

(The Jews are given yet another chance: if they overcome their ethnic pride, and accept God's latest revelation, the Holy Qur'an, they too can be forgiven, and achieve salvation.)

9. Surely this Qur'an guides to that which is most right, and gives good tidings to the believers who do deeds of righteousness that theirs will be a great reward.

10. And that those who do not believe in the Hereafter: for them We have prepared a painful penalty.

11. Yet man prays for evil as *(fervently as)* he prays for good. Truly man is ever impatient.

(Men, when angry, or bored, or confronted with difficulties, often behave impatiently to escape from them, cursing everything and anyone, including themselves.)

12. We have made the night and the day as two signs, then We have made dark the sign of night, and make the sign of the day sight-giving, that you may seek bounty from your Lord, and that you may know the number of the years and the reckoning; all things have We explained in detail.

13. Every man's augury We have fastened on his own neck; and We shall bring forth for him on the Day of Resurrection a book he shall find wide open.

14. *(It will be said to him)*: "Read your book! Your soul is sufficient this day as reckoner against you!

15. Whosoever goes right, it is only for the good of his own soul that he goes right; and whosoever goes astray goes astray to his own loss. No soul can bear another's burden. Nor do We punish until We have sent forth a messenger *(to give warning).*

(The doctrine of vicarious atonement is condemned. Salvation for the wicked cannot be attained by the punishment of the innocent. One man cannot bear the burden of another; it would be unjust, and reduce the sinner's sense of accountability.)

16. When We decree that a population should be destroyed, We *(first warn and)* command those of them that live in comfort, and yet they persist in sin so that the word is proved true against them, and then We destroy them utterly.

17. How many generations We have destroyed after Noah! Your Lord is Sufficient as Knower and Beholder of the sins of His slaves.

(as it was in this life, as they spent no time and effort for the eternal life with their Lord. In neither world is equality feasible.)

18. Whoever desires the immediate (*gains of this worldly life*), We give him here whatever We will; then We grant him Hell, where he will burn, despised and rejected.

19. And whosoever desires the Hereafter and strives for it properly, being a believer, his endeavours shall find favour.

20. Each do We supply, both these (*who desire the world*) and those (*who desire the Hereafter*) from the bounty of your Lord. And the bounty of your Lord can never be withheld.

21. See how We exalted some above another; and assuredly the Hereafter will be greater in degrees and greater in preferment.

(People are not equal in rank, wealth, health, beauty and so forth, but Allah's favours are for all, faithful or unfaithful, deserving or not. Those who wish for mere earthly good can acquire it, and will acquire a higher worldly position as a result, but this is transitory and worth little in the face of eternal life. The degree of such people in the Hereafter though, will not be as high

22. Do not associate another deity with Allah; lest you sit down reproved, forsaken.

23. Your Lord has decreed that you worship none but Him, and that you show kindness to your parents. If either or both of them attain old age with you, (*show no sign of impatience, and*) do not (*even*) say "fie to them; nor rebuke them, but speak kind words to them.

24. And lower unto them the wing of humility and tenderness and say: "Lord, be merciful to them both, as they did care for me when I was small.

25. Your Lord best knows what is in your minds. If you are righteous, He surely was ever Forgiving to those who turn (*to Him*).

26. Give to the near of kin their due, and also the destitute and the wayfarer, and do not squander your substance wastefully.

27. For the wasteful are Satan's brothers; and Satan is ever ungrateful to his Lord.

28. But if you turn away from them *(the needy),* because you are still waiting for your Lord's bounty that you are expecting, then *(at least)* speak to them a kind word.

(Some needy people of Madîna used to maintain themselves with financial help from the Blessed Prophet. But when, as sometimes happened, the Prophet had nothing to give them, he would pray to Allah to enable him to help them. When he could not help, he would feel so embarrassed that he could find no word to say to them, and averted his gaze in silence.)

29. Do not tie your hand to your neck *(do not be miserly)* nor stretch it without any restraint *(i. e. do not be extravagant)* for then you should sit down rebuked, denuded.

(In charity, the golden mean is to be pursued. Our giving should not be niggardly to the point where it becomes rebuked by the righteous, nor extravagant to the extent that our families are denuded of means.)

30. Your Lord gives abundantly to whom He will, and witholds *(His provision from whom He pleases).* He is ever Aware, Seeing of His slaves.

31. Do not slay your offspring for fear of want. It is We who provide for them, and for you. Indeed their killing is a great sin.

(The pagan Arabs were addicted to female infanticide. In a society perpetually at war sons were a source of strength, and daughters of vulnerability. In our times, too, the practice is widespread in some non-Muslim cultures, practiced both before and after birth. There is nothing new under the sun.)

32. Do not approach adultery, for it is an indecent thing and an evil way.

(There are cultures today, which shall here remain nameless, where sixty percent of men, and forty percent of women, are unfaithful to their marriage vows, with all the dangers that this poses to trust, family stability, and knowledge of paternity.)

33. Do not take the life which Allah has rendered sacrosanct, except for a just cause. And if one is slain unjustly, We have granted power to his heir. But let him not exceed bounds in slaying, for he *(his victim)* will *(in turn)* be assisted *(and avenged).*

(For the legal right to retaliation *(qisâs),* see 2:178.)

34. Do not approach the property of an orphan except in the way that is best *(responsible investment)* until he attains majority. Keep your covenants, for one is responsible for one's covenant.

35. Give full measure when you measure, and weigh with even scales *(when you weigh).* This is better, and will be the best in the end.

36. Do not go after that of which you have no knowledge, for *(man's)* eyes, ears and heart, each of these *(senses)* shall be closely questioned.

37. Do not walk proudly on the earth. You cannot cleave the earth, nor can you rival the hills in stature.

38. The evil of all these *(mentioned crimes)* is hateful in the sight of your Lord.

41. We have made plain *(Our warnings)* in this Qur'an so that they *(the disbelievers)* may take heed, but it increases them in nothing but aversion.

42. Say *(O Muhammad, to the heathen):* If there were other gods besides Him, as they say, they would certainly have sought out a way to the Lord of the Throne.

(Another devastating exposure of the contradictions of polytheism. There can be only one transcendant will.)

43. Glorified is He, and High Exalted above all that they say!

44. The seven heavens and the earth, and all who dwell in them give glory to Him. There is not a single thing that is not chanting His praise, yet you cannot understand their praises. He is ever Clement, Forgiving.

(All creation, animate and inanimate, celebrates Allah's glory, and bears witness to His power, wisdom and goodness. It was one of the miracles given to our Prophet, may God bless him and grant him peace, that he was able to hear this praise. Once, when he was with his Companions, he took some pebbles in his hand, and those present could hear them praising God.)

45. When you recite the Qur'an We place a hidden barrier between you and those who do not believe in the Hereafter.

46. And We cast veils over their hearts and a deafness in their ears, so that they understand not. *(That is why)* when you make mention of your One and Only Lord, they turn their backs in aversion.

47. We are best informed of what they wish to hear when they listen to you, and what they say when they converse in private; when the wrongdoers declare, "The man you follow is simply bewitched.

48. See what similitudes they coin for you. They have surely gone astray and cannot find a path.

49. And they say: "What! When we are bones and dust, shall we really be raised up again into a new creation?

39. These *(injunctions)* are a part of the wisdom which your Lord has revealed to you. Do not associate any other deity with Allah, or else you are cast into Hell, despised and abandoned.

(The moral law, as expounded in 17:23-39 is far in advance of the bare Ten Commandments which were given to the hard-hearted and refractory Israelites, in that it searches out motives, and draws attention to the weak and helpless. It opens and closes with the injunction to recognise only One God, for all the ethics of religion exist as reflections and affirmations of the underlying understanding of His ceaseless presence. Next the sacred text turns to the theological arguments against those who cannot recognise His presence and unity.)

40. What! Has your Lord then favoured you *(O men of Makka)* with sons and Himself adopted females from among the angels? A monstrous blasphemy is that which you utter.

(Here the Makkans are faced with the incompatibility of their morals, which held that female offspring were inferior, and their religious doctrines, which imagined that the Lord has preferred female offspring.)

50. Say *(to them: "Yes, you shall)* whether you turn to stone or iron,

(Calcium, the stuff of human bones, is a major component of chalk and limestone, and can be used in steelmaking.)

51. Or any other substance which you may think unlikely to be given life. Then they will ask: "Who will restore us? Say: "He that created you at first. They will shake their heads and ask: "When will this be? Say: "It will perhaps be soon.

(Islam, as the final link in the great cycle of revelations, places a necessary emphasis on the final Denouement, and its undoubted imminence.)

52. On the day when He will call you, you shall answer Him with praises. You shall think that you had stayed only for a brief while.

53. And *(O Muhammad)* tell My servants that they should utter only that which is the best of all. Satan is ever the plain enemy of man.

54. Your Lord is fully aware of you. He may show you mercy if He will, and punish you if He will. We have not sent you *(O Muhammad)* as a guardian over them.

(Man should never for a second entertain a thought that would imply that he is wiser than his Maker. The Lord's knowledge is complete. If He grants mercy to some that you consider wicked, or punishment to some that you consider righteous, it is your knowledge or assumptions that are at fault, not His Plan. Even the Messengers of the Lord are not sent to arrange or dispose of men's affairs, but only to teach His message. How much less can ordinary men presume to judge their fellows?)

55. And your Lord is best aware of all who are in the heavens and the earth. And We preferred some of the prophets above others; and unto David We gave the Psalms.

(Not only may we not judge others and criticise them, we may not set up false standards for judging

God's Prophets. If one was born of the unlearned Arab race, he yet was a mercy to all the nations.

If one spoke to God as "God's Spokesman , or another as "God's Spirit , this does not imply superiority in the spirit. But those who are sent to one people are in a historical sense "lesser than those who are sent to all mankind.)

56. Say: "Pray if you will to those whom you assume *(to be gods)* beside Him. They cannot relieve your troubles, nor can they change *(anything)*.

57. Those to whom they pray, themselves seek to approach their Lord *(vying with each other as to)* which of them shall be the nearest; they hope for His mercy and fear His punishment, for your Lord's punishment is something to be shunned.

58. There is no nation but that We shall destroy it, before the Day of Resurrection, or severely punish it. That is inscribed in the Book *(of Our decrees).*

59. Nothing has hindered Us from sending signs *(miracles)* except that the former people denied them. *(For example)* We sent to Thamoud the she-camel as a visible sign, yet they did wrong in respect of her. We send signs only by way of warning.

(Signs, miracles and portents are sent by Allah as a warning, to remind and strike terror into the hearts of evildoers and reclaim them for the right path. But there are some hearts which are so hard that even a miracle such as the She-camel of Thamoud cannot soften them. Of such men, the earth must be purified if the world is not to be corrupted entirely.) .

60. And *(it was a warning)* when We told you that your Lord has encircled these people, and We appointed the vision which We showed you as an ordeal for mankind, as well as the tree cursed in the Qur'an. We seek to put fear in their hearts but it only increases their wickedness.

(Commentators take the "encircling" as a reference to 72:28, and the word "vision" as a reference to the Mi'râj, the Prophet's Ascension from Jerusalem to the Seven Heavens mentioned at the start of the present Sûrah. These events are an ordeal, or trial, which demand sincere and unadulterated faith. The Cursed Tree is the Zaqqûm (37:62-5), which grows in hell, and which is also described as a trial (37:63), because of its vile taste to those who must eat it, finding no other nourishment, and also because it cannot be seen in this world, belonging to the realm of faith and acceptance of the Message from the Unseen.)

61. When We said to the angels: "Prostrate yourselves before Adam! they all prostrated themselves except Iblîs, who said: "Shall I bow to him whom You have made of clay?

62. He *(Iblîs said):* "Do You see this *(creature)* whom You have honoured above me, if You give me respite until the Day of Resurrection I surely will seize his descendants, all but a few.

63. *(Allah)* said: "Go your way! And whosoever of them follow you, assuredly Hell will be the reward of you *(all),* an ample reward.

64. You may try to allure with your *(seductive)* voice whomsoever you can. Rally against them with your cavalry and infantry, be a partner in their wealth and children, and make promises to them. But Satan makes promises for them only to deceive.

65. "But over My *(true)* servants you shall have no power. Your Lord is sufficient as Guardian.

66. It is your Lord Who drives your ships across the sea, so that you may seek of His bounty. For your Lord is ever Merciful towards you.

67. When a misfortune befalls you on the sea, all of those whom you invoke for help fail you, but He *(is there to help)*, yet when He brings you safe to land you turn away from Him. Indeed man is ever ungrateful.

68. Are you confident that He will not cause a slope of the land to engulf you or let loose a storm upon you? Then you shall find none to protect you.

69. Or are you confident that He will not sent you back to sea a second time and send against you a hurricane of wind and drown you for your thanklessness, so that you find no helper therein against Us?

70. We have honoured the children of Adam, and carried them on land and sea, and provided them with good things, and preferred them greatly over many of those We created.

(This is true humanism, a vision of man that sees him as God's noble deputy in the cosmos, borne on land and sea and mastering the earth, under Him, and enjoying the good things which have been set in it for His benefit. Secularity, by contrast, advocates a pseudo-humanism, in which, although man is seen as the measure of all things, he is at root no more than a clever monkey, destined to a life which he tries to make pleasant, but which is in reality devoid of sense, and which will end in darkness. Such are infra-human, they are blind in this world, and have no inkling of man's true glory.)

71. On the Day when We shall call all people with their leaders; those who will be given their records in their right hands, will read it, and they will not be wronged in the least.

(The word *imâm*, translated here as "leader", can also denote a "book", here either the revelation which they were given, or the record of their actions.)

72. But he who was blind in this world will be blind in the Hereafter, and more astray from the path.

73. And they indeed sought to entice you *(O Muhammad)* from what We revealed to you hoping that you might invent some other *(scripture)* in Our name, and then would they have accepted you as a close friend.

74. And had We not made you wholly firm, you would almost have inclined to them, just a little.

75. In that case We should have made you taste a double *(punishment)* in this life and in the next. Then you should have found none to protect you from Our wrath.

(The sign of the true Prophet is that he makes no concessions, however small, in order to attract those whose deliverance he seeks. The temptation is a mighty and understandable one, but the Prophets have a God-given strength to overcome it, and to present the message without the least distortion.)

76. And they indeed sought to provoke you and thus drive you out of the land, and then they would have stayed (*there*) only a little after you.

77. (*Such was Our*) way with the messengers We sent before you. And you will find no change in Our ways.

78. Establish the Prayer at the sun's decline until the darkness of the night; and the recital of dawn, for the recital (*in the prayer*) at dawn has its witnesses.

(The Muslim is asked to express his devotion by praying, preferably with his brothers and sisters in Islam, at five times each day. Certain times are especially blessed, which is why we seize the opportunity they present for spiritual practice. In particular, the early dawn is a time of tranquillity when the mind is free of agitating notions, and the spiritual environment is filled with angels, who witness the act of devotion and placid submission to the Lord.)

79. And some part of the night, awake for it (*this would be*) an optional prayer (*or spiritual*

profit) for you; it may be that your Lord will exalt you to a Praiseworthy Station.

(This applies particularly to the Blessed Prophet, who usually prayed more than the five canonical prayers. The *Tahajjud* mentioned here is an optional, though popular, prayer, observed in the fifth sixth of the night.

The Praiseworthy Station (*al-Maqâm al-Mahmûd*) is the blessed rank of our Prophet, the Messenger of the End of Time, who shall stand at the Judgement on an eminence which bears this name.)

80. And say: "My Lord, cause me to enter with truth, and cause me to go out with truth, and grant me a power from Your presence, to help me.

(This refers to any or all of the following: (1) death; (2) the Prophet's entry into Madîna; (3) entry and exit at every stage of life.)

81. And say: Truth has come and falsehood has vanished away. For falsehood is ever bound to vanish.

82. We send down in the Qur'an that which is a healing and a mercy for believers. Though to the evil-doers it adds nothing but ruin.

(The believers know that there is a spiritual healing in the Qur'an, and hence read and listen to it accordingly. But those who oppose the truth are like those who are ill but refuse to recognise the efficacy of a medicine. Consequently their illness worsens, both bodily and spiritually. Cf. also vv.45-6 above.)

83. When We bestow Our favours unto man he turns away and becomes remote. But when evil befalls him he gives himself up to despair.

84. Say: "Everyone acts according to his own manner (*or: disposition, or rule of conduct*). But your Lord best knows who is best guided on the way.

85. They ask you about the Spirit. Say: "The Spirit is of my Lord's command, and of knowledge you have been given but little.

86. And if We willed We could certainly take away that which We have revealed to you; then you should find none to plead with Us on your behalf.

87. Except for Mercy from your Lord. His goodness towards you has been great indeed.

(Verses 85-7 are said to have been revealed in answer to the third question which some rabbis prompted the idolaters to ask, the first two questions being answered in the following verse.)

88. Say: "If all men and jinn gathered together to produce the like of this Qur'an they could not produce one like it, though they were helpers one of another.

89. And We have explained to man, in this Qur'an, every kind of similitude; but most men refuse anything but disbelief.

90. They say: "We will not believe in you until you make a spring gush from the earth for us!

91. Or (until) you possess a garden of palms and vines, and cause rivers to gush forth abundantly amongst it!

92. Or (until) you cause the sky to fall upon us in pieces, as you say (will happen). Or you bring Allah and the angels as a warrant!

93. Or until you have a house of gold! Or until you ascend into heaven; and even then we will not believe in your ascension till you bring down for us a book that we can read. Say (O Muhammad): "My Lord be glorified. Am I aught but a human messenger?

94. And nothing prevented mankind from believing when the guidance came unto them but that they said: "Has Allah sent a human as (His) messenger?

(One of the reasons that the disbelievers rejected faith was their inability to understand why the Prophet was a human and not an angel. Allah tells him to respond as follows.)

95. Say: "Had there been in the earth angels walking at peace, We would have sent down for them from heaven an angel as messenger.

(To each people is sent a messenger from among themselves, so that they may understand. Their faith must not be based on spectacular manifestations of the Unseen, which leave no room for moral or intellectual choice, but on their free and considered acceptance of the Reminder. This is the only kind of faith and acknowledgement which is valid in God's sight)

96. Say: "Sufficient is Allah as witness between me and you. Surely He is aware of, and sees, His servants.

97. Whomsoever Allah guides, he is rightly guided; and those whom He leads astray, you will find no protector for them besides Him. We shall gather them all, on the Day of Resurrection, on their faces blind, dumb and deaf. Their abode will be Hell, whenever it abates, We will increase the flame for them.

98. That is their recompense because they disbelieved Our revelations and said: "What, when we are bones and broken dust shall we really be raised up as a new creation?

99. Have they not seen that Allah Who created the heavens and the earth is able to create the like of them, and has appointed for them an end about which there is no doubt. But the wrongdoers refuse anything but disbelief.

100. Say (unto them): "Had you possessed the treasures of my Lord's mercy, you would have held them back for fear of spending. For man was ever grudging.

101. And assuredly We gave to Moses nine clear signs. Do but ask the Children of Israel how he came unto them, then Pharaoh said unto him: "I consider, O Moses, that you are bewitched.

(For these signs see 7:133.)

102. Moses replied: "You know full well that none but the Lord of the heavens and the earth has revealed these things as evidence, and surely (for my part), O Pharaoh, I consider you doomed.

103. So Pharaoh sought to scare them from the land, but We drowned him and those with him, altogether.

104. And We said threafter to the Children of Israel: "Dwell in the land (of Canaan). When the promise of the Hereafter (or: the second of the promises) comes to be fulfilled, We shall bring you as a mingled crowd.

(Perhaps a reference to the intermingling of the Jews with the other nations which transpired after their dispersal, and the effects of which can be seen in the varied racial types found in any crowd of Jews, in the place where they are presently gathered together.)

105. With the truth We have sent it down (*the Qur'an*), and with the truth has it come down. We have sent you only as a bringer of good news and a warning.

106. And a Qur'an We have divided for you to recite it to mankind at intervals, and We have sent it down by stages.

107. Say: "Believe in it or do not believe; those who were given the knowledge before it, when it is recited to them, fall down upon their faces in humble prostration.

108. They say: "Glory be to our Lord, the promise of our Lord has been fulfilled!

109. They fall down upon their faces weeping, and it increases them in humility.

110: Say: "Call upon Allah or call upon the Compassionate: by whatever name you call upon Him *(it is well);* for to Him belong the most beautiful Names, neither raise your voice in your prayer nor lower it too much but choose a way in between.

111. Say: "Praise belongs to Allah, Who has never taken to Himself a son, and Who has no partner in sovereignty. Nor *(needs)* He anyone to protect Him from humiliation. And magnify Him with all magnificence!

SÛRAH XVIII
AL-KAHF (THE CAVE)

Revealed at Makka

(This Sûrah, which deals with the question of spiritual insight and instruction, takes its name from the story of the youths who took refuge from persecution in a cave (vv.10-27), and were preserved there as if asleep for a long period, identified by some writers with the Seven Sleepers of Ephesus (now in Turkey). But a strong tradition in the Muslim world asserts that this story, and that of Dhû'l-Qarnayn (vv.83-98), and possibly also that of Moses and his companion, were revealed to the Blessed Prophet to enable him to answer certain questions which the Jewish rabbis of Madîna had instructed the idolaters to ask him, as a test of Prophethood.

The date of revelation is the middle Makkan period.)

THE CAVE

In the name of Allah, the Compassionate, the Merciful.

1. Praise be to Allah who has revealed the Book to His servant and has not placed in it any crookedness.

2. *(But has made it)* straight, to give warning of stern punishment from Him, and to proclaim to the believers who do righteous deeds that they will have an excellent recompense,

3. Wherein they will remain for ever.

4. And to warn those who say that Allah has chosen a son.

(One or all of the following three may be intended: (1) the Jews, certain of whom called Uzair the "Son of God ; (2) the Christians, most of whom called Christ the "Son of God ; (3) the Makkan idolaters, who called their idols the "Daughters of God .)

5. Of this they have no knowledge, nor *(had)* their fathers. Dreadful is the word that comes out of their mouths. They utter nothing but a lie.

6. Well, *(O Muhammad)* it may be that you will torment your soul with grief for their sake, if they do not believe in this Message.

7. We have placed all that is in the earth as an ornament for it that We may try them: which of them is best in conduct.

8. Yet We will surely reduce all that is on it to barren dust.

9. Do you consider that the Companions of the Cave and the Bearers of the Inscription were a wonder among Our signs?

10. When the young men took refuge in the Cave they said: "Lord, grant us mercy from Your presence, and guide us to right conduct in our plight.

11. Then We sealed up their hearing (*made them sleep*) in the Cave for a number of years.

12. Then We raised them up in order to test which of the two parties were able to calculate correctly the period of their stay there.

13. *(Now)* We tell you their story with truth. They were young men who had believed in their Lord, and We increased them in guidance.

14. And We strengthened their hearts, when they rose up and declared, "Our Lord is the Lord of the heavens and the earth, we will not call upon any god beside Him, or then we had spoken an outrage.

15. These, our people, have adopted other gods beside Him. Why do they not bring any clear argument (*in support of their creed*)? Well who can be more wicked than the one who invents a falsehood against Allah?

16. *(It was said to them):* "When you depart from them and from that they worship other than Allah, go to the Cave for shelter; your Lord will spread for you of His mercy and will prepare for you a means of safety .

17. You would have seen the sun when it rose moving away from their Cave to the right and when it set, passing them by, on the left; and they were in the cleft thereof. That was one of the signs of Allah. He whom Allah guides is rightly guided; but he whom He misleads shall find no friend to guide him.

18. You might have thought them awake, though they were sleeping. We turned them about to right and left while their dog lay at the *(Cave's)* entrance with legs outstretched. Had you looked upon them you would have surely turned your back and fled, filled with terror.

19. In like manner We awakened them that they might question one another. One of them

said: "How long have you remained *(here)?* "A day, or but a few hours, replied some; and others said: "Your Lord knows best how long you have stayed here. Let one of you go to the city with this your silver coin and let him see what food is purest there, and bring you a supply from it. Let him conduct himself with care and gentleness, and let no man know of you.

20. For if they find you out, they will stone you, or force you back into their cult, and then you would never find success.

(One of the men went to the city to buy food. It is said that when he paid with ancient money, the people in the city were amazed, and took the man to their king, who was now living and ruling in a age of monotheism. The young man narrated their story to them, and the king and city dwellers went to the Cave and, seeing that his words were true, they marvelled at God's power and good providence.)

after them, disagreed over petty details, arguing about the construction of a shrine on the site, or about the number of the sleepers. In the Western tradition, as represented for instance by Gibbon, the number of sleepers was seven. But the point is immaterial to the lesson.)

21. Thus We disclosed them *(to the people of the city)* so that they might know that Allah's promise was true, and that the Hour *(of final Resurrection)* was sure to come. When *(the people of the city)* disputed of their case among themselves they said: "Build over them a building. Their Lord knows best concerning them. Those who won their point said: "We assuredly shall build a place of worship over them.

22. *(Some)* will say: "They *(the sleepers)* were three, their dog was the fourth. Others guessing at the unknown, will say: "They were five, their dog was the sixth. And some say: "Seven and their dog the eighth. Say *(O Muhammad)*: "My Lord is best aware of their number, none knows them but a few. Therefore do not enter into controversies concerning them except on a matter that is clear, nor consult any of them about *(the affair of)* the sleepers.

(Despite the magnitude of the sign that had been given them, the people of the city, and then mankind

23. Do not say of anything: "I will do it tomorrow,

24. Without adding "If Allah wills . When you forget remember your Lord, and say, "May Allah guide me and bring me nearer to the truth.

25. So they stayed in their Cave three hundred years and *(some)* add nine *(more)*.

(The sleepers of the Cave would thus have stayed there for 309 years. If this is according to the lunar calendar, it would amount to three centuries in the solar calendar. But again, this is a pointless diversion.)

26. Say: Allah knows best how long they stayed. To Him belongs the Unseen in the heavens and in the earth. How well He sees how well He hears! They have no protector apart from Him, nor does He make anyone to share in His government.

27. And recite *(and teach)* that which has been revealed unto you in the Book of your Lord. No one can change His words. You shall find no refuge beside Him.

28. Restrain yourself together with those who pray to their Lord, morning and evening, seeking His pleasure. Do not turn eyes away from them in quest of the good things of this life; nor obey any whose heart we have made heedless of Our remembrance, who follows his own lust and gives a loose rein to his desires.

(In this verse, the important principles of spiritual method are laid down: (1) The spiritual seeker must keep the company of the righteous, who pray to their Lord constantly, so that he may be reformed by their presence; (2) He should not pay attention to the delights of the world, for one cannot serve God and mammon; (3) He must not submit to the will of the forgetful, lest he acquiesce in, and hence be influenced by, their state; (4) Forgetfulness of the divine Reality results in, and is intensified by, following one's own caprices.)

29. Say: "(It is) the Truth from your Lord . Now whosoever will, may believe, and whosoever will, may disbelieve. For the wrong-doers We have prepared a fire (whose flames) will encircle them like the walls of a tent. If they ask for a drink they shall be showered with water as (hot as) melted brass, which will scald their faces. How terrible a drink, how evil the resting-place!

30. As for those who believe and work righteousness We do not let go waste the reward of any who do a (single) righteous deed.

31. For them will be Gardens of Paradise; beneath them rivers will flow. Reclining there upon soft couches they shall be adorned with bracelets of gold, and they will wear green garments of fine silk and rich brocade; how excellent a reward and how beautiful a resting-place!

32. And give them this parable: (Once there were) two men, to one of whom We gave two vineyards and surrounded with date palms; in between the two We placed corn-fields.

33. Each of the two gardens yielded its produce and did not fail any wise (in yielding its produce). In the midst of them We caused a river to gush forth.

34. This man had an abundant produce and he said to his companion while conversing with him: "I am richer than you and mightier in respect of men (servants).

35. And when, having thus wronged his soul he entered his vineyard, and he said: "I do not think that this will never perish.

36. Nor do I believe that the Hour (of Judgement) will ever come; and even if I am returned to my Lord I should surely find better than this as a resort.

37. His companion said, while he was conversing with him: "Have you disbelieved in Him Who created you from dust, then from a sperm-drop and then fashioned you into a man?

(The man who was proud of his wealth and his men under his command denied the life to come. Here in this verse his friend points out that He Who created man of a sperm-drop is surely Able to recreate him from anything He may please.)

38. But (as for myself, I know that) Allah alone is my Lord and I set up no partners with Him.

39. When you entered your garden why did you not say: 'That which Allah wills (will surely come to pass), there is no power but with Allah'? Though you see me poorer than yourself and blessed with fewer children,

40. Yet it may be that my Lord may give me (something) better than your garden and send down thunderbolts from heaven (upon your vineyards) turning into a barren waste,

41. Or drain its water deep into the earth so that you can find it no more.

42. So (it came to pass that) his fruits were encompassed (with ruin). Then he began to wring his hands with grief at what he had spent on his property which was now ruined on its trellises, and he would only say, "Woe is me! Would that I had never ascribed partners to my Lord!

43. And he had no troop of men to help him against Allah, nor could he save himself.

44. In such (ordeals) protection comes only from Allah, the True. No reward is better than His reward, and no recompense more generous than His.

45. And coin for them a similitude of the life of the world, like water which We send down from the sky, and the vegetation of the earth mingles with it, but soon it becomes dry stubble, which the winds scatter abroad. Allah has power over all things.

46. Wealth and children are the ornament of this life. But the good deeds which endure are better in your Lord's sight as rewards and best as *(the foundation for)* hope.

47. One day We shall remove the mountains and you will see the earth as a barren waste, and We shall gather them altogether nor shall We leave out any of them.

48. And they are set before your Lord in ranks *(and He will say to them)*: "Now assuredly you have returned to Us as We created you at first. Yet you thought We shall not fulfill Our promise.

49. And the Book *(of deeds)* will be placed and you will see the sinners fearful of that which is *(inscribed)* in it. And they say: "Woe to us! What kind of a book is this that omits nothing small or great but all are noted down? They will find all that they did, placed before them, and your Lord will wrong no one.

50. And *(remember)* when We said to the angels: "Prostrate yourselves before Adam, all prostrated themselves, except Satan. He was of the jinn, and he rebelled against his Lord's command. Will you then choose him and his offspring for your protecting friends instead of Me despite their enmity towards you? Evil would be the exchange for the wrongdoers!

51. I did not call them to witness at the creation of the heavens and the earth, nor at their own creation; nor choose I misleaders for My helpers.

52. One day He will say: "Call on those whom you thought to be My partners. And they will call on them, but they will not hear their prayer, and We shall set a gulf of destruction between them.

53. And the sinful shall see the fire and will realise that they are to fall into it; no means will they find to turn away from it.

54. And assuredly We have displayed for mankind in this Qur'an all manner of similitudes. But man is, more than anything, contentious.

55. Nothing can prevent men from having faith and seeking forgiveness of their Lord, when the guidance has been revealed to them; unless *(it be that they wish)* that the judgement of the men of old should come upon them or *(that)* they should be confronted with the Chastisement.

56. We only send the messengers as bearers of good news and as warners. But with false arguments the disbelievers seek to confute the truth, treating My revelations and My warnings as a jest.

57. Who is more wicked than he who has been reminded of the signs *(revelations)* of his Lord, then turns away from them and forgets what his hands have done? We have placed coverings over their hearts so that they do not understand this and set a deafness in their hearing, and though you call them to the guidance they shall never be guided.

58. Your Lord is the Forgiving, Full of Mercy. Had it been His will to scourge them for their sins, He would have hastened their punishment. But *(He has set)* for them an appointed hour which they shall never escape.

59. And all those nations, We destroyed them when they did wrong, and We appointed a fixed time for their destruction.

60. And when Moses said unto his attendant: "I will not give up until I reach the place where the two seas meet, though I march on for ages."

(In this section of the Qur'an, which deals with spiritual and initiatic instruction, there is a necessary obscurity over the meaning of these seas, which are commonly interpreted as denoting the two great streams of knowledge represented by Moses (the outward Law) and his companion, Khidr (the esoteric, direct apprehension of metaphysical realities), both of which are only perfect when combined. Some geographically-minded commentators hold that the two seas may be the Black Sea and the Caspian, or the Blue and the White Niles in the Sudan.)

61. But when at last they came to the place where the two seas met, they forgot their fish which made its way into the water, as if through in a tunnel.

(Moses had been told to search for the Mystical Teacher, Khidr, whose presence would be indicated by the loss of a fish he had brought as provision for his worldly needs. As elsewhere in this section, there are symbolic depths present which in the present commentary cannot be explored.)

62. And when they had gone further, Moses said to his servant: "Bring us our breakfast, truly we have suffered much fatigue at this (*stage of*) our journey.

63. He replied: "Did you see that I forgot the fish when we took refuge on the rock. I forgot the fish and none but Satan caused me to forget to mention it. The fish made its way into the sea in a bizarre fashion.

(As the journey towards new knowledge proceeds, the seeker feels increasingly exhausted, especially when there is a part of him that does not want it. The disciple had seen the fish come to life again and escape in what was surely a memorable way, yet "forgot to tell his master. Thus does inertia lead us astray: new knowledge can be missed because of culpable negligence. Hence the need to realise the mistake, retrace one's steps.)

64. "This is what we have been seeking, said Moses. So they retraced their steps again.

65. Then they found one of Our servants on whom We had bestowed mercy from Ourselves, and whom We had taught knowledge from Our own Presence.

(The spiritual guide is the recipient and disburser of the divine Mercy; whence the love in which he is held, despite his majesty. He is also the recipient and disburser of the Knowledge from the Divine Presence (*al-'ilm al-ladunnî*), which Moses sought. Now comes the request for initiation, and the trials.)

66. Moses said to him: "May I follow you so that you may teach me the right-guidance which you have been taught?

67. "You will not be able to have patience with me, said the other.

68. "For how can you bear with that which is beyond your knowledge?

(Moses was versed in the Law, yet desired the mystical consummation: the classic paradox of the spiritual seeker, who by definition does not know what he seeks to know.)

69. Moses said: "Allah willing, you shall find me patient; I shall not in anything disobey you.

70. He said: "If, then, you would follow me, then ask me no questions about anything until I myself speak to you concerning it.

71. So they both set forth but as soon as they were in the ship he made a hole in its bottom. "A strange thing you have done! exclaimed Moses. "Have you made a hole in it to drown its passengers?

72. "Did I not tell you, he replied "that you would not have patience with me?

73. Moses said: "Forgive my forgetfulness, and do not grieve me by raising a difficulty in my case.

74. They both journeyed on until, when they met a young man, he (*Moses' companion*) slew him. And Moses said: "What! have you slain an innocent soul though he had killed nobody? Truly you have done a foul thing.

75. "Did I not tell you, he replied "that you would not have patience with me?

76. (*Moses*) said: "If I ever question you again about anything do not let me accompany you, for then you would have received (*full*) excuse from myself.

77. So they both journeyed on until when they came to the inhabitants of a town. They asked them for food, but they refused to make them guests. And they found there a wall on the point of falling down, and he restored it. Moses said: "Had you wished, you could have demanded payment for this.

78. He answered: "This is the parting between you and me. (*But first*) I will tell you the interpretation of that which you could not bear with patience.

79. As for the boat, it belonged to poor people working on the sea, and I wished to render it unserviceable, because in their rear, there was a king who was seizing every ship by force.

80. As for the youth, his parents were believers, and we feared that he would oppress them by rebellion and disbelief.

81. So we desired that their Lord would give them in exchange (*a son*) better in purity (*of conduct*) and closer in affection.

82. As for the wall, it belonged to two orphan boys in the city. There was beneath it a (*buried*) treasure belonging to them, and their father had been a righteous man. So your Lord desired that they should attain their age of full strength and bring out their treasure as a mercy from their Lord. I did it not upon my own command. Such is the interpretion of (*those things*) which you were unable to bear with patience.

(Fearing the dishonesty of the wicked townsmen, the children's father had buried their inheritance so that they could recover it when they came of age. Had Khidr not repaired it, it would have fallen apart, and the treasure would have been looted.

The purpose of all three lessons is of course to demonstrate the limitations of the Law. While we are all bound by the Law, we must recognise that esoteric wisdom can sometimes see beyond it.)

83. They will ask you about Dhû'l-Qarnayn. Say: "I shall recite unto you a remembrance of him.

(Dhû'l-Qarnayn, or the king with the two horns, is often identified with Alexander the Great, although his exact identity is unimportant in the context of the present parable. He is here a Priest-King, a man who, as God's Vicegerent, is master of this world and honoured in the next. Three of his expeditions are described in the text, each embodying a great ethical idea involved in the possession of kingship or power. Thus is completed the cycle of the Sûrah, which has provided a characterisation of four spiritual possibilities: (1) reliance on God succoured by Him; (2) self-reliance leading to annihilation; (3) the Law encountering the Spirit; (4) the glories of divine kingship.)

84. Assuredly, We made him mighty in the land, and gave him the means to (*achieve*) all things.

85. One such way, he followed.

86. Until he reached the setting-place of the sun, he found it setting in a pool of opaque water, and found a people around it. We said: "O Dhû'l-Qarnayn! You must either punish them or show them kindness.

(Some identify this place with the most westerly point in Alexander's dominions: Lake Ohrid in Macedonia, which is fed by opaque springs from limestone rock formations.)

87. He said: "Whoever does wrong we shall punish him. Then he shall be sent back to his Lord, who will punish him with a fearsome punishment.

88. But whoever believes and works righteousness, he shall have a goodly reward and We shall speak to him a mild command.

(The Priest-King, despite his power, must be mild, and know always that above him is the Supreme Judge. Such is the lesson of the first episode.)

89. Then he followed (*another*) way.

90. Until, when he came to the rising-place of the sun, he found the sun rising upon a people for whom We had provided no covering protection against the sun.

91. So he did (*leave them as they were*). And We had full knowledge of all that was with him.

(God's Viceroy, when confronted with people of all types, will leave them alone, unless they are engaged in viciousness.)

92. Then followed he (*another*) way.

93. Until when he reached (*a tract*) between the two mountains, he found beneath them a people who scarcely understood a word.

(The third type of people in submission to him was more technically advanced than the second; they were skilled in metalwork. But they were regularly attacked by the wild tribes called Gog and Magog, and were

ready to pay him tribute in return for his closure of the mountain gap through which they came: possibly the Iron Gates near Bukhara, which stood between Transoxiana and Mongolia. Yet he would not accept any tribute.)

94. They said: "O Dhû'l-Qarnayn! Gog and Magog are working corruption in the land, so may we pay you tribute on condition that you set a barrier between us and them?

95. He said: "(*The power*) that My Lord has given me is better (*than any tribute*). Help me with a force of labourers and I will erect a (*strong*) barrier between you and them.

96. Bring me blocks of iron! At length, when he had levelled up (*the gap*) between the cliffs he said: "Blow (*with your bellows*). Then, when he had made it a fire, he said: "Bring me molten copper to pour on it.

97. And (*Gog and Magog*) were not able to surmount it, nor could they dig (*their way*) through it.

98. He said: "This is a mercy from my Lord, but when the promise of my Lord has been fulfilled, He will level it to dust. The promise of my Lord is ever true.

(After this third episode, Dhû'l-Qarnayn claims no credit for himself, but instead praises his Lord, in Whose name he rules. He increases his own and the people's humility by recalling that all the works of man, however imposing, shall be scattered into dust by the Resurrection, when only purity of heart is of account. The Sûrah takes up this cue, and finishes with some short declarations on the Last Day, recalling its opening verses.)

99. And on that day We shall cause them to surge like waves upon one another. The trumpet will be blown and We shall collect them all together.

100. We shall bring Hell on that day before the disbelievers, plain to view.

101. Those whose eyes had been under a veil from My remembrance, and who had been unable to hear.

102. Do the disbelievers think that they can make My servants into protectors besides Me? We have prepared Hell as a dwelling-place for the disbelievers.

103. Say: "Shall We tell you who will be the greatest losers by their works?

104. Those whose efforts have been wasted in the life of the world while they thought they were doing good.

(There are people whose smug self-righteousness is so powerful that they go through life making mischief, believing that they are acquiring merit. The case of those who campaign for certain vices is an instance of this.)

105. Those are they who disbelieve in the revelations of their Lord in the encounter with Him. Therefore their works are vain, and on the Day of Resurrection We assign no weight to them.

106. That is their reward, Hell: because they rejected faith and took My revelations and My messengers for a jest.

107. As for those who believe and do good works: they have the Gardens of Paradise as a dwelling-place.

108. Where they shall dwell forever, desiring no change to befall them.

109. Say: "If the ocean were ink for the words of My Lord, assuredly the sea would be used up before the Words of My Lord were finished, even if We brought another (ocean) like it, for its aid.

(However astonishing and far-reaching the narratives granted in Scripture may be, they are less than a drop in the ocean, for His attributes, wisdom and knowledge are without limit.)

110. Say: "I am but a man like yourselves. It is revealed to me that your Lord is only One God. Whoever hopes to meet his Lord, let him work righteousness, and let him not associate anyone with Him in worship.

SÛRAH XIX

MARYAM (MARY)

Revealed at Makka

(This takes its name from the extended reference to the Blessed Virgin Mary, mentioned in verses 16ff. It was revealed before the departure of the first Emigrants to Ethiopia in the ninth year before the Hijra, an event caused by increasing persecution by the pagan Quraish in Makka. The verses pertaining to Zachariah and Mary were recited by the emigrants to the Christian King of Ethiopia, who was deeply moved, and refused to listen to Quraish's requests that they be deported.)

MARY

In the name of Allah, the Compassionate, the Merciful.

1. Kâf. Hâ. Yâ. 'Ayn. Sâd.

2. A mention of your Lord's mercy unto His servant Zachariah.

3. When he invoked Him with a secret call.

4. Saying: "My Lord, my very bones have become rotten and my head is shining with grey hair. My Lord! I have never been disappointed in my prayer to you.

5. I now fear *(the consequences of the actions of)* my kinsmen after me, and my wife is barren. So give me, from Your presence, an heir.

6. Who shall inherit of me and inherit *(also)* of the house of Jacob; and make him, O my Lord, acceptable *(unto You)*.

7. *(And it was said to him):* "O Zachariah! We bring you good news of a son whose name is John. We have not given this name to anyone before.

8. He said: "My Lord! How shall I have a son when my wife is barren and I am well-advanced in years?

9. He said: "So *(it will be).* Your Lord says: "It is easy for Me, for I created you before whom you were nothing.

10. Zachariah said: "O my Lord! Give me a sign! He said: "Your sign is that you shall speak to no man for three nights, although you are not dumb.

11. So Zachariah came out to his people from the shrine, and signified to them: "Glorify your Lord at break of day and fall of night.

("A place looking East may also be translated to mean a place east of Mary's house, or to the east of Jerusalem's Temple Mount.)

17. She placed a screen to seclude herself from them. Then We sent to her Our spirit (*Gabriel*), and he appeared before her as a man without fault.

18. She said: "I seek refuge in the Compassionate God from you; (*do not come near*) if you fear the Lord.

19. He said: "I am only a messenger of your Lord (*to announce*) to you the gift of a pure son.

20. She said: "How can I have a son when no man has touched me; neither have I been unchaste?

21. (*The angel*) replied, "So shall it be; your Lord says: 'This is an easy thing for Me. And We shall make him a sign for mankind and a blessing from Us.' It is a matter decreed.

22. Thereupon she conceived (*the child*); and (*with it*) she went away to a distant place.

23. And the pains of childbirth drove her to a trunk of a palm-tree. She said: "Would that I had died before this, and had become a thing of naught, forgotten!

24. But (*a voice*) cried unto her from below her saying: "Do not be sad; your Lord has provided a rivulet at your feet.

25. (*As for your food*) shake the trunk of the palm-tree towards yourself; you will cause ripe dates to fall upon you.

12. (*And it was said unto his son*): "O John! Hold fast the scripture! And We gave him wisdom when a child,

13. And compassion from Our presence, and purity; and he was devout.

14. And kind towards his parents; and he was not arrogant, rebellious.

15. So peace be upon him on the day he was born and the day of his death; and the day when he is raised to life.

(John the Baptist did not live long, being beheaded by Herod. But even in his short life, he was granted (1) divine wisdom; (2) gentle pity and love for God's creatures; (3) purity of life, for he renounced the world and lived in the wilderness.)

16. And make mention of Mary in the Scripture; when she had withdrawn from her people to a place looking east.

26. So eat and drink, and be consoled; and if you meet any mortal say: 'I have vowed a fast (*of silence*) to the Compassionate God, and will not speak with any human being this day.'

27. At length she brought the (*infant*) to her people carrying him. They said: "O Mary! Truly an amazing thing you have brought.

28. O sister of Aaron! Your father was not a wicked man, nor was your mother unchaste.

(Aaron, the brother of Moses, was the first in the line of Israelite priesthood. Mary and her cousin Elisabeth (the mother of John), came of a priestly family, and were therefore in the Hebrew idiom "sisters of Aaron .)

29. She made a sign (*to them, pointing to the child*). But they replied: "How can we speak with a babe in a cradle?

30. (*Whereupon*) he (*the babe*) spoke out: "I am indeed a servant of Allah. He has given me the Scripture and has appointed me a prophet.

31. And He has made me blessed wheresoever I may be and has commanded me to pray and to give alms to the poor as long as I live.

32. And (*He*) has made me dutiful to my mother and has not made me oppressive, wicked,

33. So peace be upon me the day I was born and the day that I die and the day that I shall be raised up to life (*again*).

34. Such was Jesus, the son of Mary; a statement of the truth about which they (*vainly*) dispute.

(Such was the birth of Jesus, an event over which so much ink and blood has been spilled between rival churches, wrestling with the impossible paradox of a divine baby. The Qur'an explains that his birth, while accompanied by miracles and portents, was the birth of an ordinary human being, as Christ says in verse 30 above: the final resolution of all Christological wrangling.)

35. It is not befitting to (*the majesty of*) Allah that He should beget a son. Glory be to Him!

When He determines a matter, He only says to it "Be! and it is.

36. (*And Jesus had declared*): "Assuredly Allah is my Lord and your Lord. Therefore serve Him. That is the straight path.

37. Yet the sects differed among themselves concerning Jesus; and woe to those who disbelieve because of the witnessing of a great Day.

(Few events in history were so momentous and so malign as the invention of the myriad doctrines and suppositions which grew up over the doctrine of Jesus's divinity, something he himself never preached. It was inevitable that spectacular Christian disunity, which has given rise to more than 23,000 denominations in the modern world, should have opened the gates to secularity and spiritual death among a confused and disillusioned Western intelligentsia.)

38. On that day when they will appear before Us, how plainly will they see and hear; but transgressors are this day in manifest deviation.

39. But *(O Muhammad)*; warn them of the day of distress and anguish, when Our decrees shall be fulfilled whilst they are still heedless, and they still do not believe.

40. We shall inherit the earth and all who dwell upon it. To Us they shall be returned.

41. And make mention *(O Muhammad)* in the Book *(the story)* of Abraham. He was a man of truth, a prophet.

42. When he said unto his father: "O my father, how can you worship that which does not hear nor see, nor avail you in anything?

43. O my father, there has come unto me of knowledge which did not come to you. So follow me; I will guide you to a right Path.

44. O my father, do not serve Satan. For Satan is ever rebellious against the Compassionate God.

45. O my father, I fear that the penalty of the Compassionate God will fall upon you, and you will become a friend to Satan.

(Compare the gentle, respectful words of Abraham with the following response of his idolatrous father:)

46. *(His father)* replied: "Do you reject my gods, O Abraham? If you do not stop, I will stone you *(to death)*. Now depart from me a long while.

47. Abraham said "Peace be with you; I will pray to my Lord for your forgiveness. For He was ever gracious to me.

48. I turn away from you and from those whom you invoke besides Allah. I will pray to my Lord, perhaps in my prayers to my Lord I shall not be unblest.

49. When Abraham had turned away from them and from those whom they worshipped besides Allah, We gave him Isaac and Jacob. Each of them We made a prophet.

50. And We gave them of Our mercy and bestowed on them a high and true renown.

(The two images of isolation and withdrawal deployed in this Sûrah, those of Mary and Abraham, are now followed with brief reminders of other Prophets, "at whose mention God's grace descends , whose lives also recall the principle of *sidq*: holy fulfillment of a pledge, made to the Compassionate God, as Allah is frequently referred to in this Sûrah.)

51. Also mention in the Book *(the story of)* Moses. For he was chosen, and was a Messenger, a Prophet.

52. And We called him from the right side of Mount *(Sinai)* and made him drawn near to Us in communing.

53. And We gave him of Our mercy his brother Aaron, a Prophet.

54. And make mention in the book *(the story)* of Ishmael. He was true to what he was promised. And he was a messenger *(of Allah)*, a Prophet.

(He had promised his father that he would unflinchingly accept the sacrifice ordered by the Lord, after which he was redeemed with the ram.)

55. He used to enjoin upon his people worship and alms-giving and was acceptable in the sight of his Lord.

56. And make mention in the book, Idrîs *(Enoch)*. He was a man of truth *(and sincerity)*, and a prophet.

57. And We raised him to a high position.

58. These are those to whom Allah has bestowed His favours: the prophets from among the descendants of Adam and of those whom We carried *(in the ark)* with Noah; the descendants of Abraham and of Israel, and of those whom We guided and chosen. When the revelations of the Compassionate God were recited to them they would fall down in prostration, adoration, and tears.

59. But after them there came a generation which neglected prayer and followed passions. They will meet deception.

60. Except those who repent and embrace the faith and work righteousness. Such will enter the Garden, and they will not be wronged in the least.

61. Gardens of Paradise, which the Compassionate God has promised His servants, while they have not seen them, and most surely His promise shall be fulfilled.

62. There they shall hear no idle talk, but only greetings of peace. And there they will have their sustenance morning and evening.

63. That is the Garden which We will give as an inheritance to those of Our servants who lead a pious life.

64. *(The angels say:)* "We do not descend *(from Heaven)* but by command of your Lord. To Him belong what is before us and behind us and all that lies between, and your Lord never does forget.

(The pagans once asked some questions of the Blessed Prophet, who promised to answer them at a certain time, when he was expecting Gabriel to come and bring a new revelation. Gabriel, however, did not come at the expected time, and the pagans did not miss the opportunity to laugh at him, and to say that his Lord forgot.)

65. *(He is)* the Lord of the heavens and the earth and all that is between them. Therefore worship Him and be *(constant and)* patient in worship. Do you know any being that can be named along with Him?

(As He is the Unique, His name is shared by none other.)

66. And man says: "What! When I am *(once)* dead, shall I then be brought to life?

67. But does not man remember that We created him before when he was nothing?

68. So by your Lord, assuredly We shall assemble them and the devils. Then We shall bring them on their knees, around Hell.

69. Then We shall certainly drag out from every sect whichever of them was most stubborn in rebellion to the Compassionate God.

70. And certainly We know best who deserves most to be burnt there.

71. There is not one of you who shall not come to it. This is the absolute decree of your Lord.

(All people, sinful or righteous will pass through Hell, even if only for an instant. But the righteous will be protected from the flame.)

72. Then We shall rescue those who kept from evil and leave the evil-doers therein crouching.

73. And when Our clear revelations are recited to them, the disbelievers say to those who believe: "Which of the two parties *(yours or ours)* is better in position and more imposing as an army?

74. How many a generation have We destroyed before them who were even better in equipment and in splendour to the eye!

75. Say: "If any men go astray, then the Compassionate God extends *(the rope)* to them, until, when they witness the fulfillment of His warnings, either in punishment *(in the world)* or in *(the approach of)* the hour, they will realise who is worse in position and *(who is)* weaker in forces.

76. Allah increases in right guidance those that walk aright, and the deeds of lasting merit are best in the sight of your Lord for reward, and best in respect of *(their)* eventual return.

(These lines are the same as in 18:46 (second clause), except for the word *maraddâ*, which is here substituted for *amal* (hope). The meaning is practically the same, but "hope is more appropriate in the passage dealing with this world's goods, and "eventual return in the passage dealing with the sinner's specific investments and commitments in worldly position and organised cliques.)

77. Have you seen the *(sort of)* men who disbelieves in Our revelations and says: "I shall certainly be given wealth and children ?

78. Has he perused the Unseen; or has he made a pact with the Compassionate God?

79. By no means! We will record what he says, and We will add and add to his punishment.

80. We shall inherit from him all that he talks of, and he shall come before Us alone *(without his wealth and children).*

81. And they have chosen *(for worship)* gods other than Allah, that they may be a power for them.

82. Instead they shall reject their worship and turn against them.

83. Do you see *(O Muhammad)* We have set the devils on the disbelievers to incite them urgently *(to oppose the truth)?*

84. So make no haste against them, for We are counting out to them a *(limited)* number *(of days).*

85. The day when We shall gather the righteous like honoured guests before the Compassionate God.

86. And when We drive the sinners to Hell like thirsty cattle.

87. None *(then)* shall have the power to intercede except the one who had made a covenant with the Compassionate God.

(In rounding off the Sûrah we now return to its principle theme: the glorious status of the prophet Jesus Christ. Again the Lord reminds us of the terrible metaphysical effects of blaspheming against Him, and exalting His messengers to divine status.)

88. They say: "The Compassionate God has begotten a son!

89. Indeed you *(people)* have put forth a monstrous falsehood.

90. At which the skies are ready to burst; the earth to split asunder, and the mountains to fall down in ruins.

91. That they should ascribe unto the Compassionate God a son.

92. It does not behove *(the majesty of)* the Compassionate God that He should adopt a son.

93. There is none in the heavens and the earth but shall come to the Compassionate God as a servant.

94. He takes an account of them *(all)*; and has numbered them exactly.

95. And each of them will come to Him on the Day of Resurrection, alone.

بِسْمِ اللّٰهِ الرَّحْمٰنِ الرَّحِيمِ

﴿طه ١﴾ مَا أَنْزَلْنَا عَلَيْكَ الْقُرْآنَ لِتَشْقَى ﴿٢﴾ إِلَّا تَذْكِرَةً لِمَنْ يَخْشَى ﴿٣﴾ تَنْزِيلًا مِمَّنْ خَلَقَ الْأَرْضَ وَالسَّمَاوَاتِ الْعُلَى ﴿٤﴾ الرَّحْمٰنُ عَلَى الْعَرْشِ اسْتَوَى ﴿٥﴾ لَهُ مَا فِي السَّمَاوَاتِ وَمَا فِي الْأَرْضِ وَمَا بَيْنَهُمَا وَمَا تَحْتَ الثَّرَى ﴿٦﴾ وَإِنْ تَجْهَرْ بِالْقَوْلِ فَإِنَّهُ يَعْلَمُ السِّرَّ وَأَخْفَى ﴿٧﴾ اللّٰهُ لَا إِلَهَ إِلَّا هُوَ لَهُ الْأَسْمَاءُ الْحُسْنَى ﴿٨﴾ وَهَلْ أَتَاكَ حَدِيثُ مُوسَى ﴿٩﴾ إِذْ رَأَى نَارًا فَقَالَ لِأَهْلِهِ امْكُثُوا إِنِّي آنَسْتُ نَارًا لَعَلِّي آتِيكُمْ مِنْهَا بِقَبَسٍ أَوْ أَجِدُ عَلَى النَّارِ هُدًى ﴿١٠﴾ فَلَمَّا أَتَاهَا نُودِيَ يَا مُوسَى ﴿١١﴾ إِنِّي أَنَا رَبُّكَ فَاخْلَعْ نَعْلَيْكَ إِنَّكَ بِالْوَادِ الْمُقَدَّسِ طُوًى ﴿١٢﴾

٣١١

96. On those who believe and work deeds of righteousness, the Compassionate God shall bestow love.

97. We have revealed to you the Qur'an in your own tongue that you may thereby proclaim good tidings to the righteous and give warning to a contentious nation.

98. But how many generations have We destroyed before them! Can you find one of them still alive, or hear so much as a whisper from them?

SÛRAH XX
TÂ HÂ
Revealed at Makka

This Sûrah is mostly concerned with the career of Moses, which is rehearsed in some detail. It concludes with an account of how man's personal responsibility shall be enforced at the Judgement, for which we are to prepare ourselves carefully.

The first few verses are connected with a celebrated incident in the life of 'Umar ibn al-Khattab, who had been a fierce opponent of Islam in Makka. He set out one day, sword in hand, intending to slay the Prophet, when someone told him that his own sister had

converted. Enraged, he went to her house, where she had been listening to the Qur'an, and demanded to know what she had been hearing. She refused to yield, and he struck and wounded her. At this she announced, "Yes, we are Muslims; so do as you will! Sobered somewhat, he asked to see the text they had been reading from, and she gave him the leaf on which Tâ Hâ was written. Deeply moved, he asked to be taken to the Blessed Prophet, where his conversion caused much joy.)

TÂ HÂ

In the name of Allah, the Compassionate, the Merciful

1. Tâ. Hâ.

2. We have not revealed to you *(O Muhammad)* the Qur'an to distress you.

3. But only as a reminder to those who fear Allah.

4. *(It is)* a revelation from Him Who has created the earth and the high heavens.

5. The Compassionate God, Who is established on the throne *(of authority).*

6. To Him belongs what is in the heavens and on earth and all between them and all that lies beneath the soil.

7. And if you speak aloud *(it is no matter)* for assuredly He knows what is secret and what is yet more hidden.

8. Allah! There is no god but Him. His are the most beautiful names.

9. Has the story of Moses reached you *(O Muhammad)*?

10. When he saw a fire and said to his family: "Stay here, for I can see a fire. Perhaps I can bring you a burning brand or find some guidance at the fire .

(Moses and his family had gone forth from Midian towards Egypt, where his mother was living. During the journey, on a cold night, a baby was born. They needed a fire, and Moses saw a light burning in the distance. This fire, in fact, turned out to be a sign, to prepare him to receive the divine revelation.)

11. But when he reached that place a voice was heard: "O Moses!

12. I am your Lord. So take off your sandals; for you are in the sacred valley of Tuwâ.

13. *(Know that)* I have chosen you. Therefore, listen to what is revealed.

14. I, even I, am Allah; there is no god but Me. So serve Me and establish the Prayer for My remembrance.

15. The Hour is surely coming. But I choose to keep it hidden, so that every soul may be rewarded for its labours.

(Ukhfî also means: "I am about to make it manifest. Both interpretations are regarded as acceptable.)

16. Therefore let not any person who does not believe in it and follows his caprice, turn you away from it, lest you perish.

17. What is that in your right hand, O Moses?

18. He said: "It is my staff; upon it I lean and with it I beat down leaves for my flock, and I have other uses for it.

19. *(Allah)* said: "Throw it down, O Moses!

20. So he threw it down, and lo! it was a snake, gliding.

21. He said: "Catch hold of it and do not fear. We shall return it to its former state.

22. And put your hand under your armpit it shall come forth white, without harm. *(This will be)* another sign.

23. That We may show you *(some)* of Our greater signs.

24. Go to Pharaoh for he has indeed transgressed all bounds.

25. Moses said: "My Lord open my breast for me,

26. Ease my task for me,

27. And remove the impediment from my tongue,

28. So that they may understand me.

29. And appoint a minister for me from my *(own)* family.

30. Aaron, my brother;

31. Confirm my strength with him.

32. And make him share my task.

33. That we may glorify you much,

34. And remember you much,

35. Indeed, you are ever watching over us.

36. He said: "Your request is granted, O Moses.

37. And indeed another time already We have shown you favour,

(Joseph had entered Egypt as a slave boy, then became a minister to the Pharaoh of the day. That Pharaoh and his people had been grateful to Joseph, But generations went by, and there acceded to the throne of Egypt a Pharaoh who hated the Israelites, so much that he wanted them annihilated. He ordered all the Israelite male children to be killed as soon as they were born. The mother of Moses was able to hide him for a while, but feared capture. Then the Lord spoke to her, and told her what to do.)

people of Midian for many years, and at length came here as was ordained.

(Moses had smitten an Egyptian who was ill-treating an Israelite, and, because of his great strength, slew him unintentionally. This became public, and he was forced to flee to the land of Midian.)

41. And I have attached you to Myself.

42. Go, you and your brother, with My signs and do not, either of you, cease to remember Me.

43. Go, both of you, to Pharaoh, for he has indeed transgressed all bounds.

44. Speak to him with gentle words, that perhaps he may take warning, or fear *(Allah)*.

45. They *(Moses and Aaron)* said: "Our Lord! We fear that he will hasten with insolence against us, or transgress all bounds.

46. He said: "Have no fears; I shall be with you, Hearing and Seeing.

47. Go to him and say: "We are the messengers of your Lord. Let the Children of Israel depart with us, and do not oppress them. We have come to you with a revelation from your Lord: and peace will be upon him who follows the guidance.

48. It has been revealed to us that the Chastisement will be upon him who denies and turns away.

49. *(Pharaoh)* said: "Who then is your Lord, Moses?

50. He replied: "Our Lord is He Who has given unto everything its nature and guided it.

(Moses's answer is straightforward and to the point. He will not dispute about "my Lord or "your Lord , the God of Egypt or the God of Israel. He will only speak of the One God, Who, as maker and guide, is Lord of all.)

51. Pharaoh asked: "What, then, is the state of previous generations?

(Pharoah will not respond to this, but instead attempts to lure Moses into a denunciation of Pharoah's ancestors.)

38. When We revealed *(Our Will)* to your mother by inspiration,

39. *(Saying:)* "Place *(the child)* into the chest and throw *(the chest)* into the river, then the river should cast it up to the bank, where he shall be taken by an enemy to Me and an enemy to him. And I endued you with love from Me, so that you might be reared under My eye.

(By making the baby so attractive as to be adopted into Pharoah's household, not only was Moses brought up in the best way possible from an earthly point of view, but Divine Providence looked after him in bringing his mother to him, as stated in the next verse, and thus nourishing him on his mother's milk and keeping in touch, in his inner growth, with the feelings and sentiments of his people.)

40. When your sister went and said: "Shall I show you one who will nurse him? Thus We restored you to your mother that her eyes might be cooled and she should not grieve. Then you did kill a man but We saved you from trouble, and We tried you in various ways. You stayed among the

٣١٤

52. He replied: "The knowledge of that is with my Lord, *(recorded)* in a book. My Lord never errs, nor forgets.

53. He Who has made, for you, the earth like a bed, and has threaded in it roads for you, and has sent down water from the sky, with which have We produced pairs of various plants.

(Here God seems to be speaking through Moses in the first person. Again, he refuses to be trapped by Pharoah's insinuations, but returns to the subject of the divine signposts in nature. Note the mention of plant gender, unfamiliar before modern times.)

54. Eat *(for yourselves)* and feed your cattle. Surely in this there are signs for men of understanding.

55. From *(the earth)* did We create you, to it shall We return you, and from it shall We bring you out once again.

56. We showed Pharaoh all Our signs, but he rejected and refused.

57. He said: "Have you come to drive us from our land with your magic, O Moses?

58. We will surely produce magic like it. So appoint a day between us and you which none of us should fail to keep, and a place convenient *(for both of us)*.

59. Moses said: "The day of the encounter will be the Day of the Festival, and let all people assemble when the sun has risen high.

(Moses chose a Temple Festival, when the streets were decorated, and the people were on holiday, with the intention of collecting as large a number as possible.)

60. So Pharaoh withdrew, gathered his devices, and came *(to the appointed tryst)*.

61. Moses said to them: "Woe to you! Invent no falsehoods against Allah, or He will destroy you with a scourge. He who lies, fails miserably.

62. So they *(the magicians)* disputed with each other over their affair, but they kept their talk secret.

63. *(Then)* they said *(to Pharaoh):* "These two are magicians who intend to expel you out of your land by their magic, and destroy your best ideals.

64. So arrange your plan and come in battle line. Whoever gains the upper hand today has surely triumphed.

65. They said: "Either throw first, or shall we be the first to throw?

66. "Throw! he answered. And by the power of their magic, their cords and staffs appeared to his eyes as though they were gliding.

67. And Moses conceived a fear in his mind.

68. We said to him: "Do not fear. For you are the higher.

69. Throw that which is in your right hand. Quickly will it swallow up that which they have made. What they have made is but a magician's trick. Magicians shall not prosper, wherever they go.

(Moses obeyed the command of Allah, and threw down his staff. Then the miracle occurred: the staff turned into a real serpent and swallowed up the other snakes, which were in fact the sticks and the ropes of the magicians.)

70. So the magicians prostrated themselves, crying: "We believe in the Lord of Aaron and Moses.

71. Pharaoh said: "Do you (dare) believe in Him before I give you leave? Surely this man is your master who taught you witchcraft. I will surely cut off your hands and feet on alternate sides, and crucify you on the trunks of palm-trees. Then you shall know for certain whose punishment is more terrible and more lasting.

72. They said: "We will not prefer you over the clear signs that have come to us, nor over Him Who created us. So do whatever you will do. You can only decree (touching) this worldly life.

73. We have put our faith in our Lord, that He may forgive us our sins and the witchcraft you have forced us to practise. Allah is better, and more lasting.

74. He that comes before his Lord as a sinner; for him awaits hell, where he shall neither live nor die.

75. But he that comes before Him with faith and good works, shall be exalted to the highest rank;

76. Gardens of Paradise, beneath which rivers flow, where they will abide forever. Such is the reward of those that purify themselves.

77. And verily We inspired Moses saying: "Set forth with My servants in the night and strike for them a dry path across the sea, without fear of being taken *(by Pharaoh)* and without the fear *(of being drowned).*

(Having received this order Moses set out by night to leave Egypt with his people. But Pharaoh was informed about this by his secret police. He pursued them, but he and his troops were overwhelmed by the sea, and perished.)

78. Then Pharaoh pursued them with his forces, but the waters completely overwhelmed them and covered them up.

79. Pharaoh misled his people, and guided them not.

80. O Children of Israel! We delivered you from your enemy, and We made a covenant with you on the right side of Mount Sinai, and We sent down to you manna and quails.

(The right side: cf. 19:52. The Arabian side of Sinai was the place where Moses first received his commission before going to Egypt, and also where he received the Law after the Exodus.)

81. Eat of the good things with which We have provided you; but do not transgress therein, or My wrath shall descend on you. And on whomsoever My wrath descends, he has perished.

82. Yet I am Forgiving to him who repents and believes *(in Me)* and does righteousness, then follows the right path.

(When Moses took his people out of Egypt and entered the Sinai peninsula, he went to the Mount to receive Allah's revelations, leaving Aaron behind him in charge of his people.)

83. When Moses was upon the Mount, Allah said: "O Moses, what made you come with such haste from your people?

84. He replied: "They are close behind me. I hastened to you that I might earn Your pleasure.

(As he was in the presence of his Lord on the Mount, his people were enacting strange scenes down

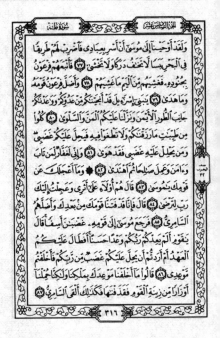

below. They were tested and tried, but they failed in the trial. A man called Sâmirî, a name which is perhaps an echo of the old Egyptian *shemer* ("a stranger"), suggested that the Israelites make the golden image of a calf for worship. Thus did they go astray and commit a great sin. Aaron was helpless to prevent them.)

85. Allah said: "We have tested your people in your absence, and *(the man called)* Sâmirî has led them astray.

86. Moses returned to his people, angry and sad. He said: "O my people! Did not your Lord promise you a fair promise? Did the time appointed then seem too long for you, or did you wish that wrath from your Lord should come upon you, that you broke your promise to me?

87. They said: "We did not break the promise to you of our own will, but we were made to carry the weight of the ornaments of the people *(of Egypt)* and we threw them *(into a fire-pit),* and that was what Sâmirî *(suggested and)* did as well.

88. Then he produced for them (*from what was in the fire, an image of*) a calf, a body that could low. "This, they said, "is your god and the god of Moses, whom he has forgotten.

89. Could they not see that it could not return them a word (*for answer*), and that it had no power either to harm them or to do them good?

90. Yet Aaron had told them beforehand: "O my people! You are being tested in this. Assuredly your Lord is the Compassionate God. So follow me, and obey my order.

91. But they had replied: "We will not cease in our devotion to it until Moses returns.

92. (*Moses*) said: "O Aaron, what kept you back, when you saw them going astray,

93. From following me? Did you then disobey my command?

94. Aaron replied: "O son of my mother, do not take me by the beard or the head. I was fearful that you would say: 'You have divided the Children of Israel and you have not observed my word'.

95. (Moses said:) "And you, O Sâmirî, what was your business?

96. He said: "I saw what they saw not. I took a handful of dust from the trail of the messenger and flung it: thus did my soul prompt me.

(The Sâmirî lies, and claims that he saw the Angel Gabriel, and picked up some dust from his footprints, cast it upon the calf, which thereby became blessed and a product of the same revelation which had come to Moses.)

97. "Begone cried Moses. "Your (*punishment*) in this life will be that you will say 'do not touch me!' And thereafter a tryst awaits you that you cannot fail to keep. Now look upon your god to whom you have become a devoted worshipper. We will certainly (*melt*) it in blazing fire and scatter it about in the sea.

("Do not touch me : he and his kind became social outcasts. Ultimately, we may suppose, the Sâmirî's descendants founded the kingdom of Samaria, whose inhabitants, having their own version of the Pentateuch and Targum, were shunned by orthodox Jews.)

98. But the god of you all is only Allah. There is no god but He alone. All things He comprehends in his knowledge.

99. Thus We recount to you the stories of what has gone before. We have given you a reminder from Our own presence.

("The reminder mentioned in the verse is the Qur'an, which narrates the past events which are worthy of contemplation.)

100. Whosoever turns away from it will bear a burden on the Day of Resurrection.

101. Abiding forever; how evil upon the Day of Resurrection that burden for them.

102. On the day when the Trumpet will be sounded. That day We shall assemble all the sinners white eyed *(with terror)*.

103. In whispers will they say each other: "You have stayed away but ten days .

104. We know full well what they will say. The most upright among them will then declare: "You have stayed away but one day!

(People at last will realize the shortness of the life in the world.)

105. They will question you *(O Muhammad)* about the mountains *(on that day)*. Say: "My Lord will crush them to fine dust.

106. He will leave them as a desolate waste, smooth and level.

107. Nothing crooked or curved will you see in their place.

108. On that day men will follow the summoner *(Isrâfîl)* in whom is no crookedness *(towards anyone)*. All voices will be hushed before the Compassionate God, and you hear no sound but a faint murmur.

109. On that day no intercession will be of benefit, save for him to whom the Compassionate

God gives leave, and whose word is acceptable to Him.

(The Prophets will each stand before Almighty God, and plead forgiveness for their peoples. The greatest Intercession shall be granted to our beloved Prophet, may God bless him and grant him peace. This is distinct from the Second Intercession, by which he brings out sinners from Hell after a certain time.)

110. He knows *(all)* that is before them and *(all)* that is behind them, but they themselves cannot comprehend it with their knowledge.

111. *(All)* faces shall be humbled before *(Him)* the Living, the Self-Subsistent. And he has failed that carries iniquity *(on his back)*.

112. But those who have believed and done good works shall fear neither iniquity nor any begrudging.

113. Thus *(O Muhammad)* We have sent this down as an Arabic Qur'an, and displayed in it some of the warnings, so that they may perhaps take heed, or may renew their remembrance.

him not drive you both out of the Garden, lest you plunge into affliction.

118. In it you shall not hunger, nor be naked.

119. You shall not thirst, nor feel the sun's heat.

120. But Satan whispered evil to him, saying: "O Adam, shall I show you the tree of immortality and a kingdom that never decays?

121. They both ate of its fruit, and so their nakedness appeared to them. They began to cover themselves with leaves from the Garden. Thus Adam disobeyed his Lord, and went astray.

122. Then his Lord chose him (for His Grace): He relented towards him, and rightly guided him.

(Note that the Fall is, in the Qur'anic account, coupled with a degree of grace, for "He relented towards him . Hence, in the Islamic vision of man, the human creature, despite his exile from the primordial Home of beauty and union, is not inherently evil. Islam rejects decisively any doctrine of "original sin , as taught by some religions, for it cannot be just that succeeding generations are held accountable for Adam's sin. Man is, in the Islamic vision, born good, not evil: it is only his cultural environment which may misguide him.)

123. He said: "Go down, both of you, from the Garden, with enmity one to another. But if there comes to you Guidance from Me, then whosoever follows My Guidance will not lose his way, nor fall into misery.

124. But whosoever turns away from My remembrance, assuredly he will have a life of narrowness, and on the Resurrection Day We shall raise him up blind.

125. He will say: "Why have You raised me up blind while I had sight (in my life-time)?

114. High above all is Allah, the True King! Do not be quick to recite the Qur'an before its revelation to you is completed; but rather say: "My Lord, increase me in knowledge!

115. We had made a covenant with Adam before, but he forgot, and We found on his part no firm resolve.

(The spiritual fall of two individual souls, Pharoah and the Sâmirî, having been described, the one through arrogance and the other through a spirit of deception, our attention is now called to the prototype of evil, who tempted Adam, the original Man, and to the fact that though man was clearly warned that Evil is his enemy and will effect his ruin, he showed so little firmness that he succumbed to it at the first opportunity.)

116. When We said to the angels: "Prostrate yourselves to Adam! They prostrated themselves, but not Iblîs: he refused.

117. Then We said: "O Adam, assuredly this (Satan) is an enemy to you and your wife, so let

126. Allah will say: "So *(it must be)*. Our revelations came to you but you disregarded them; so will you this day be disregarded.

127. Thus do We recompense him who is excessive, and does not believe the revelations of his Lord. But the punishment of the Hereafter is more terrible, and more lasting.

128. Is it not a guidance for them *(to know)* how many generations we destroyed before them in whose dwelling-places they walk? Surely in this there are signs for men of judgement.

129. But for a decree that had already gone forth from your Lord, and a term already fixed *(for their punishment in the Hereafter)*; the judgement would have been certain *(in this life)*.

130. Therefore *(O Muhammad)*, be patient with what they say. Praise your Lord's glory before sunrise and before sunset. And glorify Him some hours of the night and at the two ends of the day, that you may find joy.

(The commentators find in this verse a reference to the five statutory prayers, which are said at first light, noon, afternoon, sunset, and nightfall. But the exact times are not specified in the Qur'an, whose purpose is not to lay down liturgical detail: it may be found in the Sayings of the Blessed Prophet.)

131. Do not strain your eyes by looking at *(the worldly property)* which we have given some of them to enjoy; the splendour of the life of the world, through which We only test them. The provision of your Lord is better and more lasting.

132. Enjoin prayer on your people, and be diligent in its observance. We ask of you no provision; We provide for you. And the sequel is for righteousness.

133. And they say: "Why does he *(Muhammad)* give us no sign from His Lord? Has not a clear sign come to them of all that was in the former books *(of revelation)*?

134. And if We had destroyed them with some punishment before it, they would certainly have said: "Our Lord! If only you had sent us a messenger, so that we might have followed your revelations before we were *(thus)* humbled and disgraced .

(The living messenger they flout, because they want a sign; the sign they flout, because they want a living messenger. Human resistance to a Prophet is desperate and irrational.)

135. Say: "All are waiting: so wait if you will. You shall come to know who are the people of the Path of Equity, and who is guided.

SÛRAH XXI
AL-ANBIYÂ' (THE PROPHETS)
Revealed at Makka

This Sûrah consists of 112 verses. It belongs to the middle Makkan period, having been revealed during the years 5 and 6 before the Hijra. It deals with stories of different Messengers and prophets. It begins with the external obstacles placed by evil against purification, and gives the assurance of God's power to defend men, illustrating this with reference to Abraham's fight against idolatry, Lot's fight against unnatural wickedness, Noah's against unbelief, that of David and Solomon against injustice and failure to proclaim God's glory by making full use of man's God-given faculties and powers, that of Job against impatience and want of self confidence, that of Ishmael, Idris, and Zul-kifl against want of steady perseverance, that of Jonah against hasty anger, that of Zachariah against spiritual isolation, and that of Mary against the passions of this world. The common point is that the Prophets were not, as the profane suppose, just irresistible men. They had to win their ground inch by inch against all kinds of resistance from evil.

THE PROPHETS

In the name of Allah, the Compassionate, the Merciful.

1. Their reckoning has drawn near for mankind, while they turn away in care-lessness.

2. Every time a new reminder comes to them they hear it only while they play.

3. *(They listen to the new revelation)* with hearts preoccupied in play. The wrong-doers confer in secret, saying "Is not this man a human being like you? Will you then yield to the sorcery while you clearly see and perceive it?

4. He said: "My Lord knows every word spoken in the heavens and on the earth. He is All-Hearing, All-Knowing.

5. "Nay , they said, " *(these are)* muddled and incoherent dreams. Nay, he forged it. Nay, he is a poet. Let him bring us a sign with which the former prophets were sent.

6. Before them not one of the populations which We destroyed believed. Will these believe?

7. Before you *(also)*, the messengers We sent were only men, to whom We had granted revelation. If you do not know this, ask those who have the Reminder.

(Those "who have the Reminder , in Arabic *ahl al-dhikr*, are those scholars who are versed in sacred Writings, such as the Torah and the Qur'ân. Such scholars can be either Muslims or non-Muslims.)

8. We did not give them *(the Prophets)* bodies that could do without food, and they were not to live forever.

9. Then We fulfilled the promise to them, and delivered them and whoever We pleased. And We destroyed the transgressors.

10. (O People!), We have sent down to you the book in which is your reminder. Will you still not use your intelligence?

11. How many a city that was cruel have We destroyed, and after it We raised up another people!

12. When they felt Our punishment *(coming)*, behold, they at once began to flee from there.

13. *(It was said unto them:)* "Flee not, but return to the luxury which was given you, and to you dwellings, that you may be questioned.

14. They said: "Alas for us! We were indeed wrongdoers!

15. They went on with this cry until We rendered them like a mown field, extinct.

16. We did not create the heaven and the earth and all that is between them in play.

17. Had it been Our wish to find a game We could surely have found it in Our presence, if We ever did.

18. Nay, We hurl the truth against falsehood and it breaks its head, and behold! It vanishes. And woe betide you for what you utter *(you describe of us)*.

19. To Him belongs all that is in the heavens and the earth. And all those who are in His presence disdain not to worship Him, nor do they weary.

20. They glorify *(Him)* by night and day without tiring.

21. Or have they chosen gods from the earth who can raise the dead?

22. If there were, in the heavens and the earth, other gods besides Allah, there would have been confusion in both! Glorified be Allah, who is Lord of the Throne, above what they ascribe *(to Him)*.

23. He cannot be questioned for his acts, but they be shall questioned.

24. Or have they obtained other gods besides Him? Say: "Bring forth your proofs. This is the reminder of those who are with me and the reminder who were before me. But most of them know not the truth, and they are turning away.

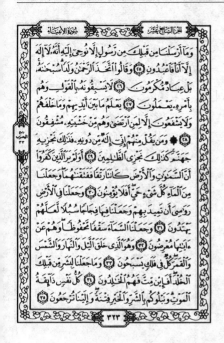

25. We did not send any messenger before you, but that We revealed to him, "there is no god but Me; therefore worship Me alone!

26. They say: "The Beneficent has taken a son! Glory be to Allah! Nay, they are only His honoured servants.

27. They speak not until He has spoken, they act by His order.

28. He knows what is before them and what is behind them. They do not intercede for anyone except for the one whom Allah accepts. And (so angels) are in awe and reverence of Him.

29. If any one of them were to say, "I am a deity apart from Him, We would reward him with Hell. Thus do We reward the wrongdoers.

30. Do not the unbelievers see that the heavens and the earth were at first one piece, then We parted them, and made every living thing from water. Will they not then believe?

31. And We have set on the earth mountains standing firm, lest it should shake with them (mankind), and We have made therein valleys as paths so that they may find their way.

32. And We have made the heavens as a well guarded canopy, yet they turn away from the signs (which these things point to).

33. And it is Allah who created the night and the day, and the sun and the moon. Each swims in its orbit.

34. (O Muhammad!) We granted not to any man a permanent life. If you then will die, will they live on for ever?

35. Every soul shall taste death. And We test you with evil and with good as a trial. And unto Us shall you be returned.

وَإِذَا رَآكَ الَّذِينَ كَفَرُوٓا إِن يَتَّخِذُونَكَ إِلَّا هُزُوًا
أَهَٰذَا الَّذِي يَذْكُرُ آلِهَتَكُمْ وَهُم بِذِكْرِ الرَّحْمَٰنِ
هُمْ كَٰفِرُونَ ٣٦ خُلِقَ الْإِنسَٰنُ مِنْ عَجَلٍ سَأُوْرِيكُمْ
ءَايَٰتِى فَلَا تَسْتَعْجِلُونِ ٣٧ وَيَقُولُونَ مَتَىٰ هَٰذَا الْوَعْدُ
إِن كُنتُمْ صَٰدِقِينَ ٣٨ لَوْ يَعْلَمُ الَّذِينَ كَفَرُوا حِينَ
لَا يَكُفُّونَ عَن وُجُوهِهِمُ النَّارَ وَلَا عَن ظُهُورِهِمْ وَلَا
هُمْ يُنصَرُونَ ٣٩ بَلْ تَأْتِيهِم بَغْتَةً فَتَبْهَتُهُمْ فَلَا
يَسْتَطِيعُونَ رَدَّهَا وَلَا هُمْ يُنظَرُونَ ٤٠ وَلَقَدِ اسْتُهْزِئَ
بِرُسُلٍ مِّن قَبْلِكَ فَحَاقَ بِالَّذِينَ سَخِرُوا مِنْهُم مَّا كَانُوا بِهِۦ
يَسْتَهْزِءُونَ ٤١ قُلْ مَن يَكْلَؤُكُم بِالَّيْلِ وَالنَّهَارِ مِنَ
الرَّحْمَٰنِ بَلْ هُمْ عَن ذِكْرِ رَبِّهِم مُّعْرِضُونَ ٤٢ أَمْ
لَهُمْ ءَالِهَةٌ تَمْنَعُهُم مِّن دُونِنَا لَا يَسْتَطِيعُونَ نَصْرَ
أَنفُسِهِمْ وَلَا هُم مِّنَّا يُصْحَبُونَ ٤٣ بَلْ مَتَّعْنَا هَٰٓؤُلَآءِ
وَءَابَآءَهُمْ حَتَّىٰ طَالَ عَلَيْهِمُ الْعُمُرُ أَفَلَا يَرَوْنَ أَنَّا نَأْتِى
الْأَرْضَ نَنقُصُهَا مِنْ أَطْرَافِهَا أَفَهُمُ الْغَٰلِبُونَ ٤٤

٣٢٤

36. When those who disbelieve see you, they take you only in jest, *(saying to one another)* "What! Is this the man who mentions your gods? And they disbelieve in the mention of the Beneficent *(God)*.

37. Man is made of haste. I will show you My signs, so do not make Me hasten.

38. And they say: "When will this promise *(be fulfilled)* if you are truthful?

39. If only those who disbelieved knew the time when they will not be able to ward off the fire from their faces, and from their backs, and they will not be helped.

40. Nay, it may come to them abruptly and confound them. They shall not be able to avert it and they shall not be reprieved.

41. Surely Messengers before you were mocked, and then those who were scoffing at them were encompassed by what they were scoffing at.

42. *(O Muhammad)* say: "Who is there to protect you by night and day from the Beneficent? Nay, yet they turn away from the mention of their Lord.

43. Or have they gods that can guard them from Us? They have no power to aid themselves nor can they be defended from Us.

44. Nay, We gave good things *(of this life)* to those men and their fathers until life grew long for them. Do they not see that We come to the land to reduce it from its outlying borders. Are they then the victors?

(According to the commentators, the "land that God will reduce was the territory then occupied by the pagans. Revealed at Makka, this passage was a joyful prophecy, a miracle of the Qur'ân. Other commentators, it may be noted, believe that this verse was revealed at Madîna, in which case it is not a prophecy of the future, but a statement of political fact, as the Muslim fortunes progressed.)

45. *(O Muhammad!)* say to them: "I only warn you according to revelation. "But the deaf will not hear the call when they are warned.

46. However, if a breath of your Lord's punishment were to touch them, they assuredly would say: "Alas for us! Because we, indeed, were wrong doers.

47. And We set up a just balance *(scales)* for the Day of Resurrection. Thus, no soul will be treated unjustly. Even though it be the weight of one mustard seed, We shall bring it forth to be weighed; and Our reckoning will suffice.

(The statement "We set up a just balance for the day of resurrection is interpreted by the commentators as follows:

(1) On the Day of judgment, injustices perpetrated in the world will finally be righted;

(2) On that Day, a great luminous pair of Scales will be set up, on which mens deeds are weighed.

48. We gave Moses and Aaron the Criterion *(of right and wrong)* and a light and Reminder for those who keep from evil

(The word "Criterion *(Furqan)* cited here can mean either the divinely inspired capacity to discriminate truth from falsehood, or the Qur'ân itself, which is itself such a discrimination.)

49. Those who fear their Lord though they have not seen Him are in dread of the Hour.

50. This is a blessed Reminder that We have revealed to you *(O idolators of Makka!)*. Will you then reject it *(saying: It is not from Allah!)?*

51. We gave Abraham his rectitude *(discretion and his proper course)* before *(Moses)*, and We knew him *(that he was qualified and worthy of prophethood.)*

52. When he said to his father and his people: "What are these images to which you are devoted in worship?

53. They said: "We found our fathers worshipping them.

54. He said: "Verily, you and your fathers were in plain error.

55. They said: "Have you brought us the truth or are you jesting?

56. He said: "Nay, your Lord is the Lord of the Heavens and the earth. He created them from nothing, and I am a witness *(to this truth.)*

57. By Allah! I shall circumvent your idols after you have gone away and turned your backs.

(It is said that Abraham uttered this in secret, and only one person heard him.)

58. Then he broke them into pieces, all except the large one, so that they might turn to it.

(Having broken the idols, Abraham hung his axe on the neck of the chief of them, as is described in the commentaries. And the people, who had gone away for a public entertainment, returned and saw that the idols had been broken.)

59. *(When they returned and saw the state of their idols,)* they said: "Who has done this to our gods? Surely it must be some evildoer.

60. They said: "We have heard a youth talk of them; he is called Abraham.

61. They said: "Then *(at once)* bring him before the eyes of the people, so that they may testify.

62. *(When Abraham was there)* they said: "Is it you who has done this to our gods, O Abraham?

63. He said: "Nay, this one, who is their chief has done it, so ask them, if they can speak.

64. At once they turned to themselves *(to discuss the position)* and said: "You, you are the wrongdoers!

65. Then they were utterly confounded, and said: "O Abraham! You have known that these do not speak!

66. Abraham said: "Do you then worship, besides Allah, those things that cannot profit you in anything at all, nor harm you?

67. "Fie upon you, and all that you worship instead of Allah! Do you not use your intelligence?

68. They said: "Burn him *(immediately)* and protect your gods, if you are doing anything.

(Abraham's people agreed with the offer and kindled a fire in order to burn him. Then they threw him into the fire with his hands and arms bound. Abraham then said: "It is enough for me to be protected by Allah; and surrendered to Him.)

69. We said: "O fire! Be coolness and peace for Abraham!

70. Then they wished to snare him, but We frustrated them and made them the ones that lost most.

(On the order and will of Allah, the fire did not burn Abraham; consequently those who planned this torture for him were utterly frustrated.)

71. And We rescued him and Lot *(who was his nephew and prophet in another country)* and directed them to the land which We have blessed for all peoples.

(Abraham, his wife and his uncle's son Lot were saved from the pagans and transferred to a country where they were to go on with their preaching.)

72. And We bestowed upon him Isaac, and Jacob as a grandson and We made each of them righteous.

(According to the commentators, the fruitful prosperous land is the districts of Damascus and Palestine. And, the fruitfulness of it arises from the fact that many prophets were sent there, and there too they started to preach their faith.)

evil and harmful acts. And when a people suffer from these two evils, Allah certainly damns them.)

78. And *(we bestowed the same favour upon* David and Solomon. Remember the occasion when the two were judging a case regarding a field into which the sheep of other people had strayed at night. And We were *(watching and)* witnessing their judgment.

(David and Solomon, who acted as judges in a case lodged between the owners of a flock and a cornfield, arrived at different verdicts. David, considering the value of the flock and the corn equal, concluded that the sheep should be given, to the owner of the corn as indemnity. Solomon, however, ruled that the cornfield should be entrusted to the owner of the sheep, who would be obliged to cultivate it and restore it to its former condition. In the meanwhile, the sheep were to be given to the owner of the cornfield, who would benefit from their milk, wool and lambs. David agreed with his son's judgement, and withdrew his own.)

79. We made Solomon to understand *(the case),* and to each of them We gave wisdom and knowledge, and We made the hills and the birds to hymn with David. We were the doers.

(In many passages, the Holy Qur'ân proclaims that the constituents of the physical universe, such as the sun, moon, seas, mountains and the natural phenomena associated with them, such as the day and the night, have all been disposed for the benefit and use of man, who must utilise and conserve them in the awareness that they are a trust from God. David's ability to make the hills and birds hymn God's praises merely reflects a special gift to him from God to render their praises audible, for all of creation sings His praise at all times, though commonly We cannot hear.)

80. And We taught him the art of making garments *(of mail)* to protect you from each other's violence. Are you then thankful?

81. And to solomon *(we subdued)* the wind in its raging. By his command it flowed towards the land which We had blessed. And of all things We are aware.

73. And We made them leaders to guide people in accordance with Our command, and We inspired in them the doing of good deeds and to establish the prayer and pay the zakat, and they were always worshippers of Us *(only).*

74. And We gave judgement and knowledge to Lot, and We delivered him from the community which practised abominations. Truly they were people of indecent acts and corruption.

75. And We admitted him to Our mercy, for he was one of the righteous.

76. *(Remember! with the same favour We blessed)* Noah when he cried to Us before *(those prophets),* We heard his prayer and delivered him and his family from great distress.

77. We helped him against the people who rejected Our signs. Truly, they were a wicked people. So we drowned them all together.

(According to Baydâwî, a commentator, Noah's people not only rejected the truth but also committed

82. And of the devils were some who dived for him *(to extract pearls from the sea)* and did other work besides; and it was We who guarded them.

83. And remember Job, when he cried to his Lord and said, "Truly distress *(disease and tribulation)* has seized me. But You are the most merciful of all who are merciful.

(Job *(Eyyûb)* was, as the commentator Baydâwî relates, a prosperous man with a large family. But his house collapsed and most of the members of his family lost their lives. His possessions and property were lost, also. He suffered a physical illness for ten years. In spite of all these troubles, however, he avoided any appeal to God for good health because he feared to be one who complains of his distress and is inconsistent in surrendering to the divine will. But, upon the request of his wife, he finally consented to pray to Allah, as expressed in the verse above.)

84. Then We heard and responded to him, and removed what was upon him of distress *(and tribulations)*. We gave him his family and restored his people to him and doubled their number with them, as a mercy from Us and a remembrance for the worshippers.

85. And Remember Ishmael, and Idris, and Dhu'l-Kifl. All were men of fortitude and patience.

86. And We brought them into Our mercy, because they were of the righteous.

87. And remember also Dhûn-Nûn, when he departed in anger and deemed that We had no power over him, but he cried out in the darkness, saying: "There is no god but You, I glorify you, and I was one of the wrongdoers.

(Dhû'n-Nûn, which is Arabic for "owner of the Fish , is a name of the prophet Jonah. He received this name because of his celebrated encounter with a large fish. Having invited his people to faith for a while, and

finally despairing of being heard, he deserted them in anger in order to save himself from a calamity which would befall them. According to one account, he left prematurely, and did not hear of their conversion. During a stormy sea-passage, he was obliged to jump overboard, in order to lighten the ship's cargo. Swallowed by a huge fish, he prayed to the Lord with the above prayer.)

88. Then We heard and responded to him, and We delivered him from distress. Thus do We deliver the believers.

89. And remember Zachariah, when he called upon his Lord: "My Lord! Leave me not solitary *(childless)*, though You are the best of inheritors.

90. Then We heard and responded to him, and We granted him John *(Yahyâ)*, and cured his wife *(to bear a child)* for him. They used to vie with one another in good deeds, and called upon Us with love and fear, and they remained humble before Us.

91. And *(remember that blessed woman)* who guarded her chastity. Then We breathed into her of Our spirit, and We made her and her son a sign for all peoples.

92. Surely this your community is one community, and I am your Lord; so worship Me.

93. And they have broken *(into fragments)* their *(religious)* affairs among them. *(Yet)* all of them are returning to Us.

94. Then whoever does any act of good while he is a believer, there is no ungratefulness for his efforts. Surely We shall record it in his favour.

95. And there is a ban upon any community which We have destroyed: that they shall not rise again.

96. This *(is to be continued)* until Gog and Magog are let loose, and they shall hasten out of every hill *(and slope).*

97. And the true promise has drawn nigh, *(as a result).* Then behold! The eyes of the unbelievers will fixedly stare in terror; saying "Ah! Woe to us! We were indeed heedless of this. Ah! we truly were wrongdoers.

(In the 94th verse it is stated that the believers will not be frustrated in their efforts; in the 95th, we find the fact that those who are destroyed because of their lack of faith and evil deeds will not have any opportunity to behave well and put forth decent efforts any longer, because they are not able to return to life again and repent. In the 96th it is noted that the deprivation of these people will continue until the wall of God and Magog which is noted as the sign of the day of resurrection, is opened, and they, coming out of every hill, spread all over the earth; or, as it is noted in another commentary, until men come out of their graves. The 97th verse warns that those who are disbelievers and lead a depraved life shall come to understand that they strayed from the right path only when the predestined day of judgement arrives; yet, then, they will be unable to do any thing except blame themselves.)

98. Surely you *(idolators)* and what you worship beside Allah are the fuel of hell. You will surely come there.

99. *(O idolators)* if these had been gods, they would not have come there! Forever all of them will abide therein.

100. There is a wailing for them, but they shall not hear anything there.

101. Those for whom the good *(record)* from Us has gone before, will be removed far therefrom.

102. They will not hear the slightest sound of it *(hell)*, they shall forever abide in what their souls longed for.

103. The great Horror *(of the resurrection or judgement)* shall not grieve them, and the angels will meet them *(with mutual greetings, saying)* "this is your day; the day that you were promised.

104. On that day We shall roll up the heavens like a scroll rolled up for books. As We originated the first creation, so We shall bring it forth again. It is a promise *(binding upon)* Us. Truly We shall fulfil it *(as We promised it)*

("So We shall bring it forth again means "We shall annihilate everything, and having annihilated, We shall recreate it as it formerly was .)

105. And verily We have written in the Zabûr *(Scripture)* after the reminder: "My righteous slaves shall inherit the earth .

(The word "reminder that occurs in this verse is usually taken to refer to the Torah. Some interpeters, however, believe that it denotes the Tablet of Allah's Decrees, which is preserved until the end of time, while the "Zabûr is a general term for all the books revealed by God.

As a prophecy which assures us that goodness shall triumph in the end, this is a good evocation of Islam's optimistic view of life.)

106. Verily in this *(Qur'ân)* is a message for people who would truly worship *(Allah)*.

107. *(O Muhammad)*! We have only sent you as a mercy for all worlds.

108. Say to them: "What has come to me by inspiration is that your God is one God. So will you surrender to Him?

109. But if they turn back, then say: "I have proclaimed to you all alike. And I know not whether what you are promised is near or far.

110. It is He who knows what is open in speech, and what you conceal.

111. And I know not, perhaps it may be a trial for you, and a grant of worldly livelihood for a time.

112. O Muhammad! Say: "My Lord! Judge with the truth! And Our Lord is the Beneficent, whose help is to be implored against that which you ascribe.

(The disbelievers said that misfortune, degradation and defeat would befall the Muslims. They assumed that the Islamic brotherhood would disintegrate, and that Islam would thus decline and vanish in a short time. The Blessed Prophet, however, put his trust in his Lord, as the verse reveals. According to another commentator, the disbelievers ascribed sorcery to the Qur'ân, or described it as fantasy. It is against these false accusations that the Blessed Prophet appeals, trusting that God will ensure the success of the Qur'ân.)

SÛRAH XXII

AL-HAJJ (THE PILGRIMAGE)

Revealed at Makka

(Al-Hajj), "The Pilgrimage , takes its name from vv.26-38, relating to the pilgrimage to Makka. This Sûrah is ascribed by some authorities to the Makkan, by others to the Madînan period. The Sûrah is concerned mainly with the spiritual implications of the Sacred House, the Pilgrimage, the Sacrifices, striving and fighting in defence of Truth when attacked, and other acts that make for unselfishness and uproot falsehood.

Some parts were probably revealed in the later Makkan period, while others came in Madîna. But the chronological question has no significance here.

THE PILGRIMAGE

In the name of Allah, the Compassionate, the Merciful

1. O mankind! Fear (*venerate*) your Lord! For the quake of the Hour (*of judgement*) is a mighty thing.

2. On the Day when you see it, every suckling women shall forget her suckling-babe and every pregnant one shall drop her burden. And you shall see mankind as drunken, yet they not drunk, but the doom of Allah will be strong (*upon them*).

3. And among the people there are some who dispute about Allah without knowledge, and they follow every rebellious devil.

4. It is decreed that whoever makes the devil his friend, surely he will mislead him and guide him the punishment of the Flame.

5. O Mankind! If you are in doubt concerning the Resurrection, *(consider that)* We created you of dust, then of semen, then of a clot of blood, then of a lump of flesh shaped and unshaped, so that We demonstrate to you Our power. And We keep in the wombs what We please to an appointed term, and afterwards We bring you forth as infants, then We cause you to grow up, that you reach your prime. And among you some die (young) and some are sent back to the feeblest old age so that they know nothing after they had knowledge. *(And O Muhammad!)* You sometimes see the earth dry and barren. But where We pour down rain on it, it trembles, and swells, and grows of every pleasant pair.

(First, if they really have doubts in their minds about life after death, they have only to turn their attention, either to their own nature, or to the nature around. How wonderful is their own physical growth from lifeless matter to seed, fertilised ovum, fetus, child, youth, age, and death! How can they doubt that the author of all these wonderful stages in their life here-below can also give them another kind of life after the end of this life? If they look at external nature, they see the earth dead and barren, and Allah's fertilising showers bring it to life, growth and beauty in various forms. The creator of this great pageant of beauty can surely create yet another and a newer world.

Second, the stages of a man's physical growth from nothing until he completes the cycle of this life are described in words whose accuracy, beauty and comprehensiveness can only be fully understood by biologists. Parallel to the physical growth may be understood man's inner growth, also by stages and by Allah's creative artistry.

Third, in this passage the mystery of our life is used to illustrate Allah's abundant mercy and favour to us. Here it is used to illustrate Allah's power in giving us a future life of even greater promise.)

6. That is so because Allah is the Truth, and it is He who gives life to the dead, and it is He who has power over all things.

7. And the Hour *(of Resurrection)* will come. There is no doubt about it. And Allah will raise up those who are in the graves.

8. Some there are amongst men who dispute about Allah without knowledge, or guidance, or an enlightening Book.

9. Turning aside in order to lead people astray from the path of Allah. For him in this world there is ignominy, and on the Day of Resurrection We shall make him taste the doom of burning.

10. *(O man!)* This *(torment of burning)* is because of your handiwork of old! For Allah is not unjust to His servants.

11. Some there are amongst people who worship Allah *(hesitantly)* on the verge. If good comes upon him he rests in it, but if an ordeal befalls him he turns himself round *(to infidelity)*. He loses both the world and the hereafter. That is the clear perdition.

(This verse aims to reproach those who seem to be believers, not sincerely but expecting some worldly good of it. So it is related in the commentary that it was revealed in relation to a tribe called *(Aârib)*, who had migrated to Madîna. One of them used to utter statements such as, "How cleverly I behaved in joining the believers in this religion! I have gained so many things in virtue of it! His wife gave birth to healthy children and his wealth increased; and he rejoiced in it. Yet, when in controversy and loss, he returned to infidelity, with such complaints as "So many misfortunes befell me because of it.)

12. He calls, apart from Allah, what does not harm him or benefit him. That is the far aberration.

13. He calls unto him whose harm is nearer than his benefit; what a bad protector! And what a bad companion!

14. Surely Allah will cause those who believe and work righteous deeds to enter gardens underneath which rivers flow. Surely Allah does what He pleases.

15. If any man thinks that Allah will not help him *(His Messenger)* in the world and in the hereafter, let him stretch out a rope to Heaven (*to the ceiling of his house*); then let him cut it off. Then let him behold whether his plan will remove what enrages him.

(Perhaps the meaning of this verse is: If any man thinks that Allah will not give victory in the world and in the Hereafter, let him take a ladder and visit Heaven to cut off the revelation that comes to the Prophet; then let him behold whether this activity will obstruct the help of Allah.)

16. Thus We sent it down as clear signs, and surely Allah guides whom He will.

17. Surely those who believe *(in Islâm),* and those who are Jews, and the Sabaeans and the Christians and the Magians, and those who become polytheists, assuredly, Allah will judge between them on the Day of Resurrection. And Allah is witness over all things.

18. Have you not seen and *(perceived)* that to Allah prostrate all who are in the heavens, and who are on the earth, and the sun and the moon, and the stars, and the mountains, and the trees, and the beasts and many of mankind? And many of mankind deserve punishment. And whoever Allah makes lowly, there is none to give him honour. Assuredly, Allah does what He will.

(All the universe is divided into parts: One of them is the material world, and the other is the spiritual world. All created things, animate and inanimate, depend on Allah for their existence, and this dependence can be construed as their *sajda* or prostration in worship. Their very existence proclaims

their dependence. How can they be objects of worship?)

19. These are two antagonists, who disputed about their Lord. As for those who disbelieve, garments of fire will be cut out for them, while boiling water will be poured down on their heads.

(Men of Faith, who confess their Lord and seek to carry out His will, and men who deny their Lord and defy His will, are implied here.)

20. Whatever is in their bodies and skins are melted by it. (*The punishment, expressed in physical terms, will be all-pervading, not merely superficial.*)

21. And for them are goads of iron.

22. Whenever they desire to go forth from Hell in distress, they are returned to it. And it will be said: "Taste the torment of burning .

23. Surely Allah will cause those who believe and do good works to enter Gardens underneath which rivers flow; therein they will be adorned with bracelets of gold, and pearls, and their attire therein will be of silk.

(In: 22:14 above, was described the destiny of the Righteous as compared with the time-servers and those who worshipped false gods (vv. 10-13). Here we have the case of those who were persecuted, abused, prevented from entering the Ka'ba and deprived of all that makes life smooth, agreeable and comfortable. For them the destiny is described in metaphors that negate all these afflictions: costly adornments, purity of speech which is the Path of the Lord of Praise.)

24. And they have been guided unto good speech *(in this life):* they have been guided unto the path of Him who is Worthy of all praise.

(The meaning of "good speech is, according to the commentators of the Holy Qur'ân, the monotheistic declaration that " there is no god but Allah).

25. Surely those who disbelieve, while they keep back men from the way of Allah and the Inviolable Sanctuary *(al-Masjid al-Haram)* which We have made open to all men, the dweller therein and the nomad *(are condemned there).* Whoever desires with infidelity injustice, We shall cause him to taste of a most grievous penalty.

26. And *(remember)* when We appointed for Abraham the site of the House; *(we said to him):* "Do not associate with Me anything, and purify My House for those who circumambulate *(the Ka'ba)* and those who stand, and those who bow and prostrate.

27. And proclaim among the people the pilgrimage! They will come to you, on foot and on lean camels, coming from every deep ravine.

28. *(They will come)* so that they may witness benefits for them, and during the known appointed days they mention the name of Allah, over the beasts of cattle He has provided them. Then eat thereof, and feed the unfortunate and distressed poor.

(There are benefits here both for our material life and for our spiritual life. Of the former kind are those associated with social intercourse, which furthers trade and increases knowledge. Of the latter kind are the opportunities of realizing some of our spiritual yearnings in sacred associations that go back to the most ancient times. Of both kinds may be considered the opportunities which the pilgrimage provides for strengthening our international brotherhood.

The three special days of Hajj are the 8th, 9th, and 10th of the month of Dhu al-Hijjah, and two or three subsequent days of Tashriq: see 2:197. The great day of commemorative Sacrifice *('îd al Adhâ)* is the 10th of Dhu al-Hijjah: the meat of cattle is to be eaten for food and distributed to the poor and needy.)

29. Then they should end their unkemptness, fulfil their vows and go round *(circumambulate)* the Ancient House.

(*Tafath,* superfluous growth on one's body, such as nails, hair, etc. which one is not permitted to remove in *ihrâm.* These may be removed on the 10th. day, when the Hajj is completed.

The spirit of the pilgrimage is one not completed by the performance of the outward rites. The pilgrim should carry in mind some vow or spiritual service and endeavor to perform it. Then comes the final *tawâf.*)

30. And *(the principle of Hajj is)* that whosoever glorifies the sacred things of Allah, it will be best for him in the sight of his Lord. And the cattle are lawful to you except what has already been mentioned to you; therefore guard yourselves against the idols and shun false testimony.

31. *(Perform your duties of Hajj)* being men of pure faith who are righteous to Allah, without associating any partner with Him. For the man who serves other gods besides Allah is like the man who falls from the sky and the birds had snatched him, or the wind had blown him to a far-off place

(A parable full of meaning. The man who falls from the worship of the one True God, is like a man who falls from heaven. His being taken up with false objects of worship is like the falling man being picked up in the air by birds of prey. But the false objects of worship cannot hold him permanently in their grip. A fierce blast of wind *(the wrath of Allah)* comes and snatches him away and throws him into a place far, far away from any place he could have imagined, into the hell of those who defied Allah.)

32. That *(is the behaviour of disbelievers)*. And whosoever glorifies the rites of Allah, that is from the devotion of hearts.

33. To you there are benefits *(in the livestock)* for a named term, then the place of sacrifices is the area of the Ancient House.

34. And for every nation We have appointed a ritual for sacrifice so that they should mention the name of Allah over the beasts of cattle which He has provided for them. So your God is one God. So to Him surrender. *(O Muhammad!)* Give glad tidings to the devotees of worship,

35. Whose hearts fear when Allah is mentioned before them, and those who are patient in what befalls them, and these who perform the Prayer *(salât)*, and those expend from what We provide them.

36. And the camels, We have appointed them for you as among the ceremonials of Allah; therein is good for you. So mention the name of Allah over them standing in rows. And when they fall down on their sides *(dead)*, eat of them and feed the poor and the beggar. Thus We have subjugated them to you; that perhaps you will be grateful.

37. *(Note it well that)* neither their flesh nor their blood shall reach Allah. But it is your piety *(and veneration)* that reaches Him. Thus has He subjugated them to you so that you should glorify Him for the guidance He has given you. And give glad tidings to the doers of good.

(The essence of sacrifice has been explained in 22: 34. No one should suppose that meat or blood are acceptable to the One True God. It was a pagan fantasy that Allah could be appeased by blood sacrifice. But Allah does accept the offering of our hearts, and as a symbol of such, some visible institution is necessary. He has given us power over the brute creation, and permitted us to eat meat, but only if we pronounce His name at the solemn act of taking life, for without this solemn invocation, we are apt to forget the sacredness of life. By the invocation we are reminded that wanton cruelty is not in our thought, but only the need of food.)

38. Allah defends those who have believed, *(but)* surely Allah does not like every treacherous ingrate.

39. *(Fighting is)* permitted to those who are fought against, because they were wronged; and surely Allah is Able to help them.

40. Those who have been expelled unjustly from their homes only for the reason that they said: "Our Lord is Allah. For had it not been for Allah's repelling some men by means of others, monasteries churches, synagogues, and mosques, wherein the name of Allah is often mentioned, would have been demolished. Allah will surely help those people who help Him. Truly, Allah is Strong, Almighty.

41. Those who, if We give them power in the earth, establish the Prayer and pay the Zakât, and enjoin kindness and forbid iniquity. And to Allah is the sequel of all affairs.

("Enjoining the right and forbidding the wrong is an essential duty of the Muslim Community, and one of the main purposes for which it has been raised. For Islâm is precisely the submission to the will of Allah. This demands both faith and doing right.)

42. If they deny you *(Muhammad!)*, *(you should remember that)* before them the folk of Noah, and the tribes of Âd and Thamûd, denied *(Our messengers)*.

43. And the people of Abraham, and of Lot,

44. And the dwellers of Midian had denied *(also our messengers)*. And Moses was denied.

But I indulged the disbelievers a long while, then seized them; and how terrible was My abhorrence!

(It is nothing new if a prophet of Allah is accused of imposture. This was done in all ages.)

45. How many a town have We destroyed while it was sinful, so it is now fallen down on its pillars, and *(how many)* a desert well and lofty tower!

46. Have they not travelled in the land, and have they hearts to comprehend with, or ears to hear with? For indeed eyes do not become blind, but hearts which are in the chest become blind.

(The word for "heart" in Arabic *(qalb)*, imports both the seat of intelligent faculties and understanding as well as the seat of affections, intuition and emotions. Those who reject Allah's message may have their physical eyes and ears, but their hearts are blind and deaf. If their faculties of understanding were active, would they not see the signs of His providence and His wrath in nature around them and in the cities and ruins, if they travel intelligently?)

47. And they ask you to hasten the torment. Allah shall never fail His promise. Truly a day with Allah is as a thousand years of what you reckon.

(If Allah gives respite, those to whom it is given have a real chance of repentance and amendment. He will not curtail His promise of respite. But on the other hand He has promised to call everyone to account for his deeds, and this involves justice and punishment for sin. This promise will also come true. It is foolish to try to hasten it. Time with Him is nothing. We keep count of time for our relative calculations. His existence is absolute, and not conditioned by time or place: what we call a thousand years may be nothing more than a day or a minute to Him.)

48. And how many a town I gave respite to while it was sinful. Then I grasped it. Unto Me is the return (the destination of all).

49. Say (Muhammad!): "O men! I am only a manifest warner unto you.

50. Those who believed and did righteous deeds, for them is forgiveness and a generous provision.

51. But those who strive against our signs to frustrate them, look! They are the companions of the Fire.

52. And We never sent a messenger or prophet before you, but (without doubt) when he framed a desire, Satan cast into his desire some affair. But Allah abrogates what Satan casts. Then Allah establishes (perfects) His signs (revelations), and Allah is All-Knowing, All-Wise.

(Prophets and messengers are but human. Their actions are righteous and their motives pure, but in judging things from a human point of view the suggestion may come to their mind that it would be good to have power or wealth or influence for furthering Allah's cause, or that it may be good to conciliate some faction which may be irreconcilable. In fact, in Allah's plan, it may be the opposite. Allah, in His mercy and inspiration, will cancel any false or vain suggestions of this kind and confirm and strengthen His own commands, and make known His will in His signs or revelations.)

53. (Allah allowed the devil to do this) because He wanted to make what Satan cast a trial (a temptation) for those in whose hearts is a disease, and those whose hearts are hardened. And surely the wrong-doers are in fargone dissension and discord.

(If any suggestion comes to the human mind that is not in accordance with Allah's will and plan, it has two opposite effects: to evil minds it is a trial and a temptation from the evil one, but to the mind well instructed in faith, it stands self-condemned at once, and becomes a means of strengthening faith and stimulating redoubled efforts to conform to the Will of Allah.)

54. And that those who have been given knowledge may know that it is the truth from your Lord, so that they may believe therein and their hearts may submit humbly unto Him. And surely Allah guides those who believe to the straight Path.

55. But those who disbelieve will persist in doubt of it, until the Hour comes upon them suddenly, or there comes upon them the doom of a disastrous day

(The penalty of deliberately rejecting Faith is that the person doing so closes the channels of mercy that flow from Allah. He will always be subject to doubts and superstitions, until the time comes when all earthly scales fall from his spiritual eyes. But then there will be no time for repentance. It will be too late to profit by the guidance of Allah given through revelation.)

56. The Sovereignty on that day belongs to Allah. He will judge between them. Then those who believed and did righteous deeds will be in Gardens of Delight.

57. And those who disbelieved and denied Our Signs *(revelations)*, for them will be a shameful doom.

58. And those who left their homes for the sake of Allah and then were killed or died, Allah verily will provide for them a good provision. For truly Allah is the best of providers.

(*Rizq*: Sustenance, provision. We have preferred the latter word here, because after death we can only think of *rizq* in a large, metaphorical sense.)

59. Verily He will cause them to enter a place with which they shall be well pleased. For Allah is Knower, Gentle.

60. That *(is so)*. Whoever punishes with the like of that with which he was punished, and then is *(again)* oppressed, Allah will indeed succour him. Allah is Relenting, Forgiving.

(Ordinarily Muslims are enjoined to bear injuries with patience and return good for evil *(23:96)*. But there are occasions when human feelings get the better of our wise resolutions, or when, in a state of conflict or war, we return "as good as we get . In that case our retaliation is permissible, provided the injury we inflict is not greater than what we receive. After such retaliation, we are even, but if the other side again acts aggressively and goes beyond all bounds in attacking us, we are entitled to protection from Allah in spite of all our faults; for Allah is the One that blots out our sins, and forgives again and again.)

61. That is because Allah makes the night pass into the day and makes the day pass into the night. And Allah is Hearer, Seer.

62. That is because Allah, He is the Truth, and that which they call instead of Him, is the False; and because Allah, He is the High, the Great.

63. Have you not seen that Allah brings down water from heaven? Thus the earth becomes green. Surely Allah is Subtle, All-Aware.

(*Latif*, as a name of Allah, is as difficult to define in words as the idea it seeks to represent. It implies (1)

fine, subtle *(the basic meaning)*; (2) so fine and subtle as to be imperceptible to human sight; (3) so pure as to be incomprehensible; (4) with sight so perfect as to see and understand the finest subtleties and mysteries; (5) so kind and gracious as to bestow gifts of the most subtle kind; extraordinarily gracious and understanding.)

64. To Him belongs what is in the heavens and what is in the earth. And Allah is indeed the Independant, the Praiseworthy.

(Each of the verse 61-63 mentioned two attributes of Allah with reference to the contents of that verse. This verse now sums up the whole argument, and the two attributes with which it closes sum up the idea by which we can understand Allah's goodness. Allah's loving kindness and mercies are not like those of human creatures who all depend upon one another, and often expect some kindness or recognition in return. Allah is above all wants, and depends in no way whatever on His creatures. His mercies have therefore a special quality, which we cannot describe except by gratefully singing the praises of Allah.)

65. Have you not seen that Allah has subjected *(made serviceable)* to you all that is in the earth, and the vessels that run upon the sea by His command, and He holds back the heaven *(sky, or rain)* from falling on the earth unless by His leave? Surely Allah is Kind and Merciful to mankind.

66. And it is He who gave you life, then He will cause you to die, then He again will give you life. Truly man is ever ungrateful

67. For every nation have We appointed a Law *(rites and ceremonies)* that they observe. So let them not dispute the matter with you. And invite them to your Lord, for you are surely following a straight guidance.

(Rites and ceremonies may appear to be an unimportant matter compared with "weightier matters of the Law and with the higher needs of man's spiritual nature. But they are necessary for social and religious organisation, and their effect on the individual himself is not to be despised. In any case, as they are visible external symbols, they give rise to the most heated controversies. Such controversies are to be deprecated. That does not mean that our rites and ceremonies are to be made light of. Those of Islâm rest on the highest social and religious needs of man, and if we are convinced that we are on the Right Way, we should invite all to join us, without entering into controversies about such matters.)

68. And if they wrangle with you, say: "Allah knows best what you are doing.

69. Allah will judge between you on the Day of Resurrection concerning that in which you differ.

70. Have you not known that Allah knows what is in the heaven and the earth? Indeed this is in a Book *(a record)*. This is indeed easy for Allah.

71. And they worship, apart from Allah, things for which He sent down no authority and of which they have no knowledge. And for the iniquitous there is no helper.

72. And when Our clear revelations *(signs)* are recited unto them you can recognize the denial on the face of those who disbelieve. They are almost jumping to assault those who recite Our revelations to them. Say: "Shall I tell you of worse than that? The Fire. Allah has promised it to those who disbelieve. Evil is the destination!

(There is irony here. "You think Allah's revelations and signs are distasteful to you! There will be something far more distasteful to you if you do not repent! What do you say to the inevitable Punishment?)

٣٤٠

73. O mankind! A parable is set forth, so listen to it: Surely, those whom you invoke, apart from Allah, will never create a fly even if they combine together for the purpose. And if the fly took something from them they could not rescue it from him. Hence, weak are both the seeker and the sought! *(the worshipper and the worshipped.)*

74. They do not esteem Allah His rightful measure. Truly Allah is Strong, Almighty.

75. Allah chooses from the angels messengers, and from mankind. Truly Allah is Hearer, Seer.

76. He knows what is before them and what is behind them; and to Allah all affairs are returned.

77. O you who believe! Bow and prostrate yourselves, and worship your Lord, and do good, that perhaps you may prosper.

78. And fight for Allah, the right fight for Him. He has chosen you, and has not laid upon you in religion any hardship; the faith of your father Abraham. He named you Muslims previously, and in this *(Scripture)*, that the Messenger may be a witness against you, and that you may be witnesses against all people. Therefore, observe the prayer, and pay the Zakât, and hold fast to Allah, for He is your Patron. An excellent Patron, and an excellent Helper!

(As far as the striving is concerned in the narrow sense, see the limitations set forth in 2: 190-191. But the words are perfectly general and apply to all true and unselfish striving for spiritual good. The Jews were hampered by many restriction, and their religion was racial. Christianity, as originally preached, was a hermit religion: "Sell whatsoever thou hast *(Mark x.21);* "take no thought for the morrow *(Mat. vi.34).* Islâm, as originally preached, gives freedom and full play to man's faculties of every kind. It is universal, and claims to date from Adam: the patriarch Abraham is mentioned as the great Ancestor of those among whom Islâm was first preached: Jews, Christians, and the Arab Quraish.)

SÛRAH XXIII.
AL-MU'MINÛN (THE BELIEVERS)
Revealed at Makka

This is so named from a word occurring in the first verse or, it may be said, from its subject, which is the triumph of believers. It is considered to be the last of the Sûrahs revealed at Makka, immediately before the prophet's migration to Yathrib *(Al-Madîna)*.

THE BELIEVERS
In the name of Allah, the Compassionate, the Merciful

1. Successful indeed are the believers;

2. Who are humble in their prayers,

3. And those who shun vain conversation,

4. And those who are payers of the Zakât.

5. And those who guard their chastity *(their hidden parts);*

6. Except from their wives, and what their right hands possess *(slaves),* for then they are not blamed,

7. But whoever craves what is beyond that, such are transgressors,

8. And those who keep their trusts and their pledge *(like shepherds),*

9. And those who observe their prayers *(Salât).*

10. These are the inheritors,

11. Who inherit the Garden, where they shall abide for ever.

(In the next passage, Allah's creative work, as far as man is concerned, is recapitulated, in order to show man's real position in this life, and the certainty of the future: to which he was referred for his reward in verses 10-11 above. Here we are not concerned with the earliest stage, the creation of primeval matter out of nothing. It is also a process of creation when inorganic matter becomes living matter. Thus inorganic constituents of the earth are absorbed into living matter by way of food, and living matter reproduces itself by means of sperm. This is deposited in the ovum and fertilises it, and rests for a time in security in the mother's womb.)

12. And verily We created man from a product of wet earth;

13. Then We placed him as a drop *(of seed)* in a safe lodging,

14. Then We fashioned the drop into a clot of blood, then We fashioned the clot into the shapeless lump, then We turned the shapeless lump into bones, then We clothed the bones with flesh, and then produced it as another creation. So blessed be Allah, the Best of Creators!

15. Then after that you surely die.

16. Then on the Day of Resurrection you are raised *(again).*

17. And We have created above you seven paths, and We are never unmindful of creation.

(*Tarâ'iq*: tracts, roads, orbits or paths of motion in the visible heavens. These seven are regular and clearly marked to our eyes, in the immense space that we see around us. We must go to astronomy to form any plausible theories of these motions. But their simplest observation gives us a sublime view of beauty, order, and grandeur in the universe.)

18. And We sent down from the sky water in *(perfect)* measure, and We gave it lodging in the earth, and surely We are able to withdraw it.

(Normally the rain comes well distributed; it soaks into the soil; the moisture is retained for a long time; it soaks and penetrates through many layers of soil and forms the architecture of physical geography; the retentive powers of higher soil enable rivers to flow perennially even where, as in parts of Turkey, the rainfall is seasonal and confined to a few months in the year. Another form in which water comes down from the sky according to due measure is in snow and hail: these also have their place in the economy of air and soil, for were it not for snow and glaciers in the higher mountain regions, some of the rivers would fail in their abundant flow. As wonderful as the supply of water and moisture is its drainage. It returns to the sea and air in all sorts of ways, and the formation of mist and clouds repeats the cycle.)

19. Then We produced for you therewith gardens of datepalms and grapes, wherein is much fruit for you and whereof you eat.

20. And a tree that sprouts forth on Mount Sinai that yields oil and relish for the eaters.

21. And in the cattle there is verily a lesson *(an instructive example)* for you. We give you to drink of that which is in their bellies, and in them you have many benefits, and of them you eat

('*Ibra*: the root meaning of the verb is "to interpret, to expound, to instruct as in 12:43; the noun means an interpretation, or example or sign that instructs as here and in 16:66, or gives a warning, as in 3:13.)

22. And on them and on the ships you are borne.

23. And We sent Noah unto his people, and he said: "O my people! Serve *(worship)* Allah, for

you have no other god than He. Do you not fear Him?

24. But the chieftains of his people, who disbelieved, said: "This *(Noah)* is only a mortal like you, he wishes to make himself superior to you. Had Allah willed, He surely could have sent down angels. We heard not of this in the case of our fathers of old.

25. He is only a man in whom is a madness, so watch him for a while.

26. He said, "My Lord! Succour me, because they deny me.

27. Then We inspired in him, saying: "Make the Ark under Our eyes and Our inspiration, then when Our command comes, and the oven gushes water, introduce therein of every kind two spouses, and also the members of your own family, except those against whom the word has already been passed. And plead not with Me on behalf of those who have done wrong. Surely they will be drowned.

28. "And when you and those with you settle in the Ark, say: "Praise be to Allah, who has rescued us from the iniquitous folk.

29. And say: "My Lord! Cause me to land in a blessed place *(deliver me from drowning, bestow on me a multitude of Children, of goodly viands, and of Your blessing),* for You are the best of all who bring to land.

30. Surely in that are signs, though We are surely testing *(by blessing and retribution).*

31. Then We created *(brought forth)* after them another generation.

32. And We sent to them a messenger from among themselves, *(saying):* "Worship Allah! You have no god other than He. Will you not venerate *(Him).* *(that is, either Âad or Thamûd.)*

33. And the notables of his people who disbelieved and denied the meeting of the hereafter, and whom We caused to revel in this world's life, said: "This is only a man like you. He eats what you eat, and he drinks what you drink.

34. And if you obey a mortal like yourselves, then you shall surely be losers.

(The type of narrow sybarite, who enjoys the good things of this life, denies a future life, and is jealous of any one who presumes to widen his horizon, is here described in a few masterly strokes. He is bored by any mention of the serious things beyond his ken. What good is it, he says, to talk about the future? Enjoy the present. The gain is all in the present. The loss is all in the future.)

35. Does he promise you that when you die and became dust and bones, you shall be brought forth?

36. Begone! begone *(Far, very far!),* with that which you are promised.

37. There is no life other than this wordly life; we die and live and we will not be raised again.

(They seem to say: "There no future life: That we shall die is certain; that we have this life is certain: some die, some are born, some live; and so the cycle continues: but how can dead men be raised to life?)

38. He is only a man who has invented a lie about Allah. We shall not believe in him.

39. He said, "My Lord! Succour me, for they deny me.

40. He said: "In a little while they will surely become penitent.

41. Then the Clamour overtook them rightfully. Then we reduced them to rubble; so, away with the iniquitous people!

42. Then after them We brought forth other generations.

43. No nation can outstrip its appointed term, neither can they delay it.

44. Then We sent Our messengers in succession. Whenever its messenger came to a nation they denied him; then We caused them to follow one another, and We made them into stories *(only their names survived)*. So away with a people who do not believe!

45. Then We sent Moses and his brother Aaron with Our signs and a plain, clear authority,

46. To Pharaoh and his notables, but they were arrogant, and they were haughty people.

47. They said: "Shall we believe in two men like us *(human beings)*, whereas their people are servants to us?

48. So they denied them, and became of those who were destroyed.

(Racial arrogance made the Egyptians say; "This man belong to a race which we hold in subjection as our slaves: How can we accept them as messengers of Allah?)

49. And We gave Moses the Scripture, that perhaps they would be guided.

(Here the reference is to the second part of the mission of Moses, that to the Israelites, which the Israelites rendered ineffective by their want of faith.)

50. And We made the son of Mary and his mother as a sign to mankind, and We gave them refuge on a height, a sheltered place with a water spring.

(The virgin birth of Jesus was a miracle both for him and his mother. She was falsely accused of unchastity, but the child Jesus triumphantly vindicated her by his own miracle *(19: 27-33),* and showed by his life the meanness of the calumny directed against his mother.

There is no need to look far for the place where mother and child were given secure shelter. It is described in 19:22-26. It was the place to which she withdrew to be delivered when the time drew near. There was a fruitful palm tree, evidently growing on high ground, for beneath it flowed a spring. She retired therein into seclusion, and she and her child rested there until it was time for her to go to her people with her child.)

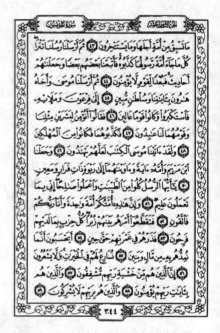

51. O messengers! Eat of the wholesome *(and lawful)* things, and act with righteousness. I am Knower of what you are doing.

52. Assuredly, this nation of yours is a single Nation, and I am your Lord; so fear me.

53. But they split their affairs between them into sects, each sect rejoicing in what it had.

54. So leave them in their error for a time.

55. Do they reckon that in what We provide them of wealth and children,

56. We hasten to them with good things? Nay, they do not perceive.

57. Those who feel the fear of their Lord, being in awe,

58. And those who believe in their Lord's signs,

59. And those who do not ascribe partners unto their Lord.

60. And those who give what they give while their hearts are in awe, because they are returning to their Lord;

61. Those race for the good things, and they shall win them in the race.

62. And We do not burden any soul with more than it can bear. And We have a book which speaks the truth *(all things about every one)*, and they are not treated unjustly.

(The record speaks clearly, and shows exactly what each soul has done and thought, and what is due to it in justice.)

63. Nay, their hearts are in deep ignorance of this, and they have other works besides, which they are doing.

64. Until, when We grasp their luxurious ones with the punishment, behold! they supplicate *(call for help)*.

65. Do not supplicate this day! Assuredly, you will not be helped by Us.

66. My verses were recited to you, but on your heels you recoiled.

67. In scorn thereof. Nightly did you rave.

68. Have *(the disbelievers)* never considered the word? Or have they received what their forefathers received not?

69. Or do they not know their messenger, and so reject him?

70. Or say they: "There is a madness in him? Nay, he came to them with the truth, and most of them are haters of truth.

71. And if the Truth had followed their desires, the heaven and the earth and whoever is in it would have been corrupted. Nay, We have brought them their Reminder, but from their Reminder they now turn away.

(Allah is All-Wise and All-Good, and His architecture of the universe is on the perfect plan. If these poor, low, selfish, ignorant creatures were to plan it according to their hearts' desires, it would be a dreadful world, full of confusion and corruption.)

72. Or do you *(Muhammad)* ask of them a tribute. Surely your Lord's tribute is better, for He is the best of providers.

73. And surely you call them to the straight path,

74. And those who do not believe in the hereafter indeed are deviating *(astray)* from the path.

75. If We took compassion on them and relieved them of the harm afflicting them, they would still persist blindly in their rebellion.

76. We grasped them with punishment, but they humble not themselves to their Lord, nor do they pray.

77. Finally, when We open against them a gate of stern torment, behold! they then are bewildered thereat.

78. And it is He who has originated for you hearing *(ears)* and sight *(eyes)*, and hearts. Small thanks do you give!

79. And it is He who spread you *(all)* through the earth, and unto Him you will be gathered.

80. And it is He who gives life and causes death, and His is the difference of night and day. Do you not comprehend?

81. Nay! They say the likes of what the ancients said.

82. They said: "When we die, and become dust and bones, shall we be raised again?

83. We and our fathers were promised this before. Surely this is merely the legends of the ancients.

84. Say: "Unto whom belongs the earth and whoever is on it; answer, if you have knowledge?

85. They will say: "to Allah. Say: "Will you not then remember?

86. Say: "Who is the Lord of the seven heavens and the Lord of the great Throne?

87. They say: "All that belongs to Allah. Ask them: "Do you not fear Him?

88. Say: "In whose hand is the dominion over all things and He protects while none can seek protection against Him? *(Answer that)* if you have knowledge.

89. They say, "Unto Allah *(all that belongs).* Ask then, "How then are you deluded?

(As these verses clearly explain, the pre-Islamic Arabs did in fact acknowledge the existence of Allah; they merely disbelieved in the prophethood of Muhammad, peace be upon him, and the blessed Book which he was given for their guidance. As the passage also shows (cf.v.82), they also denied the Resurrection and the Hereafter.)

90. Nay, We brought them the truth, and surely they are liars.

91. Allah has not acquired (or chosen) a son, neither is there a god with Him, otherwise every deity would have become (an independent) ruler over its creation, and surely some of them would raise themselves above others. Glory be to Allah, above what they describe.

(In this verse, the fact that polytheism is not compatible with the creation of the universe and its order is proved. Consequently the existence of the universe and the excellence of its order is the reflection and the proof of existence of Allah and His unity.)

92. He is Knower of the unseen and the seen. And exalted is Allah and free from the sort of things they attribute to Him.

(The "unseen" and the "seen" are two separate areas of knowledge. Knowledge of the unseen is not possible through the employment of the mind and senses, although it is attainable to a certain degree by means of certain intuitive faculties, and is conveyed to us more perfectly via revelation. In general, the "unseen worlds are to be accepted in faith, as is indicated in the opening and closing verses of Sûrah al-Baqarah.)

93, 94. (O Muhammad!) Say: "My Lord! If You would show me what they are promised (of punishment), my Lord! Place me not with the iniquitous people.

95. (O Muhammad!) Surely We are able to show you what We have promised them.

96. Repel evil with what is better, for We know best what they describe.

97. And say: "My Lord! I seek refuge in you from the promptings of the Satans.

98. And I seek refuge in you, my Lord, lest they should be present with me.

99. Finally, when death comes unto one of them he says: "My Lord, send me back!

100. That I may do righteous deeds in what I had left undone, but it is but a word he speaks. And there behind them is a barrier till the day they will be raised.

(Barzakh: a partition, a bar or barrier; the place or state in which people will be after death and before judgment.)

101. But when the trumpet is blown, there shall be no kinship among them on that day, nor will they ask of one another

102. Then those whose scales are heavy, they are the successful.

103. And those whose scales are light have lost themselves, they shall abide in hell forever.

104. The fire shall scorch their faces, and they are sullen therein.

105. *(It will be said:)* "Were not My verses *(revelations)* recited to you, and then you denied them?

106. They say: "Our Lord! Our wretchedness prevailed over us, and we were a people astray.

107. Our Lord! Bring us forth from hence! If we return *(revert to evil)* then indeed we shall be wrong-doers.

108. He said: "Fall back therein, and do not speak to Me!

109. Lo! There was a party of My servants *(slaves)* who say: "Our Lord! We believed, therefore forgive us and have mercy on us, for you are the best of the merciful.

110. *(Allah said to them),* "But you took them for a mockery, until they caused you to forget remembrance of Me, while you laughed at them.

111. "Surely this day I shall give them the reward for their perseverance. They are truly the triumphant.

112. He will say: "How long have you tarried on the earth, counting by years?

113. They will say: "We tarried a day or a part of a day. Ask of those who keep count.

(This question and answer about time implies two things (1) The attention of the ungodly is drawn to the extremely short time of the life in this world, compared to the eternity which they face. They are made to see this, and to realise how mistaken they were in their comparative valuation of things spiritual and material. (2) Time, as we know it, will have faded away and appear as almost nothing. It is just a matter relative to this life of temporary probation.)

114. He will say: "You tarried but a little, if you only knew.

115. Did you reckon that We only created you in jest, and that to Us you would not be returned?

(Allah's Creation is not without a high and serious purpose. It is not vain, or for mere play or sport. As far as man is concerned, the highest issues for him hang on his behavior in this life. "Life is real, life is earnest, and the grave is not its goal , Longfellow truly says. We must therefore earnestly search out Allah's Truth, encouraged by the fact that Allah's truth is also, out of His unbounded mercy, searching us out and trying to reach us.)

116. So, exalted is Allah, the King, the True. There no god but He; Lord of the Noble Throne.

117. And whoever invokes another god with Allah, of which he has no proof, then his reckoning shall be with his Lord. Surely the unbelievers will not be successful.

118. And say: "My Lord! Forgive and relent, for You are the best of the relenting!

SÛRAH XXIV
AN-NÛR (THE LIGHT)
Revealed at Madîna

This Sûrah was revealed between the fifth and the sixth years of the Hijrah, i.e. five years before the death of the Prophet Muhammad. It takes its title from verses 35-40, which deal with a description of God's light. Some commentators say that the title is derived from the illuminating codes of behaviour laid down for the good behaviour of mankind. With the exception of a few verses that describe God's light and power of creation, this Sûrah is an excellent reflection of Islâmic laws.

THE LIGHT
In the name of Allah, the Compassionate, the Merciful

1. This is a sûrah which We have sent down and enjoined, and in which We have sent down clear signs, that perhaps you may remember.

2. The adulteress and the adulterer, flog each of them a hundred stripes, and let not any pity *(mercy)* for them withhold you from supporting Allah's religion, if you believe in Allah and the last day. And let a party of believers witness their punishment.

(This punishment is only applied to the unmarried male or female. In the case of a married man or woman, punishment by stoning is applied, provided that certain conditions are met, the most important of which are: (a) Both the adulterer and the adulteress are caught in the actual act of intercourse, (b) There should be four witnesses to the act, of good character; (c) a confession free of any pressure by either the adulterer and the adulteress that should be repeated four times.

Commentators say that either the confirmed usage *(sunna)* of the Prophet Muhammad, upon him be peace, or a commandment received from God, has rendered the punishment of married adulteress, set at stoning to death, distinct from the punishment of the unmarried, which is flogging at one hundred stripes. This verse has abrogated verse 15 of Sûrah 4.)

3. The adulterer shall not marry save an adulteress or an idolatress. And as for the adulteress, none shall marry her except an adulterer or an idolater. All that is forbidden to the believers.

4. And those who defame chaste women, and then do not bring four witnesses; flog them with eighty stripes, and never accept their testimony *(thereafter)*, for they are perverse persons.

5. Save those who afterwords repent and make amends, for truly Allah is Forgiving, Merciful.

6. And those who accuse their wives, and have no witnesses but themselves, then the testimony of each of them shall be a testimony sworn by Allah four times repeated, that he is indeed of those that speak the truth;

7. And the fifth *(oath)* is that Allah's curse be upon him if he be of those that lie.

8. But it shall avert chastisement from her if she testify a testimony four times repeated, sworn by Allah, that he is of those that lie.

9. And a fifth *(time)* that the wrath of Allah be upon her, if he has spoken the truth.

10. If it were not for the kindness of Allah and His mercy towards you, *(you would be in ruination because of defaming your wives).* And Allah is Forgiving and All-Wise.

11. Surely those who advanced the slander are a gang among you. Regard it not as evil for you. Nay, it is good for you. To every man among them shall it be done according to the sin he has committed. As for him that had the greater part of it among them, he shall have a painful chastisement.

(The particular incident here referred to occurred on the return from the expedition to the Banu Mustaliq, in A.H. 5-6. When the march was ordered, Hazrat 'Aishah was not in her tent, having gone to search for a valuable necklace she had dropped. As her litter was veiled, it was not noticed that she was not in it. The next morning she was found by Safwan, a Muhajir, who had been left behind the camp expressly to pick up anything inadvertently left behind. He put her on his camel and brought her, leading the camel on foot. This gave occasion to enemies to raise a malicious scandal. The ringleader among them was the chief of the Medîna Hypocrites, 'Abdullah Ibn Ubayy, who is referred to in the last clause of this verse. He had other sins and enormities to his debit, and he was left to the spiritual punishment of an unrepentant sinner, for he died in that state. The minor tools were given the legal punishment of the law, and after penitence mended their lives.)

12. If only the faithful men and women, when you heard of it, had formed a favourable judgment in their own minds, and said, "This is a manifest slander.

13. If only they had brought four witness of it (to prove their charge). Since they failed to bring the witnesses, they verily are the liars in the sight of Allah

14. And had it not been for the grace of Allah and His mercy on you in this world and the hereafter, a great punishment would have befallen you, because of that which you spread abroad.

15. You received it with your tongues (and passed it around) and uttered with your mouths that of which you had no knowledge. But you counted it a trifle, while it was serious in the sight of Allah.

16. Should you not have said, when you heard of it, "It is not right of us to talk about this. Glory be to You. This is a grievous calumny.

(The right course would have been to stop any further currency of false slanders by ignoring them and at least refusing to help in their circulation. The exclamation "Glory be to You! is an exclamation of surprise and disavowal, as much as to say, "We do not believe it, and we shall have nothing to do with you, O slanderers!)

17. Allah has admonished you that you never repeat the like of this, if you are (in truth) believers.

18. And Allah makes the signs clear to you, for Allah is All-Knowing, All-Wise.

19. As for those who love that indecency (adultery) should spread amongst believers, a painful punishment awaits them in this world and the hereafter. Allah knows, and you know not.

20. Had it not been for the grace of Allah and His mercy towards you (you would have been undone). Yet Allah is Kind, Merciful.

Bakr wished to stop that aid, but according to the highest standards of Muslim ethics he was asked to forgive and forget, which he did, with the happiest results for the peace and unity of the Muslim community. But the general application holds good for all time. A generous patron should not, in personal anger, withdraw his support even for serious faults if the delinquent repents and mends his ways. If God forgives us, who are we to refuse forgiveness to our fellows?)

23. Those who slander chaste women, ignorant even of sin, who are believers, are cursed in the world and the hereafter. And for them awaits a terrible torment.

24. On the day when their own tongues and their own hands and their feet shall bear witness against them as to what they used to do.

25. On that day Allah will give them the full recompense they deserve, and they will realize that Allah is the manifest Truth;

26. Vile women are for vile men, and vile men for vile women. Good women are for good men, and good men for good women. Such are innocent of that which people say: for them is forgiveness and generous provision.

(In conformity with Allah's law of the attraction of things, people of the same qualities, type, character or interest, come together in full harmony. This verse, however, stresses the fact that the Prophet Muhammad was married to a virtuous and upright lady. This is also an exoneration of Aishah from the calumny the hypocrites tried to smear her with. The word "such refers to the Prophet's family, men and women, including his wife Aishah, as is clear from the verse)

27. O you who believe! Do not enter houses, other than your own houses, until you ask for permission, and salute those in them (greet their dwellers). That is best for you. Perhaps you will remember (observe this).

21. O you who believe! Follow not the steps of Satan, for whosoever will follow the steps of Satan; surely he will enjoin on him what is indecent and blameworthy (wickedness). Had it not been for Allah's grace unto you and His mercy none of you would have ever been purified. But Allah causes whom He will to be purified. And Allah is Hearer, Knower.

22. Let not those endowed with dignity (grace) and means among you swear that they will not give to their kindred and to the needy and to emigrants in the cause of Allah; let them rather forgive and ignore the offence (show indulgence). Do you not wish that Allah may forgive you? And Allah is Forgiving, Merciful.

(The immediate reference is to Hazrat Abû Bakr, the father of Hazrat 'Aishah. He is He was blessed both with spiritual grace from God and with ample means, which he always used in the service of Islâm and the Muslims. One of the slanderers of Hazrat 'Aishah turned out to be Mistah, a cousin of Hazrat Abû Bakr, whom he had been in the habit of supporting. Naturally Hazrat Abû

سورة النور

فَإِن لَّمْ تَجِدُوا فِيهَآ أَحَدًا فَلَا تَدْخُلُوهَا حَتَّىٰ يُؤْذَنَ لَكُمْ وَإِن قِيلَ لَكُمُ ارْجِعُوا فَارْجِعُوا هُوَ أَزْكَىٰ لَكُمْ وَاللَّهُ بِمَا تَعْمَلُونَ عَلِيمٌ ۝ لَّيْسَ عَلَيْكُمْ جُنَاحٌ أَن تَدْخُلُوا بُيُوتًا غَيْرَ مَسْكُونَةٍ فِيهَا مَتَاعٌ لَّكُمْ وَاللَّهُ يَعْلَمُ مَا تُبْدُونَ وَمَا تَكْتُمُونَ ۝ قُل لِّلْمُؤْمِنِينَ يَغُضُّوا مِنْ أَبْصَارِهِمْ وَيَحْفَظُوا فُرُوجَهُمْ ذَٰلِكَ أَزْكَىٰ لَهُمْ إِنَّ اللَّهَ خَبِيرٌ بِمَا يَصْنَعُونَ ۝ وَقُل لِّلْمُؤْمِنَاتِ يَغْضُضْنَ مِنْ أَبْصَارِهِنَّ وَيَحْفَظْنَ فُرُوجَهُنَّ وَلَا يُبْدِينَ زِينَتَهُنَّ إِلَّا مَا ظَهَرَ مِنْهَا وَلْيَضْرِبْنَ بِخُمُرِهِنَّ عَلَىٰ جُيُوبِهِنَّ وَلَا يُبْدِينَ زِينَتَهُنَّ إِلَّا لِبُعُولَتِهِنَّ أَوْ آبَائِهِنَّ أَوْ آبَاءِ بُعُولَتِهِنَّ أَوْ أَبْنَائِهِنَّ أَوْ أَبْنَاءِ بُعُولَتِهِنَّ أَوْ إِخْوَانِهِنَّ أَوْ بَنِي إِخْوَانِهِنَّ أَوْ بَنِي أَخَوَاتِهِنَّ أَوْ نِسَائِهِنَّ أَوْ مَا مَلَكَتْ أَيْمَانُهُنَّ أَوِ التَّابِعِينَ غَيْرِ أُولِي الْإِرْبَةِ مِنَ الرِّجَالِ أَوِ الطِّفْلِ الَّذِينَ لَمْ يَظْهَرُوا عَلَىٰ عَوْرَاتِ النِّسَاءِ وَلَا يَضْرِبْنَ بِأَرْجُلِهِنَّ لِيُعْلَمَ مَا يُخْفِينَ مِن زِينَتِهِنَّ وَتُوبُوا إِلَى اللَّهِ جَمِيعًا أَيُّهَ الْمُؤْمِنُونَ لَعَلَّكُمْ تُفْلِحُونَ ۝

٣٥٢

---

28. If you do not find anyone therein, do not enter until you have been given permission, and if it is said to you "Go back , then go back, for that is purer for you. And Allah has full knowledge of whatever you do.

(Entry into an empty house is not allowed unless permitted by the owner of the house.)

29. There shall be no harm in your entering uninhabited houses wherein is supply for your needs, and Allah knows what you do openly and what you hide.

(The phrase "uninhabited house means places for public use which are not allocated to certain group of people, such as inns, hotels, shops, market places, baths, etc.)

30. Say to the believers that they should restrain their eyes and guard their modesty.That will be purer for them. Allah is well aware of what they do.

31. And say to the believing women that they should restrain their eyes, and guard their modesty (virtue), and that they display not their ornaments except what appears of them. And that they draw their veils over their bosoms and display not their ornaments except to their husbands, or their fathers, or their husbands fathers, or their sons, or their husband's sons, or their brothers, or their brother's sons, or their sister's sons, or their women, or their slaves, or male domestics who have no natural sexual force, or children who know nothing of women's nakedness. And let them not strike their feet together so as to reveal their hidden ornaments. And repent you all to Allah, O you believers, that you may succeed.

(Commentators have agreed that the clause "cast veils over their bosoms means that the dress they wear should cover the whole body except the face, the two hands and the feet. This means that the hair, the neck and what is below the neck should be completely covered. Muslim scholars have agreed that the clause "show not their ornaments , is a command to abstain from showing the places of ornament of the body and the adornment itself, except to the husband, lest this lead to allurement. However, the commentators have differed on whether it is permissible or abhorred to show outward adornment like wearing rings, using eye antimony ,etc.)

32. And marry those among you who are single *(male or female)* and the righteous of your male and female slaves. If they are poor, Allah of His bounty will enrich them. And Allah is All-Embracing, All-Knowing.

33. And let those who cannot find a way to marriage be chaste until Allah of His bounty enrich them. And if those whom your right hands possess ask for a deed of manumission, write it down for them if you know good in them. And give them a portion of the wealth of Allah which He has given you. And force not your female slaves into prostitution, in order to acquire the goods of this worldly life; if they wish to preserve their chastity; yet if any one force them, surely Allah will be Merciful to them *(the women)* after their compulsion.

(A Muslim marriage requires some sort of a dower for the wife. If a man cannot afford it, he must wait and keep himself chaste. It is no excuse for him to say that he must satisfy his natural cravings, within or outside marriage.

The law of slavery, in the legal sense of the term, is now obsolete. During the time when it had a meaning, Islâm made the slave's lot as easy as possible. A slave, male or female, could ask for conditional manumission by a written deed fixing the amount required, and allowing the slave to earn money by lawful means and perhaps to get married and bring up a family. Such a deed was not to be refused if the request was genuine and the slave had a good character. Besides, the master is directed to help with money out of his own resources in order to enable the slave to earn his or her own liberty.)

34. And verily We have sent down to you explanatory verses, and an example of those who passed away before you; an exhortation *(caution)* for the God-fearing.

(The meaning probably is that the scandal raised against 'Âishah resembled the scandal in the caseof Joseph in Egypt and of the Virgin Mary, rehearsed in previous Sûrahs.)

35. Allah is the Light of the heavens and of the earth. The similitude of His light is as a niche wherein is a Lamp. The Lamp is in a glass, the glass, is as it were a glittering star, lighted from a blessed tree, an olive, neither of the east, nor of the west, whose oil would almost glow forth, even if no fire touched it. It is light upon Light. Allah guides whom He wills to His light; and Allah sets forth parables to men, for Allah is knower of all things.

(This verse may mean that Allah is the very Essence of existence of the universe, and that the word "light here may denote the eternal and sole Sustainer of all existence. It may also mean that Allah is the light of the universe through the cosmic signs, and through the signs He sent down upon man to make manifest His existence, oneness, omnipotence and all His Excellent Attributes that may lead man to the upright path and the best sequel.)

36. In houses which Allah has allowed to be raised up, that His name may therein be remembered. In them is He glorified morning and evening.

37. Men whom neither merchandise nor sale beguile from the remembrance of Allah, and from the observance of prayer, and paying to the poor their due, because they fear a day when hearts and eyes will be overturned;

38. That Allah may recompense them for the best of what they did, and increase reward for them of His bounty. Allah provides for whom He will without measure.

39. As for those who disbelieve, their deeds are like a mirage in a desert which the thirsty thinks to be water, till he comes unto it, he finds it nothing, but finds Allah there, Then Allah fully pays him his account, and Allah is swift at reckoning.

(We have had various metaphors to give us an idea of the beneficent light of Allah in the spiritual world. Now we have contrasted metaphors to enable us to see those who deny or refuse that light, and are overwhelmed in utter darkness. The Light of Allah is an absolute Reality, and is mentioned first, and the souls that follow that light are a reflected reality and are mentioned after the Light. On the other hand, the darkness is not a reality in itself, but a negation of reality; the reflected existences that refuse the Light are mentioned, and then their state, which is unreality. Two metaphors are given: a mirage, in this verse, and the depths of darkness in the sea, in the next.)

40. Or like darkness on a deep sea covered by waves riding upon waves, above which are clouds; darkness upon darkness. When a man reaches forth his hand, he can hardly see it. And he to whom Allah shall not give light, he has no light at all.

(What a graphic picture of darkness is the depths of the ocean, wave upon wave, and on top of all, dense dark clouds! There is so little light even in ordinary depths of the ocean that fishes that live there lose their eyes as useless organs.

The true source of light in the world of Reality is Allah, and anyone who cuts himself off from the light is in utter darkness, for it is the negation of the only true Light, and not merely relative darkness, like that which we see, say, in the shadows of moonlight.)

41. Have you not seen that all that is in the heavens and the earth glorifies Allah? The birds as they spread their wings? Every creature knows its prayer and its praise, and Allah knows what they do.

42. Allah's is the Kingdom of the heavens and of the earth; and unto Allah is the (final) return.

43. Have you not seen how Allah drives clouds lightly forward, then gathers them together, then piles them in masses? And then you see the rain coming forth from their midst; and He causes clouds like mountains charged with hail to descend from the heaven, and He makes it to fall on whom He will, and from whom He will He turns it aside. The brightness of His lightning all but takes away the sight!

44. Allah alternates the night and the day. Truly, in this is a teaching for men of insight.

45. And Allah has created every creature of water; some of them go upon their bellies; and some of them go upon two feet, and some of them go on four feet. Allah creates what He pleases. Surely Allah has power over all things.

46. Verily We have sent down distinguishing signs, and Allah guides whom He will unto the straight path.

47. And they *(the hypocrites)* say, "We believe in Allah and in the Messenger, and we obey , yet, later, a party of them turn away. These are not of the faithful.

(The Hypocrites, far from profiting from Allah's light and Revelation, or declaring their open hostility, play fast and loose according to their selfish worldly aims. They only wanted to go to the judge who they thought was likely to give judgement in their favour. If their case was incontestable, and justice was on their side, they came to the prophet, knowing that he was just and would judge in their favour, even against his own adherents.)

48. And when they are called before Allah and His Messenger that He may judge between them, behold! a party of them turn away.

49. But had the truth been on their side, they would have come to him willingly.

50. Is there a disease in their hearts? Or do they doubt? Or are they afraid that Allah and His messenger will deal unfairly with them? Nay, they themselves are evildoers.

51. The words of the believer, when summoned to Allah and His messenger that he may judge between them, are only to say, "we have heard and we obeyed. These are they with whom it shall be well.

52. And whoever obeys Allah and His messenger and fears Allah and venerates Him; such indeed are the victorious.

53. They have sworn by Allah with a most solemn oath that if you bid them, they will certainly march forth. Say: "Do not swear! Obedience is more worthy. Verily Allah is well aware of what you do.

(Some people, especially hypocrites, give hyperbolic assurances, as did the Madîna Hypocrites to the holy Prophet, that they would do any bidding, even to the forsaking of their hearths and homes. To this they were ready to swear their most solemn oaths, which mean nothing. They are asked to spare their oaths, and quietly do at least such unheroic duties as they are asked to do in everyday life. Idle words are not of the least value. Allah will judge by your actions, and He knows all, whether it is open or secret.)

54. Say: "Obey Allah and obey the messenger. But, if you turn away, then only the burden of his duty is on him, and the burden of your duty is on you. If you obey him *(Muhammad)* you shall have guidance, But the Messenger's only duty is plainly to convey.

55. Allah has promised to those of you who believe and do good works that He will cause them to succeed others in the land, as He gave succession to those who were before them, and that He will establish for them that religion which He has approved for them, and that after their fears He will give them security in exchange. They worship Me; they ascribe nothing as partner unto Me. And whoever disbelieves after that, such are miscreants, impious.

(If you disobey the commands of Allah as explained by His messengers, you are not going to be forced to comply. The messenger's mission is to train your will and explain clearly all the implications of your conduct. The responsibility for your conduct rests entirely on yourselves.

In this verse three things are promised to those who have faith and obey Allah's Law:

1) They will inherit power and authority in the land, not for any selfish purpose of theirs nor by way of favouritism, but in order that they may maintain the Divine Law.

2) The Religion of Right, which Allah has chosen for them, will be openly established, and will suppress all wrong and oppression.

3) The righteous will live in peace and security, instead of having to suffer persecution, or leave their hearths and homes for the cause of Allah, or practise the rites of their faith in secret.)

56. Establish the Prayer and pay the Zakât and obey the messenger, that perhaps you may find mercy.

57. *(O Muhammad!)*, do not think that the disbelievers can weaken Allah on His own earth: their dwelling place shall be the fire! An evil journey's end!

58. O you who believe! Let your slaves, and those of you who have not come of age *(puberty)*, ask leave of you, at three times a day, before they

come into your presence: before the prayer of dawn, and when you lay aside your garments at midday, and after the prayer of night. These are your three times of privacy. No blame shall attach to you or to them, if after these times, when you go your rounds of visiting on one another, *(they come in without permission)*. Thus does Allah make clear to you His signs. Allah is Knower, Wise.

(We now come to rules of politeness within the family circle in decent society. Servants and children have rather more freedom of access, as they come and go at all hours, and there is less ceremony with them. But even in their case there are limitations. During the night, before morning prayer, i.e., before dawn, they must discreetly ask for permission before they enter, partly because they must not unnecessarily disturb people asleep, and partly because the people are then undressed. The same applies to the time for the midday siesta, and again to the time after night prayers, when people usually undress and turn in to sleep. For grown-ups the rule is stricter: they ask permission to come in at all times).

59. And when the children among you come of age *(puberty)*, let them ask leave *(to come into your presence)*, as they who were before them asked it. Thus does Allah make clear to you His signs, and Allah is Knower, Wise.

60. As for women who are past childbearing, and have no hope of marriage; no blame *(sin)* shall attach to them if they lay aside their *(outer)* garments in such a way as not to show adornments. But to refrain *(from that)* is better for them. Allah is Hearer, Knower.

(According to verse 31 it is obligatory for women to cover themselves. We are also told who they should hide their charms from, in order to preserve purity of intention.

There are some women who never admit to themselves that they have grown old, and still like to paint themselves and attempt to make themselves look young. Although it is strongly advised that women should look attractive to her husband, it is unlawful for them to paint themselves for the amusement of passers-

by. Older women without the hope of marriage and having reached to a sexless stage are allowed not to wear their outer garments. But it is still preferable for them not to show their ornaments and keep their outer garments.)

61. No blame is there upon the blind nor any blame upon the lame nor any blame upon the sick nor on yourselves if you eat from your houses, or the houses of your fathers, or the houses of your mothers, or the houses of your brothers, or the houses of your sisters, or the houses of your fathers' brothers, or the houses of your fathers' sisters, or the houses of your mothers' brothers, or the houses of your mothers' sisters, or *(from that whereof you hold the keys, or from *(the house of)* a friend. No sin shall it be for you whether you eat together or apart. But when you enter houses, salute one another with a greeting from Allah, blessed and sweet. Thus Allah makes clear His revelations *(signs)* for you, that perhaps you may understand.

62. They only are believers who believe in Allah and His messenger, and, when they are with him upon any affair of common interest *(important things like war),* depart not until they have asked leave of him. Those who ask leave of you are those who believe in Allah and His messenger. So if they ask your leave for some affair of theirs, give leave to whom you will of them, and ask for them forgiveness of Allah, for Allah is Forgiving, Merciful.

63. Make not the calling of the messenger among you as your calling one of another. Allah knows those of you who steal away, hiding themselves. And let those who conspire to evade orders beware lest grief or painful punishment befall them.

(Three significations are possible; one is that adopted in the translation which agrees with the view of most Commentators. Another would be: "Do not think that the prayer of the prophet of Allah is like your ordinary requests to another; the prophet's prayer will be about serious matters and will be accepted by Allah . A third interpretation would be: "Do not address the prophet familiarly as you would address one another: use proper terms of respect for him.

64. Assuredly, unto Allah belongs whatsoever is in the heavens and the earth. He knows your condition. And *(He knows)* the Day when they are returned unto Him so that He may inform them of what they did. Allah is Knower of all things.

SÛRAH XXV

Al-FURQÂN (THE CRITERION)

Revealed at Makka

This Sûrah was revealed (except for verses 68-70) during the fifth and the sixth year before the Hijrah. It derives its title from verse 1. Al-Furqân is one of the names of the Qur'ân, and means the distinguisher between the righteous and the evil. It deal with the folly of superstitions among the idolaters, and their disputation concerning Muhammad's prophethood.

THE CRITERION

In the name of Allah, the Compassionate, the Merciful

1. Blessed is He who has sent down the Criterion unto His slave, that he may be a warner to the peoples *(creatures).*

2. His is the sovereignty of the heavens and of the earth! No son has He begotten! No partner has He in His sovereignty! All things has He created, and has decreed their destinies.

6. Say: "He has sent it down Who knows the secrets of the heavens and the earth. He truly is the Forgiving, the Merciful.

7. And they say: "What sort of messenger is this? He eats food and he walks in markets. Why is an angel not sent down to him, to take part in his warnings?

8. Or *(Why is not)* a treasure thrown down to him, or why does he not have a paradise whence he eats? And those unjust persons say: "You follow but a man who is enchanted *(bewitched).*

9. See how they coin allegories for you, but they have gone astray and cannot find their way.

10. Blessed He who, if He will, can give you better than that *(of which they speak)*: gardens beneath which rivers flow, and palaces will He assign for you.

(This phrase is usually regarded as symbolical of the bliss in the Hereafter. If it were Allah's plan, He could give His messengers complete felicity and power in this life also. Instead of being persecuted, mocked, driven out of their homes, and having to exert their utmost powers of body, mind and character to plant the flag of Truth in an unbelieving world, they could have lived in ease and security. But that would not have given the real lessons they came to teach struggling humanity by their example).

3. But they take, apart from Him, gods that create nothing, while they themselves are created. And they possess themselves neither harm nor benefit, nor do they possess power of death nor of life nor of raising.

4. And those who disbelieve say: "This Qur'ân is nothing but a fraud he has invented, and other people have helped him with it. So they have come with a slander and a lie.

5. And they say: "Legends of the ancients that he has put into writing, for they are dictated to him in the early morning and evening.

(In their misguided arrogance they say: We have heard such things before; they are pretty tales which have come down from ancient times; they are good for amusement, but who takes them seriously? When the beauty and power of the revelation are pointed out, and its miracle as coming from an unlearned man, they again hint at other men who wrote it, though they could not produce anyone who could write anything like it)

11. Nay, but they have treated *(the coming of* the Hour as a lie. We have prepared a flaming fire for these who deny the Hour.

(Denying the Hour of Judgement means denying the power of Justice and Truth to triumph; it means asserting the dominion of evil. But reality itself will punish them, as is shown in the following verses).

12. When it will see them from afar, they will hear its raging and roaring.

(Here the Fire is personified. It is raging with hunger and fury, and as soon as it sees them from afar, it emits a sigh of desire. Till then they had not realised their full danger. Now, just as their heart begins to tremble with terror, they are bound together and cast into the roaring flames).

13. And when they are flung into a narrow space thereof, chained together, they shall invoke destruction on the spot.

14. Call not this day for one destruction, but call for many destructions!

15. Say: "Is this, or the garden of eternity which was promised to the godfearing best? It shall be for them a reward and a destination."

(To the righteous, the final Bliss will in one sense be a reward. But the word "reward" does not truly represent facts, for two reasons:

1) The Bliss will be greater than they deserved.

2) Righteousness is its own reward.

The best way of expressing the result would be to say that their highest wish will now have been attained. The goal will have been reached. They will be in God's presence. That is the highest, purest salvation.)

16. Therein abiding for ever, they shall have in it all that they desire. It is for your Lord a promise that must be fulfilled.

(That is the sort of thing, the goal of Allah's presence, to be prayed for from Allah and not ephemeral things, even though they may be good. And that is the sort of thing that Allah has promised and undertaken to give.)

17. And on the day when He shall gather them together, and those whom they worship beside Allah, He will say: "Was it you who led these my servants astray, or did they themselves stray from the path?

18. They will say: "Glory be to You! It is not for us to take other Lords than You. But You gave them and good things (in life), till they forgot to remember you, and became a lost people.

19. (The Lord will say:) "They have now proved you liars in what you say, so you cannot avert (the punishment), nor obtain help. And We shall make those among you who did wrong taste a great punishment.

20. And We never sent messengers before you who did not eat food, and walk in the markets. And We test you by means of one another: will you be steadfast ? And your Lord is ever Watching.

(In Allah's universal Plan, each unit serves a purpose. If some are rich, the poor should not envy them: it may be that the rich man's proximity is itself a trial of their virtue. If some are poor, the righteous rich should not despise or neglect them. It may be that their coming within their sight is a trial for their compassion.)

21. And those who do not expect Our meeting say: "Why are not the angels sent down upon us, or do we not see our Lord? They indeed have scorned with haughtiness within themselves, and exceeded in their iniquity with great excess.

22. On the day when they shall see the angels, there shall be no good tidings on that day for the culprits. And they shall say: "A barrier that is impassable .

(The Arabic words used are "hijran mahjûran which is an old Arabic expression that may also mean "at a total loss).

23. And we shall turn to the deeds they have did, then We shall make them as scattered dust.

(That is, their righteous deeds and acts of piety, will be of no avail to them in the hereafter for their rejection of the One Lord, but they will be rewarded for them in this worldly life.)

24. The people of the Garden shall on that day be better as to their lodging, and fairer still shall be their resting place.

25. And a day when heaven will be rent asunder with the clouds, and the angels will be sent down, descending.

26. The sovereignty on that day will in truth belong to the Beneficent One; and it will be a hard day for the unbelievers.

27. And that day the wrong-doer bites his hands and says, "O! Would that I had taken the same path with the messenger!

28. Alas for me! Would that I had not taken such a one for a friend.

29. It was he who led me astray from the reminder which had reached me! And Satan is man's betrayer *(deserter).*

30. And the Messenger said: "O! my Lord! Surely my people have taken this Qur'ân as something abandoned.

31. And thus We have given to every prophet an enemy from among the wicked ones; but your Lord is a sufficient guide and helper.

32. And those who disbelieve say: 'If only the Qur'ân would be sent down upon him all at one time! Thus do We establish your heart with it, and We have recited it in a distinct recitation.

33. And they never bring to you any example but that We bring you the truth and a better interpretation

(That is, the idolaters would not bring to you the likeness of this Qur'ân; rather they bring negative disputation, against which Allah brings the truth).

34. Those who will be gathered on their faces unto Hell: such are worse in plight and further straying from the right road.

35. And We gave Moses the Book, and We appointed with him his brother Aaron as a supporter.

36. Then We said: "Go together unto the people who have denied Our signs. Then We destroyed them, a complete destruction.

37. And Noah's folk, when they denied the messengers, We drowned them and made of them a portent for mankind. We have prepared a painful doom for evil-doers.

38. And (the tribes of) Âd, and Thamûd, and the dwellers of ar-Rass, and many generations in between.

(The word "Rass means the "enclosed well . It is said that a remote people were living around such a well, worshipping different idols. Some commentators, say, however, that they were living in the remains of Thamûd in Yamama, others said that it was a village on the site of Antioch, which is now a city on the borders between Syria and Turkey).

39. To each of them We coined similitudes, and each of them We caused to perish utterly.

40. And indeed they have come across the town upon which an evil rain had rained. Did they not see it? Nay, but they do not expect resurrection.

(This refers to Lot's story and the destruction of Sodom and Gomorrah, the wicked cities of the plain near the Dead Sea, by a shower of brimstone. The site lies on the highway between Arabia and Syria. Cf 15: 74-76.)

41. And when they see you they take you only for a mockery (saying): "Is this he whom Allah has sent forth as a messenger?

42. "He would have led us away from our gods if We had not been staunch to them. They will know when they behold the doom, who is more astray from the path.

43. Have you seen him who has taken his whims for his god? Will you become a guardian over him?

(The man who worships his own passions or impulses or desires is the most hopeless person to teach or lead or guide. If anything else were the matter with him, the teacher could argue with him. But reason cannot prevail over blind passion. It is vain to hope that such a man could be led, until his mad desires are killed. No one could undertake any responsibility for him, for he obeys no law and follows no advice. He is worse then brute beasts, which may not understand, but at least follow the wholesome instincts implanted in them by Allah.)

44. Or do you reckon that most of them hearken or comprehend? They are like cattle. Nay, but they are even further astray from the path.

45. Have you not seen how your Lord stretches out the shadow? And if He had willed, He could have made it still; then We have made the sun its pilot.

(In our artificial life and surroundings we fail to see some of the finest mysteries of light and shade. We praise, and rightly so, the wonderful colours of sunset and sunrise. There is first the false dawn, with its curious uncertain light and the curious long uncertain shadows which it casts. Then there are the streaks of black in the East, succeeded by the true dawn, with its delicate tones of colours, and light and shade. The light of this true or false dawn is not given by direct rays of the sun. In a sense it is not light, but the shadows or reflections of light. They gradually merge into actual sunrise, with its more substantial or more defined shadows, which we can definitely connect with the sun.)

46. Then We withdraw it unto us, a gradual withdrawal?

47. And it is He who has made the night a garment for you, and sleep for rest, and He made the day a raising up *(resurrection)*.

48. And He it is who has sent the winds, bearing good tidings, heralding His mercy. And We sent down from heaven pure water.

49. That We may revive thereby a dead land, and that We gave it as drink to many beasts and men whom We created.

50. And assuredly We have repeated it among them that they may remember. But most of mankind refuse to be anything but thankless.

51. And had We willed, We could have sent a warner in every village.

52. So obey not the unbelievers, and strive against them thereby with a great effort.

53. And it is He who has separated the two seas, this one is fresh, palatable to the taste, and this one is saltish, piquant. And He set a barrier between them, and an insurmountable bar.

(The water is distributed all over the world, in order that all life may receive its support, according to its needs. In 25: 48-50, we have the argument of contrasts stated in another way. Water is life, and is made available to sustain life all over the world. This is a physical fact which all can see. But water is also the symbol of spiritual life, whose sustaining principle is the will of Allah as made known to us through revelation.)

54. And it is He who has created man of water, and He made him kindred by blood and marriage. And your Lord is omnipotent.

55. And they worship apart from Allah that which neither avails them, nor hurts them. And the unbeliever is ever a helper *(of evil)* against his Lord.

56. And We sent you not but as a bearer of good tidings and a warning.

57. Say: "I ask you not a wage for this, save *(the work of)* him who desires to take a way to his Lord.

58. And put your trust in the Living One who dies not, and extol His praise. And He suffices as knower of His servants' sins.

59. It is He who created the heavens and the earth, and whatever is between them in six days, then He established Himself on the throne; the Compassionate God, ask any informed one of Him.

60. And if it is said to them, "prostrate yourselves to the Compassionate God" they said: "And who is the Compassionate God? Shall we prostrate ourselves to whatever you bid us? And it increased them in aversion.

61. Blessed be He who has made in the heaven constellations, and has set there a lamp and a light-giving moon.

62. And He it is who has made the night and the day a succession, for whoever desired to remember or to be thankful.

63. And the servants of the Compassionate God are they who walk on the earth in modesty.

And if the ignorant address them, they say, "Peace!

64. And those who spend the night prostrating themselves, and standing before their Lord.

65. And who say: "Our Lord! Turn away from us the torment of Hell, for surely its torment is a constant anguish.

66. Indeed it is a wretched abode and lodging place.

67. And those who, when they expend, neither squander, nor are parsimonious, but keep straight between the two.

(In ordinary spending, this is a wise rule. But even in charity, in which we give of our best, it is not expected that we should be extravagant, i.e. that we should either do it for show (to impress others), or do it thoughtlessly, which would be the case if we "rob Peter to pay Paul . We should certainly not be niggardly, but we should remember everyone's rights, including our own, and strike a perfectly just balance between them.)

68. And those who do not invoke another god with Allah, and who do not slay the living soul that Allah has forbidden, except by right, nor commit adultery, for whoever does that shall receive the penalty.

69. For him shall the torment be doubled on the day of resurrection, and therein he shall abide for ever, disgraced.

70. Save him who repents and believes, and does righteous work; such, Allah shall change their misdeeds into good works. And Allah is Forgiving, Merciful.

71. And whoever repents and does righteous works, he surely turns to Allah in repentance.

72. And those who do not bear false witness, and when they pass by idle chatter, pass by with grace.

73. And those who, when they are reminded of their Lord's signs, do not fall down at them, deaf and blind.

74. And those who say: "Our Lord, grant us of our wives and offspring the delight of our eyes, and make us an example to the godfearing.

(The "Chamber is said to be the highest and most spiritually exalted reach of the Garden.)

75. Such shall have their reward, the chamber for their diligence, and there they shall receive a greeting and peace.

76. There they shall abide forever; it is good as an abode and a lodging place.

77. Say: "My Lord will not be concerned for you, were it not for your supplication, yet you were mendacious, so retribution shall be inescapable.

(That is, had it not been for your supplication, belief, worshipping, and your expressing of gratitude, you would be no concern to Allah. Yet the idolaters cried lies against Allah's ordinance, and so retribution will befall them in the life to come, as a sequel for falsifying Allah's religion.)

SÛRAH XXVI

ASH-SHU'ARÂ' (THE POETS)

Revealed at Makka

This takes its title from verse 224, where the difference between poets and prophets is tersely pointed out; poets being those who say what they do not mean, while a prophet always practises what he preaches. The pagan Arabs and their poets believed the poetic inspirations to be the work of Jinn.

The story of a number of former prophets is here given to console the believers at a time of persecution, with the assurance that it is no new thing for a messenger of Allah to be persecuted, but that the persecutors always suffer in the end. It shows also that all the messengers of Allah came with the same message.

It belongs to the middle group of Makkan Sûrahs, with exception of vv. 224-277, which were revealed at Madîna.

THE POETS

In the name of Allah, the Compassionate,
the Merciful

1. Tâ. Sîn. Mîm.

2. These are signs of the scripture that makes plain.

3. It may be that you torment yourself *(O Muhammad!)* because they believe not.

4. If We will, We can sent down on them from the sky a sign, so that their necks would remain bowed before it.

5. Never comes there unto them a fresh reminder from the Beneficent One, but they turn away from it.

6. Now they have denied the truth, but there will come unto them tidings of that whereat they used to scoff.

7. Have they not seen the earth, how much of every fruitful kind We make to grow therein?

8. Assuredly, in this is a sign; yet most of them are not believers.

9. And lo! Your Lord! He is indeed the Mighty, the Merciful.

10. And when your Lord called Moses, saying: "Go unto the wrongdoing people.

11. The people of Pharaoh. Will they not ward off evil?

12. He said: "My Lord! verily I fear that they will deny me.

13. And I shall be embarrassed, and my tongue will not speak plainly, therefore send for Aaron *(to help me).*

14. And they have a crime against me, so I fear that they will kill me.

15. He said: "Nay, verily. So go you twain with Our signs. Assuredly, We shall listen to you.

16. And come together unto Pharaoh and say, verily we are the messengers of the Lord of the worlds.

17. Let the Children of Israel go with us.

18. Pharaoh said unto Moses: "Did we not rear you among us as a child? And you dwelt many years of your life among us.

19. And you did that your deed which you did, and you were of one of the ingrates.

(Pharaoh reminds Moses of his having slain the Egyptian, and taunts him: "You are not only a murderer: you are an ungrateful wretch , using *kâfir* again in a double sense, "to have killed one of the race that brought you up.)

20. He said: "I did it then, when I was of those who are astray.

21. Then I fled from you when I feared you, and my Lord has given me judgement, and has made me one of His messengers.

22. And this is a past favour wherewith you reproach me; that you have enslaved the Children of Israel.

23. Pharaoh said: "And what is the Lord of the Worlds?

24. *(Moses)* said: "Lord of the heaven and the earth and all that is between them, if you only believed.

(Pharaoh had called Moses ungrateful and reproached him with all the favours which Moses had received from Egyptians. "What favours?" he says: "Do you count it also as a favour to me that you have enslaved my brethren, the Children of Israel? Moses was now speaking as a Prophet of Allah, not as an individual.)

25. *(Pharaoh)* said unto those around him: "Do you not hear?

26. *(Moses)* said: "He is your Lord, and the Lord of your fathers.

27. *(Pharaoh)* said: "Behold! Your messenger who has been sent unto you is indeed a madman.

28. He said: "*(My Lord is)* Lord of the East and the West and all that is between them, if you did but understand.

29. *(Pharaoh)* said: "If you choose a god other than Me, I assuredly shall place you among the prisoners.

30. He said: "Even though I show you something plain?

31. *(Pharaoh)* said: "Produce it then, if you are of the truthful!

32. Then he flung down his staff, and it became a serpent manifest,

33. And he drew forth his hand, and behold! it was white to the beholders.

34. *(Pharaoh)* said, unto the chiefs about him: "Behold, this is verily a knowing wizard,

35. Who would drive you out of your land by his magic. Now what counsel you?

36. They said: "Put him off *(keep him)* and his brother, and send into the cities summoners,

37. Who shall bring unto you every knowing wizard.

38. So the wizards were gathered together at a set time on a day appointed.

39. And it was said unto the people: "Are you also gathering?

40. *(They said):* "Yes, so that we may follow the wizards, if they are the winners .

41. And when the wizards came they said unto Pharaoh: "Will there surely be a reward for us if we are the winners?

42. He said: "Yes, and you will then surely be of those brought near to me.

43. Moses said unto them: "Throw what you are going to throw!

44. Then they threw down their cords and their staves and said: "By Pharaoh's might, we verily are the winners.

45. Then Moses threw his staff and behold! It swallowed that which they did falsely show.

46. And the wizards were flung prostrate.

47. They said, "We believe in the Lord of the Worlds.

48. The Lord of Moses and Aaron.

49. *(Pharaoh)* said: "You put your faith in him before I give you leave. Behold! He doubtless is your chief who taught you magic! But verily you shall come to know. Verily I will cut off your hands and your feet alternately, and verily I will crucify you every one.

50. They said: "It matters not, for assuredly, we are returning to our Lord.

51. Assuredly, we hope that our Lord will forgive us our sins, because we are the first of the believers.

52. And we inspired Moses, saying: "Take away My slaves by night, for you will be pursued.

53. Then Pharaoh sent into the cities summoners.

54. "Assuredly these are but a little troop.

55. And they are offenders against us.

56. And we are a ready host.

57. Thus did We take them away from gardens and water-springs,

58. And treasures and a fair estate.

59. Thus *(were those things taken from them)* and We caused the Children of Israel to inherit them.

60. And they overtook them at sunrise.

61. And when the two hosts saw each other, those with Moses said: We are surely overtaken.

62. He said: "Verily my Lord is with me. He will guide me.

63. Then We inspired Moses, saying: "Strike the sea with your staff . And it parted, and each part was like a mountain vast.

64. Then brought We near the others to that place.

65. And We saved Moses and those with him, every one.

66. Then We drowned the others.

67. Truly herein is a sign, yet most of them are not believers.

68. And verily your Lord, He is indeed the Mighty, the Merciful.

69. Recite unto them the story of Abraham.

70. When he said unto his father and his people: "What do you worship?

71. They said: "We worships idols, and we are ever devoted unto them.

(They want to show their true and assiduous devotion. But Abraham goes at once to the heart of the matter by asking: "To whom is your devotion paid? Is the object worthy of it?")

72. He said: "Do they hear you when you cry?

73. Or do they benefit or harm you?

74. They said: "Nay, but we found our fathers acting in this way.

75. He said: "Do you then see whom you have been worshipping?

76. You and your forefathers!

77. Behold! They are *(all)* an enemy unto me, save the Lord of the Worlds.

(The things that you worship are enemies to mankind: Let me testify from my own personal experience: They are enemies to me, they can do me no good, but would lead me astray. Contrast with their importance or to their power of mischief the One True God whom I worship. He created me and all the worlds. He cherishes me and guides me. He takes care of me, and, when I die, He will give me new life. He will forgive me and grant me final salvation. Will you then come to this true worship? How can you doubt, after seeing the contrast of the one with the other? Is it not as the contrast between Light and Darkness?)

78. Who created me, and who guides me.

79. And who feeds me and waters me.

80. And when I sicken, then He heals me.

81. And who causes me to die, then gives me life again.

82. And who, I ardently hope, will forgive me my sin on the Day of Judgement.

83. My Lord! Bestow wisdom on me and unite me to the righteous.

(Having shown clearly the distinction between truth and falsehood, Abraham now shows in the form of a prayer what his innermost wishes are.)

84. And give unto me a good report in later generations.

85. And place me among the inheritors of the Garden of Delight.

86. And forgive my father, for he was one of those who go astray.

87. And abase me not on the day when they are raised,

88. The day when wealth and sons avail not any man.

(Nothing will then avail except a pure heart; all "good deeds of this world, without the motive of purity, will be useless. The contrast of the Garden of Bliss with the fire of Misery will be plainly visible. Evil will be shown in its true colours.)

89. Save him who brings unto Allah a whole heart.

(The good will only see good, and the evil will only see evil. This type of contrast is shown to us in the world of our spiritual sense in this life.)

90. And the Garden will be brought near for those who ward off evil.

91. And hell will appear plainly to the erring.

92. And it will be said unto them: "Where is all that you used to worship,

93. Instead of Allah? Can they help you, or help themselves?

94. Then they will be hurled therein, they and the seducers.

95. And the hosts of Iblis, together.

96. And they will say, when they are quarrelling therein,

97. "By Allah, of a truth we were in error manifest,

98. When we made you equal with the Lord of the Worlds.

99. It was but the guilty who misled us.

100. Now we have no intercessors.

101. Nor any loving friend.

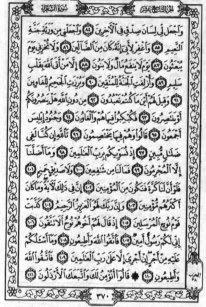

102. Oh, that if only we had another turn on earth, that we might be of the believers.

103. Assuredly, in this is indeed a sign, yet most of them are not believers.

104. And lo, your Lord! He is indeed the Mighty, the Merciful.

105. Noah's folk denied the messengers (of Allah).

106. When their brother Noah said unto them: "Will you not ward off evil?

107. Behold! I am a faithful messenger unto you.

108. So keep your duty to Allah, and obey me.

109. And I ask of you no wage for this; my wage is the concern only of the Lord of the Worlds.

110. So keep your duty to Allah, and obey me.

111-They said: "Shall we put faith in you, when the lowest of the people follow you?"

112. He said: "I have no knowledge of what they have been doing *(in the past).*

113. Their reckoning is only my Lord's concern, if you but knew.

114. And I am not to repulse believers.

115. I am only a plain warner.

116. They said: "If you cease not, O Noah, you will surely be among those stoned to death.

117. He said: "My Lord! Lo! my own folk deny me.

118. Therefore judge You between us, a judgement, and save me and those believers who are with me.

119. And We saved him and those with him in the laden ship.

(The story of Noah's flood is told in 11:36-48. Here, the point emphasised is Noah's patience and constancy against threats, and the triumph and preservation of Allah's truth even though the world was ranged against it.)

120. Then afterward We drowned the others.

121. Surely, in this is indeed a sign, yet most of them are not believers.

122. And assuredly your Lord, He is indeed the Mighty, the Merciful.

123. *(The tribe of)* 'Âd denied the messengers *(of Allah).*

124. When their brother Hûd said unto them: "Will you not ward off evil? *(Will you not fear Allah?)*

125. Because I am a faithful *(trustworthy)* messenger unto you,

126. So keep your duty to Allah and obey me.

127. And I ask of you no wage for this; my wage is the concern only of the Lord of the Worlds.

128. Do you build on every high place a monument for vain delight?

(Any measly material civilisation prides itself on show and parade. Its votaries scatter monuments for all sorts of things in conspicuous places - monuments which commemorate deeds and events which are forgotten in a few generations!)

129. And seek you out strongholds, that haply you may last for ever?

130. And if you seize by force, seize you as tyrants?

131. Rather keep your duty to Allah, and obey me.

132. Keep your duty toward Him who has aided you with *(the good things)* that you know,

133. Has aided you with cattle and sons

134. And gardens and watersprings.

135. Indeed I fear for you the punishment of an awful Day.

136. They said: "It is all one to us whether you preach or not.

137. This is but a fable of the men of old.

(They said, as our modern enemies of religion say, "You are only reviving an ancient superstition, an opiate of the masses; there is no such thing as a hereafter, or the sort of punishments you announce!")

138. And we shall not be doomed.

139. And they denied him; therefore We destroyed them. Assuredly, in this is indeed a sign, yet most of them are not believers.

140. And verily your Lord, He is indeed the Mighty, the Merciful.

141. (The tribe of) Thamûd denied the messengers (of Allah);

142. When their brother Sâlih said unto them: "Will you not ward off evil?

143. Indeed I am a faithful (trustworthy) messenger unto you.

144. So keep your duty to Allah and obey me.

145. And I ask of you no wage for this; my wage is the concern only of the Lord of the Worlds.

146. Will you be left secure in that which is here before us,

147. In gardens and watersprings,

148. And tilled fields and heavy-sheathed palm-trees,

149. And you carve houses out of rocky mountains, being skilful?

150. Therefor keep your duty to Allah and obey me,

151. And obey not the command of the prodigal (extravagant).

152. Who spread corruption in the earth, and reform not.

153. They said: "You are but one of the bewitched;

154. You are but a mortal like us. So bring some sign if you are of the truthful.

155. He said: "(Behold) this she-camel. She has the right to drink at the well, and you have the right to drink, each on an appointed day,

156. And touch her not with ill lest the penalty of a great day seize you.

157. But they hamstrung her, and then were penitent.

(Their regrets were too late. They had themselves asked for a sign. The sign had been given them in the she-camel, which their prophet Sâlih had put forward as a test case. Would they, through that symbol, respect the law of equity by which all people had right in water and in the gifts of nature? They refused to respect that law, and committed sacrilege by deliberately killing the she-camel. They themselves came to an evil end.)

158. So the retribution came on them. Assuredly, in this is indeed a sign, yet most of them are not believers.

159. And verily your Lord! He is indeed the Mighty, the Merciful.

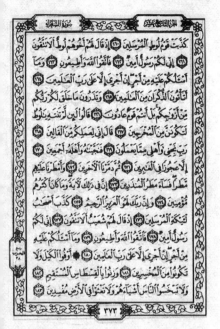

160. The people of Lot denied the messengers *(of Allah).*

161. When their brother Lot said unto them: "Will you not ward off evil?

162. Lo! I am a faithful *(trustworthy)* messenger unto you,

163. So keep your duty to Allah and obey me.

164. And I ask of you no wage for this; my wage is the concern only of the Lord of the Worlds.

165. What! Of all creatures do you come unto the males?

166. And leave the wives your Lord created for you? Nay, but you are people who transgress the limits.

167. They said: "If you cease not, O Lot, you will soon be of the outcast.

168. He said: "I am in truth of those who hate your conduct.

(He was only among them from a stern sense of duty. The whole atmosphere there was detestable to him, and he was glad to escape when duty no longer demanded his presence there. He prayed for deliverance from such surroundings.)

169. My Lord! Save me and my household from what they do.

170. So We saved him and his household, every one,

171. Except an aged woman among those who stayed behind.

172. Then afterward We destroyed the others.

173. And We rained on them a rain. And dreadful is the rain of those who have been warned.

(Perhaps a shower of ashes and cinders from a volcanic eruption. These people were the same as those already mentioned.)

174. Assuredly, in this is indeed a sign, yet most of them are not believers.

175. And your Lord, He is indeed the Mighty, the Merciful.

176. The dwellers in the wood *(of Midian)* denied the messengers *(of Allah).*

177. When Shu'ayb said unto them: "Will you not ward off evil?

178. I am a trustworthy messenger unto you,

179. So keep your duty to Allah, and obey me.

180. And I ask of you no wage for it; my wage is the concern only of the Lord of the Worlds.

181. Give full measure, and be not of those who give less *(than the due).*

(They were a commercial people but they were given to fraud, injustice, and wrongful mischief. They are asked to fear Allah and follow his ways; it is He who also created their predecessors among mankind, who never prospered by fraud and violent wrongdoing, but only justice and fair dealing.)

182. And weigh with the true balance.

183. Wrong not mankind in their goods, and do not commit evil, making mischief, in the earth.

184. And keep your duty unto Him Who created you and the generations of the men of old.

185. They said: "You are but one of the bewitched;

186. You are but a mortal like us, and indeed we deem you of the liars.

187. Then make fragments of the heaven fall upon us, if you are of the truthful.

188. He said: "My Lord is best aware of what you do.

189. But they denied him, so there came on them the retribution of the day of gloom. Behold! It was the retribution of an awful day.

(Perhaps a shower of ashes and cinders accompanying a volcanic eruption. If these people were the same as the Midianites, there was also an earthquake.)

190. Assuredly, in this is indeed a sign; yet most of them are not believers.

191. And your Lord, He is indeed the Mighty, the Merciful.

192. And verily it is a revelation of the Lord of the Worlds,

193. With it came down the Spirit of Truth (Gabriel).

194. Upon your heart, that you may be one of the warners,

195. In plain Arabic speech.

196. And it is in the Scriptures of the men of old.

(The word Zubur, used here, is a plural of Zabûr, which is mentioned in the Qur'ân as the Book revealed to the prophet David. It has also been used in the Qur'ân in the generic sense of a "Book (54:52) Here the word refers to the earlier revelation.)

197. Is it not a sign for them that the doctors of the Children of Israel know it?

(The Jews knew, from their Scripture, that a Prophet had been promised to Arabia.)

198. And if We had revealed it unto one of any nation other than the Arabs,

199. And he had read it unto them, they would not have believed in it.

200. Thus have We caused it to enter the hearts of the sinners.

201. They will not believe in it till they behold the painful punishment,

202. So that it will come upon them suddenly, when they perceive not.

203. Then they will say: "Are we to be reprieved?

204. Would they (now) hasten on Our punishment?

205. Had you then seen, if We content them for (long) years,

206. And then comes that which they were promised,

207. It will profit them not that they enjoyed this life.

208. And We destroyed no township but it had its warners.

209. As a reminder, for We were never oppressors.

210. The devils did not bring it down.

(When anything extraordinary happens, there are always people desirous of putting the worst construction on it, and saying that it is the work of the evil ones, the devils. So when the Qur'ân came with its message in astonishing Arabic, its enemies could only account for its power by attributing it to evil spirits.)

211. It is not meet for them, nor is it in their power,

212. Assuredly, they are banished from the hearing.

213. Therefore invoke not with Allah another god, lest you be one of the punished.

214. And warn your tribe of near kindred,

215. And lower your wing *(in kindness)* unto those believers who follow you.

216. And if they *(your kinsfolk)* disobey you, say: "I am innocent of what they do.

217. And put your trust in the Mighty, the Merciful.

218. Who sees you when you stand up *(to pray)*

219. And *(sees)* your movements among those who fall prostrate *(in worship)*.

(Literally, the standing and prostration which are postures of Muslim prayer. The holy prophet was equally earnest, sincere, and zealous in prayer for himself and for all his people. The Prophet's behavior was exemplary, in all the turns of fortune, and however foolish men may cavil, his purity and uprightness are fully known to Allah.)

220. Lo! He, only He, is the Hearer, the Knower.

221. Shall I inform you upon whom the devils descend?

222. They descend on every sinful, false one.

223. They listen eagerly, but most of them are liars.

224. As for poets, the erring follow them.

225. Have you not seen how they stray in every valley,

226. And how they say that which they do not do?

227. Save those who believe and do good works, and remember Allah much, and vindicate themselves after they have been wronged. Those who do wrong will come to know by what a *(great)* reverse they will be overturned!

(In this sense a perfect artist should be a perfect man; perfection may not be attainable in this life, but should be the aim of every man and especially, of one who wishes to become a supreme artist, not only in technique but in spirit and essentials. Contemporary with the Holy Prophet may be mentioned Hassan and Lebîd. The latter had the honour of being one of the seven whose poems were especially prized in the Days of Ignorance.)

SÛRAH XXXVII

AN-NAML (THE ANT)

Revealed at Makka

An-Naml, "The Ant, takes its name from the ant mentioned in v. 18. Some commentators, objecting to the miraculous, seek to explain the ants, in the story of Solomon, as an old Arab tribe, the birds as cavalry, the Hudhud *(the hoopoe)* as a man's name, and the Jinn as foreign troops. It belongs to the middle group of Makkan Sûrahs.

THE ANT

In the name of Allah, the Compassionate, the Merciful

1. Tâ. Sîn. These are signs of the Qur'an and a lucid Book.

2. A guidance and good tidings for believers.

3. Who establish the Prayer and pay the Zakât, and they are sure of the Hereafter.

4. As for those who believe not in the Hereafter, We have made their works fair-seeming unto them so that they are all astray.

5. Those are they for whom is the worst of punishment, and in the Hereafter they will be the greatest losers.

6. Truly you receive the Qur'ân from the presence of one Wise, Omniscient.

7. *(Remember)* when Moses said unto his household: "I have perceived a fire; I will bring you tidings thence, or bring to you a borrowed flame that you may warm yourselves.

(Cf. 20:9-24. Both there and here there is a reference to the dawn of Revelation in the heart of Moses. Here the emphasis is on the wonderful nature of the Fire and the remarkable way in which Moses was transformed at the touch of spiritual Light. He was travelling in the Sinai desert with his family. Seeking ordinary light, he came upon a Light which took him to the highest mysteries of Allah. No doubt all his inner history had prepared him for his great destiny. It is inner history that matters, and not the place or position of a man in the eyes of his ordinary fellows.)

8. But when he reached it, he was called, saying: "Blessed be Whosoever is in the fire and whosoever is round about it! And glorified be Allah, the Lord of the Worlds!

9. O Moses! Lo! it is I, Allah, the Mighty, the Wise.

10. And throw down your staff! But when he saw it moving as if it were a serpent, he turned to flee headlong, and retraced not his steps; *(but it was said unto him)*: "O Moses! Fear not! Lo! the messengers fear not in My presence,

11. Save him who has committed an injustice and afterward has changed evil for good. For truly, I am Forgiving, Merciful.

12. And put your hand into the bosom of your robe, it will come forth white but unhurt. *(This will be one)* among nine tokens unto Pharaoh and his people. Surely they were ever evil-living folk.

13. But when Our signs came unto them, plain to see, they said: "This is mere magic.

۳۷۷

14. And they denied them *(the signs)*, though their souls acknowledged them, for spite and arrogance. Then see the nature of the consequence for the wrong-doers!

15. And We verily gave knowledge unto David and Solomon, and they said:"Praise be to Allah, Who has preferred us above many of His believing slaves!

16. And Solomon was David's heir. And he said: "O mankind! We have been taught the language of birds, and have been given *(abundance)* of all things. This surely is evident favour."

(The point is that Solomon not only inherited his father's kingdom but his spiritual insight and the prophetic office, which do not necessarily pass from father to son. The spoken word of human speech is different from the means of communication which birds and animals have between each other. But no man can doubt that they have means of communication with each other, if he only observes the orderly flight of migratory birds or the regulated behaviour of ants, bees, and other creatures who live in communities.)

17. And there were gathered together unto Solomon his armies of the jinn and humankind, and of the birds, and they were set in battle order;

18. Till, when they reached the Valley of the Ants, an ant exclaimed: "O ants! Enter your dwellings lest Solomon and his armies crush you, unperceiving."

19. And *(Solomon)* smiled, laughing at her speech, and said: "My Lord, arouse me to be thankful for your favour wherewith you have favoured me and my parents, and to do good that shall be pleasing unto You, and include me in *(the number of)* Your righteous slaves."

20. And he sought among the birds, and said: "How is it that I see not the hoopoe, or is he among the absent?

21. I verily will punish him with hard punishment or I verily will slay him, or he verily shall bring me a plain excuse."

22. But he was not long in coming, and he said: "I have found out *(a thing)* that you apprehend not, and I come unto you from Sheba with sure tidings.

23. Lo! I found a woman ruling over them, and she has been given *(abundance)* of all things, and hers is a mighty throne.

(The Queen of Sheba *(by name, Bilqis, in Arabian tradition)* came apparently from Yemen, but she had affinities with Abyssinia and possibly ruled over Abyssinia also. The Habasha tribe *(after whom Abyssinia was named)* came from Yemen. Between the southern coast of Yemen and the north-eastern coast of Abyssinia there are only the Straits of Bâb al-Mandab, barely twenty miles across. In the 10th or 11th century B. C. there were frequent invasions of Abyssinia from Arabia, and Solomon's reign of 40 years is usually synchronised with B. C. 992 to 952. The Sabaean and Himyarite alphabets, in which we find the South Arabian pre-Islamic inscriptions, passed into Ethiopic, the language of Abyssinia. The Abyssinians possess a traditional history called "The Book of the Glory of Kings *(Kebra Nagast),* which has been translated from Ethiopic into English by Sir E. A. Wallis Budge (Oxford, 1932). It gives an account of the Queen of Sheba and her only son Menyelek I, as founders of the Abyssinian dynasty.)

24. I found her and her people worshipping the sun instead of Allah: and Satan has made their deeds seem fair unto them, so he has barried them from the way *(of Truth)* so that they go not aright:

25. So that they worship not Allah, Who brings forth the hidden in the heavens and the earth, and knows what you hide and what you proclaim,

26. Allah; there is no God save Him, the Lord of the tremendous Throne.

27. *(Solomon)* said: "We shall see whether you speak truth or whether you are of the liars.

28. Go with this my letter and throw it down unto them; then turn away and see what *(answer)* they return,

29. *(The Queen of Sheba)* said when she received the letter: "O chieftains! Lo! there has been thrown unto me a noble letter.

30. Lo! it is from Solomon, and it is: In the name of Allah the Compassionate the Merciful;

31. Exalt not yourselves against me, but come unto me as those who surrender.

32. She said: "O chieftains! Pronounce *(advise)* for me in my case. I decide no case till you are present with me.

33. They said: "We are lords of might and lords of great prowess, but it is for you to command; so consider what you will command.

34. She said: "Behold! kings, when they enter a township, ruin it and make the honour of its people into shame. Thus do they do.

35. But surely I am going to send a present unto them, and to see with what answer the messengers return.

"smokeless fire. Some are believers in the Divine Law; others are not.)

40. One with whom was knowledge of the Scripture said: "I will bring it you before your gaze returns unto you. And when he saw it set in his presence, Solomon said: "This is of the bounty of my Lord, that He may try me whether I give thanks or am ungrateful. Whosoever gives thanks he only gives thanks for *(the good of)* his own soul: and whosoever is ungrateful *(is ungrateful only to his own soul's hurt.)* For my Lord is Absolute in independence, Bountiful.

(Commentators say that this might be his chief minister, an angel, or Solomon himself. The Book here means the knowledge that Allah had imparted to him, which gave him control over physical forces so that everything was subjected to his command by God's leave.)

41. He said: "Make her throne unrecognizable to her that we may see whether she is guided to knowing it, or whether she will not be among the guided.

42. So, when she came, it was said *(unto her)*: "Is your throne like this? She said: "It is as though it were the very one. And Solomon said: "We were given the knowledge before her and we had surrendered *(to Allah.)*

43. But *(the gods)* she had worshipped instead of Allah had led her astray: for she was of a people who believed not.

44. It was said unto her: 'Enter the hall'. And when she saw it she deemed it a pool and bared her legs. Solomon said: "It is a hall, made smooth, of glass. She said: "My Lord! I have wronged myself, and I surrender with Solomon unto Allah, the Lord of the Worlds.

(The symbolic meaning would take us far afield. Let us here confine ourselves to the literal sense. Bilqis, having been received with honour on her arrival, and having accepted the transformation of her throne, placed presumably in an outer building of the Palace, is asked to enter the great Palace itself. Its floor was made of slabs of smooth polished glass, that glistened like water She thought it was water, and tucked up her clothes to pass through it, showing her legs.)

36. So when *(the envoy)* came to Solomon he said: "What!Would you help me with wealth? But that which Allah has given me is better than that which He has given you. Nay, it is you who exult in your gift.

37. Return unto them. We verily shall come unto them with hosts that they cannot resist, and we shall drive them out from there with shame, and they will be abased.

38. He said: "O chiefs! Which of you will bring me her throne before they come unto me, surrendering?

39. A stalwart of the Jinn said: "I will bring it to you before you rise from your place. I verily am strong and trusty for such work. "

(The race of jinn is divided into two types: (a) 'Ifrît jinn, who are unbelievers and rebellious against any divine law. (Some interpreters, however, say that 'Ifrît means a stalwart of the jinn.)

b) More commonly, Jinn are a species of sentient being, usually unseen by men, who are created of

45. And We verily sent to Thamûd their brother Salih, saying: "Worship Allah . And they became parties, quarrelling.

(The account here is of the secret plot of nine men against the man of God, whose teaching, they thought, brought them ill-luck; but what they called ill-luck was the just punishment from God for their own ill-deeds. Their plot was foiled, and the whole community, which was involved in evil, was destroyed. Cf. 26:141-159 for more details.)

46. He said: "O my people! Why will you hasten on the evil rather than the good? Why will you not ask pardon of Allah, that you may receive mercy?

47. They said: "We augur evil of you and those with you." He said: "Your evil augury is with Allah. Nay but you are people that are being tested.

(That is, the cause of your ill augury is known to Allah, for it is He who has decreed it.)

48. And there were in the city nine persons who made mischief in the land, and reformed not.

(They had made up their minds to wage a relentless war against justice. They did not destroy justice, but justice destroyed them.)

49. They said: "Swear one to another (a mutual oath) by Allah that we will attack him and his household by night, and afterward we will surely say unto his friend (protector): 'We witnessed not the destruction of his household'. And we are truthtellers.

50. So they plotted a plot: and We plotted a plot, while they perceived not.

51. Then see the nature of the consequence of their plotting, for We destroyed them and their people, every one.

52. Those are their dwellings empty and in ruins because they did wrong. Truly herein is a sign for a people who have knowledge.

53. And We saved those who believed and used to ward off evil.

54. And Lût! when he said unto his people: "Will you commit abomination knowingly?

(The story of Lût is referred to elsewhere. But the point emphasised here is that the crime of the Cities of the Plain was against their own nature, and they saw its enormity, and yet they indulged in it. Can degradation go further? His wife was not apparently a Believer. Her previous sympathy with the sinful people "destined her (verse 57 below) to a miserable end, as she lagged behind and shared in the destruction of her kinsfolk.)

55. Must you practise lust with men instead of women? Nay, you are but a people that are ignorant.

(The ignorance referred to here is the spiritual ignorance of how grossness and sins that bring shame on their own physical and moral nature are doomed to destroy them: it is their own loss. That they knew the iniquity of their sins has already been stated in the last verse.)

56. But the answer of his people was naught save that they said: "Expel the household of Lot from your township, for they are people who would keep clean!

57. Then We rescued him and his household, save his wife: We destined her to be of those who stayed behind.

(The Arabic word use for lingered is "ghâbirin , which may mean either among those who tarried or among those who perished. Lût's wife is said to have been left behind with his people, who were annihilated by a rain of stones of fire.)

58. And We rained a rain of stone upon them. Dreadful is the rain of those who have been warned.

59. Say (O Muhammad): "Praise be to Allah, and peace be on His slaves whom He has chosen! Is Allah best, or all that you ascribe as partners unto Him?

(Allah's revelation having been described as Light, Guidance, and Mercy, we ought all to be grateful to

God for vouchsafing His revelation. We ought also to appreciate the services of God's Messengers, who are chosen to deliver His Message: we ought to send salutations of peace on them, instead of plotting, as the wicked do, for their removal or persecution, or banishment or death. For these men of God undergo every kind of hardship and forego every kind of advantage or pleasure in life for serving mankind.)

60. Is not He Who created the heavens and the earth (best), and who has sent down for you water from the sky wherewith We cause to spring forth joyous orchards whose trees it never has been yours to cause to grow? Is there any God beside Allah? Nay, but they are people who ascribe equals (unto Him).

61. Is not He (best) Who made the earth a fixed abode and placed rivers in the folds thereof, and placed firm hills therein, and has set a barrier between the two seas? Is there any God beside Allah? Nay but most of them know not!

62. Is not He (best) Who answers the oppressed one when he cries unto Him and takes off their ills and has made you vice-regents of the earth? Is there any God beside Allah? Little do you remember!

63. Is not He (best) Who guides you in the darkness of the land and the sea, He Who sends the winds as heralds of His mercy? Is there any God beside Allah? High exalted be Allah from all that they ascribe as partner (unto Him)!

(After external nature, our attention is drawn to our inner consciousness; after that, it is drawn here to our social and collective life, in which we use the forces of nature for international intercourse, trade, agriculture, production, and economic well-being generally. In the next verse, we are asked to contemplate creation from its primeval stages, through its intermediate processes, to the final Destiny in a new Creation - a new heaven and a new earth.)

64. Is it not He Who originates the creation, then renews it, and Who provides for you from the heaven and the earth? Is there any God beside Allah? Say: "Bring your proof, if you are truthful!

65. Say *(O Muhammad):* "None in the heavens and the earth knows the Unseen save Allah; and they know not when they will be raised again.

66. Nay, but does their knowledge reach to the Hereafter? Nay, for they are in doubt concerning it. Nay for they cannot see it.

67. And those who disbelieve say: "When we have become dust like our fathers, shall we be brought forth again?

68. We were promised this, we and our fathers. This is nothing but fables of the men of old.

69. *(Unto them, say, o Muhammad!)* "Travel in the land and see the nature of the sequel for the guilty!

70. And grieve you not for them, nor be in distress because of what they plot *(against you.)*

71. And they say: "When will this promise be fulfilled, if you are truthful?

72. Say: "It may be that a part of that which you would hasten on is close behind you.

73. Surely your Lord is full of bounty for mankind, but most of them do not give thanks.

74. Truly your Lord knows all that their bosoms hide, and all that they proclaim.

75. And there is nothing hidden in the heaven or the earth but it is in a clear Record.

76. Truly this Qur'ân narrates unto the Children of Israel most of that concerning which they differ.

(The Jews had numerous sects. Some were altogether beyond the pale, e. g., the Samaritans, who had a separate Torah of their own. They hated the other Jews and were hated by them. But even in the orthodox body, there were several sects, of which the following may be mentioned: (1) the Pharisees, who were literalists, formalists, and fatalists, and had a large body of traditional literature, with which they overlaid the Law of Moses; (2) the Sadducees, who were rationalists, and seemed to have doubted the doctrine of the Resurrection or of a Hereafter; (3) the Essenes, who practised a sort of communism and asceticism and prohibited marriage. About many of their doctrines they had bitter disputes, which were settled by the Qur'ân, which supplemented and perfected the Law of Moses. It also explained clearly the nature of God and of Revelation, and the doctrine of the Hereafter.)

them. Commentators are at sharp variance concerning the word "beast". They have said that it may be an animal of abnormal shape, an enormous fowl, an insect, or a human being that will signal the end of life on earth and will come out talking to people of matters of God's faith.)

83. And *(remind them of)* the Day when We shall gather out of every nation a host of those who denied Our revelations, and they will be set in array *(in a separate disposition)*.

84. Till, when they come before their Lord, He said: "Did you deny My revelations when you could not compass them in knowledge, or what was it that you did?

85. And the Word shall fall on them because they have done wrong, and they will not speak.

86. Have they not seen how We have appointed the night that they may rest therein, and the day sight-giving? Surely therein, verily are portents for a people who believe.

87. And *(remind them of)* the Day when the Trumpet will be blown, and all who are in the heavens and the earth will be stricken with terror, save him whom Allah wills. And all come unto Him, humbled.

(It is said that when the archangel Israfil blows the trumpet the first time, it will be to herald the end of life, and the second will be to raise the dead for reckoning. Some commentators hold that the second blow of the trumpet is used as a metaphor for raising people for the Doomsday and that there is no real blowing. Other commentators say that the trumpet means 'souls', and so it may mean blowing life into the dead.)

88. And you see the hills you deem solid, but they are flying with the flight of clouds: such is the doing of Allah Who perfected all things. Surely, He is Informed of what you do.

(*Atqana*: to arrange or dispose of things with art, or so as to obtain the most perfect results. The present phenomenal world and the future that is to be, all have a definite object and purpose in the Plan of God, Who knows perfectly what we are, what we do, who we think, and what we need. Who can praise His artistry enough?)

77. And it is a guidance and a mercy for believers.

78. Assuredly your Lord will judge between them by His wisdom, and He is the Mighty, the Wise.

79. Therefore, *(O Muhammad)* put your trust in Allah, for you stand on the plain Truth.

80. Surely you cannot make the dead to hear, nor can make the deaf to hear the call when they have turned to flee;

81. Nor can you lead the blind out of their error, for you can make none to hear, save those who believe Our revelations, and who have surrendered.

82. And when the word fall on them, We shall bring forth a beast of the earth to speak unto them because mankind had not faith in Our revelations.

(That is, when the doom or retribution which they were promised falls on them, We shall bring forth out of the earth a beast that shall speak to them or injure

89. Whoever brings a good deed will have better than its worth; and such are safe from fear that Day.

90. And whoever brings an ill deed, such will be flung down on their faces in the Fire. Are you rewarded aught save what you did?

91. (O Muhammad, say:) "I am commanded only to serve the Lord of this land which He has hallowed, and unto whom all things belong. And I am commanded to be of those who surrender (unto Him).

92. And to recite the Qur'ân. And whoever goes right, goes right only for the good of his own soul; and as for him who goes astray, unto him say: I am only a warner.

93. And say: "Praise be to Allah Who will show you His portents so that you shall know them. And your Lord is not unaware of what you (mortals) do.

SÛRAH XXVIII
AL-QASAS (THE STORY)
Revealed at Makka

Al-Qasas takes its name from a word in v. 25. The name is moreover justified by the nature of the Sûrah, which consists mostly of the story of Moses, his early struggles and ultimate triumph, revealed at a time when the prophetic case seemed desperate. It is one of the last Makkan Sûrahs. Some Arabic writers even say that it was revealed during the Hijrah, while others are of opinion that v. 85 only was revealed during the migration.

A late Makkan Sûrah, except v. 85 which was revealed during the Prophet's flight from Makka to Al-Madîna, and vv. 52-55 revealed at Madîna. This Sûrah consists of eighty-eight verses.

THE STORY

In the name of Allah, the Compassionate, the Merciful.

1. Tâ. Sîn. Mîm.

2. These are verses of the Scripture that makes plain. (Or: of the lucid Book.)

3. We narrate unto you something of the history of Moses and Pharaoh with truth, for people who believe.

4. Pharaoh exalted himself in the earth and made its people castes. A tribe among them he oppressed, killing their sons and sparing their women. He was indeed one of the corruptors.

(For a king or ruler to make invidious distinctions between his subjects, and especially to depress or oppress any particular class of his subjects, is a dereliction of his kingly duties, for which he is responsible to God. Pharaoh and his clique were intoxicated with pride of race and pride of material civilization, and grievously oppressed the Israelites. Pharaoh decreed that all male sons born to his Israelite subjects should be killed, and the females kept alive for the pleasure of the Egyptians. Moses was saved in a remarkable way, as related further.)

5. And We desired to show favour unto those who were oppressed in the earth, and to make them leaders, and to make them the inheritors,

6. And to establish them in the earth, and to show Pharaoh and Haman and their hosts that which they feared.

7. And We inspired the mother of Moses, saying: "Suckle him and, when you fear for him then cast him into the river and fear not nor grieve. For We shall bring him back unto you and shall make him one of the messengers. *(The river was a branch of the river Nile.)*

8. Then the family of Pharaoh took him up, that he might become for them an enemy and a sorrow. Surely Pharaoh and Haman and their hosts were ever sinning *(perfidious)*.

9. And the wife of Pharaoh said: "He will be a delight to the eye for me and for you. Kill him not. Peradventure he may be of use to us, or we may choose him for a son. And they perceived not.

(In all life Providence so orders things that Evil is defeated by its own weapons. Not only is it defeated, but it actually, though unwittingly, advances the cause

of good! In non-religious language this is sometimes called the work of the Ironic Fates.)

10. And the heart of the mother of Moses became void, and she would have betrayed him if We had not fortified her heart that she might be of the believers.

(That is, deprived of reason because of the fear and anxiety that followed her knowing that Moses had been picked up by Pharaoh's family.)

11. And she said to his sister: "Trace him. So she observed him from afar, and they perceived not.

12. And We had before forbidden fostermothers for him, so she said: "Shall I show you a household who will rear him for you and take care of him?

13. So We restored him to his mother that she might be comforted and not grieve, and that she might know that the promise of Allah is true. But most of them know not.

14. And when he reached his full age *(strength)* and was ripe, We gave him wisdom and knowledge. Thus do We reward the doers of good.

("Full age may be taken to be mature youth, say between 18 and 30 years of age. By that time a person is fully established in life: his physical build is completed, and his mental and moral habits are formed. In this case, as Moses was good at heart, true and loyal to his people, and obedient and just to those among whom he lived, he was granted wisdom and knowledge from on high, to be used for the times of conflict which were coming for him. His internal development being complete, he now goes out into the outer world, where he is again tried and proved, until he receives his divine commission.)

15. And he entered the city at a time of carelessness of its folk, and he found therein two men fighting, one of his own caste and the other of his enemies; and he who was of his caste asked him for help against him who was of his enemies. So Moses struck him with his fist and killed him. He said: "This is of the devil's doing. Lo! he is an enemy, a clear misleader.

(This may have been either the time of the noontide siesta, when all business is suspended even now in Egypt, or the time of night, when people are usually asleep. The latter is more probable, in view of verse 18 below. But there is also another suggestion. A guest in a Palace is not free to wander about at will in the plebeian quarters of the City at all sorts of hours, and this applies even more to an inmate of the Palace brought up as a son. Moses was therefore visiting the City privately and eluding the guards. His object may have been to see for himself how things were going on; perhaps he had heard that his people were being oppressed, as we may suppose that he had retained contact with his mother.)

16. He said: "My Lord! I have wronged myself, so forgive me." Then He forgave him, for He is the Forgiving the Merciful.

17. He said: "My Lord! Since You have, favoured me, I will nevermore be a supporter of the guilty."

18. And morning found him in the city, fearing, vigilant *(watchful)*; when behold! He who had appealed to him the day before cried out to him for help. Moses said unto him: "You are indeed a mere hothead *(mad, furious).*

19. And when he would have fallen upon the man who was an enemy unto them both, he said: "O Moses! Would you kill me as you did kill a person yesterday? You would be nothing but a tyrant in the land; you would not be of the reformers.

20. And a man came from the uttermost part of the city, running. He said: "O Moses! Now the chiefs take counsel against you to slay you, therefore escape. Indeed I am of those who give you good advice.

21. So he escaped from thence fearing, vigilant. He said: "My Lord! Deliver me from the wrongdoing folk.

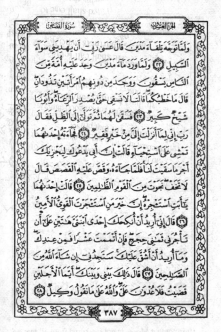

22. And when he turned his face toward Midian, he said: "Perhaps my Lord will guide me in the right road.

(His object was apparently to strike him so as to release the Israelite, not to kill the Egyptian. In fact he killed the Egyptian. This was unfortunate in more ways than one. His visit to the City was clandestine; he had taken the side of the weaker and despised party; and he had taken the life of an Egyptian.)

23. And when he came unto the water of Midian he found there a whole tribe of men, watering. And he found apart from them two women keeping back *(their flocks)*. He said: "What is your trouble? The two said: "We cannot give our flocks to drink till the shepherds return from the water; and our father is a very old man.

24. So he watered their flock for them. Then he turned aside into the shade, and said: "My Lord! I am needy of whatever good You send down for me.

(The maidens are gone, with smiles on their lips and gratitude in their hearts. What were the reflections of Moses as he returned to the shade of the tree? He returned thanks to God for the bright little vision which he had just seen. Had he done a good deed? Precious was the opportunity he had had. He had slaked his thirst. But he was a homeless wanderer and had a longing in his soul, which he dared not put into words. Those shepherds were no company for hem. He was truly like a beggar in desperate need. For any little good that came his way, he was grateful. But what was this?- this vision of a comfortable household, presided over by an old man rich in flocks and herds, and richer still in two daughters, as modest as they were beautiful? Perhaps he would never see them again! But Providence was preparing another surprise for him.)

25. Then there came unto him one of the two women, walking shyly. She said: "Lo! my father invites you, that he may reward you with a payment for that you did water the flock for us. Then, when he came unto him and told him the whole story, he said: "Fear not! you have escaped from the wrongdoing folk.

26. One of the two women said: "O my father! Hire him! For the best man that you can hire is the strong, the trustworthy.

27. He said: "Indeed I desire to marry you to one of these two daughters of mine, on condition that you hire yourself to me for the term of eight years. Then if you complete ten it will be of your own accord, for I would not make it hard for you. Allah willing, you will find me of the righteous.

28. He said: "That *(is settled)* between you and me. Whichever of the two terms I fulfil, there will be no injustice to me, and Allah is guardian over what we say.

29. Then, when Moses had fulfilled the term, and was traveling with his housefolk, he saw in the distance a fire, and said unto his housefolk: "Stay you here, for I see in the distance a fire; perhaps I shall bring you tidings thence, or a brand from the fire that you may warm yourselves.

(The episode in the desert, full of human interest, now closes, and we come to the threshold of the sacred Call to the divine ministry of Moses. Here we may compare this passage with that in 27: 7-14 and previous passages. Note that a speech in such cases is not a literal report of spoken words, but a general rendering in human words of Commands, Events, and Thoughts, such as may be relevant in connection with any particular episode and its context. In this passage we are told, after reference to Moses's preparation for his high destiny, of the particular sin of arrogance and sacrilege of which Pharaoh was guilty (28: 38-39), how it was punished, and with what instruments in the hands of Moses and Pharaoh.)

30. And when he reached it, he was called from the right side of the valley in the blessed field, from the tree: "O Moses! Lo! I, even I, am Allah, the Lord of the Worlds;

31. Throw down your staff. And when he saw it writhing as it had been a demon, he turned to flee headlong, (and it was said unto him): "O Moses! Draw nigh and fear not. Lo! you are of those who are secure.

32. Put your hand into the bosom of your robe, it will come forth white without hurt. And guard your heart from fear. Then these shall be two proofs from your Lord unto Pharaoh and his chiefs: Assuredly, they are evil-living folk.

33. He said: "My Lord! I killed a man among them, and I fear that they will kill me.

(It is not that Moses is not reassured from all fear on account of the apparent snake which his rod had become, or from the sacred and unfamiliar surroundings in which he found himself. On this point his heart has been completely assured. But he is still new to his mission, and the future is obscure to his mind. Pharaoh was after him, to take his life, and apparently with good cause, because one of Pharaoh's men had been slain at his hands. And now he is commanded to go to Pharaoh and rebuke him and his chiefs. The inner doubts and difficulties of his human mind he frankly lays before his Lord, and asks for a little human and visible support, which is grated him at once, namely, his brother Aaron.)

34. My brother Aaron is more eloquent than me in speech. Therefor send him with me as a helper to confirm me. For I fear that they will give the lie to me.

35. He said: "We will strengthen your arm with your brother, and We will give unto you both power so that they cannot reach you for Our portents. You two, and those who follow you, will be the winners.

36. But when Moses came unto them with Our clear signs, they said: "This is nothing but invented magic. We never heard of this among our fathers of old.

37. And Moses said: "My Lord is best aware of him who brings guidance from His presence, and whose will be the sequel of the Home (of bliss). Lo! wrong-doers will not be successful.

38. And Pharaoh said: "O chiefs! I know not that you have a god other than me. So, Hâmân, kindle me a fire upon the clay, then set up for me a tower that I may ascend to the God of Moses. I deem him of the liars.

39. And he and his hosts were arrogant in the land without right, and deemed that they would never be brought back to Us.

40. Therefore We seized him and his hosts, then We flung them into the sea. Behold, how was the consequence for evil-doers.

41. And We made them leaders that invite unto the Fire; and on the Day of Resurrection they will not be helped.

42. And We made a curse to follow them in this world, and on the Day of Resurrection they will be among the hateful.

(Power and patronage may be admired by sycophants and selfish place-hunters; but when they are misused, and when their exposure causes their fall, they suffer ignominy even in this life. If they manage to escape exposure while alive, it often happens that they are found out after their death, and the curses of many generations follow those whose oppressions and wrong-doing spoiled the fair face of God's earth. But even this is nothing to the true punishment that will come in the Hereafter. There, true values will be restored, and some of the highest and mightiest will be in the lowest depths of degradation.)

43. And We verily gave the Scripture unto Moses after We had destroyed the generations of old: clear testimonies (proofs) for mankind, and a guidance and a mercy, that perhaps they might reflect.

(After the destruction of the Pharaonic tyranny and other similar tyrannies before them, God began a new age of Revelation, the age of Moses and his Book. Humanity began as it were with a clean slate again. It was a full Revelation (or Shari'a) which may be looked at from three points of view: (1) as Light or Insight for men, so that they should not grope in darkness; (2) as a Guide to show them the Way, so that they should not be misled into wrong Paths; and (3) as a Mercy from God, so that by following the Way they may receive God's forgiveness and grace.)

44. And you *(Muhammad)* were not on the western side *(of the Mount)* when We decreed to Moses the commandment, and you were not among those witnessing.

(The Sinai Peninsula is in the north-west corner of Arabia. But the reference here is, we think, to the western side of the valley of Tuwâ. Mount Tur, where Moses received his prophetic commission, is on the western side of the valley.)

45. But We brought forth generations, and their lives dragged on for them. And you were not a dweller in Midian reciting unto them Our revelations, but We kept sending *(messengers to men).*

46. And you were not beside the Mount when We did call; but *(the knowledge of it is)* a mercy from your Lord, that you might warn a folk unto whom no warner came before you, that perhaps they might give heed.

(This people was the Quraish. 'Though you did not see how Moses was invested with the prophetic office at Mount Tur, you have had a similar experience yourselves, and We have sent you to the Quraish to warn them of all their sins, and to repent and come into the Faith.')

47. Otherwise, if disaster should afflict them because of that which their own hands have sent before them, they might say: "Our Lord! Why sent You no messenger unto us, that we might have followed Your revelations and been of the believers?

(Now that a warner has come among them with all the authority that previous apostles possessed, and with all the knowledge which can only come by divine inspiration, they have no excuse left whatever. They cannot say, "No warner came to us. If any evil comes to them, as the inevitable result of their ill-deeds, they cannot blame God and say that they were not warned.)

48. But when there came unto them the Truth from Our presence, they said: "Why is he not given the like of what was given unto Moses? Did they not disbelieve in that which was given unto Moses of old? They said: "Two magics that support each other ; and they said: "Lo! in both we are disbelievers.

49. Say *(unto them, O Muhammad):* "Then bring a Scripture from the presence of Allah that yields better guidance than these two, *(that)* I may follow it, if you are truthful.

50. And if they answer you not, then know that what they follow is their caprice. And who goes farther astray than he who follows his caprice without guidance from Allah? Behold! Allah guides not wrongdoing people.

51. And now We have caused the Word to reach them, that perhaps they may give heed.

(Before this, the Quraish might have said that the Word of God had come to the Hebrews in their tongue or in Greek, which was used by the Hebrews in the time of Jesus. Now that Word is brought to their own doors, in their own Arabic tongue, by a man of their own race and family, surely they have no excuse now for remaining strangers to the higher moral and spiritual law.)

52. Those unto whom We gave the Scripture before it, they believe in it,

53. And when it is recited unto them, they say: "We believe in it. Surely it is the Truth from our Lord. Even before it we were of those who surrender unto Him.

54. These will be given their reward twice over, because they are steadfast and repel evil with good, and spend of that wherewith We have provided them.

55. And when they hear vanity they withdraw from it and say: "Unto us our works and unto you your works. Peace be unto you! We desire not the ignorant.

56. *(O Muhammad:)* "You do not guide whom you like, but Allah guides whom He wills. And He is best aware of those who walk aright.

(The immediate occasion for this was the death of Abu Talib, an uncle whom the Holy Prophet loved dearly and who had befriended and protected him. The Prophet was naturally anxious that he should die in the profession of the true Faith, but the pagan Quraish leaders appear to have persuaded him to remain true to the faith of his fathers. This was an occasion of disappointment and grief to the Prophet.)

57. And they said: "If we were to follow the guidance with you we should be torn out of our land . Have We not established for them a sure sanctuary *(Makka)*, whereunto the produce of all things is brought *(in trade)*, a provision from Our presence? But most of them know not.

58. And how many a community have We destroyed that was thankless for its means of livelihood! And those are their dwellings, which have not been inhabited after them save a little. And We, even We, were the inheritors.

(A life of ease and plenty is nothing to boast of. Yet people or cities or civilisations grow insolently proud of such things. There were many such in the past, which are now mere names! Their very sites are deserted in most cases, or buried in the debris of ages.)

59. And never did your Lord destroy the townships, till He had sent to their mother town a messenger reciting unto them Our revelations. And never did We destroy the townships unless the folk thereof were evil-doers.

60. And whatsoever you have been given is a comfort of the life of the world and an ornament thereof; and that which Allah has is better and more lasting. Have you then no sense?

61. Is he whom We have promised a fair promise which he will find *(true)* like him whom We suffer to enjoy awhile the comfort of the life of the world, then on the Day of Resurrection he will be of those who are brought for retribution?

(The two classes of people are:

1) those who have faith in the goodly promise of Allah to the righteous, and who are doing everything in life to reach the fulfilment of that promise.

2) those who are ungrateful for such good things in this life as Allah has bestowed on them, by worshipping wealth or power or other symbols or idols of their fancy.)

62. On the Day when He shall call unto them and say: "Where are My partners whom you imagined?"

63. Those upon whom the Word shall come to pass will say: "Our Lord! These are they whom we led astray: We led them astray even as we ourselves were astray. We declare our innocence before you: us they never worshipped.

(False worship often names others, but really it is the worship of the Self. The others whom they name will have nothing to do with them when the awful Penalty stands in the sight of both. Then each wrongdoer will have to look to his own case. The wicked will then realise the gravity of the situation and wish that they had accepted the true guidance of Allah's Messengers.)

64. And it will be said: "Cry unto your *(so-called)* partners of Allah!" And they will cry unto them, and they will give no answer unto

them and they will behold the punishment. Ah, if they had but been guided!

65. And on the Day when He will call unto them and say: "What answer gave you to the messengers?

66. On that day *(all)* tidings will be dimmed for them, nor will they ask one of another,

67. But as for him who shall repent and believe and do right, he may be one of the successful.

68. Your Lord creates what He wills and chooses. They have never any choice. Glorified be Allah, and exalted above all that they associate *(with Him)!*

69. And your Lord knows what their breasts conceal, and what they make public.

70. And He is Allah; there is no God save Him. His is all praise in the former and the latter state, and His is the command, and unto Him you will be brought back.

71. Say: "Have you thought, if Allah made night everlasting for you till the Day of Resurrection, who is a God beside Allah who could bring you light? Will you not then hear?

72. Say: "Have you thought, if Allah made day everlasting for you till the Day of Resurrection; who is a God beside Allah who could bring you night wherein you rest? Will you not then see?

73. Of His mercy has He appointed for you night and day, that you may rest, and that perhaps you may be thankful.

74. And on the Day when He shall call unto them and say: "Where are My partners whom you pretended?

75. And We shall take out from every nation a witness, and We shall say: "Bring your proof." Then they will know that Allah has the Truth, and all that they invented will have failed them.

76. Now Korah (Qârûn) was of Moses' people, but he oppressed them; and We gave him so much treasure that the keys thereof would verily have been a burden for a troop of mighty men. When his own folk said unto him: "Exult not; Allah loves not the exultant.

(Qârûn's boundless wealth is described in the Midrashim, or the Jewish compilations based on the oral teachings of the Synagogues, which, however, exaggerate the weight of the keys to be the equivalent of the load of 300 mules!

'Usbah: a body of men, here used indefinitely. It usually implies a body of 10 to 40 men. The old-fashioned keys were big and heavy, and if there were hundreds of treasure chests, the keys must have been a great weight.)

77. But seek the abode of the Hereafter in that which Allah has given you, and forget not your portion of the world, and be you kind even as Allah has been kind to you, and seek not corruption in the earth; for Allah loves not corrupters.

(That is, 'spend your wealth in charity and good works. It is Allah Who has given it to you, and you should spend it in Allah's cause. Nor should you forget the legitimate needs of this life, as misers do, and most people become misers who think too exclusively of their wealth.')

78. He said: "I have been given it only on account of knowledge I possess. Knew he not that Allah had destroyed already of the generations before him men who were mightier than him in strength and greater in respect of following? The guilty are not questioned of their sins. *(Because Allah knows them well.)*

79. Then he went forth to his people in his pomp. Those who were desirous of the life of the world said: "Ah, would that unto us had been given the like of what has been given unto Qârûn! Indeed he is lord of rare good fortune.

(When he was in the hey-day of his glory, worldly people envied him and thought how happy they would be if they were in his place. Not so the people of wisdom and discernment. They knew a more precious and lasting wealth, which is described in the next verse.)

80. But those who had been given knowledge said: "Woe unto you! The reward of Allah for him who believes and does right is better, and only the steadfast will obtain it.

81. So We caused the earth to swallow him and his dwelling-place. Then he had no host to help him against Allah, nor was he of those who can save themselves.

82. And in the morning, those who had desired to be in his place the day before cried,

"Assuredly, Allah enlarges the provision for whom He wills of His slaves and straitens it for whom He will. If Allah had not been gracious unto us He would have caused it to swallow us also. Assuredly the disbelievers never prosper.

(Provision or sustenance, both literally and figuratively: wealth and material things in life as well as the things that sustain our higher and spiritual faculties.)

83. As for that Abode of the Hereafter, We assign it unto those who seek not oppression in the earth, nor yet corruption. The sequel is for those who ward off evil.

(Oppression, as opposed to submission to the Will of Allah, Islam. Corruption, as opposed to doing good, bringing forth fruits of righteousness. It is the righteous who will win in the end.)

84. Whoso brings a good deed, he will have better than the same; while as for him who brings an ill deed, those who do ill deeds will be requited only what they did.

and be not of those who ascribe partners (to Him).

88. And cry not unto any other god along with Allah. There is no God save Him. Everything will perish save His countenance. His is the command, and unto Him you will be brought back.

(This sums up the lesson of the whole Sûrah. The only Eternal Reality is Allah. The whole phenomenal world is subject to flux and change and will pass away, but He will endure forever.)

SÛRAH XXIX

AL-'ANKABÛT (THE SPIDER)

Revealed at Makka

Al-'Ankabût, "The Spider, "takes its name from v. 41 where false beliefs are likened to the spider's web for frailty. Most of this Sûrah belongs to the middle or last Makkan period. Some authorities consider vv. 7 and 8, others the whole letter portion of the Sûrah, to have been revealed at Madîna. It gives comfort to the Muslims in a time of persecution.

THE SPIDER

In the name of Allah, the Compassionate,
the Merciful.

1. Alif. Lâm. Mîm.

2. Do men imagine that they will be left (at ease) because they say, "We believe and will not be tested with affliction?

3. We tested those who were before you. Thus Allah knows those who are sincere, and knows those who are liars.

4. Or do those who do ill-deeds imagine that they can outstrip Us? Wretched is what they judge!

5. Whoever hopes to meet Allah (let him know that) Allah's reckoning is surely coming, and He is the Hearer, the Knower.

6. And whosoever strives, strives only for himself, for Allah is altogether Independent of (His) creatures.

85. Lo! He Who has given you the Qur'ân will surely bring you back to a place of return. Say: "My Lord is best aware of him who brings guidance and him who is in error manifest.

(Place of Return: (1) a title of Makka; (2) the occasion when we shall be restored to the Presence of our Lord. It is said that this verse was revealed at Juhfa, on the road from Makka to Madîna, a short distance from Makka, on the Hijrah journey. The Prophet was sad at heart, and this was given as consolation to him. If this was the particular occasion, the general meaning would refer the Place of Return to the occasion of the Resurrection, when all true values will be restored, however greatly they may be disturbed by the temporary interference of evil in this life.)

86. And you had no hope that the Scripture would be inspired in you, but it is a mercy from your Lord, so never be a helper to the disbelievers.

87. And let them not divert you from the signs (revelations) of Allah after they have been sent down unto you, but call mankind to your Lord,

396   AL-'ANKABÛT   Part 20, Sûrah 29

7. And as for those who believe and do good works, We shall remit from them their evil deeds and shall repay them the best that they did.

8. We have enjoined on mankind kindness to parents; but if they strive to make you join *(associate)* with Me that of which you have no knowledge, then obey them not. Unto Me is your return, and I shall tell you what you used to do.

9. And as for those who believe and do good works, We shall make them enter in among the righteous.

10. Of mankind is he who says: "We believe in Allah", but, if he be made to suffer for the sake of Allah, he mistakes the persecution of mankind for Allah's punishment; and then, if victory comes from your Lord, will say: "Lo! we were with you *(all the while)*. Is not Allah best aware of what is in the bosoms of *(His)* creatures?

(The man who turns away from Faith in adversity and only claims the friendship of the Faithful when there is something to be gained by it, is worthy of a double condemnation: first because he rejected Faith and Truth, and secondly because he falsely pretended to be one of those whom he feared or hated in his heart. But nothing in all creation is concealed from Allah.)

11. Verily, Allah knows those who believe, and verily He knows the hypocrites.

12. Those who disbelieve say unto those who believe: "Follow our way *(of religion)* and we verily will bear your sins *(for you)*. They cannot bear aught of their sins. Lo! they verily are liars.

13. But they verily will bear their own loads and other loads beside their own, and they verily will be questioned on the Day of Resurrection concerning that which they invented.

(Besides the hypocrite there is another type of man who openly scoffs at faith. 'Take life as we take it', he says: 'we shall bear your sins'. As if they could! Each soul bears its own burdens, and no one else can bear them. The principle also applies to the type of man who preaches vicarious atonement, for, if followed to its logical conclusion, it means both injustice and irresponsibility, and puts quite a different complexion on the nature of sin.)

14. And verily We sent Noah as Our messenger unto his people, and he continued with them for a thousand years save fifty years; and the flood engulfed them, for they were wrongdoers.

15. And We rescued him and those with him in the ship and made of it a portent for the peoples.

16. And Abraham! *(Remember)* when he said unto his folk: "Serve Allah, and keep your duty unto Him; that is better for you if you did but know:

17. You serve instead of Allah only idols, and you only invent a lie. Lo! those whom you serve instead of Allah own no provision for you. So seek your provision from Allah, and serve Him, and give thanks unto Him, *(for)* unto Him you will be brought back.

18. But if you deny, then nations have denied before you. The messenger is only to convey *(the Message)* plainly.

19. See they not how Allah produces creation, then reproduces it? For Allah, that is easy.

20. Say *(O Muhammad)*: Travel in the land and see how He originated creation, then Allah bringes forth the later growth. Assuredly, Allah is Able to do all things.

(Travel through the earth: again, literally as well as symbolically. If we actually go through this wide earth, we shall see the wonderful things in His Creation- the Grand Canyon and the Niagaras in North America, beautiful harbours like that at Sydney in Australia, mountains like Fujiyama, the Himalayas, and Elburz in Asia, the Nile with its wonderful cataracts in Africa, the Fiords of Norway, the Geysers of Iceland, the city of the midnight sun in Tromsoe, and innumerable wonders everywhere. But wonders upon wonders are disclosed in the constitution of matter itself, the atom, and the forces of energy, as also in the instincts of animals, and the minds and capacities of man. And there is no limit to these things.)

21. He punishes whom He wills and shows mercy unto whom He wills, and unto Him you will be turned.

(Preferable, I think, is the translation, "unto Him you will be turned , to "towards Him will be your return , as it implies not only the return of man to God in the Hereafter *(turja'un)* in verse 17 (above) but also the fact explained in verse 22 that man's needs are always to be obtained from God: man cannot frustrate God's designs, and can have no help or protection except from God: man has always to face God, whether man obeys or tries to ignore Him.)

22. You cannot escape *(from Him)* in the earth or in the sky, and beside Allah there is for you no friend nor helper.

23. Those who disbelieve in the revelations of Allah and in *(their)* Meeting with Him, such have no hope of My mercy. For such there is a painful chastisement.

24. But the answer of his folk was only that they said: "Kill him or "Burn him! Then Allah saved him from the fire. Behold, herein are signs for people who believe.

25. He said: "You have chosen idols instead of Allah. The love between you is only in the life of the world. Then on the Day of Resurrection you will deny each other and curse each other, and your abode will be the Fire, and you will have no helpers.

(In sin and wickedness there is as much log-rolling as in politics. Evil men humour each other and support each other; they call each other's vices by high-sounding names. They call it mutual regard or friendship or love; at the lowest, they call it toleration. Perhaps they flourish in this life by such arts. But they deceive themselves, and they deceive each other. What will be their relations in the Hereafter?)

26. And Lot believed him, and said: "I am a fugitive unto my Lord. Indeed He, only He, is the Mighty, the Wise.

(Lot was a nephew of Abraham. He adhered to Abraham's teaching and faith and accepted voluntary exile with him, for Abraham left the home of his fathers in Chaldaea and migrated to Syria and Palestine, where God gave him increase and prosperity, and a numerous family, who upheld the flag of Unity and the Light of God.)

27. And We bestowed on him Isaac and Jacob, and We established the Prophethood and the Scripture among his seed, and We gave him his reward in the world, and in the Hereafter he verily is among the righteous.

28. And Lot! *(Remember)* when he said unto his people: "Indeed you commit obscenity such as no creature did before you.

29. Do you come unto men, and sever the road, and practise wickedness in your meetings? But the answer of his folk was only that they said: "Bring Allah's doom upon us if you are a truth-teller!

(They infested highways and committed their horrible crimes not only secretly, but openly and publicly, even in their assemblies. Some commentators understand "severing the road to refer to highway robberies: this is possible, and it is also possible that the crimes in their assemblies may have been injustice, rowdiness, etc. But the context seems to refer to their own special horrible crime, and the point here seems to be that they were not ashamed of it and that they practised it publicly. Degradation could go no further.)

30. He said: "My Lord! Give me victory over people who work corruption .

31. And when Our messengers brought Abraham the good tidings, they said: "We are about to destroy the people of that township, for its people are wrongdoers.

(The angels, who were coming on the mission to destroy the people who were polluting the earth with their crimes, called on their way on Abraham to give the good tidings of the birth of a son to him in his old age.)

32. He said: "Lot is there. They said: "We are best aware of who is there. We are to deliver him and his household, all save his wife, who is of those who stay behind.

33. And when Our messengers came unto Lot, he was troubled upon their account, for he could not protect them; but they said: "Fear not, nor grieve! For we are to deliver you and your household, save your wife, who is of those who stay behind.

34. Behold! We are about to bring down upon folk of this township a fury from the sky because they are evil-livers.

35. And verily of that We have left a clear sign for people who have sense.

(The whole tract on the east side of the Dead Sea *(where the cities were situated)* is covered with sulphureous salts and is deadly to animal and plant life. The Dead Sea itself is called in Arabic the Bahr Lût (the sea of Lot). It is a scene of utter desolation, that should stand as a symbol of the destruction that awaits sin.)

36. And unto Midian We sent Shu'aib, their brother. He said: "O my people! Serve Allah, and look forward to the Last Day, and do not evil, making mischief, in the earth.

37. But they denied him, and the Blast took them, and morning found them prostrate in their dwelling place.

(The story of Shu'aib and the Madyan people is only referred to here (it is told more fully at: 11:84-95). Their besetting sin was fraud and commercial immorality. Their punishment was a mighty Blast, such as accompanies volcanic eruptions. The point of the reference here is that they went about doing mischief on the earth, and never thought of the Ma'âd or the Hereafter, the particular theme of this Sûrah.)

38. And *(the tribes of)* 'Âd and Thamûd! *(Their fate)* is manifest unto you from their *(ruined and deserted)* dwellings. Satan made their deeds seem fair unto them, and so debarred them from the Way, though they were keen observers.

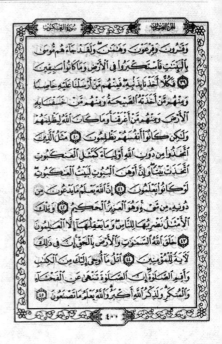

39. And Korah, Pharaoh and Haman! Moses came unto them with clear proofs *(of Allah's sovereignty)*, but they were boastful in the land. And they were not winners *(in the race)*.

40. So We seized each one in his sin; of them was he on whom We sent a hurricane, and of them was he who was overtaken by the *(Awful)* Cry, and of them was he who We caused the earth to swallow, and of them was he whom We drowned. It was not for Allah to wrong them, but they wronged themselves.

41. The likeness of those who choose other patrons than Allah is as the likeness of the spider when she takes unto herself a house, and assuredly the frailest of all houses is the spider's house, if they but knew.

(The spider's house is one of the wonderful signs of God's creation. It is made up of fine silk threads spun out of silk glands in the spider's body. There are many kinds of spiders and many kinds of spider's houses. Two main types of houses may be mentioned. There is the tubular nest or web, a silk-lined house or burrow with one or two trap-doors. This may be called his residential or family mansion. Then there is the more usual kind of spider's web: a central point and radiating threads running out in all directions.)

42. Verily Allah knows what thing they invoke instead of Him. He is the Mighty, the Wise.

43. As for these similitudes, We coin them for mankind, but none will grasp their meanings save the wise.

44. Allah created the heavens and the earth with truth. Behold, therein is indeed a sign for believers.

45. Recite that which has been inspired in you of the Scripture, and establish the Prayer. For the Prayer preserves from lewdness and iniquity, but verily remembrance of Allah is more great. And Allah knows what you do.

46. And argue not with the People of the Book unless it be in a way that is better, save with such of them who are iniquitous; and say: "We believe in that which has been revealed unto us and revealed unto you; our God and your God is One, and unto Him we surrender.

47. Thus We have revealed unto you the Book, and those unto whom We gave the Book, they believe therein; and of these *(also)* there are some who believe therein. And none deny Our revelations save the disbelievers.

(The sincere Jews and Christians found in the holy Prophet a fulfilment of their own religion. Embassies were sent by the holy Prophet in the 6th and 7th years of the Hijra to all the principal countries round Arabia, viz., the capital of the Byzantine Empire *(Constantinople)*, the capital of the Persian Empire *(al-Madâ'in)*, Syria, Abyssinia, and Egypt. All these *(except Persia)* were Christian countries. In the same connection an embassy was also sent to Yamâma in Arabia itself *(east of the Hijâz)* where the Banu Hanifa tribe was Christian, and also the Hârith tribe of Najrân who voluntarily sent an embassy to Madîna. All these

countries, except Abyssinia, eventually became Muslim, and Abyssinia itself has a considerable Muslim population now and sent some Muslim converts to Madîna in the time of the Prophet himself.)

48. And you *(O Muhammad)* did not recite a Book before it, nor did you write it with your right hand, for then the mendacious ones would have had misgivings.

(The holy Prophet was not a learned man. Before the Qurân was revealed to him, he never claimed to proclaim a Message from God. He was not in the habit of preaching eloquent truths as from a Book, before he received his Revelation, nor was he able to write or transcribe with his own hand. If he had had these worldly gifts, there would have been some plausibility in the charge of the talkers of vanities that he spoke not from inspiration but from other people's books, or that he composed the beautiful verses of the Qurân himself and committed them to memory in order to recite them to people. The circumstances in which the Qurân came bear their own testimony to its truth as from God.)

49. But it is clear revelations in the hearts of those who have been given knowledge, and none deny Our revelations save wrong-doers.

50. And they said: "If only signs were sent down upon him from his Lord? Say: "Signs are indeed with Allah, and I am but a plain warner.

51. Is it not enough for them that We have sent down unto you the Scripture which is read unto them? Indeed herein verily is mercy, and a reminder for folk who believe.

52. Say *(unto them, O Muhammad)*: Allah suffices for witness between me and you. He knows whatsoever is in the heavens and the earth. And those who believe in vanity and disbelieve in Allah, they it is who are the losers.

53. And they ask you to hasten the doom. And if a term had not been appointed, the doom would assuredly have come unto them *(already)*. And verily it will come upon them suddenly when they perceive not.

54. They bid you hasten on the doom, when hell verily will encompass the disbelievers.

55. On the day when the doom will overwhelm them from above them and from underneath their feet, and He will say: "Taste what you used to do!

56. O My bondsmen who believe! My earth is spacious. Therefore serve Me only.

(This is not merely a reproach, but a justification of the Punishment. "It is you who brought it on yourselves by your evil deeds: blame none but yourselves. God's Mercy gave you many chances: His Justice has now overtaken you!)

57. Every soul will taste of death. Then unto Us you will be returned.

(There is no excuse for any one to plead that he could not do good or was forced to evil by his circumstances and surroundings, or by the fact that he lived in evil times. We must shun evil and seek good, and God's Creation is wide enough to enable us to do that, provided we have the will, the patience, and the constancy to do it. It may be that we have to change our village or city or country; or that we have to change our neighbours or associates; or to change our habits or our hours, our position in life or our human relationships, or our callings.)

58. Those who believe and do good works, them verily We shall house in lofty dwellings of the Garden, underneath which rivers flow. There they will dwell secure. How excellent shall be the wage of those who labour.

59. Those who persevere, and put their trust in their Lord!

60. And how many an animal there is that bears not its own provision! Allah provides for it and for you. He is the Hearer, the Knower.

(If we look at the animal creation, we see that many creatures seem almost helpless to find their own food or sustain their full life, being surrounded by many enemies. Yet in the Plan of God they find full sustenance and protection.)

61. And if you were to ask them: "Who created the heavens and the earth, and constrained the sun and the moon *(to their appointed work)?* they would say: "Allah. How then are they turned away?

62. Allah makes the provision wide for whom He wills of His bondmen and straitens it for whom He wills. Verily Allah is Aware of all things.

63. And if you were to ask them: "Who causes water to come down from the sky, and therewith revives the earth after its death? they verily would say: "Allah. Say: "Praise be to Allah! But most of them have no sense.

64. This life of the world is but a pastime and a game. Lo! the home of the Hereafter, that is Life if they but knew.

65. And when they mount *(embark)* upon the ships they pray to Allah, making their faith pure for Him only, but when He brings them safe to land, behold! They ascribe partners *(unto Him)*.

66. That they may disbelieve in that which We have given them, and that they may take their ease. But they will come to know.

67. Have they not seen that We have appointed a sanctuary secure *(from violence)* while mankind are ravaged all around them? Do they then believe in falsehood and disbelieve in the bounty of Allah?

(The reference is to the sacred precincts of Makka the Ennobled, where violence, even against animals, is outlawed.)

68. Who does greater wrong than he who invents a lie concerning Allah, or denies the truth when it comes unto him? Is there not a home in hell for disbelievers?

69. As for those who strive in Us, We surely guide them to Our paths; and verily Allah is with the good.

SÛRAH XXX

AR-RÛM (THE ROMANS)

Revealed at Makka

Ar-Rûm, "The Romans , takes its name from a word in the second verse.

The armies of the Eastern Roman Empire had been defeated by the Persians in all the territories near Arabia. In the year AD 613 Jerusalem and Damascus fell and in the following year Egypt. A Persian army invaded Anatolia and was threatening Constantinople itself in the year AD 615 or 616, the sixth or seventh year before the Hijrah when, according to the best authorities, this Sûrah was revealed at Makka. The pagan Arabs triumphed in the news of Persian victories over the Prophet and his little band of followers, because the Christian Romans were believers in the One God, whereas the Persians were not. They argued that the power of Allah could not be supreme and absolute as the Prophet kept proclaiming it to be, since the forces of a pagan empire had been able to defeat His worshippers.

It belongs to the middle group of Makkan Sûrahs.

THE ROMANS

In the name of Allah, the Compassionate,
       the Merciful.

1. Alif. Lâm. Mîm

2. The Romans have been defeated.

3. In the nearer land, and they, after their defeat, will be victorious.

4. Within ten years. Allah's is the command in the former case and in the latter, and in that day believers will rejoice

5. In Allah's help to victory. He helps to victory whom He wills. He is the Mighty, the Merciful.

("Whom He will. As explained elsewhere, God's Will or Plan is not arbitrary: it is full of the highest wisdom.)

6. It is a promise of Allah. Allah does not break His promise; but most of mankind know not.

(The promise refers to the decision of all things by the command of God, Who will remove all troubles and difficulties from the path of His righteous Believers, and help them to rejoice over the success of their righteous Cause. This refers to all times and all situations.)

7. They know only some appearance of the life of the world, and are heedless of the Hereafter.

(Men are misled by the outward show of things, though the inner reality may be quite different.)

8. Have they not pondered upon themselves? Allah created not the heavens and the earth, and that which is between them, save with truth and for a destined end *(an appointed term)*. But truly many of mankind are disbelievers in the meeting with their Lord.

9. Have they not travelled in the land and seen the nature of the consequence for those who were before them? They were stronger than these in power, and they dug the earth and built upon it more than these have built. Messengers of their own came unto them with clear proofs *(of Allah's Sovereignty)*. Surely Allah wronged them not, but they did wrong themselves.

(To those who journeyed out from Makka, northward into Mesopotamia and Syria, or southward to the Yaman and Hadramaut, appeared the ruins of old civilisations which, tradition said, had been destroyed on account of their corruption and disobedience to the will of God.)

10. Then evil was the consequence to those who dealt in evil, because they denied the revelations of Allah and made a mock of them.

11. Allah originates creation, then He brings it back; then unto Him you will be returned.

12. And in the day when the Hour rises, the unrighteous will despair.

(The "Hour will be established : in due time the Hour will come when Judgment will be passed, and the seeming disturbance of balance in this world will be redressed. Then the good will rejoice, and the guilty, faced with the realities, will lose all their illusions and be struck dumb with despair.)

13. There will be no intercessors for them of those whom they made equal with Allah. And they will reject their partners *(whom they ascribed unto Him)*.

14. In the day when the Hour comes; in that day they will be sundered.

15. As for those who believed and did good works, they will be made happy in a Garden.

16. And as for those who disbelieved and denied Our revelations and denied the meeting of the Hereafter, such will be brought to torment.

17. So glory be to Allah when you enter the night and when you enter the morning.

(The special times for God's remembrance are so described as to include all our activities in life, -when we rise early in the morning, and when we go to rest in the evening: when we are in the midst of our work, at the decline of the sun, and in the late afternoon. It may be noted that these are all striking stages in the passage of the sun through our terrestrial day, as well as stages in our daily working lives. On this are based the hours of the five canonical prayers afterwards prescribed in Madîna; viz. (1) early morning before sunrise (Fajr); (2) when the day begins to decline, just after noon (Zuhr); (3) in the late afternoon, midway between noon and sunset ('Asr); and (4) and (5) the two evening prayers, one just after sunset (Maghrib), and the other after the evening twilight has all faded from the horizon, the hour indicated for rest and sleep ('Ishâ.)

18. Unto Him be praise in the heavens and the earth!-and at the twilight decline and in the noonday.

19. He brings forth the living from the dead, and He brings forth the dead from the living, and He revives the earth after her death. Thus is it that you too shall be brought forth.

(From dead matter, God's creative act produces life and living matter, and even science has not yet been able to explain the mystery of life. Life and living matter again seem to reach maturity and again die, as we see every day.)

20. And of His signs is this: He created you of dust and behold, you are human beings, scattered.

21. And of His signs is this: He created for you helpmeets (wives) from yourselves that you might find rest in them, and He set between you love and mercy. Lo, herein indeed are portents for folk who reflect.

22. And of His signs is the creation of the heavens and the earth, and the difference of your languages and colours. Lo! herein indeed are portents for men of knowledge.

(The variations in languages and colours may be viewed from the geographical aspect, or from the aspect of periods of time.)

23. And of His signs is your slumber by night and by day, and your seeking of His bounty. Lo! herein indeed are portents for people who hearken.

24. And of His signs is this: He shows you the lightning for a fear and for a hope, and sends down water from the sky, and thereby He gives life to the earth after her death. Lo! herein indeed are portents for people who understand.

25. And of His signs is this: The heavens and the earth stand firm by His command and afterward when He summons you, behold, from the earth you will emerge.

26. Unto Him belongs whosoever is in the heavens and in the earth. All are obedient unto Him.

27. He it is who originates creation, then causes it to return again, and it is easier for Him. His is the Sublime Similitude in the heavens and in the earth. He is the Mighty, the Wise.

28. He has coined for you a similitude of yourselves. Have you from among those whom your right hands possess, partners in the wealth We have bestowed upon you, equal with you in respect thereof, so that you fear them as you fear each other *(that you ascribe unto Us partners out of that which We created)?* Thus We display the signs for people who have sense.

(One way in which we can obtain some idea of the things higher than our own plane is to think of parables and similitudes drawn from our own lives and experience. And such a similitude or parable is offered to us now about false worship.)

29. Nay, but those who do wrong follow their own lusts without knowledge. Who is able to guide him whom Allah has left astray? For such there are no helpers.

30. So set your purpose *(face)*, *(O Muhammad)* for religion as a man by nature upright *(the nature framed)* of Allah, in which He has created mankind. There is no altering *(the laws of)* Allah's creation. That is the right religion, but most men know not.

(As turned out from the creative hand of God, man is innocent, pure, true, free, inclined to right and virtue, and possessed of true understanding about his own position in the Universe and about God's goodness, wisdom, and power. That is his true nature, just as the nature of a lamb is to be gentle and of a horse is to be swift. But man is caught in the meshes of customs, superstitions, selfish desires, and false teaching. This may make him pugnacious, unclean, false, slavish, hankering after what is wrong or forbidden, and deflected from the love of his fellow-men and the pure worship of the One True God.)

31. Turning unto Him *(only)*, and be careful of your duty unto Him, and establish worship and be not of those who ascribe partners *(unto Him)*;

32. Of those who split up their religion and have become sects, each sect exulting in what they have.

33. And when harm or affliction touches men they cry to their Lord, turning to Him in repentance; then, when He has made them taste mercy from Him, behold! a party of them attribute partners to their Lord.

34. So as to disbelieve in that which We have given them. *(Unto such it is said)*: Enjoy yourselves *(awhile)*, but you will soon know.

35. Or have We sent down unto them any warrant *(authority)* which speaks of that which they associate with Him?

36. And when We cause mankind to taste of mercy they rejoice therein; but if an evil thing befall them as the consequence of their own deeds, lo! they are in despair!

37. Have they not seen that Allah enlarges the provision for whom He wills, and straitens it *(for whom He wills)*. Therein indeed are signs for people who believe.

38. So give to the kinsman his due, and to the needy, and to the wayfarer. That is best for those who seek Allah's countenance; and such are they who are successful.

39. That which you give in usury in order that it may increase on people's property has no increase with Allah; but that which you give in charity, seeking Allah's countenance, has increase manifold.

(*Ribâ* is any increase sought through illegal means, such as usury, bribery, profiteering, fraudulent trading, etc. Economic selfishness and many kinds of sharp practices, individual, national, and international, come under this ban.)

40. Allah is He Who created you and then sustained you, then causes you to die, then gives life to you again. Is there any of your so- called partners that does anything of that? Praised and exalted be He above what they associate with Him.

41. Corruption has appeared on land and sea because of the evil which men's hands have earned, that He may make them taste a part of that which they have done, in order that they may return.

(God's Creation was pure and good in itself. All mischief or corruption is introduced by Evil, viz., arrogance, selfishness, etc. As soon as the mischief has come in, God's mercy and goodness step in to stop it. The consequences of Evil must be evil, and this should be shown in such partial punishment as "the hands of men have earned," so that it may be a warning for the future and an invitation to enter the door of repentance.)

42. Say *(O Muhammad, to the disbelievers)*: Travel in the land, and see the nature of the consequence for those who were before you! Most of them were idolaters.

43. So set your face to the right religion, before the inevitable day comes from Allah. On that day mankind will be sundered.

44. Whoso disbelieves must *(then)* bear the consequences of his disbelief, while those who do right make provision for themselves.

45. That He may reward out of His bounty those who believe and do good works. Lo! He loves not the disbelievers *(in His guidance)*.

46. And of His signs is this: He send winds bearing good tidings from His mercy, and that the ships may sail at His command, and that you may seek His favour, and that perhaps you may be thankful.

(In the physical world, the winds not only cool and purify the air, and bring the blessing of rain, which fertilises the soil, but they help international commerce among men through sea-ways, and now by air-ways.)

47. Verily We sent before you *(Muhammad)* messengers to their own folk. They brought them clear proofs *(of Allah's Sovereignty)*. Then We took vengeance upon those who were guilty *(in regard to them)*. To help believers is incumbent upon Us.

48. Allah is He who send the winds so that they raise *(drive)* clouds, and spreads them along the sky in the way He pleases, and causes them to break and you see the rain downpouring from within them. And when He makes it fall on whom He will of His bondsmen, lo! they rejoice *(They are filled with joy)*.

(Again the parable of the winds is presented from another aspect, both physical and spiritual. In the physical world, see their play with the clouds; how they suck up the moisture from terrestrial water, carry it about in dark clouds as needed, and break it up with rain as needed.)

49. Though before that, even before it was sent down upon them, they were in despair.

50. Look, therefore, at the prints *(traces)* of Allah's mercy *(in creation)*: how He gives life to the earth after her death. Lo! He verily is the Quickener of the Dead, and He is Able to do all things.

(After the two parables about the purifying action of the winds and their fertilising action, we now have the parable of the earth that dies in winter or drought and lives again in spring or rain, by God's grace)

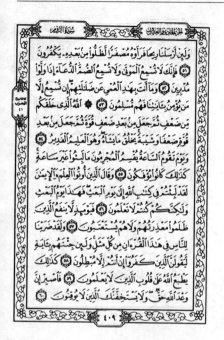

51. And if We sent a wind and they saw it yellow, they verily would still continue in their disbelief.

(Another parable from the forces of nature. We saw how the winds gladdened, vivified, and enriched those who utilised them in the right spirit.)

52. For verily you *(Muhammad)* cannot make the dead to hear, nor can you make the deaf to hear the call when they have turned to flee.

53. Nor can you guide the blind out of their error *(aberration)*. You can make none to hear save those who believe in Our revelation so that they surrender *(they are Muslims)*.

54. Allah is He who shaped you out of weakness, then appointed after weakness strength, then, after strength, appointed weakness and grey hair. He creates what He will. He is the Knower, the Mighty.

55. And on the day when the Hour rises, the guilty will swear that not even an hour did they linger; thus were they ever deceived.

56. But those to whom knowledge and faith are given will say: The truth is, you have tarried, by Allah's decree, until the Day of Resurrection. This is the Day of Resurrection, but you used not to know.

57. In that day their excuses will not profit those who did injustice, nor will they be allowed to make amends.

(It will be no use for those who deliberately rejected the clearest warnings in God's Message to say: "Oh! we did not realise this! The excuse will be false, and it would be unreasonable to suppose that they would then be asked to seek grace by repentance. It will then be too late.)

58. Verily We have coined for mankind in the Qur'ân all kinds of similitudes; and indeed if you came unto them with a miracle, those who disbelieve would verily exclaim: You are but tricksters!

59. Thus does Allah seal the hearts of those who know not.

60. So have patience *(O Muhammad)!* Allah's promise is the very truth, and let not those who have no certainty make you impatient.

(The prophet of God does not slacken in his efforts or feel discouraged because the unbelievers laugh at him or persecute him, or even seem to succeed in blocking his Message. He has firm faith, and he knows that God will finally establish His Truth. He goes on in his divinely entrusted task, with patience and perseverance, which must win against the levity of his opponents, who have no faith or certainty at all to sustain them.)

SÛRAH XXXI

LUQMÂN
Revealed at Makka

Luqmân takes its name from v. 12, which makes mention of the wisdom of Luqmân, a sage whose memory the Arabs reverenced, but who is unknown to Jewish scripture. He is said to have been a negro slave and the fables associated with his name are so like those of Aesop that the usual identification seems justified. The Sûrah conveys assurance of success to the Muslims at a time of persecution.

It belongs to the middle or last group of Makkan Sûrahs; except vv. 27 and 28, which were revealed at Madîna.

LUQMÂN

In the name of Allah, the Compassionate, the Merciful.

1. Alif. Lâm. Mîm.

2. These are the verses of the Book of wisdom.

3. A guidance and a mercy for those who do good.

4. Those who establish worship and pay the Zakât, and have sure faith in the Hereafter.

5. Such have guidance from their Lord. Such are the successful (*prosperers*).

6. And of mankind there are some who buy idle tales without knowledge, to mislead people from Allah's way, and take it in jest. For such there is a shameful doom.

7. And when Our revelations are recited unto him he turns away in his pride as if he heard them not, as if there were a deafness in his ears. So give him tidings of a painful doom.

8. Surely those who believe and do good works, for them are gardens of delight,

9. Wherein they will abide. It is a promise of Allah in truth. He is the Mighty, the Wise.

10. He has created the heavens without supports (*pillars*) that you can see, and has cast into the earth firm hills, so that it quake not with you; and He has dispersed therein all kinds of beasts. And We send down water from the sky, and We cause (*plants*) of every goodly kind to grow therein.

11. This is the Creation of Allah. Now show me that which those (*you worship*) beside Him have created. Nay, but the wrong-doers are in error manifest!

12. And verily We gave Luqmân wisdom, saying: "Give thanks unto Allah ; and whosoever gives thanks, he gives thanks for *(the good of)* his soul. And whosoever refuses, verily Allah is Self-sufficient, Praiseworthy.

(The sage Luqmân, after whom this Sûrah is called, belongs to Arab tradition. Very little is known of his life. He is usually associated with a long life. It is said that he belonged to a humble station in life, being a slave or a carpenter, and that he refused worldly power and a kingdom.)

13. And *(remember)* when Luqmân said to his son, when he was exhorting him: "O my son! Ascribe no partners unto Allah, because to ascribe partners *(unto Him)* is a tremendous wrong.

14. And We have enjoined upon man concerning his parents; his mother bears him in weakness upon weakness, and his weaning is in two years. Give thanks unto Me and unto your parents. Unto Me is the journeying.

15. But if they strive with you to make you ascribe unto Me as partner that of which you have no knowledge, then obey them not. Consort with them in the world kindly, and follow the path of him who repents unto Me. Then unto Me will be your return, and I shall tell you what you used to do.

(Where duty to man conflicts with duty to God it means that there is something wrong with the human will; we should obey God rather than man.)

16. O my son! Though it be but the weight of a grain of mustard seed and though it be in a rock, or in the heavens or in the earth, Allah will bring it forth. Truly, Allah is Subtle, Aware.

17. O my son! Establish worship and enjoin kindness and forbid iniquity, and persevere whatever may befall you. For surely that is of the steadfast heart of things.

18. Turn not your cheek in scorn toward folk, nor walk with insolence in the land. For Allah loves not each arrogant boaster.

19. Be modest in your bearing *(walk)* and subdue your voice. Lo! the harshest of all voices is the voice of the donkey.

20. Have you not seen that Allah has made serviceable unto you whatsoever is in the skies and whatsoever is in the earth, and has loaded you with His favours seen and unseen? Yet of mankind is he who disputes concerning Allah, without knowledge or guidance, or a Scripture giving light.

(Allah's grace and bounties work for us at all times. Sometimes we see them, and sometimes we do not. In things which we can apprehend with our senses, we can see God's grace, but even in them, sometimes it works beyond the sphere of our knowledge. In the inner or spiritual world, sometimes, when our vision is clear, we can see it working, and often we are not conscious of it. But it works all the same.)

21. And when it is said to them: "Follow what Allah has sent down they say: "Nay, but we follow that wherein we found our fathers . What! Even though the devil were inviting them unto the punishment of the Flame?

22. Whosoever surrenders his face to Allah while doing good, he verily has grasped the firm hand-hold. Unto Allah belongs the sequel of all things.

23. And whosoever disbelieves, let not his disbelief afflict you (O Muhammad). Unto Us is their return, and We shall tell them what they did. For Allah is Aware of what is in the breasts of men.

24. We give them comfort for a little, and then We drive them to a heavy doom.

25. If you should ask them: "Who created the heavens and the earth? they would answer:

"Allah . Say: "Praise be to Allah! But most of them know not.

26. Unto Allah belongs whatsoever is in the heavens and the earth. Assuredly Allah, He is the Self-sufficient, the Praiseworthy.

27. And if all the trees in the earth were pens, and the sea, with seven more seas to help it, (were ink), the words of Allah could not be exhausted. Truly Allah is Mighty, Wise.

(Words of Allah: His wonderful signs and commandments are infinite and could not be expressed if all the trees were made into pens, and all the wide ocean, multiplied seven times, were made into ink. Any Book of His Revelation would deal with matters which man can understand and use in his life: there are mysteries beyond mysteries that man can never fathom. Nor would any praises that we could write with infinite resources be adequate to describe His power, glory, and wisdom.)

28. Your creation and your raising from the dead are only as the creation and the raising of a single soul. Truly Allah is Hearer, Knower.

29. Have you not seen that Allah causes the night to pass into the day and causes the day to pass into the night, and has subdued the sun and the moon *(to do their work)* each running unto an appointed term; and that Allah is Informed of what you do?

30. That *(is so)* because Allah, He is the True, and that which they invoke beside Him is the False; and because Allah, He is the Sublime, the Great.

31. Have you not seen that the ships glide on the sea by Allah's grace, that He may show you of His Signs? Surely therein are signs for every steadfast, thankful one.

32. And when waves overwhelm them like shadows, they cry unto Allah making their faith pure for Him only. But when He delivers them safe to land some of them compromise. None denies Our signs save every traitor ingrate.

(Unlike the people mentioned in verse 31, who constantly seek God's help and give thanks for His mercies by using them aright and doing their duty, there is a class of men whose worship is merely inspired by terror. When they are in physical danger-the only kind of danger they appreciate, e. g., in a storm at sea they genuinely think of God. But once the danger is past, they become indifferent, or wish to appear good while flirting with evil.)

33. O mankind! Keep your duty to your Lord, and fear a Day when the parent will not be able to avail the child in aught, nor the child to avail the parent. Because Allah's promise is the very truth. Let not the life of the world beguile you, nor let the deceiver beguile you in regard to Allah.

(On the Day of Reckoning no one can help another. The most loving father cannot help his son or be a substitute for him, and vice versa. Each will have his own personal responsibilities.)

34. Verily Allah! With Him is knowledge of the Hour. He sends down the rain and knows what is in the wombs. No soul knows what it will earn tomorrow and no soul knows in what land it will die. Lo! Allah is Knower, Aware.

(The question of knowledge or mystery governs both clauses here, viz: rain and wombs. In fact it governs all the five things mentioned in this verse: viz. (1) the Hour; (2) Rain; (3) the birth of a new life *(Wombs);* (4) our physical life from day to day; (5) our death.)

SÛRAH XXXII

AS-SAJDA (THE PROSTRATION)

Revealed at Makka

(This Sûrah was revealed during the fifth year
before the Hijra. It derives its title from verse 15. The
general context of this Sûrah deals with the
omnipotency of Allah, which should be a sufficient
reason to worship and venerate Him. A comparison
between what awaits the believers on the one hand, and
the unbelievers on the other in the hereafter is given as a
reminder and exhortation. Then examples of the
behaviour of the Children of Israel in the past are given
to console the blessed prophet Muhammad for what he
faced from his people.)

It belongs in the middle group of Makkan Sûrahs.

THE PROSTRATION

In the name of Allah, the Compassionate,
the Merciful.

1. Alif. Lâm. Mîm

2. *(This is)* the sending down of the Book,
wherein is no doubt, from the Lord of the Worlds.

3. Or say they: "He has invented it ? Nay, but
it is the Truth from your Lord, that you may warn
a folk to whom no warner came before you, that
perhaps they may be guided.

4. Allah it is Who created the heavens and the
earth and that which is between them, in six Days.
Then He mounted the throne. Will you not then
remember?

(The "Day does not mean a day as we reckon it,
viz. one apparent course of the sun round the earth, for
it refers to conditions which began before the earth and
the sun were created. In verse 5 below, a Day is
compared to a thousand years of our reckoning, and in
70: 4 to 50,000 years. These figures "as we reckon
have no relation to "timeless Time , and must be taken
to mean very long periods, or ages, or aeons.)

5. He directs the ordinance *(all affairs)* from
the heaven unto the earth; then it ascends unto
Him in a Day, whereof the measure is a thousand
years of what you reckon.

(It ascends unto Him means: All affairs will go

up to Him, for He will be the Judge, and His restoration
of all values will be as a day or an hour or the twinkling
of an eye.)

6. Such is the Knower of the invisible and the
visible, the Mighty, the Merciful,

7. Who made all things good which He
created, and He began the creation of man from
clay;

8. Then He made his seed from a extract of
despised water *(fluid),*

9. Then He fashioned him and breathed into
him of His spirit; and appointed for you hearing
and sight and hearts. Small thanks give you!

10. And they say: "When we are lost in the
earth, how can we then be recreated? Nay, but
they are disbelievers in the meeting with their
Lord

11. Say: "The angel of death, who has been
charged concerning you, will gather you, and
afterward unto your Lord you will be returned.

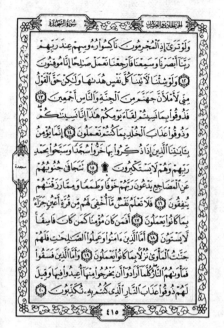

12. If only you could see when the guilty bow their heads before their Lord, *(saying)* "Our Lord! We have now seen and heard, so send us back; we will do right, now we are sure.

13. And if We had so willed, We could have given every soul its guidance, but the word from Me concerning evil-doers took effect: that I will fill hell with the jinn and mankind together.

(Could evil have been avoided? Certainly everything is in God's power. If it had been His Will and plan, He could have created a world in which there would have been no choice or will in any of His creatures. But that was not His will and plan. In the world as we see it, man has a certain amount of choice and free-will. That being so, He has provided signs and means of instruction for man, in order that man's will may be straight and pure. A necessary corollary will be punishment for the infraction of His Law. That Punishment must come to pass, for God's Word is true and must be fulfilled.)

14. So taste *(the evil of your deeds).* Forasmuch as you forgot the meeting of this your

day, We forget you. Taste the doom of immortality because of what you used to do.

15. Only those believe in Our revelations who, when they are reminded of them, fall down prostrate and extol the praise of their Lord, and they are not scornful,

16. Who forsake their beds to cry unto their Lord in fear and hope, and spend of what We have bestowed on them.

17. No soul knows what is kept hid for them of joy *(delights of the eyes),* as a reward for what they used to do.

(Delights of the eye: an idiom for that which pleases most and gives most satisfaction. In our present state we can scarcely imagine the real bliss that will come to us in the future.)

18. Is he who is a believer like unto him who is an evil-liver? They are not equal.

(The future of the two classes-the Blessed and the Wicked-is described in verses 19-22.)

19. But as for those who believe and do good works, for them are the Gardens of Retreat: a welcome in reward for what they used to do.

(A home brings before our minds a picture of peace and happiness. When to it are added honour and hospitality, it adds further to the idea of happiness.)

20. And as for those who do evil, their retreat is the Fire. Whenever they desire to issue forth from thence they are brought back to it. Unto them it is said: "Taste the torment of the Fire which you used to deny.

21. And verily We make them taste the lower punishment before the greater, that perhaps they may return.

(The final penalty is to come in the Hereafter. There is no doubt about it. But before it comes, a minor penalty comes in this very life. It may be in some kind of misfortune, or it may be in the pangs of a tortured conscience or secret sorrow. But this minor Penalty may be really a mercy, as it gives them a chance of repentance and amendment.)

22. And who does greater wrong than he who is reminded of the revelations of his Lord, then turn away from them? Surely We shall take vegeance from such criminals.

23. We verily gave Moses the Book; so be not you in doubt of his receiving it; and We appointed it a guidance for the Children of Israel.

24. And when they became patient and believed firmly in Our revelations, We appointed from among them leaders who guided by Our command.

25. Surely your Lord will judge between them on the Day of Resurrection concerning that wherein they used to differ.

26. Is it not a guidance for them *(to observe)* how many generations We destroyed before them, amid whose dwelling places they do walk?

Assuredly, there are signs in this. Will they not then listen?

27. Have they not seen how We lead the water to the barren land and therewith bring forth crops whereof their cattle eat, and they themselves? Will they not then see?

28. And they say: "When come this victory *(of yours)* if you are truthful?"

29. Say *(unto them)*: "On the day of the victory the faith of those who disbelieve *(and who then will believe)* will not avail them, neither will they be reprieved.

30. So withdraw from them *(O Muhammad)* and await *(the event)*. Lo! they *(also)* are awaiting *(it)*.

(There it is said to the Unbelievers: "Wait you: we too are waiting. Here the Righteous are told: "Wait *(you)*: they too are waiting The reversal of the order is appropriate: in each case the person *(or persons)* addressed is mentioned first.)

SÛRAH XXXIII

AL-AHZÂB (THE CLANS)

Revealed at Makka

This Sûrah was revealed near the end of the sixth and the beginning of the seventh year of the Hijra. It derives its title from verses 9 to 25, which deal with the provocation by the Jewish tribe of Banû al-Nadîr of Madîna against the Moslems, which finally led to their expulsion. They tried to incite the desert tribe of Ghatafân, the Quraishites, and some clans at Tâif to attack the Moslems with the help of another Madinah Jewish tribe, Banû Quraizah. However, the Moslems dug trenches on the outskirts of Madîna, which resulted in the failure of the attack after twenty days of siege.

THE CLANS

In the name of Allah, the Compassionate, the Merciful.

1. O Prophet! Keep your duty to Allah, and obey not the disbelievers and the hypocrites. For Allah is Knower, Wise.

2. And follow that which is inspired in you from your Lord. Truly, Allah is Aware of what you do.

3. And put your trust in Allah, for Allah is sufficient as Trustee.

4. Allah has not made for any man two hearts within his body, nor has he made your wives whom you declare *(to be your mothers)* your mothers, nor has he made those whom you claim *(to be your sons)* your sons. This is but a saying of your mouths. But Allah says the truth and He guides on the way.

(If a man called another's son "his son", it might create complications with natural and normal relationships if taken too literally. It is pointed out that it is only a "façon de parler" in men's mouths, and should not be taken literally. The truth is the truth and cannot be altered by men's adopting "sons". "Adoption" in the technical sense is not allowed in Muslim Law. Those who have been "wives of your sons proceeding from your loins" are within the Prohibited Degrees of marriage.)

5. Call them by *(the names of)* their fathers. That is more equitable in the sight of Allah. And if you know not their fathers, then *(they are)* your brethren in the faith and your clients. And there is no sin for you in the mistakes that you make unintentionally but what your hearts purpose *(that will be a sin for you)*. Allah is Forgiving, Merciful.

6. The Prophet is closer to the believers than theirselves, and his wives are *(as)* their mothers. And the owners of kinship are closer one to another in the ordinance of Allah than *(other)* believers and the fugitives *(who fled from Makka)*, except that you should do kindness to your friends. This is written in the Book *(of nature)*.

(This Sûrah establishes the dignity and position of the Holy Prophet's wives, who had a special mission and responsibility as Mothers of the Believers. They were not to be like ordinary women: they had to instruct women in spiritual matters, visit and minister to those who were ill or in distress, and do other kindly offices in aid of the Prophet's mission.)

7. And *(remember when)* We took from the prophets their Covenant, and from you *(O Muhammad)* and from Noah and Abraham and Moses and Jesus son of Mary. We took from them a solemn covenant;

8. That He may ask the loyals of their loyalty. And He has prepared a painful doom for the unfaithful.

(The men to whom God's truth has been committed for promulgation will be asked in the Hereafter as to how the Truth fared in the world -how it was received, who opposed it, and who assisted it. Like all trustees, they will have to give a full account of their trust. God knows all, and it will not add to His information. But it will be evidence for and against those to whom it was preached, so that the responsibility of those who dishonoured it may be duly enforced.)

9. O you who believe! Remember Allah's favour unto you when there came against you hosts, and We sent against them a great wind and hosts you could not see. And Allah is ever Seer of what you do.

10. When they came upon you from above you and from below you, and when eyes grew wild and hearts reached to the throats and you were imagining vain thoughts concerning Allah.

11. There were the believers sorely tried, and shaken with a mighty shock.

12. And when the hypocrites and those in whose hearts is a disease were saying: "Allah and His messenger promised us nothing but vain hope.

(Before this year's mass attack on Madîna, the Muslims had successfully reached the Syrian border on the north, and there were hopes of reaching Yemen in

the south. The holy Prophet had seen clear signs of expansion and victory for the Muslims. Now that they were shut in within the Trench on the defensive, the Hypocrites taunted them with having indulged in delusive hopes. But the event showed that the hopes were not delusive. They were realised beyond expectations in a few years.)

13. And when a party of them said: "O folk of Yathrib! There is no lodging for you, therefore turn back. And a party of them ask permission of the Prophet, saying: "Our homes lie open to the enemy *(Our homes are lying naked and exposed to the enemy.)* And they lay not open. They but wished to flee.

14. If the enemy had entered from all sides and they had been exhorted to treachery, they would have committed it, and would have hesitated thereupon but little.

15. And verily they had already sworn unto Allah that they would not turn their backs *(to the foe).* An oath to Allah must be answered for.

16. Say: "Fleeing will not avail you if you flee from death or killing, and then you dwell in comfort but a little while.

17. Say: "Who is he who can preserve you from Allah if He intend harm for you, or intend mercy for you? They will not find any friend or helper other than Allah.

18. Allah already knows those of you who hinder, and those who say unto their brethren: "come you hither unto us! and they come not to the stress of battle save a little.

19. Being covetous over you (believers). But when the fear comes, then you (Muhammad) see them regarding you with rolling eyes like one who faints unto death. Then, when the fear departs they scald (smite) you with sharp tongues in their greed for wealth (from the spoil). Such have not believed. Therefore Allah makes their deeds fruitless. And that is easy for Allah.

(Ashihhatan: covetous, grasping, niggardly. Here the meaning is twofold: (1) they spare themselves in the fight as compared with you; they are niggardly with themselves as against you; they contribute little either in personal effort or with their money and resources; and (2) they covet any gains made or booty won, on the part of the real fighters.)

20. They reckoned that the clans would never leave, and when the clans come, they will wish that they were in the desert with the wandering Arabs, asking for the news of you; and if they were among you, they would not give battle, save a little.

21. Verily in the messenger of Allah you have a good example for him who hopes for Allah and the Last Day, and has remembered Allah much.

(We now have the psychology of the Believers, - God-fearing men, led by that pattern of men and of leaders, Muhammad.)

22. And when the true believers saw the clans, they said: "This is what Allah and His messenger promised us. Allah and His messenger are true. It only increased them in faith and submission to Allah.

(This is in contrast to what the Hypocrites said in verse 12 above. The divine promise of help and success is contingent upon our striving and faith. Nothing comes to the poltroon and the sceptical idler. Dangers and difficulties, and conflict with evil, are foretold us, and we must meet them with fortitude and courage.)

23. Of the believers there are men who fulfilled what they covenanted with Allah. Some of them have paid their vow by death *(in battle),* and some of them still are waiting; and they have not altered in the least;

(In the fight for Truth there were *(and are)* many who sacrificed their all - resources, knowledge, influence, life itself - in the Cause, and never wavered. If they won the crown of martyrdom, they were blessed. Such a one was Sa'd Ibn Mu'adh, the chief of the Aws tribe, the intrepid standard-bearer of Islam, who died of a wound he had received in the Battle of the Trench. Other heroes fought valiantly and lived, always ready to lay down their lives. Both classes were staunch: they never changed or wavered.)

24. That Allah may reward the true men for their truth, and punish the hypocrites if He will, or relent toward them *(if He will).* Truly Allah is Forgiving, Merciful.

25. And Allah repulsed the disbelievers in their wrath; they gained no good. Allah averted their attack from the believers. Allah is Strong, Mighty.

26. And He brought down those of the People of the Scripture who supported them down from their strongholds, and cast panic into their hearts. Some you slew, and you made captive others.

(The reference is to the Jewish tribe of the Banû Quraiza. They were counted among the citizens of Madîna and were bound by solemn engagements to help in the defence of the City. But on the occasion of the siege by the Quraish and their allies they intrigued with the enemies and treacherously aided them.)

27. And He caused you to inherit their land and their houses and their wealth, and land you have not trodden. Allah is Able to do all things.

28. O Prophet! Say unto your wives: "If you desire the world's life and its adornment, come! I will content you and will release you with a fair release.

29. But if you desire Allah and His messenger and the abode of the Hereafter, then Allah has prepared for the good among you an immense reward.

(They were all well-doers. But being in their exalted position, they had an extra responsibility, and they had to be specially careful to discharge it. In the same way their reward would be "great , for higher services bring higher spiritual satisfaction, though they were asked to deny themselves some of the ordinary indulgences of this life.)

30. O you wives of the Prophet! Whosoever of you committed manifest lewdness, the punishment for her will be doubled, and that is easy for Allah.

31. And whosoever of you is submissive *(devout)* to Allah and His messenger and does right, We shall give her reward twice over, and We have prepared for her a rich provision.

32. O you wives of the Prophet! You are not like any other women. If you keep your duty to Allah, be not soft of speech, lest he in whose heart is a disease aspire to you, but utter customary speech.

(This is the core of the whole passage. The Prophet's Consorts were not like ordinary women, nor was their marriage an ordinary marriage, in which only personal or social considerations enter. They had a special position and special responsibilities, in the matter of guiding and instructing women who came into the fold of Islam. Islam is a Way of Life, and the Muslims are a family: women have as much place in Islam as men, and their intimate instruction must obviously be through women.)

33. And stay in your houses. Bedizen not yourselves with the bedizenment of the Time of Ignorance. Be regular in prayer, and pay the Zakât, and obey Allah and His messenger. Allah's wish is but to remove uncleanness far from you, O people of the Household, and to cleanse you with a thorough cleansing.

(Obedience to God's Law sums up all duties. Regular Prayer *(seeking nearness to God)* and Regular Charity *(doing good to fellow-creatures)* are mentioned as specially symbolical of our Religion.)

34. And remember what is recited in your houses of Allah's verses, and wisdom. Truly Allah is Subtle, Aware.

35. Behold; men who surrender to Allah, and women who surrender, and men who believe and women who believe, and men who obey and women who obey, and men who speak the truth and women who speak the truth and men who persevere *(in righteousness)* and women who persevere, and men who are humble and women who are humble, and men who give alms and women who give alms, and men who fast and women who fast, and men who guard their modesty and women who guard *(their modesty)*, and men who remember Allah much and women who remember, Allah has prepared for them forgiveness and a vast reward.

36. And it is not for a believing man or a believing woman to have any choice in their affairs when Allah and His messenger have decided an affair for them; and whoso is rebellious to Allah and His messenger, he verily goes astray in error manifest.

37. And when you said to him on whom Allah has conferred favour and you have conferred favour: "Keep your wife to yourself and fear Allah. And you hide within yourself that which Allah was to bring to light, and you fear mankind whereas Allah had a better right that you should fear Him. So when Zaid had performed the necessary formality *(of divorce)* from her, We gave her unto you in marriage so that *(henceforth)* there may be no sin for believers in respect of wives of their adopted sons, when the latter have performed the necessary formality *(of release)* from them. The commandment of Allah must be fulfilled.

(Zaid's marriage with the Prophet's cousin Zainab daughter of Jahsh did not turn out happy. Zainab the high-born looked down upon Zaid, who had been a slave. Both were good people in their own way, and both loved the Prophet, but there was mutual incompatibility and this is fatal to married life. Zaid wished to divorce her, but the Prophet asked him to hold his hand, and he obeyed. She was closely related to the Prophet; he had given a handsome marriage gift on her marriage to Zaid; and people would certainly talk if such a marriage was broken off, and poor Zainab's reputation would be ruined. This was the fear in the mind of the Prophet.)

38. There is no reproach *(difficulty)* for the Prophet in what Allah has made his due. That was Allah's way with those who passed away of old, and the commandment of Allah is certain destiny,

39. It is the practice of those who delivered the messages of Allah and feared Him, and feared none save Allah. Allah keeps good account.

40. Muhammad is not the father of any man among you, but he is the messenger of Allah and the Seal of the Prophets; and Allah is Aware of all things.

(When a document is sealed, it is complete, and there can be no further addition. The holy Prophet Muhammad closed the long line of Apostles. God's teaching is and will always be continuous, but there has been and will be no Prophet after Muhammad. The later ages will want thinkers and reformers, not Prophets.)

41. O you who believe! Remember Allah with much remembrance.

42. And glorify Him early and late.

43. He it is who blesses you, and His angels *(bless you)*, that He may bring you forth from darkness unto light; and He is Merciful to the believers.

touched them, then there is no period that you
should reckon. But content them and release
them handsomely.

44. Their salutation on the day when they shall
meet Him will be: Peace. And He has prepared for
them a goodly recompense.

45. O Prophet! We have sent you as a witness
and a bringer of good tidings and a warner.

46. And as a summoner to Allah by His
permission, and as a lamp that gives light.

47. And announce to the believers the good
tidings that they will have great bounty from
Allah.

48. And obey not the disbelievers and the
hypocrites. Disregard their noxious talk (heed
not their annoyances), and put your trust in
Allah. Allah is sufficient as Trustee.

49. O you who believe! If you marry believing
women and divorce them before you have

50. O Prophet! We have made lawful unto you
your wives whom you have paid their dowries,
and those whom your right hand possesses of
those whom Allah has given as spoils of war, and
the daughters of your uncle on the father's side
and the daughters of your aunts on the father's
side and the daughters of your uncles on the
mother's side and the daughters of your aunts on
the mother's side who emigrated with you, and a
believing woman if she gives herself unto the
Prophet and the Prophet desire to ask her in
marriage, a privilege for you only, not for the
(rest of) believers. We are aware of that which
We enjoined upon them concerning their wives
and those whom their right hands possess, that
you may be free from blame, for Allah is
Forgiving, Merciful.

بِسْمِ اللّٰهِ الرَّحْمٰنِ الرَّحِيْمِ

51. You can defer whoever you desire of them and you can lodge with you whom you please, and whomsoever you desire of those whom you have set aside *(temporarily),* it is no sin for you *(to receive her again);* that is better; that they may be comforted and not grieve, and may all be pleased with what you give them. Allah knows what is in your hearts *(O men),* and Allah is Forgiving, Clement.

(Marriage is an important relationship not only in our physical life, but in our moral and spiritual life, and its effects extend not only to the parties themselves but to children and future generations. A number of special problems arise according to special circumstances. Every man and woman must seriously consider all sides of the question and must do the best that lies in his or her power to temper instincts and inclinations with wisdom and guidance from God.)

52. It is not allowed to you to take other women henceforth, nor that you should change them for other wives even though their beauty pleased you, save those whom your right hands possess, and Allah is Watcher over all things.

53. O you who believe! Enter not the dwellings of the Prophet for a meal without waiting for the proper time, unless permission be granted you. But if you are invited, enter, and, when your meal is ended, then disperse. Linger not for conversation. For that would cause annoyance to the Prophet, and he would be shy of *(asking)* you to go; but Allah is not shy of the truth. And when you ask of them *(the wives of the Prophet)* anything, ask it of them from behind a curtain. That is purer for your hearts and for their hearts. And it is not for you to cause annoyance to the messenger of Allah, nor that you should ever marry his wives after him. Lo! that in Allah's sight would be an enormity.

(The rules of refined social ethics are as necessary to teach today as they were with the rude Arabs whom the holy Prophet had to teach in his day. Those mentioned in this verse may be briefly recapitulated thus: (1) Enter not a friend's house without permission; (2) if invited to dine, don't go too early; you are asked to dine, not to wait for the preparation of the food; (3) be there at the time appointed; (4) after the meal, don't get familiar with your host; (5) don't waste time in tittle-tattle; (6) understand what is proper behaviour for you; he may be too polite to ask you to depart.)

54. Whether you divulge a thing or keep it hidden, surely Allah is ever Knower of all things.

55. It is no sin for them *(your wives)* to *(converse freely)* with their fathers, or their sons, or their brothers, or their brothers' sons, or the sons of their sisters or of their own women, or their slaves. O women! Keep your duty to Allah. For Allah is Witness over all things.

56. Indeed Allah and His angels shower blessings on the Prophet. O you who believe! Ask *(and send)* blessings on him and salute him with a worthy salutation.

(God and His angels honour and bless the holy Prophet as the greatest of men. We are asked to honour and bless him all the more because he took it upon himself to suffer the sorrows and afflictions of this life in order to guide us to God's Mercy and the highest inner life.)

57. Those who malign Allah and His messenger, Allah has cursed them in the world and the Hereafter, and has prepared for them the doom of the disdained.

58. And those who malign believing men and believing women undeservedly, they bear the guilt of slander and manifest sin.

(It was necessary to put down all kinds of unseemly conduct in the Prophet's City. And here is the warning in the plainest terms. And the warning had its effect. The "Hypocrites were men who pretended to be in Islam but whose manners and morals were anti-Islamic. Those "with diseased hearts may have been the ones that molested innocent women. "Those who stirred up sedition put false rumours in circulation to excite the crowd. Alas! we must ask ourselves the question: "Are these conditions present among us to-day?)

59. O Prophet! Tell your wives and your daughters and the women of the believers to draw their cloaks close round them *(when they go abroad)*. That will be better, that so they may be recognised and not annoyed. Allah is ever Forgiving, Merciful.

60. If the hypocrites, and those in whose hearts is a disease, and the alarmists in the city do not cease, We verily shall urge you on against them, then they will be your neighbours in it but a little while.

61. Accursed, *(they shall suffer a curse)*. They will be seized wherever found and slain with a *(fierce)* slaughter.

62. That was the way of Allah in the case of those who passed away of old; you will not find for the way of Allah any changing.

63. Men ask you of the Hour. Say: The knowledge of it is with Allah only. What shall make you aware of it? It may be that the Hour is nigh.

64. Surely! Allah has cursed the disbelievers, and has prepared for them a flaming fire,

65. Wherein they will abide for ever. They will find (then) no protecting friend nor helper.

66. On the day when their faces are turned over in the fire, they say: "Oh, would that we had obeyed Allah and had obeyed His messenger!

67. And they say: "Our Lord! We obeyed our princes and great men, and they misled us from the Way.

68. Our Lord! Oh, give them double torment, and curse them with a mighty curse.

69. O you who believe! Be not as those who slandered Moses, but Allah proved his innocence of what they said, and he was well esteemed in Allah's sight.

(The people of Moses often vexed him and rebelled against him and against God's Law. It is said that Moses's own sister Miriam and his brother Aaron spoke against Moses because Moses had married an Ethiopian woman. Allah cleared Moses of the charge of having done anything wrong: "My servant Moses is not so, who is faithful in all mine house. Miriam was afflicted with leprosy for seven days as a punishment, after which she was forgiven, as also was Aaron. This is the Old Testament story. The holy Prophet was also attacked because of his marriage with Zainab bint Jahsh.)

70. O you who believe! Guard your duty to Allah (fear Allah) and speak words straight to the point;

71. He will make whole your works for you and will forgive you your sins. Whosoever obeys Allah and His messenger, he verily has gained a signal victory.

72. Surely We offered the trust unto the heavens and the earth and the hills, but they shrank from bearing it and were afraid of it. And man assumed (undertook) it. But he has proved a tyrant and a fool.

(The Heavens, the Earth, and the Mountains, i.e. other creatures of God, besides man, refused to undertake a Trust or a responsibility, and may be imagined as happy without a choice of good or evil being given through their will. In saying that they refused, we imply a will, but we limit it by the statement that they did not undertake to be given a choice between good and evil. They preferred to submit their will entirely to God's Will, which is All-Wise and Perfect, and which would give them far more happiness than a faculty of choice, with their imperfect knowledge.)

73. So Allah punishes hypocritical men and hypocritical women, and idolatrous men and idolatrous women. But Allah pardons believing men and believing women, and Allah is Forgiving, Merciful.

SÛRAH XXXIV

SABA'

Revealed at Makka

This Sûrah *(Saba')* (with the exception of verse 6) was revealed in the eighth year before the Hijra. It takes its title from verse 15. It starts by proclaiming the Omniscience of God; then asserts the coming of the Hour when all beings will come to a meeting with God to receive the reward they deserve. An answer is given to those who contend that there shall be no return to life after death. Then a reference is given to the boons bestowed on David and Solomon to show the difference between grateful servants and those who are ungrateful. Finally, an argument is advanced on the tongue of the Prophet to prove the folly of those who disbelieve in the Qur'ân.)

THE SHEBA

In the name of Allah, the Compassionate,
the Merciful.

1. Praise be to Allah, unto Whom belongs whatsoever is in the heavens and whatsoever is in the earth. His is the praise in the Hereafter, and He is the Wise, the Aware.

2. He knows whatever goes down into the earth and whatever comes forth from it, and what descends from the heaven and what ascends into it. He is the Merciful, the Forgiving.

3. Those who disbelieve say: "The Hour will never come unto us . Say: "Nay, by my Lord, but it is coming unto you surely. He is the Knower of the Unseen. Not an atom's weight, or less than that or greater, escapes Him in the heavens or in the earth, but it is in a clear Record,

(The last two verses have prepared us to realise the position of unbelievers in God's great Universe. They are the discord in the universal harmony of Prayer and Praise. Their existence is due to the grant of a limited free-will, the Trust which the Unbelievers have betrayed. But they must and will be eliminated: see verse 5 below. For there is nothing more certain in the world, physical, moral, and spiritual, than that every cause, great or small, must have its corresponding consequences.)

4. That He may reward those who believe and do good works. For them is pardon and a rich provision.

5. But those who strive against Our revelations, challenging Us, theirs will be a painful doom of wrath.

6. Those who have been given knowledge see that what is revealed unto you from your Lord is the truth, and leads unto the path of the Mighty, the Owner of Praise.

(Against the doubts and vain imaginings of the ignorant is the certainty of knowledge of the Enlightened: that God reveals Himself, and that His Revelation is true, and leads to the Path of true guidance. That is the Path of God, Who, in His infinite Love and Mercy, is Worthy of all praise.)

7. Those who disbelieve say: "Shall we show you a man who will tell you *(that)* when you have become dispersed in dust with a most complete dispersal, still, even then, you will be created anew?

8. Has he invented a lie concerning against Allah, or is there in him a madness *(inspired by a demon)*? Nay, but those who disbelieve in the Hereafter are in torment and far error.

9. Have they not observed *(seen)* what is before them and what is behind them of the sky and the earth? If We will, We can make the earth swallow them, or cause a piece from the sky to fall on them. Herein surely is a portent *(a sign)* for every slave who turns *(to Allah)* repentant.

10. And assuredly We gave David grace from Us, *(saying)*: "O you hills and birds, sing the praises of Allah *(with David)*! And We made the iron supple unto him,

(Iron or steel is hard: but in the hands of a craftsman it becomes soft and pliable, and with it can be made instruments for the defence of righteousness. These, in the literal sense, are coats of mail, and defensive armour, and the manufacture of them is traditionally attributed to David.)

11. Saying: "Make long coats of mail and measure the links *(thereof)*. And do right. Lo! I am Seer of what you do.

12. And unto Solomon *(We gave)* the wind, whereof the morning course was a month's journey and the evening course a month's journey, and We caused the fount of copper to gush forth for him, and *(We gave him)* certain of the jinn who worked before him by permission of his Lord. And such of them as deviated from Our command, them We caused to taste the punishment of flaming fire.

(In the Old Testament, (II. Chronicles, Chapters iii. and iv., are described the various costly materials) with which Solomon's Temple was built, and it was than furnished with vessels, candle-sticks, lamps, censers, etc. "Solomon made all these vessels in great abundance: for the weight of the brass could not be found out *(II. Chronicles, iv. 18).*)

13. They made for him what he willed: synagogues and statues, basins like wells and boilers built into the ground. Give thanks, O House of David! Few of My bondsmen are thankful.

14. And when We decreed death for him, nothing showed his death to them save a creeping creature of the earth which gnawed away his staff. And when he fell the jinn saw clearly how, if they had known the unseen, they would not have continued in despised toil.

15. There was indeed a sign for Saba (Sheba) in their dwellingplace: Two gardens on the right hand and on the left (as who should say): Eat of the provision of your Lord and render thanks to Him. A fair land and an indulgent Lord!

16. But they turned away, so We sent upon them the Flood of Arim, and in exchange for their two gardens gave them two gardens bearing bitter fruit: the tamarisk, and a few lote-trees.

("Arim (=Dams or Embankments) may have been a proper noun, or may simply mean the great earth-works lined with stone, which formed the Ma'rib dam, of which traces still exist. The French traveller T. J. Arnaud saw the town and ruins of the Dam of Ma'rib in 1843, and described its gigantic works and its inscriptions: See Journal Asiatique for January 1874: the account is in French. The dam as measured by Arnaud was two miles long and 120 ft. high. The date of its destruction was somewhere about 120 A.D., though some authorities put it much later.)

17. Thus We awarded them because of their ingratitude. Punish We ever any save the ingrates?

18. And We set, between them and the towns which We had blessed, conspicuous cities, and We made the journey there by easy stages (saying): Travel in them safely both by night and day.

19. But they said: "Our Lord! Make the stage between our journeys longer. And they wronged themselves, therefore We made them bywords (in the land) and scattered them abroad, a total scattering. Lo! herein verily are portents for each steadfast, grateful (heart).

(The covetous Saba people, in order to get more profit from travellers' supplies by concentrating them on a few stations which they could monopolise, tended to choke off traffic. Selfishness often runs counter to true self-interest. It is a historical fact that the great Yemen-Syria route in Arabia declined with the decline of Yemen.)

20. And Satan indeed found his calculation true concerning them, for they follow him, all save a group of true believers.

(Satan out of arrogance had said, when he asked for a respite from the Most High: "I will bring (Adam's) descendants under my sway, all but a few. This was now proved true for the Saba people. He had no power to force them. It was their own will that went awry and put them into his power.)

21. And he had no warrant whatsoever against them, save that We would know him who believes in the Hereafter from him who is in doubt thereof; and your Lord (O Muhammad) takes note of all things.

22. Say (O Muhammad): Call upon those whom you set up beside Allah! They possess not an atom's weight either in the heavens or the earth, nor have they any share in either, nor has He an auxiliary among them.

23. No intercession avails with Him *(in His presence)* save for him whom He permits. Yet, when fear is banished from their hearts, they say: "What was it that your Lord said? They say: "The Truth. And He is the Sublime, the Great.

("Their hearts : the pronoun "their refers to the angels nearest to Allah. On the Day of Judgement there will be such an irresistible manifestation of Power that even they will be silent for a while, and will scarcely realise what is happening.)

24. Say: "Who gives you provision from the sky and the earth? Say: "Allah. We or you assuredly are rightly guided or in error manifest.

25. Say: "You will not be asked of what we committed, nor shall we be asked of what you do.

26. Say: "Our Lord will gather us all together, then He will judge between us with truth. He is the All-knowing Judge.

27. Say: "Show me those whom you have joined unto Him as partners. Nay *(you dare not)!* For He is Allah, the Mighty, the Wise.

28. And We have not sent you *(O Muhammad)* save as a bringer of good tidings and a warner unto all mankind; but most of mankind know not.

29. And they say: "When is this promise *(to be fulfilled)* if you are truthful?

30. Say *(O Muhammad):* "Yours is the promise of a Day which you cannot postpone, nor hasten by an hour.

31. And those who disbelieve say: "We believe not in this Qur'ân nor in that which was before it; but oh, if you could see, when the wrong-doers are brought up before their Lord, how they cast the blame one to another; how those who were despised *(in the earth)* say unto those who were proud: "Had it not been for you, we should have been believers.

(To the Pagans all scriptures are taboo, whether it be the Qur'ân or any Revelation that came before it. The people of the Book despised the Pagans, but in their arrogant assumption of superiority, prevented them, by their example, from accepting the latest and most universal Scripture when it came in the form of the Qur'ân. This relative position of men who fancy themselves on their knowledge, and men whom they despise but exploit and mislead, always exists on this earth.)

32. And those who were proud say unto those who were despised: "Did we drive you away from the guidance after it had come unto you? Nay, but you were guilty.

33. Those who were despised say unto those who were proud: "Nay but *(it was your)* scheming night and day, when you commanded us to disbelieve in Allah and set up rivals *(equals)* unto Him. And they fill with remorse when they behold the doom; and We place carcans on the necks of those who disbelieved. Are they requited aught save what they did?

34. And We sent not unto any township a warner, but its pampered ones declared: Lo! we are disbelievers in that which you bring unto us.

35. And they said: "We are more than you in wealth and children. We are not the punished!

36. Say *(O Muhammad)*: "Surely my Lord enlarges the provision for whom He will and narrows it for whom He will. But most of mankind know not.

(Provision *(or Sustenance)*: good things of all kinds in this life, material goods as well as power, opportunities, influence, mental gifts, etc. These do not necessarily all go to the good, nor is their denial to be interpreted to mean that it is a withdrawal of Allah's favour.)

37. And it is not your wealth nor your children that will bring you near unto Us, but he who believes and does good *(he draws near)*. As for such, theirs will be a twofold reward for what they did, and they will dwell secure in lofty halls.

(All worldly goods are but a shadow that will pass away. Their intrinsic and eternal value is small. But those who work righteousness in Faith are on the true path of self-development. The rewards they will get will be infinitely more than their merits entitle them to. For they will partake of the boundless favours of Allah.)

38. And as for those who strive against Our revelations, challenging, they will be brought to the punishment.

39. Say: "Indeed my Lord enlarges the provision for whom He wills of His bondsmen, and narrows *(it)* for him. And whatsoever you spend *(for good)* He replaces it. And He is the Best of Providers.

(Even in the seeming inequality of distribution of the good things of life, Allah has a wise and merciful purpose: for nothing arises by chance. He is the best to give us, now and evermore, just those things which serve our real needs and advance our inner development.)

40. And on the day when He will gather them all together, then He will say unto the angels: "Did these worship you?"

41. They will say: "Glory be to You! You are our Protector from them! Nay, but they worshipped the jinn; most of them were believers in them.

42. That day you will possess no use nor hurt one for another. And We shall say unto those who did wrong: "Taste the doom of the Fire which you used to deny.

43. And if Our revelations are recited unto them in plain terms they say: "This is naught else than a man who would turn you away from what your fathers used to worship; and they said: "This is naught else than an invented lie . Those who disbelieve say of the truth when it reaches them: "This is naught else than mere magic.

(Apart from the worship of Evil in the guise of the Powers of Light, there is another form of false worship, which depends on ancestral tradition. "Why it is said "should we not do as our fathers did? They reject a new prophet of Truth simply because his teaching does not agree with the ways of their ancestors.)

44. And We have given them no Scriptures which they study, nor sent We unto them, before you, any warner.

45. Those before them denied, and these have not attained a tenth of that which We bestowed on them *(of old)*; yet they denied My messengers. How intense then was My abhorrence *(of them)*.

46. Say *(unto them O Muhammad)*: "I exhort you unto one thing only: that you awake for Allah's sake, by twos and singly, and then reflect: There is no madness in your comrade. He is nothing else than a warner unto you in face of a terrific doom.

(Note that in verses 46, 47, 48, 49 and 50, arguments are suggested to the Prophet, by which he can convince any right-thinking man of his sincerity and truth. Here the argument is that he is not possessed or out of his mind. If he is different from ordinary men, it is because he had to give a warning of a terrible spiritual danger to the men whom he loves but who will not understand his Message.)

47. Say: "Whatever reward I might have asked of you is yours. My reward is the affair of Allah only. He is Witness over all things.

48. Say: "Surely my Lord hurls the truth. He is the knower of hidden things.

49. Say: "The Truth has come, and falsehood shows not its face and will not return.

50. Say: "If I err, I err only to my own loss, and if I am rightly guided it is because of that which my Lord has revealed unto me. Surely He is Hearer, Nigh.

51. If you could see when they are terrifed with no escape, and are seized from near at hand.

(After the arguments for the reality and triumph of Truth, we are asked to contemplate the position of the opposers of Truth when Truth is established. They will be struck with terror: For Truth is all-compelling.)

52. And say: "We now believe in him. But how can they reach (faith) from far away?

53. They had disbelieved in it before. They aim at the unseen from afar off.

54. And a gulf (barrier) is set between them and that which they desire, as was done for people of their kind of old. Lo! they were in hopeless doubt.

SÛRAH XXXV

AL-FÂTIR (THE ORIGINATOR)

Revealed at Makka

(This Sûrah is an early Makkan one that was revealed during the seventh year before the Hijra. It takes its title from verse 1. Some interpreters, however, call it "The Angels , a word also found in this verse. The general theme of it is an admonition to the people of Makka to worship the One God and do works of righteousness. It gives a comparison between those who follow Satan's footsteps, and those who follow God's Ordinance, and refers to the recompense that awaits each of them.)

THE ORIGINATOR

In the name of Allah, the Compassionate, the Merciful.

1. Praise be to Allah, the Creator of the heavens and the earth, Who appoints the angels messengers having wings two, three and four. He multiplies in creation what He pleases. For Allah is Able to do all things.

(As man's knowledge of the processes of nature advances, he sees how complex is the evolution of matter itself, leaving out the question of Life and the spiritual forces, which are beyond the competence ken of experimental science.)

2. That which Allah opens to mankind of mercy none can withhold it; and that which He withholds, none can release thereafter. He is the Mighty, the Wise.

3. O mankind! Remember Allah's grace toward you! Is there any creator other than Allah who provides for you from the sky and the earth? There is no God save Him. Whither then are you turned?

4. And if they deny you (*O Muhammad*), messengers (*of Allah*) were denied before you. Unto Allah all things are brought back.

5. O mankind! Verily the promise of Allah is true. So let not the life of the world beguile you, and let not the beguiler beguile you with regard to Allah.

6. Truly the devil is an enemy for you, so treat him as an enemy. He only summons his faction to be owners of the Blaze.

7. Those who disbelieve, theirs will be an awful doom; and those who believe and do good works, theirs will be forgiveness and a great reward.

8. Is he, the evil of whose deeds is made fair-seeming unto him so that he deems it good, (*equal to one who is rightly guided?*). Allah verily misleads whom He wills and guides whom He wills, so let not your soul expire in sighings for them. For Allah is Aware of what they do.

9. And Allah it is who sends the winds and they raise a cloud; then We lead it unto a dead land and revive therewith the earth after its death. Such is the Resurrection.

(The allegory here is double. (1) Dry, unpromising soil may seem, to all intents and purposes, dead; there is no source of water near; moisture is sucked up by the sun's heat from a far-off ocean, and clouds are formed; winds arise; it seems as if the wind is really Allah's Providence that drives it to the dead land; the rain falls, and behold! there is life and motion and beauty everywhere! So in the spiritual world, Allah's Revelation is His Mercy and His Rain; (2) So again, may be the general Resurrection (*Nushûr*), the unfolding of a new World in the Hereafter.)

10. Whoso desires power (*should know that*) all power belongs to Allah. Unto Him good words ascend, and the righteous deed He exalts; but those who plot iniquities, theirs will be an awful doom; and the plotting of such (*folk*) will come to naught.

11. Allah created you from dust, then from a little fluid, then He made you pairs (*the male and female*). No female conceives or gives birth save with His knowledge. And no one grows old who grows old, nor is aught lessened of his life, but it is recorded in a Book. Surely that is easy for Allah.

(Here the argument is that man's physical origin is lowly; his physical body is but dust; his life-sperm issues from a part of his body which he hides and considers as a place of shame; and the mystery of sex shows that no one individual among mankind is sufficient for himself.)

12. And two seas are not equal; this, fresh, sweet, good to drink, this *(other)* bitter, salt. And from them both you eat fresh meat and derive the ornament that you wear. And you see the ship cleaving them with its prow that you may seek of His bounty, and that haply you may give thanks.

13. He makes the night to pass into the day and He makes the day to pass into the night. He has subdued the sun and moon to service. Each runs to an appointed term. Such is Allah your Lord; His is the Sovereignty; and those unto whom you pray instead of Him own not so much as the white spot on a date-stone.

(The phases of light in nature may have other uses. But for man they mark periods of rest and activity, and have great influence on his physical, moral, and spiritual life.)

14. If you pray unto them they hear not your prayer, and if they heard they could not grant it

you. On the Day of Resurrection they will disown association with you. None can inform you like One Who is Aware.

15. O mankind! You are the poor in your relation to Allah. And Allah! He is the Rich, the Owner of Praise.

16. If He will, He can be rid of you and bring *(instead of you)* some new creation.

17. That is not a hard thing for Allah.

18. And no burdened soul can bear another's burden, and if one heavy laden cries for help with his load, naught of it will be lifted even though he *(unto whom he cries)* be of kin. You warn only those who fear their Lord in secret, and have established worship. He who grows in goodness grows only for himself, *(he cannot by his merit redeem others)*. Unto Allah is the journeying.

19. The blind man is not equal with the seer;

20. Nor is darkness with the light;

21. Nor is the shadow equal with the sun's full heat;

22. Nor are the living equal with the dead. Surely Allah makes whom He will to hear. But you can never cause to hear those who are in the graves.

(The final contrast between the Living and the Dead; those whose future has in it the promise of growth and fulfilment, and those who are inert and on the road to perish. With Allah everything is possible: He can give life to the dead.)

23. You are but a warner.

24. Truly we have sent you with the Truth, a bearer of glad tidings and a warner; and there is not a nation but a warner has passed among them.

(It is Allah Who sends the Revelation. While there is warning in it for the heedless, there is good news (in Christian terms, the 'gospel') for those who listen and repent. The warning always came to all peoples before punishment.)

25. And if they deny you, those before them also denied. Their messengers came unto them with clear proofs (of Allah's sovereignty), and with the Psalms and the Scripture giving light.

26. Then seized I those who disbelieved, and how intense was My abhorrence!

27. Have you not seen that Allah causes water to fall from the sky, and We produce therewith fruit of divers hues; and among the hills are streaks white and red, of divers hues and (others) raven-black;

28. And among men and beasts and cattle there are those of divers hues? The learned among His bondsmen fear Allah alone. And Allah is Mighty, Forgiving.

(In outer nature we can, through colours, understand and appreciate the finest shades and gradations. But in the spiritual world, that variation or gradation is even more subtle and more comprehensive. Who can truly understand it? Only Allah's servants, who know, have the inner knowledge which comes through their acquaintance with the spiritual world. It is such people who truly appreciate the inner world, and it is they who know that the fear of Allah is the beginning of wisdom.)

29. Surely those who read the Scripture of Allah, and establish worship, and spend of that which We have bestowed on them secretly and openly, they look forward to imperishable gain,

30. That He will pay them their wages and increase them of His grace. Truly He is Forgiving, Responsive.

31. As for that which We inspire in you of the Scripture, it is the Truth confirming that which was *(revealed)* before it. Surely Allah is indeed Observer, Seer of his slaves.

32. Then We gave the Scripture as inheritance unto those whom We elected of Our bondsmen. But of them are some who wrong themselves, and of them are some who follow a middle course, and of them are some who outstrip *(others)* through good deeds, by Allah's leave. That is the great favour!

(The custodians of the Qur'ân after the Holy Prophet were the People of Islam. They were chosen for the Book, not in any narrow sense, but in the sense that the Book was given for their age and they were charged to obey it and preserve and propagate it, so that all mankind should receive the Message. But it does not follow that they are all true and faithful to their charge, as indeed we see too painfully around us today.)

33. Gardens of Paradise! They enter them wearing armlets of gold and pearl, and their raiment therein is silk.

34. And they say: "Praise be to Allah, who has put grief away from us. Surely Our Lord is Forgiving, Bountiful,

35. Who, of His grace, has installed us in the mansion of eternity, where toil touches us not nor can weariness affect us.

36. But as for those who disbelieve, for them is fire of hell; it takes not complete effect upon them so that they can die, nor is its torment lightened for them. Thus We punish every ingrate.

37. And they cry for help there, *(saying)*: "Our Lord! Release us; we will do right, not *(the wrong)* that we used to do. Did We not grant you a life long enough for him who reflected to reflect therein? And the warner came unto you. Now taste *(the flavour of your deeds)*, for evil-doers have no helper.

38. Truly, Allah is the Knower of the Unseen of the heavens and the earth. Surely He is Aware of the secret of *(men's)* breasts.

(They had had a long enough respite for repentance and amendment.)

39. He it is who has made you succeed one another in the earth (or: God's vicegerents on earth); so he who disbelieves, his disbelief be on his own head. Their disbelief increases, for the disbelievers, in their Lord's sight, nothing save abhorrence. Their disbelief increases for the disbelievers naught save loss.

40. Say: "Have you seen your partner-gods to whom you pray beside Allah? Show me what they created of the earth! Or have they any portion in the heavens? Or have We given them a Scripture so that they act on clear proof therefrom? Nay, the evil-doers promise one another only to deceive.

41. Surely Allah grasps the heavens and the earth that they deviate not, and if they were to deviate there is not one that could grasp them after Him. Truly He is ever Clement, Forgiving.

42. They used to swear on solemn oaths by Allah that if a warner had come unto them, they would certainly have been better guided than any other nation in the world. But when a warner came unto them, it increased them in nothing but aversion to the Truth.

(In the first instance this referred to the Quraish. Their attitude to the People of the Book had been one of lofty superiority or of insincere excuses.

They accused the Jews and Christians of deviating from their revelations; and for themselves, they said they had received no direct revelation from Allah, or they would have shown themselves the most amenable to discipline, the most ready to follow Allah's Law. This was before the Holy Prophet received his mission from Allah. When he received it and announced it, they turned away .)

43. (Shown in their) behaving arrogantly in the land and plotting evil; and the evil plot encloses only the men who make it. Then, can they expect aught save the treatment of the folk of old? You will not find for Allah's way of treatment any substitute, nor will you find for Allah's way of treatment aught of power to change.

44. Have they not travelled in the land and seen the nature of the consequence for those who were before them, and they were mightier than these in power? Allah is not such that aught in the heavens or in the earth escapes Him. For He is the Wise, the Mighty.

45. If Allah took mankind to task by that which they deserve, He would not leave a living creature on the surface of the earth; but He reprieves them unto an appointed term, and when their term comes then verily *(they will know that)* Allah is ever Seer of His slaves.

SÛRAH XXXVI
YÂ SÎN

Revealed at Makka

Yâ Sîn takes its name from the two letters of the Arabic alphabet which stand as the first verse and are generally held to signify Ya Insân *("O Man")*. This Sûrah is regarded with special reverence, and is recited in times of adversity, illness, fasting and on the approach of death.

It belongs to the middle group of Makkan Sûrahs.

YÂ SÎN

In the name of Allah, the Compassionate, the Merciful.

1. Yâ Sîn

2. By the wise Qur'ân

3. Truly you are of those sent,

4. On a straight path,

5. A revelation of the Mighty, the Merciful,

6. That you might warn a folk whose fathers were not warned, so they are heedless.

7. Indeed, the word was proved true against the greater part of them, for they believe not.

8. Surely we have put on their necks yokes reaching unto the chins, so that they are made stiff-necked.

(Man's misdeeds inevitably call forth the operation of Allah's Law, and therefore the result is, in Qur'ânic language, attributed to Allah.)

9. And We have set a bar before them and a bar behind them, and *(thus)* have covered them so that they see not.

10. Whether you warn them or you warn them not, it is alike for them, for they believe not.

11. You warn only him who follows the Reminder *(message)* and fears the Beneficent in secret. To him bear tidings of forgiveness and a rich reward.

12. Surely, We bring the dead to life. We record that which they send before them and their footprints. And all things We have kept in a clear register.

(Our deeds, good and bad, go to Allah's Judgement-Seat before us. They will of course be brought to our account; but our account will also be swelled by the example we left behind us and the consequences of our deeds, that will come into play or continue to operate after our earthly life has ceased.)

13. Coin for them a similitude: The *(story of)* the companions of the city when the messengers came to them.

14. When We sent unto them two, and they denied them both, so We reinforced them with a third, and they said: "Lo! we have been sent unto you.

15. They said: "You are but mortals like ourselves. The Beneficent has not revealed any thing. You do but lie!

16. They answered: "Our Lord knows that we are indeed sent unto you,

17. And our duty is only to proclaim the clear message.

18. *(The people of the city)* said: "We augur ill of you: If you desist not, we shall surely stone you, and grievous torture will befall you at our hands.

(Tâ'ir means a bird. Like the Roman augurs, the Arabs had a superstition about deriving omens from birds. Cf. the English word "auspicious , from the Latin *avis*, a bird. From Tâ'ir *(bird)* came *tatayyara*, or *ittayyara*, to draw evil omens. Because the prophets of Allah denounced evil, the evildoers thought that they brought ill-luck to them.)

19. They said: "Your evil augury be with you! Is it because you are reminded *(of the truth)*? Nay, but you are a people transgressing all bounds.

20. And there came from the uttermost part of the city a man running. He cried: "O my people! Follow those who have been sent!

21. Follow those who ask of you no fee, and who are rightly guided.

22. For what cause should I not serve Him Who has created me, and unto Whom you will be brought back?

23. Shall I take *(other)* gods in place of Him when, if the Beneficent should wish me any harm, their intercession will avail me naught, nor can they save?

24. Then truly I should be in error manifest.

25. Indeed I have believed in your Lord, so hear me!

26. It was said *(unto him):* "Enter Paradise. He said: "Would that my people knew,

27. With what *(munificence)* my Lord has pardoned me and made me of the honoured ones!

(For he had heard and obeyed the call of the prophets and obtained his spiritual desire .)

34. And We have placed therein gardens of the date-palm and grapes, and We have caused springs of water to gush forth therein

35. That they may eat of the fruit thereof, and their hands made it not. Will they not, then, given thanks?

36. Glory be to Him Who created all the *(sexual)* pairs, of that which the earth grows and of themselves, and of that which they know not *(till now.)*

37. A sign for them is night. We strip it of the day, and behold! they are in darkness.

(Withdrawing the Day from the Night is a striking phrase and very apt. The Day, or the Light, is the positive thing. The Night, or Darkness, is merely negative. We cannot withdraw the negative. But if we withdraw the real thing, the positive, which filled the void, nothing is left but the void. The whole of this section deals with Signs and Symbols - things in the physical world around us, from which we can learn the deepest spiritual truths if we earnestly apply ourselves to them.)

38. And the sun runs on unto a resting-place for him. That is the measuring of the Mighty, the Wise.

39. And for the moon We have appointed mansions till she return like an old shrivelled palm-leaf.

40. It is not for the sun to overtake the moon, nor does the night outstrip the day. They float, each in an orbit.

28. We sent not down against his people after him a host from heaven, nor do We ever send.

29. It was but one Shout, and behold! they were extinct *(like ashes).*

(Allah's Justice or Punishment does not necessarily come with pomp and circumstance. A single mighty Blast - either the rumbling of an earthquake, or a great and violent wind-was sufficient in this case.)

30. Ah, the anguish for the bondsmen! Never came there unto them a messenger but they did mock him!

31. Have they not seen how many generations We destroyed before them? They indeed will not return unto them;

32. But all, without exception, will be brought before Us.

33. A sign for them is the dead earth. We revive it, and We bring forth from it grain so that they eat thereof;

41. And a token unto them is that We bear their offspring in the laden ship,

42. And We have created for them similar *(vessels)* thereof on which they ride.

43. And if We will, We drown them, and there is no help for them, neither can they be saved;

44. Unless by mercy from Us, and a comfort for a while.

45. When it is said unto them: "Beware what is before you and what is behind you, that haply you may find mercy , *(they are heedless).*

(Man should consider and beware of the consequences of his past, and guard against the consequences in his future. The present is only a fleeting moment poised between the past and the future, and gone even while it is being mentioned or thought about.)

46 - Never came a sign of the signs of their Lord to them but they did turn away from it!

47. And when it is said unto them: "Spend of that wherewith Allah has provided you , those who disbelieve say unto those who believe: "shall we feed those whom Allah if He willed would feed? You are in naught else than error manifest.

48. And they say: "When will this promise be fulfilled if you are truthful?

49. They await but one Shout which will surprise *(seize)* them while they are disputing.

50. Then they cannot make bequest, nor can they return to their own folk.

(Then they will neither be able to make a will, nor be able to return to their families.)

51. And the trumpet is blown, and lo! from the graves they hie unto their Lord,

52. Crying: "Woe upon us! Who has raised us from our place of sleep? This is what the Beneficent did promise, and the messengers spoke the truth,

(The dead will rise as in a stupor, and they will be confused in the new conditions. They will gradually regain their memory and their personality. They will be reminded that Allah in His grace and mercy had already announced the Hereafter in their probationary lives, and the word of Allah's messengers, which then seemed so strange and remote, was true and was now being fulfilled.)

53 - It is but one Shout, and behold them brought together before Us!

54. This day no soul is wronged in aught; nor are you requited aught save what you used to do.

55. Surely the Garden's people this day are happily employed,

56. They and their wives, in pleasant shade on thrones reclining;

57. Much fruit (and enjoyment) will be there for them,

58. The word from a Merciful Lord (for them) is: Peace (salâm).

59. And keep apart on this day, O you perfidious(criminals)!

60. Did I not command you, you sons of Adam, that you worship not the devil; surely he is your open foe!

(This is a gentle reproach to the wrongdoers, more in sorrow than in anger. They are addressed as "children of Adam , to emphasise two facts, (1) that they have disgraced their ancestry, for Adam after his Fall repented and was forgiven, and the high destiny of mankind has been the prize open to all his descendants, and (2) that Allah the Most Merciful has throughout the ages continued to warn mankind against the snares laid by Satan, the avowed enemy of our race.)

61. And that you should worship Me? That was the right path.

62. And yet he has led astray of you a great multitude. Had you then no sense?

63. This is hell which you were promised (if you followed him).

64. Burn therein this day for that you disbelieved.

65. This day We seal up mouths, and hands speak out, and feet bear witness as to what they used to earn.

66. And had We willed, We verily could have quenched their eyesight so that they should struggle for the way. Then how could they have seen?

67. And had We willed, We verily could have fixed them in their place, making them powerless to go forward or turn back.

68. He whom We bring unto old age, We reverse him in creation (making him regress to weakness after strength). Have you then no sense?

69. And we have not taught him (Muhammad) poetry, nor is it meet for him. This is naught else than a Reminder and a Lecture (Qur'ân) making plain,

70. To warn whosoever is alive, and that the word may be fulfilled against the disbelievers.

("Alive , both in English and Arabic, means not only "having physical life , but having all the active qualities which we associate with life. In religious language, those who are not responsive to the realities of the spiritual world are no better than those who are dead. The Message of Allah penetrates the hearts of those who are alive in the spiritual sense.)

71. Have they not seen how We have created for them of Our handiwork the cattle, so that they are their owners,

72. And We have subdued them unto them, so that some of them they have for riding, and some for food?

73. Benefits and *(divers)* drinks have they from them. Will they not then give thanks?

74. And they have taken *(other)* gods beside Allah in order that they may be helped.

75. It is not in their power to help them; but they *(the worshippers)* are unto them a host in arms.

76. So let not their speech grieve you *(O Muhammad);* for We know what they conceal and what they proclaim.

77. Has man not seen that We created him from a drop of seed? Yet lo! he is an open opponent.

(Man's disobedience and folly are all the more surprising, seeing that - apart from Allah's greatness and mercy - man is himself such a puny creature, created out of something that is less than a drop in the vast ocean of Existence. Yet man has the recklessness to stand out and dispute with his Maker, and institute idle comparisons, as in the next verse!)

78. And he has coined for Us a similitude, and has forgotten the fact of his creation, saying:

"Who will revive these bones when they have rotted away?

79. Say: "He will revive them Who produced them at the first, for He is Knower of every creation,

80. Who has appointed for you fire from the green tree, and behold! you kindle from it.

81. Is not He Who created the heavens and the earth Able to create the like of them? Aye, that He is! for He is the All-Wise Creator,

(Which is the more difficult to create - man, or the heavens and the earth, with all creatures? Allah created the heavens and the earth, with all the creatures, and He can create worlds like these in infinity. To him it is a small matter to raise you up for the Hereafter!)

82. But His command, when He intends a thing, is only that he says unto it: Be! and it is.

83. Therefore glory be to Him in Whose hand is the dominion of all things! Unto Him you will be brought back.

SÛRAH XXXVII

AS-SÂFFÂT

(THOSE WHO SET THE RANKS)

Revealed at Makka

As-Sâffât takes its name from a word in the first verse. The reference in the first three verses is to the angels, as is made clear by vv. 164-166, where the revealing angel speaks in person. Tradition says that soothsayers and astrologers throughout the East were bewildered at the time of the Prophet's coming by the appearance in the heavens of a comet and many meteors which baffled all their science and made them afraid to sit at nights on high peaks to watch the stars, as was their general custom. They told enquirers that their familiars could no longer guide them, being themselves completely at a loss and terrified.

It stands early in the middle group of Makkan Sûrahs.

THOSE WHO SET THE RANKS

In the name of Allah, the Compassionate,
the Merciful.

1. By those who set the ranks in battle order

2. And those who drive away *(the wicked)* with reproof

3. And those who read *(the word)* for a reminder,

4. Truly your Lord is One;

5. Lord of the heavens and of the earth and all that is between them, and Lord of the sun's risings.

(Allah is the Lord of everything that exists - the heavens and the earth, and all between them. He is the Lord of the *Mashâriq*-of every point at the rising of the sun. As the Commentators tell us, there are in the solar year only two equinoctial days, when the sun rises due east: on every other the sun rises at a shifting point either north or south of due east.)

6. Lo! We have adorned the lowest heaven with an ornament, the planets;

7. We protect it with security from every froward devil.

8. They cannot listen to the Highest Chiefs for they are pelted from every side,

9. Outcast, and theirs is a perpetual torment;

10. Save him who snatches a fragment, and there pursues him a piercing flame.

11. Then ask them *(O Muhammad)*: Are they stronger as a creation, or those whom We created? Truly We created them of sticky clay.

12. Nay, but you do marvel when they mock.

13. And when they are reminded, They heed not

14. And they seek to scoff when they behold a portent.

15. And they said: "This is mere magic;

16. When we are dead and have become dust and bones, shall we then, forsooth, be raised *(again)*?

17. And our forefathers?

18. Say *(O Muhammad)*: "Yea, in truth; and you will be brought low.

19. There is but one Shout, and behold! *(they begin to see)*.

20. And say: "Ah, woe for us! This is the Day of Judgement.

21. This is the Day of Separation, which you used to deny.

22. *(And it is said unto the angels)*: "Assemble those who did wrong, together with their wives and what they used to worship,

23. Instead of Allah, and lead them to the path to hell;

24. And stop them, for they must be questioned.

25. Why do you not assist one another?

26. Nay, but this day they make full submission.

27. And some of them draw near unto others, mutually questioning.

28. They say: "Lo! you used to come unto us at the right hand *(of authority, swearing that you spoke the truth).*

29. They answer: "Nay but you *(yourselves)* were not believers.

30. We had no power over you, but you were wayward folk.

31. Now the word of our Lord has been fulfilled concerning us. Assuredly, we are about to taste *(the punishment).*

32. Thus we misled you. Truly, we were *(ourselves)* astray.

33. Surely on that day they *(both)* are sharers in the doom.

34. Lo! thus We deal with the guilty.

35. For when it was said unto them, "There is no god save Allah they were scornful.

(Selfish arrogance was the seed of sin and rebellion: 2:34 *(of Satan);* 27:39 *(of Pharaoh);* etc. It is that kind of arrogance which prevents man from mending his life and conduct. When he speaks of ancestral ways, or public opinion, or national honour, he is usually thinking of himself or of a small clique which thrives on injustice. The recognition of Allah, the one true God, as the only standard of life and conduct, the Eternal Reality, cuts out Self, and is therefore disagreeable to Sin. If false gods are imagined, who themselves would have weaknesses that fit in with sin, they give countenance to evils, and it becomes difficult to give them up, unless Allah's grace comes to our assistance.)

36. And they say: "Shall we forsake our gods for a mad poet?

37. Nay, but he brought the Truth and he confirmed those sent *(before him).*

38. *(Now)* verily you taste the painful doom.

39. You are requited naught save what you did;

40. Save single-minded slaves of Allah;

41. For them is a known provision,

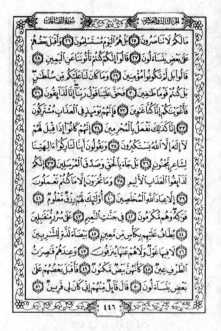

42. Fruits. And they will be honoured

43. In the Gardens of delight,

44. On couches facing one another;

45. A cup from a gushing spring is brought round for them,

46. White, delicious to the drinkers,

47. Wherein there is no headache, nor are they made mad thereby.

48. And with them are those of modest gaze, with lovely eyes *(women.)*

49. *(Pure)* as though they were hidden eggs *(of the ostrich).*

50. And some of them draw near unto others, mutually questioning.

51. A speaker of them said: Lo! I had a comrade

(This companion was a sceptic, who laughed at Religion and the Hereafter. How the tables are now turned! The devout man backed up his Faith with a good life and is now in Bliss: the other was a cynic and made a mess of his life, and is now burning in the Fire.)

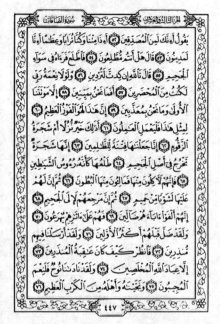

62. Is this better as a welcome, or the tree of Zaqqûm?

(This bitter tree of Hell is a symbol to contrast with the beautiful Garden of Heaven with its delicious fruits.)

63. We have appointed it a torment for wrong-doers.

64. Surely it is a tree that grows in the heart of hell.

65. Its crop is as it were the heads of devils.

66. And they verily must eat thereof, and fill their bellies therewith.

(The parable of fruits and drinks in the contrasted fortunes of the Good and the Evil is further elaborated in 47:15, where the boiling water given to the evil ones cuts up their entrails.)

67. And afterward, thereupon they have a drink of boiling water

68. And afterward, their return is surely unto hell.

69. They indeed found their fathers astray,

70. But they make haste (to follow) in their footsteps.

71. And verily most of the men of old went astray before them,

72. And verily We sent among them warners.

73. Then see the nature of the consequence for those warned,

74. Save single-minded slaves of Allah.

(But there is always a band of sincere and devoted men who serve Allah, and the highest spiritual life is open to them.

Note that this verse occurs at 37:40 above, where the argument of the difference between the fates of the righteous and the unrighteous was begun. Here it is rounded off with the same phrase, and now we proceed to take illustrations from the early Prophets.)

75. And Noah verily prayed unto Us, and gracious was the Hearer of his prayer.

(The story of Noah occurs in many places; here the point is that when men gird themselves against evil, Allah protects them, and Evil cannot triumph against Allah's Plan.)

76. And We saved him and his household from the great distress,

52. Who used to say: "Are you in truth of those who put faith (in his words)?

53. Can we, when we are dead and have become mere dust and bones, can we (then) verily be brought to book? (or shall we indeed receive rewards and punishments?)

54. He said: "Will you look?"

55. Then looks he, and sees him in the depth of hell.

56. He said: "By Allah, you verily did all but cause my ruin,

57. And had it not been for the favour of my Lord, I too had been of those brought forth to doom.

58. Are we then not to die.

59. Saving our former death, and are we not to be punished?

60. Truly this is the supreme triumph.

61. For the like of this, then, let the workers work.

77. And We made his seed the survivors,

78. And We left for him among the later folk *(the salutation):*

79. Peace be unto Noah among the peoples!

80. Thus do We reward the doers of good,

81. Truly, he is one of Our believing slaves.

82. Then We did drown the others.

83. And surely from his party was Abraham.

(The main story will be found in 21:51-73; but the episode about his readiness and that of his son to submit to the most extreme form of self-sacrifice under trial *(in verses 102-107 below)* is told here for the first time, as this Sûrah deals with the theme, "Not my will, but Thine be done! In "followed his way, the pronoun "his refers to Noah, "he, of verse 81 above.)

84. When he came unto his Lord with a whole heart;

85. When he said unto his father and his folk: "What is it that you worship?

86. Is it a falsehood; gods beside Allah, that you desire?

(False worship, worship of idols or stars or symbols, or Mammon or Self - is due either to false and degrading conceptions of Allah, or to a sort of make-believe, where practice is inconsistent with knowledge or ignores the inner promptings of conscience. Abraham's challenge to his people is: 'Are you fools or hypocrites?')

87. What then is your opinion of the Lord of the Worlds?

88. And he glanced a glance at the stars

89. Then said: "I feel sick!

90. And they turned their backs and went away from him.

91. Then turned he to their gods and said: "Will you not eat?

92. Why do you not speak?

93. Then he attacked them, striking with his right hand.

94. And *(his people)* came toward him hastening.

95. He said: "Worship you that which you yourselves do carve

96. When Allah has created you and what you make?

97. They said: "build up for him a building, and fling him in the red-hot fire.

98. And they designed a snare for him, but We made them the undermost.

99. And he said: "Lo! I am going unto my Lord, Who will guide me

(This was the Hijrah of Abraham. He left his people and his land, because the Truth was dearer to him than the ancestral falsehoods of his people. He trusted himself to Allah, and under Allah's guidance he laid the foundations of great peoples.)

100. My Lord! Grant me one of the righteous.

101. So We gave him tidings of a gentle son.

102. And when *(his son)* was old enough to walk with him, *(Abraham)* said: "O my dear son, I have seen in a dream that I must sacrifice you, so look, what think you? He said: "O my father! Do that which you are commanded. Allah willing, you shall find me of the steadfast.

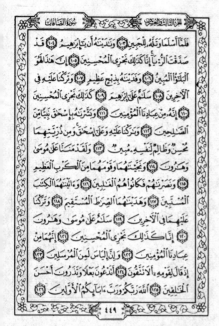

103. Then, when they had both surrendered to Allah, and he had flung him down upon his face,

(Note that the sacrifice was demanded of both Abraham and Ishmael. It was a trial of the will of the father and the son. By way of trial the father had the command conveyed to him in a vision. He consulted the son. The son readily consented, and offered to stand true to his promise if his self-sacrifice was really required. The whole thing is symbolical. Allah does not require the flesh and blood of animals (22:37), much less of human beings.)

104. We called unto him: "O Abraham!

105. You have already fulfilled the vision. Lo! thus do We reward the doers of good.

106. That verily was a clear test *(trial)*.

107. Then We ransomed him with a tremendous sacrifice

108. And We left for him among the later folk *(the salutation)*:

109. Peace be unto Abraham!

110. Thus do We reward the doers of good.

111. Surely he is one of Our believing slaves.

112. And We gave him tidings of the birth of Isaac, a Prophet of the righteous.

113. And We blessed him and Isaac. And of their seed are some who do good, and some who plainly wrong themselves.

114. And We verily gave grace unto Moses and Aaron,

115. And saved them and their people from the great distress,

116. And We helped them so that they became the victors.

117. And We gave them the clear Scripture.

118. And showed them the right path.

119. And We left for them among the later folk *(the salutation):*

120. Peace be unto Moses and Aaron!

121. Surely thus do We reward the doers of good.

122. Truly they are two of our believing slaves.

123. And Elias was of those sent to warn

(Elias is the same as Elijah, whose story will be found in the Old Testament in 1 Kings xvii-xix. and 2 Kings i-ii. Elijah lived in the reign of Ahab *(B. C. 896-874)* and Ahaziah *(B. C. 874-872)*, kings of the *(northern)* kingdom of Israel or Samaria. He was a prophet of the desert, like John the Baptist-unlike our Holy Prophet, who took part in, controlled, and guided all the affairs of his people.)

124. When he said unto his folk: "Will you not ward off *(evil)?*

125. Will you cry unto Baal and forsake the best of Creators,

126. Allah, your Lord and Lord of your forefathers?

127. But they denied him, so they surely will be called up *(for the doom)*

128. Save single-minded slaves of Allah.

129. And We left for him among the later folk *(the salutation):*

130. Peace be unto Elias!

131. Surely thus do We reward the doers of good.

132. Truly he is one of our believing slaves.

133. And Lot verily was of those sent *(to warn),*

(The best illustration of this passage about Lût will be found in 7: 80- 84. He was a prophet sent to Sodom and Gomorrah, Cities of the Plain, by the Dead Sea. The inhabitants were given over to abominable crimes, against which he preached.)

134. When We saved him and his household, every one,

135. Save an old woman among those who stayed behind;

136. Then We destroyed the others.

137. And you verily pass by *(the ruin of)* them in the morning

138. And at night-time; have you then no sense?

139. And Jonah verily was of those sent *(to warn)*

(For illustrative passages, see 21:87-88, and 67:48-50. Jonah's mission was to the city of Nineveh, then steeped in wickedness. He was rejected and he denounced Allah's wrath on them, but they repented and obtained Allah's forgiveness. But Jonah "departed in wrath *(21:87)*, forgetting that Allah has Mercy as well as forgiveness.)

140. When he fled unto the laden ship,

141. And then drew lots and was of those rejected;

142. And the fish swallowed him while he was blameworthy;

(The rivers of Mesopotamia have some huge fishes. The word used here is Hût, which may be a fish or perhaps a crocodile. If it were in an open northern sea, it might be a whale. The locality is not mentioned: in the Old Testament he is said to have taken ship in the port of Joppa *(now Jaffa)* in the Mediterranean.)

143. And had he not been one of those who glorify *(Allah)*

144. He would have tarried in its belly till the day when they are raised;

145. Then We cast him on a desert shore while he was sick;

146. And We caused a tree of gourd to grow above him;

147. And We sent him to a hundred thousand *(folk)* or more

148. And they believed, therefore We gave them comfort for a while.

149. Now ask them *(O Muhammad):* "Has your Lord daughters whereas they have sons?

150. Or created We the angels females while they were present?

151. Lo! it is of their falsehood that they say:

152. Allah has begotten children. And lo! verily they tell a lie.

153. *(And again of their falsehood):* "He has preferred daughters to sons.

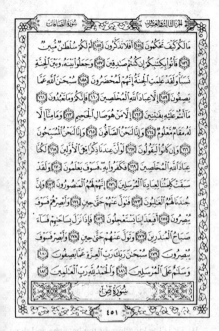

154. What ails you? How judge you?

155. Will you not then reflect?

156. Or have you a clear warrant? *(authority).*

157. Then produce your Book, if you are truthful.

158. And they imagine kinship between him and the jinn, whereas the jinn know well that they will be brought before Him

(The angels are at least pure beings engaged in the service of Allah. But the Pagan superstitions not only connect them with Allah as daughters but even connect Allah by relationship with all kinds of spirits, good or evil! In some mythologies the most evil powers are gods or goddesses as if they belonged to the family of Allah the Creator and had some semblance of equality with Him! This, too, is repudiated in the strongest terms.)

159. Glorified be Allah from that which they attribute *(to Him.)*

160. Save single-minded slaves of Allah.

161. Lo! verily, you and that which you worship,

162. You cannot excite *(anyone)* against Him

163. Save him who is to burn in hell.

164. There is not one of Us *(the angels)* but has his known position.

(To round off the argument of the Sûrah we go back to the idea with which it began. Those who range themselves in ranks for the united service of Allah, whether angels or men of God, are content to keep their ranks and do whatever service is assigned to them.)

165. Truly We are only the rankers.

166. And We are only glorifiers.

167. And indeed they used to say:

168. "If only we had had before us a Reminder from the men of old.

169. We would be single-minded slaves of Allah.

170. But *(now that it is come)* they disbelieve therein; but they will come to know.

171. And verily Our word went forth of old unto Our bondsmen sent *(to warn)*

172. That they verily would be helped,

173. And that Our host, they verily would be the victors.

174. So withdraw from them *(O Muhammad)* awhile,

175. And watch, for they will *(soon)* see.

176. Would they hasten on Our doom?

177. But when the doom comes home to them, then it will be a hapless morn for those who have been warned.

178. Withdraw from them awhile.

179. And watch for they will *(soon)* see.

180. Glorified be your Lord, the Lord of Majesty, from that which they attribute *(unto Him)*

181. And peace be unto those sent *(to warn)*

182. And praise be to Allah, Lord of the Worlds!

SÛRAH XXXVIII
SÂD
Revealed at Makka

This Sûrah takes its name from the letter of the Arabic Alphabet which stands alone as the first verse. Tradition says that the first ten verses were revealed when the leaders of Quraish tried to persuade Abû Tâlib to withdraw his protection from the Prophet, or when Abû Talib died. The former is the more probable.

Its place is in the middle group of Makkan Sûrahs.

SÂD

In the name of Allah, the Compassionate, the Merciful.

1. Sâd. By the renowned Qur'ân,

2. Nay, but those who disbelieve are in false pride and schism.

(Teaching, Warning, Signs have been given by Allah to all nations and at all times, and yet nations have rebelled and gone wrong, and suffered destruction. If only later generations could learn that wrongdoing results in self-destruction! For the justice of Allah merely carries out the result of their own choice and actions.)

3. How many a generation We destroyed before them, and they cried out when it was no longer the time for escape!

4. And they marvelled that a warner from among themselves has come unto them, and the disbelievers say: "This is a wizard, a charlatan.

5. Makes he the gods One God? Lo! that is an astounding thing.

6. The chiefs among them go about, exhorting: "Go and be staunch to your gods! Lo! this is a thing designed.

7. We have not heard of this in later religion. This is naught but an invention.

('If a Message had to come, why should it come to him, the orphan son of 'Abd Allah, and not to one of our own great men?')

8. Has the reminder *(message)* been revealed unto him *(alone)* among us? Nay, but they are in doubt concerning My reminder; nay but they have not yet tasted My doom.

9. Or are theirs the treasures of the mercy of your Lord, the Mighty, the Bestower?

10. Or is the kingdom of the heavens and the earth and all that is between them theirs? Then let them ascend by ropes!

(Of course they cannot frustrate Allah's purpose. In that world -the spiritual world- they will be ignominiously routed, even if they form the strongest confederacy of the powers of evil that ever could combine.)

11. Any host of confederates there, will be defeated.

12. The folk of Noah before them denied *(their messenger),* and also Aad, and Pharaoh firmly planted.

13. And *(the tribe of)* Thamoud, and the folk of Lot and the dwellers in the wood: these were the factions.

14. Not one of them but did deny the messengers, therefore My doom was justified,

15. These wait for but one Shout, there will be no second thereto.

16. They say: "Our Lord! Hasten on for us our fate before the Day of Reckoning.

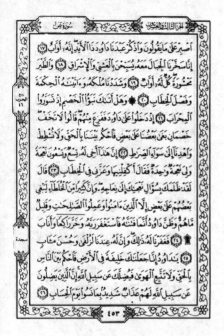

19. And the birds assembled; all were turning unto Him.

20. We made his kingdom strong and gave him wisdom and decisive speech.

21. And has the story of the litigants come unto you? How they climbed the wall into the royal chamber;

(David was used to retiring to his private chamber at stated times for his devotions. One day, suddenly, his privacy was invaded by two men, who had obtained access by climbing over a wall. David was frightened at the apparition. But they said: "we have come to seek your justice as king: we are brothers, and we have a quarrel, which we wish you to decide.)

22. When they burst in upon David, and he was afraid of them, they said: "Be not afraid! *(We are)* two litigants, one of whom has wronged the other, therefore judge aright between us; be not unjust; and show us the fair way.

23. Behold, this my brother has ninety and nine ewes while I had one ewe and he said: 'Entrust it to me' and he conquered me in speech.

24. *(David)* said: "He has wronged you in demanding your ewe in addition to his ewes, and lo! many partners oppress one another, save such as believe and do good works, and they are few. And David guessed that We had tried him, and he sought forgiveness of his Lord, and he bowed himself and fell down prostrate and repented.

25. So We forgave him that; and indeed he had access to Our presence and a happy journey's end.

26. *(And it was said unto him)*: "O David! Lo! We have set you as a viceroy in the earth; therefore judge aright between mankind, and follow not desire lest it beguile you from the way of Allah. Surely those who wander from the way of Allah have an awful doom, forasmuch as they forgot the Day of Reckoning.

17. Bear with what they say, and remember Our bondsman David lord of might. Lo! he was ever turning in repentance *(toward Allah)*

(All nature sings in unison and celebrates the praises of Allah. David was given the gift of music and psalmody, and therefore the hills and birds are expressed as singing Allah's praises in unison with him. The special hours when the hills and groves echo the songs of birds are in the evening and at dawn, when also the birds gather together, for those are respectively their roosting hours and the hours of their concerted flight for the day.)

18. Truly We subdued the hills to hymn the praises *(of their Lord)* with him at nightfall and sunrise,

(Note the mutual echo between this verse and verse 17 above. The Arabic *awwâb* is common to both, and it furnishes the rhyme or rhythm of the greater part of this Sûrah, thus echoing the main theme: 'Turn to Allah in Prayer and Praise, for that is more than any worldly power or wisdom.')

27. And We created not the heaven and the earth and all that is between them in vain. That is the opinion of those who disbelieve. And woe unto those who disbelieve, from the Fire!

28. Shall We treat those who believe and do good works as those who spread corruption in the earth; or shall We treat the pious as the wicked?

(Revelation is not a mere chance or haphazard thing. It is a real blessing - among the greatest that Allah has bestowed on man. By meditation on it in an earnest spirit man may learn of himself, and his relation to nature around him and to Allah, the Author of All. Men of understanding may, by its help, resolve all genuine doubts that there may be in their minds, and learn the true lessons of spiritual life.)

29. *(This is)* a Scripture that We have revealed unto you, full of blessing, that they may ponder its revelations, and that men of understanding may reflect.

30. And We bestowed on David, Solomon. How excellent a slave! Lo! he was ever turning in repentance *(toward Allah).*

31. When there were shown to him at eventide light-footed coursers

(The story is not found in the Old Testament. I interpret it to mean that, like his father David, Solomon was also most meticulous in not allowing the least motive of self to be mixed up with his spiritual virtues. He was fond of horses: he had great armies and wealth; but he used them all in Allah's service. Cf. 27:19, 27: 40).

32. And he said: "Truly I have preferred the good things *(of the world)* to the remembrance of my Lord; till they were taken out of sight behind the curtain.

33. *(Then he said):* "Bring them back to me, and fell to slashing *(with his sword their)* legs and necks.

(What was the trial of Solomon? All the power, wealth, and glory, which were given to him were a spiritual trial to him. They might have turned another man's head, but he was staunch and true, and while he enjoyed and used all the power he had -over spirits, men, and the forces of nature, *(see below),* he kept his mind steady to the service of Allah.)

34. And verily We tried Solomon, and set upon his throne a *(mere)* body. Then did he repent.

35. He said: "My Lord! Forgive me and bestow on me sovereignty such as shall not belong to any after me. Surely you are the Bestower.

36. So We made the wind subservient unto him, setting fair by his command wheresoever he intended.

37. And the unruly *(satanic ones)* every builder and diver *(made We subservient).*

38. And others linked together in chains,

39. *(Saying):* "This is Our gift, so bestow you, or withhold, without reckoning.

40. And he enjoyed indeed a near approach to Us, and a happy journey's end.

41. And make mention *(O Muhammad)* of Our bondman Job, when he cried unto his Lord *(saying):* "Surely the devil does afflict me with distress and torment.

42. *(And it was said unto him):* "Strike the ground with your foot. This *(spring)* is a cool bath and a refreshing drink.

43. And We bestowed on him *(again)* his household and therewith the like thereof, a mercy from Us, and a memorial for men of understanding.

(In his worst distress, Job was patient and constant in faith, but apparently his wife was not. According to the book of Job *(ii. 9-10,* "Then said his wife unto him, dost thou still retain thine integrity? Curse God, and die. But he said unto her, you speakest as one of the foolish women speaketh. What? Shall we receive good at the hand of God, and shall we not receive evil? In all this did not Job sin with his lips. He must have said in his haste to the woman that he would beat her: he is asked now to correct her with only a wisp of grass, to show that he was gentle and humble as well as patient and constant.)

44. And *(it was said unto him)*: "Take in your hand a twig and smite therewith and break not your oath. Lo! We found him steadfast; how excellent a slave! Truly he was ever turning in repentance *(to his Lord).*

45. And make mention of Our bondsmen Abraham, Isaac and Jacob, men of power and vision.

46. Indeed We purified them with a pure thought, remembrance of the Home *(of the Hereafter).*

47. Lo! in Our sight they are verily of the elect, the excellent.

(Ismael, the Patriarch of the Arab race, was also mentioned *(37:101-107)* as a pattern of self-sacrifice; now he is mentioned in the company of the Good, i.e., of those who were a blessing to their people.)

48. And make mention of Ishmael and Elisha and Dhû'l-Kifl. All are of the chosen.

49. This is a reminder. And surely for those who ward off evil is a happy journey's end,

50. Gardens of Paradise whereof the gates are opened for them,

51. Wherein reclining they call for plenteous fruit and cool drink *(that is)* therein.

52. And beside them will be chaste women restraining their glances. *(They are companions)* of equal age.

53. This it is that you are promised for the Day of Reckoning.

54. Lo! this in truth is Our provision, which will never waste away.

55. This *(is for the righteous).* And for the transgressors there will be an evil journey's end,

56. Hell, where they will burn, an evil resting place.

57. This is a boiling and an ice-cold draught, so let them taste it,

58. And other torment of the kind in pairs.

59. Here is an army rushing blindly with you. *(Those who are already in the fire say)*: No word of welcome for them. Lo! they will roast at the fire.

60. They say: "Nay but you *(misleaders)*, for you there is no word of welcome. You prepared this for us *(by your misleading).* Now evil is this place of abiding.

61. They say: "Our Lord! Whoever did prepare this for us, oh give him a double portion of the Fire.

62. And they say: "What ails us that we behold not men whom we were wont to count among the wicked?

63. Did we take them *(wrongly)* for a laughing-stock, or have our eyes missed them?

64. Lo! that is very truth: the wrangling of the dweller in the Fire.

(When Joseph preached to his fellow - prisoners, he recalled that the one supreme Message of importance to mankind was *(and is)* the Unity of Allah: that He is the Creator and Sustainer of all: that His Will is supreme: that He can carry out His Will without question, and no powers of evil can defeat it: and that He forgives by His grace again and again. This Message the Holy Prophet came to deliver; and he delivered it.)

65. Say *(unto them, O Muhammad)* : "I am only a warner, and there is no God save Allah, the One, the Irresistible.

66. Lord of the heavens and the earth and all that is between them, the Mighty, the Pardoning.

67. Say: "It is tremendous tidings.

68. Whence you turn away!

(The hierarchy in Heaven, under Allah's command, discuss questions of high import in the Universe. Those are not necessarily revealed to men, except insofar as it is good for men to know, as in verses 71-85 below. But the chief thing for man is to know that Allah is Most Merciful, that He forgives again and again, and that Evil has no power over those who trust in Allah.)

69. I had no knowledge of the Highest Chiefs when they disputed;

70. It is revealed unto me only that I may be a plain warner.

71. When your Lord said unto the angels: "I am creating a mortal out of mire,

72. And when I have fashioned him and breathed into him of My spirit, then fall down before him prostrate,

73. The angels fell down prostrate, every one.

74. Except Iblîs; he was scornful and became one of the disbelievers.

75. He said: "O Iblîs! What hinders you from falling prostrate before that which I have created

with both My hands? Are you too proud, or are you of the high exalted?

(The Muslim mystics explain this as meaning that Man was made with both the beautiful and the rigorous attributes of God, whereas the angels were created by the exercise of only one class of attributes.)

76. He said: "I am better than him. You created me of fire while him you did create of clay.

77. He said: "Go forth from hence, for you are outcast,

78. And My curse is on you till the Day of Judgement.

79. He said: "My Lord! Reprieve me till the day when they are raised.

80. He said: "Lo! You are of those reprieved

81. Until the day of the time appointed.

82. He said: "Then by Your might, I surely will beguile them every one,

83. Save Your single-minded slaves among them.

84. He said: "The Truth is, and the Truth I speak,

85. That I shall fill hell with you and with such of them as follow you, all together.

86. Say *(O Muhammad, unto mankind)* : "I ask of you no fee for this, and I am no impostor.

87. Lo! it is naught else than a reminder for all peoples.

88. And you will come in time to know the truth thereof.

SÛRAH XXXIX
AZ-ZUMAR (THE TROOPS)

Revealed at Makka

This takes its name from a word meaning troops or companies, which occurs in verses 71 and 73. The verses 53-55 were revealed at Madîna.

In the name of Allah, the Compassionate, the Merciful

1. The revelation of the Book is from Allah the All-Mighty, the All-Wise.

2. Lo! We have sent down this book to you *(Muhammad)* in truth; so worship Allah alone, making religion pure for Him.

3. Pure Religion is for Allah only! And those who have taken protecting friends beside Him *(say:)* "We worship them only that they may bring us closer to Allah . Lo! Allah will judge between them concerning all that in which they differ. Surely Allah does not guide any liar and denier of the truth.

4. If Allah had willed to take a son, He could have chosen anyone He pleased out of His creation: but Glory be to Him ! *(He is above such things.)* He is Allah, the One, the Omnipotent.

5. He has created the heavens and the earth in truth. He makes night to succeed day, and day to succeed night. He has so subjected the Sun and the Moon that each is moving till an appointed time. Is not He the All-Mighty, All - Forgiving ?

6. He created you *(all)* from a single being, then from that being, He created its mate. He has given you eight heads of cattle in pairs, male and female. He created you in the wombs of your mothers, in stages, one after another, in a threefold gloom. This same Allah *(Whose works are these)* is your Lord. His is the Sovereignty. There is no god save Him. How, then, are you turned away *(from Him)?*

(The eight heads of cattle are the camel, cow, sheep and goat, male and female. The three veils of darkness which cover the unborn child are: the belly, the womb and the caul or membrane. It is clear that you owe your very existence and your maintenance, growth and preservation to Allah. He is the essence of your being: how is it that you are turned away by casual things from Him?)

7. If you are thankless, yet Allah is Independent of you, though He is not pleased with thanklessness for His bondsmen ; and if you are thankful He is pleased therewith for you. No soul will bear the burden of another; ultimately, to your Lord is your return, when He will declare to you the truth of all you have been doing *(in this life).* Lo ! He knows even the secrets of the hearts.

(Allah is independent of all wants; therefore man's thanklessness does not affect Allah. But He cares for man, and therefore man's thankfulness earns Allah's good pleasure, and man's ingratitude and rebellion are displeasing to Him.

The account is between you and Allah. No one else can take your burden or carry your sins.)

8. When harm touches man, he cries unto his Lord, turning to Him in repentance; yet no sooner does He bestow on him a favour from Him then he forgets that for which he had cried before and sets up rivals to Allah, in order to lead astray from His way. Say *(O Muhammad):* "Enjoy your blasphemy for a while; Lo! you are of the companions of the Fire.

(Those who practise evil, and those who teach evil and blasphemy, may seem to flourish in this world. But their satisfaction will be of very short duration. They are treading all the while the path that leads to Hell.)

9. Is one who worships devoutly during the hours of night, prostrating or standing *(in*

خَلَقَكُمْ مِّنْ نَّفْسٍ وَّاحِدَةٍ ثُمَّ جَعَلَ مِنْهَا زَوْجَهَا وَأَنْزَلَ لَكُمْ مِّنَ الْأَنْعَامِ ثَمَانِيَةَ أَزْوَاجٍ يَخْلُقُكُمْ فِي بُطُونِ أُمَّهَاتِكُمْ خَلْقًا مِّنْ بَعْدِ خَلْقٍ فِي ظُلُمَاتٍ ثَلَاثٍ ذَلِكُمُ اللَّهُ رَبُّكُمْ لَهُ الْمُلْكُ لَا إِلَهَ إِلَّا هُوَ فَأَنَّى تُصْرَفُونَ ۝ إِنْ تَكْفُرُوا فَإِنَّ اللَّهَ غَنِيٌّ عَنْكُمْ وَلَا يَرْضَى لِعِبَادِهِ الْكُفْرَ وَإِنْ تَشْكُرُوا يَرْضَهُ لَكُمْ وَلَا تَزِرُ وَازِرَةٌ وِزْرَ أُخْرَى ثُمَّ إِلَى رَبِّكُمْ مَّرْجِعُكُمْ فَيُنَبِّئُكُمْ بِمَا كُنْتُمْ تَعْمَلُونَ إِنَّهُ عَلِيمٌ بِذَاتِ الصُّدُورِ ۝ ۞ وَإِذَا مَسَّ الْإِنْسَانَ ضُرٌّ دَعَا رَبَّهُ مُنِيبًا إِلَيْهِ ثُمَّ إِذَا خَوَّلَهُ نِعْمَةً مِّنْهُ نَسِيَ مَا كَانَ يَدْعُو إِلَيْهِ مِنْ قَبْلُ وَجَعَلَ لِلَّهِ أَنْدَادًا لِّيُضِلَّ عَنْ سَبِيلِهِ قُلْ تَمَتَّعْ بِكُفْرِكَ قَلِيلًا إِنَّكَ مِنْ أَصْحَابِ النَّارِ ۝ أَمَّنْ هُوَ قَانِتٌ آنَاءَ اللَّيْلِ سَاجِدًا وَقَائِمًا يَحْذَرُ الْآخِرَةَ وَيَرْجُو رَحْمَةَ رَبِّهِ قُلْ هَلْ يَسْتَوِي الَّذِينَ يَعْلَمُونَ وَالَّذِينَ لَا يَعْلَمُونَ إِنَّمَا يَتَذَكَّرُ أُولُوا الْأَلْبَابِ ۝ قُلْ يَا عِبَادِ الَّذِينَ آمَنُوا اتَّقُوا رَبَّكُمْ لِلَّذِينَ أَحْسَنُوا فِي هَذِهِ الدُّنْيَا حَسَنَةٌ وَأَرْضُ اللَّهِ وَاسِعَةٌ إِنَّمَا يُوَفَّى الصَّابِرُونَ أَجْرَهُمْ بِغَيْرِ حِسَابٍ ۝

٤٥٨

adoration)* and who dreads the terrors of the life to come and hopes for the mercy of his Lord *(like one who does not)?* Say *(to them, O Muhammad):* "Can those who know and those who do not know ever be equal? But only men of understanding will pay heed.

(It is a great thing when a man attains the attitude of humble devotion to the Creator. To him the life to come is a real thing, and he prepares for it with good works. He doesn't build his hopes on the vanities of this world, but on Allah's Grace and Mercy. Such a man is a man of understanding and receives the Creator's Message with fervour and alacrity. It is not possible to compare him with a disbeliever or a cynic who knows nothing about the real value of the inner life.)

10. *(O Muhammad)* Say: "O My servants who have believed, fear your Lord. For those who do good in this world there is good, and Allah's earth is spacious. Verily those who endure with patience will be rewarded without measure.

(We must always do right. If our conditions do not allow us to act according to our belief, we must be prepared to suffer ostracism or even exile.)

11. Say (O Muhammad): "Verily I am commanded to worship Allah, making religion pure for Him (only).

12. And I am commanded to be the first of those who are Muslims (surrender to Him).

(Islam means submission, and Muslim means one who surrenders to God, obeys His orders, thus standing in harmony with the universe which obeys the laws of God also.)

(Laws of nature are called in Islam, Sunnetullah, Allah's way of handling the affairs of the universe.)

13. Say: "Lo! If I should disobey my Lord, I fear the doom of a tremendous Day.

14. Say: "I shall worship Allah alone, making my religion sincerely His.

15. As for you, worship what you will, beside Him. The real losers will be those who lose themselves and their housefolk on the Day of Resurrection. Ah, that will be the real bankruptcy.

16. They shall be covered with layers of fire from above and from beneath. This is the doom with which Allah frightens His bondsmen. So, O my servants, avoid My wrath!

17. (Contrary to this), those who put away false gods lest they should worship them, and turn to Allah in repentance, for them there are glad tidings. Therefore give good tidings (O Muhammad) to My bondsmen!

18. Who listen to the word and follow what is best in it. Such are those whom Allah has shown guidance, and such are men of understanding.

19. Who can protect the person for whom the torment has already been decreed? Can you (O Muhammad) rescue him who has already fallen into the Fire?

20. But those who truly feared their Lord, for them there are high mansions, built with storey upon storey, beneath which there will be rivers flowing. This is Allah's promise: Allah never fails in His promise.

21. Have you not seen that Allah has sent down water from the sky and has caused it to penetrate the earth as watersprings, then He brings forth thereby a variety of crops of different kinds, and afterward they wither and you see them turn yellow; then He makes them crumble away. Truly, in this is a reminder for men of understanding.

22. Is he whose breast Allah has expanded for Islam, so that he follows a light from his Lord, *(as he who disbelieves)?* Woe to those whose hearts are hardened against the remembrance of Allah. They are in manifest error.

(Those who listen to Allah's message find at each stage His grace helping them more and more to expand their spiritual understanding and to receive His light. They walk in the Light shown by the Creator. They are not to be compared to those who shut out Allah's Light from their hearts.)

23. Allah has sent down the most beautiful Message in the form of a Book, consistent with itself *(wherein promises of reward are)* paired *(with threats of punishment),* whereat the skins of those who fear their Lord tremble, and then their skins and hearts soften to Allah's remembrance. Such is Allah's guidance: He guides to the Right Way whom He wishes. But whomsoever Allah sends astray has no guide whatever.

24. Is, then, he who has to fear the severe punishment on the day of Resurrection on his face *(as he who does right)* ? And it will be said to the wrongdoers: "Taste *(the fruit of)* what you had been earning.

(The unrepentant sinners' whole being will be affected by the severe punishment on the Day of Resurrection. Their hands will not have the power to guard them. They are helpless.)

25. Those before them *(also)* denied, and so the scourge overtook them unawares.

26. Thus Allah made them taste disgrace in the life of the world, but the punishment of the Hereafter will be more terrible, if they only knew!

27. And verily We have given mankind in this Qur'an every kind of parable, so that they may take heed.

28. It is a Qur'an in Arabic, without any crookedness, that they may guard themselves against evil.

29. Allah sets forth a parable: There is a man who is shared by many *(harsh)* masters, each pulling him to himself; and there is the other man who entirely belongs to one master. Can the two be equal in comparison? Praise be to Allah! But most of them have no knowledge.

30. *(O Prophet!)* Truly you will die *(one day)* and they *(also)* will die.

31. Then on the Day of Judgement in your Lord's presence you will settle your disputes.

32. And who does greater wrong than one who utters a lie concerning Allah and denies the truth when it comes to him? Is there not in Hell an abode for disbelievers?

33. And he who came with the truth and he who confirmed it; they indeed shall be Godfearing

34. They shall have everything that they desire from their Lord: Such is the reward of those who do good.

35. That Allah will erase from their account their worst deeds, and recompense them according to the best of what they have done.

36. (O Prophet:) Will not Allah defend His slave? Yet they threaten you with other (gods) beside Him. He whom Allah lets go astray, there is no guide for him.

37. And he whom Allah guides, for him there can be no misleader. Is not Allah Mighty, and Capable of revenge?

38. And assuredly, if you should ask them who created the heavens and the earth, they will surely say, "Allah . Say: "Do you think then, of those you worship beside Allah, if Allah willed some hurt for me, could they remove from me His hurt; or if He willed some mercy for me, could they restrain His mercy? Say: "Allah is my sufficiency. In Him do the trusting repose their trust.

39. Say: "O my people! Act in your manner. So shall I. Thus you will come to know,

40. Who it is to whom comes a penalty that will abase him, and on whom descends an abiding doom.

41. *(O Prophet!)* We have sent down to you the Scripture for all mankind with the truth. Then whosoever adopts the right way, will do so for his own soul, and whosoever goes astray, injures his own soul. And you are not a warder over them.

42. Allah receives the souls at the time of their death, and those that have not yet died, during sleep. Then He witholds those for whom He has ordained death and restores the souls of others till an appointed term. Verily in this are signs for people who reflect.

43. What! Have they taken besides Allah others as intercessors? Say: *"(Will they intercede)* even if they have no power whatever, nor intelligence?

44. Say: "Intercession is wholly in the power of Allah. His is the Sovereignty of the heavens and the earth. Afterward to Him you will be brought back.

45. And when Allah the One and Only is mentioned the hearts of those who do not believe in the Hereafter are filled with repulsion and horror; and when those *(whom they worship)* beside Him are mentioned, behold! they are filled with joy.

46. Say: "O Allah, Creator of the heavens and the earth! Knower of the Invisible and the Visible! You will judge between your slaves in those matters about which they have been differing.

47. Even if the wrong-doers possessed all the wealth of the earth, and as much more, they would be prepared to offer it all as ransom to escape the terrible punishment on the Day of Resurrection; but something will appear before them which they had never anticipated.

48. There, all the evil results of their deeds will confront them, and that whereat they used to mock will surround them.

49. Now, when hurt touches man, he calls upon Us, and when We bestow a favour on him, he says; "I have been given this because of my knowledge! Nay, it is a trial. But most of them do not know.

50. Thus the *(generations)* before them said it, but whatever they earned did not avail them.

51. So, the evil results of their deeds overtook them. And the wrong-doers of this *(generation)*: the evil results of their deeds will soon overtake them *(too)*. They cannot escape.

52. And do they not know that Allah enlarges providence for whom He wills, and restricts it

(for whom He wills)? Verily, in this there are signs for people who believe.

53. *(O Prophet!)* Say: "O my slaves who have transgressed against their souls! Do not despair of Allah's mercy! Surely Allah forgives all sins; for He is the All - Forgiving, the Most Merciful.

54. Turn to your Lord repentant, and submit to Him, before the scourge overtakes you when you shall not be helped.

55. And follow the best aspect of what is sent down to you from your Lord, before the punishment comes on you suddenly while you perceive not.

56. Lest any soul should say: "Alas, my grief, that I was unmindful of Allah, and I was among those who mocked.

أَوْ تَقُوْلَ لَوْ أَنَّ اللّٰهَ هَدٰىنِيْ لَكُنْتُ مِنَ الْمُتَّقِيْنَ ۝

أَوْ تَقُوْلَ حِيْنَ تَرَى الْعَذَابَ لَوْ أَنَّ لِيْ كَرَّةً فَأَكُوْنَ

مِنَ الْمُحْسِنِيْنَ ۝ بَلٰى قَدْ جَآءَتْكَ اٰيٰتِيْ فَكَذَّبْتَ بِهَا

وَاسْتَكْبَرْتَ وَكُنْتَ مِنَ الْكٰفِرِيْنَ ۝ وَيَوْمَ الْقِيٰمَةِ

تَرَى الَّذِيْنَ كَذَبُوْا عَلَى اللّٰهِ وُجُوْهُهُمْ مُّسْوَدَّةٌ أَلَيْسَ فِيْ

جَهَنَّمَ مَثْوًى لِّلْمُتَكَبِّرِيْنَ ۝ وَيُنَجِّى اللّٰهُ الَّذِيْنَ اتَّقَوْا

بِمَفَازَتِهِمْ لَا يَمَسُّهُمُ السُّوْءُ وَلَا هُمْ يَحْزَنُوْنَ ۝ اللّٰهُ

خَالِقُ كُلِّ شَيْءٍ وَّهُوَ عَلٰى كُلِّ شَيْءٍ وَّكِيْلٌ ۝ لَهُ مَقَالِيْدُ

السَّمٰوٰتِ وَالْأَرْضِ وَالَّذِيْنَ كَفَرُوْا بِاٰيٰتِ اللّٰهِ أُولٰئِكَ

هُمُ الْخٰسِرُوْنَ ۝ قُلْ أَفَغَيْرَ اللّٰهِ تَأْمُرُوْنِّيْ أَعْبُدُ أَيُّهَا

الْجٰهِلُوْنَ ۝ وَلَقَدْ أُوْحِيَ إِلَيْكَ وَإِلَى الَّذِيْنَ مِنْ قَبْلِكَ لَئِنْ

أَشْرَكْتَ لَيَحْبَطَنَّ عَمَلُكَ وَلَتَكُوْنَنَّ مِنَ الْخٰسِرِيْنَ ۝ بَلِ اللّٰهَ

فَاعْبُدْ وَكُنْ مِّنَ الشّٰكِرِيْنَ ۝ وَمَا قَدَرُوا اللّٰهَ حَقَّ قَدْرِهِ

وَالْأَرْضُ جَمِيْعًا قَبْضَتُهُ يَوْمَ الْقِيٰمَةِ وَالسَّمٰوٰتُ

مَطْوِيّٰتٌ بِيَمِيْنِهِ سُبْحٰنَهُ وَتَعٰلٰى عَمَّا يُشْرِكُوْنَ ۝

٤٦٤

57. Or should say: "If only Allah had guided me I should certainly have been among the Godfearing .

58. Or should say when it *(actually)* sees the torment: "If only I had another chance, I should certainly be among the doers of good!

59. *(But now the reply will be:)* "Nay, My signs did come to you; and you denied them and showed arrogance, and you were among the disbelievers.

60. And on the day of Resurrection you will see those who lied concerning Allah with their faces blackened. Is there not in Hell enough room for the arrogant?

61. But Allah will deliver those who ward off *(evil)* because of their deserts. No evil shall touch them neither will they grieve.

62. Allah is the Creator of everything; and He is the Guardian over all things.

63. His are the keys of the heavens and the earth; and the losers are only those who reject the signs of Allah.

64. Say *(O Prophet, to the disbelievers):* "Is it someone other than Allah that you bid me worship, O you ignorant ones?

65. *(Tell them this plainly because)* The Revelation sent to you and to all the Prophets before you has been this: "if you ascribe a partner to Allah, all your works will be rendered vain, and you indeed will be among the losers.

66. Therefore, *(O Prophet)* you should worship only Allah and be among *(His)* grateful *(servants).*

67. And they have not esteemed Allah as He has the right to be esteemed; when the whole earth is His handful on the Day of Resurrection, and the heavens will be rolled up in His right hand. Glory to Him! And High is He above the partners which, in their idolatry, they associate with Him.

68. And the Trumpet will be sounded, and all those who are in the heavens, and the earth will swoon, except those whom Allah may allow (to live). Then the Trumpet will be blown a second time, and they will all stand up, looking.

69. And the earth will shine with the light of her Lord, and the book will be placed open, and the Prophets and the witnesses will be brought, and the people will be judged with full equity, and none will be wronged.

70. And each soul will be paid in full for whatever it had done. And He is Best Aware of what they do.

71. (After this judgement) those who had disbelieved will be driven to Hell in groups, till, when they reach it, its gates will be opened, and its keepers will say to them: "Did not messengers of your own come to you, reciting to you the revelations of your Lord, and warning you of the meeting of this your Day? They will say: "Yes, they did come, but the Decree of punishment has proved true against the disbelievers.

72. It will be said to them: "Enter the gates of Hell to dwell therein for ever. What an evil abode for the arrogant!

73. And those who had feared their Lord will be led to the Garden in groups till, when they arrive there, and its gates will already have been opened, its keepers will say: "Peace be with you! You have done well. Enter here to dwell forever.

74. They will say: "Praise be to Allah, Who has fulfilled His promise to us, and has made us inherit the land; now we can dwell in the Garden wherever we like. How excellent a reward for the doers (of right)!

75. And you *(O Muhammad)* will see the angels circling the Throne, glorifying their Lord with His praises; and the people will be judged with full equity, and it will be said: "Praise is for Allah, the Lord of the Worlds!

SÛRAH XL

AL-MU'MIN (THE BELIEVER)
Revealed at Madîna

Also known as Ghâfir, this Sûrah was revealed at Makka, with the exception of verses 56 and 57, which were revealed at Madîna. This Sûrah takes its name from verses 28-45, which describe the attempt of a believer, in the house of Pharaoh, to dissuade his people from opposing Moses and Aaron.

THE BELIEVER

In the name of Allah, the Compassionate, the Merciful

1. Hâ. Mîm.

(See surah Baqarah, verse 1 for explanation of these letters.)

2. The revelation of the Book is from Allah, the Mighty, the Knower.

3. The Forgiver of sins, the Acceptor of repentance, the Stern in punishment, the Bountiful. There is no deity beside Him. To Him is the journeying.

4. None dispute concerning the Signs of Allah except those who have disbelieved: so let not their strutting about in the land deceive you.

(Disbelievers' strutting about is a respite from Allah, and they are going to face punishment in the Hereafter.)

5. Before them the people of Noah also denied, and so did many a host after them. And every people purposed to seize their Messenger and tried to defeat the Truth by means of falsehood, but I seized them, and how *(fearsome)* was My punishment!

(Disbelievers' are reminded of those perished peoples, as their ruined dwellings were known to the disbelievers. They are warned of a similar consequence.)

6. Thus was the Decree of your Lord proved true against the disbelievers; that truly they are companions of the Fire!

7. The *(angels)* who bear the *(Divine)* Throne and those around it, all are glorifying their Lord with His praises. They affirm faith in Him, and ask forgiveness for the believers, *(saying):* "Our Lord! You embrace everything in Your mercy and knowledge, so forgive those who repent and follow Your Way: and preserve them from the torment of the Fire!

(Those who bear the Divine Throne-The Throne of Allah are the angels. They surround the Throne on all sides, singing Glory and Praise to their Lord, They cry on all sides: "Praise be to Allah, The Lord of the Worlds! The number of these angels will be about eight as it is indicated in 69/17 in Sûrah Al-Hâqqa.

the true life on this earth. And the second death is the end of life on earth which is the physical death - or the cessation of our physical life. The second life is the Resurrection. The disbelievers will ask: "Is there any way out of this?- Can we get out of hell-fire and go back to the world for a while and be a believer and die in faith and come back in the Hereafter as a believer.)

12. *(They will be answered:)* "You have incurred this *(fate)* because when Allah was invoked as the only *(object of worship)* you disbelieved, but when some partner was ascribed to Him, you were believing. Now the judgement belongs only to Allah, the Sublime, the Majestic.

13. He it is Who shows you His Signs and sends down for you provision from the sky; but only those receive admonition who turn *(to Allah)* repentant.

(The Allah's Signs shown here are vouchsafed every where and continue, and every kind of means are provided for man's "sustenance and physical, mental, and spiritual development and growth. For this Allah has mentioned in many sûrahs over and over many times. These are rain, sun and air without these nothing will grow.)

14. Therefore, *(O believers)* pray to Allah with sincere devotion, even though the disbelievers may detest it.

15. The Exalter of Ranks, the Master of the Throne. He lets the Spirit descend at His behest upon whom He will of His slaves, that He may warn of the Day of Meeting.

(Allah is the fountain of all honour, dignity, and authority, therefore, He is the One who exalts or raises ranks or degrees. He is the "Râfî . He bestows His blessing to His creatures and raises the ranks and degrees of His slaves, His angels. The "Spirit discussed in the above verse is the revelation - the Divine revelation given to his slaves. And the Day of Meeting is the day of "Meeting of all of creatures of Allah. All men will meet together and meet their Lord at the Resurrection, no matter how far scattered thay may be in this life or in the Hereafter. The ones created before will meet the latter ones. The oppressed will meet the oppressor. The created will meet his Creator.)

16. The Day when they shall rise up *(from their graves)* with nothing hidden from Allah, *(On that Day it will be asked:)* "Whose is the Sovereignty today? *(The whole universe will cry out:)* "It belongs to Allah the One, the Almighty.

8. Our Lord! Admit them to the Gardens of Paradise which You have promised them, and *(admit therein also)* of their parents and wives and children who are righteous. For You, only You, are the Mighty, the Wise.

9. And ward off from them *(all)* evils, for whomsoever You preserve from evils on the Day of Resurrection, to him You have showed great mercy. And that is indeed the supreme success.

10. The disbelievers will be addressed *(on that Day):* "Allah's wrath against you was greater than is your own anger against yourselves today, seeing that you were called to faith and you used to refuse.

11. They will say: "Our Lord! You have made us die twice and You have made us live twice. Now we confess our sins. Is there any way *(to depart from here)*?

(First death is the non-existence before the Life on this earth or the state of man being in the form of "noutfâ - embrio Or existence as clay without life is equivalent to death. And the first life begins with birth -

17. That Day every soul shall be paid for what it has earned. On that Day none shall be wronged. And Allah is swift at reckoning.

18. *(O Prophet)* forewarn them of the approaching day, when hearts will leap up to the throats and choke them; when the wrongdoers will have no friend, nor any intercessor who will be listened to.

19. Allah is aware of the treachery of the eyes, and of the secrets that the bosoms conceal.

20. Allah will judge men with fairness, but those whom they invoke besides Him can judge nothing at all. Indeed Allah alone is the All-Hearing, the All-Seeing.

21. Have they not travelled in the land to see the end of those who had gone before them? They were stronger than they in power, and *(have left)* mightier traces in the land, yet Allah seized them because of their sins, and there was none to save them from Allah.

22. That was because their messengers kept bringing them clear signs *(of Allah's Sovereignty)* and they disbelieved; so Allah seized them. Indeed, He is Mighty, and stern is His punishment.

23. And verily We sent Moses with Our revelations and a clear warrant

24. To Pharaoh, Haman and Korah, but they said: "A lying magician.

25. And when he brought them the Truth from Our presence, they said: "Kill the sons of those who believe with him, and keep alive their females. But the plot of disbelievers was futile.

(The three people mentioned in verse 24 are: Pharaoh, Haman, and Korah (Qârûn). Of the three, Pharaoh and Hâmân were coptics, but Qârûn was from the Children of Israel. As we will understand from the following verses, it is Pharaoh who gave orders: "Kill all Israelite's male children, the unknown Prophet to be born would be amongst them so kill them all with him. It is Qârûn who gave this idea to Pharaoh. Qârûn having despised priests and men of God gave this suggestion to Pharaoh according to some narrators.)

26. And Pharaoh said: "Leave me to kill Moses, and let him invoke his Lord! I fear that he will change your religion, or will cause mischief to appear in the land.

(The fact that Pharaoh said "leave me to kill Moses indicates that he was prevented from doing so. Some of the people in the court had told Pharaoh: "Moses does not deserve your fear. If you kill him you cause a suspicion to find its way to peoples hearts. If you kill him the public might think that you are unable to cap him by reasoning . Pharaoh's expression shows how afraid he was of Moses(pbwh).)

27. Moses said: "I have taken refuge in my Lord and your Lord against every arrogant one who does not believe in the Day of Reckoning.

28. And a believing man of Pharaoh's kinsfolk, who had kept his faith hidden, said: Would you kill a man merely because he says, 'My Lord is Allah?' whereas he has brought clear (signs) to you from your Lord? If he is a liar, his lie will recoil on him; but if he is truthful, some of (the dreadful things with) which he threatens you will certainly befall you. Allah does not guide one who is a transgressor and a liar.

(It is accepted that this believer is a cousin of the Pharaoh.)

29. O my people! Yours is the kingdom today, being dominant in the land, but who will save us from the wrath of Allah should it reach us? Pharaoh said: "I show you only what I see. Nor do I guide you except to the right path.

(What Pharaoh was suggesting in the above verse was the "murder of moses , but he was avoiding to tell it openly. He was hiding what he was harboring in his heart.)

30. The man who had believed, said: "O my people! I indeed fear for you a fate like that of the factions (of old);

31. Like the fate of the people of Noah, Aad, and Thamoud, and those after them. And Allah does not seek to wrong His slaves.

32. And, O my people! I fear for you the Day of Summoning,

33. A day when you will turn to flee, having no protector from Allah; and he whom Allah sends astray, for him there is no guide.

بِسْمِ اللّٰهِ الرَّحْمٰنِ الرَّحِيْمِ

وَلَقَدْ جَآءَكُمْ يُوْسُفُ مِنْ قَبْلُ بِالْبَيِّنٰتِ فَمَا زِلْتُمْ فِيْ شَكٍّ مِّمَّا جَآءَكُمْ بِهٖ ۖ حَتّٰى إِذَا هَلَكَ قُلْتُمْ لَنْ يَّبْعَثَ اللّٰهُ مِنْ بَعْدِهٖ رَسُوْلًا ۚ كَذٰلِكَ يُضِلُّ اللّٰهُ مَنْ هُوَ مُسْرِفٌ مُّرْتَابُۨ ۙ ٣٤ الَّذِيْنَ يُجَادِلُوْنَ فِيْ اٰيٰتِ اللّٰهِ بِغَيْرِ سُلْطٰنٍ أَتٰىهُمْ ۖ كَبُرَ مَقْتًا عِنْدَ اللّٰهِ وَعِنْدَ الَّذِيْنَ اٰمَنُوْا ۚ كَذٰلِكَ يَطْبَعُ اللّٰهُ عَلٰى كُلِّ قَلْبِ مُتَكَبِّرٍ جَبَّارٍ ٣٥ وَقَالَ فِرْعَوْنُ يٰهَامٰنُ ابْنِ لِيْ صَرْحًا لَّعَلِّيْۤ أَبْلُغُ الْأَسْبَابَ ٣٦ أَسْبَابَ السَّمٰوٰتِ فَأَطَّلِعَ إِلٰى إِلٰهِ مُوْسٰى وَإِنِّيْ لَأَظُنُّهُ كَاذِبًا ۚ وَكَذٰلِكَ زُيِّنَ لِفِرْعَوْنَ سُوْءُ عَمَلِهٖ وَصُدَّ عَنِ السَّبِيْلِ ۚ وَمَا كَيْدُ فِرْعَوْنَ إِلَّا فِيْ تَبَابٍ ٣٧ وَقَالَ الَّذِيْۤ اٰمَنَ يٰقَوْمِ اتَّبِعُوْنِ أَهْدِكُمْ سَبِيْلَ الرَّشَادِ ٣٨ يٰقَوْمِ إِنَّمَا هٰذِهِ الْحَيٰوةُ الدُّنْيَا مَتَاعٌ وَّإِنَّ الْاٰخِرَةَ هِيَ دَارُ الْقَرَارِ ٣٩ مَنْ عَمِلَ سَيِّئَةً فَلَا يُجْزٰىۤ إِلَّا مِثْلَهَا ۚ وَمَنْ عَمِلَ صَالِحًا مِّنْ ذَكَرٍ أَوْ أُنْثٰى وَهُوَ مُؤْمِنٌ فَأُولٰٓئِكَ يَدْخُلُوْنَ الْجَنَّةَ يُرْزَقُوْنَ فِيْهَا بِغَيْرِ حِسَابٍ ٤٠

٤٧٠

34. And verily, before this Joseph had brought to you clear proofs, but you continued to be in doubt concerning what he brought; and when he died, you said: "Allah will never send another messenger after him. Thus Allah lets the transgressors and doubters go astray.

(The interval between Joseph(pbwh) and Moses(pbwh) was not very long. Joseph's(pbwh) Pharaoh was of the people of Amalika, and Moses'(pbwh) Pharaoh of Copts. Ignoring the spiritual message, Egyptians persecuted Israelites who were in Egypt and Moses rescued them.)

35. Those who dispute Allah's signs without any authority having reached them, it is greatly hateful in the sight of Allah and in the sight of those who believe. Thus Allah seals up the heart of every arrogant tyrant.

36. And Pharaoh said: "O Hâmân, build for me a tower, that I may reach the ways.

37. The ways of *(reaching)* the heavens, and that I may mount up to the God of Moses, though I think him to be a liar. *(Pharaoh, being arrogant, thinks that the Kingdom of Heaven resembles a kingdom on earth. He envisages spiritual things in terms of material ones)* Thus was the evil that he did made seem fair to Pharaoh and he was barred from the *(Right)* Way. His plot led to nothing but *(his own)* ruin.

38. The man who had believed said: "O my people! Follow me; I shall show you the right way.

39. O my people! Verily the life of this world is nothing but a passing comfort; and the Hereafter, that is the everlasting mansion.

40. Those that do evil shall be repaid the like thereof, while those that have faith and do good works, whether male or female, shall enter the Garden, where they shall be nourished without measure.

41. And, O my people! How it is that I call you to salvation and you call me to the Fire?

42. You call me to deny Allah, and to set up with Him partners of whom I know nothing; while I call you to the Almighty, the Forgiving.

43. Without doubt, those to whom you call me have no claim in this world or in the Hereafter, and our return will be to Allah, and the transgressors are people of the Fire.

44. Soon you will remember what I say to you. To Allah I commit my cause; surely Allah is ever watchful over His servants."

45. Thus, Allah delivered him from the evils which they plotted, and the companions of Pharaoh themselves were encompassed by a dreadful scourge;

46. The Fire of Hell; they are exposed to it morning and evening; and on the day when the Hour of Resurrection comes, (a voice will cry):

"Let the people of Pharaoh enter the more awful punishment!"

(When the punishment is inflicted, it is ever present, at all times. This verse is interpreted as confirming the punishment during the period in which human being is in grave.)

47. Behold, they will dispute with each other in the Fire. The weak ones will say to those that had been haughty, "We were your followers, will you therefore save us from some portion of the Fire?"

48. Those who had been arrogant will say: "We are all in the same state here, and Allah has already judged between (His) slaves."

(Allah's judgement is to send the believers to the Paradise and disbelievers to Hell.)

49. And those in the Fire will say to its keepers, "Implore your Lord to relieve our torment for one day!"

50. They will say: "Did not your Messengers come to you with Clear Signs? They will say: "Yes . The keepers of Hell will say: "Then pray *(for help)* yourselves, although the prayer of disbelievers is in vain.

(Those in the fire) The disbelievers will turn to the angels (Keepers of Hell) asking them to pray and intercede for them. But the angels are set there to watch over them, not to intercede for them. In their innocence they ask, "Did you have no warnings from messengers, men like yourselves, in your past life? Since Prayer without faith is Delusion, it misses its mark, besides that is neither time nor place for the prayer. They (the disbelievers) should have done their prayers in their past life.)

51. We verily do help Our Messengers and those who believe, in the life of the world, and on the Day when the witnesses stand up.

(The witnesses are the angels. They will bear testimony to the fact that the messengers had preached the Truth and the disbelievers did not accept it.)

52. The day when excuses of the wrongdoers will not avail them in anything, and theirs is the curse, and theirs is the evil abode.

53. And We did give Moses the guidance and made the Children of Israel to inherit the Scripture.

54. A guide and a reminder for men of understanding.

55. Therefore have patience *(O Muhammad);* Allah's promise is true. Ask forgiveness of your fault, and glorify your Lord morning and evening with His praise.

(Allah's promise is believers' being victorians: Moses' stand against Pharaoh is a clear evidence. The Prophet sets an example for his umma: so asking Allah for forgiveness is a sunnat of him to be followed by the believers.)

56. Assuredly, those who wrangle concerning the Revelations of Allah without any authority having come to them, there is nothing but pride in their hearts; but they will never attain to their ambitions. Therefore take refuge in Allah. It is He Who hears and sees.

57. Surely the creation of the heavens and the earth is a greater thing than the creation of mankind; but most of mankind know it not.

58. And the blind and the seeing are not equal, nor are those who believe and do good works *(equal to)* the evil-doers, but you understand only a little.

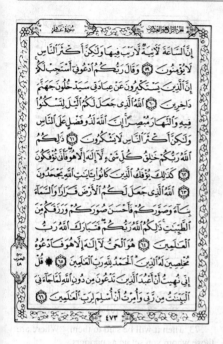

59. The Hour of Resurrection will certainly come, there is no doubt about it, yet most of mankind do not believe.

(Just like this world has beginning it will definetly have ending. The end will most certainly will come. That is the "Day of Reserruction and the Day of Judgement "The Hour is the consummation of man's life on this earth - and it is the gateway to the Hereafter and the beginning of the new life which is a permanent one.)

60. Your Lord has said: "Call on Me, and I will answer your prayers. But those who are too arrogant to worship Me will certainly certainly enter Hell, disgraced.

61. It is Allah Who made the night for you to rest in it, and made the day for seeing. Allah is full of grace and bounty to mankind, yet most people do not give thanks.

62. Such is Allah, your Lord, the creator of all things. There is no God but Him. How, then, are you being deluded?

63. Likewise are those who deny the Signs of Allah deluded.

64. It is Allah who appointed for you the earth as a dwelling-place and the sky a canopy over it, and fashioned you and made your shapes beautiful, and has provided you with pure and good things. Such is Allah, your Lord. So, Blessed is Allah, the Lord of the Worlds!

65. He is the Living One. There is no god but Him. So, pray to Him, making religion pure for Him only. Praise be to Allah, the Lord of the Worlds!

66. Say (O Muhammad) to the people: "I am forbidden to worship those whom you call upon instead of Allah, now that clear proofs have been given me from my Lord, and I have been commanded to surrender to the Lord of the Worlds.

67. He it is who created you from dust, then from a drop *(of sperm),* then from a leech-like clot, then He brings you forth as a child, then *(He ordains)* that you attain full strength and afterward that you become old men, though some of you may die before. This is done so that you may reach an appointed term, and may perhaps understand.

(The various stages of human being's physical life are mentioned in this verse. They are: 1. Simple matter, dust; 2. The sperm-drop in the father; 3. The fertilized owum in the mother's womb; 4. Coming out as a human child; 5. Youth and maturity; 6. Decay; and 7. Death. There is indication to the fact that the first human being Adam(pbwh) was created from dust, and the other stages of life is mentioned.)

68. It is He Who ordains life and death. When He decrees a thing, He only says: Be! and it is.

69. Do you not see those who dispute concerning Allah's Signs, how they are turned away ?

70. Those who have denied the Scripture and the Message with which We have sent Our Messengers will soon know:

71. When with chains and shackles round their necks they will be dragged,

72. Through boiling waters; then they are cast into the Fire.

73. Then it will be said to them: "Where are those whom you set up as partners,

74. Besides Allah? They say: "They have been lost to us; nay, we did not invoke before anything *(that had real existence.)* Thus Allah leaves the disbelievers to stray.

(The idolaters will deny that they had worshipped idols. But when they face the idols, they will be bewildered.)

75. *(And it will be said to them: "You have met this fate)* because you rejoiced in the earth in things other than the truth, and because you were insolent.

76. Enter the gates of Hell to stay therein forever. Evil is the abode of the arrogant!

77. Therefore have patience *(O Muhammad).* For the promise of Allah is true. Whether We let you witness a part of the *(evil consequences)* with which We are threatening them, or recall you *(from the world in death)* before it is fulfilled, to Us they will all return.

78. Verily We sent many a Messenger before you; of some We have already related to you the story, of others We have not. Yet it was not in the power of any Messenger to bring a sign without Allah's leave. Then when Allah's command came, the judgement was passed with justice and those who followed falsehoods then incurred loss.

(It is accepted that Allah has sent 124.000 Messengers. It is pointed out that the Messengers were 'sent' and they did not come forward through their own effort, and they were supported by miracles.

In the Holy Qur'an only 25 prophets' names mentioned and their stories are told.)

79. It is Allah Who has provided you with cattle, that you may ride on some, and eat flesh of others.

80. And you have (many) benefits from them; you may satisfy through them a desire in your hearts, and you are carried on them as well as on ships.

81. And He shows His signs. Which, then of the signs of Allah will you deny?

(Allah's signs are superiority and absoluteness of His Power.)

82. Have they not travelled in the earth to see the fate of those who had gone before them? They were more numerous and stronger in might and have left greater traces of their power in the earth; yet what they earned did not avail them in anything.

83. And when their messengers brought them clear signs (of Allah's sovereignty) they exulted in the knowledge that they already had, but soon the scourge at which they were wont to scoff encompassed them.

84. When they saw Our doom, they said: "We believe in Allah only, and reject all those gods which we used to associate with Him.

85. But when they saw Our doom, their belief could not avail them, because the same has been the (standing) law of Allah to deal with His slaves; and then the disbelievers will be ruined.

SÛRAH XLI

FUSSILAT (THEY ARE EXPOUNDED)
Revealed at Makka

This Sûrah takes its name from a word occurring in verse 3. It is also known as "Hâ-Mîm, and "al-Masâbîh .

In the name of Allah, the Compassionate, the Merciful

1. Hâ. Mîm.

2. This is a revelation from the Compassionate, the Merciful.

3. A scripture the verses of which are well expounded, a Qur'an in Arabic for people who understand,

4. Giving good news and warning, yet most of them have turned away, so that they do not hear.

(The Qur'an is explicit and not ambiguous.)

5. And they say: "Our hearts are shielded against that to which you are inviting us; our ears have become deaf, and between us and you there is a veil: so do as you will; we, too, shall do as we will.

(The tribe of Quraish expressed their unwillingness to hear Qur'an.)

6. *(O Prophet)*, say *(to them)*, "I am only a man like you. I am told by Revelation that your God is only One God; so take the straight path to Him and implore Him to forgive you. And woe to those who associate others with Him.

(Taking the straight path to Allah is possible only through belief, sincerity, obedience, and worshipping.)

7. Those who do not practise the Zakât, and are disbelievers in the Hereafter.

8. As for those who have believed and done good works, for them there is surely a reward enduring.

9. Say *(O Muhammad, to the idolaters):* "Do you indeed disbelieve in Him who created the world in two days? *(in two stages.)* And do you set up equals with Him? He is the Lord of the Worlds.

10. He set upon the earth firm mountains towering high above it, and blessed it and measured therein its sustenance in four days *(four stages)* in accordance with the needs of *(all)* those who ask;

11. Then He comprehended in His design the sky, which was smoke at that time; He said to it, and to the earth: "Come *(into being)* both of you, willingly or unwillingly. They answered: "We do come willingly.

(Allah (swt) commanded both the earth and the sky to perform their duties from what expected from them.)

12. Then He ordained them seven heavens in two Days. *(A day, in this context, may include thousands of years.)* And in each heaven He ordained its law, and We adorned the lower heaven with lamps, and made it fully secure. Such is the decree of the Mighty, the Knower.

(Ordaining in each heaven its law means creating angels, stars and the other heavenly bodies and assigning them their duties.)

13. Now, if they turn away, say: "I have given you warning of a thunderbolt of punishment like the thunderbolt which fell of old upon the tribes of Aad and Thamoud.

14. When the Messengers came to them from before them and behind them, saying: "Worship none but Allah! they said: "If our Lord had willed, He would have sent down angels *(to us)*, therefore, we are disbelievers in what you have been sent with.

(It is understood that Messengers were sent to those peoples in continuation.)

15. As for the Aad, they behaved arrogantly in the land without right, and said: "Who is mightier than us? Did they not see that Allah Who created them, is mightier than them? Yet they continued to deny Our revelations.

16. Consequently, We sent upon them a raging wind in evil days so that We might make them taste a humiliating torment in the life of this world; but the doom of the Hereafter is even more shameful, and they will not be helped.

(The days are not 'evil' as such. The implication is that they were doomed and the days that disaster fell on them, were evil days for them.)

17. And as for the Thamoud, We gave them guidance, but they preferred to remain blind rather than follow the guidance. Consequently, a humiliating doom seized them because of what they had earned.

18. And We saved those who had believed and kept their duty to Allah.

19. *(Imagine)* the time when Allah's opponents will be gathered together to be driven to Hell.

20. Then, when all will have reached it, their ears, their eyes and their skins will testify against them concerning what they had been doing *(in this world)*.

21. And they will say to their skins: "Why have you testified against us? They will reply: "The same Allah Who has given speech to everything has given us speech. He it is Who created you in the first instance, and now to Him you are being returned.

22. *(When in the world)* you hid yourselves *(while commiting crimes),* you never thought that your own ears and your own eyes and skins would ever testify against you. Rather, you thought that Allah had no knowledge of many of your works.

23. But this thought of yours concerning your Lord has ruined you, and you have found yourselves *(this day)* among the lost.

24. As such, whether they are patient or not, the Fire will still be their abode, and if they ask for favour, yet they are not of those to whom favour can be shown.

25. We had assigned them companions, who made everything, past and future, seem fair to them. And the same Decree of punishment

proved true against them, which had proved true against nations of jinn and humankind who had passed away before them. Certainly they were the losers.

(Bad companions who made sin look fair to Jinn and humankind in this life will be in Hell sharing the regrets of those who were deceived by them.)

26. Those who disbelieve say: "Do not listen to this Qur'ân, and when it is recited, drown the hearing of it, so that you may gain the upper hand.

27. We shall certainly make those who disbelieve taste a severe punishment and shall pay them back for the worst of their misdeeds.

28. That is the reward of Allah's enemies: the Fire. Therein is their eternal home: A fit requital for that they denied Our Revelations.

29. The disbelievers will say: " Our Lord! Show us the jinn and the men who misled us; we shall trample them beneath our feet, so that they become utterly disgraced *(before all).*

33. And who could be better in speech than one who calls others to Allah, does what is right, and says: "I am one of the Muslims.

(The person described in the verse is the Messenger of Allah. According to some scholars, the verse is about the muazzins calling the people to worship the Creator. It is obvious that any believer who obeys Allah's orders, behaves well and calls the others to Allah, is in this position.)

34. Good and evil deeds are not equal. Repel evil with what is better; you will see that he with whom you had enmity has become your dearest friend.

(Evil is to be repelled with what is best: for example wrath should be repelled by patience and endurance, ignorance by tolerance and persuasion, evil by forgiveness.)

35. And none is granted this except those who endure with fortitude; and none is granted this save the owner of great happiness.

36. And if you feel an incitement from Satan, seek refuge in Allah. He is the One who hears and knows.

(Incitement from Satan is preventing human being from doing good to others and should be resisted with the help of Allah.)

37. Among His signs are the night and the day, and the sun and the moon. But do not prostrate yourselves before the sun and the moon, but prostrate yourselves before Allah Who created them all, if you would truly worship Him.

38. But (it does not matter) if these people show arrogance (and still persist in their way), (let them remember) that those who are in Allah's presence glorify Him day and night, and are never wearied.

30. Those who say: "Our Lord is Allah, and further take the right path (to Him), the angels descend on them, saying: "Fear not, nor grieve, but rejoice in the good news of the Garden that has been promised to you.

(The angels will give the good tidings to the believers during the latters' death "to take the right path(to Him) has been interpreted by Abu Bakr(may Allah be pleased with him) as "to be straight forward in speaking as well as in action , by Omar(mApwh) "not to be a hypocrite by Osman(mApwh) to be sincere in action , and by Ali(mApwh) "to comply with Allah's orders . The angels' tidings about not to be afraid is pertaining to what is coming after death, and what had been done before it. Their tidings about "not to worry is pertaining to the children and dependants of the believer.)

31. We are your protectors in this life and in the Hereafter: There you will have whatever you desire, and whatever you call for will be yours.

32. A hospitable gift from the Forgiving, the Merciful!

39. And among His signs is that you see the earth dry and barren; and when We send down rain on it, it stirs to life and swells. Surely the God Who gives the dead earth life will raise the dead also to life. Indeed, He has power over all things.

40. Those who pervert the truth in Our Signs *(either by altering the scriptures or by neglecting the Signs of God around them and neglecting their duty towards Him)* are not in any way hidden from Us. Just consider who is better: he who will be cast into the Fire, or he who will emerge safe on the Day of Resurrection? Do as you will: verily He sees clearly all that you do.

("Those who pervert the truth in Our Signs means those who alter the scriptures, and give different meanings and deviate from the straight path.)

41. These are the people who rejected the Message when it came to them. But the fact is that this is a mighty Book.

42. No falsehood can approach it from before or behind it: it is a Revelation from the Wise and Praiseworthy One.

43. O Prophet, nothing is said to you that has not already been said to the Messengers before you. Surely your Lord has at His command all forgiveness, as well as a most grievous penalty.

44. Had We revealed this Qur'ân in a foreign language, they would have said: "If only its verses were expounded! Why in a foreign language, when the Prophet is Arabian? Say: "It is a guide and a healing to those who believe, and for those who do not believe, there is a deafness in their ears and a covering over their eyes. They are like men being called from afar."

45. Before this We had given Moses the Book, but there arose disputes concerning it. And had it not been for a word that had already gone forth from your Lord their differences would have been settled. But they are in a disquieting doubt about it.

('a word that had already gone forth from your Lord' means that accounting and punishment will take place on the Day of Judgement. Because of this fact, those who dispute concerning the Book, those who deny the Book do not face their punishment in this world.)

46. Whoever does good, benefits his own soul; and whoever does evil, will himself bear its consequences; your Lord is never unjust to His servants.

47. To Allah is referred the knowledge of the Hour *(of Doom)*. He alone knows all the fruits that come out from their sheaths: He alone knows which female has conceived and which has given birth. On the Day He will call mankind to Him and say: "Where are the partners you set up with Me? they will reply: "We confess that none of us can bear witness to that .

48. At that time all those gods whom they used to invoke before this will be lost to them, and they will realize that they have no way of escape.

49. Man never wearies of praying for good things. But when an evil befalls him, he loses hope and becomes desperate.

("Praying for good is asking for wealth, health, and happiness and peace and all other blessings to be bestowed by Allah. "Evil is poverty, sickness, difficulties in life and hopelessness.)

50. And if We give him a taste of mercy from Ourselves after some adversity has touched him,

he is sure to say: "This is due to my merit. I do not think the Hour of Doom will ever come. But if I am brought back to my Lord, I have much good stored in His sight! We shall certainly tell the disbelievers what they had done, and We shall make them taste a severe penalty.

(When a man acquire health and happiness after difficulties in his life. He believes that this is his own success rather than thanking God, his success is from Allah because of His mercy. And he disbelieves in the Hereafter. The above verse brings this important point to our attention.)

51. When We bestow favours on man, he turns away and holds aloof; but when evil touches him, he is long in prayer.

52. *(O Prophet)*, say to them: "Think: if this Qur'ân is indeed from Allah and you reject it, who can be more astray than one who openly defies *(Him)*?

53. We shall show them Our Signs in the world around them, as well as in their own souls, till it becomes manifest to them that *(this Qur'ân)* is indeed the Truth. Is it not enough that your Lord is watching over all things?

('Âfâq' means 'outer world', the regions around human being, 'fi anfusihim' means 'in their own souls' 'in their own biological existence'. All facts related to the Universe and innermost of human being indicates oneness of the Creator, Allah.)

54. Yet they are in doubt concerning the meeting with their Lord. Surely, He encompasses all things.

SÛRAH XLII

ASH-SHÛRÂ (THE COUNSEL)

Revealed at Makka

This Sûrah takes its name from a word in v. 38 which indicates that Muslims should make use of the principle of mutual consultation in carrying out their affairs. Verses 23-26 were revealed at Madîna.

In the name of Allah, the Compassionate, the Merciful.

1. Hâ. Mîm.

2. 'Ain. Sîn. Qâf.

3. Thus Allah the Mighty, the Wise inspires you *(O Muhammad)* as *(He inspired)* those before you.

(The Lord explained in the previous Scriptures He sent down to other prophets just like He did in the Holy Qur'an. The Letters Hâ. Mîm, 'Ain, Sin. Qâf, the mystical letters (Look p. 1 of Sûrah Al-Baqara) of al-Hurûf al Muqatta'ât are open warning to bring an attention to the readers and a mercy given to all other prophets.)

4. To Him belongs all that is in the heavens and on earth: He is the Sublime, the Tremendous.

5. The heavens are almost rent asunder above them *(by His Glory),* and the angels hymn the praise of their Lord and ask forgiveness for those on earth. Verily, Allah, He is the Forgiver, the Merciful.

(The highest heavens are almost ready to burst asunder by His Glory.)

6. And as for those who take other protectors besides Him, Allah does watch over them, and you are in no way a disposer of their affairs.

(The Prophet's duty is only to convey the message.)

7. Thus We revealed to you *(O Prophet)*, this Arabic Qur'ân so that you may warn the Mother of Cities *(Makka)* and those around it, and warn them of the Day of Gathering which is sure to

come: when some will be in the Garden, and some in the Flame.

(Makka is the centre of Islam, and "all around her' is the whole world. Implication is that Qur'an has been sent to the people of Makka and to whole humanity.)

8. Had Allah so willed, He could have made all of them one community, but He admits into His mercy whom He wills; and the wrongdoers have no protector, nor helper.

(It is one of the Signs of Allah that He has made us different, that we may be tried in the exercise of our wills.)

9. What! Have the foolish people taken other guardians besides Him? Allah alone is the Guardian: He alone gives life to the dead, and He has power over everything.

10. In whatsoever you differ, the judgement thereof belongs to Allah. Such is Allah my Lord. In Him I put my trust, and to Him I turn in repentance.

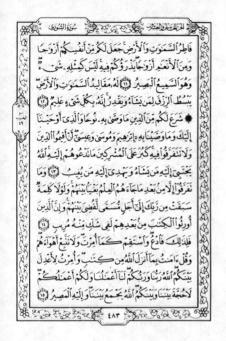

11. Creator of the heavens and the earth; He made for you pairs from your own kind, and pairs also of the cattle *(from their own kind)* so as to multiply you. There is nothing like Him *(in the universe, nothing can be compared with Him)*, and He is the Hearer, the Seer.

12. His are the keys of the heavens and the earth: He gives abundantly to whomsoever He will and sparingly to whomsoever He will; He is Knower of all things.

(the keys of the heavens and the earth are rain, plants etc.)

13. He has ordained for you the same Way of Religion which He had enjoined on Noah, and that *(O Muhammad)* We have now revealed to you, and which We had already enjoined on Abraham and Moses and Jesus, saying: "Establish the Religion and be not divided in it : Dreadful for the idolaters is that to which you *(O Muhammad)* are calling them. Allah chooses for Himself whomever He will, and guides to His way only him who turns to Him in penitence.

14. Yet they became divided only after knowledge had reached them, out of envy among themselves. And had it not been for a word that had already gone forth from your Lord, reprieving them till an appointed term, the matter would have been settled between them. Those who inherited the Book after them, have their suspicious doubts too.

(Knowledge was about punishment in Hereafter, sending of the Last Messenger. Because of a decision by Allah to punish the disbelievers in Hereafter that they do not get their punishment immediately in this world.)

15. Therefore, *(O Muhammad)* call them *(to the true faith)*, and hold fast to it yourself as you have been commanded, and do not follow their whims, but say: "I believe in whatever Book Allah has sent down, and I have been commanded to do justice between you. Allah is our Lord as well as your Lord; for us is the responsibility for our deeds, and for you for your deeds. Let there be no argument between us. Allah will bring us all together, and to Him we shall return.

(Here, the method to be followed by the Messenger has been set: Calling to Truth is to be maintained and vain proposals of disbelievers are not to be entertained.)

16. And those who argue concerning Allah after He has been acknowledged, their argument has no weight with their Lord, and His wrath will fall upon them. They will be severely punished.

(The arguments of the (Jews) have no weight with their Lord after the miracles of Allah (The Holy Qur'an) has been revealed to them. Allah's wrath will be on them in this life, and the terrible punishment in the Hereafter.)

17. It is Allah Who has revealed the Scripture with truth and the balance *(by which to weigh conduct);* and what will make you understand that the Hour of Judgement might well have drawn near?

18. Those who do not believe in its coming, seek to hasten it, but those who believe in it, dread it, and know that it is sure to come. Indeed, those who dispute concerning the coming of the Hour, in order to create doubts about it, have gone far astray.

19. Allah is kind to His slaves. He gives whatever He pleases to whom He will. He is the Invincible, the Almighty.

(As we understand from above verse Allah provides both for the believers and the disbelievers because of His Mercy. But the disbelievers will be deprived of His Mercy in the Hereafter.)

20. Whoever seeks the harvest of the Hereafter, We increase his harvest; and whoever seeks the harvest of this world, We give him of it here, but in the Hereafter he will have no portion.

(Here in the above verse Allah promises to reward those who do good deeds in this world, both in Hereafter as well as in this world. The resemblance is here is the man who ploughs and prepares the land, sows the seed and later on harvests when the season comes. The reward is sometime one to ten and sometimes one to seven hundred and sometimes even more. Allah will add manifold rewards both in material and as well as spiritual gain. But those who are only interested in the vanities of this world, they will have no portion in the Hereafter.)

21. What! Do they have partners of Allah who have made lawful for them in religion that which

Allah has not allowed? Had the decisive word not *(been pronounced already),* their fate would surely have been settled in this life. The wrongdoers will endure a painful doom.

(Allah (s.w.t.) here asking a guestion to those disbelievers who assign partners to God and deny the Resurrection and the Day of Judgement and follow the satan and those who make the lawful unlawful in religion.)

22. You will see the wrongdoers fearful of the consequence of their deeds, and it will certainly befall them. Whereas, those who have believed and done righteous deeds, will be in the meadows of the Garden : having what they wish from their Lord. This is the great favour.

23. This is what Allah announces to true believers who do good works. Say *(O Muhammad:)* "I do not ask of you any reward *(for this work)* except love of relatives. Whoever earns a good deed, We shall increase its good for him. Indeed, Allah is All-Forgiving, Appreciative.

(Prophet Muhammad is here told to tell his people to love his relatives. Since the word "Gourbâ" mentioned here means in arabic "to come close. Allah (s.w.t.) also commending prophet Muhammad to tell his people to come close to Allah (s.w.t.)

24. Or do they say: "He has forged a lie about Allah? If Allah so wills, He may seal up your heart *(against them)*. Allah will reduce falsehood to nothing and vindicate the truth by His words. Lo! He is Aware of what is hidden in the breasts *(of men)*.

(The disbelievers here accuse Prophet Muhammad to forge a lie about Allah. The Messenger of Allah is free from these kind of accusations. If the Messenger

would attempt something of that sort his heart would be sealed up against them.

25. He is the One who accepts repentance from His servants and pardons the evil deeds. And He knows all that you do.

(One should repent without losing time. Apart from wrongdoings towards other human beings, whatever the sin, Allah's Mercy is open to sincere Repentance, at all times. One should: 1. Keep away from that sinful action completely, 2. Regret for that sin, 3. Not return again to that action.)

26. He answers those who believe and do good works and gives them even more out of His bounty. But for the disbelievers there is a terrible punishment.

27. If Allah were to enlarge the provision for His servants, they would surely rebel in the earth, but He sends down in due measure what He wills. For He is of His servants Well- acquainted, Watchful.

28. He is the One who sends down the saving rain after they have despaired, and spreads abroad His mercy. He is the Protecting Friend, the Praiseworthy.

29. Among His Signs is the creation of the heavens and the earth, and the living things which He dispersed through them. And He is Able to gather them whenever He will.

30. Whatever misfortune befalls you, is for what your own hands have earned, and for many *(of them)* He grants forgiveness.

(The people in mind here are the sinful believers. The misfortune that befalls on believers that are not sinful raises their degrees in the Heaven if they are patient and they do not rebel.)

31. You are not beyond *(His)* reach in this earth, nor do you have any protector or helper besides Allah.

32. And among His portents are the ships, like banners on the sea;

33. If He wills He can calm the wind so that they keep still upon its surface. In this there are many signs for every steadfast grateful heart.

34. Or He can cause them to perish on account of that which they have earned. And He forgives much.

(It may be that a ship sinks because of sins committed by some on board. Many of them may be forgiven and saved.)

35. And that those who argue about Our Revelations may realize that they have no refuge.

36. Whatever you have been given is merely a passing comfort for the life of the world, and that which is with Allah is better and more lasting for those who believe and put their trust in their Lord.

(When Abu Bakr(mApwh) spent all his property for the cause of Islam, some criticised him, and this verse was revealed upon that occasion.)

37. And those who refrain from gross sins and shameful deeds, and when they are angry, forgive,

38. And those who answer the call of their Lord and establish worship, and whose affairs are a matter of counsel between them, and who spend of what We have given them as sustenance,

(This verse indicates form of administration and government in Islâm through counselling among themselves.)

39. And those who, when great wrong is done to them, defend themselves,

40. The recompense of an ill-deed is an ill-deed like thereof. But whosoever pardons and seeks reconciliation, his reward is with Allah. Lo! He does not love the wrong-doers.

41. And those who avenge themselves after they have been wronged, cannot be held blameworthy.

42. The way (of blame) is only against those who oppress mankind, and wrongfully rebel in the earth. For such people there is a painful doom.

43. However, the one who practices patience and is forgiving, these indeed are works of great courage and resolution.

(It is difficult to be patient and to forgive, but it is the highest and noblest form of courage and resolution.)

44. The one whom Allah sends astray, has no protector after Him. You will see the evil-doers when they see the torment, how they say: Is there any way of return?

45. And you will see them exposed *(to Hell)*, made humble by disgrace, and looking with stealthy glances. And those who believe will say: Lo! the *(eternal)* losers are they who lose themselves and their housefolk on the Day of Resurrection. Beware! Wrong-doers will suffer an everlasting torment.

(The eternal losers are those who will dwell in the Hell and will be deprived of the blessings of the Heaven.)

46. And they will have no protecting friends to help them instead of Allah. The one whom Allah sends astray, for him there is no way of escape.

47. Answer the call of your Lord before there comes the Day of which there is no chance of being averted by Allah. On that day you will have no place of refuge, nor any power of refusal.

48. Now if they turn away, We have not sent you *(O Prophet)* as a warder over them: your only responsibilty is to convey the Message. Man is such that when We let him taste Our mercy, he exults in it, and if an evil befalls him because of that which his own hands have sent before, he turns utterly ungrateful.

(Here Prophet Muhammad is warned not to worry over his people if they turn away from him. His mission is only to convey the message to them. He is not a guardian over them. The second point here is when a good falls on man he exults in it but, when misfortune befalls on him because of what his hands committed he turns ungrateful.)

49. To Allah belongs the Sovereignty of the heavens and the earth. He creates whatever He wills. He gives daughters to whom He wills, and sons to whom He wills;

50. Or He gives both sons and daughters to whom He will and makes barren whom He will. Indeed He is Knower, Powerful.

51. And it is not given to any mortal that Allah should speak to him unless it be by revelation or from behind a veil, or that He sends a messenger *(an angel)* who, by His Command, reveals whatever He wills. He is Exalted, Wise.

(Here, the forms of revelation are told. There are three ways in which Allah, in His infinite Mercy, Communicates with man as described in verses 51: (1) Speaking with Lord without seeing him from behind a veil. (2) He sends a messenger (Arch angel-Gabrial), who by His command, reveals whatever He Wills. (3) Or the inspiration put to prophets' heart by Allah.)

52. And thus We have *(O Muhammad)* revealed a Spirit to you by Our Command. You did not know what was the Scripture, nor what the Faith was, but We have made it a light whereby We guide whom We will of Our bondsmen. You are indeed guiding to a Right Way.

(The "Spirit mentioned here also means that through the command of Allah the spirit (Arch-Angel Gabrial) is sent to Muhammad. Here it is also emphasized that Prophet Muhammad is rightly guided.)

53. The way of Allah, to Whom belongs everything that is in the heavens and in the earth. Beware! All affairs shall return to Allah at last!

(Here, the believers are given glad-tidings of the rewards in the Hereafter and the disbelivers and sinners are given the warning of the punishment in the Hereafter. All affairs will be settled then.)

SÛRAH XLIII

AZ--ZUKHRUF
(ORNAMENTS OF GOLD)

Revealed at Makka

This Surah takes its name from a word which occurs in verse 35. In this Sûrah it is stressed that man's value does not depend on what he possesses of worldly riches, but on his spiritual standing.

In the name of Allah, the Compassionate, the Merciful

1. Hâ. Mîm!

2. By the Book that makes things clear,

3. We have made it a Qur'ân in Arabic so that you may understand.

4. And, verily, it is inscribed in the Mother of the Book, which We possess, sublime and full of wisdom.

(The "Mother of the Book is the original tablet preserved in Heaven from which all the Books revealed to the Prophets have been derived.)

5. Shall We then withhold, and stop sending the Reminder to you because you are a corrupt people?

6. How many a Prophet have We sent among the ancient peoples too.

7. And never came there a Prophet to them but they used to mock him.

8. So, We destroyed them though they were mightier than these in prowess; And *(thus)* has passed on the parable of the peoples of old.

9. If you ask them: "Who has created the heavens and the earth? they will surely answer: "The All-Mighty, the All-Knowing has created them.

10. Who made the earth a resting-place for you, and made in it roads for you so that you may find your way;

11. Who sent down water from heaven in due measure, and We revived thereby a dead land. Even so will you be brought out *(from the earth)*;

(In due measure: according to needs. Reviving dead land is a reminder of reviving dead people.)

12. Who created all the pairs, and appointed for you ships and cattle whereupon you ride.

13. That you may mount upon their backs, and may remember your Lord's favour when you mount thereon, and may say: "Glorified be He who has subjected these to us, otherwise we could not have brought them under control;

14. And *(one day we have to)* return to our Lord!

(Mounts should remind people of the Creator Who subdued them to human beings. The Companions thought of Hereafter when set out on a journey, they remembered the great journey which they had been taking to Eternity. The Messenger recited those verses whenever set out on a journey.)

15. Yet they attribute to some of His bondsmen a share with Him *(in His godhead)!* Truly man is manifestly ungrateful.

(Indication here is to the fact that some of the Jews accept Uzair(pbwh) as son of Allah; Christians accept Jesus(pbwh) as son of Allah and idolators of Makka had accepted angels as daughters of Allah.)

16. What! Has He chosen daughters out of what He Himself creates, and blessed you with sons?

17. Whereas, when the birth of the *(female child the like of which)* they ascribe to the Merciful God, is announced to any of them, his face grows black and he is filled with grief.

(As it is indicated in the above verses, when the birth of the female child reached them (the idolators) their faces would grow black and they would be in grief. Because of the shame! They would bury their daughter alive.)

18. *(Would they assign to Allah the offspring)* who is brought up among ornaments and is unable even to make itself clear in disputation?

(Here, the desire of the women for ornaments is indicated. And the women are weak in striving.)

19. And they regard the angels, who are themselves slaves of the Beneficent God, as females. Did they witness their creation? Their testimony will be recorded and they will be called to account.

20. And they say: "If the Beneficent One had willed *(that we should not worship them),* we should not have worshipped them. Of that they have no knowledge! They do nothing but guess.

21. Or have We given them a Book before this of which they hold an authority *(for their angel-worship)?*

22. Nay! but they say only: "We found our fathers on a *(religious)* way, and we are only walking in their footsteps.

(Thus, it is obvious that there is no base at all to worship angels; and needless to say that imitating the ancestors blindly has no value whatsoever.)

23. And even so, whenever before you We sent a warner to any township, its luxurious ones said: "We have found our fathers on a *(religious)* way, and we are only following in their footsteps.

(Here, the disbelievers claiming to imitate their forefathers and they say: "we are only following in their footsteps.)

24. *(Every Prophet)* asked them, "Will you still go on following the same old way, even if I guide you to a more right way than what you found your fathers following? They answered: "Lo! in what you bring we are disbelievers."

25. Consequently, We took vengeance on them. Consider what was the end of those who denied *(the Truth)!*

26. Recall the time when Abraham had said to his father and his people, "Lo! I am innocent of what you worship.

27. Save Him Who created me: He alone will guide me.

28. And he left behind the same Word among his descendants so that they might return.

(Prophet Abraham did not follow the footsteps of his father by setting the example that all believers should believe in One True God mainly Allah. The word "Hanif means in believing in One True God. Without doubt, at that time there were people who believed in One True God, and they were called "Hanif.)

29. *(In spite of that, when those people started worshipping others, I did not annihilate them),* but I went on providing sustenance of life to them, and to their fathers until the Truth came to them and a Messenger who expounded everything clearly.

30. But when the Truth came to them they said: "This is a sorcery, and we are disbelievers therein.

31. And they say: "If only this Qur'ân had been sent down to one of the great men of the two cities *(Makka and Tâ'if)?*

(The head of the idolotars known as Velid b. Mugire insultingly claimed : "I am the wealthiest and the ruler of Mekkâ and the wealthiest of Taif was Urva as Sakafi. While we are superior in every way to Muhammad Qur'an cannot be revealed to Muhammad.

In the eyes of Allah, the superiority is the righteousness, Prophet Muhammad although he was

an orphan he was the noblest of them because he was the descendant of Abraham-from a generation who believed in "Hanif -One True God. Despite that he was not rich.)

32. Is it they who distribute the mercy of your Lord? We have distributed their livelihood in the life of this world, and raised some of them above others in rank so that they may take one another in service; and the mercy of your Lord is better than *(the wealth)* which they amass.

(Human beings created by Allah can not decide who the prophets will be! It is Allah Who chooses the prophets. The division of wealth and positions is decided by Allah alone, who will be rich, who will be poor, strong and weak, ignorant or learned, ruler or ruled. All these are The Divine Division.)

33. And were it not that mankind would have become one community *(through love of riches)* We would have made for those who disbelieve in the Compassionate, houses with roofs of silver and stairways *(of silver)* by which they go to upper chambers,

34. And for their houses doors *(of silver)* and couches of silver whereon to recline,

35. And ornaments of gold. But all that would have been merely a provision of this worldly life; and the Hereafter with your Lord is only for the Godfearing.

36. And he whose sight is dim to the remembrance of the Compassionate, We set a devil upon him, who becomes his comrade.

37. And lo! they surely turn them from the way of Allah, and yet they deem that they are rightly guided;

38. Until, when he comes to Us, he will say *(to his comrade)*: "Would that between me and you there were the distance of the East and the West: *(you turned out to be)* a most evil comrade!

(In the Hereafter, a bad companion who misleads his friend in the life of the world he will be denounce

his friend and will say: "would that between me and you there were the distance of the East and the West: (you turned out to be) a most evil comrade!)

39. *(Then it will be said to them)*: "Now you have done wrong, it avails you nothing today that *(you and your satans)* are partners in the torment.

40. Now *(O Muhammad),* can you make the deaf hear you, or show the way to the blind and those who are in manifest deviation?

41. And if We take you away from the world, We surely shall take vengeance on them,

42. Or, *(if)* We show you their end, which We promised them; We have full power over them. *(And indeed, the doom which they were threatened befell them and the Prophet saw their end.)*

43. So, hold fast to the Book that has been revealed to you: you are surely on a Straight Way.

44. And lo! this *(Book)* is a great honour for you and your people, and you will be called to account *(for it).*

45. And ask all other Prophets whom We sent before you if We had ever appointed any other gods to be worshipped beside the Beneficent?

(None of the prophets sent before Muhammad worshipped any other god except Allah.)

46. And verily We sent Moses with Our revelations to Pharaoh and his chiefs, and he said: "I am a Messenger of the Lord of the worlds.

47. Then, when he showed Our Tokens to them, they laughed at them.

48. We showed them Token after Token, each greater than the one which went before it, and We grasped them with the torment that they might return.

49. *(Whenever a torment visited them)*, they said: "O sorcerer, entreat your Lord for us by virtue of the pact that He has made with you: we shall surely take the right way.

(The nation of Moses, the children of Israel, whenever was inflicted by a torment, they said: "O sorcerer (meaning Moses), entreat your Lord for us by virtue of the pact that He has made with you: we shall surely take the right way. But whenever Allah removed the torment from them, they went back on their word.)

50. But whenever We removed the torment from them, they went back on their word.

51. And Pharaoh proclaimed among his people: "O my people: Is not mine the sovereignty of Egypt and these rivers flowing under me? Can you not see?

(Pharaoh meant that he was better than Moses and he owned wealth, palaces, and power over his people. He also wanted to degrade Moses because he had a speach defect.)

52. I am surely better than this contemptible fellow, who can hardly express himself clearly!

53. Why, then, have bracelets of gold not been set upon him, or angels sent along with him?

54. Thus he persuaded his people to make light *(of Moses)*, and they obeyed him, for they were indeed a wanton folk.

55. So, when they angered Us, We took vengeance on them and drowned them all together.

56. And We made them a precedent from the past, and an example for later generations.

57. And when the son of Mary is quoted as an example, behold! your people laughed out,

58. And say: "Are our gods better or is he? They raise the objection only in a spirit of dispute. Truly, they are a quarrelsome people.

(Those who call themselves 'Christian' have made Jesus(pbwh) into a god. In fact, Jesus was a human being and was sent as a prophet to the children of Israel. The pagan Arabs conceived Jesus in the same category as their gods, and they wondered why a foreign god, as they saw him, should be considered better than their idols.)

59. He is nothing but a slave *(Abd Allah, "Slave of Allah , is the proudest designation among the Muslims, bondage to the Creator implying liberation from all earthly servitudes.)* whom We rendered an example for the Children of Israel.

(There is reiteration of the fact that Jesus(pbwh) was a Prophet to the Children of Israel.)

60. And if We had willed We could have set among you angels to be viceroys in the earth.

61. And (the second coming of Jesus shall be) a sign of the Hour: therefore, do not have any doubt about it, and follow Me. This is the Straight Way.

(There is indication to Jesus' descension before the Day of Judgement.)

62. And let not Satan hinder you from this: he is an open enemy for you.

63. And when Jesus came with clear proofs (of Allah's Sovereignty), he said: "I have brought wisdom to you, and have come to make plain to you the reality of those things in which you differ: so fear Allah and obey me.

64. Truly, Allah is my Lord and your Lord. So worship Him. This is the Straight Way.

65. But the factions among them differed. So, woe to those who do wrong from the doom of a painful Day.

(Some of those who call themselves 'Christian' and some of Jews claimed that Jesus(pbwh) was 'god' or 'son of God'. The indication in the verse is that they are going to be held responsible for this wrong belief.)

66. Do they now only await the Hour (of Resurrection) that it should come upon them suddenly while they are unaware?

67. Friends on that day shall be foes to one another, except those who kept their duty (to Allah).

68. O My slaves! Today you have nothing to fear, nor will there be any cause for you to grieve.

(Devotion and service to Allah result in the liberation of soul from all fear and sorrow, as regards past, present and future. Such devotion and service are shown by believing in Allah's signs, His Will, and by merging our will completely in His universal Will, which means being in tune with the Infinite, and acting in everything to further His Sovereignty.)

69. (You) who believed in Our tokens and were self-surrendered,

70. Enter the Garden, you and your wives, to be made glad.

71. For them will be passed round dishes and goblets of gold; and there will be therein all that souls could desire, all that eyes could delight in. And you are immortal therein.

72. You have inherited this Paradise by virtue of the deeds you did (in the world).

73. You have abundance of fruit here, which you will eat.

74. As for the criminals, they shall endure forever the torment of Hell.

75. It is not relaxed for them, and there they will remain despairing.

(Criminals mentioned above means, those who reject God and assign pantners to Allah s.w.t.)

76. We did not wrong them, but they themselves were the wrongdoers.

77. They will cry: "O Mâlik! *(The angel who guards Hell.)* Let your Lord make an end of us! He says: "Here you must remain.

(The disbelievers will cry: "O Malik! (The angel who guards Hell) Let your Lord make an end of us since the punishment is so severe and unbearable. They will prefer to die instead of being alive and constantly being punished. But Malik will answer to them: "Here you must remain-There is no way out!)

78. Verily, We had brought the Truth to you, but you were, most of you, averse to the Truth.

79. What! Have they settled some plan *(to conspire against the Blessed Prophet)* among themselves? But it is We who settle things.

(The reference is to the plans that the chiefs of Quraish were devising in their secret assemblies, hoping to take a decisive action against the Holy Prophet. In fact, man cannot settle the high affairs of the universe. If they plot against the Truth, the Truth will destroy them, just as, if they accept the Truth, the Truth will make them free. It is Allah Who deals with affairs.)

80. Do they think that We do not hear their secret talk and private confidences? *(We hear everything and)* Our angels at their sides are recording it.

81. Say *(O Muhammad):* "If *(Allah)* the Compassionate had a son, I would be first among his worshippers. *(But there is no son.)*

82. Glory to the Lord of the heavens and the earth, the Lord of the Throne *(of Authority)!* *(He is free)* from the things they attribute *(to Him)!*

83. So let them babble and play *(with vanities)* until they meet the Day which they are promised.

84. And He it is Who in the heaven is God, and in the earth is God. He is the Wise, the Knower.

85. And blessed is He to whom belongs the dominion of the heavens and the earth, and all that is between them, and with Whom is knowledge of the Hour *(of Judgement).* And to Him you will be returned.

86. And those whom they invoke besides Him have no power of intercession, except him who bears witness to the Truth knowingly.

(Contrary to the belief of the idolators, the idolotars who assign partners to God have no power of intercession. But prophets Jesus, Uzair and angels will have the power of intercession with permission of Allah for the believers who bear witness to the truth knowingly.)

87. And if you ask them who created them, they will surely say: "Allah . How then are they deluded away *(from the Truth)?*

88. *(Allah has knowledge)* of the *(Prophet's* cry: "O my Lord! Truly these are a people who don't believe! .

89. Well, bear with them *(O Muhammad)* and say: "Peace to you . Soon they shall know.

SÛRAH XLIV

AD-DUKHÂN (SMOKE)

Revealed at Makka

This revelation explains clearly how worldly pride and power are humbled if they resist spiritual forces, and how Evil and Good find their true context in the Hereafter.

In the name of Allah, the Compassionate, the Merciful

1. Hâ. Mîm.

2. By the Lucid Book.

3. We sent it down in a blessed night, for We are ever warning.

(Usually accepted to be a night in the month of Ramadân, probably the 27th. This is the Night of Glory, or Power. The night that a Message comes down from the Creator is indeed a blessed night, like a day of rain for a parched land.)

4. In that night every affair of wisdom is made distinct.

5. As a command from Our presence, for We *(ever)* send *(revelations),*

6. As a Mercy from your Lord. For He hears and knows *(all things).*

(It is because Allah is the friend of the friendless and the helper of the helpless that He hears all sincere prayers, and as His knowledge embraces all things, He grants to us whatever is best for us, not as we see it, but as He knows it in His perfect knowledge.)

7. Lord of the heavens and the earth and all that is between them, if you would really believe.

8. There is no god but He. *(Allah is the real God, Who alone deserves to be rendered every species of service and worship.)* It is He Who gives life and death. He is your Lord, and Lord of your forefathers.

9. Nay, but they play in doubt.

10. But watch you *(O Muhammad)* for the day when the sky will produce visible smoke,

11. That will envelop the people. This will be a painful punishment.

12. *(Then they will say:)* "Our Lord, relieve us of the torment. For we are really believers!

(The commentators have two interpretations about this smoke - Ad - Duhân(1) The smoke means famine and drought. At the time of prophet Muhammad there was a famine and drought and the people of Quraish came to the prophet and asked to be relieved of this torment.(2) This smoke is one of the signs of the end of the world "the Final Hour. According to the narration Prophet Muhammad (s.a.w.) This smoke will cover from East to West.)

13. How can there be remembrance for them, when a messenger making plain *(the Truth)* had already come to them,

14. And they had turned away from him and said: "One taught *(by others),* a man possessed ?

15. We shall indeed remove the torment for a while, *(but)* you will revert *(to your ways).*

(Allah gives every chance to all His creatures, however rebellious. He gives them a trial, perhaps personal, perhaps economic, to see if it would bring them to their senses.)

16. On the day when We seize them with the greater seizure, *(then)* in truth We shall punish.

17. And verily We tried before them Pharaoh's folk, when there came to them a noble messenger,

18. Saying: "Give up to me the slaves of Allah. I am to you a faithful messenger.

19. And be not arrogant against Allah. For I bring you a clear warrant.

("Clear warrant here, is the miracles that Moses (p.u.h.) was able to show with the permission of God.)

20. And I have taken refuge in my Lord and your Lord, lest you should assault me *(by stoning).*

(Prophet Moses did not pay attention to the threats of the Pharaoh's people; he told them: "I have taken refuge in my Lord.)

21. If you do not believe in me, keep away from me.

22. *(But they were aggressive.)* And he cried to his Lord, saying: "These are indeed a guilty folk.

23. Then *(his Lord commanded):* "Take away My servants by night; for you will be followed.

24. And leave the sea as a furrow *(divided):* for they are a host *(destined)* to be drowned.

(For the passage of Moses and his people, the sea had divided: they were to pass through the furrow and leave it alone, to lure on the Egyptian host, on which the sea afterwards closed in, destroying them.)

25. How many were the gardens and watersprings they left behind.

26. And the cornlands and the noble buildings,

27. And pleasant things wherein they took delight!

28. Thus *(was their end)!* And We made it an inheritance for other folk.

29. And neither heaven nor earth wept for them, nor were they reprieved.

30. And We delivered the Children of Israel from the shameful doom;

31. *(We delivered them)* from Pharaoh. For he was arrogant *(even)* among inordinate transgressors.

(Pharaoh had enslaved the Chidren of Israel. He used to kill their sons.)

32. And We chose them, purposely, above the nations,

33. And We gave them portents wherein was a clear trial.

(From its degrading servitude, Israel was delivered, and taken to a land flowing with milk and honey, where later they established the glorious

kingdoms of David and Solomon. But their being chosen did not mean that they could do what they chose. In this sense there is no "chosen race before Allah. But Allah gives every race and every individual a chance, and when they fail to live up to it, they fall and give place to others. Among the portents given to Israel were their own Revelation under Moses, their prosperous land of Canaan. their splendid Kingdom under David and Solomon, and the advent of Jesus to reclaim the lost ones among them. All these were trials. When they failed in the trials, they were left to wander through the earth.)

35. "There is nothing beyond our first death, and we shall not be raised again.

36. Bring back our fathers, if what you say is true!

37. What! are they better than the people of Tubba' *(a name for many kings of Himyar, i.e. the South Arabians)* and those before them? We destroyed them, for surely they were guilty.

38. And We did not create the heavens and earth, and all that is between them, in play.

39. We did not create them except with truth; but most of them do not understand.

40. Assuredly the Day of Decision is the term for all of them.

(In the Day of Judgement, the distinction between right and wrong will be made. The word "fasl" is used here to indicate the separation of the friends and relatives. Those who believe will go to paradise those who disbelieve go to Hell.)

41. A day when no protector can avail his client in aught, and no help can they receive,

42. Save him on whom Allah has mercy: for He is Exalted in Might, Most Merciful.

43. Verily the tree of Zaqqûm

(A tree which grows in Hell, the exact counterpart of the exquisite fruits of the Garden.)

44. Is the food of the sinner!

45. Like molten brass; it will boil in their bellies,

46. Like the seething of scalding water.

47. (And it will be said:) Take him and drag him to the midst of the Blaze!

48. Then pour over his head the torment of boiling water.

49. (Saying:) Taste! Truly you were the mighty, the noble!

50. Truly this is what you used to doubt.

51. As to the righteous, (they will be) in a place secure.

52. Among gardens and watersprings;

53. Dressed in fine silk and in rich brocade, facing one another.

54. Even so (it will be). And We shall wed them to fair ones with wide, lovely eyes.

55. There they call for every kind of fruit in safety.

56. There they will not taste death, except the first death; and He will preserve them from the punishment of hell.

57. As a bounty from your Lord! That is the supreme triumph!

58. Verily, We have made this (Qur'ân) easy in your language, that they may heed.

59. So wait (O Muhammad and watch); for they (too) are waiting.

SÛRAH XLV

AL-JÂTHIYA (CROUCHING)

Revealed at Makka

This Sûrah derives its name from a word occurring in v.28, which describes the condition of our race on the Final Day.

In the name of Allah, the Compassionate, the Merciful.

1. Hâ. Mîm.

2. The revelation of the Scripture is from Allah, the Mighty, the Wise.

3. There are signs for believers in the heavens and in the earth.

(There signs indicate Unity of Allah and His Absolute Power.)

4. And in your own creation, and all the beasts that He scatters *(all over the earth)*, there are signs for a folk whose faith is sure.

(The most interesting of these signs is creation of human being and the stages he passes through during coming into being.)

5. And the succession of night and day, and the provision that Allah sends down from the sky, whereby He revives the earth after its death, and in the circulation of the winds, are signs for people who have sense.

6. These are the Signs of Allah, which We recite to you *(Muhammad)* with truth. Then what is there, after Allah and His Signs, in which they will believe?

7. Woe to each sinful liar,

8. Who hears the Signs of Allah recited, yet persists in his disbelief arrogantly as if he never heard them. Give him tidings of a painful punishment.

9. When something of Our Signs comes to his knowledge, he takes it as a jest. For all such people there is an abasing torment.

10. Beyond them there is hell, and that which they have earned will naught avail them, nor those whom they have chosen for protecting friends beside Allah. Theirs will be an awful doom.

(Their gains, children, property and the objects of their worshipping will be of no avail to them in Hereafter.)

11. This *(Qur'ân is true)* guidance, and for those who have refused to believe in the Signs of their Lord, there is a painful doom of wrath.

12. Allah it is Who has made the sea of service to you, that the ships may sail in it by His command, and that you may seek of His bounty *(through trade)*, and that haply you may be grateful to Him;

13. And He has subjected to you everything that the heavens and the earth contain; it is all from Him. There are many signs in this for those who reflect.

14. *(O Prophet)*, tell the believers to pardon the errors of those who do not fear the days of Allah, so that Allah may Himself recompense a group for what they have earned.

(The "Days of Allah" are the stages through which man passes towards inner purity; or, alternatively, the days of the coming Kingdom.)

15. Whoever does good, does so for himself, and whoever does evil will himself bear its burden. And afterward to your Lord you will be brought back.

16. Before this, We had bestowed on the Children of Israel the Book and the Command and the Prophethood, and provided them with good things, and favoured them above (all) peoples.

(The Children of Israel had been given Torah, they were made sovereigns of the Earth, and Moses and Aaron were sent as Messengers to them.)

17. And gave them plain commandments. Then they differed among themselves *(not because of ignorance but)* after the Knowledge had come to them, through rivalry among themselves. Your Lord will judge between them on the Day of Resurrection concerning that in which they used to differ.

(The Children of Israel knew about the Prophethood of Muhammad(pbwh). They thought that the Last Messenger would have been sent among them. Therefore, because of jealousy they did not accept him.)

18. And now We have set you *(O Muhammad)* on a clear road of *(Our)* commandment; so follow it, and do not follow the whims of those who have no knowledge.

(The notables of Quraish had been trying to make the Prophet relinquish his duty. The verse warns him against their desires and foolish proposals.)

19. They cannot avail you at all against Allah *(That is, "If you make changes in Allah's Religion only to please these people, they will not be able to save you from Allah's judgement and punishment.")* The wrongdoers are companions of one another while the Companion of the righteous is Allah.

20. These are lights of discernment for mankind, and guidance and mercy for those who are certain.

(This Qur'an is undeceiving.)

21. Or do those who commit evil deeds suppose that we shall make them as those who believe and do good works, the same in life and death? Bad indeed are the judgements they pass!

(Disbelievers will be punished in Hereafter, no matter how affluent they are in this world; and believers will be rewarded abundantly.)

22. And Allah has created the heavens and the earth with truth in order that every soul be rewarded for what it has earned. And they shall not be wronged at all.

23. Then, have you ever considered the case of the person who made his desire his god, and Allah let him go astray in spite of (his) knowledge, and set a seal upon his heart and ears and laid a covering on his eyes? Then who will lead him after Allah *(has condemned him)*? Do you learn no lesson?

24. And they say: "Life is only this worldly life of ours. Here we shall die and live and nothing but time destroys us. In fact, they have no knowledge concerning this: they merely guess.

(Some who deny revival and Hereafter think that time or nature causes death, being unable to perceive the real cause, beyond time and nature: The Creator of time and nature. They have no proof whatsoever. They only guess.)

25. And when Our clear revelations are recited to them, their only argument is that they say: "Bring *(back)* our forefathers if you are truthful.

26. Say *(to them, O Muhammad):* "Allah gives you life, then He causes you to die, then gathers you together on the day of Resurrection, which is sure to come. But most people do not know.

27. And to Allah belongs the sovereignty of the heavens and the earth, and when the Day of the Hour of Resurrection arrives, on that day those who follow falsehood will be lost.

28. At that time you will see each nation crouching, each nation summoned to its record. *(It will be said to them):* "This day you are requited for what you used to do.

(Each community will be brought to the Presence of Allah and their records will be given to them, and then the individuals will be rewarded or punished according to their deeds in the worldly life.)

29. This Our Book pronounces against you with truth. Assuredly, We have caused *(all)* that you did to be recorded.

(The angels record all human beings' actions. These records will testify against those who do wrong against others.)

30. Then, as for those who believed and did good works, their Lord shall admit them to His mercy; this is the manifest success!

31. And as for those who disbelieved, *(it will be said:)* "Were not My Revelations recited to you? But you showed arrogance, and became criminals.

32. And when it was said, 'Allah's promise is true, and there is no doubt about the coming of the Hour *(of Armageddon)*, you used to say, 'We do not know what the Hour is; we only guess; we are not certain.'

('Promise' is interpreted as revival after death.)

33. And the evils of what they did will appear to them and they will be encompassed by what they used to mock.

(Whatever the disbelievers committed will appear to them in the Hereafter. Because of the evils they have committed they will be encompassed by what they used to mock.)

34. It will be said to them: "This day we forget you, even as you forgot the meeting of this your day; and your habitation is the Fire, and there is none to help you.

35. *(You have met this fate)* because you took Allah's Revelations in jest, and the life of the world deluded you. Therefore, neither shall they be taken out of Hell today, nor shall they be asked to make amends.

(Those who deserve torture are disbelievers who did not accept Hereafter and mocked with Qur'an. Their repentance in Hereafter will be of no avail to them.)

36. So, praise be to Allah alone, Lord of the heavens and Lord of the earth, the Lord of the Worlds.

37. To Him belongs Majesty in the heavens and the earth, and He alone is the Mighty, the Wise.

SÛRAH XLVI
AL-AHQÂF
(THE WIND-CURVED SANDHILLS)

Revealed at Makka

Takes its name from the word al-Ahqâf, which occurs in verse 21, refering to a characteristic of the region in which the tribe of 'Aad had lived.

In the name of Allah, the Compassionate, the Merciful.

1. Hâ. Mîm.

2. The revelation of the Scripture is from Allah, the Mighty, the Wise.

3. We have created the heavens and the earth and all that lies between them only with truth and to last for an appointed term, but the disbelievers are turning away from that of which they have been warned.

(The verse states that all that has been created, proves the Absolute Power of the Creator.)

4. *(O Prophet)*, say to them: "Have you thought on all that you invoke beside Allah? Show me what they have created in the earth. Or have they any portion in the heavens? Bring me a Book revealed before this, or produce some remnants of knowledge *(in support of your beliefs)* if you are truthful.

(In fact, all the objects of worship besides Allah have no effect whatsoever in the creation.)

5. And who is further astray than the one who invokes, instead of Allah, those who cannot answer him till the day of Resurrection, and are unconscious of their prayer.

(Because idols are without life and intellect, they are man-made objects.)

6. And when mankind are gathered *(to the judgement)* will become enemies for them, and will become deniers of having been worshipped.

(In Hereafter, idols become enemy of those who worship them in this world.)

7. And whenever Our clear revelations are recited to them, and the Truth comes before them, the disbelievers say: "This is plain magic.

8. Do they mean to say that the Messenger himself has fabricated it? Say *(O Muhammad):* "If I have fabricated it myself, you will *(still)* not be able to do anything to save me from Allah. He is best aware of whatever you utter. He is enough as a witness between me and you; and He is the Forgiving, the Merciful.

(This is the most silencing reply to all those who claim that the Messenger fabricated it.)

9. Say to them: "I am no new thing among the Messengers. *(Just as all the former Prophets were mortals who had no share in Divine attributes and powers, so am I.)* I do not know what shall befall you tomorrow or what shall befall me. I only follow that which is revealed to me, and I am no more than a plain warner.

(Prophet Muhammad here, is warning the idolotars of Mekkâ that he does not know what shall befall them in the future and what shall befall him. He is not first of the prophets but he is the last of the prophets who has come as a plain warner. It is up to the people of Mekkâ to learn lessons from the past. All the prophets came before him were mortals and so was he.)

10. *(O Prophet),* say to them: "Have you ever considered that if this *(Qur'an)* were really from Allah, and yet you denied it, *(what would be your end)?* And a witness from among the Children of Israel has already borne witness to the like of it; he believed while you showed arrogance. Allah does not show guidance to wrongdoers.

(The important point here is that Qur'an has been sent down by Allah (s.w.t.) without any doubt. The best witness to this is prophet Moses as it was told in Torah who believed that there will a *prophet* after him. So did Jesus. Since Moses is from the Children of Israel - The Jews should believe in Prophet Muhammad and accept The Holy Qur'an to be the Word of Allah.)

11. And those who disbelieve say of those who believe: "If it had been *(any)* good, they

would not have been before us in attaining it. As they have not accepted any guidance from it, they will surely say: "This is an ancient falsehood.

(Among the first Muslims there were slaves and poor people. The notables of Quraish refers to this fact.)

12. Yet before it there came the Book of Moses as a guide and a mercy; and this Book has been revealed to confirm it in the Arabic language so as to warn the wrongdoers and to give good news to those who do good.

(The verse reiterates that there was Torah before Qur'an as a Book of Guidance, and Qur'an endorses the previous books.)

13. Indeed those who said: "Allah is our Lord then remained steadfast, no fear shall come upon them, neither shall they grieve.

14. They are people of the Garden, wherein they shall live for ever, as a reward for the deeds they used to do.

15. We have enjoined man to treat his parents with kindness. His mother bore him with trouble and she gave him birth with trouble, and his bearing and his weaning took thirty months, until, when he attained to his full strength and became forty years old, he said: "O my Lord, grant me the grace to thank You for the favours You have bestowed on me and on my parents, and to do such good works as may please You. And be gracious to me in my progeny. I turn to You in penitence, and I am of those who have surrendered to You (as Muslims).

(It is been narrated by interpreters of the Holy Qur'an that the cause of revelation of this verse is Hz. Abu Bak (R.A.) Abu Bakr. (R.A.) completed his fortieth birthday after two years when Muhammad (S.A.W.) received his prophethood. The age of full strength and manhood is the age of forty. His spiritual faculties also grow and gain upper hand after forty. Man should treat his parents kindly that is what exactly what Abu Bakr R.A. did prayed for his parents and saved many people who were being persecuted by the

idolotars. He bought their freedom out. The greatest blessing is to enter into Islâm and do good deeds that will please Allah.)

16. From such people We accept the best of their deeds and overlook their evils. They will be among the dwellers of the Garden according to the true promise that has been made to them (in the world).

(Allah will accept and reward people like Abû Bakr and the believers like him because of the best of their deeds. And Allah will overlook their evil deeds.)

17. And who says to his parents: "Fie upon you! What, do you frighten me with this, that I shall be taken out (of the grave after death)? Whereas many a generation has passed away before me (and none has risen from among them). And they both cry for Allah's help and say: "Believe, O wretch! Allah's promise is true. But he says: "These are nothing but tales of the ancient times.

(The argument between father and mother and their child is presented. The disobedient child who rejects God. And does not believe in his parents.)

18. Such are the people against whom the decision of torment has already been decreed. They will also join those hosts of the jinn and men (of their own kind) who have passed away before them. Indeed, they are the losers.

19. And for all there will be ranks according to their deeds, so that Allah may reward them fully for what they have done, and they will not be wronged.

(The believers will be high, in the paradise the disbelievers will be deep in Hell.)

20. And on the day when those who disbelieve are exposed to the Fire, it will be said to them: "You have exhausted your share of the good things in your life of the world and sought comfort in them. Now today you are rewarded with the punishment of disgrace because you were arrogant in the land without any right, and because you used to transgress.

21. And *(O Muhammad)* relate to them the story of the brother of Âad *(the Prophet Hud)* - when he warned his folk among the wind - curved sandhills - and verily warners came and went before and after him *(saying):* "Worship none but Allah. I fear for you the torment of a mighty day.

(The people of Âad used to live in the sandhills overlooking the sea. This area was called "Al-Ahqâf.)

22. They said: "Have you come to seduce us away from our own gods? Well, bring that with which you threaten us, if you are really truthful.

23. He said: "The knowledge of this is with Allah only. I convey to you the message with which I have been sent. But I see that you are a people sunk in ignorance.

(In answer to his people prophet Hûd told them "the knowledge of time when the punishment will come is with Allah only.)

24. Then, when they saw the torment coming towards their valleys, they said: "This is a cloud that will give us much rain. Nay, but it is that which you asked to be hastened: a wind bringing a painful torment.

25. Destroying all things by commandment of its Lord. Thus, there remained nothing to be seen except their *(empty)* dwellings. Thus do We recompense the guilty.

(Only Prophet Hud(Âad) and the believers were saved.)

26. And verily We had empowered them with that wherewith We have not empowered you, and had assigned them ear s and eyes and hearts; but nothing did their ears and eyes and hearts avail them, because they denied the Revelations

of Allah, and what they used to mock befell them.

27. And verily We have destroyed habitations around you. We showed them the signs in various ways that they might return.

(Those habitations were those of the people of Samud, Âad and Lot.)

28. Then why did not those *(beings)* help them, whom they had made their gods instead of Allah, and regarded them as a means of attaining nearness to Him? *(They had put faith in those beings with the idea that they were favourite servants of Allah through whom they would attain nearness to Him, but then, gradually, they made them their gods: they started invoking them for help and praying to them.)* Nay, they were lost from them: and this was *(the end of their)* lies and *(their false beliefs that)* they had invented.

(In this verse Allah (s.w.t.) rejects the idea that their false gods will bring them close to Allah.)

29. And recall the event (O Muhammad) when We brought to you a group of the jinn so that they might listen to the Qur'ân. (This happened during the Holy Prophet's return from Tâ'if to Makka.) When they reached the place they said to each other: "Give ear! and when the recitation was over, they returned to their people as warners.

(When prophet Muhammad was performing morning prayer in the valley of Nahl on his return from Taif Expedition. A group of people of the Jinn (seven or nine) came to listen the recitation of the Holy Qur'an by prophet Muhammad. They listened and when they returned to their own people of Jinn they testified the Truth about the Holy Qur'an.)

30. They said to them: "O our people! We have just listened to a Book that has been sent down after Moses. It confirms what came before it, and it guides to the Truth and to a Straight Road.

(This indicates that these jinn had already had faith in the Prophet Moses and the Holy Books. On hearing the Qur'ân, they understood that it was from the same

Divine Source, and believed in it and the Holy Prophet.)

31. O our people! Respond to Allah's summoner and believe in Him. He will forgive you your sins and guard you from a painful torment.

(In this verse the people of Jinn are commanded to respond to invitation of Prophet Muhammad to enter into Islâm.

The condition of the people of Jinn is a matter of argument by different scholars. According to Abû Hanîfe, although the Jinn will be saved from the punishment of Hell-fire-They will not be rewarded. Where as the other scholars like Imâm Mâlik, Abu Leylâ, Abu Yûsuf and Muhammad argue that they will be saved from the Hell-fire and also will be rewarded.)

32. And he who does not respond to Allah's summoner neither possesses any power in the earth to make Allah helpless nor has any protector to save him from Him. Such people are in manifest error.

33. Have they not seen that Allah, Who created the heavens and the earth and was not wearied by their creation, is Able to give life to the dead? Yes, surely He has power over everything.

34. The day when those who disbelieve are exposed to the Fire, they will be asked: "Is not this the Truth? They will say: "Yes, by our Lord, this is the very Truth! . Allah will say: "Then taste the punishment in consequence of your denying the Truth.

35. Therefore, have patience (O Muhammad) as did the Messengers endowed with firmness of purpose, and do not be in haste concerning them. On the day when they see that which they are threatened, it will appear to them that they had not stayed in the world for more than an hour of a day. The Message has been conveyed. Now, shall any other than the disobedient people be destroyed?

(Here in the above verse Prophet Muhammad is advised to have patience with the difficulties that he was facing at his time. The other prophets came before him faced also many difficulties but they stayed firm in their purpose and never gave up.)

SÛRAH XLVII

MUHAMMAD

Revealed at Madîna

This Sûrah takes its name from the mention of the blessed Prophet in verse 2.

In the name of Allah, the Compassionate, the Merciful

1. Those who disbelieved and debarred others from Allah's Way; He rendered their actions vain.

(People of Makka resisted Islam, and persecuted those who entered Islam. The verse states that because of their disbelief, their good deeds were rendered vain. Through belief one becomes in harmony with oneself and the whole universe.)

2. And those who believed, and did good works, and accepted that which has been sent down to Muhammad - and it is the very Truth from their Lord - Allah removed their sins from them and set their condition right.

3. That is because the disbelievers followed falsehood and the believers followed the Truth which has come from their Lord. Thus does Allah coin their similitudes for mankind.

4. Now, when you meet the disbelievers in the battle-field, first smite their necks; then, when you have crushed them completely, bind *(the prisoners)* tight. Then either grace or ransom, until war lays down her burdens. That is the ordinance. And if Allah had willed, He would Himself have dealt with them. But *(He has adopted this way)* so that He may test some of you by means of others. And those who are slain in the way of Allah, He will not render their actions vain.

(According to this verse the disbelievers who follows falsehood, have to be smited by their necks when they are faced in the battle-field. When they are crushed or subdued completely, they have to be bound tight. At the end of the war they can be either freed by grace or exchanged for a ransom. That is the commandment of Allah. Those who are slain for striving for the *cause of* Allah, their efforts will not be vain and they will be rewarded.)

5. He will guide them and improve their state.

6. And will admit them to the Garden with which He has acquainted them.

7. O you who have believed; if you help Allah, He will help you, and make your footsteps firm.

8. As for those who have disbelieved, for them is destruction; and Allah has set their deeds astray.

9. That is because they have hated what Allah has sent down; therefore did He make their deeds fruitless.

10. Have they not travelled in the earth, that they could see the end of those who had gone before them? Allah obliterated them; and the disbelievers are destined for a similar end.

(The disbelievers here are warned how the other nations came before them were destroyed because of their disobedience and wrongdoing so the disbelievers of Mekkâ are reminded to take lessons from these historical evidences and travel in thè land take lessons from the evidences of the destroyed nations.)

11. That is because Allah is the Protector of the believers, and the disbelievers have no protector at all.

12. Allah shall admit those who have believed and done good works into Gardens beneath which rivers flow; while the disbelievers take their comfort in this life and eat even as the cattle eat; and the Fire is their final abode.

(The verse defines here the behavior of the disbelievers in the life of this world how they indulge themselves in eating (like cattle) and enjoying illegal and promiscuous sex, and enjoying the comforts of this life.)

13. (O Prophet), how many a township stronger than your township which has expelled you, have We destroyed, and they had no helper!

(The township in this verse is Mekkâ. The disbelievers are reminded that the townships stronger than Mekkâ were destroyed in the past.)

14. Can it ever be that he who is on a clear guidance from his Lord be like those whose evil deed has been made to seen fair to them, and who are following their own caprices?

15. The Garden that has been promised to the righteous is such that rivers will be flowing in it,

of unpolluted water, and rivers will be flowing in it of milk of unchanged flavour, and rivers will be flowing in it of wine which will be delicious to the drinkers, and of honey, clear and pure. (According to the explanation given in a Hadith, the wine in Paradise will not have been distilled from rotten fruit, the honey will not have been drawn from the bees' bellies, but all these drinks will flow in the form of natural springs.) In it there will be fruits of every kind for them, and pardon from their Lord. (Are those who enjoy all this) like those who are immortal in the Fire, and are given boiling water to drink so that it tears their bowels?

16. Among them are some who give ear to what you say, and when they leave you, they ask those who have been blessed with knowledge: "What did he say just now? Those are they whose hearts Allah has sealed, and they follow their own caprices.

(The hypocrites' behaviors are discribed here. When they are in the presence of Prophet Muhammad they listen his sermons and talks but, when they leave they ask the islamic scholars what did the prophet say. Of course their purpose is to mock. Because of their hypocrcy their heart is sealed.)

17. While as for those who have received guidance, Allah increases their guidance and grants them their piety.

18. Do they then only await the Resurrection, that it should come upon them unawares? And the beginnings thereof have already come. But when it overtakes them, what chance will there be for them to accept admonition?

(Here in the above verse, the beginning of the "Final Hour has already come. The signs for them are: The coming of the last Prophet Muhammad, the split of the moon into two halves, the famine and the black cloud which will appear.)

19. So, know (O Prophet), that there is none worthy of worship but Allah, and ask forgiveness for your fault, and for the believing men and women, too, for Allah is aware of your busy movements and also your resting place.

(Allah (s.w.t.) is aware of our busy movements 'this world' and the resting place 'Hereafter'.)

20. And those who believe say: "If only a Sûrah were revealed! But when a decisive Sûrah is revealed in which fighting is mentioned, you see those in whose hearts is a disease looking at you like *(someone)* under the shadow of death. Therefore, woe unto them!

(Here a decisive verse is revealed about fighting with the idolotars of Mekkâ. Allah (s.w.t.) is disgracing those in whose hearts there is a disease 'hypocrisy'.)

21. *(On their tongue is)* the promise of obedience and civil word. Then, when the matter is determined, if they are loyal to Allah it will be well for them.

(When the decision is taken about jihad, the believers should not hesitate nor they should shun.)

22. Would you then, if you were given the command, work corruption in the land and sever your ties of kinship?

(Those who do not keep their word when they enter in to Islam are guilty of hypocrisy and disobedience they would be going back as if they are going to live the life of ignorance before Islâm.)

23. Such are they whom Allah cursed, and made them deaf and blind.

24. Will they then not meditate on the Qur'ân, or are there locks upon their hearts?

25. Those who turn back after guidance has become clear to them, for them Satan has made their way easy and prolonged for them false hopes.

(Indication here is that if people who have believed, turn back or become hypocrites, their actions are governed by Satan and they are the losers.)

26. That is because they say to those who hate what Allah has revealed: "We shall obey you in some matters. Allah knows their secret affairs well.

(Indication is to the hypocrites.)

27. Then how *(will it be with them)* when the angels take their souls, smiting their faces and their backs!

28. That will be because they followed the way that made Allah wrathful, and hated to adopt the way of His pleasure. Therefore, He has made all their works fruitless.

(This refers to all those works they performed as hypocritical Muslims. Their prayers, their fasting, their payments of Zakât and all other acts of worship and goodness, which in appearance and form are counted among good works, were rendered void, for they failed to adopt the attitude of sincerity and loyalty towards Allah and Islam and the Muslim community, even though they professed to be Muslims; but on the contrary, they conspired with the enemies of Islam merely for worldly gains).

29. Or do those in whose hearts is a disease deem that Allah will not expose their rancour?

30. And if We would, We could show them to you, and then you should know them surely by their faces. But you will certainly know them from the manner of their speech. And Allah is fully aware of your actions.

(After the revelation of this verse, the Messenger recognised all the hypocrites.)

31. And verily We shall try you till We know those of you who strive hard, and the steadfast, and till We test your record.

(The believers will be tested for their firmness of faith.)

32. Those who disbelieve and hinder others from Allah's Way and dispute with the Messenger after the guidance has been manifested to them, can in no way harm Allah, but Allah indeed will render all their works of no effect.

(Those who disbelieve and hinder others from Allah's way and dispute with the Messenger are the Jews of Quraish and Nadir and the idolotars that were

killed in the battle of Badr. It is indicated in the above verse that Allah will indeed render all their works of no effect.)

33. O you who believe! Obey Allah and obey the Messenger and render not your actions rain.

34. And as for those who disbelieve and hinder others from Allah's Way and die as disbelievers, Allah will never pardon them.

35. Therefore, do not be faint-hearted, and do not beg for peace, for you will surely gain the upper hand. *(It should be remembered that when this discourse was revealed, only a handful of the Muslims consisting of some hundreds of the Muhajirin and the Ansâr living in the small habitation that was Madîna were upholding the standard of Islam although faced by the whole of pagan Arabia. Such were the conditions prevailing when they were exhorted "not to be faint - hearted and not to implore the enemy for peace , but to make preparations for a decisive conflict.)* Allah is with you and will never let your works go to waste.

36. The life of the world is but a sport and a pastime. If you believe, and follow the way of piety, He will give you your rewards and will not ask you for your wealth.

(That is, 'Allah is Self-Sufficent: He does not need to take anything from you for himself. If He tells you to spend something in His way, He does so not for Himself, but only for your own good).

37. If He were to ask it of you, and press you, you would be niggardly, and He would bring your malice out.

(The test that man faces in regard to wordly belongings is discussed here.)

38. Behold, you are those who are called to spend in the way of Allah, yet among you there are some who hoard, whereas the one who is niggardly is, in fact, being niggardly only to himself. Allah is Rich; it is you who are the needy. If you turn away, Allah will replace you with another folk, and they will not resemble you.

(The believers are supposed to spend what is prescribed to them.)

SÛRAH XLVIII
AL-FATH (VICTORY)

Revealed at Madîna

The Fath refers to the truce of Al-Hudaibiyyah, which proved a very great victory in terms of spreading Islam. This Sûrah was revealed between Makka and Madîna in the sixth year of the Hijrah.

In the name of Allah, the Compassionate, the Merciful.

1. *(O Prophet)*, We have indeed given you a manifest victory,

2. That Allah may forgive you of your sin that which is past and that which is to come, and may perfect His favour upon you, and may guide you on a right way,

(Perfecting heavenly favour upon the Messenger has been seen in the fact that he was victorious in his struggle, he has become the most prominent human being in history, his name is mentioned along with the name of Allah on many occasions.)

3. And that Allah may help you with strong help.

(The victory mentioned in this verse is the conquest of Makka and Taif. Two majors cities that opposed prophet Muhammad. Those who opposed the prophet also were defeated. The prophet gained dignity and honour through the Mercy of Allah against his enemies. The prophet is the most Beloved person by Allah (s.w.t.) He is blessed with the "Midnight Journey His name is been mentioned in many places besides Allah in prayers. Many other blessings are given to him.)

4. He it is who sent down tranquillity into the hearts of the believers so that they may have more Faith added to their Faith. *(Sakinah denotes tranquillity and peace of mind. This implies the patience and calm that the Muslims displayed at Hudaibiyyah in spite of provocative circumstances, and thanks to their complete faith in the leadership of the Holy Prophet which enabled them to overcome the difficult situation. This was yet another favour of Allah).* Allah's are the hosts of the heavens and the earth, and Allah is ever Knower, Wise.

5. That He may bring the believing men and the believing women into Gardens underneath which rivers flow, wherein they will abide, and may remit from them their evil deeds - That, in the sight of Allah, is the supreme triumph -

6. And may punish the hypocritical men and the hypocritical women, and the idolatrous men and the idolatrous women, who think an evil thought concerning Allah. For them is the evil turn of fortune, and Allah is wroth against them and has cursed them, and has made ready for them hell, a hapless journey's end.

7. Allah's are the hosts of the heavens and the earth, and Allah is ever Mighty, Wise.

8. *(O Prophet)*, We have sent you as a witness, as a bearer of good news and as a warner.

9. So that you, *(O mankind)*, may believe in Allah and His Messenger, and may help him *(i.e. the Messenger)* and honour him, and glorify Allah morning and evening.

(The duties of the prophet are to witness those who believed in him in the Hereafter. To give glad-tidings to the believers of Heaven and to warn the disbelievers of Hell-fire.)

10. *(O Prophet)*, those who swear allegiance to you, swear allegiance only to Allah. The Hand of Allah is above their hands. *(That is, the hand on which the Muslims were swearing fealty was not the hand of the Prophet's person, but of Allah's representative, and thus allegiance was in fact being sworn to Allah through His Messenger.)* Now, whosoever breaks this pledge breaks it at his own peril, and whosoever keeps his pledge that he has made with Allah, Allah will grant him a great reward. *(The reference is to the oath of allegiance that the Holy Prophet took from his Companions at Hudaibiyyah, following the rumour that Hadrat Uthmân had been killed at Makka. This oath was taken so that if the news of Hadrat Uthmân's martyrdom proved to be true, the Muslims would settle their account with the Quraish there and then, even if they were cut to pieces in the clash.)*

11. Those of the wandering Arabs who were left behind will tell you: "Our properties and our households kept us occupied; so ask forgiveness for us. *(This refers to the people living in the suburbs of Madîna whom the Holy Prophet had invited to accompany him while making preparations for 'Umrah, but who had not left their homes despite their claim to faith, because they were afraid of death. They thought that going for 'Umrah to Makka, the stronghold of the Quraish, on that occasion was merely to walk to their own deaths.)* They say with their tongues that which is not in their hearts. Say to them: "Well, if it is so, who then can have any power to withold Allah's decree on your behalf if He intends to do some harm to you or bring to you some good? Allah is well aware of your actions.

12. *(But the truth is not what you say:)* Nay, you rather thought that the Messenger and the believers would never return to their families, and this fancy delighted your hearts and you harboured evil thoughts, and you were a worthless folk.

13. And whoever does not believe in Allah and His Messenger, for such disbelievers We have prepared a blazing Fire.

14. To Allah belongs the Sovereignty of the heavens and the earth. He may pardon whomever He will and punish whomever He will. And Allah is ever Forgiving, Merciful.

15. Those who were left behind will say, when you set out to take the spoils: "Allow us too to go with you. They wish to change Allah's decree. Tell them plainly: "You will not come with us. Allah has already said this before. They will say: "Nay, but you are jealous of us. *(Whereas there is no question of jealousy)*, but they understand little.

(On the sixth year of the Islamic Calender Hijrah after returning from Hudaibiyyah the prophet took off to capture Khayber. After this victory, lots of spoils were captured. Those who stayed behind wanted to have share in the spoils. Since they did not take part in fighting, they did not take shares in the spoils as it is explained in the above verse.)

16. Tell the desert Arabs who were left behind: "You will soon be called upon to fight a mighty people. You will have to fight them, or they will submit. Then if you obey, Allah will give you a good reward, but if you turn your backs as you did before, Allah will punish you with a painful torment.

(Those who stayed behind 'from fighting' will be tested again by being called to fight mightier people 'Persians, Romans, and after the death of Prophet Muhammad those who went back to disbelief: Yamana, Musaylamat-ul Kazzab and those who followed them Children of Hanafi.)

17. However, there is no blame if the blind and the lame and the sick do not come forth *(for Jihâd)*. Whosoever obeys Allah and His Messenger, Allah will admit him into Gardens underneath which rivers flow; and the one who turns away, He will punish him with a painful doom.

18. Allah was well pleased with the believers when they swore allegiance to you under the tree. And He knew what was in their hearts; therefore, He sent down peace of reassurance on them and rewarded them with a near victory;

(The alliance mentioned above is the 'Alligiance of Rıdvan' under the tree of Samra at Hudaibiyah. About 1400 of the prophet's companions swore to fight to death with Quraish until the end. Allah sent down peace of reassurance on them and rewarded them with a near victory 'conquest of Khaibar'.)

19. And much booty that they will capture. *(The reference is to the conquest of Khaibar.)* Allah is ever Mighty, Wise.

(Muslims captured Khaibar and acquired lots of spoils.)

20. Allah promises you rich spoils which you will acquire. *(This refers to the other victories that the Muslims achieved after Khaibar).* Presently He has granted you this *(victory, i.e. the treaty of Hudaibiyyah)*, and has restrained the hands of the people from you *(He restrained the disbelieving Quraish from attacking you at Hudaibiyyah although to all appearances they*

were in a much better position and yours was much weaker) so that it may be a sign to the believers, and that He may guide you to a right way.

21. Besides, He promises you other spoils as well, which you are not as yet able to take, and Allah has encompassed them *(most probably the conquest of Makka);* Allah is Able to do all things.

22. If the disbelievers fight you, then they with certainly turn their backs and will find no protector or helper.

(If the disbelievers would choose to fight instead of signing the 'Treaty of Hudaibiyah'. They would loose the war and run away and no one to find to help them.)

23. This is the way of Allah that has been followed in the past, and you will find no change in the way of Allah.

24. It is He who restrained their hands from you, and your hands from them, in the valley of Makka, after He granted you victory over them, and Allah is Seer of what you do.

(Indication is to Hudaibiyyah, where the Muslims caught armed Makkans and set them free.)

25. They are the ones who disbelieved and debarred you from the Inviolable Place of Worship, and hindered the sacrificial animals from reaching their place of sacrifice. Had there not been certain believing men and women *(in Makka)* whom you did not know that you were trampling them and for whom a crime would have been incurred, *(the fighting would not have been allowed to stop. It was stopped)* so that Allah may admit into His mercy whom He will. Had the believers stood apart *(from the people of Makka),* We would have severely punished the disbelievers among them.

(This was the reason why Allah did not allow fighting to take place at Hudaibiyyah. At that time there were quite a number of Muslims living in Makka, who were either hiding their Faith or were being persecuted

as they had no means to migrate. If there had been fighting, and the Muslims had pushed back the disbelievers and entered Makka, those Muslims might also have been killed in ignorance along with the disbelievers.)

26. When the disbelievers had set up in their hearts zealotry, the zealotry of the Age of Ignorance, then Allah sent down His peace of reassurance upon His Messenger and the believers, and obliged the believers to adhere to the word of piety, for they were most worthy and deserving of it. And Allah is Aware of all things.

(The importance of piety is the most important point to pay attention to. This verse is related to the incident happened at the time of signing the "Treaty of Hudaibiyah" The idolotars of Mekkâ refused to recognize the prophet's signature as the 'Messenger of Allah.' The believers were very sad about this, but remembering the adherence of piety in above verse calmed them down. The prophet dictated Hd. Ali to write as "This treaty is between Muhammad son of Abdullah and the people of Makkâ." The idolators accepted and signed the treaty.)

27. Indeed Allah had shown His Messenger a true vision, according to the truth: "You will surely enter the Inviolable Place of Worship, if Allah wills, in full security; you will have your heads shaved, your hair shortened, and you will have nothing to fear. He knows what you do not know. Therefore, He granted you this near victory before *(the fulfiment of the vision).*

28. He it is Who has sent His Messenger with guidance and the religion of truth, that He may cause it to prevail over all religion. And Allah is enough for a witness.

(Prophet Muhammad before he left for Hudaibiyyah he saw a dream that he and his companions (as their heads shawed) were entering in Makkâ victoriously. His componions were very happy about his dream which they (as usual) might come true. When the believers were prevented from entering into Makkâ that year they were disappointed. Some of the hipocrites took advantage of this and started to talk to believers about this that prophet's dream did not come through, not knowing that the next year the prophet's dream did come through and the believers entered into Makkâ without blood-shed. This is the wisdom and plan of Allah that-the hypocrites can not conceive.)

29. Muhammad is the Messenger of Allah, and those who are with him are stern against the disbelievers and merciful among themselves. When you see them you will find them bowing down and falling prostrate and craving for Allah's bounty and grace. They have the marks of prostrations on their faces by which they are distinguished. This is their description in the Torah; and in the Gospel they have been likened to a crop which put out its shoot, then strengthened it, then swelled and then stood on its own stem, filling the sowers with delight and the disbelievers with rage at them. Allah has promised those of them who believe and do good works, forgiveness and an immense reward.

(In this verse the comparison of the companions of the prophet at the beginning of Islam and later years is made. The Muslims were few in number and they were weak at the beginning, but later on they grew in number and became strong. The resemblence is made to a crop which puts out its shoot (from a seed) then becomes strong and swells and stands on its stem. That is the growth of Islâm.)

SÛRAH XLIX

AL-HUJURÂT

(THE PRIVATE APARTMENTS)

Revealed at Madîna

This Sûrah deals with manners, and particularly with behaviour toward the Holy Prophet. It takes its name from the word "Hujurât in verse 4.

In the name of Allah, the Compassionate, the Merciful.

1. O you who believe, do not be forward in the presence of Allah and His Messenger (but follow behind: do not precede them but be subordinate to them. Do not decide your matters yourselves by your own initiative, but look for the guidance given in Allah's Book and the Way of Life of His Prophet concerning these matters) and keep your duty to Allah. Allah is Hearer, Knower.

2. O you who believe, do not raise your voices above the Prophet's voice, nor shout when speaking to him as you shout one to another, lest your works be rendered void while you do not perceive.

3. Those who subdue their voices in the presence of the Messenger of Allah, are, in fact, those whose hearts Allah has proven to righteousness. For them is forgiveness and a great reward.

4. (O Prophet), those who call out to you from behind the apartments, most of them have no sense.

(A group of Bedouins came while the Messenger was sleeping in his room at noon. They shouted to him to come out. The verse was revealed on that occasion.)

5. And if they had had patience until you came out to them, it had been better for them. *(Some of the people who came to see the Holy Prophet from different parts of Arabia were so uncouth and impolite that instead of informing him of their arrival through some attendant they would start shouting, to call him from outside the apartments of his wives. This sort of behaviour troubled the Holy Prophet much, but he was tolerant on account of his natural clemency. At last, Allah had to intervene, Who reproved the people for their uncivilized behaviour and gave this instruction: Whenever they came to see the Holy Prophet and did not find him, they should wait for him patiently until he came out to them himself, instead of shouting to call him out.)* And Allah is Forgiving, Merciful.

6. O you who believe! If a wicked person brings you some news, inquire into it carefully lest you should harm others unwittingly and afterwards be sorry for what you did.

(Walid, son of Oqbah, was sent by the Messenger of Allah to the tribe of Mustaliq. There was enmity between Walid and that tribe from the time of jahiliy-yah.So, Walid became apprehensive and returned and stated that tribe of Mustaliq had apostated. The Messenger sent Halid son of Walid to make inquires. The verse was revealed on that occasion and it sets a guideline for muslims.

The Muslims should follow this guiding principle: whenever you receive an important piece of news, you should not accept it immediately but should first examine the person who brings it. If he is an unrighteous person whose report may not be normally trusted, you should inquire into it carefully to find out the truth, instead of accepting it and acting on it immediately.)

7. And know that the Messenger of Allah is among you. If he were to obey you in many matters, you would surely fall into distress. But Allah has endeared the Faith to you and beautified it in your hearts, making unbelief, wrongdoing and disobedience abhorrent to you. Such are they who are rightly guided.

8. *(It is)* a bounty and a grace from Allah; and Allah is Knower, Wise.

9. And if two parties of the believers fall to mutual fighting *(mutual fighing is not the character of Muslims, nor should it be. However, if, such a thing ever happens the procedure that follows should be adopted:)* make peace between them. And if one party of them does wrong to the other, fight that which does wrong till it returns to the ordinance of Allah. Then if it returns, make peace between them justly and act equitably. Allah loves those who do justice.

10. The believers are naught else than brothers. Therefore make peace between your brethren and observe your duty to Allah, that you may obtain mercy.

11. O you who believe! Let not a group mock another group; it may be that these are better than they; nor should women mock other women, it may be that these are better than they. *(Mocking does not only imply mocking with the tongue but also includes mimicking somebody, making pointed references to him, laughing at his words, or his work, or his appearance or his dress, or calling people's attention to some defect in him so that others also may laugh at him).* Do not taunt one another nor call one another by nicknames. It is an evil thing *(to be called a)* bad name after faith. Those who do not desist are wrongdoers.

12. O you who believe! Avoid much suspicion, for in some cases suspicion is a crime. Do not spy *(on one another)*, nor backbite one another. Would any of you like to eat the flesh of his dead brother? Surely you would abhor it. Have fear of Allah. He is Forgiving and Merciful.

(The Prophet defined backbiting thus: "It is speaking of your brother in a way that is irksome to him. It was asked: "What if the defect being talked of is present in my brother? The Holy Prophet answered: "If it is present in him, it would be backbiting, and if it is not present, it would be slander. The sole exception here are cases where talking ill of a person in his absence may be a real necessity, which cannot be met without resort to backbiting, and if backbiting is not resorted to, there is a likelihood of this resulting in a bigger evil.)

13. O mankind! We have created you from a male and a female, and then rendered you nations and tribes so that you might know one another. Indeed, the most honourable among you in the sight of Allah is he who is the most pious. Allah is Knower, Aware.

(All human beings are equal at birth. Since all of them are descendants of Adam and Eve. So, no one should brag about his ancestary being superior to other. The only superiority among human beings is piety.)

14. The Arabs of the desert say: "We believe! Say *(to them O Muhammad):* "You do not; rather say: 'We profess Islam', for faith has not yet entered your hearts. If you obey Allah and His Messenger, He will not diminish anything from your works. Surely Allah is Forgiving, Merciful.

(The Arabs of the desert mainly Children of Asad came to Prophet and said to him. "We entered into Islâm." And we did not fight against you like the

other." The verse indicates that they only said with their tongue whereas their faith have not entered into their hearts. It was time of the famine they asked charity from the prophet by pretenting that they entered in Islâm.)

15. The true believers are those who have faith in Allah and His Messenger, and do not doubt, and who fight for His cause with their wealth and their lives. They indeed are the truthful ones.

16. Say *(to them, O Prophet):* "Would you teach Allah your religion, when Allah knows what the heavens and the earth contain, and He has knowledge of all things?

17. They regard it as a favour to you that they embraced Islam. Say: "Count not your Islam as a favour to me. It was Allah who bestowed a favour on you, in guiding you to faith, if you are sincere.

18. Allah has knowledge of every hidden thing in the heavens and the earth; and He sees whatever you do.

SÛRAH L

QÂF

Revealed at Makka

Takes its name from a letter in the first verse.

In the name of Allah, the Compassionate, the Merciful.

1. Qâf. By the glorious Qur'ân.

2. Nay, but they marvel that a warner of their own has come to them; and the disbelievers say: "This is a strange thing:

3. When we are dead and have become dust *(shall we be brought back again)?* That would be a far return!

4. *(Whereas)* We know very well whatever the earth consumes of *(their bodies)*, and with Us is a recording Book.

5. Nay, but they denied the Truth when it came to them. That is why they are confused now.

6. Have they never observed the sky above them *(and marked)* how We built it up and furnished it with ornaments, leaving no crack *(in its expanse)?*

7. We spread out the earth and set upon it immovable mountains. We brought forth in it all kinds of delightful plants.

8. An enlightenment and reminder for every penitent slave.

9. And We have sent down from the sky blessed water with which We have brought forth gardens and the harvest grain.

10. And lofty date-palms with ranged clusters:

11. Provision *(made)* for men; thereby giving new life to a dead land. Even so shall be the Resurrection.

(The dead land is revived by water, a new life comes to plants and trees. Human being also will come out of the land on the Days of Resurrection. The One Who revives the earth, is surely Able to revive the people.)

12. Before them, the people of Noah and the people of the Rass denied the Truth; and so did Thamoud,

13. And *(the tribe of)* Âad, and Pharaoh, and the brethren of Lot.

14. And the dwellers of the Forest *(Midian)* and folk of Tubba' *(the famous dynasty in the Yaman):* all disbelieved their messengers and thus brought down upon themselves My threatened warning.

(There is consolation to the Messenger reminding him of the other Messengers whose people did not obey them and thus incurred punishment.)

15. Were We then worn out by the first creation? Yet they are in doubt about a new creation.

(Allah is not tired of the first creation, so, He is Able to create again, and this is not a difficult task for Him.)

16. We created man, and We know the promptings of his soul, and We are nearer to him than his jugular vein.

17. *(And beside this direct knowledge of Ours)*, two scribes, sitting on his right and on his left, are recording *(everything)*.

18. Each word he utters is noted down by a vigilant guardian.

19. And when the agony of death justly comes, "This is what you have striven to avoid.

20. And the Trumpet is blown. This is the threatened Day.

21. Every person comes, a driver with it and a witness.

(The word "driver" means here is one of the two angels assigned to each person who records the bad deeds and takes him to the Day of Judgement. And the "witness" is the other angel on the right, who records the good deeds of every person 'or soul' in the Day of Judgement.)

22. *(To the evil-doer will it be said:)* "You were heedless of this. Now We have removed your veil from you, so your sight this day is sharp.

23. And his comrade *(one of the two angels, or a faculty)* will say: "My testimony is ready.

24. *(And it is said:)* "Cast into hell every stubborn disbeliever,

25. Hinderer of good, transgressor, doubter,

26. Who has set up another god besides Allah. Hurl him to the terrible doom.

27. His comrade *(the devil chained to him)* will say: "Our Lord! I did not mislead him. He was already gone far astray.

28. Allah will say: "Do not dispute in My presence. I gave you warning.

29. My word cannot be changed, nor am I unjust to My servants.

30. On that day We shall ask Hell: "Are you full? and Hell will answer: "Is there any more?

31. And the Garden is brought close to the righteous, no longer distant.

32. It will be said: "Here is all that you were promised; it is for every penitent and heedful one,

33. Who fears the Compassionate in secret and comes with a contrite heart.

34. Enter Paradise in Peace. That will be the Day of Eternity.

35. There they have all that they desire, and there is more with Us.

("There is more with Us" in this verse means: Allah (s.w.t.) will make it possible for that righteous person to see his Creator in the Hereafter. Some interpreters also say that it means blessings that never seen by any human eye or never heard by any human being. It can also means that blessings that have no limit.)

36. And how many a generation We destroyed before them, who were mightier than these in prowess so that they overran the lands! Had they any place of refuge *(when the judgement came)?*

37. Surely in this there is a lesson for every man who has a heart or gives ear with full attention.

38. And verily We created the heavens and the earth, and all that is between them, in six days *(XXII, 47; XXXII, 5; LXX, 4),* and never were We touched by fatigue.

(There refutation of the jew's claim that Allah created the universe in six days and He rested on Saturday. It is out of question that He would be tired and rested.)

39. Therefore *(O Muhammad)* bear with what they say, and glorify your Lord before sunrise and before sunset.

(The verse here means the daily prayers of morning, noon and midafternoon.)

40. And in the night-time, hymn His praise, and after the *(prescribed)* prostrations.

41. And listen on the day when the crier will call from nearby;

(The word "Mighty Blast" is used for Resurrection Men will rush out from all corners of the world to answer the call 'Mighty Blast'.)

42. The Day when they will hear the *(Awful)* Cry in truth. On that day they will rise up *(from their graves).*

(The Angel Israfil will blow the horn twice. On second blow people will rise up from their graves come to the place of Judgement.)

43. It is We Who ordains life and death. And to Us all shall return.

44. On that day when the earth will be rent asunder from them, *(and they shall rush forth)* in haste. That is a gathering which is easy for Us.

45. We are best aware of what they say, and you *(O Muhammad)* are in no wise a compeller over them. But warn by the Qur'an whoever fears My warning.

SÛRAH LI
ADH-DHÂRIYÂT
(THE SCATTERING WINDS)

Revealed at Makka

The "Scattering Winds takes its name from the word Adh-Dhâriyât, which occurs in the first verse.

In the name of Allah, the Compassionate, the Merciful.

1. By those *(winds)* that scatter *(dust),*

2. And those that bear the burden *(of the rain),*

3. And those *(ships)* that glide with ease *(upon the sea),*

4. And those *(angels)* who distribute *(blessings)* by command,

5. That which you are threatened is indeed true,

6. And the Judgement will indeed befall.

7. By the heaven with its starry highways,

8. You have discordant opinions!

(The idolaters could not unite in misnaming the Messenger: some called him magician, some called poet, some sorcerer.)

9. None but those who are made perverse turn away *(from the true faith).*

10. Woe to the lie-makers,

11. Who are careless in a pit.

12. They ask: "When is the day of Judgement?

13. On that Day they will be tormented at the Fire.

14. *(And a voice will say to them):* "Taste your torment. This is what you have sought to hasten!

15. The righteous will dwell amid gardens and watersprings,

16. And will receive what their Lord shall give them. For they were aforetime doers of good.

17. They used to sleep but little of the night.

18. Praying at dawn for Allah's pardon.

19. And in their wealth the beggar and the outcast had due share.

20. And in the earth are portents for those whose faith is sure.

(Everything indicates to the existence of the Creator.)

21. And *(also)* in yourselves. Can you not see?

22. And in the heaven is your providence and that which you are promised;

23. And by the Lord of the heavens, and the earth, this is true, as true as you are speaking now!

(Man should not doubt hearing the truth, as he would not doubt hearing his own voice.)

24. Have you heard *(O Muhammad)* the story of Abraham's honoured guests?

25. When they came in to him and said: "Peace! he answered: "Peace! *(and thought):* Folk unknown *(to me).*

26. He betook himself to his family and returned with a fatted calf.

27. And he set it before them, saying: "Will you not eat?

28. Then he grew afraid of them, but they said: "Have no fear, and gave him tidings of *(the birth of)* a wise son.

(This son was Isaac(pbwh).)

29. Then his wife came crying and beating her face. "Surely I am a barren old woman, she said.

30. "Such is the will of your Lord, they replied. "He is the Wise One, the All-Knowing.

(The person meant here is the aged wife of Prophet Abraham when she heard the news of having a son, she was bewildered and surprised. She said "I am a woman of old age (meant that she cannot have a baby) but for Allah nothing is impossible. He is the Mighty.)

31. "Messengers", said Abraham, "What is your errand?"

32. They said: "We are sent forth to a wicked nation.

33. That we may bring down on them *(a shower)* of clay-stones.

34. Marked by your Lord for the destruction of the sinful."

35. Then We saved all the faithful that were there,

36. We found in it but one household of Muslim believers.

37. And We left behind therein a portent for those who fear a painful doom.

(The portent was: stones, accumulated rocks and black water.)

38. In Moses too *(there was a portent)*. We sent him forth to Pharaoh with clear authority.

39. But he turned his back, he and his nobles, saying: "He is either a sorcerer or a madman."

40. So We seized him and his hosts and flung them in the sea, for he was reprobate.

(The pharaoh was seized when he was reprobating for claiming to be the Lord, for rejecting th Lord of Moses, and being stubborn about it.)

41. And in *(the fate of)* 'Âad *(there is a portent)*, when We sent the fatal wind against them.

42. Which turned to dust all that it swept before it.

43. And in *(the tribe of)* Thamoud *(was another portent)*, when it was told them: "Take your ease awhile."

44. But they disobeyed the command of their Lord, and so the thunderbolt struck them while they were looking on;

45. And they were unable to get up, nor could they save themselves.

46. And the folk of Noah aforetime. They too were corrupt men.

47. We built the heaven with might, and We it is who make the vast expanse.

48. And We have laid out the earth. Gracious is He Who spread it out!

49. And all things We have created by pairs, that haply you may reflect.

("Pairs" means-everything is created in pairs. For example: man and woman, earth and sky, sun and the moon, valley and mountain, land and sea, summer and winter, life and death, sweet and bitter, dark and light etc. By thinking the opposite creations one can contemplate the greatness of God and believe in him.)

(Reflection on the creature in pairs guides to perceiving Unity of the Creator.)

50. Therefore flee to Allah. I am a warner to you from Him.

51. Set up no other gods besides Allah. I am a warner to you from Him.

(The Prophet of God, Muhammad is inviting his people to believe in One True God and not to assign partners to Him.)

52. Even so, whenever a messenger came to those that were before them they cried: "Sorcerer!" or "Madman!"

53. Have they handed down this *(cry)* from one generation to the next? Surely they are transgressors.

54. *(O Muhammad)* Withdraw from them; you will incur no blame.

(Because the Messenger had carried out his duty for a long time.)

55. And warn, for warning profits believers.

56. I created the jinn and humankind only that they might worship Me.

57. I seek no livelihood from them, nor do I ask that they should feed Me.

58. Allah! He it is that gives livelihood, the Lord of unbreakable might.

(It is Allah who gives livelihood. He does not need man and Jinn for livelihood. He is "Rezzaq". He is the Giver.)

59. The lot of the wrongdoers is like the lot of their companions *(of earlier generations).* Let them not challenge Me to hurry it on.

(The Nations of the past who assigned partners to Allah and disobeyed, they got their punishment by being destroyed. The idolators of Makkâ will get the same punishment like their companions of earlier generations.)

60. And woe to those who disbelieve, because of the day which they have been promised!

SÛRAH LII
AT- TÛR (THE MOUNT)
Revealed at Makka

This Sûrah takes its name from the word Al-Tûr which occurs in the first verse.

In the name of Allah, the Compassionate, the Merciful.

1. By the Mount *(Sinai.)*
2. And a Scripture inscribed.
3. On fine parchment unrolled.

4. And the House frequented *(the Ka'ba).*

5. And the roof, exalted *(the sky),*

6. And the sea kept filled,

7. Lo! the doom of your Lord will surely come to pass;

8. There is none that can ward it off.

(The mountain discussed in above verse is the Mount Sinai where Moses met with His Lord. The Scripture inscribed is Torah, and The Holy Qur'an, and the place in the heaven where permenant records are being kept. And the House mentioned here is Ka'bah.)

9. On that day the heaven will shake and reel.

10. And the mountains move and pass away.

11. Then woe that day unto the deniers.

12. Who play in talk of grave matters;

13. The day when they are thrust with a *(disdainful)* thrust, into the fire of Hell.

14. *(And it is said to them):* This is the fire which you denied.

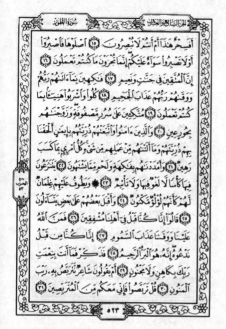

(Raising of Children is very important. Those children who are raised as believers will join their parents in the Heaven provided that their parents also died as believers. Every individual will receive what is due to him.)

22. And we provide them with fruit and meat such as they desire.

23. There they pass from hand to hand a cup inspiring no idle talk, no sinful urge.

24. And there go round, waiting on them, menservants of their own, as though they were hidden pearls.

25. They will advance to each other, and ask each other:

26. Aforetime, we were not without fear for the sake of our people.

(A man may be good, and may within limits have found goodness in his own spiritual life, but may still have anxieties about his family or friends whom he loves. All such shadows are removed in heaven by divine grace.)

27. But Allah has been gracious to us, and delivered us from the torment of the breath of Fire.

28. Truly, we have prayed to Him. He is the Kind, the Merciful.

(Some commentators of the Holy Qur'an interpret that the word "gilman" used in verse 24 means they are the children who died before their parents will serve as menservants.)

29. Therefore, give warning (O Muhammad). By the grace of Allah, you are neither a soothsayer nor a madman.

30. Or do they say: "He is a poet; we are waiting for some misfortune to befall him?"

31. Say (to them): "Wait if you will; I too am waiting along with you!"

(Those who wait the death of Prophet Muhammad forgetting themselves that they will also die. Here the disbelievers are warned that they will receive the punishment they deserve after they die. Prophet Muhammad and the believers will receive the reward of Paradise after they die.)

15. Is this magic or do you not see?

16. Endure the heat thereof, and whether you are patient of it or impatient of it is all one for you. You are only being paid for what you used to do.

17. Surely the Godfearing will dwell in gardens and delight.

18. Happy because of what their Lord has given them, and (because) their Lord has warded off from them the torment of Hell-fire.

19. (And it is said to them): "Eat and drink in joy because of your good deeds."

20. They shall recline on couches ranged around. And We shall wed them to houris (ladies of heaven) with large and lovely eyes.

21. Those who believe and are followed in faith by their descendants, We cause their descendants to join them. And We deprive them of nothing of their work. Every individual is a pledge for what he does.

32. Do their minds prompt them to say this? Or is it merely that they are wicked men?

33. Do they say: "He has invented it *(the Qur'ân)* himself?" Indeed, they have no faith.

34. Let them produce a speech like it, if what they say be true!

35. Or were they created out of the void? Or were they their own creators?

36. Or did they create the heavens and the earth? Surely, they have no faith!

37. Do they own the treasures of your Lord, or have control over them?

38. Or have they any stairway *(to heaven)* by means of which they overhear *(decrees)*? Then let their listener produce some warrant manifest!

(Here the disbelievers asked the question of whether they own a stairway to Heaven to overhear the decrees. If they (the disbelievers) do then they should produce evidence!)

39. Is He to have daughters and you sons?

40. Are you demanding payment of them that they should fear to be weighed down with debts?

41. Or have they knowledge of the Unseen so that they write it down?

42. Or do they intend a plot *(against you, O Muhammad)*? But those who disbelieve are themselves the victims of the plot.

43. Or have they a god other than Allah? Exalted be He above what they associate with Him!

44. And if they were to see a fragment of the heaven falling, they would say: "A heap of clouds."

(The disbelievers had wanted a fragment of the Heaven to fall as punishment. But if that happened they would have interpreted the event, out of obstinacy, in a different way.)

45. Then leave them alone until they encounter the day in which they will be thunder-stricken.

46. A day in which their plot will avail them nothing and none will help them.

47. And verily, for those who do wrong, there is a punishment beyond that. But most of them do not know.

48. So wait patiently *(O Muhammad)* for your Lord's decree, for verily you are in Our sight; and glorify your Lord when you wake;

49. And in the night-time also, hymn His praise, and at the setting of the stars.

(These times are for prayers of Maghrib, Ishâ and Fajr.)

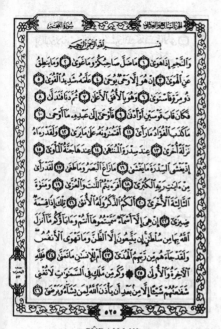

SÛRAH LIII

AN-NAJM (THE STAR)

Revealed at Makka

The Star takes its name from the word *An-Najm*, which occurs in the first verse.

In the name of Allah, the Compassionate, the Merciful.

1. By the star when it sets,

2. Your companion *(Muhammad)* is neither in error, nor is he deceived,

3. Nor does he speak out of his caprice,

4. This is no other than an inspired revelation.

5. He is taught it by one who is mighty in power.

6. And vigorous *(Gabriel)*; and he grew clear to view.

7. When he was on the uppermost horizon,

8. Then he approached and came nearer,

9. Till he was *(distant)* two bows' length, or even nearer.

10. And He *(Allah)* revealed to his servant that which He revealed.

(Gabriel is just a messenger, who can do no more than convey Allah's Message to Allah's Messenger).

11. The *(Prophet's)* *(mind and)* heart in no way falsified that which he saw.

12. Will you *(disbelievers)*, then, question what he saw?

13. And verily he beheld him yet another time *(when the Prophet ascended through the seven heavens)*.

14. Near the Lote-tree of the utmost boundary,

15. Near it is the Garden of Refuge.

16. Behold, the Lote-tree was shrouded *(in mystery unspeakable!)*

17. *(His)* sight swerved not, nor did it go wrong!

18. Verily he saw one of his Lord's greatest signs.

(In these verses night journey of Last Messenger is referred to. During Mi'raj He experienced glory, He was shown some Signs of Allah. Now, from the heights of divine Glory, we come back again to this sorry earth, with its base idolaters. We are asked to "look at this picture, and at that!")

19. Have you thought upon Al-Lât and al - 'Uzzâ.

20. And Manât, the third, the other? *(The three principal idols of the pagan Arabs, who called them 'the daughters of Allah').*

21. What! for you the male sex, and for him, the female?

22. This is indeed an unfair division!

23. They are but names which you invented, you and your fathers; Allah has sent no authority for them. They follow vain guesses and the whims of their own souls, although the guidance of their Lord has come to them.

24. Is man to attain all that he desires?

25. But to Allah belongs the Hereafter and the present life.

26. And how many angels are in the heavens whose intercession will avail nothing until Allah gives leave to whom He chooses and accepts!

27. Those who disbelieve in the life to come call the angels by the names of females.

28. Yet of this they have no knowledge; they follow a mere guess, and a guess avails nothing against truth.

29. *(O Muhammad)* Give no heed, then, to those who ignore Our remembrance and seek only the life of this world.

30. Such is their sum of knowledge. Your Lord knows best who has strayed from His path, and who is rightly guided.

31. To Allah belongs whatsoever is in the heavens and whatsoever is in the earth, that He may reward those who do evil with that which they have done, and reward those who do good with goodness.

32. Those who avoid enormities of sin and abominations, and commit only small offences, *(for them)* your Lord is of vast mercy. He is Best-Aware of you from the time when He created you from the earth, and when you were hidden in the bellies of your mothers. Therefore do not justify yourselves; He knows best those who guard themselves against evil.

(We are reminded of the fact that Adam(pbwh) was created from the earth, of our weakness; human being should remember his creation and should not be proud and haughty.)

33. Did you *(O Muhammad)* observe him who turned away *(from the faith),*

34. Giving little at first, then was grudging?

35. Has he knowledge of the Unseen, and therefore can see?

(Those verses were revealed about Walid son of Mughiyrah who entered Islam then turned away from the faith. When Walid entered Islam, one of the idolaters blamed him. Walid replied that he entered Islam, because he was afraid of Allah's punishment. The idolater said that he would take over his punishment if Walid paid him some amount. Upon this,

Walid turned away from faith and paid that man some part of the amount which was agreed upon. The verse states that event.)

36. Or has he not had news of what is in the books of Moses,

37. And Abraham who fulfilled his duty:

38. That no soul shall bear another's burden.

39. And that each can have nothing save what he strives for,

40. And that his effort will be seen.

41. And afterward he will be repaid for it with fullest payment;

42. And that your Lord, He is the goal;

43. And that He it is who moves to laughter and to weeping.

44. And ordains death and life;

(Individual is responsible himself for all his actions.)

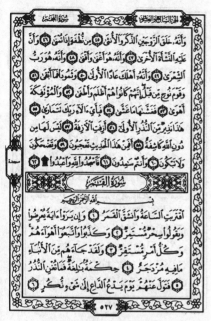

56. This is a warner like the warners of old.

(The destruction of the previous nations is reminded. The old (the nations before) means Aad, Sadom and Gomorro, Lot's peoples and the people of Noah. The disbelievers are warned by Allah. The idolotars of Makkah can have the same punishment.)

57. The coming *(judgement)* is near at hand;

58. None beside Allah can disclose its hour.

59. Do you marvel then at this discourse,

60. And laugh: instead of weeping,

61. While you amuse yourselves?

62. Rather prostrate yourselves before Allah, and worship Him.

SÛRAH LIV

AL-QAMAR (THE MOON)

Revealed at Makka

Al-Qamar, 'The Moon', takes its name from the first verse: "The hour is drawing near and the moon is cleft in two." A strange appearance of the moon in the sky, as if it had been torn asunder, is recorded in the traditions of several Companions of the Prophet as having astonished the people of Makka at about the time when the idolaters were beginning to persecute the Muslims.

THE MOON

In the name of Allah, the Compassionate, the Merciful.

1. The hour *(of judgement)* is drawing near, and the moon is cleft in two.

(The idolaters of Makka had asked the Last Messenger for a miracle. When He pointed to the moon, it came into two parts.)

2. Yet when they see a sign they turn away and say: "Prolonged magic."

3. They deny the truth and follow their own fancies. But every matter will be settled.

4. Surely there has come to them news which will deter.

5. And full of wisdom; but warnings are unavailing.

6. So withdraw from them *(O Muhammad)* on the day when the Summoner summons to a hard task.

45. And that He created the sexes, the male and the female,

46. From a drop of ejected semen.

47. And He must accomplish the other bringing-forth,

48. That it is He Who gives wealth and contentment;

49. That He is the Lord of Sirius *(The Dog - Star, worshipped by the pagan Arabs);*

50. And that He destroyed the former *(tribe of)* 'Aad.

(There was still in existence a tribe of that name.)

51. And *(the tribe of)* Thamûd, He didn't spare;

52. And the folk of Noah aforetime, verily they were more unjust and more tyrannical;

53. And the Mu'tafikah *(the ruined cities where Lot's people lived)* He destroyed,

54. So that there covered them that which did cover.

55. Concerning which, then, of the blessings of your Lord, can you dispute?

7. With downcast eyes, they come forth from graves as if they were scattered locusts.

8. Hastening toward the Summoner; the disbelievers say: "This is a hard day."

9. Long before them the people of Noah denied Our slave, and said: "A madman! and he was repulsed.

(To be *Abd Allah* a slave of Allah', is the proudest rank the Muslim can claim, bondage to Allah implying liberation from all other servitudes. All, especially devoted men, are called, slaves of Allah, in the Qur'ân.)

10. Then he invoked his Lord, *(saying)* "I am vanquished, so help me!"

11. So We opened the gates of heaven with pouring water.

12. And caused the earth to burst with gushing springs, so that the waters met for a predestined purpose.

13. And we carried him upon a thing of planks and nails.

14. That ran *(upon the waters)* in Our sight, as a reward for him who was rejected.

(Prophet Noah and his followers in Allah's sight, safely proceeded in their Journey upon the waters.)

15. And verily We left it as a token; but will anyone take heed?

(Noah's Ark was left as a token on top of the mountain after the flood for people to see and take a heed.)

16. How terrible were My punishment and warnings!

17. And in truth We have made the Qur'ân easy to remember, but will any take heed?

(It is a fact that the Qur'an is marvellously easy for believers to commit to memory. Millions of Muslims know the whole Book by heart.)

18. Aad too denied *(their prophet)*. Then how terrible were My punishment and warnings!

19. On a day of unremitting woe, We let loose on them a howling wind.

20. Sweeping men away as though they were uprooted palm trunks.

21. Then see how terrible were My punishment and warnings!

22. And in truth We have made the Qur'an easy to remember; but will any take heed?

23. Thamoud, too, disbelieved the warnings.

24. They said: "Are we to follow a man who stands alone among us? We would surely then fall into error and madness.

(The prophet Salih(pbwh) was rejected by his own tribe and Thamoud.)

25. Did he alone among us receive the remembrance? He is indeed a rash liar."

26. *(To their warner it was said)*: "Tomorrow they will know who is the rash liar."

27. We are sending the she-camel as a test for them; so watch them and have patience;

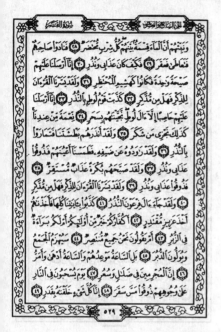

34. We let loose on them a stone-charged whirlwind which destroyed them all, except the family of Lot, whom We saved in the last watch of the night.

35. As a grace from Us. Thus We reward the thankful.

36. And he indeed had warned them of Our blow, but they disputed about the warnings.

37. They even asked of him his guests for an ill purpose. Then We blinded their eyes (and said:) "Taste now My punishment after My warnings!"

(The angels were in the form of youths. The folk of Lot tried to molest them.)

38. And in truth the punishment decreed befell them early in the morning.

39. Now taste My punishment after My warnings!

40. And in truth We have made the Qur'ân easy to remember; but will any take heed?

41. And in truth warnings came to the house of Pharaoh.

42. But they disbelieved all Our signs and We smote them with the grasp of one Mighty, and Powerful.

43. Are your disbelievers better than those, or have you some immunity in the Scriptures?

44. Or do they say: "We are a victorious army"?

45. Their army will be routed and put to flight.

46. Nay, but the Hour (of doom) is their appointed time, and the Hour will be more wretched and more bitter (than their earthly failure).

47. Truly, the wrongdoers persist in error and madness.

48. On the day when they are dragged into the Fire with faces downwards, (We shall say to them): "Feel the touch of the Flame!"

49. We have created all things according to a measure.

28. And inform them that the water is to be shared between (her and) them. Every drinking will be witnessed."

(According to Divine allocation, the camel would consume the water one day and the tribe of Thamoud would use it the next day.)

29. But they called their comrade and he took and hamstrung (her).

(The person who hamstrung the Camel was a man named Kudar b. Saleh, a cruel disbeliever.)

30. Then how terrible were My punishment and warnings!

31. Then We sent against them one cry, and they became like the dry twigs of the cattle fold builder.

32. And in truth We have made the Qur'ân easy to remember; but will any take heed?

33. The folk of Lot rejected the warnings.

50. We command but once: *(Our will is done in the twinkling of an eye.*

51. And verily We have destroyed your fellows; but will any take heed?

52. And every thing they did is in the scriptures.

53. And every small and great thing is recorded.

54. The righteous are in gardens and rivers.

55. Honourably seated in the presence of a Mighty King.

SÛRAH LV

AR-RAHMÂN (THE COMPASSIONATE)

Revealed at Makka

This Sûrah takes its name from the first verse. In this Sûrah "which of your Lord's blessings would you two deny?" is repeated several times, in the dual form, addressing mankind and the Jinn.

In the name of Allah, the Compassionate, the Merciful.

1. The Compassionate

2. Has taught the Qur'ân,

3. Has created man,

4. Has taught him speech.

5. The sun and the moon are made punctual.

6. The plants and the trees bow down in adoration.

7. And the sky He has uplifted; and He has set the measure,

(Among all creatures, only the human being has been given ability to think and talk.)

8. That you do not exceed the measure,

(Here, Allah (s.w.t.) is commanding us not to upset the balance (measure). Man today has already upset the balance, and because of that we have the serious problems of air pollution, water pollution, nuclear pollution, destruction of forests, soil erosion, floods and other catastrophies. If man follows the commandment of Allah (s.w.t.) not to upset the balance (measure) of this world. He will be able to prevent this catastrophies. And live happily.)

9. But observe the measure strictly, nor fall short therein.

10. He laid the earth for His creatures,

11. Therein are fruits and sheathed palmtress,

12. Husked grain and scented herb.

13. Which of your Lord's blessings would you two *(men and jinn)* deny?

14. He created man of clay like the potter's,

15. And then jinn He created of smokeless fire.

16. Which of your Lord's blessings would you two deny?

وَرَبُّ الْمَشْرِقَيْنِ وَرَبُّ الْمَغْرِبَيْنِ ۞ فَبِأَيِّ الَآءِ رَبِّكُمَا تُكَذِّبَانِ ۞ مَرَجَ الْبَحْرَيْنِ يَلْتَقِيَانِ ۞ بَيْنَهُمَا بَرْزَخٌ لَا يَبْغِيَانِ ۞ فَبِأَيِّ الَآءِ رَبِّكُمَا تُكَذِّبَانِ ۞ يَخْرُجُ مِنْهُمَا اللُّؤْلُؤُ وَالْمَرْجَانُ ۞ فَبِأَيِّ الَآءِ رَبِّكُمَا تُكَذِّبَانِ ۞ وَلَهُ الْجَوَارِ الْمُنْشَئَاتُ فِي الْبَحْرِ كَالْأَعْلَامِ ۞ فَبِأَيِّ الَآءِ رَبِّكُمَا تُكَذِّبَانِ ۞ كُلُّ مَنْ عَلَيْهَا فَانٍ ۞ وَيَبْقَى وَجْهُ رَبِّكَ ذُو الْجَلَالِ وَالْإِكْرَامِ ۞ فَبِأَيِّ الَآءِ رَبِّكُمَا تُكَذِّبَانِ ۞ يَسْأَلُهُ مَنْ فِي السَّمَوَاتِ وَالْأَرْضِ كُلَّ يَوْمٍ هُوَ فِي شَأْنٍ ۞ فَبِأَيِّ الَآءِ رَبِّكُمَا تُكَذِّبَانِ ۞ سَنَفْرُغُ لَكُمْ أَيُّهَ الثَّقَلَانِ ۞ فَبِأَيِّ الَآءِ رَبِّكُمَا تُكَذِّبَانِ ۞ يَا مَعْشَرَ الْجِنِّ وَالْإِنْسِ إِنِ اسْتَطَعْتُمْ أَنْ تَنْفُذُوا مِنْ أَقْطَارِ السَّمَوَاتِ وَالْأَرْضِ فَانْفُذُوا لَا تَنْفُذُونَ إِلَّا بِسُلْطَانٍ ۞ فَبِأَيِّ الَآءِ رَبِّكُمَا تُكَذِّبَانِ ۞ يُرْسَلُ عَلَيْكُمَا شُوَاظٌ مِنْ نَارٍ وَنُحَاسٌ فَلَا تَنْتَصِرَانِ ۞ فَبِأَيِّ الَآءِ رَبِّكُمَا تُكَذِّبَانِ ۞ فَإِذَا انْشَقَّتِ السَّمَاءُ فَكَانَتْ وَرْدَةً كَالدِّهَانِ ۞ فَبِأَيِّ الَآءِ رَبِّكُمَا تُكَذِّبَانِ ۞ فَيَوْمَئِذٍ لَا يُسْأَلُ عَنْ ذَنْبِهِ إِنْسٌ وَلَا جَانٌّ ۞ فَبِأَيِّ الَآءِ رَبِّكُمَا تُكَذِّبَانِ ۞

17. Lord of the two Easts, and Lord of the two Wests.

(The points where the sun rises and sets in winter and summer.)

18. Which of your Lord's blessings would you two deny?

19. He has let loose the two seas; they meet one another.

(The salt water and the sweet.)

20. Between them stands a barrier which they cannot overrun.

21. Which of your Lord's blessings would you two deny?

22. Pearls and corals come from both.

23. Which of your Lord's blessings would you two deny?

24. His are the ships that sail like mountains upon the sea.

25. Which of your Lord's blessings would you two deny?

26. All that is upon the earth shall pass away

27. And the face of your Lord will abide forever, full of majesty and glory.

28. Which of your Lord's blessings would you two deny?

29. All that are in the heavens and the earth entreat Him. Every day He exercises His *(universal)* power.

(The created ones entreat Allah who has created all the Universe and has been exercising His Power over it.)

30. Which of your Lord's blessings would you two deny?

31. We shall dispose of you, O you two dependents *(man and jinn)*.

32. Which of your Lord's blessings would you two deny?

33. O company of jinn and men, if you have power to penetrate *(all)* regions of the heavens and the earth, then penetrate *(them)*! You will never penetrate them except with *(Our)* sanction.

34. Which of your Lord's blessings would you two deny?

35. Flames of fire will be unleashed upon you, and brass. No defence will you have.

36. Which of your Lord's blessings would you two deny?

37. And when the heaven splits asunder and becomes rosy like red hide,

38. Which of your Lord's blessings would you two deny?

39. On that day neither man nor jinn will be questioned of his sin.

(Because they will be known by their faces, and there will be no need to question them.)

40. Which of your Lord's blessings would you two deny?

41. The wrongdoers will be known by their marks, and will be seized by the forelocks and the feet.

42. Which of your Lord's blessings would you two deny?

43. This is Hell, which the sinners deny.

44. They go circling round between it and fierce, boiling water.

45. Which of your Lord's blessings would you two deny?

46. And for those that fear the standing before their Lord there are two gardens.

47. Which of your Lord's blessings would you two deny?

48. *(Gardens)* with many branches.

49. Which of your Lord's blessings would you two deny?

50. Therein are two flowing fountains.

51. Which of your Lord's blessings would you two deny?

52. Therein is every kind of fruit in pairs.

53. Which of your Lord's blessings would you two deny?

54. They will recline on couches lined with thick brocade, and within their reach will be the fruits of both gardens.

55. Which of your Lord's blessings would you two deny?

56. Therein are maidens of modest gaze, whom neither man nor jinn will have touched before them.

(These maidens of modest gazed never touched by human beings and Jinns will be found in Paradise in palaces and kiosks.)

57. Which of your Lord's blessings would you two deny?

58. *(In beauty)* they are like rubies and corals.

59. Which of your Lord's blessings would you two deny?

60. Is the reward of goodness anything but goodness?

61. Which of your Lord's blessings would you two deny?

62. And beside them there are two other gardens.

63. Which of your Lord's blessings would you two deny?

64. Dark green with foliage.

65. Which of your Lord's blessings would you two deny?

66. Therein are two flowing fountains.

67. Which of your Lord's blessings would you two deny?

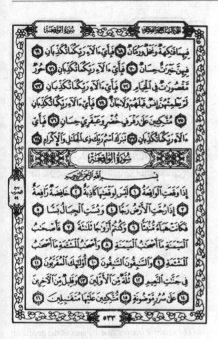

78. Blessed be the Name of your Lord, the Lord of majesty and glory!

SÛRAH LVI

AL-WÂQI'A (THE EVENT)

Revealed at Makka

Takes its name from the word which occurs in the first verse.

In the name of Allah, the Compassionate, the Merciful.

1. When the event befalls!

2. And no soul will then deny its coming.

3. Some will be abased and others exalted.

4. When the earth is shaken with a violent shock,

5. And the hills are ground to powder.

6. So that they become scattered dust,

7. You will be divided into three groups:

8. Those on the right what of those to the right;

9. Those on the left *what of* those on the left;

10. And the Foremost *(in faith)* will be the Foremost *(in the Hereafter)*.

11. Such are they that shall be brought near *(to their Lord)*.

12. In the gardens of delight:

13. A whole multitude from the men of old,

14. But only a few from the later generations.

15. On lined couches.

16. Reclining therein face to face.

(In those verses, some aspects of life in Hereafter is described. Human beings will be in three groups: two of which will be in Paradise, one group, the disbelievers and sinners will be in Hell. The Foremost are the first believers and they are the favorite ones.)

68. In them are fruits; palms and pomegranate.

69. Which of your Lord's blessings would you two deny?

70. In them will be chaste and fair ones.

71. Which of your Lord's blessings would you two deny?

72. Houris sheltered in pavilions.

73. Which of your Lord's blessings would you two deny?

74. Neither man nor jinn will have touched them before.

75. Which of your Lord's blessings would you two deny?

76. Reclining on green cushions and fine carpets.

77. Which of your Lord's blessings would you two deny?

17. There wait on them immortal youths.

18. With bowls and ewers, and a cup from a pure spring.

(One of the blessings of Paradise is a sort of drink called "Mâ'in" which never gives a head-ache.)

19. That will neither pain their heads nor take away their reason;

20. With fruits of their choice.

21. And flesh of fowls that they desire.

22. And fair ones with wide, lovely eyes.

23. Like unto hidden pearls.

24. As a reward for what they used to do.

25. There they will hear no idle talk, no sinful speech.

26. But only the greeting, 'Peace! Peace!'

27. Those on the right hand what of those on the right hand?

28. They will be among thornless lote- trees.

29. And clustered plantains.

30. And spreading shade.

31. And water gushing.

32. And fruit in plenty.

33. Neither limited nor forbidden.

34. And (they will sit) on raised couches.

35. We created (the women) again,

36. And made them virgins,

37. Loving companions of the same age,

38. For those on the right hand:

39. A multitude from the men of old.

40. And a multitude from the later generations.

(The verses above discribe the ages of the people of Paradise is to be between the ages 30 to 33. The women of Paradise will be virgins without the period of pregnancy and birth.)

41. As for those on the left hand what of those on the left hand?

42. (They will dwell) amidst scorching winds, and seething water:

43. In the shadow of pitch-black smoke.

44. Neither cool nor refreshing.

45. They had previously lived in luxury.

46. And persisted in the awful sin.

47. And they used to say: 'When we are dead, and turned to dust and bones, shall we be restored to life?

48. And also our forefathers?'

49. Say (to them, O Muhammad): 'Those of old and those of later times

50. Will be all brought together on an appointed day.

51. As for you sinners who deny (the truth)

52. You will eat the fruit of the Zaqqûm - tree.

53. And fill your bellies with it.

54. You will drink seething water:

55. Yet you will drink it as the thirsty camel drinks.'

56. This will be their welcome on the Day of Judgement.

57. We created you: will you not believe?

58. Behold (the semen) you emit:

59. Do you create it or are We the Creator?

60. We mete out death among you, and We are not to be outrun.

61. That We may transfigure you and make you what you know not.

62. And verily you know the first creation. Why, then, do you not reflect?

63. Have you seen that which you cultivate?

64. Is it you who foster it, or are We the Fosterer?

65. If We willed, We verily could make it chaff, then would you cease not to exclaim:

66. 'We are laden with debts!

67. Surely we are deprived!'

68. Have you observed the water which you drink?

69. Is it you who brought it down from the cloud, or We?

70. If We pleased, We verily could make it bitter. Why then do you not give thanks?

71. Have you observed the fire which you light;

72. Was it you who made the tree thereof to grow, or were We the Grower?

73. We have made it a reminder and a comfort for the dwellers in the wilderness.

74. Therefore (O Muhammad), praise the name of your Lord, the Tremendous.

(Verses above discribe the life of the people of the left in Hell-fire. Allah is all Mighty and He is capabable of recreating a man from nothing in the Hereafter just like He created man from a simple sperm in this world. He is also capabable of making it rain from the sky and growth of plants. These are all the signs of His Might. And He is the Tremendous.)

75. Nay, I swear by the places of the stars -

(Today's researchers attribute, in positive, sciences the "places stars" as to be the "Black spots" in the space.)

76. A mighty oath, if you but knew it -

77. That this is indeed a noble Qur'ân,

78. *(Inscribed)* in a hidden book.

79. Which none may touch except the purified;

(No one can touch the Holy Qur'an unless he is purified. Purification means according to some interpreters: a muslim has to have ablution before touching the Qur'an; according to others purification means he has to purified by entering into Islâm and becoming a beliver plus having ablution.)

(Only those with ablution may touch the Holy Qur'an.)

80. A revelation from the Lord of the Worlds.

81. Is it this discourse that you scorn?

82. And have you made its denial your means of livelihood?

83. Why, then, when *(man's soul)* comes up to the throat *(of the dying)*

84. While you are looking

85. And We are nearer to him than you are, but you do not see

(When man's soul comes up to the throat of the dying. Allah is closer to the person of dying with knowledge, but the humans beings cannot understand this close relationship with the man about to die and his Lord.)

86. Why, then, if you are not in bondage *(to Us),*

87. Do you not force it back, if you are truthful?

88. Thus, if he is of those brought nigh,

89. His lot will be repose and plenty, and a Garden of delight.

90. If he is of those on the right hand,

91. Then *(the greeting)* 'Peace be to you!' from those on the right hand.

92. But if he is of the rejecters, the erring.

93. Then the welcome will be boiling water,

94. And roasting at hell-fire.

95. This is certain truth.

96. Praise then the name of your Lord, the Tremendous!

SÛRAH LVII

AL-HADÎD (IRON)

Revealed at Madîna

This Sûrah takes its name from the word *Al-Hadîd* which occurs in verse 25.

In the name of Allah, the Compassionate, the Merciful.

1. All that is in the heavens and the earth glorify Allah. He is the Mighty, the Wise.

2. His is the Sovereignty of the heavens and the earth; He ordains life and death; and has power over all things.

3. He is the First and the Last and the Outward and the Inward; and He is Knower of all things.

(Allah is the first, He has created everything, there was nothing before Him. He is the Last, His existence is Eternal, When everyone is dead He still is. He is the Outward; His existence and unity is manifest in everything for those who can think. He is the Inward; the senses and intellect can not comprehend Him.)

4. He it is Who created the heavens and the earth in six days *(a day with Allah is as a thousand years of what you reckon: XXII, 47),* then He mounted the Throne. He knows all that enters the earth and all that emerges from it, all that comes down from the sky and all that ascends in it; and He is with you wheresoever you may be. And Allah is Seer of what you do.

(His mounting Throne means exercise of His Power upon the Universe.)

5. His is the Sovereignty of the heavens and the earth, and to Him will all things return.

6. He causes the night to pass into the day and the day to pass into the night. And He has knowledge of what is in the hearts of men.

(He causes the night to pass into the day and the day to pass into the night. This also means days get longer in summer and shorter in winter. And the nights get longer in winter and shorter in summer.)

7. Believe in Allah and His messenger, and give in alms of that which He has made you to inherit; for whoever of you believes and gives in alms will be richly rewarded.

(This verse was revealed during the battle of Tabûk Exepidition. The person intented in this verse was Hd. Othman (R.A.) who was very generous in donating for the expedition.)

8. And what cause have you not to believe in Allah, when the Messenger calls on you to have faith in your Lord, and He has already made a covenant with you, if you are true believers?

(Although Prophet Muhammad called people to way of Allah, some did not believe in him. In the world of "Ervah" spirits Allah made covenant with His creatures. People still don't keep their covenant. They have to use their intelligence to obey Allah and keep their covenant with Him.)

9. He it is Who sends down clear revelations to His servant, so that He may lead you out of darkness into light; Allah is Compassionate and Merciful to you.

10. And why should you not give in the cause of Allah, when He alone will inherit the heavens and the earth? Those of you that gave of their wealth before the victory and took part in the fighting are not equal *(to those who gave ana fought thereafter).* Their degree is greater. Yet Allah has promised each a good reward; He has knowledge of all your actions.

(Those who spent for the sake of Allah before the conquest of Makkâ is more virtuous than those who spent after the conquest of Makkâ. In this verse Abu Bakr R.A. was pointed out indirectly for spending for the cause of Allah and also being the first in beleiving in Allah and Prophet Muhammad.)

11. Who will give a generous loan to Allah? He will pay him back twofold, and he will receive a rich reward.

(Meaning of 'giving loan to Allah' is giving loan to those who are in need, and being lenient with them as for getting back the amount, and helping others only to please Allah.)

12. On the day when you *(O Muhammad)* will see the believers, men and women, their light shining forth before them and on their right hands, *(and a voice saying to them):* 'Rejoice this day. You will enter gardens watered by running streams in which you will abide forever. That is the supreme triumph.

13. On that day the hypocrites, both men and women, will say to the true believers: 'Wait for us that we may borrow some of your light' It will be said: 'Go back and seek some *(other)* light. Then a wall with a gate will be set before them. Inside there will be mercy, and out, to the fore, the scourge *(of Hell)*.

(This verse points out the condition of the hypocrites both men and women. In the Hereafter they will be distinguished by a gate, those who will stay inside of the gate will have the mercy of their Lord and will have light. Those who stay outside of the gate will have the punishment of Hell-fire.)

14. They will call out to them, saying: 'Were we not with you?' They will reply: 'Yes, verily; but you tempted yourselves, you wavered, you doubted and were deceived by your own wishes until Allah's will was done and the deceiver *(Satan)* deceived you concerning Allah.

(Those hypocrites who will regret in the Hereafter will say "were we not with you?" But having followed their own desires and being deceived by satan will taste torment of the Hell-fire.)

15. So this day no ransom can be taken from you, nor from those who disbelieved. Your home is the Fire; that is your patron, and a hapless journey's end!'

16. Is not the time ripe for the hearts of those who believe to submit to Allah's reminder and to the truth which is revealed, that they become not

as those who received the Scripture of old but the term was prolonged for them and so their hearts were hardened, and many of them are evil-livers?

(Implication is that the Jews and Christians, people of Scripture, of whom hearts were hardened because of the fact that the term was prolonged for them. The Muslims who suffered at Makka and became relaxed and lanquished at Madîna, after hijrah are warned of similar situation and they are advised to invoke Allah.)

17. Know that Allah restores the earth to life after its death. We have made plain to you Our revelations that you may understand.

18. Those that give alms, be they men or women, and those that give a generous loan to Allah, will be repaid twofold. They will receive a noble recompense.

(In order to understerant what "generous loan" means look in this Sûrah, Verse 11)

19. And those who believe in Allah and His messengers, they are the loyal; and the martyrs are with their Lord; they have their reward and their light; while as for those who disbelieve and deny Our revelations, they are owners of hell-fire.

20. Know that the life of this world is only play, and idle talk, and pageantry, and boasting among you, and rivalry in respect of wealth and children; as the likeness of vegetation after rain: the tillers rejoice in it, but then it withers and turns yellow, soon becoming worthless stubble. In the life to come there is grievous punishment, and also forgiveness from Allah and His good pleasure, whereas the life of the world is but the comfort of illusion.

(Worldly life is transitory, and one should not forget the fact that he is here being tested, he should not indulged in vain affairs.)

21. Race one with another for forgiveness from your Lord and for a Paradise as vast as heaven and earth, prepared for those who believe in Allah and His messengers. Such is the grace of Allah: He bestows it on whom He will. His grace is infinite.

(No one will enter into Heaven without the forgiveness of Allah and without His grace.)

22. No misfortune can befall in the earth, or your own persons, but it is recorded in a book before We bring it into being. That is easy for Allah.

23. So that you may not grieve for the good things you miss or be overjoyed at what you gain. Allah does not love the haughty, the vainglorious;

24. Who hoard, and who enjoin upon the people avarice. And whosoever turns away, still Allah is the Absolute, the Owner of Praise.

(We are warned against being miser.)

25. We verily sent Our messengers with clear proofs, and revealed with them the Scripture and the Balance, that mankind may observe right measure; and He revealed iron, wherein is mighty power and *(many)* uses for mankind, and that Allah may know those who support Him, though unseen, and support His messengers. Powerful is Allah, and Mighty.

(It is necessary to have power to maintain law and order. Sources of justice, law and order were provided through the Messengers. Without power, justice can not be maintained. Iron is a main source of power as well as it is the basic element of the heavy industry.)

26. And We verily sent Noah and Abraham, and bestowed on their offspring prophethood and the Scriptures. Some were rightly guided, but many were evildoers.

(The four holy books that are mentioned in the Qur'an was revealed to the offspring of these Prophets.)

27. Then We caused Our messengers to follow in their footsteps; and We caused Jesus, son of Mary, to follow, and gave him the Gospel, and placed compassion and mercy in the hearts of those who followed him. But monasticism they invented - We did not ordain it for them - only seeking Allah's pleasure, and they observed it not with right observance. So We give those of them who believe their reward, but many of them were evildoers.

(Monasticisizm was not ordained by Allah, but it was invented by those who followed by Jesus. Source of them relinquished worldly pleasure, but many left the teachings of Jesus, followed the rulers, distorted the Gospel, inserted trinity and denied the Last Messenger.)

28. O believers, have fear of Allah, and put your trust in His messengers. He will grant you a double share of His mercy, and will give you a light to walk in, and will forgive you. Allah is Forgiving and Merciful.

29. Let the People of the Book *(Jews and Christians)* know that they have no control over the gifts of Allah; that these gifts are in His hands alone, and that He vouchsafes them to whom He will. And Allah is of tremendous bounty.

(Here the People of the Book 'Jews and Christians' are reminded that it is up to Allah who will vouchsafe or decide who will be the prophets. Allah is the Lord of tremendous bounty, it is He who decides whom He will bestow His Mercy.)

SÛRAH LVIII

AL-MUJÂDILA (SHE WHO DISPUTED)
Revealed at Madîna

This Sûrah takes its name from a word which occurs in the first verse.

In the name of Allah, the Compassionate, the Merciful.

1. Allah has heard the words of her[1] who disputed with you *(O Muhammad)* concerning her husband and made her plaint to Allah. Allah has heard the arguments of both of you. He hears all and observes all.

2. Those of you who divorce their wives *(by saying they are as their mothers)* should know that they are not their mothers. Their mothers are only those who gave birth to them. The words they utter are unjust and false: but Allah is Pardoning, Forgiving.

---

[1] Khawla daughter of Tha'laba.

(Islam has abolished an old custom of Arabs in divorcing their wives by saying they are as their mothers. That practise was called *zihâr*.)

3. Those that divorce their wives *(by saying they are as their mothers)* and afterwards retract their words shall free a slave before they touch each other again. This you are enjoined to do: Allah is cognizant of all your actions.

4. He that does not have *(a slave)* shall fast two successive months before they touch one another. If he cannot do this, he will feed sixty of the poor. This is enjoined on you so that you may have faith in Allah and His Messenger. Such are the limits set by Allah. And Allah's grievous punishment awaits the disbelievers.

5. Those who oppose Allah and His messenger will be abased as were those before them. We have sent down clear tokens; and a shameful punishment awaits the disbelievers.

6. On the day when Allah restores them all to life He will inform them of their actions. Allah has kept account of it, while they forgot it. And Allah is Witness over all things.

7. Are you not aware that Allah knows what the heavens and the earth contain? There is no secret counsel between three but He is the fourth of them; nor between five but He is the sixth of them, nor between fewer or more but He is with them wherever they are. Then, on the Day of Resurrection, He will inform them of their doings. Allah has knowledge of all things.

8. Do you not see those who were forbidden secret counsels, then they return to that which they are forbidden and hold secret counsels for iniquity and hostility, and disobedience of the Messenger? When they come to you they salute you in words with which Allah does not greet you, and ask themselves: 'Why does Allah not punish us for what we say?' Hell is scourge enough for them: they will burn in its flames, a wretched fate.

(Those who were forbidden to hold secret councels were Jews and hypocrites. They "the Jews and the hypocrites would create mischief between the believers. They had another crime that they would commit. When they would see the prophet, they would use the phrase "As sâmâ alayk" which meant "death to you (o prophet). Knowing this the prophet of Allah would answer to them. "Alaykûm" meaning "to you" would never change his polite and gentle attitude toward them.)

9. O believers, when you converse in private do not speak with wickedness and enmity and disobedience towards the Messenger, but with justice and piety. Have fear of Allah, before Whom you will be brought together.

(Some of the interpreters of the Holy Qur'an here disagree to the point whether the party intended here are believers or the hypocrites.)

10. Secret counsels are the work of the devil, who thereby seeks to annoy the faithful. Yet he can harm nothing at all except by Allah's leave. In Allah let the faithful put their trust.

(Secret counsels and whispering are prohibited in Islam. They are considered to be the causes of enmity between the believers. And the most important secret counsels are the work of the devil.)

11. Believers, make room in your assemblies when you are bidden to do so: Allah will make room for you. Again, rise up when you are told to rise: Allah will raise to high ranks those that have faith and knowledge among you. He is cognizant of all your actions.

(When the believers are asked to make room for the new comers they should do so, and when they are asked to rise again they should abide the rules of kindness and nice manners. Those who possess the knowledge of faîth and practice it will achieve higher degrees.)

12. Believers, when you consult the Messenger in private, give alms before such consultation. That is best and purest for you. But if you lack the means, know that Allah is Forgiving and Merciful.

(This action implies regard for the Prophet. The poor also is favoured.)

13. Do you hesitate to offer alms before your consultations with him? If you do not and Allah will pardon your offence then recite your prayers and pay the Zakât, and show obedience to Allah and His Messenger. Allah is cognizant of all your actions.

(With this verse Allah has lightened the burden of the believers to offer alms before consultations with the prophet. Allah will pardon the offence of not giving alms.)

14. Do you see those that have befriended a people *(the Jews)* who have incurred Allah's wrath? They belong neither to you nor to them. They knowingly swear to falsehoods.

(Those are the hypocrites. They claimed faith, but they had been concealing disbelief.)

15. Allah has prepared for them a grievous scourge. Evil indeed is that which they have done.

16. They use their faith as a disguise and thus debar others from the path of Allah. A shameful punishment awaits them.

17. Neither their wealth nor their children will in the least protect them from Allah. They are the people of the Fire, and there they will abide forever.

18. On the day when Allah restores them all to life they will swear to Him as they now swear to you, thinking that their oaths will help them. Surely they are liars.

(The disbelievers in the Day of Judgement will swear to being believers, but their oaths will do them no good since they are liars.)

19. The devil has gained possession of them and caused them to forget Allah's warning. They are the devil's party; and the devil's party will assuredly be lost.

20. Those who oppose Allah and His Messenger will be among the lowest.

21. Allah has decreed: 'I will surely triumph, Myself and My Messengers.' Powerful is Allah, and Mighty.

22. You will find no believers in Allah and the Last Day on friendly terms with those who oppose Allah and His messengers, even though they be their fathers, their sons, their brothers, or their kindred. Allah has written faith in their very hearts, and strengthened them with a spirit of His own. He will admit them to gardens watered by running streams where they will dwell for ever. Allah is well pleased with them and they with Him. They are the party of Allah: and Allah's party will surely triumph.

(The Companions of the Last Messenger set the best example for this attitude.)

SÛRAH LIX
AL-HASHR (EXILE)

Revealed at Madîna

Al-Hashr (Exile) takes its name from verses 2-17 where the exile of the Jewish tribe Banî Nadîr is related. They were exiled because of attempting to murder the Prophet by treason. The hypocrites had secretly sympathised with those Jews, and had promised to side with them should there be a war with the Muslims; and to emigrate with them if they were constrained to be exiled. But the hypocrites did not help them when the Muslims marched against them. And when they were exiled, the hypocrites did not go with them.

In the name of Allah, the Compassionate, the Merciful.

1. All that is in the heavens and all that is in the earth glorifies Allah, and He is the Mighty, the Wise.

2. He it is that drove the disbelievers among the People of the Book[1] out of their dwellings into the first exile. You did not think that they would go, and they, for their part, fancied that their strongholds would protect them from Allah. But Allah overtook them whence they did not expect, casting such terror into their hearts that their dwellings were destroyed by their own hands as well as by those of the faithful. So learn a lesson, O you who have eyes!

3. Had Allah not decreed evacuation for them, He would surely have punished them in this world, and theirs in the Hereafter is the punishment of the Fire.

---

[1]Jews and Christians. Here it refers to Jews.

4. That is because they were opposed to Allah and His messenger; and he that is opposed to Allah should know that Allah is stern in retribution.

5. Whatever palm-tree you cut down or leave standing upon its roots, it is by Allah's leave, so that He might humiliate the evil - doers.

(The unnecessary cutting down of fruit trees or destruction of crops, or any wanton destruction whatever in war is forbidden by the law and practice of Islam. But some destruction may be necessary to put pressure on the enemy, and to that extent it is allowed. Yet so far as possible, and consistently with that objective of military operations, such trees should not be cut down. Both these principles are in accordance with the Divine will, and were followed by the Muslims in their expeditions.)

6. And that which Allah gave as spoil to His messenger from them, you did not make for this any expedition with either cavalry or camelry;

but Allah gives His messenger lordship over whomsoever Allah pleases: and Allah is able to do all things.

(The Jewish tribe of Nadir at Madîna had concluded an agreement with the Last Messenger. But they breached it and they were expelled from Madîna. The first 6 verses refer to this event.)

7. That which Allah gives as spoil to His messenger from the people of the townships, it is for Allah and His messenger *(for the State)* and for the near of kin and the orphans and the needy and the wayfarer, so that they will not become the property of the rich among you. Whatever the Messenger gives you, accept it; and whatever he forbids you, abstain from it. Have fear of Allah; He is stern in retribution.

(The spoils that taken from the enemies of Islâm have to be divided according to the above verse. The spoils have to be devided into five portions. And the portion divided for Allah and his prophet are is the sign of respect to Allah (s.w.t.))

8. And *(spoil is)* for the poor fugitives who have been driven out from their homes and their belongings, who seek bounty from Allah and help Allah and His Messenger. They are the true believers.

9. Those, before them, who had homes in the City *(Madîna)* and embraced the Faith before them love those who have sought refuge with them; they entertain no desire in their hearts for what they are given, but rather prefer them above themselves, though poverty become their lot. And whoever is saved from his own avarice will surely prosper.

(Attitude of Ansar(Helpers, people of Madîna) towards Muhajirin was exactly as stated in the verse. They were excellent Muslims.)

10. And those who came into the faith after them say: 'Our Lord! Forgive us and our brethren who were before us in the faith, and do not place in our hearts any rancour toward those who believe. Our Lord! You are Compassionate and Merciful,

(Those who came into the faith after them are all the Muslim generations up to the end of this worldly life. All muslims should respect the Companions, not criticise them.)

11. Have you not seen the hypocrites?' They say to their fellow-disbelievers among the People of the Book: 'If you are driven out, we surely shall go out with you, and we shall never obey anyone against you, and if you are attacked you verily shall help you. 'And Allah bears witness that they are lying.

(Reference is to Abdullah b. Ubay, the chief hypocrite and to his correspondence with the Nadirite jews.)

12. If they are driven out, they will not go with them, nor, if they are attacked, will they help them. Indeed, if they go to their help, they will turn their backs in flight, and then they will not be helped.

13. Their dread of you is more intense in their hearts than their fear of Allah: so devoid are they of understanding.

(The fear of hypocrites from the believers is more than Allah is because Allah has postponed their punishment for later.)

14. They will never fight against you in a body, save in fortified cities from behind high walls. Their hostility among themselves is very great; you think of them as one, yet their hearts are divided. That is because they are a folk who have no sense.

(When Jews and hypocrites would be engaged in a battle with the prophet of Allah, they would not act in one body. Because of their disbelief, Allah put fear in their hearts. They were unable to find in open land because of their cowardness. They preferred to fight in fortified cities.)

15. On the likeness of those who suffered a short time before them, they taste the ill-effects of their own conduct; and a grievous scourge awaits them.

(The pagan Arabs were defeated at Badr, in Shawwal, A.H.2. The Jews evidently did not take that lesson to heart.)

(The condition of the Jews were same as the condition of the idolators of Makkâ who were defeated short time before at the battle of Badr.)

16. And the hypocrites are like the devil when he orders man to disbelieve, then, when he disbelieves, says: 'I here and now disown you. I fear Allah, the Lord of the Worlds!'

upon a mountain, you *(O Muhammad)* would have seen it humbled, rent asunder by the fear of Allah. Such are the parables We set forth to mankind, so that they may reflect.

22. He is Allah besides whom there is no other god; knower of the visible and the unseen. He is the Compassionate, the Merciful.

(The Compassionate(Rahman) and the Merciful (Rahim) are derived in Arabic from the same root: Rahmat. Rahman's mercy covers all His creatures in this world. Rahim means He will spare only the believers on the day of Judgement.)

23. He is Allah besides whom there is no other god. He is the Sovereign Lord, the Holy One, the Source of Security the Keeper of Faith; the Guardian, the Mighty One, the All- Powerful, the Proud! Exalted be He above the partners they ascribe to Him.

24. He is Allah, the Creator, the Originator, the Modeller. His are the most beautiful names. All that is in the heavens and the earth glorifies Him. He is the Mighty, the Wise.

(The Last Messenger(pbwh) said about the last three verses of this Sûrah: "Whoever recites in the morning these three verses after saying three times Auzu billahis Semi'il Alimi min Ash Shaytanirrajim Allah assignes for him seventy thousand angels who pray for his forgiveness that day. If he dies that day, then his death is of a martyr's death. And if he recites these three verses in the evening, his situation is likewise.)

17. And the consequence for both will be that they are in the Fire, to remain there for ever. Such is the reward of evil-doers.

(It is explained in this verse the consequence of disbelievers and the Satan both are evil-doers.)

18. O believers! Observe your duty to Allah. And let every soul look to that which it sends forward for the morrow. And observe your duty to Allah, for He is cognizant of all your actions.

(Hereafter is meant by morrow. The worldly life is only one day in sight of Allah, so Hereafter. Observation duty to Allah is reiterated by repetition.)

19. And be not as those who forgot Allah, so that He caused them to forget themselves. Such men are evil-doers.

20. The people of the Fire and the dwellers of Paradise are not equal. The dwellers of Paradise are the victorious.

21. If We had caused this Qur'an to descend

SÛRAH LX
AL-MUMTAHANAH (SHE THAT IS TO BE EXAMINED)
Revealed at Madîna

Al-Mumtahanah *(She that is to be examined)* takes its name from v. 10, where the believers are told to question women who come to them as fugitives from the idolaters and, if they find them sincere converts to Islam, not to return them to the idolaters. This marked a modification of the terms of the Truce of Hudaibiyyah, by which the Prophet had undertaken to return all fugitives, male and female, while the idolaters were not obliged to give up renegades from Islam. The more terrible persecution which women had to undergo, if extradited, and their helpless social condition were the causes of the change. Instead of giving up women refugees who were sincere, and not fugitives on account of crime or some family quarrel, the Muslims were to pay an indemnity for them; while as for Muslim husbands whose wives might flee to Quraish, no indemnity was to be paid by the latter, but, when some turn of fortune brought wealth to the Islamic state, they were to be repaid by the state what their wives had taken of their property. Verse 12 .names the pledge which was to be taken from the women refugees after their examination.

The date of the revelation is the eighth year of the Hijrah.

SHE THAT IS TO BE EXAMINED

In the name of Allah, the Compassionate, the Merciful.

1. O Believers! Do not make friends with those who are enemies of Mine and yours, showing them kindness when they have denied the truth that has been revealed to you and driven the Messenger and yourselves out of your city because you believe in Allah, your Lord. If it was indeed to fight for My cause, and out of a desire to please Me that you left your city, how can you be friendly to them in secret? I well know all that you hide and all that you proclaim. Whoever of you does this will stray from the right path.

2. If they have the upper hand over you, they will be your foes, and will stretch out their hands and their tongues toward you with evil intent; and they long for you to disbelieve.

3. On the Day of Resurrection neither your kinsfolk nor your children will avail you. Allah will judge between you. He is Cognizant of all your actions.

4. There is an excellent example for you in Abraham and those who followed him. They said to their people: 'We are quit of you and that which you worship besides Allah.' We renounce you; enmity and hate will reign us until you believe in Allah only except Abraham's saying to his father: 'I shall implore Allah to forgive you, although I have no power to save you from His punishment' Lord, in You we have put our trust; and to You we turn in repentance: unto You is the journeying.

(The Prophet Abraham(pbwh) told his father, who was a disbeliever that he would implore Allah to forgive him. But he was prevented, because imploring for forgiveness of a disbeliever is not permitted.)

5. Our Lord! Do not make us a prey for those who disbelieve. And forgive us, our Lord! Verily, You, only You are the Mighty, the Wise'.

6. Truly, in those men there is a good example for you, and for him who puts his hopes in Allah and in the Last Day. He that gives no heed to you, Allah alone is Self-sufficient and Worthy of praise.

7. It may well be that Allah will put good-will between you and those with whom you have hitherto been at odds. Allah is Mighty; and Allah is Forgiving, Merciful.

(Believers are told here that not to go too extreme at being with odds with the disbelievers, there might come a day that Allah might put good-will between the believers and disbelievers. This is exactly what happened later on, the disbelievers of Makkâ became Muslims and later on strived for the cause of Islâm.)

8. Allah does not forbid you to be kind and equitable to those who have neither made war on your religion nor driven you from your homes. Allah loves the equitable.

(The cause of the revalation of this verse is the incident that when Asma, the daughter of Hd. Abu Bakr R.A. wanted to be visited by her mother who stayed behind in Makkâ as a disbeliever was refused for the visit.

According to some interpreters "those who made no war on your religion nor driven you from your homes" means the ones who embraced Islam but were unable to migrate. And according to some other interpreters those are women and children who did not fight against Muslims.

And the majority of the interpreters agreed that The tribe of Huzâa was what intended in this verse who made agreement with the prophet and stayed loyal to the treaty, and did not fight against the prophet.)

9. Allah only forbids you to make friends with those who have fought against you on account of your religion and driven you from your homes, or abetted others to do so. Those who make friends with them are wrongdoers.

10. O believers! When believing women seek refuge with you, examine them. Allah best knows their faith. If you find them true believers, do not return them to the infidels; they are not lawful to the infidels, nor are the infidels lawful to them. But hand back to the disbelievers what they have spent. Nor is it an offence for you to marry such women, provided you give them their dowries. Do not hold onto the ties of marriage with disbelieving women: demand what you have spent and let them ask for what they have spent. Such is the law which Allah lays down among you. Allah is Wise and All-Knowing.

(The conditions discussed in above verse occurred after the Hudaibiay Treaty which regulated the exchange of prisoners according to the Law of Allah.)

11. If any of your wives go over to the disbelievers and you subsequently have your turn, pay those whose wives have fled the equivalent of the dowries they have given them. Fear Allah in Whom you believe.

12. O Prophet! If believing women come to you and pledge themselves to associate in worship nothing with Allah, to commit neither theft, nor adultery, nor child-murder, to utter no monstrous falsehoods *(concerning the fatherhood of their children),* and to disobey you in nothing just, accept their allegiance and implore Allah to forgive them. Allah is Forgiving and Merciful.

(This verse was revealed on the day of conquest of Makkâ. The prophet of Allah accepted the pledge of allegiance of the beleiving women not to associate in worship nothing with Allah, to commit neither theft, nor adultery, nor child murder and also not to slander their husbands about the fatherhood of their Children.)

13. O believers! Do not make friends with those who have incurred the wrath of Allah. Such men despair of the life to come, just as the disbelievers despair of the buried dead.

SÛRAH LXI

AS-SAFF (BATTLE ARRAY)

Revealed at Madîna

This Sûrah takes its name from the word *Al-Saff* which occurs in verse 4, describing the believers who fight for Islam.

In the name of Allah, the Compassionate, the Merciful.

1. All that is in the heavens and all that is in the earth glorifies Allah, and He is the Mighty, the Wise.

2. O believers! Why do you say what you do not do?

(Some muslims said that if they had known which action was the most pleasing one to Allah they would had done it. Upon this, the verse which states that Allah loves those who fight for His cause descended. The fact that some of the muslims turned away from the battle of Uhud was the cause of this address and reproach.)

3. It is most odious in Allah's sight that you should say that which you do not do.

4. Allah loves those who fight for His cause in ranks, as if they were a solid structure.

5. And remember when Moses said to his people: 'O my people: Why do you seek to harm me, when you know that I am Allah's messenger to you?' So when they went astray Allah let their hearts go astray. Allah does not guide the evil-doers.

6. And remember Jesus, son of Mary, who said: 'O Children of Israel; I am the messenger of Allah to you, confirming that which was revealed before me in the Torah *(Books of Moses)* and bringing good tidings of a messenger who will come after me, whose name is Ahmad'[1] Yet when he has come to them with clear proofs, they say: 'This is mere magic.'

7. And who is more wicked than the man who invents a falsehood about Allah when called to Islam? Allah does not guide the wrongdoers.

(Inventing falsehood about Allah is assigning partners to Him, ascribing son to Him and calling His Signs magic.)

8. They seek to extinguish the light of Allah with their mouths; but Allah will perfect His light, much as the disbelievers may dislike it.

(Religion of Allah will prevail despite the slanders of the disbelievers.)

---

[1] Muhammad *(Ahmad being one of his names).*

9. He it is who has sent His messenger with guidance and the Religion of Truth, so that He may exalt it above all religions, much as the pagans may dislike it.

10. O believers! Shall I show you a commerce that will save you from a painful doom?

11. You should believe in Allah and His messenger, and should strive for the cause of Allah with your wealth and your lives. That is better for you, if you but knew it.

12. He will forgive you your sins, and bring you into Gardens watered by running streams: He will lodge you in pleasant mansions in Gardens of Paradise. That is the supreme triumph.

13. And He will give you another blessing which you love: help from Allah and imminent victory. Give good tidings *(O Muhammad)* to believers!

(Imminent victory was opening of Makka to Islam, defeat of the super powers(Eastern Rome and Sasanid Empires) by the Muslims.)

14. O believers! Be Allah's helpers. When Jesus son of Mary said to the disciples: 'Who will come with me to the help of Allah?' They replied: 'We are Allah's helpers.' And a party of the Children of Israel believed, while a party disbelieved. Then We strengthened those who believed against their foe, and they became the uppermost.

(Believing party is those who believed that Jesus is Allah's creature and His Prophet and that he was uplifted to the Heaven. Disbelieving party is those who claim that Jesus is son of Allah and he is the third of the three.)

SÛRAH LXII

AL-JUMU'A

(THE CONGREGATION)

Revealed at Madîna

The Revelation has come among unlearned men, to teach purity and wisdom not only to them, but to others, including those who may have an older Message but do not understand it: thus meet solemnly for the Assembly *(Friday)* Prayer, and let not worldly interests deflect you from it.

THE CONGREGATION

In the name of Allah, the Compassionate, the Merciful.

1. Whatever is in the heavens and in the earth glorifies Allah, the Sovereign Lord, the Holy One, the Mighty, the Wise.

2. He it is who has sent among the unlettered ones a messenger of their own, to recite to them His revelations and to make them grow, and to teach them the Scripture and Wisdom, though they have hitherto been in gross error.

3. Along with others of them who have not yet joined them. He is the Mighty, the Wise.

(Prophet Muhammad is a universal prophet sent to all mankind till the Day of Judgement.)

4. That is the bounty of Allah; which He gives to whom He will. His grace is infinite.

5. The similitude of those who are entrusted with the Law of Moses, yet apply it not, is that of a donkey carrying books *(which does not understand them)*. Evil is the similitude of people who falsify the revelations of Allah. And Allah does not guide wrongdoing folk.

(The Jews who are familiar with Torah do not practice with it. So the Jews are resembled to a donkey.)

6. Say *(O Muhammad)*: "O you who are Jews! If you claim that you are favoured by Allah apart from all mankind, then long for death, if you are truthful.

(Because Allah's friends prefer Hereafter to this world, and death is the beginning of Hereafter.)

(Jews should desire death more than life if they think they are really favored by Allah on the contrary . They hate death and they love life.)

7. But they will never long for it because of all that their own hands have sent before them, and Allah is Aware of evil-doers.

(The evil-doers will never long for death.)

8. Say *(to them, O Muhammad)*: "The death from which you flee will truly overtake you; and afterward you will be returned to the Knower of the invisible and the visible, and He will tell you what you used to do.

9. O believers! When the call is heard for the prayer of the day of congregation, hasten to the remembrance of Allah and cease your trading. That is better for you if you but knew it.

10. And when the prayer is ended, then disperse in the land and seek of Allah's bounty, and remember Allah much, that you may be successful.

(After the prayer is ended believers are encouraged to seek the bounty of Allah and praise Him and do other good deeds such as visiting sick and friends and other duties.)

11. Yet when they see some merchandise or entertainment, they break away to it and leave you standing. Say: 'That which Allah has in store is far better than any merchandise or entertainment. Allah is the Most Munificent Giver.'

(While the Prophet was delivering hutbah of Jumu'a caravan arrived. It was the custom that when a caravan arrived, they would beat drums showing pleasure. Only ten believers remained in the mosque listening to the Prophet and the others left.)

SÛRAH LXIII

AL-MUNÂFIQÛN (THE HYPOCRITES)

Revealed at Madîna

This Sûrah deals with the hypocrites and their behaviour, taking its name from the first verse.

In the name of Allah, the Compassionate, the Merciful.

1. When the hypocrites come to you they say: 'We bear witness that you are Allah's messenger.' Allah knows that you are indeed His messenger, and Allah bears witness that the hypocrites are lying!

2. They use their oaths as a disguise and debar others from the path of Allah. Evil is what they do.

3. That is because they believed and then renounced their faith: their hearts are sealed, so that they are devoid of understanding.

4. And when you see them their figures please you, and when they speak you listen to what they say. Yet they are like propped-up beams of timber. They deem every shout to be against them. *(Their conscience always troubles them. If any cry is raised, they immediately grow alarmed, and think it is against themselves. Such men are worse than open enemies.)* They are the enemy. So beware of them. The curse of Allah be upon them! How perverse they are!

(The hypocrites, Abdullah b. Ubayy, Mughis b. Qays and others were handsome and robust persons. They used to come to the presence of the Prophet, lean against wall and speak. They are resembled to propped-up beams of timber, having impressive figures but no heart or spirit.)

5. When it is said to them: 'Come! The Messenger of Allah will ask forgiveness for you!' they avert their faces and you see them turning away, disdainful.

6. It is alike to them whether or not you ask forgiveness for them: Allah will not forgive them. He does not guide the evil-doers.

7. It is they who say: 'Spend nothing on those that follow Allah's messenger until they have deserted him. But to Allah belong the treasures of the heavens and the earth; yet the hypocrites cannot understand.' But strength belongs to Allah and His messenger and the faithful: yet the hypocrites know it not.

8. They say: 'Surely, if we return to Madîna, the strong will soon drive out the weaker, when strength belongs to Allah and to His messenger and the believers; but hypocrites do not know.

9. O believers! let neither your riches nor your children beguile you of Allah's remembrance. Those who do so, they are the losers.

10. And spend of that with which We have provided you before death befalls any of you and he should say: 'Reprieve me, my Lord, awhile, that I may give in charity and be among the righteous.'

11. But Allah reprieves no soul when its term expires. Allah has knowledge of all your actions.

SÛRAH LXIV

AT-TAGHÂBUN
(MUTUAL DISILLUSION)

Revealed at Madîna

Mutual Disillusion takes its name from the word "At-Taghâbun, which occurs in verse 9.

In the name of Allah, the Compassionate, the Merciful.

1. Whatever is in the heavens and on earth glorifies Allah. His is the sovereignty, and His the praise. He has power over all things.

2. He it is who created you, but one of you is a disbeliever and one of you is a believer; and Allah is Seer of what you do.

3. He created the heavens and the earth with truth, and He shaped you and made good your shapes, and to Him is the journeying.

4. He knows what the heavens and the earth contain, and knows all that you hide and all that you reveal. And Allah is Aware of what is in the breasts *(of men).*

5. Has not the story reached you of those who disbelieved of old and thus tasted the ill- effects of their conduct, and theirs will be a painful doom?

(Those are folks of Noah, Hud, Salih and Lot. People of Makka is warned of a similar consequence.)

6. That was because their messengers *(from Allah)* kept coming to them with clear proofs *(of Allah's sovereignty),* but they said: 'Shall mere mortals guide us?' So they disbelieved and turned away, and Allah was independent *(of them).* Allah is Absolute, Owner of Praise.

7. Those who disbelieve assert that they will not be raised again. Say *(to them O Muhammad):* 'By my Lord, you will assuredly be raised to life! Then you will be told of all that you have done, and that is easy for Allah.'

8. Believe, therefore, in Allah and His Messenger, and the light which We have revealed. And Allah is Aware of what you do.

9. The day when He assembles you all to the Day of Assembling. That will be the day of mutual disillusion. And those who believe in Allah and do right, He will remit from them their evil deeds and will bring them into Gardens watered by running streams, where they will dwell for ever. That is the supreme triumph.

(The Day of Assembling will be day of disillusion for the disbelievers. They will be punished for their disbelief and misdeed by being thrown into Hell.)

10. But those who disbelieve and deny Our revelations will be the people of the Fire, and will abide therein - a hapless journey's end!

11. No calamity befalls except by Allah's leave. And whosoever believes in Allah, He guides his heart. And Allah is Knower of all things.

(No calamity, no disease can reach human being without Allah's knowledge and permission. Therefore, who believes in Allah and destiny, perceives that whatever befalls him, it is by a Heavenly Decree, and he recovers easily.)

12. Obey Allah and obey His messenger; but if you turn away, then the duty of Our messenger is only to convey *(the message)*.

13. Allah! There is no god save Him. In Allah, therefore, let believers put their trust.

14. O believers, among your wives and your children there are enemies for you, therefore beware of them. And if you overlook their offences and forgive and pardon them,then know that Allah is Forgiving and Merciful.

(Some of the Muslim's wives and children tried to prevent them from emigrating to Madîna asserting that they would be in a very awkward situation. When the

muslims learned about high degrees attained by emigration(Hijrah), they wanted to punish their household. This verse was descended and urged them not to punish their household, but to forgive them. Nevertheless, the verse indicates to the fact that at some crucial situations wives and children may be a hindrance.)

15. Your wealth and your children are only a temptation, whereas with Allah is an immense reward.

16. So keep your duty to Allah as best you can, and listen, and obey, and spend; that is better for your souls. And those who are saved from their own greed will surely prosper.

17. If you give a generous loan to Allah, He will pay you back twofold and will forgive you, for Allah is Responsive, Clement.

(A loan without interest or any thought of gain or loss.)

18. Knower of the invisible and the visible, the Mighty, the Wise.

SÛRAH LXV

AT-TALÂQ (DIVORCE)

Revealed at Madîna

The relations of the sexes are an important factor in social life. This Sûrah deals with some of its aspects. The Prophet *(peace be with him)* said: "In the sight of Allah, divorce is the most hateful of the permitted things. Thus the sanctity of marriage is safeguarded, because it is the essential basis of family life. On the other hand, this sanctity should not be made into a fetish at the expense of human life.

DIVORCE

In the name of Allah, the Compassionate, the Merciful.

1. O Prophet! If you *(believers)* divorce your wives, divorce them at the end of their waiting period, and keep your duty to Allah, your Lord. Do not expel them from their homes or let them go away unless they commit a proven immora-

lity. Such are the bounds set by Allah; and he that transgresses Allah's bounds wrongs his own soul. You never know; after that Allah may bring to pass some new situation.

(Although divorce is lawful it is disliked by Allah (s.w.t.) Allah addresses to Prophet Muhammad, but the believers are also responsible just like the prophet. If the divorce has to take place it has to be at the end of their waiting period and they should not be expelled from their homes until proper arrangements are made. During the waiting period one of the parties might regret and wish to return to the other party. Then he or she might want to return to one another.)

2. When they have reached their prescribed time, either keep them honourably or part with them honourably. Call to witness two honest men among you and keep your testimony upright for Allah. Whoever believes in Allah and in the Last Day is exhorted to do this. And whoever keeps his duty to Allah, He will appoint a way out for him.

3. And will provide for him from whence he did not reckon. Allah is sufficient for the man who puts his trust in Him. He will surely bring about what He decrees. He has set a measure for all things.

(Toward the end of the waiting period, the husband either keep his wife honourably or part with honourably. He should keep two witnesses at either case. The divorce should take according to the Sunnah: It should be at the end of the prescribed period, not to expel the woman from her house. Make two witnesses present, and be just while doing all these.)

4. If you are in doubt concerning those of your wives who have ceased menstruating, know that their waiting period is three months. And let the same be the waiting period of those who have not yet menstruated. As for pregnant women, their term will be the time they deliver their burden. Allah will ease the hardship of the man who fears Him.

5. That is the commandment of Allah which He has revealed to you. And whoever keeps his duty to Allah, He will remit from him his evil deeds and will enlarge his reward.

6. Lodge them in your own homes, according to your means. Do not harass them so as to make life intolerable for them. If they are with child, maintain them until they deliver their burden; and if, after that, they give suck to their children, give them their sums and consult together in all reasonableness. But if you cannot bear with each other, let other women suckle for you.

7. Let the rich man spend according to his wealth and the poor man according to what Allah has given him. Allah does not charge a man with more than He has given him; He will bring ease after hardship.

8. And how many a community revolted against the ordinance of its Lord and His messengers, and We called it to a stern account and chastised it with dire punishment.

9. So that it tasted the ill-effects of its conduct, and the consequence of its conduct was loss.

10. Allah has prepared for them stern punishment; so keep your duty to Allah, O men of understanding! O you who believe! Now Allah has sent down to you a reminder,

11. A messenger reciting to you the revelations of Allah made plain, that He may bring forth those who believe and do good works from darkness into light. And whosoever believes in Allah and does right, He will bring him into Gardens watered by running streams, where he will abide for ever. Allah has appointed for him a generous provision.

12. Allah it is who has created seven heavens, and of the earth a similar number. His commandment descends through them, so that you may know that Allah has power over all things, and that He has knowledge of all things.

(Just as there are grades one above the other in the spiritual kingdom, so too there are similar grades in our life on this earth. If we adopt the literal meaning, then just as we see the heavenly too spheres one above another over our heads, so we can see that the crust of the earth is built up of geological strata one above another.)

SÛRAH LXVI

AT-TAHRÎM (PROHIBITION)

Revealed at Madîna

This Sûrah takes its name from an incident in which the Prophet banned some food for himself.

In the name of Allah, the Compassionate, the Merciful.

1. O Prophet! Why do you forbid that which Allah has made lawful to you, seeking to please your wives? And Allah is Forgiving, Merciful.

(The cause of revelation of this verse is the incident that took place while Prophet Muhammad was at the home of one his wifes Zaynab. His other wifes Aisha and Hafza got jeaulous about this incident and they told the prophet a bad smell came from his breath. Having heard from this prophet swore not to drink honey sherbet 'Juice made with honey'. The prophet here is commanded to Allah to break his oath.)

2. Allah has made lawful for you *(Muslims)* absolution from your oaths *(of such a kind)*, and

Allah is your Protector. He is the Knower, the Wise.

3. When the Prophet confided a secret to one of his wives; and when she disclosed it and Allah informed him of this, he made known one part of it and said nothing about the other. And when he told it her she said: 'Who has told you?' He replied: 'The Knower, the Aware, has told me.'

(The prophet confided to one of his wifes 'Havsa' about the order of Khalifate after his death. The order would be Abu Bakr, and Omar R.A. after him. His wife Hafsa disclosed this secret to Aisha R.A. The prophet was informed about this by Allah (s.w.t.) through revelation.)

4. If you two[1] turn to Allah in repentance for your hearts were inclined *(to the prohibition)* you will be pardoned; but if you back up each other against him, know that Allah is his protector, and Gabriel, and the righteous among the faithful. The angels too are his helpers.

5. It may happen that his Lord, if he divorces you, will give him in your place better wives than yourselves, submissive to Allah and full of faith, devout, penitent, obedient, and given to fasting; both formerly married and virgins.

6. O you who believe! Guard yourselves and your kindred against the Fire which has fuel of men and stones, whose keepers are fierce and mighty *(angels)* who never disobey Allah's command, and promptly do His bidding.

7. *(Then it will be said):* 'O you who disbelieve! Make no excuses for yourselves this day. You will be rewarded according to your deeds.'

---

[1] Hafsa and Aisha.

8. O believers! Turn to Allah in true repentance. Your Lord may forgive you your sins and admit you to gardens watered by running streams, on a day when the Prophet and those who believe with him will suffer no disgrace at the hands of Allah. Their light will shine in front of them and on their right, and they will say: 'Our Lord, perfect our light for us and forgive us. You have power over all things.'

(Those who make repentance should not go back to committing same crime. "Nasouh" means, to advise oneself, to regret not to committ the same crime again.)

9. O Prophet! make war on the disbelievers and the hypocrites, and deal sternly with them. Hell will be their home, evil their fate.

10. Allah has given as example to the disbelievers the wife of Noah and the wife of Lot. They were married to two of Our righteous servants, but they deceived them, so that their husbands availed them nothing against Allah, and it was said (to them): "Enter the Fire along with those who enter.

(Noah's wife used to tell the people that he was a madman.)

11. But to the faithful Allah has given as example Pharaoh's wife, who said: 'My Lord! Build for me a home with You in the Garden, and deliver me from Pharaoh and his misdeeds. Deliver me from a wicked nation.'

(The wife of Pharaoh, Asiye was a believer when Pharaoh tied Asiye's hands and legs and put o heavy rock on her chest under the sun she prayed to her Lord the prayer in the above verse.)

12. And Allah has given as example Mariam, Imran's daughter, who preserved her chastity and into whose womb We breathed of Our spirit; who put her trust in the words of her Lord and His Scriptures, and was truly devout.

SÛRAH LXVII

AL-MULK (THE SOVEREIGNTY)

Revealed at Makka

This Sûrah takes its name from the word '*Al-Mulk*' in the first verse.

In the name of Allah, the Compassionate, the Merciful.

1. Blessed is He in whose hand is the Sovereignty, and He is Able to do all things.

2. Who has created life and death that He may try you, which of you is best in conduct; and He is Mighty, the Forgiving.

(Life is not a meaningless existence, nor the death is end of everything. On the contrary, life in this world is 'the near life' and continuation of it is 'life of Hereafter' and human being has been being tested in this world.)

3. Who has created seven heavens in harmony. You *(Muhammad)* cannot see any fault in the Beneficent One's creation; then look again . Can you see any rift?

4. Then look again, and yet again, your sight will return to you weakened and made dim.

5. Verily We have beautified the world's heaven with lamps, and We have made them missiles for the devils, for whom We have prepared the doom of flame.

(The missiles for the devils are "Shehabs". For further information look Surah Al Hijr Verses 16-18 and Surah As-Saffat verses 6-10.)

6. And for those who disbelieve in their Lord there is the doom of hell, a hapless journey's end!

7. When they are flung into it they hear its roaring as it boils up.

8. As though it would burst with rage. Whenever a fresh host is flung into it, its keepers ask them: 'Did no-one come to warn you?'

9. They say: 'Yes, verily, a warner came to us; but we denied and said: Allah has revealed nothing: you are in grave error.'

10. And they say: 'If only we had listened and understood, we should not now be among the people of Hell.'

11. So they acknowledged their sins; but far from Allah's mercy are the people of Hell.

12. But those who fear their Lord, although they cannot see Him, will be forgiven and richly rewarded.

13. Whether you speak in secret or aloud, He knows what is in your hearts.

14. Should He not know what He created? And He is the Gracious and All-Knowing.

15. He it is who has made the earth subservient to you, so walk in the paths of it and eat of His providence. And to Him will be the resurrection *(of the dead)*.

(Everything in earth is given to the command (use) of man for his own good. And everything on earth is subservient to man. This verse encourages man to progress especially the muslims.)

16. Are you confident that He who is in heaven will not cause the earth to cave in beneath you and *(cause you)* to be swallowed by it as it shakes?

(It is Allah who He decides about the management of affairs of the universe with His angels. But without his permission nothing happens in the world.)

17. Or are you confident that He who is in the heaven will not loose against you a sandy whirlwind? You will before long know how *(terrible)* was My warning.

18. And verily those before them denied, then *(see)* the manner of My wrath *(against them)!*

19. Have they not seen the birds above them spreading out their wings and closing them? None save the Merciful sustains them. He is Seer of all things.

20. Who is it that will defend you like an entire army, if not the Merciful? Truly, the disbelievers are in error.

21. Or who will provide for you if He withholds His sustenance? Yet they persist in arrogance and in rebellion.

22. Who is more rightly guided, he that goes grovelling on his face, or he that walks upright upon a straight path?

23. Say: 'He it is who gave you being, and has assigned to you ears and eyes and hearts. Yet you are seldom thankful.'

24. Say: 'It was He who multiplied you on the earth, and before Him you will all be assembled.'

25. They ask: 'When will this promise be fulfilled, if what you say be true?'

26. Say: 'Allah alone has knowledge of that. My mission is but to warn you plainly.'

27. But when they see it near, the faces of the disbelievers will turn black with gloom and a voice will say: 'This is the doom which you used to call.'

28. Say (O Muhammad): 'Have you thought: Whether Allah destroys me and all my followers or has mercy upon us, who will protect the disbelievers from the woeful punishment?'

29. Say: 'He is the Beneficent. In Him we believe and in Him we put our trust. You will know who is in grave error.'

30. Say: 'Think: if all the water that you have were to sink down into the earth, who would give you gushing water in its place?

SÛRAH LXVIII

AL-QALAM (THE PEN)

Revealed at Makka

The Pen takes its name from the word 'Al-Qalam', which occurs in the first verse.

In the name of Allah, the Compassionate, the Merciful.

1. Nûn. By the Pen and what they write.

(1-Nûn-is a mystical letter. These kind of letters are called al-huruf al Muqatta'ât, As it was explained at the beginning of Surah Al Baqara. The true meaning of it is not known. But some of the commentators who try to give meaning to it call it ink-container. And in Surah Al-Alaq, and in this verse pen is mentioned. This is to attract the attention of the reader to encourage man to read.)

2. By the grace of your Lord, you are not a madman.

(The attention is brought to the idolators mind to remind them the prophethood is a blessing giving to Prophet Muhammad, and he is not a mad man as they accuse of him to be. This verse is an answer to idolaters that they are the liars.)

3. An unfailing reward awaits you.

4. Surely you have a Sublime Character.

5. And you will see and they will see.

6. Which of you is the demented.

7. Verily your Lord is best aware of those who stray from His path, and of those who are rightly guided.

8. Therefore, obey not the rejecters.

9. They wish you were pliant, so that they would be pliant.

10. Nor yield to the wretch who makes many oaths.

11. Detracter, spreader abroad of slanders.

12. Hinderer of the good, transgressor, malefactor.

13. Violent *(and cruel)* with all that, base - born.

14. It is because he possesses wealth and numerous sons.

15. That when Our revelations are recited to him, he says: 'Mere fables of the men of old.'

16. Soon We shall brand him on the nose!

17. Verily We have tried them as We tried the owners of the orchard who had sworn that they would pluck its fruit next morning.

18. Without adding any reservations *(such as: if it be Allah's will).*

19. Then a visitation came down upon it while they slept.

20. And in the morning it was as black as midnight.

21. At daybreak they called out to one another.

22. Saying: 'Hurry to your orchard, if you would pick its fruit.'

23. So they went off, whispering to one another:

24. 'No needy man will enter it today against you.' *(It was a custom to allow the poor a gleaning of all harvests).*

25. Thus they went out, fixed in their resolve.

26. But when they saw it, they said: 'We have been wrong.

27. We are utterly ruined.'

28. The best among them said: 'Did I not bid you to praise Allah?'

29. They said: 'Glorified be our Lord! We have assuredly done wrong!'

30. Then some of them drew near to others, self-reproaching.

31. They said: 'Alas for us! In truth we were outrageous.

32. It may be that our Lord will give us a better orchard in its place. To our Lord we turn!'

33. Such was the punishment. And verily the punishment of the Hereafter is greater, if they did but know.

34. Verily, for the righteous are gardens of bliss with their Lord.

35. Are We to deal with the true believers as We deal with the wrongdoers?

36. What is the matter with you? How foolishly you judge!

37. Or have you a Book through which you learn,

38. That you will have through it whatever you choose?

39. Or have you covenants with Us on oath binding till the Day of Resurrection that you will have whatever you demand?

40. Ask them *(O Muhammad)* which of them will vouch for that!

41. Or have they other gods? Then let them bring their other gods, if they are truthful.

42. On the day when the dread event takes place and they are bidden to prostrate themselves, they will not be able.

(By the "dread event" means the truth will come out openly.)

43. Their eyes will be cast down, ignominy will cover them. And they had been summoned to prostrate themselves while they were yet unhurt.

44. Therefore leave to Me those that deny this revelation. We will lead them step by step to their ruin in ways beyond their knowledge.

45. I shall bear long with them: My stratagem is sure.

46. Or do you *(Muhammad)* ask a fee from them so that they are heavily taxed?

47. Or that the Unseen is in their hands, so that they can write it down?

48. So wait with patience for the judgement of your Lord and do not be like him who was swallowed by the fish *(Jonah)*, who cried out in despair.

49. Had his Lord not bestowed on him His grace, he would have been cast into the wilderness while he was reprobate.

50. But his Lord chose him and placed him among the righteous.

51. And the disbelievers would fain disconcert you with their eyes when they hear the Reminder, and they say: 'he is indeed mad;'

52. But it is nothing less than a Reminder to creation.

SÛRAH LXIX

AL-HÂQQA (THE REALITY)

Revealed at Makka

Takes its name from a word which occurs in the first three verses, and implying the Resurrection.

In the name of Allah, the Compassionate, the Merciful.

1. The Reality!

2. What is the Reality?

3. Ah, What would make you realise what the Reality is?

(The Day of Judgement or Settlement of Accounts will be a tremendous day. The importance of this day is emphasized.)

4. *(The tribes of)* Thamoud and Aad disbelieved in the judgement to come.

5. As for Thamoud, they were destroyed by the lightning.

6. And as for Aad, they were destroyed by a fierce roaring wind,

7. Which He imposed on them for seven long nights and eight long days so that you might have seen men lying overthrown, as they were hollow trunks of palm-trees.

8. Can you see any remnant of them?

9. Pharaoh, and those before him, and the ruined towns, also committed sin.

10. And disobeyed their Lord's messenger. With a terrible scourge He smote them.

11. When the Flood rose high We carried you upon the ship.

12. That We might make it a memorial for you, and that remembering ears *(that heard the story)* might remember.

(Indication is to the flood of Noah "We carried you upon the ship" means we carried your ancestors. If We had not spared them, you would not have come to existence.)

13. And when the trumpet shall sound one blast,

14. And the earth with the mountains be lifted up and crushed with one crush,

15. Then, on that day, will the Event befall.

16. And the heaven will split asunder, for that day it will be frail.

17. And the angels will be on all its sides. And eight *(of them)* will carry the throne of your Lord above them.

18. On that day you will be exposed; not a secret of you will be hidden.

19. Then, as for him who is given his record in his right hand, he will say: 'Take, read my book!

20. Surely, I knew that I should have to meet my reckoning;'

21. Then he will be in a blissful state.

22. In a high Garden.

23. With clusters of fruit within reach.

24. *(We shall say to him):* 'Eat and drink to your heart's content because of what you did in days gone by.'

25. But as for him who is given his record in his left hand, he will say: 'Oh, would that I had not been given my book.

26. Would that I knew nothing of my account!

27. Would that my death had ended all!

28. My wealth has availed me nothing,

29. My power has gone from me!

(Whatever power the disbelievers possessed in this world has no use in the Hereafter therefore they are doomed to hell-fire.)

30. *(It will be said):* 'Take him and bind him.

31. And then expose him to hell-fire,

32. Then fasten him with a chain seventy cubits long.

33. For he did not believe in Allah the Tremendous.

34. Nor did he urge the feeding of the poor.

(It is significant that not urging the feeding of the poor is mentioned immediately after disbelief, as a grave sin.)

35. Therefore, he has no lover here this day.

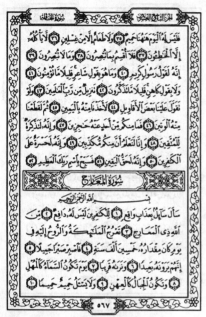

36. Nor any food except filth.

37. Which only sinners eat!

38. I swear by all that you can see,

39. And all that is hidden from your view.

40. That it is indeed the speech of a noble messenger.

(The Master of that speech is Allah (s.w.t.) the messenger is Prophet Muhammad who received the messega from Angel Gabrial.)

41. It is not poet's speech: scant is your faith!

42. Nor sooth-sayer's divination: how little you reflect!

43. It is a revelation from the Lord of the Worlds.

44. And if he had invented false sayings concerning Us,

45. We assuredly had taken him by the right hand

46. And then severed his life-artery,

47. And not one of you could have held Us off from him.

48. It is a warrant to righteous men.

49. We know that there are some among you who will deny it.

50. It is indeed an anguish for the disbelievers.

51. It is absolute truth.

52. So, glorify the name of your Lord, the Tremendous!

SÛRAH LXX

AL-MA'ÂRIJ (THE WAYS OF ASCENT)

Revealed at Makka

Takes its name from the word Ma'ârij which means stages of ascending.

In the name of Allah, the Compassionate, the Merciful.

1. A questioner questioned concerning the doom about to fall.

2. Upon the disbelievers, which none can repel,

(The disbelievers mentioned in this verse are Nadr. b. Haris and Abu Jahl)

3. From Allah, Lord of the Ascending Stairways.

4. *(Whereby)* the angels and the Spirit ascend to Him in one day, the measure of which is fifty thousand years.

(The meaning of the "day" is explained in Surah As Sajda verse 5.)

5. Therefore conduct yourself with becoming patience.

6. They think *(the Day of Judgement)* is far off;

7. While We see it near at hand.

8. On that day the sky will become as molten copper,

9. And the hills become as flakes of wool.

10. And no familiar friend will ask a question of his friend

11. Though they will be given sight of them. To redeem himself from the torment of that day the guilty man will gladly sacrifice his children

12. And his spouse and his brother,

13. And his kin that harboured him,

14. And all that are in the earth, if then this might deliver him.

15. By no means! It is a flaming Fire.

16. Eager to roast;

(The word "Shevah" used in this verse means in arabic skin of the head-or scalp. It can be also interpreted as the parts of body; the heads, the hands, and the feet and other internal organs.)

17. And it will call him who turned his back *(on the true faith).*

18. And amassed riches and covetously hoarded them.

19. Indeed, man was created impatient,

20. When evil befalls him he is despondent;

21. But blessed with good fortune he grows niggardly.

22. Not so the worshippers,

23. Who are steadfast in prayer;

24. And in whose wealth there is a right acknowledged

25. For the beggar and the destitute;

26. And those who believe in the Day of Judgement,

27. And those who are fearful of their Lord's doom.

28. For none is secure from the punishment of their Lord;

29. Who restrain their carnal desire,

30. Save for their wives and slave-girls, for thus they are not blameworthy.

31. But those who trespass beyond this are transgessors;

32. And those who keep their pledges and their covenant.

33. And those who stand by their testimony

34. And those who are attentive at their worship,

(While enumarating qualities of good people, prayer, worship is mentioned in the beginning (22) and at the end (34), because of its importance.)

35. These will dwell in Gardens, honoured.

36. Now what is the matter with the disbelievers, that they keep staring toward you *(O Muhammad),* open-eyed.

37. On the right and on the left, in groups?

38. Does every one of them seek to enter the Garden of Delight?

(The polytheists used to listen to the Prophet along with the believers. They would say to themselves that if those who believed in the Last Messenger's message, Islam entered Paradise, they would have certainly entered even before.)

39. By no means. For We have created them out of the *(base matter)* they know.

40. I swear by the Lord of the rising- places and the setting-places *(of the sun)* that We are Able

41. To replace them by *(others)* better than them. And We are not to be outrun.

42. So leave them to plunge and play until they face the day which they are promised;

43. The day when they come forth from the graves in haste, as racing to a goal.

44. With downcast eyes and countenances distorted with shame. Such is the day which they are promised.

("The goal" they (disbelievers) race is perhaps "their idols" wishing them that would be help to them.)

SÛRAH LXXI
NOAH
Revealed at Makka

In this Sûrah, the tale of the Prophet Noah and his activities is related.

In the name of Allah, the Compassionate, the Merciful.

1. We sent forth Noah to his people, saying: 'Warn your people before a woeful scourge overtakes them!'

2. He said: 'O my people! I am a plain warner to you

3. *(Bidding you):* Serve Allah and fear Him, and obey me.

4. So He may forgive you your sins and respite you to an appointed term. When the term of Allah arrives, none shall put it back. Would that you understood this!'

(The word "sins" used in this verse means the sins of the believers before they entered into Islâm or the sins committed after entering into Islâm except the rights of the others.)

5. He said: 'My Lord! Day and night I have called my people.'

6. But my call has only added to their aversion.

7. Each time I call on them to seek Your pardon, they thrust their fingers in their ears and cover themselves with their garments, persisting in sin and bearing themselves with insolent pride.

8. Further, I have called to them aloud.

9. Further, I have spoken to them in public and secretly in private.

10. Saying: Ask forgiveness from your Lord: for He is Oft-Forgiving.

11. He will send rain to you in abundance,

12. And will help you with wealth and sons, and will bestow on you Gardens and bestow on you rivers.

13. What is the matter with you that you do not hope toward Allah for dignity

14. Seeing that it is He that has created you in diverse stages?

(Diverse stages means: basic elements, combination of elements so as to be convenient food for human being, then the four basic things, then sperm, and then clot, bone and finally human being in the perfect form.)

15. Can you not see how Allah has created the seven heavens one above another.

16. Placing in them the moon as a light and the sun as a lantern?

17. Allah has brought you forth from the earth like a plant.

18. And to the earth He will restore you. Then He will bring you back afresh.

19. And Allah has made the earth a vast expanse for you

20. So that you may walk in its spacious paths!

21. Noah said: "My Lord, my people have disobeyed me and followed those whose wealth and offspring only hastened their perdition.

22. And they have devised an outrageous plot.

23. And said (to each other) 'Do not renounce your gods. Do not forsake Wadd or Suwa' or Yaghûth or Ya'ûq or Nasr.'

(These were the most important idols of that folk.)

24. They have already misled many; therefore, drive the wrongdoers only to further error.

(The disbelievers who did not believe in Noah forced Noah to make a prayer like this.)

25. And because of their sins they were overwhelmed by the Flood and cast into a Fire. They found none to help them besides Allah.

26. And Noah said: 'O my Lord! do not leave a single disbeliever in the land.

27. If you spare them they will mislead Your servants and beget none but sinners and disbelievers.

28. O my Lord! Forgive me, my parents and every true believer who seeks refuge in my house. Forgive all the faithful, men and women, and do not increase the wrong-doers save in ruin'.

(The word "house" used by Noah might be his ship or his place of worship.)

SÛRAH LXXII
AL-JINN (THE JINN)

Revealed at Makka

This takes its name from a word in the first verse, the meaning of which is 'elemental spirits' to whom, as to mankind, the Qur'ân came as a guidance. The incident occured during the Prophet's return from his unsuccessful missionary journey to Tâ'if.

THE JINN

In the name of Allah, the Compassionate, the Merciful.

1. Say *(O Muhammad):* 'It has been revealed to me that a company of the jinn gave ear, and they said: We have heard a wonderful Qur'ân,

2. Which guides to rightousness, so we believe in it and we shall not join *(in worship)* any *(gods)* with our Lord.

(On his return from Taif Prophet Muhammad led the prayers in morning prayers. The Jinn were present at that time. Prophet Muhammad did not see them. Later on it was revealed to him by above verses.)

3. And *(we believe)* that He - exalted be the glory of our Lord! - has taken neither wife nor son.

4. There were come foolish ones among us, who used to utter extravagant lies against Allah;

5. And, we had supposed that human kind and Jinn would not speak a lie concerning Allah.

6. True, there were persons among mankind who took shelter with persons among the jinns, but they increased them in folly.

7. And indeed they supposed, even as you supposed, that Allah would not raise anyone *(from the dead).*

8. *(The jinn who had listened to the Qur'ân said):* 'We had sought the heaven but had found it filled with strong warders and meteors.

9. We used, indeed, to sit there in *(hidden)* stations, to *(steal)* a hearing; but any who listens now will find a flaming fire watching him in ambush.

10. And we don't know whether ill is intended to those on earth, or whether their Lord intends guidance for them.

11. And among us there are righteous folk and among us there are far from that. We are sects having different rules.

12. And we know that we cannot escape from Allah in the earth, nor can we escape by flight.

13. And when we heard the guidance, we believed in it: he that believes in his Lord shall fear neither wrong nor harm.

14. Among us there are some who have surrendered *(to Allah)* and there are among us some who are unjust. Now those who surrendered to Allah, such have taken the right path.'

15. But those who are unjust, they will become the fuel of hell.

16. If they *(the pagans)* follow the right path, We shall vouchsafe them abundant rain.

17. And thereby put them to the proof. But if any turns away from the remembrance of his Lord, He will thrust him into ever-growing torment.

18. And the places of worship are only for Allah, so do not pray to anyone along with Allah.

(The places of worship (masjeds) are described as such:(1) places of worship built for that purpose; (2) Praying and worshipping are not limited only to masjeds, the whole face of earth is the place of worship.(3) All masjeds have qıbla and that qıbla is the Masjed Al Haram",(4) The parts of the body that touches are the places of worship.

In this verse muslims are warned not to worship anyone along with Allah, like Christians and Jews do when they enter into their churches and synogogues.)

19. And when the slave of Allah *(the Prophet)* stood up in prayer to Him, they crowded on him, almost stifling.

(When the Prophet of Allah stood up, the people of Jinn crowded on him in order to listen the Holy Qur'an being recited. Some other commentators of the Holy Qur'an interpreted this verse as idolatars both (man and Jinn) crowded on him in order to cancel the religion of the Prophet Muhammad.)

20. Say *(to them, O Muhammad)*: 'I will pray to my Lord and associate none with Him.'

21. Say: 'It is not in my power to cause you harm or to bring you to right conduct.'

22. Say: 'No one can deliver me from Allah *(If I were to disobey Him),* nor should I find refuge except in Him.

23. *(Mine is)* but conveyance *(of the truth)* from Allah, and His messages; those that disobey Allah and His Messenger, for them is Hell: they will dwell there forever.'

24. At length, when they behold the scourge with which they are threatened they will know which side had the less powerful protector and which was fewer in numbers.

25. Say: 'I cannot tell whether that with which you are threatened is imminent, or whether my Lord will set it on a far-off day.

26. He *(alone)* knows the unseen, and does not reveal to anyone His secret.

27. Except to every messenger whom He has chosen, and then He sends down guardians who walk before him and behind him.

28. That He may know that they have indeed conveyed the message of their Lord. He surrounds all their doings, and He keeps count of all things.

SÛRAH LXXIII

AL-MUZZAMMIL

(THE ENSHROUDED ONE)

Revealed at Makka

This Sûrah takes its name from the word *Al-Muzzammil* which means 'the enshrouded one': the Prophet went to his wife Khadija after his first vision and told her to 'wrap him up'.

In the name of Allah, the Compassionate, the Merciful.

1. O you *(Muhammad)* folded in garments!

(When the first revelation was revealed to Prophet Muhammad the Arch-Angel Gabrial appeared to him in the form of an angel the prophet was very frightened he was shaking all over, he wert to his wife Knatija to cover him.

After this incident happened the Angel Gabrial appeared again and addressed him as such: "O you (Muhammad) folded in garments.)

2. Keep vigil the night long, except a little,

3. Half of it, or a little less,

4. Or a little more, and recite the Qur'ân in slow, measured rhythmic tones.

5. We are about to address to you words of great gravity.

6. Truly the rising by night is *(a time)* when impression is stonger and speech more certain.

7. True you have by day a chain of business.

8. But keep in remembrance the name of your Lord and dedicate yourself to Him utterly.

9. He is the Lord of the East and the West; there is no god but Him. So choose Him alone for your defender.

10. And bear with patience what they *(the disbelievers)* say, and leave their company with dignity.

11. Leave Me to deal with the deniers, lords of ease and comfort *(in this life);* and bear with them yet a little while.

12. We have *(in store for them)* heavy fetters and a blazing fire.

13. Choking food and a painful doom.

(The "food" mentioned in this verse is considered as to be poisonous throne, zaqqum, thorn made out of fire, blood and pus and filth.)

14. *(This will be their lot)* on the day when the earth shakes with all its mountains, and the mountains crumble into heaps of shifting sand.

15. We have sent to you a messenger as witness against you, even as We sent to Pharaoh a messenger.

16. But Pharaoh disobeyed the messenger, so that We seized him with a dreadful punishment.

17. Then how, if you disbelieve, will you protect yourselves on a day which will turn children grey

18. The very heaven being then rent asunder. His promise is to be fulfilled.

19. Verily, this is a Reminder. Let him who will, then, choose a way to his Lord.

20. Your Lord knows that you (Muhammad) sometimes keep vigil nearly two thirds of the night and sometimes half or one - third of it, and so does a party of those with you. Allah measures the night and the day. He knows that you cannot count it, and turns to you mercifully. Recite from the Qur'ân as much as is easy (for you); He knows that among you there are sick men and others travelling the road in quest of Allah's bounty; and yet others fighting for His cause. Recite from it, then, as much as is easy (for you). Attend to your prayers, pay the Zakât, and give Allah a generous loan. Whatever good you do for your souls you will surely find it with Allah, better and richly rewarded by Him. Implore Allah to forgive you; He is Forgiving, Merciful.

(Some of the companions of the prophet were offering prayers in good part of the night they would get very tired and their feet would be swollen. Although the night prayer for the prophet was compulsory, it was not cumpolsory for the companions. So every person should offer salat prayers at night according to his physical condition.

Whatever good one does should do it for himself before he dies while he is living in this world. After one dies although he might have the best will it might not be carried out by his inheritors.)

SÛRAH LXXIV
AL-MUDDATHTHIR
(THE CLOAKED ONE)

Revealed at Makka

Takes its name from a word which occurs in the first verse. When the Prophet suddenly saw the angel again, he wrapped himself in his cloak. In this Sûrah the Prophet was ordered to begin preaching of Islam openly.

In the name of Allah, the Compassionate, the Merciful.

1. You (Muhammad) who are wrapped up in your vestment,

2. Arise and give warning!

3. Magnify your Lord!

4. Cleanse your garments,

5. And keep away from all pollution.

6. Don't show favour, seeking worldly gain!

7. Be patient for the sake of your Lord!

8. For when the trumpet sounds,

9. Surely that day will be a day of distress,

10. And far from easy for the disbelievers.

11. Leave Me to deal with him whom I created lonely,

12. And then bestowed on him ample means,

13. And sons abiding in his presence

14. And made life smooth and comfortable for him.

15. Yet he is greedy that I should add (yet more).

16. By no means! For to Our revelations he has been stubborn!

(Prophet Muhammad in order not to forget the revelation given to him, he was trying to repeat it with its tongue. So he is reminded here hot to be in hurry so he can memorise the whole thing first and then to repeat it.)

17. On him I shall impose a fearful doom.

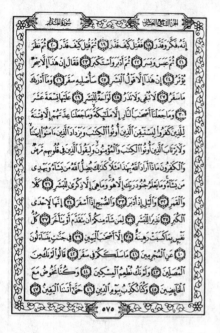

18. For he thought and plotted!

19. And woe to him! How he plotted!

20. Again, woe to him; How he plotted!

21. Then he looked round;

22. Then he frowned and showed displeasure.

23. Then he turned away in pride.

24. Then he said; 'This is nothing but magic from of old;

25. This is nothing but the word of a mortal!'

(Reference is to behaviour of Walid b. Mughira, a notable of Quraish tribe.)

26. Soon I shall cast him into Hell fire!

27. And what will explain to you what Hell fire is?

28. It leaves nothing, it spares no one;

(The person who knows that he is about to die.)

29. It burns the skins of men

30. It is guarded by nineteen *(keepers).*

(The agony of parting from this world and the agony of going to his Lord "next world" is heaped on top of one another.)

31. We have appointed none but angels to guard the Fire, and made their number a subject for dispute among the disbelievers, so that those to whom the Scriptures were given may be convinced and the true believers strengthen in their faith; that those to whom the Scriptures were given, and the true believers, may have no doubts; and that those in whose hearts there is disease, together with the disbelievers, may say: 'What could Allah mean by this?' Thus Allah leaves in error whom He will and guides whom He pleases. None knows the soldiers of your Lord but Him.This is nothing but an admonition to mankind.

32. Nay, by the moon!

33. And by the receding night!

34. And the forthcoming dawn!

35. This is one of the greatest portents.

36. As a warning to mankind

37. To any of you that would like to march on and those that would like to remain behind.

38. Each soul is held in pledge for what it earns

39. Except the companions of the right hand;

40. They will be in Gardens *(of Delight);* they will question each other,

41. And *(ask)* of the sinners:

42. 'What led you into Hellfire?

43. They will say: 'We were not of those who prayed

44. Nor were we of those who fed the wretched;

45. But we used to talk vanities with vain talkers,

46. And we used to deny the Day of Judgement,

47. Till the inevitable *(death)* overtook us.'

48. No intercessor's plea will avail them.

49. Why then do they turn away from admonition?

50. As if they were frightened asses.

51. Fleeing from a lion!

52. Indeed, each one of them desires a scripture *(of his own)* to be unrolled *(before him).*

53. By no means! Verily they have no fear of the Hereafter.

54. No, this is an admonition.

55. Let him who will, take heed!

56. But none takes heed except by the will of Allah. He is the Lord of Righteousness and the Lord of Forgiveness.

SÛRAH LXXV

AL-QIYÂMA (THE RESURRECTION)

Revealed at Makka

Takes its name from the word *al-Qiyâmah* which occurs in the first verse.

In the name of Allah, the Compassionate, the Merciful.

1. Nay, I swear by the Day of Resurrection;
(Man's development from a single sperm to birth and the period of gestation.)

2. Nay, I swear by the accusing soul *(that this Scripture is true).*

3. Does man think that we shall never put his bones together again?

4. Indeed, We can remould the very tips of his fingers.

5. Yet man would ever deny what is to come.

6. He asks: 'When will be this Day of Resurrection?'

7. At length, when the sight is confounded,

8. And the moon is buried in darkness,

9. And the sun and moon are joined together.

10. That day man will say: 'Where is the refuge?'

11. By no means! No place to flee!

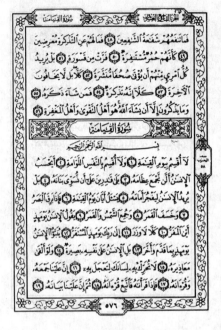

12. To your Lord is the recourse that day.

13. On that day man will be informed of all that he has sent before and left behind.

14. Oh, but man will be evidence against himself.

15. Even though he were to offer excuses.

16. Do not move your tongue *(with the revelation)* so that you may hasten *(committing)* it *(to memory).*

(Prophet Muhammad in order not to forget the revelation given to him, he was trying to repeat it with his tongue. So he is reminded here not to be in hurry so he can memorise the whole thing first and then to repeat it.)

17. It is for Us to collect it and to promulgate it.

18. But when We have promulgated it, follow its recital *(as promulgated):*

19. We shall Ourself explain its meaning.

(The agony of parting from this world and the agony of going to his Lord 'next world' is heaped on top of another.)

31. So he gave nothing in charity, nor did he pray!

32. But on the contrary, he rejected Truth and turned away!

33. Then he went to his folk with glee.

34. Well have you deserved (this doom);

35. Well have you deserved it.

36. Does man think that he will be left uncontrolled (without purpose)?

37. Was he not a drop of fluid which gushed forth?

38. Then he became a clinging clot; then (Allah) shaped and fashioned

39. And made of him a pair, the male and female.

40. Is He then not able to raise the dead to life?

SÛRAH LXXVI

AL-DAHR OR AL-INSÂN

(TIME OR MAN)

Revealed at Makka

Takes its name from words which occur in the first verse.

In the name of Allah, the Compassionate, the Merciful.

1. Has there come over man a period of time when he was nothing, not mentioned?

(Man's development from a single sperm to birth and the period of gestation.)

2. We have created man from sperm mixed *(with ovum)* to put him to proof. So We have endowed him with sight and hearing.

3. We have shown him the right path, whether he be grateful or ungrateful.

4. We have prepared for disbelievers chains and fetters, and a blazing Fire.

5. But the righteous will drink of a cup tempered with Kâfûr *(Camphor)*.

20. Yet you *(men)* love this fleeting life.

21. And you are heedless of the life to come.

22. On that day there will be fresh faces.

23. Looking towards their Lord.

24. And on that day there will be mournful faces,

25. Knowing that a great calamity will be inflicted on them.

(Verse 25 mentions the morning, noon and midafternoon prayers; and verse 26 mentions evening and night prayer in the second sentence of the verse the obligatory night prayer which is only for the prophet as mentioned.)

26. But when *(man's soul)* reaches the throat,

27. And it is said: 'Is there a magician to save him?'

28. And he knows that it is the parting:

(The person who knows he is about to die.)

29. And agony is heaped on agony;

30. To your Lord that day will be the driving.

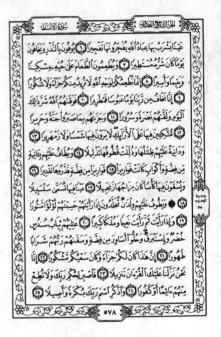

6. A fountain where the slaves of Allah drink, making it gush forth abundantly.

7. *(Because)* they fulfill the vow and fear a day whose evil flies far and wide.

8. And they feed, for the love of Allah, the indigent, the orphan, and the captive.

9. Saying, 'We feed you for the sake of Allah alone. No reward do we desire from you, nor thanks.'

10. We only fear a day of distressful wrath from our Lord.

11. Therefore, Allah has warded off from them the evil of that day, and has made them find brightness and joy

12. And has awarded them for all that they endured, a Garden and *(garments of)* silk.

13. Reclining in the *(Garden)* on raised thrones, they will see there neither the sun's excessive heat nor the biting cold.

14. Trees will spread their shade around them, and fruits will hang in clusters over them,

15. They will be served with silver dishes, and goblets of crystal,

16. Crystal-clear, but made of silver, which they themselves will measure:

(The comparison is made here between the blessings of this world and the rewards of the next world 'heaven' to believers as blessings. Although names are same they are different in nature.)

17. And they will be given to drink from cups brimful with ginger-flavoured water.

18. From a fount called Salsabîl.

19. They will be attended by youths never aging, who, to the beholder's eyes, will seem like scattered pearls.

20. When you gaze upon that scene you will behold blessings and a glorious kingdom.

21. Their raiment will be fine green silk and gold embroidery. And they will be adorned with bracelets of silver. And their Lord will give them a pure beverage to drink.

22. *(And it will be said to them)*: 'Verily this is a Reward for you, and your endeavour is accepted and recognised.'

23. We, even We, have revealed to you the Qur'ân by stages.

24. Therefore submit patiently to your Lord's command, and do not obey of them any sinner or disbeliever.

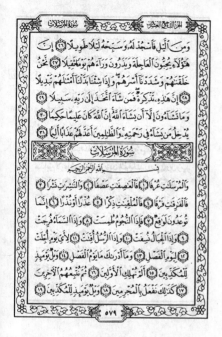

25. And celebrate the name of your Lord morning and evening.

(Verse 25 mentions the morning, noon and midafternoon prayers; and verse 26 mentions evening and night prayer in the second sentence of the verse the obligatory night prayer which is only for the prophet is mentioned.)

26. And prostrate to Him *(a portion)* of the night. And glorify Him through the long night.

27. As to these, they love the fleeting life, and put away behind them *(the remembrance of)* a grievous day.

28. We created them, and endowed their limbs and joints with strength. And when We will, We can substitute the like of them by a complete change.

(Allah is all powerful who can create man again when he so desires. It is His will to do so in the Hereafter.)

29. This is an admonition: whosoever will, let him take a *(straight)* path to his Lord.

30. Yet you will not, unless Allah wills: for Allah is full of knowledge and wisdom.

31. He will admit to His mercy whom He will: but for the wrongdoers He has prepared a grievous penalty.

SÛRAH LXXVII

AL-MURSALÂT (THE EMISSARIES)

Revealed at Makka

Takes its name from the word *al-Mursalât* which occurs in the first verse. Verses 1,2 and 3 are interpreted as referring to winds; verses 4 and 5 to angels.

In the name of Allah, the Compassionate, the Merciful.

1. By the winds sent forth in swift succession *(to man's profit)*.

2. By the raging hurricanes.

3. By those which cause earth's vegetation to revive.

4. By those who winnow with a winnowing.

5. By those who bring down the Reminder

6. To excuse or to warn.

7. Surely what you are promised will befall.

8. Then when the stars become dim,

9. When the sky is cleft asunder,

10. And when the mountains are blown, away

11. And when Allah's messengers are brought together on the appointed day;

12. For what day is the time appointed?

13. For the Day of Judgement!

14. Would that you knew what the Day of Judgement is!

15. Woe on that day to the deniers!

16. Did We not destroy the former folk?

17. And cause others to follow them?

18. Thus We deal with the guilty.

19. Woe on that day to the deniers!

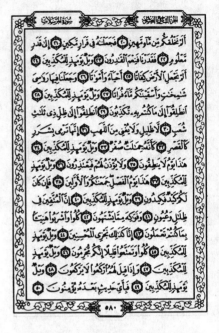

20. Haven't We created you from an unworthy fluid,

21. Which We kept in a safe receptacle,

22. For an appointed time?

23. Thus We have arranged. How excellent is Our arranging!

24. Woe on that day to the deniers!

25. Have We not made the earth a receptacle,

26. Both for the living and the dead,

27. And placed upon it mountains standing firm, and given you fresh water for your drink?

28. Woe on that day to the deniers!

29. *(It will be said to them)* Begone to that *(torment)* which you used to deny!

30. Depart into shadow that will rise high in three columns,

31. Giving neither shade nor shelter from the flames,

32. And throwing up sparks like castles,

33. As though it were yellow camels!

34. Woe on that day to the deniers!

35. On that day they will not be able to speak,

36. Nor will it be open to them to make pleas.

37. Woe on that day to the deniers!

38. This is the Day of Judgement. We have brought you and the past generations together.

39. Now, if you have any wit, outwit Me.

40. Woe on that day to the deniers!

41. The righteous will dwell amidst cool shades and fountains

42. And such fruits as they desire.

43. *(It will be said to them):* 'Eat and drink, and may every joy attend you! This is the reward of your labours.'

44. Thus do We reward the Doers of Good.

45. Woe on that day to the disbelievers!

46. Eat and enjoy yourselves awhile. You are wicked men.

47. Woe on that to the deniers!

48. When they are bidden to kneel down, they do not kneel.

49. Woe on that day to the deniers!

50. In what statement, after this, will they believe?

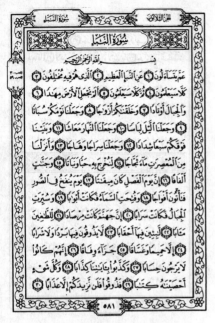

SÛRAH LXXVIII
AN-NABA' (THE TIDING)

Takes its name from the word *Al-Naba* which occurs in the second verse, and deals with the Hereafter.

In the name of Allah, the Compassionate, the Merciful

1. About what do they question one another?

2. About the awesome tiding,

3. Concerning which they are in dispute.

4. Verily, they will soon know!

5. Verily, verily they will soon know!

6. Have We not made the earth as a wide expanse,

7. And the mountains as pegs?

8. We have created you in pairs (*males and females*).

9. We have appointed your sleep for repose,

10. And have appointed the night as a cloak (*a cover of darkness for sleep and rest*),

11. And have appointed the day for livelihood,

12. And We have built above you seven strong (*heavens*),

13. And We have made a lamp blazing with splendour (*the Sun*),

14. And have sent down from the rainy clouds abundant water,

15. So that We may bring forth grain and plants,

16. And gardens thick with foliage.

17. Verily the Day of Judgement is a fixed time.

18. A day when the Trumpet is blown, and you come in multitudes.

19. And the heaven is opened and becomes as gates,

20. And the mountains are set in motion and become as a mirage,

21. Then Hell will lie in ambush,

22. A place of return for the rebellious!

23. They will remain in it for countless ages.

24. There they will taste neither coolness nor any drink,

25. Except boiling water and intense cold:

26. A suitable recompense!

27. This is because they did not expect reckoning;

28. They called Our revelations false with strong denial.

29. But We have recorded all their doings in a Book.

30. Taste, therefore, for We shall not increase you save in torment!

31. As for the righteous, they will surely triumph.

32. Theirs will be gardens and vineyards.

33. Youthful maidens of equal age with firm breasts,

34. And a cup full.

35. There they will hear neither vain talk nor falsehood.

36. A recompense from your Lord; a gift in payment,

37. Lord of the heavens and the earth and all that lies between them, the Compassionate; with Him no one can speak,

38. On that day, when the Spirit and the angels stand up in their ranks, they will not speak; except him who will receive the sanction of the Beneficent and say what is right.

39. That day is true. Let him who will, seek recourse to his Lord.

40. We warn you of a doom at hand. On that day every man will look on his works, and the rejector of faith will say: 'Would that I were dust!'

SÛRAH LXXIX

AN-NÂZI'ÂT (THE SNATCHERS)

Revealed at Makka

This Sûrah deals with the Resurrection.

In the name of Allah, the Compassionate, the Merciful

1. By the angels who violently snatch away the souls of the wicked!

2. And those who gently draw out the souls of the blessed,

3. By the lone stars floating,

4. By the angels hastening,

5. And by those that govern the event,

6. On the day when the Trumpet sounds its first blast,

7. Followed by the second,

8. On that day hearts will be throbbing.

9. While eyes are downcast,

10. They will say: 'Shall we really be restored back to life in the grave,

11. Even after we have become crumbled bones?'

12. They say: 'Then that would be a vain proceeding.'

13. It will be a single cry,

14. And behold, they will all be awakened.

15. Has the story of Moses reached you?

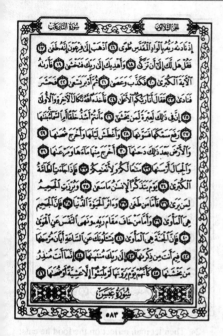

26. Verily in this there is an instructive warning for whosoever fears (Allah):

27. What! are you harder to create than the heaven which He has built?

28. He raised it high and fashioned it.

29. He made dark its night and brought out its light.

30. And after that He spread the earth,

31. And then drew from it water and pastures.

32. Then the mountains He fixed:

33. A provision for you and for your cattle.

34. But when the great disaster comes

35. The day when man will call to mind his labours

36. And when Hell is brought in sight for all,

37. Those who transgressed all bounds

38. And chose this present life

39. Will find themselves in Hell;

40. But those who feared to stand before their Lord and curbed their souls' desires

41. The Garden will be their dwelling place.

42. They question you (Muhammad) about the Hour of Doom: 'When will it be?'

43. But how are you to know?

44. Your Lord alone knows when it will come.

45. You are but a warner for those who fear it.

46. The Day they see it (it will be) as if they had remained only a single evening or the morning of the following day.

(In this surah life after death is discussed, death, life in the grave, rising from the grave, the Day of Judgement, and the place to arrive after the settlement of accounts.)

16. How his Lord called out to him in the sacred valley of Tuwa,

17. (Saying): "Go to Pharaoh: he has transgressed all bounds!

18. And say: 'Have you the desire to purify yourself

19. And that I guide you to your Lord and that you will fear Him?'

20. And he showed him the tremendous token.

21. But he denied and disobeyed,

22. Then he turned away in haste,

23. And gathering his people, he cried out

24. And proclaimed: 'I am your supreme Lord'

25. But Allah seized him with the torment of both the next world and this.

SÛRAH LXXX

'ABASA (HE FROWNED)

Revealed at Makka

(While the Prophet was talking to notables of Quraish, a blind man, Abdullah b. Ummi Maktum came to him and asked to learn about Islam. The Prophet as a human being, did not like the interruption. When the blind man repeated his action, the Prophet frowned. The verses refers to that incident which is one of the proofs of his prophethood, as no one would reproach oneself in this way.)

In the name of Allah, the Compassionate,
the Merciful

1. He *(Muhammad)* frowned and turned away

2. Because the blind man approached him.

3. How can you *(Muhammad)* know? perhaps he might purify himself.

4. Or be mindful, and the Reminder might profit him.

5. As for him who regards himself as self-sufficient.

6. To him you eagerly attend.

7. Though it is not your concern if he does not purify himself.

8. But as for him who eagerly hastens to you,

9. And is in fear of Allah,

10. You are heedless of him.

11. By no means *(should it be so)! (The Qur'ân)* is surely an Admonishment.

12. So let whosoever will, pay heed to it.

13. It is set down on honoured pages,

14. Exalted and purified,

15. *(Borne)* by the hands of emissaries *(angels)*,

16. Noble and righteous.

17. Woe to man! How ungrateful he is!

18. From what stuff did He create him?

19. From a drop of seed. He created and proportioned him.

20. Then made the way easy for him.

21. Then caused him to die, and buried him.

22. Then, when He pleases, He will bring him back to life.

23. Yet he declines to do His bidding.

24. Then let man reflect on the food he eats:

25. How We pour water in showers,

26. Then split the earth in clefts,

27. And cause the grain to grow on it,

28. And grapes, and fresh herbage,

29. And olive-trees and palm-trees

30. And enclosed gardens, dense with lofty trees,

31. And fruits and pasture,

32. Provision for you and your cattle.

33. But when the Shout comes,

34. On the day when a man flees from his brother.

35. His mother and his father,

36. And his wife and his children;

37. For each one of them will on that day have enough concern of his own.

38. On that day, there will be faces radiant,

39. Smiling, rejoicing at good news;

40. And there shall be other faces, on that day, with dust upon them.

41. Veiled in darkness,

42. These are the disbelievers, the wicked.

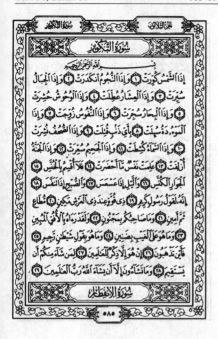

SÛRAH LXXXI

AT-TAKWÎR (THE FOLDING UP)

Revealed at Makka

Takes its name from the 'folding up of the sun'.

In the name of Allah, the Compassionate,
the Merciful

1. When the sun is folded up,

2. And when the stars fall, losing their lustre;

3. And when the mountains are moved;

4. And when the ten-month pregnant camels are abondoned;

5. And when the wild beasts are herded together;

6. And when the seas are set boiling,

7. And when souls are reunited,

8. And when the girl-child that was buried alive is asked

9. For what sin she was slain;

10. And when the records of men's deeds are laid open;

11. And when the heaven is torn away;

12. And when the Hell is set blazing;

13. And when the Garden is brought near;

14. Then every soul will know what it has done.

15. Oh, I swear by the turning planets,

16. And by the stars that rise and set;

17. And by the night as it falls,

18. And by the morning as it breathes:

19. Verily this is the word of a gracious messenger *(Gabriel).*

20. Mighty, established in the presence of the Lord of the Throne.

21. *(One)* to be obeyed, and trustworthy;

22. No, your companion *(the prophet)* is not mad.

23. He saw him *(Gabriel)* on the clear horizon.

24. He does not withold the unseen;

25. Nor is this *(the Qur'ân)* the utterance of an accursed satan.

26. Where then are you going?

27. This *(the Qur'ân)* is but a reminder to all men:

28. To those among you that have the will to be upright.

29. And you cannot will, unless Allah wills, who is Lord of the Worlds.

SÛRAH LXXXII

AL-INFITÂR (THE CLEAVING)

Revealed at Makka

Revealed at Makka after the Sûrah Nâzi'ât, this deals with the cleaving of the sky on the Last Day.

In the name of Allah, the Compassionate, the Merciful

1. When the sky is cleft asunder,

2. And when the planets are dispersed,

3. And when the oceans are poured forth

4. And when the graves are overturned,

5. Each soul will know what it has sent forward and what it has kept back.

6. O man! what has beguiled you from your Lord, the Bountiful,

7. Who created you, then fashioned, then proportioned you?

8. In whatever form He wished, He formed you.

9. No, you deny the Last Judgement.

10. Yet there are guardians watching over you,

11. Noble recorders

12. Who know of all that you do.

13. The righteous surely will dwell in bliss.

14. While the wicked surely will be in blazing Fire.

15. In it they will burn on the Day of Judgement.

16. They will not escape it.

17. What will convey to you what the Day of Judgement is!

18. Again, what will convey to you what the Day of Judgement is!

19. A day on which no soul has power at all for any other. The absolute command on that day is Allah's.

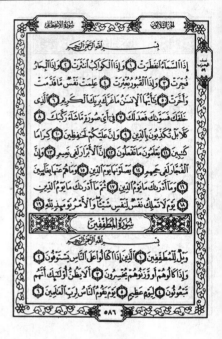

SÛRAH LXXXIII

AL-MUTAFFIFÎN (DEALERS IN FRAUD)

Revealed at Makka

Takes its name from a word in the first verse.

In the name of Allah, the Compassionate, the Merciful

1. Woe to those that deal in fraud;

2. Those who, when others measure for them, exact in full,

3. But when they measure or weigh for others, defraud them!

4. Do they not think that they will be raised to life

5. For a fateful day,

6. A day when all mankind will stand before the Lord of the Worlds?

(Ibn Omar burst into tears when this verse was being recited. If one hides the faults of the products he sells, the wrath of Allah and the curse of angels will be on that person.)

18. But the record of the righteous will be in Illiyyîn.

19. What will convey to you what Illiyyîn is!

20. It is a sealed book,

21. Seen by those who are closest, to Allah.

22. The righteous will surely dwell in bliss.

(Although the idolators fought against the prophet they were defeated by the armies of the prophet. The Arabs who disbelieved already knew this despite that they fought him. The Qur'an they rejected is kept as a permenant record in the sight of Allah. But man still do not take lesson from these incidents.)

23. Reclining upon soft couches, they will look around them;

24. In their faces you recognize the glow of joy.

25. They will be given to drink of a pure wine.

26. Whose seal is musk. For this let all men aspire.

27. And mixed with water of Tasnîm

(Tasnîm is a spring of the water of Paradise.)

28. A spring at which those brought near to Allah will drink.

29. The evil-doers used to laugh at the faithful.

30. And wink at another as they passed them.

31. When they returned to their people; they spoke of them with jests.

32. And when they saw them, they used to say: 'These are erring men!'

33. Yet they were not sent as keepers over them.

34. But on this day the faithful will laugh at the disbelievers

7. Truly, the record of the sinners is in Sijjin.

8. Would that you knew what Sijjin is!

9. It is a book inscribed.

10. Woe on that day to the repudiators!

11. Those who deny the Day of Judgement

12. And non can deny it except every transgressing sinner,

13. When our revelations are recited to him, he says: 'These are fables of the ancients.'

14. No! Their own deeds have cast a veil over their hearts.

15. No! surely on that day they will be veiled from their Lord;

16. They will burn in Hell.

17. Then it will be said to them: 'This is the scourge that you denied!'

35. As they recline upon their couches gazing around them.

36. Are not the disbelievers paid for what they used to do?

SÛRAH LXXXIV

AL-INSHIQÂQ (THE SUNDERING)

Revealed at Makka

This takes its name from a word which occurs in the first verse.

In the name of Allah, the Compassionate, the Merciful

1. When the heaven is split asunder,

2. And attentive to her Lord in fear,

3. And when the earth is spread out

4. And cast out all that is in it, and has voided itself.

5. And attentive to her Lord in fear!

6. O man! You are indeed toiling towards your Lord painfully, and you will meet Him.

7. He that is given his book in his right hand

8. Will have a lenient reckoning,

9. And go back rejoicing to his people.

10. But he that is given his book from behind his back,

11. Will call down destruction on himself.

12. And burn in the fire of Hell;

13. For he was happy among his people,

(In these verses, position of the rich who is egotistic and does not care for others, is described. Those who do not learn from these verses the necessary lessons, will find themselves in that regrettable situation.)

14. And thought he would never return *(to Allah).*

15. Yet his Lord is ever beholding him.

16. Oh, I swear by the glow of sunset;

17. And by the night and all that it brings home,

18. And by the moon, in its full perfection:

19. Surely you will journey on from state to state.

20. Why, then, do they not have faith,

21. And, when the Qur'ân is recited to them, do they not prostrate?

22. But on the contrary, the disbelievers deny it.

23. Yet Allah knows best what they are hiding.

24. So announce to them a woeful doom!

25. Except those who embrace the true faith and do good works; theirs will be a reward unfailing.

SÛRAH LXXXV

AL-BURÛJ (THE CONSTELLATIONS)
Revealed at Makka

It includes a reference to the massacre of the Christians of Najran by the Jewish king Dhû Nuwâs of the Yemen, who incinerated them in a trench.

In the name of Allah, the Compassionate, the Merciful

1. By the heaven with its constellations!

2. And by the Promised Day!

3. And by the witness and the witnessed!

4. Woe to the people of the trench!

5. It was a fire blazing with fuel.

6. When they sat over it.

7. Watching what they were doing to the believers.

8. And they had nothing against them save that they believed in Allah; the Mighty, the Praiseworthy.

9. Sovereign of the heavens and earth; and Allah is witness over all things.

10. Those who persecuted the believing men and women and never repented will suffer the punishment of Hell and the torture of burning.

11. But those who believe and do good works, theirs will be gardens beneath which rivers flow. That is the greatest triumph.

12. Surely the punishment of your Lord is severe.

13. He it is who originates and brings back to life.

14. He is the Forgiving, the Loving,

15. Lord of the Throne, the Glorious,

16. Doer of whatever He wills.

17. Has the story of the hosts come to you,

18. Of Pharaoh and *(the tribe of)* Thamûd?

19. And yet the disbelievers persist in rejecting *(the Truth)*.

20. But Allah surrounds them all.

21. Indeed this is a glorious Qur'ân,

22. Preserved in a well-guarded Tablet.

SÛRAH LXXXVI
AT-TÂRIQ (THE NIGHT STAR)
Revealed at Makka

This takes its name from the word *At-Târiq* which occurs in the first verses meaning the shining star which appears towards dawn. Metaphorically it means the Prophet himself, emerged from the darkness of the Age of Ignorance.

In the name of Allah, the Compassionate, the Merciful

1. By the heaven, and by the night visitant!
2. What will convey to you what the night visitant is!
3. It is the piercing star.
4. There is no soul that has no guardian over it.
5. Now let man reflect from what he is created.
6. He is created from an ejected fluid
7. That issues from between the loins and the ribs.
8. Surely He is able to bring him back to life
9. On a day when all innnermost thoughts will be searched out.
10. Then he will be helpless and without any supporter.
11. By the heaven which gives the returning rain,
12. And by the earth ever bursting with new growth;
13. This *(Qur'ân)* is the conclusive utterance.
14. It is not uttered in jest.
15. They are devising great schemes.
16. And I am Myself devising great schemes!
17. So give a respite to the disbelievers. And let them be alone for a while.

SÛRAH LXXXVII
AL-A'LÂ (THE MOST HIGH)
Revealed at Makka

In the name of Allah, the Compassionate, the Merciful

1. Glorify the name of your Lord, the Most High,
2. Who has created all things and well proportioned them;
3. Who has ordained *(their)* destinies and guided *(them)*;
4. And who brings forth the pasturage,
5. Then turns it into russet stubble.
6. We shall make you recite *(Our revelations)*, so that you will not forget *(any of them)*
7. Except what Allah pleases. He has knowledge of all that is manifest, and all that is hidden.
8. We shall guide you to the easiest path.
9. Therefore give admonition, in case the admonition profits *(the hearer)*.
10. The admonition will be received by those who fear *(Allah)*:
11. But it will be avoided by those most unfortunate ones,
12. Who will enter the greatest Fire,
13. In it he will neither die nor live.
14. Prosperous indeed are those who purify themselves,
15. And glorify the name of their Lord and perform the prayers.

1. Has the account of the Overwhelmer come to you?

2. On that day faces will be humble,

3. Toiling, weary,

4. Burning in a scorching fire,

5. Drinking from a stream of boiling water!

6. They will have no food except bitter thorn-fruit,

7. Which does not nourish, nor release from hunger.

8. On that day other faces will be blissful.

9. Glad for their labours,

10. Dwelling in a lofty garden,

11. Where they hear no idle talk.

12. There will be a gushing fountain:

13. And raised soft couches

14. And goblets set at hand

15. And cushions arrayed

16. And rich carpets spread out.

17. Do they not look at the camels, how they were created?

18. And at the sky, how it was raised?

19. And at the mountains, how they were erected?

20. And the earth, how it was levelled?

21. Therefore, remind, for you are one to remind:

22. You are not at all a warder over them.

23. But who turns away and rejects faith,

24. Allah will punish him with a most terrible torment.

25. Surely to Us will be their return,

26. Then it will be for Us to do the reckoning.

16. But you *(humankind)* prefer the life of this world,

17. While the life to come is better and more lasting.

18. All this is contained in earlier scriptures;

19. The scriptures of Abraham and Moses.

SÛRAH LXXXVIII

AL-GHÂSHIYA (THE OVERWHELMER)

Revealed at Makka

Al-Ghashiyah takes its name from a word in verse 1. An early Makkân Surah. It deals with the matter of destinies of Good and Evil in the Hereafter. The Life goes on according to the plans of Allah. The man's final end is he meets with his Lord to give an account.

In the name of Allah, the Compassionate, the Merciful

SÛRAH LXXXIX

AL-FAJR (THE DAWN)
Revealed at Makka

This takes its name from a word occurring in the first verse.

In the name of Allah, the Compassionate, the Merciful

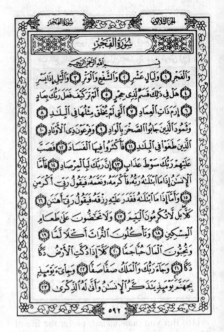

1. By the dawn,

2. And ten nights, *(of the month of Pilgrimage),*

3. And the Even and the Odd,

4. And the night when it passes away;

5. There surely is an oath for thinking man.

6. Have you not considered how your Lord dealt with *(the tribe of)* 'Aad.

7. *(The people)* of the many-columned city of Iram,

8. Whose like has never been built in the lands;

9. And with *(the tribe of)* Thamûd, who clove the rocks in the valley;

10. And with Pharaoh, of *(the victims impaled upon)* stakes.

11. They had transgressed in the land

12. And multiplied corruption in it.

13. Therefore your Lord let loose on them the scourge of His punishment;

14. For your Lord is ever watchful.

(According to some commentators when pharaoh would want to punish some people he would drive four sticks into the ground and would tie their hands and legs to these sticks and would punish them this way. Because of this way of cruelty he was practicing on people he was called "zul-avtâd the owner of the sticks.")

15. As for man, whenever his Lord tests him by honouring him and bestowing favours on him, he says: 'My Lord has honoured me.'

16. But whenever He tests him by restricting his subsistence; he says: 'My Lord has humiliated me.'

17. No! But you do not honour the orphan.

18. Nor do you urge one another to feed the needy.

19. Rather, you devour the inheritance *(of the orphan)* unsparingly.

20. And you love wealth with an exceeding love.

(During the period of ignorance before Islâm Arabs used to have the practice of depriving of their inheritance of their women 'not necessarily wifes' alone but also children, and orphans.)

21. No! But when the earth is crushed to fine dust,

22. And your Lord comes with angels, rank upon rank,

23. And Hell is brought near, on that day man will remember. But what will remembrance avail him?

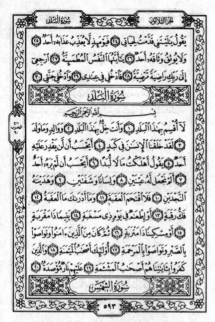

24. He will say: 'Would that I had done good works in my lifetime!'

25. For on that day no-one will punish as He will punish.

26. Nor will anyone bind with chains like His.

27. O serene soul!

28. Return to your Lord, pleased and well pleasing.

29. Enter among My servants.

30. And enter My Garden!

SÛRAH XC
AL-BALAD (THE TOWN)
Revealed at Makka

This takes its name from a word which occurs in the first verse, denoting Makka.

In the name of Allah, the Compassionate, the Merciful

1. No! but I swear by this town *(Makka);*

2. And you *(Muhammad)* are a dweller in this town,

3. And by the begetter, and that which he begat,

4. Indeed We have created man in hardship.

5. Does he think that none has power over him?

6. He *(boastfully)* says: 'I have squandered abundant wealth!'

7. Does he think that none observes him?

8. Have We not given him two eyes,

9. A tongue and two lips,

10. And shown him the two highways *(of good and evil)?*

11. Yet he would not assault the steep road.

12. Would that you knew what the steep road is!

13. It is the freeing of a bondsman;

14. Or feeding, on a day of famine.

15. Of an orphaned relation.

16. Or a needy man in distress;

17. And also that he be one of those who believe, and counsel one another to patience and mercy.

18. Those who do this will be the people of the right hand!

(In order to understand better what the "people of right" or the "people of the left" means look in Surah Al-Wâqi'a verses: 8, 9, 16.)

19. But those who deny Our revelations will be the people of the left hand.

20. With Hell-fire closed over them.

SÛRAH XCI
ASH-SHAMS (THE SUN)
Revealed at Makka

This takes its name from a word which occurs in the first verse.

In the name of Allah, the Compassionate, the Merciful

1. By the sun and its morning brightness,
2. And the moon when it follows it,
3. And the day when it displays it,
4. And the night when it covers it,
5. And the heaven, and Him that built it,
6. And by the earth and Him that spread it;
7. And by the soul and Him that formed it,
8. Then inspired it with *(knowledge of)* sin and piety:
9. He has indeed prospered who purifies it
10. And he who stunts it is ruined.
11. *(The tribe of)* Thamûd rejected *(their prophet)* in their rebellious pride.
12. When the most wicked of them rose up.
13. And the messenger of Allah *(the Prophet Sâlih)* said to them: 'This is Allah's she - camel. Let her drink.'

(The she-camel of the Prophet Sâlih was a miraculous animal which Allah brought forth from a rock. The Prophet Sâlih agreed with his people that one day the tribe of Thamûd and their animals would drink at the water, while the next day only the she-camel would drink. Thamûd wanted to slaughter the camel and did so. Allah became wrathful with them in consequence, and destroyed the tribe.)

14. But they denied him, and slaughtered her. So their Lord doomed them for their sin and rased their town to the ground.
15. He does not fear the consequences.

SÛRAH XCII
AL-LAYL (THE NIGHT)

Revealed at Makka

Takes its name from a word in the first verse.

In the name of Allah, the Compassionate, the Merciful

1. By the night when it lets fall its darkness,
2. And by the day when it shines in glory,
3. And by Him who has created the male and the female,
4. Your effort is surely to diverse ends.
5. As for him that gives *(in charity)* and guards himself *(by obeying Allah)*
6. And believes in the best,
7. We shall surely ease his way to the best.
8. But as for him who is miserly and thinks himself self - sufficient,
9. And disbelieves in the best,
10. We shall surely ease his way to hardship *(the way to evil)*.
11. His riches will not save him when he perishes.
12. Surely with Us rests guidance,
13. And verily to Us belong the hereafter and this world.
14. Therefore I do warn you of the blazing Fire!

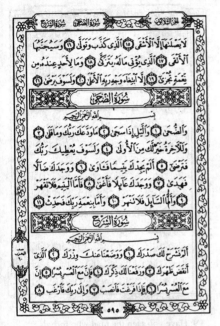

1. By the morning hours,

2. And by the night when it is still:

3. Your Lord has neither forsaken you, nor is He displeased.

(Revelation ceased for a while and the idolaters mocked the Prophet saying that his Lord had forsaken him. These verses explain the situation.)

4. And verily the hereafter will be better for you than this world;

5. And your Lord will surely give to you, and you will be satisfied.

6. Did He not find you an orphan, and give you, shelter?

7. Did He not find you wandering, and guide you?

8. Did He not find you needy, and enrich you?

9. As for the orphan, do not oppress him;

10. And as for the beggar, do not repel him;

11. And as for the bounty of your Lord, proclaim it.

15. None will burn in it but the most wretched,

16. Who denies the truth and turns away.

17. But the most pious one shall be removed from it:

18. He who gives his wealth in alms to purify himself,

19. Not in return for any favour done to him,

20. Seeking only the Countenance of his Lord Most High.

21. He will surely be content.

SÛRAH XCIII
AD-DUHÂ (THE MORNING HOURS)
Revealed at Makka

This takes its name from the word Ad-Duhâ.

In the name of Allah, the Compassionate, the Merciful

SÛRAH XCIV
AL-INSHIRÂH (SOLACE)
Revealed at Makka

This takes its name from a word in the first verse.

In the name of Allah, the Compassionate, the Merciful

1. Have We not relieved your breast for you,

2. And removed from you your burden

3. Which had weighed heavily upon your back,

4. And exalted your fame?

5. Surely every hardship is followed by ease.

6. Surely every hardship is followed by ease.

7. So, when you are relieved, resume your toil,

(When you are free from daily cares, exert yourself in prayers).

8. And strive to please your Lord.

SÛRAH XCV
AT-TÎN (THE FIG)
Revealed at Makka

This Sûrah, which refers to man's spiritual stiuation, takes its name from a word occurring in the first verse.

In the name of Allah, the Compassionate, the Merciful

1. By the fig and the olive,

2. By Mount Sinai,

3. And by this inviolate city *(Makka):*

4. Surely We have created man in the most noble mould,

5. Then We reduced him to the lowest of the low.

(Human being is the best one and the perfect among the creatures. On top of this he has been given intellect. "Ahsani Taqwim means the "perfection . So, he is responsible for it(intellect), if he does not use it in the right way, he will find himself at the lowest level.)

6. Except those who believe and do good works: for they will have an unfailing reward.

7. What can, after this, contradict you as to the Judgement *(to come)?*

8. Is not Allah the wisest of all Judges?

SÛRAH LCVI
AL-'ALAQ (THE CLINGING CLOT)
Revealed at Makka

The first five verses of this Sûrah were revealed at Hira, and were the first verses of the Qur'ân to be revealed.

In the name of Allah, the Compassionate, the Merciful

1. Read: In the name of your Lord who created,

2. Created man from a clinging clot.

3. Read: Your Lord is the Most Bountiful.

4. Who taught by the pen.

5. Taught man what he did not know.

6. No, indeed man is rebellious.

7. For he thinks himself self-sufficient,

8. Verily, to your Lord is the return of all.

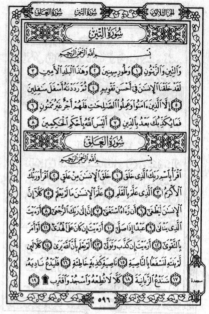

9. Have you seen the man who forbids

10. A servant when he prays?

(Abu Jahl, who disturbed the Prophet while he was praying.)

11. Have you considered if he fol ows the right guidance,

12. Or enjoins piety?

13. Think: if he denies the truth and gives no heed,

14. Does he not know that Allah sees all things?

15. Let him beware! If he does not cease, We shall drag him by the forelock.

16. A lying, sinful forelock!

17. Then let him call his helpmates.

18. We, in Our turn, shall call the guardians of Hell!

19. No! never obey him! But prostrate yourself and draw near *(to Allah).*

(Human being is nearest to his Creator when he is in the form of prostration .)

SÛRAH XCVII
AL-QADR (GLORY)
Revealed at Makka

This Sûrah refers to the night on which the Prophet began receiving the verses of the Qur'an. It is believed that Allah's decrees for the year are brought down to the earth on this night.

In the name of Allah, the Compassionate, the Merciful

1. We have indeed sent it *(the Qur'ân)* down on the Night of Qadr.

2. Would that you knew what the Night of Qadr is like!

3. The Night of Qadr is better than a thousand months,

4. On that night angels and the Spirit come down by their Lord's leave, with all His decrees.

5. *(That night is)* Peace, until the rising of the dawn.

SÛRAH XCVIII
AL-BAYYINA (THE CLEAR PROOF)
Revealed at Madîna

In the name of Allah, the Compassionate, the Merciful

1. Those who disbelieve among the People of the Scripture and the idolaters will not desist until a clear proof comes to them.

2. A messenger from Allah, reading purified pages.

3. Containing correct scriptures.

4. Nor did the People of the Book disagree among themselves until the Clear Proof was given them.

5. And they have been ordered no more than this: To worship Allah, offering Him sincere devotion, being True *(in faith),* to establish regular prayer; and to give obligatory alms *(zakât).* And that is the true religion.

(Look for "Being True (in faith-Hanıf" in Surah Ar-Rûm verse 30.)

6. Surely those who reject faith among the People of the Scripture and the idolaters will burn for ever in the fire of Hell. They are the worst of created beings.

7. But those who embrace faith and do good works are the best of created beings.

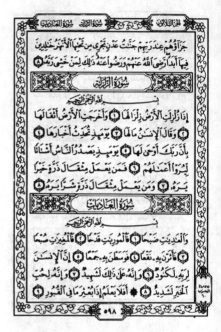

8. Their reward is with their Lord: Gardens of Paradise, beneath which rivers flow; where they will dwell forever. Allah is well pleased with them and they are well pleased with Him. This is for him who fears his Lord.

SÛRAH XCIX
AL-ZALZALA (THE EARTHQUAKE)

Revealed at Madîna

This deals with the Day of judgement..

In the name of Allah, the Compassionate, the Merciful

1. When the earth is shaken with its *(final)* earthquake

2. And the earth yields up its burdens,

(The Earth extracts the dead, the minerals, lava etc. on the Last Day.)

3. And man says: 'What is the matter with it?'

4. That day it will proclaim its tidings

5. Because your Lord inspired it.

6. That day mankind will come forth in scattered groups to be shown their deeds.

7. And whoever does good an atom's weight will see it then.

8. And whoever does ill an atom's weight will see it then.

SÛRAH C
AL-'ÂDIYÂT (THE COURSERS)

Revealed at Makka

In the name of Allah, the Compassionate, the Merciful

1. By the snorting coursers!

2. Striking sparks of fire,

3. And scouring to the raid at dawn,

4. Raising thereby a trail of dust,

5. Forcing their way into the centre *(of the enemy),*

6. Surely man is ungrateful to his Lord.

7. And to this he himself is a witness.

8. Surely he is violent in the love of wealth.

9. Does he not know that when those in the graves are raised,

10. And the secrets of the breasts are laid open,

11. On that day their Lord will be fully appraised of them!

SÛRAH CI

AL-QÂRI'A (THE CALAMITY)

Revealed at Makka

In the name of Allah, the Compassionate, the Merciful

1. The Calamity!

2. What is the Calamity?

3. Would that you knew what the Calamity is!

4. It is a day on which men will become like scattered moths,

5. And the mountains will become like carded wool.

6. Then, as for him whose scales are heavy *(with good deeds)*

7. He will be in a pleasing life.

8. But as for him whose scales are light,

9. The bottomless pit will be his home.

10. What will convey to you what this is like!

11. It is raging Fire.

(Scales' being heavy means good deeds; being light means lack of good deeds.)

SÛRAH CII

AT-TAKÂTHUR (RIVALRY IN WORLDLY INCREASE)

Revealed at Makka

Takes its name from a word which occurs in the first verse.

In the name of Allah, the Compassionate, the Merciful

1. Mutual rivalry in worldly increase has distracted you

2. Until you visit the graves.

3. But no, you will know!

4. Again no, you will know!

5. No indeed, if you only knew the truth with certainty;

6. You will see the blazing Fire.

7. You will see it with certain vision.

8. Then, on that day, you will be questioned about the pleasures *(you indulged in).*

(Human being is responsible for what he does in this world: how spent his time, money, etc.)

SÛRAH CIII

AL-'ASR (TIME)

Revealed at Makka after Sûrah Al-Inshirâh, this Takes its name from the word Al-Asr which occurs in the first verse and means time.

In the name of Allah, the Compassionate, the Merciful

1. By *(the token of)* time *(through the ages)*!

2. Surely man is in a state of loss;

3. Except those who believe and do good works, and exhort one another to truth, and exhort one another to steadfastness.

SÛRAH CIV

AL-HUMAZA (THE SLANDERER)

Revealed at Makka

In the name of Allah, the Compassionate, the Merciful

1. Woe to every slanderer and backbiter

2. Who gathers wealth and counts it

3. Thinking his wealth will render him immortal!

4. By no means! but verily he will be flung to the Consuming One.

5. What will convey to you what the Consuming One is!

6. It is the Fire of Allah, set ablaze,

7. Which rises up to the hearts of men.

8. It will close in upon them from every side.

9. In outstretched columns.

SÛRAH CV

AL-FÎL (THE ELEPHANT)

Revealed at Makka

It is related that Abraha al-Ashram, the Abyssinian (Christian) general, who had driven out the Jewish Himyarite rulers from Yaman, built a church in San'a, wishing to divert pilgrimage from the Ka'ba to this

church., Abraha led a large expedition against Makka, intending to destroy the Ka'ba. He had with him an elephant, or elephants, which much impressed the Arabs. Tradition says that the elephant refused to advance on the last stage of the march, and that swarms of flying creatures pelted the Abyssinians with stones. This happened in the year in which the Prophet Muhammad (peace be with him) was born.

THE ELEPHANT

In the name of Allah, the Compassionate, the Merciful

1. Have you not seen how your Lord dealt with the owners of the Elephant?

2. Did He not foil their evil scheming?

3. And send against them flocks of birds,

4. Which pelted them with stones of baked clay,

5. And made them like plants cropped by cattle?

SÛRAH CVI

QURAISH

Revealed at Makka

In the name of Allah, the Compassionate, the Merciful

1. For the protection-covenant of Quraish;

2. For their protection -covenant during the winter and summer journeys.

(Muslims are commanded to sacrifice animals on certain days and for certain purposes only for the sake of Allah but nothing else according to this verse.)

3. So let them worship the Lord of this House,

4. Who has fed them against hunger, and has made them safe from fear.

(The Quraish tribe enjoyed security in their journeys to the North in summer and to the South, to Yemen in winter because they were custodians of Kaba, while the other tribes were struggling for survival and were at each others' throats. This was a great favour of Allah to Quraish and they were well off because of their position which enabled them to engage commercial activities.)

SÛRAH CVII

AL-MÂ'ÛN (NEIGHBOURLY ASSISTANCE)

Revealed at Makka

Takes its name from a word in the last verse.

In the name of Allah, the Compassionate, the Merciful

1. Have you observed him who denies the Religion?

2. Such is he who repulses the orphan,

3. And who does not urge others to feed the poor.

4. Woe to the worshippers

5. Who are absent-minded to their prayer;

6. Those who make a show *(of piety)*

7. And refuse neighbourly assistance.

(Believers are warned both in verse 6 and 7 not pray for a show-off or cheat on their prayers.)

SÛRAH CVIII

AL-KAWTHAR (ABUNDANCE)

Revealed at Makka

This takes its name from a word in the first verse. It includes a reply to the disbelievers who used to taunt the Prophet with the fact that he had no son to uphold his religion after him.

In the name of Allah, the Compassionate, the Merciful

1. We have surely given you abundance!

(Kawsar has several meanings. The idolaters called the Prophet 'ebter' implying that having no sons, he was not going to be remembered. But his name is mentioned five times a day, when muazzins recite azan, and this takes place round the clock.)

2. So, pray to your Lord and sacrifice to Him.

3. Surely he who hates you will be cut off.

SÛRAH CIX

AL-KÂFIRÛN (THE DISBELIEVERS)

Revealed at Makka

In the name of Allah, the Compassionate,
the Merciful

1. Say: 'O disbelievers!

2. I do not worship what you worship,

3. Nor do you worship what I worship.

4. I shall never worship what you worship.

5. Nor will you ever worship what I worship.

6. To you belongs your religion, and to me, mine.

SÛRAH CX

AN-NASR (THE HELP)

Revealed at Madîna

Takes its name from the word *Nasr,* which means help. Though ascribed always to Madîna tradition says that it was actually revealed at Makka in the tenth year of the Hijrah. It is accepted to have been the first announcement of the Prophet's approaching death.

In the name of Allah, the Compassionate,
the Merciful

1. When Allah's help comes, and the victory,

2. And you see mankind entering the religion of Allah in multitudes,

3. Then celebrate the praise of your Lord and seek His forgiveness. He is ever disposed to show mercy.

SÛRAH CXI

AL-LAHAB (THE FLAME)

Revealed at Makka

The Prophet's uncle Abû Lahab (The Father of Flame) made it his business to torment the Prophet. Here he and his wife are denounced.

In the name of Allah, the Compassionate, the Merciful

1. May the hands of Abû Lahab perish! May he himself perish!

2. His wealth and gains will not avail him.

3. He will be plunged into flaming fire,

4. And his wife, the carrier of firewood:

5. Around her neck shall be a rope of palm fibre.

(The Prophet invited his relatives and preached them Islam. Among them was Abu Lahab, his uncle, who reproached the Prophet sayings: 'have you called us for this' and disrupted. Upon this occasion this surah was revealed. If a man's hand perish, he can not do anything.)

SÛRAH CXII

AL-IKHLÂS (UNITY)

Revealed at Makka

Takes its name from its subject. This Sûrah is called the 'essence of the Qur'ân'.

In the name of Allah, the Compassionate, the Merciful

1. Say: 'He is Allah, the One!

2. Allah, the eternally Besought of all!

3. He begat none. Nor was He begotten.

4. And there is none comparable to Him!

(Ikhlas means sincerity and commitment, purity in intention. Samad(besought of): Who needs no one but everyone need Him.)

SÛRAH CXIII

AL-FALAQ (DAYBREAK)

Revealed at Madîna

Takes its name from a word which occurs in the first verse. This and the following Sûrah are prayers for protection, being known as the Mu'awwadhatayn.

In the name of Allah, the Compassionate, the Merciful

1. Say: 'I seek refuge in the Lord of the Daybreak.

2. From the evil of what He created;

3. From the evil of the darkness when it is intense.

4. And from the evil of the witches blowing on knots;

5. And from the evil of an envier when he envies.'

SÛRAH CXIV

AN-NÂS (MANKIND)

Revealed at Madîna

This Sûrah also is a prayer for protection. Reciting these two Sûrahs protects one against the jinn and magic.

In the name of Allah, the Compassionate, the Merciful

1. Say: 'I seek refuge in the Lord of mankind

2. The King of mankind,

3. The God of mankind,

4. From the evil of the slinking whisperer,

5. Who whispers in the hearts of mankind,

6. Of the jinn and of mankind.'

وهذه الأوجه التى تقدمت لحفص عن عاصم ذكرها الإمام الشاطبى فى نظمه المسمى « حرز الأمانى ووجه التهانى ».

هذا ، والمواضع التى تختلف فيها الطرق ضُبطت لحفصٍ بمايوافق طريق النظم المذكور .

﴿ علامات الوقف ﴾

مـ علامة الوقف اللازم ، نحو : إِنَّمَا يَسْتَجِيبُ ٱلَّذِينَ يَسْمَعُونَ وَٱلْمَوْتَىٰ يَبْعَثُهُمُ ٱللَّهُ .

لا علامة الوقف الممنوع ، نحو : ٱلَّذِينَ تَتَوَفَّىٰهُمُ ٱلْمَلَٰٓئِكَةُ طَيِّبِينَ يَقُولُونَ سَلَٰمٌ عَلَيْكُمُ ٱدْخُلُوا ٱلْجَنَّةَ .

ج علامة الوقف الجائز جوازا مستوى الطرفين ، نحو : نَّحْنُ نَقُصُّ عَلَيْكَ نَبَأَهُم بِٱلْحَقِّ إِنَّهُمْ فِتْيَةٌ ءَامَنُوا بِرَبِّهِمْ .

صلى علامة الوقف الجائز مع كون الوصل أوْلى ، نحو : وَإِن يَمْسَسْكَ ٱللَّهُ بِضُرٍّ فَلَا كَاشِفَ لَهُ إِلَّا هُوَ وَإِن يَمْسَسْكَ بِخَيْرٍ فَهُوَ عَلَىٰ كُلِّ شَىْءٍ قَدِيرٌ .

قلى علامة الوقف الجائز مع كون الوقف أوْلى ، نحو : قُل رَّبِّى أَعْلَمُ بِعِدَّتِهِم مَّا يَعْلَمُهُمْ إِلَّا قَلِيلٌ فَلَا تُمَارِ فِيهِمْ .

∴ ∴ علامة تعانُق الوقف بحيث إذا وُقِف على أحد الموضعين لا يصح الوقف على الآخر ، نحو : ذَٰلِكَ ٱلْكِتَٰبُ لَا رَيْبَ فِيهِ هُدًى لِّلْمُتَّقِينَ .

فإن الهاء لاتوصل مطلقا ، لئلا يجتمع ساكنان .

نحو قوله تعالى : ﴿ لَهُ ٱلْمُلْكُ ﴾ ، ﴿ وَءَاتَيْنَـٰهُ ٱلْإِنجِيلَ ﴾ ﴿ فَأَنزَلْنَا بِهِ ٱلْمَآءَ ﴾ ، ﴿ إِلَيْهِ ٱلْمَصِيرُ ﴾ .

تنبيهـات :

(١) ـ فى سورة الروم ورد لفظ ﴿ ضَعْفٍ ﴾ مجرورا فى موضعين ومنصوبا فى موضع واحد .

وذلك فى قوله تعالى : ﴿ ٱللَّهُ ٱلَّذِى خَلَقَكُم مِّن ضَعْفٍ ثُمَّ جَعَلَ مِنۢ بَعْدِ ضَعْفٍ قُوَّةً ثُمَّ جَعَلَ مِنۢ بَعْدِ قُوَّةٍ ضَعْفًا وَشَيْبَةً ﴾

ويجوز لحفص فى هذه المواضع الثلاثة وجهـان : أحدهما : فتح الضاد ، وثانيهما : ضمها .

والوجهان مقروء بهما ، والفتح مقدم فى الأداء .

(٢) ـ فى لفـظ ﴿ ءَاتَىٰنِۦ ﴾ فى سورة النمل وجهـان لحفص وقفا .

أحدهما إثبات اليـاء ساكنـة ، وثانيهمـا : حذفهـا ، مع الوقف على النون .

أما فى حال الوصل فتثبت اليـاء مفتوحة .

(٣) ـ وفى لفظ ﴿ سَلَـٰسِلَا۟ ﴾ فى سورة الإنسان وجهـان أيضا وقفا .

أحدهما : إثبـات الألف الأخيرة ، وثانيهمـا : حذفهـا ، مع الوقف على اللام ساكنة .

أما فى حال الوصل فتحذف الألف .

مردودة إلى خلف بعد هاء الضمير المذكور إذا كانت مكسورة يدل على صلتها بياء لفظية فى حال الوصل أيضا .

وتكون هذه الصلة بنوعيها من قبيل المد الطبيعى إذا لم يكن بعدها همز ، فتمد بمقدار حركتين : نحو قوله تعالى ﴿ إِنَّ رَبَّهُۥ كَانَ بِهِۦ بَصِيرًا ﴾ وتكون من قبيل المد المنفصل إذا كان بعدها همز ، فتوضع عليها علامة المد ، وتمد بمقدار أربع حركات أوخمس نحو قوله تعالى : ﴿ وَأَمْرُهُۥٓ إِلَى ٱللَّهِ ﴾ ، وقوله جل وعلا :

﴿ وَٱلَّذِينَ يَصِلُونَ مَآ أَمَرَ ٱللَّهُ بِهِۦٓ أَن يُوصَلَ ﴾ .

والقاعدة أن حفصا عن عاصم يصل كل هاء ضمير للمفرد الغائب بواو لفظية إذا كانت مضمومة ، وياء لفظية إذا كانت مكسورة بشرط أن يتحرك ماقبل هذه الهاء ومابعدها ، وقد استثنى من ذلك مايأتى :

(١) – الهاء من لفظ ﴿ يَرْضَهُ ﴾ فى سورة الزمر . فإن حفصا ضمها بدون صلة .

(٢) – الهاء من لفظ ﴿ أَرْجِهْ ﴾ فى سورتى الأعراف والشعراء فإنه سكنها .

(٣) – الهاء من لفظ ﴿ فَأَلْقِهْ ﴾ فى سورة النمل ، فإنه سكنها أيضا .

وإذا سكن ماقبل هاء الضمير المذكورة ، وتحرك مابعدها فإنه لايصلها إلا فى لفظ ﴿ فِيهِۦ ﴾ فى قوله تعالى :

﴿ وَيَخْلُدْ فِيهِۦ مُهَانًا ﴾ فى سورة الفرقان .

أما إذا سكن مابعد هذه الهاء سواء أكان ماقبلها متحركا أم ساكنا

ووضـــع نقطة مدوّرة مسدودة الوسط (.)فــوق الهمزة
الثانية من قوله تعالى : ﴿ءَاْعْجَمِيٌّ وَعَرَبِيٌّ﴾ . يدل على تسهيلها بينَ
بينَ أى بين الهمزة والألف .

ووضع حرف السين فوق الحرف الأخير فى بعض الكلمــات
يدل على السكت على ذلك الحرف فى حال وصله بما بعده سكتة
يسيرة من غير تنفس .

وورد عن عاصــم السكت بلاخلاف من طريــق
الشاطبية علــى ألــف ﴿عِوَجَاْ﴾ بسورة الكهـف ، وألــف
﴿مَّرْقَدِنَاْ﴾ بسورة يـس ، ونون ﴿مَنْ رَاقٍ﴾ بسورة القيامــة ،
ولام ﴿بَلْ رَانَ﴾ بسورة المطففين .

ويجوز له فى هاء ﴿مَالِيَهْ﴾ بسورة الحاقة وجهان :
أحدهما : إظهارها مع السكت ، وثانيهما : إدغامها فى الهاء التى
بعدها فى لفظ ﴿هَلَكَ﴾ .

وقد ضبط هذا الموضع على وجه الإظهار مع السكت ، لأنه هو
الأرجح ، وذلك بوضع علامة السكون على الهاء الأولى ، مع تجريد الهاء
الثانية من علامة التشديد للدلالة على الإظهار ، ووضع حرف السين
على هاء ﴿مَالِيَهْ﴾ للدلالة على السكت عليها سكتة يسيرة بدون
تنفس ، لأن الإظهار لايتحقق وصلا إلا بالسكت .

وإلحاق واو صغيرة بعد هاء ضمير المفرد الغائب إذا كانت مضمومة
يدل على صلة هذه الهاء بواو لفظية فى حال الوصل . وإلحاق ياء صغيرة

الآية ويرقمها على عدد تلك الآية فى السورة ، نحو : إِنَّآ أَعْطَيْنَاكَ ٱلْكَوْثَرَ ۝ فَصَلِّ لِرَبِّكَ وَٱنْحَرْ ۝ إِنَّ شَانِئَكَ هُوَ ٱلْأَبْتَرُ ۝ ولا يجوز وضعها قبل الآية ألبتة فلذلك لا توجد فى أوائل السُّوَر ، وتُوجد دائما فى أواخرها .

وتدل هذه العلامة (۞) على بداية الأجزاء والأحزاب وأنصافها وأرباعها .

ووضعُ خطٍّ أُفقيٍّ فوق كلمة يدل على مُوجب السَّجدة .

ووضع هذه العلامة (۩) بعد كلمة يدل على موضع السجدة نحو: وَلِلَّهِ يَسْجُدُ مَا فِى ٱلسَّمَوَٰتِ وَمَا فِى ٱلْأَرْضِ مِن دَآبَّةٍ وَٱلْمَلَٰئِكَةُ وَهُمْ لَا يَسْتَكْبِرُونَ ۝ يَخَافُونَ رَبَّهُم مِّن فَوْقِهِمْ وَيَفْعَلُونَ مَا يُؤْمَرُونَ ۝ ۩ .

ووضع النقطة الخالية الوسط المُعيَّنة الشكل (۵) تحت الراء فى قوله تعالى : بِسْمِ ٱللَّهِ مَجْرٮٰهَا . يدل على إمالة الفتحة إلى الكسرة ، وإمالة الألف إلى الياء . وكان النُّقَّاط يضعونها دائرة حمراء فلما تعسر ذلك فى المطابع عُدِل إلى الشكل المُعيَّن .

ووضعُ النقطة المذكورة فوق آخر الميم قُبَيْل النون المشدَّدة من قوله تعالى : مَالَكَ لَا تَأْمَنَّا عَلَىٰ يُوسُفَ . يُدل على الإشمام (وهو ضم الشفتين) كمن يريد النطق بضمة إشارة إلى أن الحركة المحذوفة ضمة (من غير أن يظهر لذلك أثر فى النطق) .

المصاحف العُثمانية مع وجوب النطق بها ، نحو : ذَلِكَ ٱلْكِتَبُ.
يَلْوُونَ أَلْسِنَتَهُم . إِنَّ وَلِيِّيَ ٱللَّهُ . إِلَىفِهِمْ رِحْلَةَ ٱلشِّتَآءِ . وَكَذَلِكَ نُـجِى
ٱلْمُؤْمِنِينَ .

وكان **علماء الضبط** يلحقون هذه الأحرف حمراء بقــدر
حروف الكتابة الأصلية ولكن تعسُّر ذلك فى المطابع فاكتفى
بتصغيرها فى الدلالة على المقصود .

وإذا **كان الحرف المتروك** له بدلٌ فى الكتابة الأصلية عُوِّل فى
النطق على الحرف الملحَق لا على البدل ، نحو: ٱلصَّلَوةَ . ٱلزَّكَوٰةَ .
ٱلتَّوْرَىةِ . ونحو : وَٱللَّهُ يَقْبِضُ وَيَبْصُۜطُ . فِى ٱلْخَلْقِ بَصۜطَةً . فان وضعت
السين تحت الصاد دلَّ على أن النُّطــق بالصاد أشهر وذلك فى
لفظ : ٱلْمُصَۜيْطِرُونَ .

ووضع هذه العلامة (~) فوق الحرف يدل على لزوم مدّه
مدّا زائدا على المدّ الأصلى الطبيعى ، نحو : ءَالَ . ٱلطَّآمَّةُ . قُرُوٓءٍ .
سِىٓءَ بِهِمْ . شُفَعَـٰٓؤُا۟ . تَأْوِيلَهُۥ إِلَّا ٱللَّهُ . لَا يَسْتَحْىٓ أَن يَضْرِبَ .
بِمَآ أُنزِلَ . على تفصيل يعلم من فنّ التجويد . ولا تستعمل هذه
العلامة للدلالة على ألف محذوفة بعد ألف مكتوبة مثل آمنوا كما
وُضع غلطا فى كثير من المصاحف بل تكتب ءامنـوا بهمزة وألف
بعدها .

والدائرة المحلاة التى فى جوفها رقــم تدل بهيئتها على انتهاء

وتعريته مع عدم تشديد التالي يدُلُّ على إدغام الأوَّل فى الثاني إدغاما ناقصا نحو مَن يَقُولُ . مِن وَالٍ . فَرَّطتُمْ . بَسَطتَ . أو إخفائه عنده فلا هو مظهر حتى يقرعه اللسان ولا هو مُدغَم حتى يقلب من جنس تاليه نحو مِن تَحتِهَا . مِن ثَمَرَةٍ . إِنَّ رَبَّهُم بِهِم

ووضعُ ميم صغيرة (م) بدَلَ الحركة الثانية من المنوَّن أو فوقَ النون الساكنة بدَلَ السكون مع عدم تشديد الباء التالية يدُلُّ على قلب التنوين أو النون ميماً ، نحو : عَلِيمٌ بِذَاتِ الصُّدُورِ . جَزَآءَ بِمَا كَانُوا . مُنۢبَئًا .

وتركيب الحركتين : (ضمتين أو فتحتين أو كسرتين) هكذا : ـٌ ـً ـٍ يدُلُّ على إظهار التنوين ، نحو : سَمِيعٌ عَلِيمٌ . وَلَا شَرَابًا إِلَّا . وَلِكُلِّ قَوْمٍ هَادٍ .

وتتابُعُهما هكذا ـّٰ ـً ـٍ مع تشديد التالي يدُلُّ على الإدغام الكامل نحو : خُشُبٌ مُّسَنَّدَةٌ . غَفُورًا رَّحِيمًا . وُجُوهٌ يَوْمَئِذٍ نَّاعِمَةٌ .

وتتابُعُهما مع عدم التشديد يدُلُّ على الإدغام الناقص نحو : وُجُوهٌ يَوْمَئِذٍ . رَحِيمٌ وَدُودٌ . أو الإخفاء ، نحو : شِهَابٌ ثَاقِبٌ . يَرَاكَ اذَلِكَ . بِأَيْدِى سَفَرَةٍ كِرَامٍ . فتركيب الحركتين بمنزلة وضع السكون على الحرف . وتتابعهما بمنزلة تعريته عنه .

والحروفُ الصغيرة تدل على أعيـــان الحروف المتروكـــة فى

وأُخِذَ بيانُ مواضع السكتـات عنـد حفص من «الشاطبيـة» وشراحها وتعرف كيفيتها بالتلقى من أفواه المشايخ .

﴿اصطلاحات الضبط﴾

وَضع الصِّفر المستديِر (ه) فوق حرف عِلَّة يدل على زيادة ذلك الحرف فلا يُنْطَقُ به فى الوصل ولا فى الوقف ، نحو : يَتْلُوٓا۟ صُحُفًا . أُولَٰٓئِكَ . مِن نَّبَإِى۟ٱلْمُرْسَلِينَ . بَيْنَهَابِأَيْيْدٍ .

ووضع الصِّفر المستطيل القائم (٥) فوق ألِف بعدها متحرّك يدُلّ على زيادتها وصلا لاوقفا ، نحو : أَنَا۠خَيْرٌمِّنْهُ . لَٰكِنَّا۠ هُوَٱللَّهُ رَبِّى . وأُهملت الألف التى بعدها ساكن ، نحو : أَنَا ٱلنَّذِيرُ. من وضع الصفر المستطيل فوقها وإن كان حكمها مثل التى بعدها متحرك فى أنها تسقط وصلا وتثبت وقفا لعدم توهم ثبوتها وصلا .

ووضع رأس خاء صغيرة (بدون نقطة) (ﺣ) فوق أى حرف يدُلُّ على سكون ذلك الحرف وعلى أنه مُظهَر بحيث يقْرعه اللسانُ ، نحو : مِنْخَيْرٍ . وَيَنْهَوْنَعَنْهُ . قَدْسَمِعَ . أَوَعَظْتَ . وَخُضْتُمْ .

وتعرية الحرف من علامة السكون مع تشديد الحرف التالى يدُلّ على إدغام الأوّل فى الثانى إدغاماً كاملًا ، نحو : أُجِيبَت دَّعْوَتُكُمَا . يَلْهَث ذَّٰلِكَ . وَقَالَت طَّآئِفَةٌ . وَمَن يَكْرِههُّنَّ . وكذا قوله تعالى ﴿ أَلَمْ نَخْلُقكُّم ﴾ على أرجح الوجهين فيه .

واتُّبِعَتْ فى عد آياته طريقة الكوفيين عن أبى عبدالرحمن عبدالله ابن حبيب السُّلمىِّ عن على بن أبى طالب رضى الله عنـه على حسب ماورد فى كتاب «ناظمة الزُّهر» للإمـام الشاطبىّ ، وغيرها من الكتب المدوّنة فى علم الفواصل ، وآى القرآن على طريقتهم ٦٢٣٦ آية .

وأُخِـذَ بيـانُ أوائـل أجزائـه الثلاثين وأحزابـه الستين وأرباعهـا من كتاب «غيث النفع» للعلامة السَّفَاقُسىِّ . و «ناظمة الزهر» للإمـام الشاطبىِّ وشرحها . و « تحقيق البيان » للشيخ محمد المتولى ، و «إرشاد القراء والكاتبين» ، لأبى عيد رضوان المخلّلاتى .

وأُخِـذَ بيان مكِّيه ومدنيّه فى الجدول الملحق بآخر المصحف ، من «كتاب أبى القاسم عمر بن محمد بن عبد الكافى» و «كتب القراءات والتفسير» على خلاف فى بعضها .

وأُخِـذَ بيـان وقوفه وعلامـاتها مما قررته اللجنة فى جلسـاتها التى عقدتها لتحديد هذه الوقوف على حسب مااقتضته المعـانى التى ظهرت لها مسترشدة فى ذلك بأقوال الأئمـة من المفسرين وعلمـاء الوقف والابتداء .

وأُخِـذَ بيان السجدات ومواضعهاً من كتب الفقه والحديث على خلاف فى خمس منها لم نشر إليـه فى هامش المصحـف وهـى السجدة الثانية بسورة الحج والسجدات الواردة فى السور الآتية : صّ والنجم والانشقاق والعلق .

كُتِب **هذا المصحف** وضُبِط على مايوافق رواية حفص بن سليمان ابن المغيرة الأسَدَىّ الكُوفىّ لقراءة عاصم بن أبى النّجود الكوفىّ التابعىّ عن أبى عبدالرحمن عبدالله بن حَبيب السُلمىّ عن عثمانَ بن عفّان وعلىّ بن أبى طالب وزيد بن ثابت وأُبَىّ بن كَعْب عن النبىّ صلى الله عليه وسلم .

وأُخِذَ هجاؤه مما رواه علماء الرسـم عن المصاحف التى بعث بها الخليفة الراشد عثمان بن عفّان رضى الله عنه إلى البصرة والكوفة والشام ومكة ، والمصحف الـذى جعله لأهل المدينة ، والمصحف الذى اختص به نفسه ، وعن المصاحف المنتسخة منها . وقد روعى فى ذلك مانقله الشيخان أبو عمرو الدانى وأبوداود سليمان بن نجاح مع ترجيح الثانى عند الاختلاف .

هذا وكل حرف من حروف هذا المصحف موافـق لنظيره فى المصاحف العثمانية الستة السابق ذكرها .

وأُخِذَت طريقةُ ضبطه مما قرره علماء الضبط على حسب ماورد فى كتـاب «الطراز على ضبط الخراز» للإمـام التَّنَسِىّ مع الأخـذ بعلامات الخليل بن أحمد وأتباعه من المشارقة ، بدلا من علامات الأندلسيّين والمغاربة .

Numerical order of Sûras

Alphabetical order of Sûres

Name of suras	Number of suras	Number of âyats	Page	Name of suras	Number of suras	Number of âyats	Page	Name of suras	Number of suras	Number of âyats	Page
'Abasa	80	42	584	al-İkhlâs	112	4	604	an-Nahl	16	128	266
al-Âdiyât	100	11	599	al-İnfitâr	82	19	586	an-Nâs	114	6	604
al-Ahqâf	46	35	501	al-İnsân	76	31	577	an-Nasr	110	3	603
al-Ahzâb	33	73	417	al-İnshiqâq	84	25	588	an-Nâzilât	79	46	582
al-A'lâ	87	19	591	al-İnshirâh	94	8	596	an-Naba	78	40	581
al-'Alâq	96	19	597	al-İsrâ	17	111	281	an-Nejm	53	62	525
Âl İmrân	3	200	49	al-Jâthiya	45	37	498	an-Naml	27	93	376
al-'Ankebût	29	69	395	al-Jin	72	28	571	an-Nisa	4	176	76
al-A'râf	7	206	150	al-Jumu'a	62	11	522	an-Nûh	71	28	569
al-'Asr	103	3	601	al-Qâri'a	101	11	600	an-Nûr	24	64	349
al-An'âm	6	165	127	al-Qadr	97	5	598	ar-Ra'd	13	43	248
al-Anbiyâ'	21	112	321	al-Qâf	50	45	517	ar-Rahmân	55	78	530
al-Anfâl	8	75	176	al-Qalam	68	52	563	ar-Rûm	30	60	403
al-Baqara	2	286	48	al-Qamar	54	55	527	Sâd	38	88	452
al-Balad	90	20	593	al-Qasas	28	88	384	as-Saff	61	14	550
al-Bayyina	98	8	598	al-Quraish	106	4	602	as-Sâffât	37	182	445
al-Burûj	85	22	589	al-Kâfirûn	109	6	603	Saba'	34	54	427
adh-Dhâriyât	51	60	519	al-Kahf	18	110	292	as-Sajda	32	30	414
ad-Duhâ	93	11	595	al-Kawthar	108	3	602	aş-Şu'arâ	91	15	594
ad-Dukhân	44	59	495	al-Kıyâma	75	40	576	aşh-Şu'arâ	26	327	366
al-Fâtiha	1	7	—	al-Lahab	111	5	603	aşh-Şûrâ	42	53	482
al-Fâtır	35	45	433	al-Layl	92	21	595	Tâ-hâ	20	135	311
al-Fajr	89	30	592	al-Luqmân	31	34	410	at-Tahrîm	66	12	559
al-Falaq	113	5	604	al-Mâ'ida	5	120	105	at-Talâq	65	12	557
al-Fath	48	29	510	al-Mâ'ûn	107	7	602	at-Târıq	86	17	590
al-Fîl	105	5	601	al-Ma'ârij	70	44	567	at-Taghâbün	64	18	555
al-Furqân	25	77	358	Maryam	19	98	304	Tekâsür	102	8	600
Fussilat	41	54	476	Muhammad	47	38	506	at-Takvir	81	19	585
al-Ghâşiya	88	26	591	al-Mutaffifin	83	36	587	at-Tauba	9	129	186
al-Hajj	22	78	331	al-Mujadili	58	22	541	at-Tin	95	8	596
al-Hadîd	57	29	536	al-Muddaththir	74	56	574	at-Tûr	52	49	522
al-Hâqqa	69	52	565	al-Mulk	67	30	561	al-Vâqıa	56	69	533
al-Hashr	59	24	544	al-Mu'min	40	85	466	Yâ-sîn	36	83	439
al-Hijr	15	99	261	al-Mu'minûn	23	118	341	Yunus	10	109	207
al-Hujurât	49	18	514	al-Mumtahana	60	13	548	Yûsuf	12	111	234
Hûd	11	123	220	al-Munâfikûn	63	11	553	az-Zalzala	99	8	599
al-Humaza	104	9	601	al-Mursalât	77	50	579	az-Zuhraf	43	89	488
İbrahim	14	52	254	al-Muzzammil	73	20	573	az-Zümar	39	75	457

GENERAL INDEX